■ Because Without Cause

OXFORD STUDIES IN PHILOSOPHY OF SCIENCE

General Editor:
Paul Humphreys, University of Virginia

Advisory Board
Anouk Barberousse (European Editor)
Robert Batterman
Jeremy Butterfield
Peter Galison
Philip Kitcher
Margaret Morrison
James Woodward

The Book of Evidence
Peter Achinstein

Science, Truth, and Democracy
Philip Kitcher

Inconsistency, Asymmetry, and Non-Locality
A Philosophical Investigation of Classical Electrodynamics
Mathias Frisch

The Devil in the Details: Asymptotic Reasoning in Explanation, Reduction, and Emergence
Robert W. Batterman

Science and Partial Truth: A Unitary Approach to Models and Scientific Reasoning
Newton C.A. da Costa and Steven French

Inventing Temperature: Measurement and Scientific Progress
Hasok Chang

The Reign of Relativity: Philosophy in Physics 1915–1925
Thomas Ryckman

Making Things Happen: A Theory of Causal Explanation
James Woodward

Mathematics and Scientific Representation
Christopher Pincock

Simulation and Similarity: Using Models to Understand the World
Michael Weisberg

Systematicity: The Nature of Science
Paul Hoyningen-Huene

Causation and Its Basis in Fundamental Physics
Douglas Kutach

Reconstructing Reality: Models, Mathematics, and Simulations
Margaret Morrison

The Ant Trap: Rebuilding the Foundations of the Social Sciences
Brian Epstein

Because Without Cause: Non-Causal Explanations in Science and Mathematics
Marc Lange

Because Without Cause

Non-Causal Explanations in Science and Mathematics

Marc Lange

OXFORD
UNIVERSITY PRESS

OXFORD
UNIVERSITY PRESS

Oxford University Press is a department of the University of Oxford. It furthers
the University's objective of excellence in research, scholarship, and education
by publishing worldwide. Oxford is a registered trade mark of Oxford University
Press in the UK and certain other countries.

Published in the United States of America by Oxford University Press
198 Madison Avenue, New York, NY 10016, United States of America.

Library of Congress Cataloging-in-Publication Data
Names: Lange, Marc, 1963– author.
Title: Because without cause: non-causal explanations in science and mathematics / Marc Lange.
Description: New York, NY: Oxford University Press, [2017] |
Series: Oxford studies in philosophy of science | Includes bibliographical references and index.
Identifiers: LCCN 2016010808 | ISBN 9780190269487 (hardcover : alk. paper)
Subjects: LCSH: Probabilities—Philosophy. | Conditional expectations (Mathematics) |
Science—Philosophy. | Mathematics—Philosophy.
Classification: LCC QA273.A35 L364 2017 | DDC 511.3/1—dc23
LC record available at https://lccn.loc.gov/2016010808

Hier ist ein warum.

CONTENTS

PREFACE

WELCOME

Many explanations in science work by virtue of describing the world's network of causal relations. It is easy to find examples of "causal explanations." We explain the extinction of the dinosaurs by describing its various proximate causes, such as climate change, and we also explain it by describing its more distant causes, such as the terrestrial collision of one or more celestial bodies. According to classical physics, we explain the planets' motions by describing the gravitational influences causing those motions. In a more workaday example, we explain why a certain car fails to start by describing some respect in which its internal mechanism is malfunctioning, perhaps adding the causes of that malfunction. In other examples, we explain laws of nature. For instance, we explain why it is a law of nature that a gas's pressure climbs when it is compressed by a moveable piston under constant temperature. Our explanation describes the causal process underlying gas pressure: the collisions of gas molecules with the container's walls. Our explanation then gives certain of the laws governing that causal process, according to which molecules must collide more frequently with the container's walls as the gas is compressed under constant temperature.

This book is about some explanations that do *not* derive their explanatory power by virtue of describing the world's network of causal relations. Some of these explanations explain mathematical theorems; they are explanations *in mathematics*. Presumably, all explanations in mathematics are non-causal. The other non-causal explanations that this book will investigate are all *scientific* explanations; although many scientific explanations are causal, I contend that some are not. Non-causal explanations all involve "because without cause."[1]

Non-causal explanations in mathematics and science have generally been underappreciated in the vast recent philosophical literature about explanation. With regard to scientific explanation, causal explanation has received nearly all of the attention in recent decades.[2] Some philosophers have even declared that all scientific explanations are causal:

> [A]n explanation, I think, is an account of etiology: it tells us something about how an event was caused. Or it tells us something general about how some, or many, or all events of a certain kind are caused. Or it explains an existential fact by telling us something about how several events jointly make that fact true, and then perhaps something about how those truthmaker events were caused (Lewis 1986a, 73–74).

Even philosophers who officially leave room for non-causal scientific explanations, such as Woodward (2003, 221) and Strevens (2009, 5), devote scant attention to them. These philosophers take any non-causal explanations there may be as having to fit the models they have proposed of causal explanation—except that some sort of non-causal dependence must take the place of causal dependence. All told, then, non-causal scientific explanations have been largely neglected by philosophy of science. Likewise, explanation in mathematics has never been among the central topics in the philosophy of mathematics. Although mathematical explanation has recently begun to receive increased scrutiny, many philosophers still deny that there is any interesting sense in which certain mathematical proofs differ from other proofs of the same theorems in being able to explain why those theorems hold.

I will argue that non-causal explanations have long been recognized in both mathematics and science. I will offer many examples to persuade you not only that the task of giving explanations is an important part of mathematical practice, but also that non-causal scientific explanations play important roles that could not be played (even in principle) by causal explanations. I will not try to portray non-causal scientific explanations as working in roughly the same way as causal scientific explanations do (except that some variety of non-causal dependence appears in place of causal dependence). I will not even try to portray all non-causal scientific explanations as working in the same way as one another.

Once upon a time, many philosophers failed to acknowledge explanation over and above efficient description as a key aim of science.[3] Similarly, many philosophers today fail to see that some mathematics aims at explanation and that some important scientific explanations are non-causal. Fortunately, mathematicians and scientists never stopped looking for non-causal explanations just because some philosopher said that there is no such thing. In offering examples of non-causal explanations in mathematics and science, I will avoid examples that merely strike me (or some other philosopher) as explanatory. Rather, I will focus on examples that mathematicians and scientists themselves have proffered as explanatory. In many cases, I will look closely at their reasons for taking these examples to be explanatory. My aim throughout will be to account for these features of mathematical and scientific practice.

It would be of some value merely to have on hand a range of exemplary non-causal explanations (just as philosophy of science has settled upon some canonical examples of causal scientific explanations). However, I will not be content merely to offer some examples or even to classify them into natural kinds. Rather, I will try to elucidate how these various kinds of non-causal explanations work. If their explanatory power does not derive from their describing relevant features of the world's network of causal relations, then what does make them explanatory? To answer this question for various kinds of non-causal explanations in math and science is the principal aim of this book.

I will examine closely a great many fascinating and instructive explanations in math and science. For example, I will look at some "brute-force" mathematical proofs and contrast them with proofs of the same theorems that exploit symmetries to explain why those theorems hold. I will examine why combinatorial mathematicians regard simple bijective proofs of partition identities as explanatory, by contrast with non-explanatory proofs that appeal to generating functions out of which the simple partition identities seem to emerge miraculously from out of a welter of algebra. I will investigate proofs that explain theorems concerning the real numbers by placing them in the broader context of the complex numbers, and I will contrast these proofs with non-explanatory proofs of the same theorems that stick purely to the real numbers. I will present scattered theorems of Euclidean geometry that are explained by being unified under a single proof that uses properties from projective geometry, and I will investigate how these projective properties qualify as mathematically natural. I will present mathematical facts that have no explanations at all as well as mathematical explanations that are not proofs. I will identify mathematical explanations that reveal further, formerly invisible aspects of the theorems being explained, thereby provoking new questions about why those theorems hold. I will point out mathematical coincidences and specify the relation between being a mathematical coincidence and having a certain sort of mathematical explanation.

Turning to scientific explanations, I will describe how the minimum number of equilibrium points of any double pendulum is explained by the topology of any double pendulum's configuration space and how this explanation contrasts with a causal explanation of the same fact. This topological explanation and other "distinctively mathematical" scientific explanations work by showing how the fact being explained is inevitable considering the framework that any system *must* inhabit (regardless of whether and how it is caught up in causal relations)—where this variety of necessity transcends ordinary natural necessity. I will argue that an explanation that appeals to regression toward the mean works by depicting the phenomenon being explained as fallout from the mere fact that certain factors are statistically correlated, whatever this correlation's causal basis (if any). I will argue that explanations in evolutionary population biology that appeal to random drift are likewise "really statistical" explanations. On this view, natural selection and random drift are not different kinds of causal processes, but rather involve different kinds of explanations. In addition, I will distinguish several varieties of non-causal scientific explanation that work by showing how the fact being explained follows merely from the dimensional architecture. For instance, the reason why freely falling bodies obey Galileo's "odd number rule," rather than various alternatives to it that were proposed in Galileo's time, is that those alternatives are dimensionally impossible whereas Galileo's rule is dimensionally possible. Furthermore, I will maintain that an analogy between derivative laws of nature concerning physically dissimilar cases (such as cases in thermodynamics, electrostatics, and hydrodynamics) is physically coincidental insofar as these laws have no important common explainer among more fundamental laws. Yet this analogy between the various derivative laws is nonetheless mathematically no coincidence if their similarity arises from a similarity either in the cases' dimensional architecture or in the mathematical form of various, more fundamental laws. I will examine what would make it no coincidence that both gravitational and electric forces conserve energy, but instead for the law of energy conservation to explain this similarity between the two kinds of forces. I will also elucidate what it would take for a conservation law to be explained by a spacetime symmetry principle. I will argue that these explanations work by supplying (contextually relevant) information about the source of the especially strong necessity possessed by the fact being explained. I will use this account to understand several other non-causal scientific explanations, such as the way that the principle of relativity and other symmetry principles would explain the Lorentz transformations. These are among the topics that I will be investigating in this book.

■ WHAT THIS BOOK IS NOT ABOUT

Having sketched what this book will be about, I will now say a few words about what this book will *not* be about.

There are many non-causal explanations with which this book will not be concerned. For instance, a given base runner in a baseball game was out because he was beaten to first base by the thrown ball. Similarly, Carter can issue orders to Pyle because Carter is a sergeant and Pyle is a private. The rules of chess and the locations of various pieces on the chessboard explain non-causally why Fisher cannot move his king. The rules of a given language's grammar explain non-causally why a certain sentence is (or is not) grammatical in that language. Non-causal explanations can also be found in legal explanation. For instance, it is illegal in the United States to burn currency because a certain law is in force, and that law is a law, in turn, because certain legislative procedures were followed in its passage. Non-causal explanations can also be found in moral explanations. We might explain why a given character trait is a virtue (or a vice) or why a given action would be good (or courageous or mendacious). For example, the reason why it would be good for Alice to return the keys she borrowed is that she promised to return them and the rule of promise-keeping would maximize happiness/is a rule that no one could reasonably reject/is God's command/is (fill in your favorite moral theory here). Non-causal explanations can also be found in epistemology. Jones would be justified in believing that there are three other people joining him for dinner because of what he has been told and his background knowledge. In all of the explanations to which I have just referred, certain normative statuses are explained by other normative statuses or by certain non-normative facts together with certain norms. These diverse normative explanations are non-causal but are neither mathematical nor scientific explanations. They fall outside the scope of this book.

Likewise, some philosophers (e.g., Sturgeon 1985) have argued that a moral fact can explain a non-moral fact, such as when the rightness of Alice's returning the car keys she borrowed explains why Alice believes that it would be right for her to return them and ultimately why she returns them. I will not appeal to putative explanations of this kind in order to argue for the existence of non-causal scientific explanations. Likewise, suppose that Chris's experiencing pain is explained by his mental state's physical ground. In such a case, the instantiation of a supervening property is explained by the instantiation of a subvening property. Some philosophers (e.g., Kim 1998, 44; Gibbons 2006, 89) have characterized such an explanation as non-causal in that the subvening property's instantiation is not a *cause* of the supervening property's instantiation.

That the connection between these property instantiations is not causal, however, is insufficient to show that this scientific explanation works differently from standard examples of causal explanations. A "causal explanation" does not have to cite causes of whatever is being explained. Rather (as I will argue in chapter 1), an explanation that cites no causes of what it explains may deserve to be classified in the same category as an explanation that does cite causes of its explanatory target. They ought to be co-classified (as "causal explanations") because they work in the same way: each derives its power to explain by virtue of supplying (contextually relevant) information about the world's network of causal relations. This may well be precisely what happens in some cases where we explain a supervening property's instantiation by identifying the subvening property in which its instantiation consists. The explanation may work not merely by virtue of the supervenience relation (which could, unlike the explanatory relation, be symmetric), but also by virtue of describing an important aspect of the supervening property instantiation's place in the world's causal network. For example, by so locating the supervening property instantiation, the explanation may inform us that any cause of the supervening property instantiation operated ultimately by causing—or by supervening on events causing—the instantiation of the subvening property. For a similar reason, intentional explanations (e.g., by which an action is explained by the actor's beliefs and desires) may be causal explanations. Accordingly, I will not appeal to explanations of these kinds in order to argue for the existence of non-causal scientific explanations.

Furthermore, I will not make my case for non-causal scientific explanation by appealing to the spooky "passion at a distance" exhibited by quantum-mechanical systems. The specific peculiarities of quantum mechanics do not bear on the operation of the broad varieties of non-causal scientific explanations that I will study. Some philosophers believe that there are no causal relations in fundamental physics; if these philosophers are correct, then presumably any explanations supplied by fundamental physics are non-causal. But I will not use any argument along these lines to make the case for non-causal scientific explanations.

In addition, it has sometimes been argued that certain scientific explanations work by abstracting from, idealizing, mathematically massaging, or otherwise departing from the causal details of the case at hand and that these explanations therefore do not work by accurately describing the world's network of causal relations. I will not be relying on any such argument to show that there are non-causal scientific explanations. An explanation that works by giving an abstract description of the world's causal network still derives its power to explain by virtue of supplying information (of an abstract kind) about the world's causal network and so is (by my lights) a causal explanation. By contrast, I will look at many scientific explanations that abstract from the petty causal details but (as I will show) do *not* work by virtue of describing abstract features of the world's causal network. For instance, some non-causal scientific explanations work by identifying certain constraints to which the world must conform. These constraints (such as mathematical facts and symmetry principles) apply to causal processes, but not in virtue of their being causal processes. Rather, they apply in the same way to all aspects of the world, whether causal or not. Indeed, they would apply in the same way even if the world contained no causal network at all.

By the same token, "non-causal dependency relations" (Kim 1974, 41) were in play when Xanthippe became a widow as a result of Socrates's death, when the birth of my first child turned my father into a grandfather, and when my arrival in Paris gave the Eiffel Tower the property of being within 10 miles of me. In these cases, some A's relational properties changed because of a change in some B's properties (where A is not B). However, explanations of these "mere Cambridge changes" are not the kinds of non-causal explanations that I will be examining.

The same applies to many putative non-causal explanations involving metaphysical "grounding"—such as that the mereological sum of A and B exists because A exists and B exists, or that the disjunctive fact that it is raining or I am wearing a green shirt holds because it is raining, or that Jones and Smith have a common acquaintance because they both know Brown. I will look neither at "truthmaking" explanations (such as that p is true because p) nor at explanations of narrowly logical truths (perhaps it is the case that $(p \to p)$ or q because it is the case that $(p \to p)$). Similarly, I will not be invoking explanations according to which some relation holds between sentences (or propositions) by virtue of their logical forms, such as that "The meeting is likely to start at noon" is logically equivalent to "It is likely that the meeting will start at noon" because they have the same logical form.

Of course, some "in virtue of" explanations (as Rosen (2010) calls them) have tremendous scientific importance—such as that some fact about light holds in virtue of some fact about electromagnetic waves. But once again, I will not use such an explanation to make the case for non-causal scientific explanations because I suspect that this explanation works by describing features of the world's causal network—in particular, by tracing light's causal powers to the causal powers of electromagnetic fields. Likewise an explanation that reveals how a cube's water-solubility (or some other dispositional property instantiation) is grounded in the cube's molecular structure (or some other non-dispositional property instantiation) is a causal explanation (by the lights of chapter 1) even though the cube's molecular structure does not *cause* the cube to be water-soluble. The cube's molecular structure explains the cube's water-solubility by virtue of the fact that any manifestation of the cube's water-solubility (such as its dissolving when immersed in water) would have the cube's molecular structure as a cause. The explanation of the disposition in terms of its non-dispositional ground works by supplying information about the world's causal network. It is thus a causal explanation. Having given "causal explanation" such a broad scope, I find it especially interesting to discover that certain scientific explanations are non-causal.

There are scientific cases where facts of the form "There exists an F" are explained non-causally. But if an "in virtue of" (or "truthmaker") explanation of "There exists an F" must appeal to a fact of the form "c is F" (as in the explanation of Smith and Jones having a common acquaintance), then many non-causal scientific explanations of "There exists an F" are not "in virtue of" (or "truthmaker") explanations. For instance, Kelvin's account of why there is a lowest temperature ("absolute zero") is not that minus 273.15°C is it. (In chapter 1, I will present another example: the reason why there exists at this moment a pair of antipodal points on the Earth's equator having the same temperature.)

There are some scientifically important "in virtue of" explanations that may be non-causal but will not be examined in this book. A system may have a given electric charge in virtue of the charges of its parts. How this explanation works depends on why charges add. Although I will not look at this example, I will look carefully (in chapter 4) at how the "composition law" for forces (the "parallelogram law") is explained and what would make its explanation causal or non-causal.

Consider how a net force is explained by its component forces. This explanation might be termed a "constitutive explanation" in that the state of the whole is being explained by the states of its parts (together with a composition law: the parallelogram of forces). One might be tempted to characterize a constitutive explanation as "non-causal" in that the states of the parts do not *cause* the state of the whole; the whole's being in a certain state is not an event distinct from the parts' being in certain states. However, I will not appeal to "constitutive explanations" to argue that some scientific explanations are non-causal. At least some constitutive explanations work by supplying information about the world's causal network—as when we explain some capacity possessed by an intricate compound system (such as a machine or organism) by the diverse, simpler dispositions of its parts (together with the parts' interrelations). Such an explanation works by specifying an underlying causal mechanism. It works by telling us that (for example) any outcome of the given capacity of the system would be a manifestation of various dispositions of its parts—and thus by telling us about the world's causal network. Likewise, as I will show in chapter 4, the fact that the relation between component and net forces is a part/whole relation rather than a causal relation does not suffice to ensure that the explanation of the force composition law is non-causal. Although the net force is not distinct enough from its components to be an effect of them, an explanation of the force composition law will be a causal explanation if it works by tracing the individual effects of the component forces.

Many philosophical explanations are non-causal—including philosophical explanations of facts about the causal relation itself. For instance, a philosophical account of what causal relations consist in should explain why it is the case (if and insofar as it is indeed the case) that all token-level causal relations are transitive but some type-level causal relations are intransitive. Likewise, Kant proposed an account of why appearances stand in causal relations. Such philosophical explanations do not purport to be causal explanations; they do not work by virtue of supplying information about the particular lines of causal influence that exist, though they do purport to supply information about what causal relations are. Such philosophical explanations are not part of mathematics or science and so fall outside the purview of this book. Likewise, if God exists outside spacetime, then presumably God's properties do not cause whatever they explain, so such theistic explanation is non-causal. I do not examine theistic explanation.

There are some varieties of explanation in mathematics and some varieties of non-causal scientific explanation that I do not examine in this book (or that I merely mention briefly). For instance, that Samuel Clemens and Mark Twain are identical explains non-causally why they have the same height, weight, and birth dates. Of course, the fact that Clemens and Twain are identical conveys some information about the world's network of causal relations: it tells us, for instance, that any cause of Clemens's height is a cause of Twain's height. But that Clemens and Twain are identical does not owe its explanatory power to its supplying such information about the world's causal relations. Even if there were no causal relations at all, identities would explain in the same way. As Lycan (1981, 10) says, "What better way to explain a . . . correlation between A's and B's than by supposing . . . that in fact A's are just B's." This "identity explanation" (Achinstein 1983) of the correlation reveals that causal relations have nothing to do with why it holds.

That Clemens and Twain have the same height because Clemens is identical to Twain is thus unlike the explanation of visible light's having a certain speed in glass because visible light is identical to certain electromagnetic waves and those electromagnetic waves have that speed in glass. This explanation of light's speed is a causal explanation because it works by supplying the information that the factors causally responsible for light's speed are electromagnetic. Because this explanation is causal, it is asymmetric in the same way as causal relations are: the speed in glass of certain electromagnetic waves is not explained by the fact that those waves are identical to visible light and that visible light has the given speed in glass.

The Twain-Clemens non-causal explanation is like some purported explanations from science—which also purport to be non-causal explanations. For instance, when Wheeler proposed that an electron moving backward in time would be indistinguishable from a positron moving forward in time, so that a single electron might move both forward and backward in time, Feynman (1998, 163) reports Wheeler to have said, "I know why all electrons have the same charge and the same mass. . . . Because, they are all the same electron!"

In another kind of scientific explanation that I do not examine, we explain why p is the case by appealing to the fact that p is a law and so *had to* be the case; p was inevitable, unavoidable—necessary. For instance, the fact that every actual long, linear charge distribution with static uniform charge density λ has an electric field strength at a distance r equal (in Gaussian CGS units) to $2\lambda/r$ is explained by the fact that as a matter of natural law, every such charge distribution must have such an electric field. Although in chapter 2 I offer an account of what it would take for certain special kinds of laws (e.g., conservation laws) to possess certain special powers to explain, I do not in this book offer an account of what makes an ordinary law that p able to explain the fact that p. I have tried to offer such an account elsewhere, most recently in Lange (2009a), and I touch briefly upon that account in section 2.5. On my view, the power of p's lawhood to explain why p is the case arises from the connection between lawhood and necessity: if it is a law that p, then p holds because p must hold. In Lange (2009a), I offer an account of what this must-ness consists in. The law specifying the electric field of any static, uniform, long, linear charge distribution is explained, in turn, by Coulomb's law. This explanation is causal, on my view, because it works by describing the field's individual causes and how their separate effects compose to give the charge distribution's total electric field strength.

There are plenty of vexed questions about the role of non-causal explanation in science that I will not address. I will not study whether so-called teleological explanations in biology (e.g., mammals have hearts in order to circulate their blood) are causal explanations. I will not examine whether the apparently non-causal explanations given by extremal principles in physics (e.g., roughly speaking, that light takes a certain path from here to there in order to minimize its travel time in getting there) are actually parasitic on causal explanations (e.g., that light takes all possible paths from here to there, but the light waves taking paths near to the least-time path interfere constructively, the others canceling out). In short, I will not aim to give an exhaustive survey of non-causal explanations in science and mathematics. Rather, I will look at some varieties of non-causal explanation that have generally been overlooked by philosophers, that have significant connections with one another, and that have been especially important in science and mathematics.

■ COMING ATTRACTIONS

Although I have been describing the subject of this book as "non-causal explanation in math and science," this characterization is potentially misleading. My main concern will not be to label certain explanations as "causal" and others as "non-causal." There may be several illuminating distinctions that merit this terminology, and there may also be intermediate cases. My main concern will be to understand how various (interrelated, important, and relatively neglected) kinds of explanations in math and science work. That is, I want to understand where their power to explain comes from.[4]

The 11 chapters that follow divide into four parts.

Part I (chapters 1, 2, 3, and 4) focuses on a single prominent type of non-causal scientific explanation that I call "explanation by constraint." In chapter 1, I describe "distinctively mathematical" scientific explanations, offer an account of how they work, and identify an important respect in which they qualify as "non-causal." In chapter 2, I argue that other "constraints" can play the same role as mathematical facts do in "distinctively mathematical" explanations. Over the course of chapters 2 and 3, I offer an account of how "explanations by constraint" operate and what difference it would make that some law has such an explanation. In chapter 2, I focus on conservation laws and symmetry principles as possible "constraints," transcending the various force laws. In chapter 3, I look at the coordinate transformations (whether Galilean or Lorentz) as constituting possible constraints, and I identify what it would be for "top-down" explanations supplied by (what Einstein called) "theories of principle" to be autonomous from the "bottom-up" explanations supplied by "constructive theories." In chapter 4, I investigate what it would be for the parallelogram of forces (and other such composition laws) to transcend dynamics and how some scientists argue that the parallelogram law is explained by statics rather than dynamics.

Non-causal scientific explanations as a category are set apart merely by what they are *not*: causal explanations. Therefore, we should expect some non-causal scientific explanations to work differently from others. In part II (chapters 5 and 6), I examine several varieties of non-causal scientific explanation that are not "explanations by constraint." In chapter 5, I investigate explanations that reveal the fact being explained to be just a statistical "fact of life," such as explanations appealing to regression toward the mean. I call these "Really Statistical" (RS) explanations and argue that they are "non-causal" explanations in the sense elaborated in chapter 1. I apply my account of how "RS explanations" work to the case of explanations in population biology that appeal to random drift. In chapter 6, I look at several kinds of "dimensional explanation" in physics; I argue that they, too, are non-causal explanations by the lights of chapter 1. Some dimensional explanations are "explanations by constraint," whereas others are not. A causal explanation of a given derivative law can explain certain features of the law that a dimensional explanation cannot explain, but by the same token, a dimensional explanation can sometimes explain features of the derivative law that a causal explanation cannot explain. For instance, its dimensional explanation may reveal that one of its features results entirely from certain dimensional features of the more fundamental laws entailing it, so that other features of those more fundamental laws are not responsible for that feature of the derivative law.

Part III (chapters 7, 8, and 9) concerns explanation in mathematics rather than scientific explanations. In chapter 7, I give many examples (drawn from actual mathematical practice) of proofs that explain the theorems they prove, as well as proofs of those theorems that are not regarded in mathematical practice as explanatory. To capture these examples, I propose an account (the "big Lange theory") of what makes certain mathematical proofs not only prove their theorems, but also explain why those theorems hold. I also briefly identify some other kinds of explanation in mathematics, including explanations that do not explain theorems and explanations that do not consist of proofs. In chapter 8, I use my account to investigate explanations in mathematics that unify various mathematical facts. By virtue of having such an explanation, a given mathematical fact is no "mathematical coincidence." I also compare my account of explanation in mathematics to the accounts that have been proposed by Steiner and Kitcher. In chapter 9, I apply my account to the explanation of Desargues's theorem in Euclidean and projective geometry. I examine the status of mathematical properties such as the property of being a point in projective geometry—that is, being a Euclidean point *or* a "point at infinity." I propose an account of what makes such a property mathematically natural (that is, a genuine respect of mathematical similarity) rather than wildly disjunctive. I also investigate what makes Desargues's theorem in two-dimensional Euclidean geometry capable of being properly understood only in a broader environment: in three-dimensional projective geometry. The fact that projective geometry is where Desargues's theorem naturally belongs, the fact that the property of being a projective point is mathematically natural, and the fact that Desargues's theorem in projective geometry is no mathematical coincidence are all facts bound up with the mathematical explanation of Desargues's theorem. In this way, we can appreciate the significance of explanation in mathematics.

Finally, part IV (chapters 10 and 11) brings together ideas concerning both explanation in mathematics and non-causal explanation in science. In chapter 10, I examine scientific explanations that explain why certain physically unrelated laws of nature are so similar. These explanations work by revealing the laws' similarity to be no *mathematical* coincidence. Some of these explanations are dimensional explanations that account for dimensional similarities among otherwise unrelated laws of nature. To understand how these scientific explanations work, I will need to draw upon some of the ideas that I elaborated in connection with explanation in mathematics. Chapter 11 highlights some of the themes that ran through many of the earlier chapters, tying together different kinds of non-causal explanation and even causal explanation. I do not argue in this book that all explanations work in the same way; I do not give a single, general, abstract model of explanation that all kinds of mathematical and scientific explanations instantiate. However, it is also not the case that the explanations form an arbitrary, gerrymandered class having little or nothing in common besides our calling them "explanations." Despite their diversity, all of the different kinds of non-causal explanations deserve to be grouped with one another—and with the causal explanations—as species of the same genus. There are important respects in which they are all alike, especially in the ways that explanations can render similarities non-coincidental and properties natural. Non-causal explanations join causal explanations as all belonging to the same natural kind.

Scattered passages of this book draw on some of my previously published articles and are reproduced here with the kind permission of the publishers: "Dimensional Explanations," *Noûs* 43 (2009), 742–775; "A Tale of Two Vectors," *Dialectica* 63 (2009), 397–431; "What Are Mathematical Coincidences (and Why Does It Matter)?," *Mind* 119 (2010), 307–340; "Conservation Laws in Scientific Explanations: Constraints or Coincidences?," *Philosophy of Science* 78 (2011), 333–352; "Really Statistical Explanations and Genetic Drift," *Philosophy of Science* 80 (2013): 169–188; "What Makes a Scientific Explanation Distinctively Mathematical?," *British Journal for the Philosophy of Science* 64 (2013), 485–511; "Aspects of Mathematical Explanation: Symmetry, Unity, and Salience," *Philosophical Review* 123.4 (2014), 485–531; " 'There Sweep Great General Principles Which All the Laws Seem to Follow,' " in *Oxford Studies in Metaphysics*, vol. 7, edited by Karen Bennett and Dean Zimmerman (Oxford: Oxford University Press, 2012), 154–185; "How to Explain the Lorentz Transformations," in *Metaphysics and Science (Mind Association Occasional Series)*, edited by Stephen Mumford and Matthew Tugby (Oxford: Oxford University Press, 2013), 73–98; "How the Explanations of Natural Laws Make Some Reducible Physical Properties Natural and Explanatorily Potent," in *Laws of Nature: Metaphysics and Philosophy of Science*, edited by Walter Ott and Lydia Patton (Oxford: Oxford University Press, forthcoming); "Because Without Cause: Scientific Explanations by Constraint," in *Explanation beyond Causation*, edited by Juha Saatsi and Alexander Reutlinger (Oxford: Oxford University Press, forthcoming); "Explanation, Existence, and Natural Properties in Mathematics— A Case Study: Desargues' Theorem," *Dialectica* 69.4 (2015), 435–472.

PART I

Scientific Explanations by Constraint

1

What Makes a Scientific Explanation Distinctively Mathematical?

■ 1.1 DISTINCTIVELY MATHEMATICAL EXPLANATIONS IN SCIENCE AS NON-CAUSAL SCIENTIFIC EXPLANATIONS

Mathematics figures in many scientific explanations. But some scientific explanations are *distinctively* mathematical: they are mathematical in a different way from ordinary scientific explanations that employ mathematics. In this chapter, I will argue that these "distinctively mathematical" scientific explanations are *non*-causal explanations, unlike many other scientific explanations employing mathematics. Because distinctively mathematical scientific explanations are non-causal in an especially dramatic way, I will use them to argue that we must recognize the existence of non-causal scientific explanations.

Of course, I must specify what it takes for a scientific explanation to qualify as "causal"—and thus what it would be for a scientific explanations *not* to be causal (i.e., to be non-causal). The distinction between "causal" and "non-causal" explanations (as I will use these terms) lies in how they work—that is, in what gives them explanatory power. A "non-causal" explanation may incidentally identify (or, at least, supply information about) causes of what is being explained. But it does not derive its explanatory power by virtue of doing so.

Having used distinctively mathematical scientific explanations as my point of entry into non-causal scientific explanations, I will devote the rest of parts I and II of this book to examining non-causal scientific explanations more closely. I will argue that different kinds of non-causal scientific explanations work in different ways. "Distinctively mathematical" scientific explanations are our first example of what I will call "explanations by constraint." In the subsequent three chapters (making up the rest of part I), I will give many more examples of explanations by constraint and I will offer an account of how these non-causal explanations work. I will argue that there are other "constraints" besides mathematical facts and so there are "explanations by constraint" that are not "distinctively mathematical" explanations. I will specify what it is to be a "constraint." In part II (chapters 5 and 6) and later in chapter 10, I will investigate several kinds of non-causal scientific explanations that are *not* explanations by constraint. Ultimately,

I will try to understand how each of these kinds of non-causal scientific explanation works—that is, how explanations of these various kinds acquire their power to explain.

"Distinctively mathematical" explanations are *scientific* explanations, as distinct from explanations *in mathematics*—the subject of part III (chapters 7, 8, and 9). That is, part III is concerned with explanations in which the facts being explained (the "explananda") are theorems of mathematics, whereas the explanations with which I will be concerned in this chapter (and in the rest of parts I and II) take as their targets various facts about the natural, spatiotemporal world. However, occasionally in parts I and II it will be useful to cast an anticipatory glance at explanation in mathematics. For instance, the notion of a "coincidence" will arise in connection with both scientific explanations and explanations in mathematics. In addition, Steiner's (1978a, 1978c) account of (what I call) distinctively mathematical scientific explanations appeals to the notion of explanation in mathematics. In section 1.5, I will argue that explanations in mathematics are not connected to distinctively mathematical scientific explanations in the way that Steiner believes. I hope that these "spoiler alert" peeks at explanation in mathematics will encourage you to read part III!

In trying to characterize distinctively mathematical scientific explanations, I am not trying to explicate the meaning of the term "distinctively mathematical" so as to agree with some intuitions about its proper application. We may well have no pretheoretic notions at all regarding what a "distinctively mathematical" scientific explanation would be. Furthermore, my aim is not to explicate the meaning of "distinctively mathematical" so as to fit this term's use in scientific practice. No such term is commonly used in science. Nevertheless, the task of characterizing "distinctively mathematical" scientific explanations does aim to fit certain intuitions as well as certain features of scientific practice.

Shortly, I will present several examples of scientific explanations that are mathematical in a manner that intuitively differs profoundly from many familiar scientific explanations employing mathematics. One goal of this chapter is to explore this apparent difference in order to see whether it withstands careful scrutiny. I will use the term "distinctively mathematical" to mark this apparent difference. Ultimately, I will suggest that there is a fundamental difference between the explanations I will present and many familiar scientific explanations employing mathematics. My account of what makes certain scientific explanations but not others "distinctively mathematical" aims to accord with our intuitions about which scientific explanations are alike and which fundamentally differ.

An account of "distinctively mathematical" explanations aims to fit scientific practice by deeming to be explanatory only examples that would (if true) constitute genuine scientific explanations. But it also has a more ambitious aim: to reveal how "distinctively mathematical" explanations work.

The modern study of scientific explanation began with Hempel's and Oppenheim's 1948 proposal of the D-N model (Hempel 1965). Unfortunately, notorious counterexamples such as the flagpole, the eclipse, and the barometer (Salmon 1989, 46–50) demonstrated that the D-N model counts various non-explanations as explanatory. To avoid these problems for the D-N model, many philosophers have suggested that causal relations (which have no place in the D-N model) play a central role in scientific explanations. Indeed, many philosophers have gone on to suggest that *all* scientific explanations (or, at least, all scientific explanations of particular events or singular facts) are "causal explanations." For example, Salmon has written:

> To give scientific explanations is to show how events and statistical regularities fit into the causal structure of the world. (Salmon 1977, 162)

> Causal processes, causal interactions, and causal laws provide the mechanisms by which the world works; to understand why certain things happen, we need to see how they are produced by these mechanisms. (Salmon 1984, 132)[1]

The same note has been sounded by many other philosophers:

> Here is my main thesis: *to explain an event is to provide some information about its causal history.* (Lewis 1986b, 217; see Jackson and Pettit 1992, 12–13)[2]

> Causal explanation is the unique mode of explanation in physics. (Elster 1983, 18)

> The explanation of an event describes the "causal structure" in which it is embedded. (Sober 1984, 96)[3]

> An explanation is an adequate description of underlying causes helping to bring about the phenomenon to be explained. (Miller 1987, 60)

Recent accounts of scientific explanation (e.g., Woodward 2003; Strevens 2008) have continued to emphasize that scientific explanations work by describing causal connections.

I will argue that this view of scientific explanation cannot do justice to "distinctively mathematical" explanations. In arguing that these explanations are "non-causal," I am not appealing to some account of what makes an explanation "causal" that aims to fit either some pretheoretic intuitions about which explanations are "causal" or some scientific practice of labeling certain explanations "causal." Rather, I am trying to elaborate a notion of "causal" explanation that not only motivates many philosophers to contend that all scientific explanations are causal, but also helps us to understand how scientific explanations work. Distinctively mathematical explanations are "non-causal" because they do not work by supplying information about a given event's causal history or, more broadly, about the world's network of causal relations. A distinctively mathematical explanation works instead (I will argue) roughly by showing how the fact to be explained could not have been otherwise—indeed, was inevitable to a stronger degree than could result from the action of causal powers. If a fact has a distinctively mathematical explanation, then the modal strength of the connection between causes and effects is insufficient to account for that fact's inevitability. Accordingly, distinctively mathematical explanations do not qualify as "causal" even when the range of explanations that qualify as "causal" is broad enough to include every explanation that explains by virtue of describing the world's causal structure.

Thus, the importance of understanding how distinctively mathematical explanations work does not derive from the significance of any intuitions we may have regarding what makes an explanation "distinctively mathematical" or "causal." Rather, its importance lies in what it reveals about the kinds of scientific explanations there are and the ways they work—and, in particular, about the limits of philosophical accounts that place causal relations at the center of all scientific explanations.

Enough with the preliminaries! The best way to approach our topic is to give several examples of scientific explanations that intuitively are "distinctively mathematical." Here is a very simple example (inspired by Braine 1972, 144):

> The fact that 23 cannot be divided evenly by 3 explains why Mother fails every time she tries to distribute exactly 23 strawberries evenly among her 3 children without cutting any (strawberries—or children!).

The explanation seems no less distinctively mathematical when the "explanans" (i.e., the collection of explainers) includes certain contingent facts:

> That Mother has 3 children and 23 strawberries, and that 23 cannot be divided evenly by 3, explains why Mother failed when she tried a moment ago to distribute her strawberries evenly among her children without cutting any.

Notice that in the latter explanation, the explanandum (i.e., the fact being explained) concerns Mother's failure in a *particular* attempt, whereas in the former explanation, the explanandum is more general. In either case, the explanation is distinctively mathematical.

Here is another example along roughly similar lines. Suppose we select three jellybeans from a sample containing only red jellybeans and blue jellybeans. Why is it that of the three jellybeans we select, two are the same color? The answer is that with three objects but only two colors to distribute among them, two of the objects must share a color. This is an instance of what mathematicians call the "pigeonhole principle." Lipton (2009a, 46–47) gives a similar example: "I came to understand why my class had four students whose last birthdays fell on the same day of the week when it was explained to me that since there are only seven days in a week and twenty-two students in my class, there is no way to arrange the birthdays to avoid this result."

Here is an example given originally by Colyvan (1998, 321–322; 2001, 49–50; 2007, 120). Consider the fact that at every moment that Earth exists, on the equator (or on any other great circle) there exist two points having the same temperature that are located antipodally (i.e., exactly opposite each other in that the line between them passes through the Earth's center). Why is that? An explanation begins with the fact that temperature is a continuous function. That is, roughly speaking, as you move along the equator, temperature changes smoothly rather than jumping discontinuously. Now imagine placing your two index fingers on a globe at two antipodal points on the equator. Take the temperature on Earth at the location x that your left index finger is touching minus the temperature at the antipodal location that your right index finger is touching. This difference function $D(x)$ must change continuously as you move your two fingers eastward, keeping them at antipodal points on the equator (since a function is continuous if it is the difference between two continuous functions). Suppose without loss of generality that for the initial value of x, $D(x)$ is greater than zero (i.e., the left-finger location is warmer than the right). Then when you have moved your two fingers far enough around the equator that your left finger is where your right finger began (and vice versa), D must be less than zero. Hence, since D is continuous, there must have been a moment as you were moving your fingers when D went from positive to negative. That is, there must have been an x where $D(x) = 0$. (This step uses the intermediate value theorem: if f is a real-valued, continuous function on $[a,b]$ and u is a real number between $f(a)$ and $f(b)$, then there is a $c \, \varepsilon \, [a,b]$ such that $f(c) = u$.) Thus, there must be antipodal equatorial points at the same temperature.[4]

This explanation seems distinctively mathematical. Colyvan emphasizes that although it explains why there is always such a pair of points (rather than no such pair), it does not explain why two particular antipodal equatorial points are at the same temperature (rather than at different temperatures). To explain that fact, we would have to invoke the meteorological conditions in some neighborhoods of those points at some earlier moment. I will return to the contrast between these two explanations: one distinctively mathematical, the other not.

Pincock (2007) offers another example. Why has no one ever succeeded (or, in particular, why did a given person on a given occasion not succeed) in crossing all of the bridges of Königsberg exactly once (while remaining always on land or on a bridge rather than in a boat, for instance, and while crossing any bridge completely once having begun to cross it)? Here it is understood that the problem concerns the town's bridges as they were arranged when Euler considered this problem in 1735 (see fig. 1.1). A distinctively mathematical explanation is that in the bridge arrangement considered as a network, it is not the case

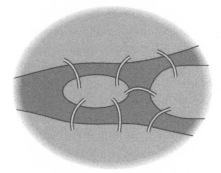

Figure 1.1 The bridges of Königsberg

that either every vertex or every vertex but two is touched by an even number of edges. (In fact, none is: one is touched by five edges, and each of the others is touched by three edges.) Any successful bridge-crosser would have to enter a given vertex exactly as many times as she leaves it unless the vertex is the start or the end of her trip. So among the vertices, either none (if the trip starts and ends at the same vertex) or two could touch an odd number of edges. Intuitively, this explanation is distinctively mathematical. It would not have been a distinctively mathematical explanation if it had instead been that no one ever tried turning left rather than right after crossing a given bridge, or that the bridges were made of a material that would immediately corrode anything in contact with them, or that someone was poised to shoot anyone who tried to cross a given bridge. By the same token, Lazare Carnot (1803, xxxvii) said: "If I propose to move a knight in the game of chess over all the squares on the chessboard, without passing twice over any given one, it doesn't concern me at all what is the mass of the knight and the force that I employ to move it." Carnot held that there is a separate science to cover such cases: "the theory of motion, considered in abstraction from the forces that produce or transmit it." This science supplies distinctively mathematical explanations.

As another example, consider why a particular attempt—or every past attempt, or every attempt ever—fails to unknot a given trefoil knot (see fig. 1.2) without cutting it. A distinctively mathematical explanation is that in three dimensions, the trefoil knot is distinct from the unknot. This explanation seems sharply different from an appeal to the fact that the knot was too tight, or that the rope was too hot to touch, or that all of those who tried to untie the knot gave up before they tried twisting the rope in a certain subtle way—each of which might explain why every attempt to disentangle some knot failed.[5]

Lipton gives the following example:

Suppose that a bunch of sticks are thrown into the air with a lot of spin so that they twirl and tumble as they fall. We freeze the scene as the sticks are in free fall

Figure 1.2 A trefoil knot

and find that appreciably more of them are near the horizontal than near the vertical orientation. Why is this? The reason is that there are more ways for a stick to be near the horizontal than near the vertical. To see this, consider a single stick with a fixed midpoint position. There are many ways this stick could be horizontal (spin it around in the horizontal plane), but only two ways it could be vertical (up or down). This asymmetry remains for positions near horizontal and vertical, as you can see if you think about the full shell traced out by the stick as it takes all possible orientations. (Lipton 2004a, 9–10; see Lipton 2004b, 31–32; 2009b, 622)

Mancosu (2008, 134) says that the mathematical explanation of physical phenomena is "well illustrated" by Lipton's example. (Shortly I will demur.)

Perhaps these few examples suffice to suggest that, as Steiner (1978b, 18) says, "one senses a striking difference" between distinctively mathematical scientific explanations and ordinary scientific explanations that use mathematics. In the following sections, I will examine various proposals for capturing this difference and understanding how these explanations work. Ultimately, I will argue that roughly speaking, these explanations explain not by describing the world's causal structure, but rather by revealing that the explanandum is *necessary*—in particular, more necessary than ordinary laws of nature are. The Königsberg bridges as so arranged were never crossed because they *couldn't* be crossed. Mother's strawberries were not distributed evenly among her children because they *couldn't* be. The three jellybeans I selected were not all of different colors because they *couldn't* have been. Four students in Lipton's class had their last birthday on the same day of the week because this fact "could not have been otherwise" (Lipton 2009a, 47). A trefoil knot was never untied because it *couldn't* be. While Earth exists, there are always antipodal equatorial points at the same temperature because there *must* be. These necessities are stronger than the variety of necessity possessed by ordinary laws of nature, setting explanations like these apart from ordinary scientific explanations. Ultimately, I will suggest that distinctively mathematical scientific explanations work by appealing only to facts (including but not always limited to mathematical facts) that are

modally stronger than ordinary laws of nature, together with contingent conditions that are contextually understood to be constitutive of the arrangement or
task at issue in the why question.

In this way, distinctively mathematical explanations are examples of what
I will dub "explanations by constraint," a kind of scientific explanation that has
received scant attention from philosophers but that I will examine at length in
the next three chapters. Explanations by constraint work not by describing the
world's causal relations, but rather by describing how the explanandum arises
from certain facts ("constraints") possessing some variety of necessity stronger
than ordinary laws of nature possess. The mathematical facts figuring in distinctively mathematical explanations possess one such stronger variety of necessity: mathematical necessity. But (I will argue in subsequent chapters) science
has taken seriously the idea that there are other varieties of necessity that are
stronger than ordinary natural necessity and so that there are other "constraints"
besides mathematical facts.

Although it has sometimes been suggested that distinctively mathematical
scientific explanations are "non-causal," this idea requires careful elaboration
(as I will show in the next section). Mancosu (2008, 135) tries to capture the
distinction between distinctively mathematical and ordinary scientific explanations by saying that the former "is explanation in natural science that is carried
out by essential appeal to mathematical facts."[6] But this criterion fails to exclude
many ordinary scientific explanations. For example, to explain why the electric
field strength at a distance r from a long, linear charge distribution with static
uniform charge density λ is equal (in Gaussian CGS units) to $2\lambda/r$, we can
integrate the contributions to the field (given by Coulomb's law) from all segments of the line charge (Purcell 1965, 28). When the integral is simplified, it
becomes $(\lambda/r)\int_{-\pi/2}^{\pi/2}\cos\theta d\theta$. The explanation then makes essential appeal to the
mathematical fact that $\int_{-\pi/2}^{\pi/2}\cos\theta d\theta = 2$. But intuitively this explanation is not
distinctively mathematical.

An account of the distinction between distinctively mathematical explanations and ordinary scientific explanations that use mathematics should do justice to the conflicting ways in which we may find ourselves pulled in trying to
classify a given explanation. For example, we may not entirely share Mancosu's
confidence that Lipton's explanation of why more tossed sticks are nearly horizontal than nearly vertical is distinctively mathematical. Perhaps what is doing
the explaining is a propensity of the stick-tossing mechanism (that it is equally
likely to produce a tossed stick having any initial orientation) together with
a propensity of the surrounding air molecules (that they are equally likely to
push a tossed stick in any direction). After all, if the tossed sticks were instead all

spinning uniformly about axes in the horizontal plane, they would be as likely at any moment to be vertical as horizontal, contrary to what we observe. If the explanans in Lipton's example includes the propensities of the stick-tossing mechanism and air molecules, then Lipton's example seems like the explanation of a fair coin's behavior in terms of the propensities of the chance setup (or the explanation of a gas's behavior in terms of the statistical-mechanical propensities of its molecules) rather than like the other examples I have given of distinctively mathematical explanations. An account of distinctively mathematical explanations should shed some light on this example. (I will return to it at the end of section 1.5.)

Most of the literature that I will cite concerning distinctively mathematical explanations has been motivated largely by "indispensability arguments" for the existence of mathematical entities. The basic thought behind these arguments is that if scientific theories must quantity over numbers, functions, sets, and other mathematical entities, then in accepting these theories, we are committed to the existence of these abstract entities just as we are committed to the existence of the concrete unobservable entities that these theories posit (such as electrons and the electromagnetic field). Some philosophers believe that this argument is strengthened by the fact that some scientific explanations are distinctively mathematical. Other philosophers believe that the mathematical entities figuring in these explanations are not doing the same kind of explanatory work as concrete unobservables do or that we do not become committed to the existence of abstract entities in accepting theories that quantify over them. In any case, this ontological debate in the philosophy of mathematics is irrelevant to my discussion. Philosophers engaged in this debate have generally paid relatively little attention to the questions I am pursuing: How do these "distinctively mathematical" scientific explanations differ from ordinary scientific explanations that use mathematics and how do they succeed in explaining?

Of course, we might say that a scientific explanation qualifies as "distinctively mathematical" exactly when it uses mathematics in the manner that indispensability arguments exploit—that is, exactly when the explanans must quantify over mathematical entities. However, on this way of using the term "distinctively mathematical," the ordinary scientific explanation of the fact that an infinite uniform line charge's electric field strength is inversely proportional to r counts as distinctively mathematical. This explanation quantifies over mathematical entities: the explanans includes the fact that there exists a function in which r appears solely as $(1/r)$ and that solves the integral generated by summing the contributions to the field from all segments of the line charge. Therefore, this way of using the term "distinctively mathematical" does not help to capture the intuitive difference between the various explanations that I have just given and ordinary scientific explanations that use mathematics.

In section 1.2, I will consider whether distinctively mathematical explanations are set apart by their failure to cite causes. I will argue that on the contrary, many ordinary scientific explanations fail to identify causes of the explanandum and at least some distinctively mathematical explanations do cite the explanandum's causes. Having adopted a broad notion of what makes an explanation "causal," I will argue in section 1.3 that distinctively mathematical explanations are non-causal. I will also argue that we must refine the explanatory target very carefully before we can agree with those philosophers who characterize certain explanations appealing to natural selection as distinctively mathematical. In sections 1.4 and 1.5, I will elaborate and defend my account of how distinctively mathematical explanations work. I will argue that even when such an explanation appeals to a contingent law of nature, it works by showing the explanandum to be necessary in a stronger sense than any causal explanation could.

■ 1.2 ARE DISTINCTIVELY MATHEMATICAL EXPLANATIONS SET APART BY THEIR FAILURE TO CITE CAUSES?

Mancosu (2008, 135) regards distinctively mathematical explanations as "counterexamples to the causal theory of explanation." Lipton (2004a, 9–10; 2009a, 47) and Kitcher (1989, 426) agree. Their remarks suggest that distinctively mathematical explanations are set apart from ordinary scientific explanations by their failure to specify the explanandum's causes. Writing about the tossed sticks, Lipton apparently thinks that an explanation is "causal" if and only if it cites causes of the explanandum: "The explanation why more sticks are near the horizontal than near the vertical is that there are two horizontal dimensions but only one vertical one. This is a lovely explanation, but apparently not a causal one, since geometrical facts cannot be causes" (Lipton 2004b, 31–32). However, there are two problems with the suggestion that distinctively mathematical explanations are non-causal by virtue of their failure to cite any causes of the explanandum: (1) many ordinary, causal scientific explanations fail to specify any causes of the explanandum, and (2) at least some distinctively mathematical explanations do cite the explanandum's causes. Although I agree with Mancosu, Lipton, and Kitcher that distinctively mathematical explanations are non-causal, we must be careful not to join Colyvan (1998, 324–325) in identifying an explanation as non-causal just when "it makes no appeal to causally active entities."[7]

For example, as Beebee (2004, 301–304) emphasizes, a typical explanation that appeals only to an omission or absence (along with laws of nature) is causal even though strictly speaking (according to many philosophers), an omission is not a cause since it is not even an event; it involves nothing happening. For example, Brandon (2006, 321) says that when we explain (according to classical physics) why a given body is moving uniformly (i.e., not accelerating) by citing the absence of any forces on it, we give a causal explanation that cites no causes since it cites no forces. Of course, on this view, the uniform motion of a body feeling no forces has no causes, strictly speaking.[8] Nevertheless, it has a causal explanation. The explanation works by citing a law that specifies how a body must move in the absence of any cause influencing its motion.

There are also causal explanations that cite no causes of the explanandum even though the explanandum has causes. For instance, many philosophers (e.g., Prior, Pargetter, and Jackson 1982) regard dispositions as causally impotent to bring about their manifestations. That is because the connection between a disposition (e.g., being water-soluble), its trigger (being immersed in water), and its manifestation (dissolving) is metaphysically necessary; the identities of these properties are enough to connect them in this way. In contrast, the link between causes and their effects is much weaker: mere natural necessity (that is, the kind of necessity possessed by ordinary laws of nature). Nevertheless, many philosophers (such as Lewis 1986b, 221; Jackson and Pettit 1992, 10) believe that a body's water-solubility, for example, causally explains why it dissolved when it was immersed in water. Though this explanation does not specify the molecular features of the body and water that caused the body to dissolve on being immersed in water, it is still informative regarding the causes of the body's dissolving. For instance, it rules out other possible causes of the body's dissolving, such as the body's being installed in a contraption that replaces the water with a different liquid—a powerful solvent—once the body is immersed in the water.

Instead of an explanation that uses a disposition to explain its manifestation, consider an explanation of the disposition itself. According to many philosophers, the possession of various categorical properties by various entities (together with some natural laws) explains why some entity possesses a given disposition. Such an explanation may be causal (I will argue) even though the disposition's categorical base does not *cause* the disposition. For instance, the categorical ground of a key's power to open a distant lock resides in the key's structure and the lock's structure, but the lock's structure is not a *cause* of the key's power (on pain of action at a distance on the cheap).

Thus, many explanations that fail to cite the explanandum's causes (even when it has causes) are nevertheless causal explanations. Accordingly, I will adopt a broad conception of what makes an explanation "causal": that it explains by virtue of describing contextually relevant features of the explanandum's causal history or, more broadly, of the world's network of causal relations. To do this, it does not need to specify any causes. When a body's water-solubility explains why it dissolved when it was immersed in water, the explanans explains without identifying the particular causally efficacious properties possessed by the immersed body and the water (having to do with various molecular forces and their causes). That the immersed body is water-soluble explains by supplying information about the explanandum's causal history. By the same token (as Jackson and Pettit 1990 argue, and Colyvan 1998, 324 also maintains), when the squareness of a rigid peg of side L explains its failure to fit through a round hole of diameter L (made through a rigid board), the peg's squareness is not itself a cause of the failure to fit. Rather, it ensures that there are such causes—namely, contact forces between the peg and the material surrounding the hole. Thus, the peg's squareness figures in a causal explanation despite not being causally efficacious.

The peg's squareness, though not itself a cause, ensures that the peg would still have failed to fit though the hole in the board even if the peg had been aligned differently with the hole so that the particular peg and board molecules that actually strongly repelled one another remained too far apart to interact. Other peg and board molecules would have strongly repelled one another instead. The peg's squareness explains not just by describing the actual causes of the outcome, but also by telling us that had different initial conditions prevailed, similar causes would have produced a failure to fit through the hole. As Jackson and Pettit (1992) emphasize, many causal explanations derive their explanatory power partly from describing what the world's network of causal relations would have been like under other conditions. Railton (1981, 251) nicely captures why such explanations are best understood as importantly like explanations that work by specifying the outcome's actual causes:

> this sort of causal process is such that its macroscopic outcomes are remarkably insensitive (in the limit) to wide variations in initial microstates. The stability of an outcome of a causal process in spite of significant variation in initial conditions can be informative about an ideal causal explanatory text in the same way that it is informative to learn, regarding a given causal explanation of the First World War, that a world war would have come about (according to this explanation) even if no bomb had exploded in Sarajevo. This sort of robustness or resilience of a process is important to grasp in coming to know explanations based upon it.

Similarly, the explanation of Mother's failure to distribute her 23 strawberries evenly (without cutting any) among her 3 children reveals that her failure is insensitive to her precise technique for distributing strawberries. However, this explanation does *not* work by describing the various causal relations that would have obtained if she had tried other ways of distributing the strawberries, and then showing that each of these causal processes would have failed to distribute the strawberries evenly. This explanation does not describe any technique of strawberry distribution. It derives its explanatory power neither by virtue of describing the actual causes nor by telling us about what the network of causal relations would have been like under other initial conditions. Rather (I will argue), this explanation shows the outcome to be inevitable to a stronger extent than facts merely about causal relations (actual and counterfactual) could make it. This explanation is distinctively mathematical.

Sober (1983; 1984, 139–142) has characterized "equilibrium explanations" that work by describing not only the actual causal relations, but also the causal relations that would have obtained under other initial conditions. Sober's chief example is R. A. Fisher's natural-selection explanation of the fact that the sex ratio at reproductive age is 1:1 in many species. The gist of Fisher's explanation is that if a population contains more males than females, then individuals who have a heritable tendency to produce more female than male offspring will tend to have more grandchildren than individuals without this tendency, and so this tendency will tend to spread and to restore the sex ratio to 1:1. If, on the other hand, a population contains more females than males, then the heritable tendency to produce more male than female offspring will be selectively advantageous, tending to restore the 1:1 ratio. Sober correctly emphasizes that such an equilibrium explanation of a population's current 1:1 ratio does not describe the particular causal path by which the population arrived at that ratio; it does not specify the varying sex ratios or selection pressures at earlier moments. Rather, the explanation works by showing how the tendency to return to a 1:1 ratio arises from various unchanging features of the population, including that the only selection pressure on the sex ratio is selection for individuals who have a tendency to overproduce the minority sex, that such a heritable tendency is present among some members of the population, and that male and female offspring require the same resources.

Sober (1983, 204) insists that a causal explanation of a population's current 1:1 ratio would differ from an equilibrium explanation in describing the actual history of the population's sex ratio and selection pressures. Sober concludes that an equilibrium explanation is not a causal explanation. But I see no reason to regard explanations that work by specifying the actual causes as fundamentally different from explanations that work by describing what the causes would have been like under certain conditions that extend significantly beyond the actual ones. Accordingly, unlike Sober in 1983, I take equilibrium explanations to be causal explanation.[9]

Both equilibrium explanations and distinctively mathematical explanations show the facts being explained to be inevitable. But equilibrium explanations (unlike distinctively mathematical explanations) work by describing the world's causal structure and so (I will argue) cannot show the fact being explained to be as inevitable as distinctively mathematical explanations do. Mother's success was *mathematically* impossible, not merely impossible by virtue of the world's causal structure. As Sober (1983, 207) remarks, an "equilibrium explanation situates [the sex ratio's] actual trajectory (whatever it may have been) in a more encompassing structure." That structure is a causal structure.[10]

Let's see another sort of causal explanation that specifies no actual causes of the fact being explained, but works by virtue of identifying the causal relations that would obtain under various conditions. Consider the explanation (given in section 1.1) of the derivative law concerning the strength of the electric field of a uniform infinite line charge. This explanation works by deducing the explanandum from Coulomb's law. This is a causal explanation even though "the explanation of a general law by deductive subsumption under theoretical principles is clearly not an explanation by causes" (Hempel 1965, 352) since laws are not causes. The explanandum is a law and so has no causes; its explainers are not causes. Nevertheless, this explanation works by describing part of the world's network of causal relations—in particular, the causes of the electric fields of uniform infinite line charges (namely, line-charge segments) and how the contributions made by the various causes of a given infinite line charge's field combine. A general regularity (whether a law, correlation, or statistical-relevance relation) is explained causally by relevant features of the causal mechanisms that produce the events figuring in the regularity. As another example, take the explanation of Kepler's "laws" by Newton's laws of motion and gravity (and some contingent features of the solar system). Harman (1986, 73) calls this explanation "non-causal" since it does not work by citing prior events that caused a given event; neither the explanans nor the explanandum specifies events. By contrast, I would emphasize that this explanation of Kepler's laws works by describing the way planetary motion is caused. Therefore, I deem it to be a causal explanation.[11]

Consider again the explanation of the derivative law concerning the strength of the electric field of a uniform infinite line charge. Perhaps there happens never to be a uniform infinite line charge. The explanation of the derivative law then cannot work by describing the causal histories of the fields of actual uniform infinite line charges. Nevertheless, the explanation remains causal. It works not by describing any actual event's causes, but rather by describing the world's network of causal relations—specifically, by describing what that network would have been like, had there been an infinite line charge.[12] In this respect, the explanation is like Sober's "equilibrium explanation": it works by describing what would cause what.

Likewise, to explain why neon is chemically inert, we could give the various causal mechanisms behind the chemical activity of other atoms and then show why atoms like neon (having filled outer electronic shells) are unable to form chemical bonds in any of these ways. This is a causal explanation of neon's inertness even though (as Kitcher 1985, 637 says) it does not describe any causal processes at work in neon. It explains by virtue of describing the world's network of causal relations (in particular, the causes of other atoms' chemical activity).

Similarly, when a disposition is explained by its categorical base (and natural laws), the categorical base does not cause the disposition (as I mentioned earlier). The explanation does not supply information about the disposition's causal history (since the disposition has none, strictly speaking). Lewis (1986b, 223–224) says that no event is being explained. But, as Lewis also says, the explanation is nevertheless causal in that it works by supplying relevant information about the world's network of causal relations. The categorical base explains the disposition by virtue of the base's role as what would cause any manifestations of the disposition.

By the same token, when we explain why some body is moving uniformly (rather than nonuniformly) by noting that the body is experiencing no forces, we are not giving the explanandum's causes (since it has none). But we are explaining by virtue of describing a relevant aspect of the world's network of causal relations. In particular, we are explaining by specifying the forces (the acceleration-causers) that are acting on the body, namely, none. That there are no forces acting on the body qualifies as explanatorily relevant by virtue of the fact that forces cause accelerations. Likewise, the explanation cites a law (Newton's first law of motion) that helps to explain by virtue of governing how bodies behave in the absence of any causes of accelerations (that is, forces). We have here a causal explanation because the facts that explain are explanatorily relevant by virtue of their significance regarding the world's network of causal relations.[13]

Likewise, we might explain why visible light has a given speed in a given medium by the fact that electromagnetic waves within a certain range of frequencies have that speed there together with the fact that visible light consists of electromagnetic waves in that frequency range. Light's speed is not *caused* by the speed of electromagnetic waves since visible light and electromagnetic waves of those frequencies are not distinct things; light is identical to electromagnetic waves in that frequency range. Nevertheless, an explanation of light's behavior that appeals to some properties of electromagnetic waves is a causal explanation because it works by supplying relevant information about the world's network of causal relations. For instance, an explanation of light's speed in a given medium that appeals to the speed of electromagnetic waves there works by telling us that light's speed in that medium is caused by whatever causes the speed of electromagnetic waves there—and that those factors cause light's speed by virtue of causing electromagnetic waves' speed. The reverse is not true; although light is an electromagnetic wave, light behaves as it does by virtue of being an electromagnetic wave, not the reverse. The laws of electromagnetism causally explain the laws of light (just as the Coulomb's law causally explains the laws giving the electric field of a long linear uniform charge distribution). Just as a machine's capacity to do something is explained causally by some of the capacities that its components possess (capacities that combine to form the capacity being explained), so likewise light's capacity to do something is explained causally by the capacities of the electromagnetic waves that constitute it. These are all causal explanations because they work by supplying information about the causes that some effects would have. For instance, light's color and intensity acquire their powers to affect the eye by virtue of being electromagnetic properties.[14]

In short, then, what makes an explanation "causal" is not that it cites the explanandum's causes, since the explanandum in a causal explanation need not have any causes, and even if it does, a causal explanation need not specify them—and (as I will show shortly) even a non-causal explanation may specify the explanandum's causes. Rather, what makes an explanation "causal" is how it works: that it derives its explanatory power by virtue of supplying relevant information about the explanandum's causes or, more broadly, about the world's network of causal relations. In other words, in a causal explanation, an explainer's explanatory credentials derive partly from the information it supplies regarding the world's network of causal relations. Any causes cited by a causal explanation explain by virtue of being causes and thereby supplying information about the network of causal relations—and since even non-causes can supply such information, they can figure in causal explanations, too. As I will show, when causes figure in non-causal explanations, the source of their explanatory power is not their status as causes.

Of course, this is not to say that in a causal explanation, any information whatever about the world's network of causal relations (or even about the explanandum's causes in particular) is explanatory. A principal aim of any account of causal explanation is to specify what makes some such information explanatorily relevant. The length of a building's shadow and the sun's angle of elevation in the sky supply some information about the cause of the building's height: that it caused a building tall enough to cast a shadow of that length when the sun is elevated to that angle. But the shadow's length and the sun's angle nevertheless do not help to explain the building's height because they do not supply the right sort of information about the world's network of causal relations. A causal explanation works by virtue of supplying the right sort of information about the world's causal nexus, and an account of causal explanation must say a good deal about what determines "the right sort" in various cases.

This conception of what it is for an explanation to be "causal" is hardly original. Lipton (2004b, 32), for example, writes that "causal explanations are explanatory *because* they are causal" (his emphasis). That is, what makes an explanation causal is not that it cites causes or that it supplies information about causes, but rather that it explains *by virtue of* doing so—that this is how the explanation manages to explain. I take this notion of "causal explanation" to be what many philosophers have had roughly in mind in holding that all scientific explanations are causal. Of course, one could use the term "causal explanation" more narrowly than I do, as when Sober (1983, 203) says "A causal explanation describes what the cause is" and concludes that equilibrium explanations are non-causal. As I mentioned earlier, I do not contend that my broader conception of "causal explanation" fits better with firm pretheoretic intuitions about the term's proper use (I doubt there are any) or with the term's widespread use in scientific practice (I doubt it has any). Rather, my conception of "causal explanation" fits the term's use by those philosophers who contend that all scientific explanation is causal and allows us to draw an important distinction between different ways in which scientific explanations work. As I have just shown, some explanations that do not "describe what the cause is" still work very much like explanations that do work by specifying the explanandum's cause. Therefore, it is illuminating to group these various explanations together—especially when we are trying to understand explanations that appear to work in a radically different way.[15] Although my conception of what it takes for an explanation to be "causal" is sufficiently broad to allow non-causes (such as laws) to supply causal explanations and even to admit causal explanations that cite no causes, it is not broad enough to encompass all scientific explanations. Not all scientific explanations derive their explanatory power from describing the world's network of causal relations.[16]

If (as I believe) Mancosu, Lipton, and Kitcher are correct in deeming distinctively mathematical scientific explanations to be non-causal, then those explanations cannot work by describing the world's network of causal relations. How, then, do they work? In section 1.4, I will propose that they work by constraining what there could be.

I have just argued that an explanation that fails to cite any causes nevertheless qualifies as causal if it explains by virtue of describing the world's network of causal relations. By the same token, some distinctively mathematical explanations, though non-causal, nevertheless happen to cite the explanandum's causes. Even so, they qualify as non-causal because they do not derive their explanatory power from their success in describing the world's network of causal relations specifically.

For instance, that Mother had 3 children and 23 strawberries were causes of her failure a moment ago when she tried to distribute her strawberries evenly among her children. That these were causes of her failure is the common verdict of many different accounts of causal relations. For instance, Lewis's counterfactual account says that C causes E exactly when there is a chain of stepwise "influence" from C to E, where C "influences" E exactly when "there is a substantial range C_1, C_2, . . . of different not-too-distant alterations of C (including the actual alteration of C) and there is a range E_1, E_2, . . . of alterations of E, at least some of which differ, such that if C_1 had occurred, E_1 would have occurred, and if C_2 had occurred, E_2 would have occurred, and so on" (Lewis 2007, 476). Such a pattern of counterfactual dependence obtains in the strawberry example: if Mother had had 24 strawberries (or 2 children and 22 strawberries), for instance, then she would not have failed. Alternatively, a manipulability account of causal relations (Gasking 1955; Woodward 2003) says roughly that C is a cause of E exactly when systematic changes in E can be brought about by suitable interventions on C. Clearly, manipulation of the numbers of strawberries or children would bring about corresponding changes in the outcome of Mother's attempt. Likewise, that there are 3 children and 23 strawberries raises the probability of the outcome from what it otherwise would be (in accordance with probabilistic accounts of causal relations), and there is a causal process of "maternal strawberry distribution" connecting the outcome to the initial conditions (in accordance with accounts inspired by Salmon 1984).

Nevertheless, I maintain that this explanation is non-causal because it does not work by virtue of describing the outcome's causes or, more broadly, the world's network of causal relations. The causal mechanism by which Mother distributed her strawberries does not enter into it. The numbers of children and strawberries do not figure in this explanation as causes of the outcome. A distinctively mathematical scientific explanation may happen to cite causes, but it does not appeal to them *as causes*. It does not work by exploiting their causal powers.[17]

That a distinctively mathematical explanation happens to cite facts about the explanandum's causes does not mean that it works by virtue of describing the explanandum's causes. In the distinctively mathematical explanation, Mother's having 3 children helps to explain her failure to distribute the strawberries evenly not by virtue of being a cause of her failure, but rather by virtue of helping to make her success mathematically impossible. By the same token, the fact that 23 cannot be divided evenly by 3 supplies information about the world's network of causal relations: it entails that there are no causal processes by which 23 things are distributed evenly (without being cut) into 3 groups. But in the distinctively mathematical explanation of Mother's failure, the fact that 23 cannot be divided evenly by 3 does not possess its power to explain by virtue of supplying this information about causal processes in particular. The distinctively mathematical explanation does not exploit what the world's *causal structure* is like as a matter of mathematical necessity. Rather, it exploits what *the world* is like as a matter of mathematical necessity: the fact that 23 things cannot mathematically possibly be divided evenly (while remaining uncut) into 3 groups explains why no collection of 23 things is in fact ever so divided. The mathematical fact entails that even a pseudoprocess rather than a causal process (and even a world without causal processes) cannot involve such a division of 23 things. The mathematical fact supplies information about the world's network of causal relations (just as any fact does: that the cat is on the mat tells us that the world's network of causal relations includes no events caused by the cat's being off the mat). But its supplying information about the world's *causal* network per se is not responsible for its explanatory power in the distinctively mathematical explanation. In contrast, in a causal explanation, a fact's supplying (the right sort of) information about the world's causal network per se is responsible for the fact's explanatory significance.

As I showed earlier, there is a non-causal explanation for the existence at a given moment of antipodal equatorial points having the same temperature. Perhaps this occurrence also has a causal explanation that appeals to whatever prior meteorological conditions (and natural laws) explain why those particular antipodal equatorial points have the same temperature (rather than different temperatures) at the given moment. Of course, the non-causal explanation shows that even if meteorological conditions had been different so that the temperatures at those particular antipodal points had been unequal, there would still have been a pair of antipodal equatorial points at the same temperature. Perhaps, then, prior meteorological conditions do not explain why a pair of antipodal equatorial points having the same temperature exists, even though the explanandum is entailed by a (contingent) fact that the meteorological conditions do explain, namely, that these particular antipodal equatorial points have the same temperature.[18] On the other hand, there are well-known examples where C causally explains E even though E would still have occurred, had C not occurred. (Standard examples include cases of preemption, as when Assassin kills Victim, but had Assassin not pulled the trigger, Backup would have done so.) Whether or not the existence of a pair of antipodal equatorial points having the same temperature has a causal explanation is a question about causal explanation and overdetermination that I will put aside.

However, even if there is such a causal explanation for the existence *at a given moment* of a pair of antipodal equatorial points having the same temperature, I contend that if we take this causal explanation and combine it with another causal explanation regarding another such pair of points *at another moment*, then we do *not* thereby explain why it is that *at both moments* there are antipodal equatorial points at the same temperature. That is because this pair of causal explanations inaccurately depicts this similarity between the two moments as utterly coincidental—as having no important common explainers—since the earlier meteorological conditions relevant to one moment are largely disjoint from those relevant to the other moment.

Let's linger momentarily on this notion of being a "coincidence." It is a coincidence that President Kennedy and President Lincoln both had vice presidents named Johnson. This fact is coincidental in virtue of its two components having no common cause—or, at least, none of any interest; in a typical context in which this Kennedy-Lincoln fact is entertained, the cosmological Big Bang (for example) is not of any interest. We can explain why Kennedy and Lincoln both had vice presidents named Johnson by causally explaining why Kennedy had a vice president named Johnson and similarly explaining why Lincoln did. These two causal explanations have nothing interesting in common, and the same goes for every explanation of the fact that Kennedy and Lincoln both had vice presidents named Johnson. That is what makes this fact coincidental.

To understand what makes it no coincidence that at each of the two moments, a pair of antipodal equatorial points having the same temperature exists, we must recognize that for a fact to qualify as coincidental, it is not enough for its components to have no interesting common *cause*. Rather, it is enough to make a fact coincidental that its components have no interesting common *because*— that is, no interesting common *explainer*. In fact, the similarity between the two moments (in that at both, there is a pair of antipodal equatorial points having the same temperature) is not coincidental. The two components of this fact have interesting common explainers (e.g., that temperature is a continuous function of position)—indeed, enough common explainers to give these two components a common explanation: the distinctively mathematical explanation.

Admittedly, then, there may be a causal explanation of the fact that *at a given moment*, two antipodal equatorial points at the same temperature exist. Nevertheless, there is no causal explanation of the fact that *at every moment* (or: at two arbitrary moments) in Earth's history, two such points exist.[19] This fact is explained only by a non-causal, distinctively mathematical explanation.

If the similarity between the two moments had indeed been coincidental (like the Kennedy-Lincoln fact), then their similarity would be explained by the combination of the two separate causal explanations (one for each moment), if there are such causal explanations. But since the similarity between the two moments is in fact no coincidence, any genuine explanation must so characterize it.

■ 1.3 MATHEMATICAL EXPLANATIONS DO NOT EXPLOIT CAUSAL POWERS

I have just suggested that distinctively mathematical explanations are non-causal, even if some of them appeal to causes of what they explain, because they do not appeal to them *as causes*; they do not exploit their causal powers. In section 1.4, I will suggest that if some association between a cause (in the explanans) and its effect (the explanandum) is invoked by a distinctively mathematical explanation, then that association holds not by virtue of an ordinary law of nature, but by virtue of something modally stronger—typically, by mathematical necessity.[20] In this way, mathematics enters distinctively mathematical explanations.

It may be objected that although a distinctively mathematical explanation appeals to mathematical facts, it also exploits the causal powers of some of the explanandum's causes. In the Königsberg bridge case, for example, the arrangement of bridges and islands initially (i.e., at the start of some attempt to cross them) helps to cause their arrangements later (while the attempt is under way), and this fact is crucial to the distinctively mathematical explanation. (After all, matters would be very different if it were a law of nature that whenever someone starts to traverse a bridge, its beginning and ending points come to be touched by an even number of bridges, perhaps by another bridge's coming into existence.)

Likewise, in the example involving Mother's attempt to distribute strawberries to her children, the numbers of children and strawberries initially (when Mother begins her attempt) are causes of their numbers later. That bridges are not brought into existence or caused to disappear by people traveling over other bridges, that strawberries are not caused to replicate by being distributed, and that (in the trefoil knot example) knotted ropes do not spontaneously break, their ends then tending to reunite, all reflect the causal powers of various things and are matters of contingent natural law, not mathematical necessity. These facts underlie the distinctively mathematical explanations I have given.

I reply that these distinctively mathematical explanations do not exploit these causal powers. Rather, the fixity of the arrangement of bridges and islands, for example, is presupposed by the why question that the explanation answers: Why did this attempt (or every attempt) to cross this particular arrangement of bridges (the bridges of Königsberg in 1735) end in failure? The bridges' arrangement does not function in the distinctively mathematical explanation as an initial condition that in fact persists during all attempts to cross the bridges (partly by virtue of various ordinary laws of nature describing various kinds of causal interactions). Rather, the why question itself takes the arrangement as remaining unchanged over the course of any eligible attempt. If, during the course of an attempt to cross all of the bridges exactly once, one of the bridges happened to collapse before it had been crossed, then the attempt in progress would simply be disqualified from counting as having managed to cross the intended arrangement of bridges. The laws determining the conditions under which the bridges' arrangement would remain fixed thus do not figure in the explanans.

If every distinctively mathematical explanation used no contingent laws of nature, then this feature would nicely distinguish these explanations from many ordinary scientific explanations that use mathematics, such as the explanation (described in section 1.1) of any infinite uniform line charge's electric field strength. However, it would not distinguish distinctively mathematical explanations from all non-causal scientific explanations. For example, the non-causal explanation of the fact that Mark Twain and Samuel Clemens have the same height (namely, because Twain and Clemens are identical) appeals to no contingent natural laws (see the preface). Furthermore, even if every distinctively mathematical explanation used no contingent laws of nature, this feature would not distinguish distinctively mathematical explanations from all causal explanations; some causal explanations likewise appeal to no contingent natural laws. For example, a given biological trait's increasing frequency in some population may be explained by the absence of mutations and migrations together with the trait's fitness exceeding the fitness of any alternative to it that was available to the population. Such an explanation appeals to no contingent natural laws, but rather to the principle of natural selection (PNS)—roughly speaking: that fitter traits are more likely to increase in frequency in the absence of mutation or migration. The PNS is a broadly logical truth. (That is, its modality belongs with narrowly logical necessity, metaphysical necessity, mathematical necessity, conceptual necessity, moral necessity, and so forth.) The PNS is not a contingent natural law, but it is also not a mathematical fact.

That one trait is fitter than another entails that there is selection *of* the fitter trait but not that there is selection *for* that trait (Sober 1984). That is, the fitter trait might not *make* various creatures more likely to have a greater number of viable offspring (so it might not be selected *for*), but might merely tend to be associated with traits that do (so that there is selection *of* creatures with that trait). A selectionist explanation of a trait's increasing frequency (or its current high frequency) might go beyond citing the trait's greater fitness to identify the particular selection pressures at work; it might specify whether or not the given trait has been selected *for* and, if so, why. It might, for instance, explain how the trait represents an optimal solution to some challenge that such a creature faces. Baker (2005, 229–235; 2009b) characterizes one such selectionist explanation as a distinctively mathematical explanation. Although Batterman (2010, 3) finds Baker's example "interesting and persuasive" and Leng (2005, 174) agrees that it qualifies as a distinctively mathematical explanation, I think we must first draw some distinctions before we can find here a distinctively mathematical explanation.

The explanandum in Baker's example is "that cicada life-cycle periods are prime" rather than composite numbers of years (Baker 2009b, 624). One possible explanation that biologists have offered is that a species with a periodic life-cycle maximizes its chance of avoiding predator species that also have periodic life-cycles exactly when the species' period in years is coprime to the most numbers close to it (where natural numbers m and n are "coprime" exactly when they have no common factors except 1). That is because if two species' periods m and n are coprime, then their coincidence is minimized (since mn is their lowest common multiple). Since a *prime* number m is coprime to the most numbers close to it (namely, to every number less than $2m$), it is evolutionarily advantageous for cicada life-cycle periods to be prime and so (if this is the only relevant consideration) they are likely to be prime.

However, if this is the reason why cicada life-cycle periods are prime numbers of years, then (it seems to me) this explanation works by describing the world's network of causal relations—in particular, the natural history of cicadas. Consider the explanation that cicadas have prime periods because prime periods have been selected for (and this is the only relevant selection pressure and the PNS holds). This is a causal explanation, since "selection *for* is the causal concept par excellence" (Sober 1984, 100). Suppose we add that prime cicada periods have been selected for over composite periods because some of the cicada's predators also have periodic life-cycles, the avoidance of predation by these predators is selectively advantageous to cicadas, and prime cicada periods tend to minimize this predation while bringing to cicadas no selective disadvantages that outweigh this advantage. This explanation is also just an ordinary causal explanation. It uses a bit of mathematics in describing the explanandum's causal history, but it derives its explanatory power in the same way as any other selectionist explanation. Taken as a whole, then, it is not a distinctively mathematical explanation, though it appeals to some mathematics and to no contingent natural laws.

But suppose we narrow the explanandum to the fact that in connection with predators having periodic life-cycles, cicadas with prime periods tend to suffer less from predation than cicadas with composite periods do. This fact has a distinctively mathematical explanation (namely, the explanation given above involving coprime numbers).[21] Analogous remarks apply to the selectionist explanation that Lyon and Colyvan (2008, 228–229) characterize as distinctively mathematical: "What needs explaining here is why the honeycomb is always divided up into hexagons and not some other polygons (such as triangles or squares), or any combination of different (concave or convex) polygons" (Lyon and Colyvan 2008, 228). The proposed explanation is that it is selectively advantageous for honeybees to minimize the wax they use to build their combs—together with the mathematical fact that a hexagonal grid uses the least total perimeter in dividing a planar region into regions of equal area (the "Honeycomb Conjecture" proved recently by Thomas Hales; see Hales 2001). Again, this explanation works (purportedly) by describing the relevant features of the selection pressures that honeybees have experienced, so it is an ordinary causal explanation, not distinctively mathematical.[22] But suppose we narrow the explanandum to the fact that in any scheme to divide their combs into regions of equal area, honeybees would use at least the amount of wax they would use in dividing their combs into hexagons of equal area (assuming combs to be effectively planar and the dividing walls' thickness to be negligible). This fact has a distinctively mathematical explanation: it is just an instance of the Honeycomb Conjecture. By the same token, "word problems" in mathematics textbooks are full of allusions to facts that have distinctively mathematical explanations—for example, the fact that if Farmer Brown, with 50 feet of negligibly thin and infinitely bendable fencing, uses his fencing to enclose the maximum area in a flat field, then he makes his fencing into a circle.

■ 1.4 HOW THESE DISTINCTIVELY MATHEMATICAL EXPLANATIONS WORK

In the previous section, I suggested that if every distinctively mathematical explanation used no contingent laws of nature, then this feature would nicely distinguish distinctively mathematical explanations from many (though not all) causal explanations that use mathematics, such as the explanation of an

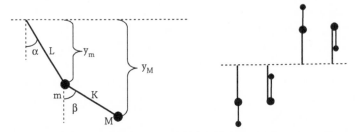

Figure 1.3 The simple double pendulum (left) and its four equilibrium configurations (right); only the first equilibrium configuration is stable.

infinite uniform line charge's electric field strength. However, some distinctively mathematical explanations appeal to contingent natural laws. Here is an example.

Suppose we make a "simple double pendulum" by suspending a simple pendulum from the bob of another simple pendulum and allowing both bobs to move under the influence of gravity (which varies negligibly with height) while confined to a single vertical plane (see fig. 1.3). (By definition, a "simple pendulum" has an inextensible cord with negligible mass and encounters negligible friction and air resistance.) Any simple double pendulum has exactly four equilibrium configurations (see fig. 1.3), where a "configuration" is fixed by the angles α and β. (An "equilibrium configuration" is a configuration where the two bobs, once placed there at rest, will remain there as long as the system is undisturbed.)

One way to explain why a simple double pendulum has these four equilibrium configurations is to identify the particular forces on the two bobs (with masses m and M, as shown in fig. 1.3) and then to determine the configurations in which both bobs feel zero net force. By Newton's second law of motion, they will then undergo no acceleration and so will remain at rest once placed in that configuration.[23] Equivalently, since the force on a system is the negation of its potential energy's gradient,[24] we can express the system's potential energy $U(\alpha,\beta)$ and then solve for the configurations where the energy's gradient is zero, that is, where $\dfrac{\partial U}{\partial \alpha} = \dfrac{\partial U}{\partial \beta} = 0$—that is to say, where U is "stationary" (i.e., at a maximum, minimum, or saddle point):

$$U(\alpha,\beta) = -mg\, y_m - Mg\, y_M$$

$$y_m = L \cos\alpha$$

$$y_M = L \cos\alpha + K \cos\beta$$

$$\text{So } U(\alpha,\beta) = -mg\, L \cos\alpha - Mg\big(L \cos\alpha + K \cos\beta\big)$$

$$\frac{\partial U}{\partial \alpha} = mgL \sin \alpha + MgL \sin \alpha$$

$$\frac{\partial U}{\partial \beta} = MgK \sin \beta.$$

Hence, U's gradient vanishes exactly when $\sin \alpha = \sin \beta = 0$, which is exactly where $(\alpha,\beta) = (0,0), (0,\pi), (\pi,0),$ or (π,π)—the four equilibrium configurations shown in figure 1.3.

This is a causal explanation.

But there is a non-causal, distinctively mathematical explanation of the fact that a simple double pendulum has at least four equilibrium configurations. Since (α,β) and $(\alpha + 2\pi n, \beta + 2\pi m)$ designate the same configuration (for any integers n, m), the configuration space of any double pendulum can be represented as the points on a toroidal surface (see fig. 1.4). Since $U(\alpha,\beta)$ is everywhere finite and continuous, it can be represented by distorting the torus so that each point (α,β)'s height equals $U(\alpha,\beta)$. Any such distortion remains a surface of genus $g = 1$ (i.e., topologically equivalent to a torus, which is a sphere with $g = 1$ holes in it). For any surface (as long as it is smooth, compact, orientable, etc.), the numbers of minima, maxima, and saddle points obey the equation $N_{\min} - N_{\text{sad}} + N_{\max} = 2 - 2g$, which equals zero for $g = 1$.[25] By compactness, there must be at least one maximum and one minimum, so by this equation, there must be at least two saddle points—and so at least four stationary points in total.

This is a non-causal explanation because it does not work by describing some aspect of the world's network of causal relations. No aspect of the particular forces operating on or within the system (which would make a difference to $U(\alpha,\beta)$) matters to this explanation. Rather, the explanation exploits merely the fact that by virtue of the system's being a double pendulum, its configuration space is the surface of a torus—that is, that U is a function of α and β. This topological explanation is similar to the distinctively mathematical explanation of the fact that there are always antipodal equatorial points of the same

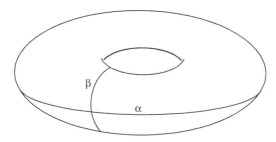

Figure 1.4 The topology of the configuration space of a simple double pendulum.

temperature—except that the relevant surface is in configuration space rather than physical space.

Since the configuration space of *any* double pendulum is a torus, the same explanation applies to any double pendulum, not just to a simple one. For example, the same explanation applies to a compound square double pendulum (see fig. 1.5). It also applies to a double pendulum where the two suspended extended masses are not uniformly dense and to a complex double pendulum under the influence of various springs forcing its oscillation. Each of these has at least four equilibrium configurations, though the particular configurations (and their precise number) differ for different types of double pendulums. Although the *causal* explanation of the system's *particular* equilibrium configurations differs for each of these kinds of pendulum (since their potential energy functions differ), the distinctively mathematical explanation of its having at least four equilibrium configurations is the same in each case.

Perhaps there is a causal explanation of a given double pendulum's having at least four equilibrium configurations (namely, an explanation that first explains why it has certain particular equilibrium configurations rather than different ones, and then points out that those equilibrium configurations number at least four). But even if there is such a causal explanation for a given double pendulum, the combination of two such explanations (e.g., for a simple double pendulum and a complex double pendulum) does not explain why the two pendulums are alike in having at least four equilibrium configurations. That is because this combination appeals to importantly different factors for the two pendulums and so inaccurately depicts as coincidental their similarity in having at least four equilibrium configurations.

The reason I have mentioned the distinctively mathematical explanation of a double pendulum's having at least four equilibrium configurations is that although this explanation does not derive its explanatory power from its

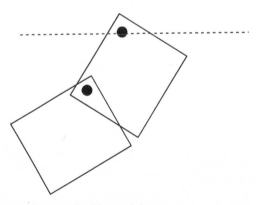

Figure 1.5 A compound square double pendulum

describing the causes operating on the system, it does appeal to a contingent natural law: that a system is at equilibrium exactly when the net force on each of its parts is zero (i.e., when its potential energy is stationary)—a particular case of Newton's second law. Why doesn't this law make the explanation causal? Because, I suggest, Newton's second law describes merely the framework within which any force must act; it does not describe (even abstractly) the particular forces acting on a given situation. Any *possible* force accords with Newton's second law. For example, had gravity been an inverse-cube force, then it would still have operated according to Newton's second law. Had there been some other (physically impossible) kind of forces in addition to the actual kinds, Newton's second law would still have held. Such counterlegals are sometimes invoked in science, as when Ehrenfest (1917) famously showed that had gravity been an inverse-cube force or fallen off with distance at any greater rate, then planets would eventually have collided with the Sun or escaped from the Sun's gravity. Ehrenfest's argument requires that Newton's second law would still have held, had gravity been an inverse-cube force or fallen off with distance at any greater rate. As I will explain further in the next three chapters, Newton's second law—like the conservation laws (to be discussed in chapter 2), the spacetime coordinate transformation laws (in chapter 3), and the parallelogram law for the composition of forces (in chapter 4)—according to many scientists "transcends" (Wigner 1972, 13) the peculiarities of the various kinds of forces that happen to exist (e.g., electromagnetic, gravitational) in that it would still have held even if those forces had been different.

Indeed, even just to say "the peculiarities of the various kinds of forces that *happen* to exist" is to recognize that although these individual force laws are matters of natural necessity, Newton's second law is *more* necessary than they. Compared with it, they *happen* to hold. In other words, although Newton's second law is not a mathematical, conceptual, metaphysical, or logical truth, it stands closer to them modally than an ordinary law does. Thus, an explanation that shows the explanandum to follow entirely from such laws thereby shows the explanandum to be necessary in a way that no explanation that depends on a force law could show it to be—or, more broadly, in a way that no causal explanation could show it to be.

Of course, Newton's second law characterizes the causal relation between force and motion: that the force experienced by a point particle (together with its mass) causes it to undergo a certain acceleration. When Newton's second law (together with the force on and mass of a point body) explains the body's acceleration, it is figuring in a causal explanation. However, that is not what it is doing in connection with the distinctively mathematical explanation of a double pendulum's having at least four equilibrium configurations. That Newton's second law describes a *causal* relation does not matter to that explanation. All that matters is that there is a certain relation between the force (or energy) function and equilibrium, regardless of whether and how one is causally related to the other—and that this relation is modally stronger than the causal details. Recall that the number of Mother's children helps to *cause* her to fail in her attempt to distribute the strawberries evenly. But that causal role is not the role that the number of Mother's children plays in the distinctively mathematical explanation. That role is to make Mother's success *impossible* (in a stronger respect than causal considerations underwrite). Likewise, the causal relation between force, mass, and acceleration helps to causally explain many features of a double pendulum's behavior. But that is not its role in the distinctively mathematical explanation of the existence of at least four equilibrium configurations. Its role there is to make the existence of at least four equilibria inevitable (in a stronger respect than causal considerations could). What matters to that explanation is the law's role in the framework that any possible double pendulum must inhabit. What the law contributes to the explanation is its strong variety of necessity, which helps to make it impossible (in that strong respect) for a double pendulum to have fewer than four equilibrium configurations. This strong necessity makes no contribution to a causal explanation of a body's acceleration; as far as such a causal explanation is concerned, Newton's second law of motion might just as well not transcend the various particular force laws.

Any causal explanation in terms of forces must go beyond Newton's second law to exploit the particular forces at work—if not specifying them fully, then at least appealing to their relevant features (such as their proportionality to the inverse-square of the distance). This is not done by the distinctively mathematical double-pendulum explanation (which is why it can apply to double pendulums that differ in the particular forces at work). Therefore, this explanation qualifies as non-causal despite including Newton's second law. By contrast, even an "equilibrium explanation" of why a given ball, released just inside the rim of a concave bowl, ends up at the bowl's bottom must appeal to something about the particular forces acting, such as the existence of friction between the ball and the bowl's surface. So this explanation is causal despite abstracting from the ball's particular trajectory in the bowl.

Any natural laws in a distinctively mathematical explanation, I will suggest, must transcend the laws describing the particular kinds of causes that exist. In chapter 2, I will make this notion of "transcendence" precise. For now, I will say merely that Newton's second law transcends the particular force laws if it is modally stronger than they. By the same token, mathematical truths (such as those figuring in the various distinctively mathematical explanations that I have examined) transcend the particular force laws in that mathematical necessity is a stronger variety of necessity than natural necessity. A distinctively mathematical explanation works (I propose) not by describing the world's actual causal structure, but rather by showing how the explanandum arises from the framework that any *possible* physical system (whether or not it figures in causal relations) must inhabit, where the "possible" systems extend well beyond those that are logically consistent with all of the actual natural laws. Both mathematical truths and contingent natural laws that transcend the force laws are therefore able to figure in distinctively mathematical explanations.

For example, suppose we had two double pendulums: one simple, the other with inhomogeneous, extended masses and oscillations driven by various springs. Why do both of these pendulums have at least four equilibrium configurations? We could specify the energy functions for both pendulums and then derive separately the particular equilibrium configurations for each, thereby showing that each has at least four of them. But this derivation would portray the explanandum as a coincidence since this derivation would fail to identify some important feature common to the two pendulums as responsible for their both having at least four equilibrium configurations. Since there is such a common feature, this derivation fails to explain why both pendulums have at least four equilibrium configurations. The explanandum has only a distinctively mathematical explanation. That these two double pendulums are alike in having at least four equilibrium configurations is no coincidence because any double pendulum, in virtue of being a double pendulum, *must* possess this property. This *must* is stronger than the necessity possessed by the force laws, and so no derivation using those laws could show that these two pendulums, just by virtue of being double pendulums, *must* have this feature. (I made a similar point at the end of section 1.2 regarding the fact that two moments in Earth's history are alike in that at each there exists two antipodal equatorial points having the same temperature; the similarity between these moments also turns out to be no coincidence by virtue of having a distinctively mathematical explanation.)

In like manner, the distinctively mathematical explanation of the repeated failure to cross the Königsberg bridges works not by describing the world's nexus of causal relations, but rather by showing that the task *cannot* be done— where this impossibility is stronger than natural impossibility. The distinctively mathematical explanation thereby reveals it to have been no coincidence that all of the actual attempts failed. The explanans consists not just of various mathematically necessary facts, but also (as I showed in section 1.3) of various contingent facts presupposed by the why question: that the arrangement of bridges and islands is fixed, that any "crossing" consists of a continuous path over them, and so forth. The distinctively mathematical explanation shows it to be necessary (more strongly so than any particular force law) that under these contingent conditions, the bridges are not crossed. By the same token, the distinctively mathematical explanation in the double pendulum example shows it to be necessary (and more than merely naturally necessary) for a given double pendulum to have at least four equilibrium configurations under certain contingent conditions that the why question presupposes (e.g., that the string does not lengthen, the bob does not explode, the pendulum remains confined to a plane). These contingent facts specify the double pendulum arrangement in question just as

various contingent facts fixing the bridge arrangement are understood to be presupposed by the task of crossing the Königsberg bridges.

Under the contingent conditions fixing the bridge arrangement in question,
that arrangement functions as an abstract, ideal, "mathematical" object: a "graph"
(or "network"). Likewise, suppose we ask (in discussing a classic problem of
geometric construction) why no one has ever trisected a 60° angle using only a
compass and an unmarked straightedge. That such a construction is mathematically impossible explains why no one has ever done it. Once again, the task in
question is understood to involve an ideal compass and straightedge (or physical
instruments that are not exploiting their departures from the ideal).

■ 1.5 ELABORATING MY ACCOUNT
OF DISTINCTIVELY MATHEMATICAL
EXPLANATIONS

Let's take stock of the foregoing proposal concerning the way that distinctively
mathematical explanations operate. I agree with Mancosu, Lipton, and Kitcher
(in the passages cited at the start of section 1.2) that distinctively mathematical
explanations are non-causal. But I do not accept Batterman's (2010, 3) diagnosis that what makes them non-causal is that they involve a "systematic throwing away of various causal and physical details." Many causal explanations do
that, too—including explanations that appeal to one trait's having greater fitness
than another (abstracting away from the detailed histories of individual mating,
reproduction, and predation events), explanations that appeal to a peg's squareness and a hole's circularity (abstracting away from the particular intermolecular forces at work), and (as Jackson and Pettit 1992 suggest) explanations of a
flask's cracking that appeal to the temperature of the hot water in it (abstracting away from the particular collisions between water and glass molecules that
caused the cracking). All of these are causal explanations because they work by
offering "information relevant to the causal history of the thing to be explained"
(Jackson and Pettit 1992, 11; see 3, 9).

A computer program explains why a computer performs some behavior by
ensuring that some electronic event or other occurs to bring about that behavior (without determining every detail of the electronic event). In like manner,
a "program explanation" of the flask's cracking specifies a property (the water's
temperature) that all but ensures that a molecular collision occurs that causes
the cracking, but without determining that collision's every detail (Jackson
and Pettit 1990). I agree with Jackson and Pettit that such a "program explanation" is causal. However, I suggest (contrary to Jackson and Pettit) that some
scientific explanations (such as distinctively mathematical explanations) are
non-causal. Like program explanations, distinctively mathematical explanations
supply modal information. But unlike distinctively mathematical explanations,

program explanations supply modal information by describing the world's causal structure—for instance, by revealing that even if the molecular collision that actually cracked the flask had not occurred, some other molecular collision would still have cracked the flask. A program explanation works by telling us that something plays a certain causal role, without identifying the specific role-filler. Distinctively mathematical explanations do not work in this way.

Likewise, I agree with Pincock's characterization of the Königsberg bridge explanation as an "abstract explanation" in that it "appeals primarily to the formal relational features of a physical system" (Pincock 2007, 257). But I do not agree with Pincock (273) that "abstract explanations are a species of what are sometimes called 'structural explanations' (McMullin 1978)," since McMullin (1978, 139) regards structural explanations as causal: as working by describing the constituent entities or processes (and their arrangement) that cause the feature being explained.[26] On my view, the order of causal priority is not responsible for the order of explanatory priority in distinctively mathematical scientific explanations. Rather, the facts doing the explaining are eligible to explain by virtue of being modally more necessary than ordinary laws of nature (as both mathematical facts and Newton's second law are) or being understood in the why question's context as constitutive of the physical task or arrangement at issue. The arrangement of bridges, the number of students in Lipton's class, the numbers of Mother's strawberries and children, the numbers of jellybeans and available colors, and so forth are explanatorily prior to the outcomes they help to explain in the various distinctively mathematical explanations I have examined—but *not* by virtue of their being *causes* of those outcomes. Rather, in the contexts of the respective why questions, these facts are explanatorily prior to the explanatory targets by virtue of being understood as constituting the situations at hand. They are the fixed parameters of the cases with which those why questions are concerned.

Plenty of explanations abstract from petty causal influences, emphasizing mathematical structure instead—but are nevertheless causal rather than distinctively mathematical explanations. For instance, let our explanandum be the fact that when something diffuses through a homogeneous, boundless, two-dimensional medium after having been released at the origin $(0,0)$ at time $t = 0$ (so the total finite quantity of the diffusing substance starts out infinitely concentrated),[27] at every subsequent time t the concentration curve $\Phi(x,y,t)$ is a Gaussian (i.e., bell-shaped) curve—in other words, the concentration is proportional to $e^{-(x^2+y^2)/c}$ for some constant c. Here is an explanation of this fact, following an argument discovered by John Herschel (1850, 19–20):

> The concentration function is proportional to the function giving the likelihood of a diffusing parcel's being at a given location. A parcel's likelihood of having managed to make its way to some point or other with a given x-coordinate is equal to its

likelihood of being then at some point or other with the negation of that x-coordinate. Therefore, the likelihood of its being at a point with an x-coordinate between x and $(x + dx)$ is dx times some probability density function $f(x^2)$ so that the likelihood is equal whether x is positive or negative. The likelihood function is rotationally symmetric and so the same for the y axis. Hence, the same f figures in the likelihood of a parcel's being at a point with a y-coordinate between y and $(y + dy)$: $f(y^2)dy$. Given the time, a parcel's being at a point with a given x-coordinate is statistically independent of its being at a point with a given y-coordinate, so the likelihood of its being at a point with an x-coordinate between x and $(x + dx)$ and a y-coordinate between y and $(y + dy)$ is the product of their separate likelihoods: $f(x^2) f(y^2) dx\, dy$. But a location (x,y) that is not on either axis can equally well be taken to lie at the coordinates $(0, [x^2 + y^2]^{1/2})$ along a pair of axes rotated relative to the x and y axes, and since the likelihood function is rotationally symmetric, we can apply the same formula to these new axes, so the likelihood of the parcel's being at this location is $f(0) f(x^2 + y^2) dx\, dy$. Therefore, $f(x^2) f(y^2) = f(0) f(x^2 + y^2)$. Any function meeting this condition must take the form $f(x^2) = Ae^{cx^2 + d}$.[28] Since the total probability must add to 1, the constant c must be negative. Hence we arrive at a Gaussian distribution.

Herschel originally used his argument to explain why the results of skillful archers aiming at a target form a Gaussian distribution. Later Maxwell (1860/ 1890, 377) used the same argument to explain why the velocity distribution of the molecules in an ideal gas form a Gaussian distribution, remarking that whether a case involves archery errors or diffusion or ideal-gas molecular velocities, "mathematical expressions of this exponential form are sure to make their appearance" (1871, 289).

How does Herschel's explanation work—that is, why do the various formal features of the concentration curve Φ to which Herschel's argument appeals (such as Φ's rotational symmetry) count as explanatorily prior to Φ's character as an exponential function? After all, we could instead have explained Φ's exponential character by starting with the diffusion equation[29] and then solving it for the concentration given the initial conditions:

$$\Phi(x,y,t) = \frac{M}{(4\pi Dt)^{1/2}} e^{\frac{-(x^2 + y^2)}{4Dt}}$$

where M is the total mass of the diffusing substance and D is the diffusion constant. Obviously, it follows from this complete solution that Φ at every moment not only is exponential, but also has the various formal features to which Herschel's derivation appeals. Why, then, don't these two facts about Φ simply have the same explanation in the diffusion equation (in the manner of two effects of a common cause)—why do the various formal features to which Herschel appeals take explanatory precedence over Φ's exponential character?

The evident answer, it seems to me, is that in apparently appealing to Φ's rotational symmetry, for example, Herschel's explanation is actually appealing to the fact that the laws governing the microcausal process underlying diffusion (such as molecular collisions) privilege no direction. Likewise, when Herschel's derivation apparently appeals to the parcel's x-coordinate being statistically independent from its y-coordinate, Herschel is actually appealing to the axes' independence in the underlying causal processes—as in the vector addition of forces. Similarly, in appealing to the fact that a parcel's likelihood of having a given x-coordinate is equal to its likelihood of having the negation of that x-coordinate, Herschel is appealing to features of the initial velocity distribution of the diffusing particles, the initial state of the diffusing medium, and the laws governing the microcausal processes. In short, the various formal features to which Herschel's derivation appeals pertain directly to the microcausal processes underlying diffusion and in this way derive their explanatorily priority over Φ's exponential character: the explanandum is an effect of causes described by the explanans. Therefore, Herschel has given us a causal explanation. Despite its abstract character (enabling it to apply to diffusion, errors,[30] and ideal gases), Herschel's explanation differs fundamentally from distinctively mathematical explanations. That the microcausal processes underlying diffusion (or archery errors or the velocity distribution in an ideal gas) have these various formal features is neither modally more necessary than ordinary laws of nature nor understood in the why question's context as constitutive of the physical task or arrangement at issue. Instead, these various formal features acquire their explanatory precedence by describing the causes at work.

As I have mentioned, a "program explanation" (Jackson and Pettit 1990, 1992) is a causal explanation that works not by citing a cause of the outcome being explained, but rather by citing a property instantiation that ensures (or renders highly probable) that there is a cause. Jackson and Pettit (1990, 114) treat a computer's having been programmed in a certain way as analogous to the possession of the property that "programs for" the realization of the cause: "The analogy is with a computer program that ensures that certain things will happen—things satisfying certain descriptions—though all the work of producing those things goes on at a lower, mechanical level." The analogy goes further. The fact that a computer now has a certain output can be given a program explanation by the fact that the computer has been programmed to produce that output under certain circumstances and that it occupies those circumstances now. Perhaps this program explanation works by ascribing a certain disposition to the computer, possessed by virtue of the computer's current internal mechanism. Alternatively, perhaps this program explanation works by describing relevant features of the computer's history—namely, what it was programmed to do. In either case, the explanation works by virtue of supplying information about causes.

Suppose that the computer is simply a calculator; it has been programmed to execute addition operations after certain keys have been pressed (under standard conditions). That the calculator displays "4" (rather than some other numeral) is explained by the fact that the keys "2," "+," "2," and "=" were depressed in succession, that the calculator was programmed to display correct answers to equations like this, and that in fact $2 + 2 = 4$. This explanation is just an example of a program explanation of a computer's having a certain output; the explanation appeals to the computer's having been programmed to produce certain outputs under certain circumstances. In this case, the output programmed consists of displaying the correct answers to equations of certain kinds and the circumstances are that the relevant components of one of those equations have been inputted. The fact that $2 + 2 = 4$ is the fact specifying the correct answer to the inputted equation in this case. So this mathematical fact figures in the explanation by virtue of helping to specify a relevant feature of the computer program. Perhaps the explanation works by ascribing a disposition to the calculator. Alternatively, perhaps it works by describing the calculator's history of having been programmed. But in either case, the explanatory role played by the fact that $2 + 2 = 4$ is to describe causal relations: either the calculator's current internal causal mechanism that carries out its programming or the causal mechanism that programmed the calculator before the equation was inputted. Thus, this explanation of the calculator's displaying "4" (namely, because $2 + 2 = 4$ and . . .) is a causal explanation even though the fact that $2 + 2 = 4$ cannot enter into causal relations. The explanation (depending on how we interpret it) is, in brief, that the calculator is disposed (or was designed) to yield the truth about certain sorts of equations fed into it and $2 + 2 = 4$ is such a truth.[31]

Now let's consider an objection aiming to show that there is actually no distinction between "distinctively mathematical" explanations and many ordinary causal explanations. Consider an ordinary causal explanation that deduces the explanandum from statements specifying various causes and natural laws (or from laws alone, as with the explanation given earlier of the law specifying a line charge's electric field strength). Such an explanation consists of an argument that is mediated by a logical truth: that those law-and-cause statements logically entail the explanandum. In involving a logical truth, this explanation is like a "distinctively mathematical" explanation.

However, there is a notable difference between them: such an ordinary causal explanation contains at least one natural law that is modally weaker—less necessary—than all of the natural laws (e.g., Newton's second law of motion) and mathematical truths that figure in distinctively mathematical explanations. (In chapter 2, I will explain this modal difference more carefully.) This difference is connected with the fact that distinctively mathematical explanations do not work in the way that causal explanations do: by supplying information about the world's causal nexus. Ordinary laws of nature have sufficient modal strength to supply that information. But greater modal strength is required to participate in distinctively mathematical explanations. That is because they work by showing the explanandum to be inevitable considering the framework that any possible physical system *must* inhabit (regardless of whether and how it is caught up in a network of causal relations)—where this species of "necessity" transcends ordinary natural necessity. Thus, the involvement of logico-mathematical necessities in ordinary causal explanations is not enough to efface the distinction between those explanations and distinctively mathematical explanations.

In describing how distinctively mathematical explanations work, I tried (in the previous section) to say why the role of Newton's second law in the double-pendulum explanation does not make the explanation causal. Now let's consider why the role of Newton's second law in the double-pendulum explanation does not keep that explanation from qualifying as "distinctively mathematical." After all, Newton's second law is not a mathematical truth; it has greater necessity than an ordinary causal law (such as the gravitational-force law), but it is modally weaker than a mathematical fact. What makes some non-causal scientific explanations (e.g., regarding the antipodal points) but not others (e.g., regarding Samuel Clemens/Mark Twain) qualify as "distinctively mathematical"? The answer cannot be that distinctively mathematical explanations appeal only to mathematical facts (along with whatever contingent facts are understood to specify the physical task or arrangement in question), making no appeal to any natural laws, since the double-pendulum explanation is distinctively mathematical but appeals to Newton's second law.

On my view, a non-causal explanation appealing to *no* mathematical facts (such as the Twain/Clemens explanation) is not a distinctively mathematical explanation. But there is no criterion that sharply distinguishes the distinctively mathematical explanations from the other non-causal explanations that appeal to mathematical facts as (what I will later call) "constraints." Whether such an explanation is "distinctively mathematical" is a matter of degree and context. To the degree that mathematical facts alone are emphasized as doing the explaining, the explanation is properly characterized as distinctively mathematical. For example, the double-pendulum explanation is aptly characterized as distinctively mathematical in a context where the role of Newton's second law is not emphasized—that is, where the explanation is described as showing that the explanandum depends merely on the structure (specifically, the topology) of the system's configuration space (as in Chang et al. 1990, 179). The mathematical ingredient's prominence in the explanans is context-sensitive—unlike the explanation's character as non-causal.

Of course, we could stipulate that "distinctively mathematical" explanations must not appeal to any contingent natural laws. Perhaps "distinctively mathematical" is a somewhat misleading term for the class of explanations I have been examining, considering that the prominence of mathematics in an explanation is not enough to make it "distinctively mathematical." However, what sets these explanations apart (on my view) is not just the prominence of mathematics in them, but also the particular role that mathematics plays in them because of how they work: by revealing the facts being explained to have an especially strong grade of necessity. No matter how prominent the mathematics in a causal explanation, that prominence does not suffice to make the explanation seem much like the distinctively mathematical explanations given at the start of this chapter.

For instance, consider a causal explanation in which mathematical considerations are in the foreground.[32] Why are the tides on Earth more strongly influenced by the Moon than by the Sun (especially considering that the Sun's gravitational influence on Earth is stronger than the Moon's—the Earth orbits the Sun, after all)? The reason is that although the tides are caused by gravity, the tide (the height of the ocean relative to the land) depends on the *difference* between the gravitational influence on the ocean and the gravitational influence on the solid earth. The difference is what matters because a high tide in the ocean nearest the Moon, for instance, results from that water's being pulled harder toward the Moon and consequently approaching nearer to the Moon than the solid earth does. Gravity falls off with the distance squared and (here comes the key mathematical fact) the $1/r^2$ curve diminishes with increasing r much faster at smaller r than at larger r. So since the Moon is much nearer than the Sun, its r is smaller and so the difference between the Moon's gravity on the ocean (at the point on Earth's surface nearest the Moon) and its gravity on the solid earth is greater than the corresponding difference for the Sun's gravity. This difference is great enough to outweigh the Sun's having much greater mass than the Moon, making the Moon's tidal influence much stronger.[33]

Here, then, we have an explanation where a mathematical fact plays a pivotal role. Yet despite the mathematical fact's front-and-center location, this explanation does not seem much like the various distinctively mathematical explanations given at the start of this chapter. Each of those explanations works by revealing the fact being explained to be mathematically inevitable given the arrangement in question, independent of the causal powers operating. By contrast, the tides explanation works precisely by describing (in mathematical terms) the causal powers operating. The mathematical fact figuring prominently in the tides explanation acquires its explanatory role by virtue of helping to describe the causes of tides—in particular, the difference between the Sun's and Moon's differential effect on ocean and solid earth. In short, we find the tides explanation to be markedly dissimilar to the distinctively mathematical explanations given earlier because the tides explanation is a causal explanation and even prominent mathematical considerations do not play the same role in a causal explanation as they do in distinctively mathematical explanations.

Likewise, the contingent facts in the tides explanation (the Sun's and Moon's masses and distances) do not play the same roles as the contingent facts figuring in distinctively mathematical explanations. The arrangement of bridges, for example, is presupposed by the question asking why no one has ever crossed that arrangement, and its causal role is not exploited by the explanation. In contrast, even if the why question regarding the tides presupposes that the Sun's mass and gravitational pull on Earth is greater than the Moon's, the why question does not presuppose the particular values of the Sun's and Moon's masses or, in particular, that the Sun's mass (though greater than the Moon's) is not enough greater to compensate in causing tidal forces for the Moon's being nearer than the Sun. The causal powers of the Sun's and Moon's masses are exploited by the explanation of the Moon's exerting greater tidal forces than the Sun.[34]

Let's return to an ordinary causal explanation: the explanation of the electric field strength of a long linear charge distribution that first uses Coulomb's law to specify the various field components caused by the distribution's various elements, and then adds those components by appealing to the solution of a definite integral—a mathematical fact. Suppose we take all of the nonmathematical facts in this explanation and incorporate them into the why question by asking why it is that when a long, linear charge distribution with static uniform charge density λ has an electric field at a distance r equal (in Gaussian CGS units) to $(\lambda/r)\int_{-\pi/2}^{\pi/2}\cos\theta\,d\theta$, then the distribution's electric field is $2\lambda/r$? The answer is that it is a mathematical fact that $(\lambda/r)\int_{-\pi/2}^{\pi/2}\cos\theta\,d\theta = \dfrac{2\lambda}{r}$. This explanation qualifies as distinctively mathematical. It works not by tracing causal relations, but rather by showing that the fact to be explained is mathematically inevitable. The main difference between this example and the distinctively mathematical explanations given at the start of this chapter is that in this example, we constructed the why question while already knowing that the fact being explained is mathematically inevitable. It then comes as no surprise that this why question is answered by a distinctively mathematical explanation. In contrast, we can easily imagine someone who repeatedly failed to untie a trefoil knot (or to cross an arrangement of bridges), asks why she failed over and over, and only subsequently discovers to her surprise that she was not doing anything wrong: her failure was mathematically unavoidable. It is difficult to imagine an analogous sequence of events occurring in the electric field example. It is hard to see how someone who understood the why question could fail to recognize that with the charge distribution's electric field given as $(\lambda/r)\int_{-\pi/2}^{\pi/2}\cos\theta\,d\theta$, any further simplification is just a matter of mathematics (rather than by way of some additional causal factor).

The philosophical literature contains very few proposals regarding the way that distinctively mathematical explanations work. Steiner (1978, 19) offers one. He suggests that such an explanation contains an argument that not only proves a given mathematical theorem, but also explains why that theorem holds—that is, constitutes a mathematical explanation *in mathematics*. Here we have our first contact between two of the main topics of this book: non-causal *scientific* explanations (such as "distinctively mathematical" explanations) and explanations *in mathematics*—in particular, proofs that explain why mathematical theorems hold. Part III of this book will be devoted to explanations in mathematics. (In section 8.5, I will examine Steiner's account of them.) Although I have not yet investigated explanation in mathematics, I can nevertheless take up Steiner's proposal that a distinctively mathematical explanation in science consists of an explanation in mathematics supplemented by a mapping from the mathematical theorem that was explained to the explanandum of the scientific explanation. In short, Steiner proposes that if all of the physics is removed from a distinctively mathematical explanation, then the remnant constitutes an explanation in mathematics.

The trouble with Steiner's proposal, I think, is that none of the distinctively mathematical explanations that I have given incorporates an explanation in mathematics. Those distinctively mathematical explanations include mathematical facts, of course, but not their proofs—much less proofs explaining why they hold. For example, that 3 fails to divide 23 evenly explains Mother's failure to distribute 23 strawberries evenly among her 3 children, but this explanation includes no account of *why* 3 fails to divide 23 evenly. The mere fact that 3 fails to divide 23 evenly is enough to explain. I am not sure that there even exists a distinction between a proof that explains why this mathematical fact holds and a proof that merely proves that it holds. (There is no such distinction for mathematical facts that have no especially striking features, according to the account of explanation in mathematics that I will give in chapter 7.) A mathematical fact's having no explanation in mathematics would not prevent it from figuring in distinctively mathematical scientific explanations.

Likewise, to explain why no trefoil knot has ever been untied, it suffices that untying one is mathematically impossible, that is, that the trefoil knot is topologically distinct from the unknot. There are many proofs that this is so. Each proof begins by identifying some knot characteristic that remains unchanged in every Reidemeister move (i.e., in every change that is allowable as part of a procedure for untying a knot); the proof then shows that the trefoil knot and the unknot differ in that characteristic. There are many such "knot invariants," including the "unknotting number," the "bridge number," the "minimal crossing number," and "tricolorability." Although each of these proofs proves that the trefoil knot is distinct from the unknot, it is not evident to me which of these proofs, if any, explains why they are distinct. None of these proofs is included in the distinctively mathematical explanation of the fact that no trefoil knot has ever been untied.[35] To explain why no trefoil knot has ever been untied, it suffices to point out that it is mathematically impossible to untie a trefoil knot. It has never happened because it cannot happen.

Let's look at another example from section 1.1 to see whether distinctively mathematical scientific explanations must incorporate explanations that mathematics gives of various theorems—but now let's choose an example where the theorem has an explanation. Consider the fact that when I selected three jellybeans from a collection consisting exclusively of red jellybeans and blue jellybeans, two of the jellybeans I selected were the same color. Here is the mathematical theorem (a special case of the "pigeonhole principle") to which this distinctively mathematical explanation appeals: when there are three objects and the same two possible states (R and B) for each of them, then two of the three objects must occupy the same state. One way to prove this theorem is to deduce it by listing all eight possible state-descriptions (RRR, RRB, RBR, RBB, BRR, BRB, BBR, BBB) and noting that in each case, at least two of the objects are in the same state. But in chapter 8, I will argue that such a brute-force proof fails to explain why the theorem holds. That is because the proof is not a single "common proof" for every case of the theorem. Rather, it treats each state description separately.

By contrast, to explain why the theorem holds, a proof must treat every case together. Indeed, the theorem's striking feature is that it identifies a respect in which each case (RRR, RRB, . . .) is alike, namely, each involves a repeated state. To explain the theorem (according to my account in part III), a proof must trace its striking feature back to a similar feature of the setup: that each case is alike in some other way. Indeed, each case is alike in distributing three objects between two states. From this respect in which each case is similar, we can show that there is another such respect: in each case, 2 objects end up in the same state. Here is the proof. Select one object of the three. Either it is in the same state as one of the others, or it is not. If it is not, then (since there are only two possible states) the other two objects must be in the same state.

This proof of the theorem, unlike the brute-force proof, treats each possible state-description the same way. Therefore (according to my account in part III), this proof explains why the theorem holds, given that the theorem's striking feature is its revealing a respect in which each case is alike. In chapter 8, I will give similar examples drawn from mathematical practice.

But for now, my point is that *the reason why* the theorem holds does not matter for explaining why two of the jellybeans that I selected are the same color. This distinctively mathematical explanation fails to incorporate any explanation (or even proof) of the mathematical theorem to which it appeals. It simply invokes the theorem's *truth*. To argue for this, let me make one final remark anticipating part III. In chapter 8, I will argue that certain mathematical facts are "mathematical coincidences" (such as the fact that the thirteenth digit in the decimal expansion of π is the same as the thirteenth digit in the decimal expansion of e). I will argue further that if a fact is a "mathematical coincidence," then it has no mathematical explanation. Now suppose that the mathematical theorem in the jellybean case had (contrary to fact) been a mathematical coincidence. In other words, suppose that although the theorem could be proved by a brute-force, case-by-case examination of all eight possible state-descriptions (as we just saw), there is no way to prove the theorem by treating all eight cases alike and at once by using a property that all eight cases have in common. The theorem would then be a mathematical coincidence; it would have no mathematical explanation. However, I contend that it could still be used to explain why two of the three jellybeans I selected are the same color—and likewise why *whenever* three jellybeans are selected under such conditions, two are the same color. Therefore, the distinctively mathematical explanation of the jellybean fact that appeals to a mathematical theorem does not work by incorporating an explanation of the theorem.

An account of how distinctively mathematical explanations work aims to fit scientific practice by deeming to be explanatory only what would (if true) constitute genuine scientific explanations. Let's see what my account makes of the following non-explanation:

> Why are all planetary orbits elliptical (approximately)? Because each planetary orbit is (approximately) the locus of points for which the sum of the distances from two fixed points is a constant, and that locus is (as a matter of mathematical fact) an ellipse.

My account correctly regards this argument as failing to qualify as a distinctively mathematical explanation (presumably, it is no other kind of scientific explanation either) because the first fact to which it appeals is neither modally more necessary than ordinary laws of nature nor understood in the why question's context to be constitutive of being a planetary orbit (the physical arrangement regarding which we were posing the why question). In the same way, I would account for the explanatory impotence of another argument. Start with the Königsberg-bridge explanation:

Q_1: Why did no one ever succeed in crossing Königsberg's arrangement of bridges as they were in 1735?

A_1: Because that arrangement, understood as a network, lacks property P, and it is a mathematical fact that a network can be crossed only if it possesses P.

Apply the same mathematical fact to a different city, where the arrangement of bridges *was* crossed:

Q_2: Why did London's bridges as they were in 1900, understood as a network, possess property P?

A_2: Because someone succeeded in crossing that arrangement of bridges and it is a mathematical fact that an arrangement can be crossed only if, understood as a network, it possesses P.

Why does A_1 answer Q_1 but A_2 fail to answer Q_2? One might be tempted to think that the order of causal priority accounts for this difference: success in an attempt to cross some bridges (by a continuous path without duplication . . .) is caused partly by the bridges' arrangement, but their arrangement is not caused by the success of some attempt to cross them. However, if the order of causal priority accounts for the difference in explanatory significance between Q_1-A_1 and Q_2-A_2, then the "non-causal" explanation given by A_1 actually depends upon the causal nexus.

I do not believe that the difference between Q_1-A_1 and Q_2-A_2, as far as constituting a distinctively mathematical explanation is concerned, arises from any fact about causal relations. (Q_2-A_2 may fail to qualify as a *causal* explanation because it runs opposite to the order of causal priority.) Rather, the difference between Q_1-A_1 and Q_2-A_2 in their distinctively mathematical explanatory powers arises from the fact that Q_1 targets the failure to accomplish a given task, and certain facts about the bridge arrangement (which straightforwardly fix whether it possesses or lacks P) are part of what define that task. (The task is roughly to cross a certain arrangement of bridges.) Nothing analogous holds of Q_2; having actually been crossed is no part of what it is for an arrangement of bridges to be the arrangement at issue in Q_2. That is, Q_1 is understood to concern an arrangement of bridges that lacks P in virtue of the particular arrangement it is. In contrast, Q_2 is understood to concern an arrangement of bridges that would still have been that arrangement even if no one had ever crossed it. Thus, A_1 appeals to a feature that is understood to be constitutive of the physical arrangement with which Q_1 is concerned, whereas A_2 appeals to a feature that is not understood to be constitutive of the physical arrangement with which Q_2 is concerned.

How is it evident that the feature to which A_2 appeals is not so understood (unlike the arrangement of Königsberg's bridges in connection with Q_1)? In some cases, the features constitutive of the physical arrangement in question are alluded to in the why question itself. But in other cases, they are not—and this may produce some ambiguity. As an example, let's return to Lipton's explanation (given in section 1.1) concerning the orientation of tossed sticks. It was unclear whether this explanation is distinctively mathematical. It is distinctively mathematical if the explanans does not include the "evenness" of various propensities (e.g., that the stick-tossing mechanism is equally likely to produce a tossed stick in any initial orientation). But if the explanans describes various propensities, then the explanation is an ordinary causal explanation. Which is it?

Lipton did not pose the why question in any particular context (other than that of a philosophy essay), so a crucial part of this question was left underspecified. Perhaps the "evenness" of the tossing (i.e., the symmetry of the various probability distributions concerning the tossing mechanism and surrounding air) is tacitly part of the why question. In that case, the question asks why, in view of these symmetries, the outcome is so asymmetric (i.e., more sticks are nearly horizontal than nearly vertical). How does this asymmetry arise from such symmetry? The explanation is then distinctively mathematical. That there are "more ways" for a stick to be horizontal than for it to be vertical is a feature of space that transcends any facts (including laws) about the particular kinds of things that inhabit space. Even if the laws of motion had been different, there would still have been more ways for a stick to be horizontal than to be vertical. On the other hand, the why question may be requesting simply an appropriate description of the result's causes—without any emphasis on how the result's asymmetry contrasts with the setup's symmetry. Various propensities must then figure in the explanans. This explanation is like Herschel's in that it appeals to some symmetries in the microcauses at work and the facts about these symmetries help explain the explanandum by virtue of pertaining to its causes. This ambiguity in Lipton's why question is the reason we find ourselves pulled in conflicting directions when we try to evaluate whether this explanation is distinctively mathematical.

■ 1.6 CONCLUSION

I have tried to understand the kind of scientific explanation represented by the examples given in section 1.1. I have suggested that these explanations work not by describing the world's network of causal relations in particular, but rather by describing the framework that any physical system (whether or not it figures in causal relations) *must* inhabit, where this variety of necessity is stronger than the necessity possessed by the ordinary laws of nature. My proposal has thus identified what these distinctively mathematical explanations contribute to science that could not be supplied, even in principle, by causal explanations.

In the next three chapters (the remainder of part I), I will look at other non-causal explanations that appeal to modally exalted facts. I will study the varieties of necessity that these facts possess—stronger than the variety possessed by ordinary laws of nature. I will propose an account of what makes one variety of necessity stronger than another while they are all varieties of the same thing (necessity). I will suggest that distinctively mathematical explanations are just one kind of "explanation by constraint," where the "constraints" figuring in these explanations may have any variety of necessity stronger than ordinary natural necessity. I will argue that many important scientific explanations are explanations by constraint. None of these explanations works by describing the world's network of causal relations. Rather, they all operate roughly like the distinctively mathematical explanations that we have been examining: by showing that the explanandum *had* to be—to a degree beyond ordinary laws of nature.

2

"There Sweep Great General Principles Which All the Laws Seem to Follow"

My title is taken from a passage in Feynman's classic book *The Character of Physical Law*: "When learning about the laws of physics you find that there are a large number of complicated and detailed laws, laws of gravitation, of electricity and magnetism, nuclear interactions, and so on, but across the variety of these detailed laws there sweep great general principles which all the laws seem to follow. Examples of these are the principles of conservation" (1967, 59). My aim in this chapter will be to explain this conception of the conservation laws and of certain other "wide principles which sweep across the different laws" (49). I will argue that science recognizes an important distinction: between conservation laws (for instance) as *constraints* on the fundamental forces there could be, on the one hand, and conservation laws as *coincidences* of the fundamental forces there happen to be, on the other hand. In the above passage, Feynman characterizes conservation laws as constraints: as laws that the force laws must follow rather than as coincidental byproducts of the force laws.[1] I will not argue that the conservation laws (and various other laws) are in fact constraints. It is for empirical science rather than metaphysics to ascertain whether they are constraints or coincidences—just as it is up to science to determine whether they are laws rather than accidental truths or even falsehoods. However, I will argue that some conservation laws (and certain other overarching laws) have justly often been taken by scientists[2] to be constraints.

Furthermore, I will argue that their status as constraints would make an important difference to their role in scientific explanations. It would allow them to figure in "explanations by constraint," an important variety of non-causal scientific explanation that I introduced in chapter 1. There I argued that various mathematical truths serve as constraints in explanations by virtue of having a stronger variety of necessity than ordinary natural laws possess. Those "distinctively mathematical explanations" are one variety of explanation by constraint. Other explanations by constraint use other constraints, such as the conservation laws. In this chapter, I will identify what it would take for not only mathematical facts, but also certain natural laws to be able to play this "constraining" role in explanations. In the following two chapters, I will look at other laws of nature besides conservation laws that have sometimes been regarded as "constraints." I will use these examples to elaborate my account of how explanations by constraint work.

In sections 2.2 and 2.3, I will contrast conservation laws as constraints with conservation laws as coincidences. As coincidences, conservation laws are naturally necessary, of course, but they are explained by the force laws. As constraints, by contrast, they help to explain certain features of the force laws. These explanations do not work by describing causal processes and interactions. Rather, they are non-causal explanations—"explanations by constraint." Certain other arguments constitute scientific explanations only if conservation laws are coincidences rather than constraints. I will also argue that if conservation laws are constraints, then certain facts have no causal explanation at all because any such explanation would mischaracterize these facts as more contingent than they actually are. These facts have only explanations by constraint. I will distinguish facts that have exclusively explanations by constraint from facts that have both causal explanations and explanations by constraint. My principal example in these sections will be the various roles that energy conservation might play in explaining Archimedes's principle.

In section 2.4, I will turn from conservation laws to some of the other "great general principles" that have sometimes been reasonably thought to "sweep across" the various force laws, explaining why they are alike in possessing certain features. As examples of potentially overarching laws, I will look at Newton's second law of motion (an example from chapter 1), the principle of virtual work, and the law that all interactions operate through fields of force (to which Hertz appealed in order to explain why, as he thought, all fundamental forces exhibit an inverse-square dependence on distance). Even if some of these principles turn out to be coincidences (or not laws at all) rather than constraints, these examples show that the distinction between constraints and coincidences has played an important role in scientific thinking. An adequate metaphysics should accordingly leave room for it. For instance, even if the particular explanation proposed by Hertz turns out to fail on empirical grounds, metaphysics alone should not have sufficed to rule it out.

In section 2.5, I will argue that conservation laws as constraints would be modally stronger than force laws (though not as necessary as mathematical truths). Here I will look at explanations in thermodynamics offered by Gibbs and Planck. These explanations are able to consider hypothetical states of affairs that are naturally impossible. That is because these states of affairs are thermodynamically possible and because these explanations succeed by showing the explanandum to be thermodynamically necessary, not merely naturally necessary.

In section 2.6, I will offer my account of what it would be for a given law of nature to constitute a constraint and what it would be for the law to constitute a coincidence. I will cash out the distinction between constraints and coincidences in terms of the facts expressed by various counterfactual conditionals. Roughly speaking, I will propose that energy conservation is a constraint exactly when it would still have held, even if there had been additional types of fundamental interactions. Thus, a constraint possesses a certain distinctive kind of invariance under counterfactual perturbations. As I will elaborate, the facts possessing a given variety of necessity are collectively as invariant under counterfactual perturbations as they could collectively be. It follows that the varieties of necessity form a hierarchy with room for different strengths of natural necessity. This picture provides a natural place for the distinction between constraints and coincidences. I will use the same apparatus to cash out the (even stronger) necessity possessed by mathematical facts. I will thereby redeem the promise that I made in chapter 1: to explicate the sense in which mathematical facts and other constraints "transcend" the force laws.

In section 2.6, I will also show how conservation laws could derive their status as constraints from being associated with symmetry principles that are metalaws. I will thereby show how symmetry principles (as metalaws) non-causally explain conservation laws. As a corollary, I will explain why those conservation laws that are constraints cannot help to account for the symmetry principles with which they are associated (because even as constraints, the conservation laws would still be first-order laws rather than metalaws, and so the conservation laws would have insufficient modal strength to explain symmetry metalaws). For a similar reason, the force laws for the forces at work in a given system cannot help to explain causally why a given quantity is conserved there, if its conservation is required by a constraint. That quantity would still have been conserved even if the forces at work had been different.

Finally, in section 2.7, I will examine two influential accounts of scientific explanation that fail to leave room for explanations by constraint: (1) Woodward's manipulationist conception of explanatory regularities and scientific explanation, and (2) the "dispositional essentialist" conception of laws and explanation that has been defended recently by Bird (2007), Ellis (2001, 2002), and Mumford (2004), among others. Woodward's account portrays explanations as specifying what would have been the case in place of the explanandum had conditions been different. But although the momentum conservation law as a constraint explains why all of the interactions taking place in a given system conserve momentum (because they must), the momentum conservation law does not identify circumstances in which an alternative to the explanandum would have held (that is, in which the system's momentum would not have been conserved), much less does it identify some alternative to momentum conservation as what would have obtained instead in such circumstances.

Thus, Woodward's account cannot recognize "explanations by constraint" as genuine scientific explanations. According to dispositional essentialism, laws are metaphysical necessities arising from the causal powers essential to the sparse fundamental properties of physics. Dispositional essentialism, I charge, is unable to allow for different strengths of necessity since all laws are metaphysically necessary and hence modally on a par. In addition, by placing causal dispositions at the bottom of the world, dispositional essentialism portrays all conservation laws as coincidences and all scientific explanations as causal. It thus uses metaphysical grounds to rule out various theories that science has (with good reason) taken seriously. This failure to accommodate scientifically respectable options strikes me as a serious count against dispositional essentialism.

■ 2.2 CONSTRAINTS VERSUS COINCIDENCES

Consider the law of energy conservation.[3] (I could just as well have chosen any of the other conservation laws that have been proposed in the history of physics, such as the conservation of linear momentum, angular momentum, electric charge, mass, parity, baryon number, or lepton number.) As Feynman emphasizes, although the various kinds of fundamental interactions differ in a host of ways (such as in their range, their strength, and the kinds of bodies that participate in them), they are all alike in conserving energy. As convenient examples of kinds of fundamental interactions, I will (following Feynman) take gravitational and electric interactions as described in classical physics by Newton's gravitational-force law and (in the static case) Coulomb's law, respectively. Despite their differences, these two types of interactions are alike in conserving energy.

Of course, gravity is not in fact a force at all according to general relativity, and electric and magnetic forces are not actually distinct kinds of force according to special relativity. But none of this matters to my argument. I appeal to these two forces only to illustrate my claim that physical theory recognizes an important distinction between two ways in which a law like energy conservation could hold: as a constraint or as a coincidence. I contend that any metaphysical account of natural law should leave room for both of these possibilities. The same distinction must be drawn whatever the fundamental forces actually are—indeed, even if there is in fact only a single kind of fundamental interaction (a "grand unified field").

Why are gravitational and electric interactions alike in conserving energy? Here are two possible explanations.[4]

1. Gravitational interactions conserve energy because the gravitational force law requires them to do so. Electric interactions conserve energy because

the electric force law requires them to do so.[5] The two interactions are therefore alike in conserving energy—but for separate reasons.

2. Both kinds of interaction conserve energy for the same reason: because the law of energy conservation requires them to do so.

On the first option, it is just a *coincidence* that both of these forces conserve energy since, roughly speaking, there is no common explanation of their doing so. Of course, an account of why one force conserves energy combined with an account of why the other force conserves energy would, strictly speaking, be a common explanation of their both doing so. But it remains coincidental that both forces conserve energy if the reasons why each conserves energy have nothing important in common. The same idea applies to less exotic examples. For instance, it is a coincidence for two friends both to be in Chicago on the same day if the reasons why each of them is there have nothing important in common (e.g., they had made no plans to meet there, they were not both attending the same convention). Similarly, it is a coincidence for various distinct forces all to conserve energy if there is no important common reason why each of them does so, but rather each conserves energy for a substantially separate reason.[6]

In contrast, on the second of the two possible explanations I just gave for why gravitational and electrical interactions are alike in conserving energy, the law of energy conservation is not a coincidence. Rather, the reason why one fundamental kind of interaction conserves energy is the same as the reason why another conserves energy. The common explanation is given by the conservation law. It is a *constraint* on the forces. The conservation law limits the kinds of forces there could have been to those that would conserve energy, and that is why every kind of force there actually is conserves energy. I will characterize this possible explanation as an "explanation by constraint," in contrast to a causal explanation (such as the first of the two possible explanations I just gave).[7]

The difference between energy conservation as a constraint and energy conservation as a coincidence is a difference in what is explanatorily prior to what. If energy conservation is a coincidence, then the various force laws are explanatorily prior to the law of energy conservation; they are partly responsible for its holding. On the other hand, if energy conservation constrains the force laws, then the conservation law is explanatorily prior to them. It does not suffice to determine the particular force laws there are. But it explains why every force law exhibits a certain feature. These two options (constraint or coincidence), then, are mutually exclusive.[8]

However, these two options are alike in one important respect: whichever option holds, the law of energy conservation is naturally (a.k.a. physically, nomically, nomologically) necessary—a law rather than an accident.[9] Even as a coincidence, a conservation law is naturally necessary in virtue of following from premises that include no accidents but only laws such as the gravitational-force law, the electric-force law, and the law that all fundamental forces are gravitational or electric or . . . (a "closure law"). Despite being naturally necessary, the law of energy conservation is still a coincidence if, for example, the fact that electric forces conserve energy has no important explainer in common with the fact that gravitational forces conserve energy. The conservation law is likewise naturally necessary if it is a constraint. But as a constraint, it transcends the grubby, pedestrian details of the various particular force laws and the closure law. It is a "great general principle which all of the [force laws] follow," as Feynman suggests. It does not depend on the kinds of forces there actually happen to be. Rather, it limits the kinds of forces there could have been. If various conservation laws are constraints, then they carve out a species of possibility: certain kinds of forces that are not among the kinds there actually are nevertheless qualify as possible in virtue of satisfying these constraints, whereas others qualify as impossible not merely in the weak sense that they are inconsistent with the closure law, but in the stronger sense that they would violate the conservation laws.

In chapter 1, I regarded various mathematical truths as constraints in "distinctively mathematical" scientific explanations. For example, Mother fails every time she tries to distribute 23 strawberries evenly among her 3 children (without cutting any) because this *cannot* be done since 3 does not divide 23 evenly. I will contend that if energy conservation is a constraint, then it is like a mathematical truth in possessing greater necessity than ordinary laws of nature do and thereby limiting the *possible* kinds of forces to those that would conserve energy. Explanations by constraint include both distinctively mathematical explanations and the explanations that conservation laws as constraints supply. These are non-causal explanations.

Whether a given conservation law is a constraint or a coincidence makes a difference not merely to whether the conservation law explains why gravitational and electric interactions both conserve energy, but also to whether various other arguments constitute scientific explanations. For example, consider the fact that any ideally incompressible, nonviscous, homogeneous fluid at rest in a container at rest and feeling no external forces besides a uniform downward (let's call it "gravitational") pull does not begin to circulate; none of its parcels at the top feels an unbalanced force pulling it downward, nor do any bottom parcels feel unbalanced forces pushing them upward. Why is that? If energy conservation is a constraint, then it explains why. For gravity or some internal force to make the fluid parcels begin to circulate from rest would violate energy conservation: in beginning to circulate, the parcels' total kinetic energy would increase but their total potential energy would be unchanged. As ascending parcels gain gravitational potential energy, descending parcels lose an equal quantity of it. Any potential energy associated with an internal force would also be unchanged by the replacement of some fluid parcels with others while exactly the same locations are occupied by qualitatively identical parcels. Energy conservation as a constraint rules out any circulation-inducing force.

However, as a coincidence, energy conservation cannot supply this explanation. If energy conservation is a coincidence, then the reason why the fluid undergoes no circulation is that electric forces fail to induce circulation (because of the electric-force law), gravitational forces fail to induce circulation (because of the gravitational-force law), and so forth for all of the kinds of forces (whether internal or external) experienced by the fluid parcels. This is a causal explanation, not an explanation by constraint. As a coincidence, the general principle of energy conservation cannot explain why various kinds of fundamental force are alike in failing to induce fluid circulation, since as a coincidence rather than a constraint, energy conservation is not explanatorily prior to the force laws. The reason why electric forces fail to induce circulation (and, more broadly, the reason why they conserve energy) is not the coincidence that all forces conserve energy; it is the electric force law. As a coincidence, energy conservation cannot explain fluid noncirculation by explaining why the electric force law is such that electric forces fail to induce circulation, why the gravitational force law is such that gravitational forces fail to induce circulation, and so forth.

Could energy conservation, despite being a coincidence, explain fluid noncirculation (simply on the grounds that energy would fail to be conserved if the fluid were to begin circulating) *without* being explanatorily prior to the force laws—namely, while being explained by the various force laws (together with other laws such as the closure law and the fundamental dynamical law linking force to motion)? Let's see. Fluid parcels feel gravitational forces, so the fact that gravitational forces conserve energy may help to explain why there are no circulation-inducing forces. But if fluid parcels feel no magnetic forces, then the fact that magnetic forces conserve energy does not help to explain why there are no circulation-inducing forces. If the conservation law is a coincidence, then it is effectively the fact that gravitational forces conserve energy, magnetic forces conserve energy, and so forth for all of the actual kinds of forces.[10] But if some of these forces are not experienced by fluid parcels, then the fact that they conserve energy is not explanatorily relevant, and so neither is the general conservation law. For a coincidence to be explanatorily relevant to an outcome, each of its components must be explanatorily relevant.[11]

For instance, the reason why the seesaw on which you and I are perched (on opposite arms) is balancing may be the coincidence that each of us weighs 150 pounds (together with the relevant laws and the fact that the seesaw's arms are equally long). Of course, the coincidence that you, I, and Frank each (coincidentally) weighs 150 pounds entails that you and I do. But the coincidence that you, I, and Frank each weighs 150 pounds is not the reason why the seesaw balances, since Frank is not on the seesaw. As a coincidence of the various kinds of fundamental forces, the conservation law explains only if all of those forces are explanatorily relevant.

Admittedly, there is a sense in which the fact that you, I, and Frank each weighs 150 pounds "contains" a fact that helps to explain why the seesaw balances. But that fact does not involve Frank. Suppose we start with the explanation that appeals to the fact that you and I each weighs 150 pounds and that we are the sole riders on the seesaw. Suppose we then add as a further premise that Frank also weighs 150 pounds. The explanandum still follows deductively. But the argument's explanatory power is lost because an explanation can include nothing that is explanatorily irrelevant.[12] Any temptation to think that the addition of the Frank fact does not ruin the explanation, but merely constitutes a harmless superfluous premise in the argument, may be accounted for by the fact that it is easy to see how to carve an explanation out of the argument the includes the superfluous premise. In that sense, the argument "contains" an explanation without itself constituting one.

Of course, an explanation that consists of a deductive argument for the explanandum typically has premises that are stronger than they need to be in order to entail the explanandum. The problem with the Frank premise is not that it is unneeded to entail the explanandum, but that it is explanatorily irrelevant.

Let's return to the conservation law as a coincidence. Suppose that in fact, fluid parcels feel *every* species of fundamental force so that every component of the energy-conservation coincidence is explanatorily relevant. Does energy conservation, despite being a coincidence, then explain fluid noncirculation? Yes, the conservation law is explained by all of the force laws (and other laws, including the closure law) and, in turn, the conservation law helps to explain why the fluid parcels do not circulate. However, the explanation by constraint succeeds even if fluid parcels do not feel every actual kind of fundamental force. In contrast, if energy conservation is a coincidence, then it helps to explain fluid noncirculation only if fluid parcels feel every actual kind of fundamental force. As a coincidence, the energy conservation law is effectively that each of the actual kinds of forces conserves energy. Fluid noncirculation depends on all of these components of the coincidence only if fluid parcels feel each of the kinds of forces there are.

Let's look again at the seesaw by way of comparison. Suppose that there is a 250-pound weight at the end of one arm of the seesaw (where the two arms are equally long) and that either you, I, or Frank (or several of us together), but nothing else, perch on the end of the other arm. Suppose that coincidentally, each of us weighs 150 pounds. These facts (together with the relevant laws) suffice to entail that the seesaw tips (in some direction or other). But only the weights of the persons actually on the seesaw help to explain the seesaw's behavior. That coincidentally each of us weighs 150 pounds helps to explain the seesaw's behavior only if we are all on the seesaw. In that case, the explanans would have to include not merely the fact that each of us weighs 150 pounds, but also that we are all sitting on the end of the seesaw's other arm.

Thus, there is a causal explanation of the fluid's noncirculation in which energy conservation, despite being a coincidence, figures (if the fluid parcels feel every actual kind of fundamental force). By contrast, the explanation that we had originally been examining does not specify or depend on anything about which kinds of fundamental forces the fluid parcels experience. Its point is precisely that the outcome does not depend on what possible forces are actually at work—where the "possible" forces extend beyond the kinds of forces listed in the closure law. No matter which possible kinds of forces were acting on the fluid parcels, the fluid would still fail to circulate.

I have just argued that the following (omitting some of the physical details) is an explanation regardless of which of the actual kinds of fundamental forces are experienced by fluid parcels if and only if energy conservation is a constraint:

> If a fluid begins to circulate, the total energy changes [equivalently: If energy is conserved, then no fluid begins to circulate]
>
> Energy conservation is a law
>
> ---
>
> No fluid begins to circulate

For this to be an explanation regardless of which of the actual kinds of fundamental forces are experienced by fluid parcels, it must be an explanation by constraint.[13] I will now argue that the following is an explanation if and only if energy conservation is a coincidence:

> Fluid parcels experience electrical forces and . . . and gravitational forces, and that's all.
>
> Electrical forces fail to induce fluid circulation (because of the electric-force law and fundamental dynamical law)
>
> ⋮
>
> Gravitational forces fail to induce fluid circulation (because of the gravitational-force law and fundamental dynamical law)
>
> Any fluid circulation requires a force to induce it
>
> ---
>
> No fluid begins to circulate

If energy conservation is a coincidence, then the reason why the fluid undergoes no circulation is that electric forces fail to induce circulation (because of the electric-force law), gravitational forces fail to induce circulation (because of the gravitational-force law), and so forth for all of the actual kinds of forces actually experienced by the fluid parcels. In contrast, if energy conservation is a constraint, then this argument fails to explain why the fluid does not begin to circulate because it depicts the explanandum as depending on which particular kinds of forces are in fact acting on the fluid parcels. But no force that would produce fluid circulation is even possible.

Of course, even if energy conservation is a constraint, the fact that no fluid circulation begins is *entailed* by the fact that neither gravitational forces nor electrical forces nor any of the other forces actually felt by fluid parcels induces fluid circulation (together with the fact that these are exactly the forces felt by fluid parcels and that any fluid circulation requires a force to induce it). But if energy conservation is a constraint, then any proposed explanation appealing to the kinds of forces that happen to exist mischaracterizes the explanandum as a coincidental upshot of those particular forces rather than as necessary in virtue of the kinds of forces there could have been. (When I look at explanation in mathematics in part III, I will present a similar idea. In chapter 9, I will show that Euclidean geometry mischaracterizes Desargues's theorem in projective geometry as a motley collection of results concerning unrelated special cases. Since there is a unified common proof of these various results [namely, a proof in projective geometry], separate Euclidean proofs of these various results combine to *prove that* but not to *explain why* Desargues's theorem in projective geometry holds. But all of that will have to wait until I take up explanation in mathematics!)

Here is an analogy to the way that energy conservation's status as a constraint would make the fact being explained no coincidence and thereby preclude certain of its derivations from having explanatory power. Consider Jones and Smith, each convicted in separate trials before separate judges of possessing (independently) 100 kg of marijuana. Why did each of them receive a sentence exceeding five years? The reason is not that Smith's judge passed this sentence because he believed that Smith's crime rose to a certain level of seriousness because of various factors including . . . , and Jones's judge passed this sentence because he believed that Jones's crime rose to a certain level of seriousness because . . . , *if* the two judges were both constrained by the same mandatory minimum sentencing law to pass sentences of at least five years for the possession of 100 kg of marijuana. If there is such a law, then it is no coincidence that the two judges handed down sentences that are alike in this respect. Rather, the law is a common explainer in requiring the sentences, so they are not the products of judicial contingencies— and any account is mistaken if it depicts the two sentences as the products of independent judicial decisions that weighed the particulars of the individual cases.

Similarly, if energy conservation is a constraint, then the absence of a circulation-inducing force is less contingent than the facts about which particular kinds of forces the fluid parcels feel. Hence, if energy conservation is a constraint, then the absence of a circulation-inducing force has no causal explanation—no explanation that appeals to the particular kinds of forces the fluid parcels feel. Rather, it has only an explanation by constraint. In the same way, the various particular force laws do not help to explain why energy is always conserved if energy conservation is a constraint. In like manner, I argued in chapter 1 that there is no causal explanation of the fact that two arbitrary moments in Earth's history are alike in that at each, there are two antipodal equatorial points at the same temperature. This fact has only a non-causal, "distinctively mathematical" explanation because only such an explanation accurately characterizes this fact as no coincidence and as no product of meteorological contingencies.

If energy conservation is a constraint, then perhaps there is a causal explanation of the fact that *electrical* forces conserve energy (namely, by an appeal to the electrical-force law and the fundamental dynamical law linking force to motion). This is like my earlier contention (at the end of section 1.2) that perhaps there is a causal explanation for the existence *at a given moment* of a pair of antipodal equatorial points having the same temperature (namely, by whatever prior meteorological conditions explain the temperatures at those particular points at that particular moment). But (I said in chapter 1) if there is such an explanation and we combine it with an analogous explanation for the existence of such a pair of points *at another moment*, then we have *not* explained why it is that *at both moments* there are antipodal equatorial points at the same temperature. That pair of causal explanations would inaccurately depict this similarity between the two moments as coincidental. Likewise, if energy conservation is a constraint, then even if there is a causal explanation (from the electrical-force law) of the fact that *electrical* forces conserve energy as well as a causal explanation (from the gravitational-force law) of the fact that *gravitational* forces conserve energy, their combination is no explanation of the fact that electrical and gravitational forces are alike in conserving energy. This combination of separate explanations would inaccurately depict the similarity between the two forces as coincidental.

There are other explanations by constraint that are very much like the explanation by constraint of the fluid's noncirculation. Consider a wooden block (of any shape) sitting on top of a post, and suppose that across the upper surface of the block is laid part of a uniform, homogeneous, perfectly flexible loop of rope (or chain), while the rest of the loop hangs below the block. Suppose the loop experiences a uniform downward force (and no other external forces besides the impenetrability of the block). Why is it that any such loop, having been laid across the block, does not begin to turn round and round the block? If energy conservation is a constraint, then it explains why no force puts the loop into circulation: any such force is ruled out by energy conservation for exactly the same reason as it precludes a force inducing fluid circulation. However, if energy conservation is a coincidence, then this explanation is unavailable, as I have argued; instead, the explanation is that one kind of force felt by the rope fails to induce circulation, another also (for independent reasons) fails to do so, and so forth for all of the kinds of forces at work on the rope. This explanation may involve different kinds of fundamental forces from the corresponding explanation of the fluid's behavior; different forces may be at work on rope parcels than on fluid parcels. Therefore, the causal explanations (if they exist) do not unify these two cases. In contrast, the explanations by constraint (if they exist) not only unify these two phenomena under the same explainer (the law of energy conservation), but also unify them further by giving them explanations of the very same form. (I will say more about this idea in chapter 10.)[14]

Energy conservation's status as a constraint rather than a coincidence makes a difference to its power to explain various other facts about the force laws besides the fact that gravitational and electric interactions both conserve energy. No law of nature posits that a certain field of force pops alternately into and out of existence every other second. (Suppose the field would produce on any point body located within it a force in a given direction that is equal to the product of the body's mass and the field's strength at the body's location, and suppose that this force would then affect the body in accordance with Newton's second law of motion.) The existence of such a field of force (in the absence of something else to compensate for it, such as another field winking into existence whenever the first field winks out and vice versa) would violate energy conservation (as long as there are bodies in the field) since at each moment it winks into existence, the potential energy of each body in the field would change but its kinetic energy would remain unchanged. If energy conservation is a constraint, then it explains why there is no such field (with bodies in it and unaccompanied by other winking fields to compensate for it): because such a field would violate energy conservation. However, if energy conservation is a coincidence, then it does not explain why there is no such field just as it does not explain why there is no circulation-inducing force. Rather, there is no such field because no such field appears in the closure law giving the inventory of the kinds of fields there are. That a winking field (with a body in it and nothing to compensate for it) would violate energy conservation is not a reason why there is no such field.

Likewise, if the conservation of mass is a constraint, then it explains why no 1 kg mass initially at rest at $x = 1$ ever experiences for the next 3 seconds a net position-dependent force $F = x^2$ directed toward increasing x—since such a body would vanish from the universe within that time, violating mass conservation.[15] But if mass conservation is a coincidence, then the order of explanatory priority is reversed: mass conservation holds because of the inventory of the kinds of forces there are, which ensures that no such event ever occurs.

My overall point is that energy conservation's status as a constraint or a coincidence makes a big difference to features of the world that science cares about: to the kinds of explanations there are and the unifications they bring.[16] These are matters that must be discovered empirically. I will not be arguing that if every single fundamental kind of force conserves energy, then this "conspiracy" is unlikely to be a coincidence—that its components probably have a common origin. Instead my focus will be on unpacking what this argument is an argument for—on understanding what it would be for energy conservation to be a constraint. I insist that it is sometimes reasonable to posit constraints, that science has frequently taken such hypotheses seriously, and that therefore metaphysics should not foreclose them.

■ 2.3 HYBRID EXPLANATIONS

I have just presented several examples where a conservation law's status as a constraint or a coincidence makes a difference to some argument's explanatory power. If the conservation law is a constraint, then the explanandum in one of these examples is more necessary than ordinary laws of nature (such as the various force laws and closure law)—but this is not the case if the conservation law is a coincidence. Therefore, if the conservation law is a constraint, the ordinary laws of nature are too contingent to help explain the explanandum. The explanandum is explained only by the conservation law (or other constraints).

However, in other cases where a conservation law's status as a constraint or a coincidence makes a difference to the explanatory power of some argument using that law, the explanandum is not more necessary than ordinary laws of nature even if the conservation law is a constraint. Accordingly, even if the conservation law is a constraint, the explanandum has an explanation that appeals to ordinary laws of nature (such as force laws) and not to any conservation laws. Such an explanation does not mischaracterize the explanandum's modal status. If and only if the conservation law is a constraint, the explanandum also has an explanation in which the conservation law serves as a constraint. Such an explanation has two parts: an explanation by constraint (appealing to the conservation law) and a causal explanation (appealing to a force law or some other fact about the force that is explained by the force law). Without the second part, the explanation could not explain a fact that is more contingent than a constraint. This "hybrid" explanation's power to explain depends on the conservation law's status as a constraint. But unlike the explanations by constraint in the examples that I have already given, the hybrid explanation does not preclude the explanandum from also having a thoroughly causal explanation.

Let's look at an example. Take the explanandum to be Archimedes's principle: that the buoyant force on a body surrounded by an ideally incompressible, nonviscous fluid in a container at rest in a uniform downward gravitational field equals the weight of the fluid displaced by the body. Hydrostatics supplies a causal explanation of Archimedes's principle. As the physicist James Trefil (2003, 22) says, "Archimedes' principle can be understood in terms of kinetic theory. . . . For a completely submerged object, the pressure will be less on its top than on its bottom—the molecules of the fluid will be hitting the bottom of

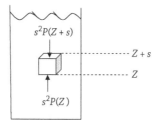

Figure 2.1 Start of hydrodynamic explanation of Archimedes's principle

the object with a greater force than those hitting the top. This is the molecular origin of the upward buoyant force."

More fully (see Pnueli and Gutfinger 1992), the hydrostatic explanation begins by defining a fluid as a continuum that cannot resist a change in its shape, so the force that one fluid parcel feels from contact with another is perpendicular to its surface. Since the fluid parcels are all at equilibrium (i.e., not accelerating), it follows (from Newton's second law of motion) that the forces exerted on all sides of a fluid parcel sum to zero. Shrinking the parcel to a point, we find that at any point in the fluid, there is a well-defined pressure P that is equal in all directions.

Take a cubical parcel of fluid (see fig. 2.1), each side of length s, its faces aligned with the coordinate axes and small enough that the pressure is uniform over any given side. Since the pressure force on a face is perpendicular to it, the total force in the z (upward) direction exerted on the parcel by contact with the surrounding fluid is the magnitude $s^2 P(Z)$ of the force on the cube's base, all points of which have Z as their z-coordinate, minus the magnitude $s^2 P(Z + s)$ of the force on the cube's top, totaling $-s^3 \dfrac{P(Z+s)-P(Z)}{s}$. Gravity is the only force on the parcel that does not act by contact; it has only a z-component: $-\rho s^3 g$, where ρ is the fluid's density. By Newton's second law, $-\rho s^3 g - s^3 \dfrac{P(Z+s)-P(Z)}{s} = ma_z$ for the parcel's mass m and z-acceleration a_z. Dividing by s^3 and taking the limit as s approaches zero, we find $-\rho g - \dfrac{dP}{dz}(Z) = \rho a_z$. Since the fluid's parcels are at equilibrium, $a_z = 0$, so $\dfrac{dP}{dz}(Z) = -\rho g$.

Suppose (for simplicity) that the submerged body is a cylinder of height h with horizontal top and bottom surfaces, each of area A (see fig. 2.2). Let Z be the bottom surface's z-coordinate. The force downward on the top surface exerted by the fluid above it at pressure $P(Z + h)$ is $AP(Z + h)$; the upward force on the cylinder's bottom surface exerted by the fluid below it at pressure $P(Z)$ is $AP(Z)$. (The pressure exerts forces only perpendicular to the cylinder's surface so no upward or downward force is exerted on the cylinder's sides.) The net

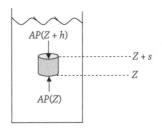

Figure 2.2 End of hydrodynamic explanation of Archimedes's principle

z-force is then $A[P(Z)-P(Z+h)]=-A\int_{Z}^{Z+h}\left(\frac{dP}{dz}\right)dz=A\rho gh.$ The cylinder's

volume is Ah, so the mass of the fluid it displaces is $A\rho h$. That fluid's weight is $A\rho gh$—which (I just showed) equals the buoyant force.[17]

That was a causal explanation of Archimedes's principle. Along with this explanation, a derivation from energy conservation may (depending on energy conservation's status as constraint or coincidence) also explain why Archimedes's principle holds. Such a "top-down" derivation is frequently characterized as explanatory; for instance, a physics journal article (Leroy 1985) says that in view of this derivation, "the origin of the buoyancy force need no longer be mysterious and therefore hidden behind a principle; it can be explained in physical terms."[18] If energy conservation is a constraint, then this derivation from energy conservation constitutes a "hybrid" explanation since it involves not only a conservation law serving as a constraint, but also a force law (or a fact explained by a force law, such as the potential energy function associated with the gravitational force).

Here is such a derivation. Suppose an applied upward force F just suffices to raise the submerged body by a vertical distance d; the body is moved arbitrarily slowly without any superfluous motion of the fluid (see fig. 2.3). By energy conservation, the work Fd thereby done on the system equals the energy added to the system. Since the fluid is ideal, none of the work goes into overcoming friction (which would have raised the fluid's internal energy) and so it all goes into changing the system's potential energy, which (in view of the kinds of forces there are) consists of its gravitational potential energy. The body's gravitational potential energy rises by $M_b gd$, where M_b is the body's mass. As the body rises, fluid flows downward to fill the space it vacates. As a result of its journey, the body effectively trades places with a fluid parcel of the body's size and shape that was initially located at a distance d above the body's initial position (see fig. 2.3). That parcel thus descends by d, so its gravitational potential energy diminishes by $M_p gd$, where M_p is the parcel's mass. Setting the work done equal to the net

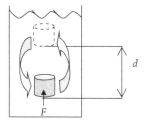

Figure 2.3 Top-down explanation of Archimedes's principle

increase in the system's potential energy, we find $Fd = M_bgd - M_pgd$. Therefore, $F = M_bg - M_pg$. By contrast, had there been no fluid, then the force just suffi-cient to raise the body would have been simply M_bg—just enough to balance the body's weight. But with the fluid present, we need less force by M_pg—the weight of the fluid displaced by the body. That upward force supplementing F is the buoyant force.[19]

Energy conservation's role in this derivation is only to explain why the work done on the system equals the energy added to it—that is (in view of the kinds of forces present), to make "gravitational potential energy" well-defined and to make the work done on the system equal to the change in its gravitational poten-tial energy. But if energy conservation is a coincidence, then (as I have argued) it cannot explain why gravitational interactions conserve energy. Thus, for the general principle of energy conservation to help explain why Archimedes's prin-ciple holds, energy conservation must be a constraint.

Having explained why the work done on the system equals the change in its gravitational potential energy, the explanation goes on to apply the formula for gravitational potential energy. This part of the argument explains by describing the world's network of causal relations; the gravitational force law accounts for the formula for gravitational potential energy. Hence, though the first part of this explanation appeals to energy conservation as a constraint, this explanation does not depict Archimedes's principle as a constraint. Rather, it reveals that the buoyant force depends on gravity in particular—just as the thoroughly causal explanation says. The two explanations are compatible.

Another hybrid explanation of Archimedes's principle begins by using energy conservation to explain why the fluid undergoes no circulation. As I showed in the previous section, that explanation requires energy conservation to be a constraint. The second part of the hybrid explanation incorporates the hydro-static explanation of Archimedes's principle. The thoroughly causal, hydrostatic explanation of Archimedes's principle begins (as I showed) by appealing to the fact that the fluid parcels are all at equilibrium. By contrast, this hybrid expla-nation begins by using energy conservation to give the fluid's equilibrium an explanation by constraint. Once again, this hybrid explanation requires energy conservation to be a constraint, but it allows Archimedes's principle also to have a thoroughly causal explanation.

If energy conservation is a constraint, then there is no causal explanation of the fact that there is no circulation-inducing force. This fact has only an explanation by constraint. Hence, a thoroughly causal, hydrostatic explanation of Archimedes's principle that involves the fact that the fluid parcels are at equilibrium must simply appeal to this fact. It cannot begin with an explanation of this fact and remain thoroughly causal. (Of course, the hydrostatic explanation works despite failing to explain this fact; every scientific explanation must begin somewhere.) It makes no difference to the hydrostatic explanation why there is no circulation-inducing force. It could be a coincidence of the kinds of forces there happen to be or the consequence of a constraint specifying what the forces have got to be like.

Even if the general law of energy conservation is a coincidence and so unable to help account for Archimedes's principle, the fact that gravitational interactions in particular conserve energy could nevertheless help to explain Archimedes's principle. The explanation could proceed along the same lines as the first hybrid explanation I gave, except that instead of beginning with the general principle of energy conservation explaining why gravitational interactions conserve energy, it would begin simply by appealing to the fact that gravitational interactions conserve energy (and that gravity is the only force at work). It would then be thoroughly causal rather than a hybrid explanation. Its appeal to gravity's conserving energy and to the formula for gravitational potential energy would be an appeal to facts explained by the gravitational force law. The gravitational force law would then help to explain both Archimedes's principle and the fact that gravitational interactions conserve energy. As a coincidence, energy conservation would not transcend the force laws.

If energy conservation is a constraint, then there are many other such "hybrid" explanations with an explanation by constraint as one component and a causal explanation as the other. Consider a classical pendulum (experiencing no air resistance or friction, in a uniform downward gravitational field, and with a rigid cord). Having initially been released from rest at height h, the bob rises no higher than h on any subsequent upswing. Why is that? A thoroughly causal explanation answers this question by using Newton's laws of motion and gravity to entail the bob's equation of motion, which in turn entails the explanandum. Can the general principle of energy conservation also be used to explain it? Not if energy conservation is a coincidence, since then (as I showed in the previous section) not every component of this coincidence is explanatorily relevant. But if energy conservation is a constraint, then although the pendulum feels only certain kinds of forces, energy conservation as a constraint explains why those forces conserve energy. The conclusion of this explanation by constraint then feeds into a causal explanation: the bob's potential energy is entirely gravitational, and given the formula for gravitational potential energy, the bob cannot rise higher than h without violating energy conservation. The explanation by constraint together with the causal explanation form a hybrid explanation of the bob's rising no higher than h.

For another example of such an explanation, consider the standard explanation of the Magnus force—the force responsible for the behavior of a curveball and slider in baseball, for example. The Magnus force is orthogonal to the direction in which a spinning ball is pitched and also orthogonal to the direction of the axis of the ball's spin:

> The creation of the Magnus force is explained as follows. As the spinning ball moves through the air . . . the boundary layer separation point [at which the air pulled along with the spinning of the ball separates tangentially from the ball's surface] will advance forward on the side of the ball that is spinning in opposition to the airflow. This is due to a reduction in pressure drag in this region [i.e., to the ball's spin dragging the adjacent air in a direction opposite to the direction that the ball was pitched]. Conversely, the boundary layer will retreat further to the back of the ball on the side where the spin is moving with the airflow, as the increased pressure drag holds the boundary layer close to the ball for longer. The asymmetry boundary layer separation due to the ball spin leads to a deflection of the wake behind the ball [so that the wake goes somewhat downward behind the ball, if the ball is pitched to the left and is spinning clockwise]. Now Newton's third law tells us that there must be a reactive force acting upward as a consequence of the downward pointing deflected wake. That is, the momentum change due to the wake deflection is balanced by a momentum change in the ball causing it to move upwards. [i.e., since the wake is deflected downward, conservation of momentum requires the ball to be deflected upward.] This is the Magnus force. (White 2011, 109; see Hoffman and Johnson 2007, 177–178)

In this explanation, the conservation law can be interpreted not as the general principle of momentum conservation, but instead as the law that momentum is conserved by the particular force acting between the air and the ball. The explanation then does not need to specify this species of force or its force law—only that it conserves momentum. That it conserves momentum could be explained by its force law. Under this interpretation, momentum conservation does not function as a constraint in this explanation, and the explanation is entirely causal. Alternatively, the conservation law in this explanation can be interpreted as the general principle of momentum conservation rather than as the law that momentum is conserved by the particular species of force between the air and the ball. The general principle of momentum conservation is then functioning in the explanation as the reason why the particular species of force acting between the air and the ball conserves momentum: because all forces have got to do so. Under this interpretation, the explanation is a hybrid: part explanation by constraint, part causal (describing how the ball's spin deflects the wake).

A conservation law does not need to be a brute fact in order for it to be a constraint. It may have an explanation. In fact, one way for a conservation law to be a constraint is for it to arise from a symmetry principle, since then it is no coincidence that each of the actual forces conserves the relevant quantity. Each does so for the same reason: because of the symmetry principle. As is well known, various classical conservation laws follow from various spacetime symmetries within a Hamiltonian dynamical framework: energy conservation follows from the laws' invariance under arbitrary temporal displacement, linear momentum conservation from their invariance under arbitrary spatial displacement, and angular momentum conservation from their invariance under arbitrary rotations.[20] If these derivations *explain why* the conservation laws hold (as they are often said to do), then the conservation laws are constraints, not coincidences. As Wigner says: "for those [conservation laws] which derive from the geometrical principles of invariance it is clear that their validity transcends that of any special theory—gravitational, electromagnetic, etc.—which are only loosely connected" (1972, 13). In other words, Wigner contends that those symmetries are not coincidences of the particular kinds of forces there happen to be, and so the associated conservation laws transcend the idiosyncrasies of the force laws figuring in causal explanations. Rather, those symmetries are constraints. In the following chapters, I will also examine the roles that such symmetries may play in explaining the coordinate transformations (chapter 3) and the parallelogram law for the composition of forces (chapter 4). These would be explanations by constraint. Greene (2005, 225) says that "the symmetries of nature are not merely consequences of nature's laws. From our modern perspective, symmetries are the foundation from which laws spring." This is a claim about the order of explanatory priority: that symmetries are constraints rather than coincidences.

■ 2.4 OTHER POSSIBLE KINDS OF CONSTRAINTS BESIDES CONSERVATION LAWS

Conservation laws and symmetry principles are not the only "great general principles" that have sometimes been reasonably thought to "sweep across" the various force laws, explaining why all of those laws share certain features. Even if some of these allegedly "great general principles" turn out to be coincidences (or false) rather than constraints, metaphysics should recognize the distinction between constraints and coincidences and leave room for explanations by constraint.

Newton's gravitational-force law is an inverse-square law. So is Coulomb's law for the electric force between two point charges at rest. So is Ampere's law for the magnetic force between two electric-current elements. In his 1884 Kiel lectures, Hertz said that (as far as science has been able to discover) all fundamental force laws are inverse-square—and that this regularity has never been thought coincidental [*zufällig*] (Hertz 1999, 68).

What could Hertz have meant by this? If he meant that this regularity among the force laws has never been thought to be accidental in the manner of all gold cubes being smaller than a cubic meter, then his observation would be true but trivial: obviously, there is no possible world with exactly the same laws as the actual world (according to Hertz's science) but where it is *not* the case that all of the fundamental force laws are inverse-square. Instead, I suggest, Hertz meant that the inverse-square character of all of the fundamental forces has always been considered to be a *constraint*, not a *coincidence*. In other words, Hertz meant that there is (by widespread consensus) some common explanation (perhaps as yet unknown) for each force's being inverse-square; they are not independently inverse-square.

This interpretation of Hertz's remark is confirmed by his characterizing this regularity among the various fundamental forces as too remarkable for its instances not to have a common explainer: "Is it not marvelous [wunderbar] that all long-range forces follow [an inverse-square] law?" (Hertz 1999, 68). Indeed, Hertz immediately suggests one possible common explainer: "Kant and many others before and after him have tried to relate this feature [the inverse-square character of the force laws] to the three-dimensional nature of space." But whereas Kant offers the inverse-square character of forces as explaining why space is three-dimensional (see Callendar 2005), Hertz proposes that explanatory priority runs in the opposite direction.

Hertz's proposed explanation begins with another regularity among the fundamental forces: that every fundamental interaction operates by contact action—that is, by a field acting at the same point in spacetime as the force it causes. The field causally mediates between the two interacting bodies (which may be far apart).[21] According to Hertz, that no fundamental interaction constitutes action at a spatiotemporal distance is a constraint on any force there might have been rather than a coincidence of the various forces there actually are. Hertz argues for this constraint not a priori, but rather by inference to the best explanation: the most plausible explanation of the "marvelous" fact that all fundamental forces are inverse-square is that all fundamental forces *must* operate by contact action.

In his Kiel lectures, Hertz does not say anything about why, in turn, all fundamental forces must operate by contact action. But to fund his explanation of the inverse-square character of all fundamental forces, this contact-action regularity must be a constraint rather than a coincidence. For if it were a coincidence, then it could not be a *common* reason why every force is inverse-square. At best, the electric-force law would be inverse-square because electric charges interact by contact (i.e., through the electric field at each charge's location), the gravitational-force law would be inverse-square because gravity acts by contact, and so forth. In that case, it would be a *coincidence* that all of the fundamental forces are inverse-square, contrary to Hertz's view (following a broad consensus, he says) that this regularity is no coincidence.

In his later work as well, Hertz emphasizes the distinction between constraints and coincidences. In his *Principles of Mechanics* (his last work, published in 1894), Hertz says that there are various features that all fundamental forces possess: conserving energy, being independent of absolute time and place, being central forces,[22] not being a function of higher time derivatives than velocity, and so forth (1950, 10–11). Hertz recognizes that some of these regularities may turn out not to hold of all fundamental forces, but he emphasizes that which of these regularities in fact holds is less important than that "we can predicate more [of the fundamental forces] than the accepted fundamental laws do" (10). He elaborates: "Although there is such difference of opinion as to the precise properties which are to be attributed to the elementary forces, there is a general agreement that more of such general properties can be assigned, and can from existing observations be deduced, than are contained in the fundamental laws. We are convinced that the elementary forces must, so to speak, be of a simple nature" (11). This *must* is a kind of necessity stronger than that possessed by the various force laws—the kind that distinguishes constraints from coincidences. According to Hertz, "we often feel, indeed sometimes are convinced, that" a force violating one of these great general principles "is by the nature of things excluded" (11). This prohibition involves an impossibility stronger than the impossibility of (e.g.) gravity's being weaker (or repulsive) or like electric charges attracting or additional kinds of forces operating. This modal strength is precisely what underwrites an explanation by constraint.

How is the constraint that all forces are inverse-square supposed to be explained by the constraint that all forces act by contact (and that space is three-dimensional)? Consider a configuration of bodies and any imaginary surface enclosing them. If a given sort of influence operates by contact action, then the influence of those bodies on any body outside of the surface must pass through the intervening surface (rather than hop "over" it). Therefore, the field at all points on the surface must fix the influence of the enclosed bodies on any body outside of the surface. Hence, any two configurations with the same field at all points on the surface must have the same field everywhere outside of the surface. The existence of such a "uniqueness theorem" (as it is commonly called today) imposes strict limits on the form that the force law can take. As Hertz (1999, 68) rightly notes, the requirement that there be a uniqueness theorem rules out a force that declines linearly with distance or with the cube of the distance. Indeed, though

Hertz does not mention this result explicitly, it is a mathematical theorem that for a $1/r^n$ force, there is a uniqueness theorem (in three-dimensional space) only for $n = 2$ (Bartlett and Su 1994). That is why (according to Hertz) all of the various fundamental forces are inverse-square forces.

On Hertz's view, then, at least two constraints are not conservation laws: that all fundamental forces are inverse-square and that all fundamental forces act by contact. Notice once again that a constraint does not have to be a brute fact; on Hertz's view, the inverse-square constraint is explained by the contact-action constraint. Hertz's proposed explanation cannot be entirely correct as it stands since an inverse-square force is not quite the only kind of central force (with a force law consisting of an analytic function that is real-valued except, perhaps, at isolated singularities) that permits a uniqueness theorem. Rather, a uniqueness theorem holds for such a force if and only if it is proportional to $1/(e^{kr} r^2)$ for some real k (Bartlett and Su 1994). This is called a "Yukawa force law" (or a force with a "Yukawa potential"). An inverse-square force is the special case where $k = 0$.

More about the various types of forces is known today than in Hertz's day. Not all of the forces that physicists today look upon as perhaps fundamental are inverse-square. However, if all of the actual fundamental forces are Yukawa forces, then perhaps an argument like Hertz's explains why this is so. A Yukawa force was famously posited by (can you guess?) Yukawa in 1935 as the strong nuclear force (i.e., the force holding protons and neutrons together in atomic nuclei). However, even if Hertz's proposed explanation fails because not all actual fundamental forces are governed by Yukawa force laws, my point still stands. Metaphysics must not foreclose explanations of the sort that Hertz proposes on pain of failing to do justice to the fact that science has rightly taken such proposals seriously.

I suggested in chapter 1 that Newton's second law of motion might reasonably be taken as transcending the particular kinds of forces there happen to be—that is, as describing the framework within which any force *must* act and hence as able to figure in explanations by constraint. Various principles of statics may do likewise.[23] Consider, for instance, the principle of virtual work (PVW) and, in particular, the way it can be used to derive Archimedes's principle (as in Mach 1960, 125). The PVW says that a mechanical system acted upon by various outside forces is in equilibrium exactly when no total work is done by those forces in any "virtual displacement"—that is, in any hypothetical infinitesimal change in the positions of the system's components in accordance with the "constraints" on the system. (Here I am *not* using the term "constraints" in the sense that I have stipulated in drawing a contrast with coincidences. Rather, I am using "constraints" in a sense that is standard in classical mechanics, namely, for limitations on a system's degrees of freedom, such as that a given body must lie on a certain surface or that two bodies must remain connected by a rigid rod. "Forces of constraint" in this sense are contrasted with external forces. Context should suffice to disambiguate any use of the term "constraint.") To derive Archimedes's principle from the PVW, suppose (for the sake of simplicity) that the submerged body is a cube of side s with horizontal top and bottom faces. If its virtual displacement consists of its descent by dh, then a body slab of volume $s^2 dh$ effectively descends by s and a fluid parcel of the same volume ascends by s. Gravity performs virtual work $g\rho_b \, s^3 dh$ on the body and $-g\rho_f s^3 dh$ on the fluid (for body density ρ_b and fluid density ρ_f), so by the PVW, the system is in equilibrium if $\rho_b = \rho_f$. Therefore, any submerged body must experience an upward force that would balance its weight if $\rho_b = \rho_f$, that is, if its weight were equal to the weight of the fluid it displaces—in other words, an upward force equal to the weight of the displaced fluid.

The PVW remains useful in structural mechanics and mechanical engineering. But whether this derivation from the PVW *explains* Archimedes's principle is recognized as depending on whether the PVW is a constraint or a coincidence. A common view (Lanczos 1986, 77; Whewell 1874, 333 [bk. 6, ch. 2, sec. 4]) is that the PVW holds in virtue of the fact that in each elementary kind of mechanical system (e.g., lever, pulley, wheel . . .), the total work done by the forces of constraint under any virtual displacement is zero. These various facts, one for each kind of simple machine, have no important common explainer. Instead, the PVW is a coincidence (albeit naturally necessary) and hence does not account for Archimedes's principle. Accordingly, Whewell (333) says of the PVW that it "serves verbally to conjoin Laws . . . [rather] than to exhibit a connexion in them: it is rather a help for the memory than a proof for the reason."[24]

Likewise, the principle of least (better: stationary) action has sometimes been interpreted as a constraint but more often as a coincidence. For instance, Planck says that it has generally been regarded as a coincidence: "In present-day physics the principle of least action plays a relatively minor role. It does not quite fit into the framework of present theories. Of course, admittedly it is a correct statement; yet usually it serves not as the foundation of the theory, but as a true but dispensable appendix, because present theoretical physics is entirely tailored to the principle of infinitesimal local effects. . . . Physics hence is inclined to view the principle of least action more as a formal and accidental curiosity than as a pillar of physical knowledge" (1948, 48). Clearly, "accidental" here does not mean "lacking in natural necessity." I suggest that it means "a coincidence rather than a constraint." (Planck himself was inclined to think it unlikely that "the dominance of such a simple law could be a mere accident.")

■ 2.5 CONSTRAINTS AS MODALLY MORE EXALTED THAN THE FORCE LAWS THEY CONSTRAIN

I have suggested that if various proposed non-causal explanations succeed by appealing to conservation laws, then they work because those conservation laws constrain the force laws figuring in causal explanations, limiting the kinds of forces that there could possibly have been. In terms of this modality, the kinds of forces and force laws there could possibly have been go beyond the kinds there actually are. For gravitational forces to exist but to be repulsive rather than attractive, for example, is *naturally* impossible (i.e., is logically inconsistent with some laws of nature). Nevertheless, it may (at least according to classical physics) possess some species of possibility that is broader than natural possibility (though narrower than logical, mathematical, conceptual, and metaphysical possibility). It would possess this species of possibility by virtue of being logically consistent with the constraints on the force laws. In contrast, if energy conservation is a constraint, then its violation is not just *naturally* impossible; it also possesses an even stronger kind of impossibility.

On this view, an explanation by constraint may expressly consider a hypothetical state of affairs that the laws of nature preclude (and that are not even approximations to or idealizations of some natural possibility). An explanation by constraint can get away with appealing to a natural impossibility as long as the impossible state of affairs is not ruled out by the constraints. The explanation works by showing how the explanandum comes to possess the constraints' distinctive species of necessity (stronger than natural necessity).

Here is an example: the standard textbook explanation (originating with Gibbs) of the law for the entropy of a mixture of two noninteracting ideal gases. The explanation uses energy conservation to account for the law giving ΔS: the difference between the mixture's entropy and the entropy of the gases when separated. Suppose N_A molecules of gas A occupy volume V_A (the left side of a container) and N_B molecules of gas B occupy volume V_B (the right side); the container is isolated and the two gases have the same pressure P and temperature T. Suppose gas A is confined behind a freely moveable membrane permeable to B but not to A, and gas B is similarly confined behind a membrane permeable to A but not to B. Initially, the two membranes divide the container along the same plane (see fig. 2.4), so the gases are entirely separated. Then the membranes are allowed to move slowly, each gas expanding quasi-statically, so that ultimately the two membranes reach opposite ends of the container and both gases fill the entire container (volume $V_A + V_B$). Each gas's expansion is a reversible isothermal process. Let W be the total work done on the system:

$$W = -\int_{V_A}^{V_A+V_B} P\,dV - \int_{V_B}^{V_A+V_B} P\,dV = -\int_{V_A}^{V_A+V_B} N_A kT\frac{dV}{V} - \int_{V_{BA}}^{V_A+V_B} N_B kT\frac{dV}{V}$$

$$= N_A kT \ln \frac{V_A}{V_A+V_B} + N_B kT \ln \frac{V_B}{V_A+V_B}.$$

Figure 2.4 Explanation of the entropy of a mixture of two noninteracting ideal gases

By energy conservation (i.e., the first law of thermodynamics), the change ΔU in internal energy and the heat Q absorbed are related by

$$\Delta U = Q + W.$$

Since the gases expand isothermically, $\Delta U = 0$, so $Q = -W$. Thus

$$Q = N_A kT \ln \frac{V_A + V_B}{V_A} + N_B kT \ln \frac{V_A + V_B}{V_B}.$$

Then since $\Delta S = Q/T$,

$$\Delta S = N_A k \ln \frac{V_A + V_B}{V_A} + N_B k \ln \frac{V_A + V_B}{V_B},$$

which is the explanandum: the formula for the entropy of a mixture of two non-interacting ideal gases.

Crucially, this explanation does not presuppose that laws make it (naturally) possible for there to exist a pair of membranes, one permeable to A but not to B, the other permeable to B but not to A. Whether there are any possible materials that could constitute such membranes depends on the particular gases involved. Generally, such membranes are impossible. For instance, if molecules of A are small and uncharged whereas molecules of B are large and charged, then typically there is nothing that could form a membrane permeable to B but not to A according to the laws specifying the molecular constitutions of A and B as well as the behavior of naturally possible membrane materials.

But remarkably, the thermodynamic explanation is not thereby undermined. That is because it proceeds entirely from *constraints* on the laws specifying the constitutions of A and B and the behavior of membranes. As far as those constraints are concerned, such membranes are possible for any molecular species. As Planck said in 1891 in commenting on Gibbs's derivation of this equation: "The enormous generalization that Gibbs has given to this tenet and which must, in and of itself, appear irresponsibly daring, rests clearly on the self-evident thought that the validity of so fundamental a tenet as that of the entropy of a mixed ideal gas, cannot depend on the arbitrary circumstance of whether we really have available in each individual case a suitable semi-permeable membrane" (translated in Seth 2010, 108). It is not obviously an "arbitrary circumstance" since, after all, it is a matter of natural necessity. Yet it is indeed "arbitrary" as far as the constraints are concerned, since whether any such membranes are possible for a particular pair of gases is a matter of what the fundamental force laws *happen to be*. Because Gibbs's explanation shows the explanandum to depend on thermodynamics alone, the explanation can afford to posit membranes that are naturally impossible.[25] The laws of thermodynamics transcend the laws concerning various particular naturally possible kinds of gas and materials out of which membranes could be constructed. That is because the laws of thermodynamics (and any explanandum they entail) would still have held, whether or not the laws permit a suitable pair of membranes for a particular pair of gases—an "arbitrary circumstance," just as Planck says. Though I would resist Planck's thought that it is "self-evident" that the mixture's entropy cannot depend on these details of the laws, I embrace Planck's thought that if the entropy does not "depend" on them (i.e., cannot partly be explained by them), then its only explanation is by constraints, and such an explanation can traffic in natural impossibilities.

Similarly, to explain various laws concerning dilute solutions, Planck in 1887 (see Fermi 1956, 115) considered what would happen were the temperature so high and the pressure so slight that the solute and solvent vaporized into a mixture of ideal gases. After explaining the equations in this way, Planck wrote: "incidentally, it is completely inconsequential [gleichgultig] if the given state can really be arrived at experimentally, and certainly whether it represents a stable state of equilibrium or not; because these expressions [the explanandum] are completely independent of this [question]" (translated in Seth 2010, 102). Later he elaborated: "In reality, such a process [vaporizing a dilute solution into a mixture of ideal gases] will admittedly often not be realizable, because in many cases, at high temperatures, as are necessary here, chemical transformations occur, and the molecules are thereby altered" (translated in Seth 2010, 108). Seth (102) comments:

> [Planck's point], introduced so casually, was, in fact, anything but incidental. Planck had clearly seen an apparent objection, and an obvious one at that. If one considers the case described (a dilute solution, say, of NaCl in water), lowering the pressure and increasing the temperature does not automatically produce the result required [a mixture of ideal gases, one of the solute and one of the solvent]. In most common cases, the water will vaporize, leaving a solid salt. For Planck's process, however, one requires both the salt and the water to vaporize *and* to maintain their molecular integrity as compounds. Whether it was at all possible to carry out such a procedure cannot have been clear to Planck. . . . The argument, however, was a thermodynamic one and the details of the process, including the very possibility of its experimental realization, did not matter for Planck. It was thermodynamically possible and hence the result followed.

"Thermodynamic possibility," as Seth nicely terms it, is broader than "natural possibility" because the laws of thermodynamics constrain the ordinary laws; like logical possibility, thermodynamic possibility includes more than just what is naturally possible. Planck's explanation succeeds, despite trafficking in natural impossibilities, because it works by showing the explanandum to be thermodynamically necessary, not merely naturally necessary. No purported causal explanation could show the explanandum to be so inevitable (and so any purported causal explanation would mischaracterize the explanandum as more contingent than it is) because no purported causal explanation, appealing to various ordinary laws, could show that the explanandum would still have held, even if the ordinary laws had been different. The force laws do not entail what the force laws would have been like, had they been different. Such subjunctive conditionals will now move to the forefront of my account of the difference between constraints and coincidences.

■ 2.6 MY ACCOUNT OF THE DIFFERENCE
BETWEEN CONSTRAINTS AND COINCIDENCES

I will now try to be more precise about what it would take for a conservation law to be a constraint rather than a coincidence. As I hinted at the close of the previous section, I will elaborate this distinction in terms of subjunctive conditionals. Energy conservation constrains the possible force laws exactly when energy would still have been conserved even if there had been an additional kind of force (that is, a force that is not electric or gravitational or any of the other actual kinds) acting together with the various actual kinds—in other words, even if there had been an additional kind of interaction experienced by some of the same entities undergoing some of the actual kinds of interaction.[26] (If the additional kinds of force were uninstantiated, then they would obviously pose no threat to energy conservation. If forces of the additional kinds were not influencing any of the actual sorts of entities, then even if there existed other sorts of entities that these additional forces did influence, these additional kinds of forces would still pose no threat to the conservation of quantities possessed exclusively by the actual sorts of entities.) The subjunctive fact associated with energy conservation as a constraint is roughly that energy's conservation is *resilient*: that energy would still have been conserved even if there had been additional kinds of force threatening to undermine its conservation.

On the other hand, to say that energy conservation is a coincidence of the actual force laws is to say that it is *not* the case that energy would still have been conserved, had there been additional kinds of force acting together with the various actual kinds. Rather, energy is conserved because as it happens, each of the actual kinds of forces conserves energy as a result of its own particular force law. So if there had been additional kinds of forces, then energy might still have been conserved, but then again, it might not still have been, depending on the force laws for the additional forces. Since those force laws might not have upheld energy conservation, it is not the case that energy would still have been conserved, had there been additional kinds of forces. In somewhat the same way, if a fair coin has been tossed 10 times and has landed heads each time, then this regularity is coincidental, and so had the coin been tossed again, it might have landed heads, but it might not—so it is false that if the coin had been tossed again, it would have landed heads. The coin's tosses are independent and the various fundamental interaction laws (without constraints on them) are, too (though the coin tosses are stochastic, unlike the fundamental interaction laws).[27]

At least some scientists believe that because each of the various known fundamental interactions conserves energy, we have strong empirical evidence that were there additional kinds of fundamental interaction (perhaps taking place only under exotic, unfamiliar conditions), then they too would conserve energy.[28] As I have just explained, this subjunctive conditional is not merely *unlikely* to be true if energy conservation is coincidental. It is *false*. Hence, scientists who accept this subjunctive conditional cannot consistently believe energy conservation to be a coincidence.[29]

I have cashed out the distinction between energy conservation as a constraint and energy conservation as a coincidence in terms of the conservation law's behavior in connection with counterfactuals. Of course, the distinction between natural laws and accidents is also standardly cashed out in this way. For example, Coulomb's law would still have held, even if there had existed additional charged bodies. By contrast, the accident that each of the families living on my block has two children might not still have held, had there been additional families living on the block. So it is not the case that had there been additional families living on the block, then all of the families on the block would still have had two children. My account of the difference between constraints and coincidences draws the same sort of distinction at a "higher level": energy conservation is a constraint exactly when energy would still have been conserved, had there been additional kinds of forces (and hence additional force laws). We saw Feynman describe the conservation laws as seeming to occupy a higher level than the force laws: as "great general principles which all the [force] laws seem to follow."

Likewise, a standard view is that laws explain their instances whereas accidents do not. For example, Coulomb's law explains the mutual electrostatic repulsion between two point charges. By contrast, the fact that my family has two children is not explained by the fact that all of the families on our block have two children, since it is just an accident that all of those families have two children. My account of the difference between constraints and coincidences draws the same sort of distinction at a higher level. The fact that various actual forces conserve energy is explained by energy conservation as a constraint on the forces, but not by energy conservation as a coincidental similarity among them.

That the constraint/coincidence distinction is drawn at a higher level than the law/accident distinction means that the distinction between constraints and coincidences is not identical to the distinction between laws and accidents. As I mentioned earlier, even as a coincidence, energy conservation would logically follow from facts all of which are laws and so would not be an accident. It would be naturally necessary. Accordingly, there is an important difference between the counterfactuals used to elaborate the law/accident distinction and the counterfactuals used to elaborate the constraint/coincidence distinction. The counterfactuals associated with the law/accident distinction have antecedents that all represent natural possibilities, such as "Had there been additional charged bodies" or "Had there been additional families living on our block." In contrast, a natural impossibility is posited by the counterfactual antecedent ("Had there been additional kinds of forces") associated with the distinction between constraints and coincidences; this counterfactual is a "counterlegal." Thus, although the distinction between constraints and coincidences is a modal distinction, like the distinction between laws and accidents, the two distinctions are not the same.[30]

In the remainder of this section, I will sketch a fuller account of the varieties of necessity (stronger than natural necessity) possessed by constraints. I will identify what it is that constraints and ordinary laws have in common in virtue of which they each possess a variety of the same thing—necessity—though of different strengths. In so doing, I will also specify what it is about mathematical truths (which, as I showed in chapter 1, can serve as constraints in "distinctively mathematical" explanations) in virtue of which they possess an even stronger variety of necessity than conservation laws and the like. By understanding these varieties of necessity, I will show how various kinds of constraints "transcend" the ordinary laws of nature and hence have the requisite necessity to function in explanations by constraint. I have defended this account in detail elsewhere (Lange 2009a). I shall not repeat those arguments here. A reader could accept much of what I say in part I about explanations by constraint without adopting my particular account of the stronger variety of necessity that constraints possess. But even such a reader may find it helpful to see how one proposed account of natural lawhood leaves a natural place for the distinction between constraints and coincidences.

As I just mentioned, laws of nature have traditionally been thought to differ from accidents in having greater perseverance under counterfactual antecedents. For instance, since it is a law that no body is accelerated from rest to beyond the speed of light, this cosmic speed limit would not have been broken even if the Stanford Linear Accelerator had now been cranked up to full power. On the other hand, since it is an accident that all gold cubes are smaller than a cubic meter, this pattern would presumably have been broken if Bill Gates had wanted to have constructed a gold cube exceeding a cubic meter.

Of course, laws are unable to persist under counterfactual suppositions with which they are logically inconsistent. This suggests that the laws would still have held under any counterfactual antecedent as long as that antecedent is logically consistent with all of the laws. Trivially, no fact that is an accident is preserved under all of these antecedents (since one such antecedent posits the accident's negation, and the accident is not preserved under that antecedent!). Making a few details more explicit, we arrive at the following proposal:

> It is a law that *m* if and only if in any conversational context, for any circumstance *p* that is logically consistent with all of the facts *n* (taken together) where it is a law that *n*, it is true that if *p* had been the case, then *m* would still have been the case (that is, $p \, \square \!\!\rightarrow m$).

In this proposal and until further notice, I reserve lowercase letters (such as *m*, *p*, and *n*) for "subnomic" claims—that is, for claims such as "The emerald at spatiotemporal location . . . is 5 g" and "All emeralds are green," as contrasted with "nomic" claims such as "It is a law that all emeralds are green" and "It is an accident that the emerald at spatiotemporal location . . . is 5 g." (On my view, a claim is "subnomic" exactly when in any possible world, what makes the claim hold [or fail to hold] is not [even partly] that a given fact in that world is a law or that a given fact in that world is an accident.) Let me also note that the account of laws I am sketching here presupposes that every logical consequence of laws qualifies as a law and that every broadly logical truth (that is, every truth holding with some broadly logical necessity, such as narrowly logical necessity, metaphysical necessity, mathematical necessity, conceptual necessity, or moral necessity) is by courtesy a natural law since it has all of the necessity of a law and then some.[31] The reference in the above proposal to the conditional's being true in *all conversational contexts* is required because the truth-values of counterfactual conditionals are notoriously context-sensitive.[32]

This proposal captures an important difference between laws and accidents in their behavior toward counterfactuals. However, even if this proposal is correct, there is an obvious limitation on how enlightening it can be. That is because the laws appear in this proposal on *both* sides of the "if and only if." That is, the proposal picks out the laws by their invariance under a certain range of counterfactual antecedents *p* (namely, under any circumstance *p* that is logically consistent with all of the facts *n* where it is a law that *n*)—but this range of antecedents, in turn, is obviously picked out by the laws. Therefore, although this proposal's truth is not thereby made trivial, this proposal fails to specify what it is in virtue of which *m* is a law. It also fails to account for what makes the laws *important*. The laws' invariance over the particular range of counterfactual antecedents identified in the proposal makes the laws special only if there is already something special about having this particular range of invariance. But since the laws are precisely what pick out this range, there is something special about being invariant over this range only if there is already something special about the laws. If there is no prior, independent reason why this particular range of counterfactual antecedents is special, then the laws' invariance under these antecedents fails to make the laws special. They merely have a certain range of invariance (just as a given accident has some range of invariance).

However, these deficiencies can be overcome by tweaking the proposal. It said roughly that the laws form a set of truths that would still have held under every antecedent with which the set is logically consistent. In contrast, take the set containing exactly the logical consequences of (for example) the accident that all gold cubes are smaller than a cubic meter. This set's members are *not* all preserved under every antecedent that is logically consistent with this set's members. For instance, had Bill Gates wanted to have constructed a gold cube exceeding a cubic meter, then such a cube might well have existed—yet that Bill Gates wants to have such a cube constructed is *logically* consistent with all gold cubes being smaller than a cubic meter.

That is the idea behind the definition of "subnomic stability":

> Consider a nonempty set Γ of subnomic truths containing every subnomic logical consequence of its members. Γ possesses *subnomic stability* if and only if for each member m of Γ and for any p where $\Gamma \cup \{p\}$ is logically consistent (and in every conversational context), it is not the case that if p had held, then m might not have held (i.e., m's negation might have held)—that is, $\sim (p \lozenge \rightarrow \sim m)$.[33]

Notice that $\sim (p \lozenge \rightarrow \sim m)$ logically entails $p \;\square\rightarrow m$. (In other words, that it is not the case that $\sim m$ might have held, had p held, logically entails that m would have held, had p held.) Therefore, a set of truths is subnomically stable exactly when its members would all still have held—indeed, not one of their negations even might have held—under any counterfactual antecedent with which they are all logically consistent. In contrast to the earlier proposal, stability does not use the laws to pick out the relevant range of counterfactual suppositions; stability avoids privileging the range of counterfactual antecedents that is logically consistent with the laws. Rather, each set picks out for itself the range under which it must be invariant in order for it to qualify as stable.

According to my earlier proposal, the set Λ of all subnomic truths m where it is a law that m is subnomically stable. In contrast, the set spanned by the fact that all gold cubes are smaller than a cubic meter is unstable because this set's members are all logically consistent with Bill Gates wanting a gold cube larger than a cubic meter, yet the set's members are not all invariant under this counterfactual supposition.

Let's look at another example. Take the accident g that whenever a certain car is on a dry flat road, its acceleration is given by a certain function of how far its gas pedal is being depressed. Had the gas pedal on a certain occasion been depressed a bit farther, then g would still have held. Can a stable set include g? Such a set must also include the fact that the car has a four-cylinder engine, since had the engine used six cylinders, g might not still have held. (Once the set includes the fact that the car has a four-cylinder engine, the antecedent that the engine has six cylinders is logically *inconsistent* with the set, so to be stable, the set does not have to be preserved under that antecedent.) But since the set includes a description of the car's engine, its stability also requires that it include a description of the engine factory, since had that factory been different, the engine might have been different. Had the price of steel been different, the engine might have been different. And so on. To see that this ripple effect propagates endlessly, take the following antecedent: had either g been false or there been a gold cube larger than a cubic meter. Under this antecedent, is g preserved? In every context? Certainly not. This counterfactual antecedent pits g's invariance against the invariance of the gold cube generalization. It is not the case that in every context, g proves more resilient. Therefore, to possess subnomic stability, a set that includes g must also include the fact that all gold cubes are smaller than a cubic meter (making the set logically inconsistent with the above antecedent, and so to be stable, the set does not have to be preserved under that antecedent). Since a stable set that includes g must include even the fact about gold cubes, I conclude that the only set containing g that might be stable is the set of *all* subnomic truths.

I conclude that *no* nonmaximal set of subnomic truths that contains an accident possesses subnomic stability. This suggests my proposal for distinguishing laws from accidents: that the set Λ of all subnomic truths m where it is a law that m is subnomically stable, whereas no set containing an accident is subnomically stable (except perhaps for the set of all subnomic truths, considering that the range of subjunctive antecedents under which this "maximal" set must be preserved in order to qualify as stable does not include any false antecedents since no subnomic falsehood is logically consistent with all of this set's members).[34]

It is a law that m, then, exactly when m belongs to a (nonmaximal) subnomically stable set. Now let's show that this account leaves a natural place for the distinction between constraints and coincidences. Are there any other nonmaximal subnomically stable sets besides Λ? The subnomic, broadly logical truths form a stable set since they would still have held under any broadly logical possibility. (I return to this point below.) I will now show that for any two subnomically stable sets, one must be a proper subset of the other. The strategy is to consider an antecedent of the sort that I just employed in connection with the example involving g and the fact about gold cubes—namely, an antecedent pitting the invariance of the two sets against each other:

1. Suppose (for reductio) that Γ and Σ are subnomically stable, t is a member of Γ but not of Σ, and s is a member of Σ but not of Γ.
2. Then ($\sim s$ or $\sim t$) is logically consistent with Γ.
3. Since Γ is subnomically stable, every member of Γ would still have been true, had ($\sim s$ or $\sim t$) been the case.
4. In particular, t would still have been true, had ($\sim s$ or $\sim t$) been the case. That is, ($\sim s$ or $\sim t$) $\square \rightarrow t$.
5. So t & ($\sim s$ or $\sim t$) would have held, had ($\sim s$ or $\sim t$). Hence, ($\sim s$ or $\sim t$) $\square \rightarrow \sim s$.
6. Since ($\sim s$ or $\sim t$) is logically consistent with Σ, and Σ is subnomically stable, no member of Σ would have been false had ($\sim s$ or $\sim t$) been the case.
7. In particular, s would not have been false, had ($\sim s$ or $\sim t$) been the case. That is, $\sim(($\sim s$ or $\sim t$) $\square \rightarrow \sim s)$.
8. Contradiction from 5 and 7.

Thus, the subnomically stable sets must form a nested hierarchy.

I was asking about nonmaximal subnomically stable sets besides Λ. Since no nonmaximal *superset* of Λ is subnomically stable (since it would have to contain accidents), we must look for subnomically stable sets among Λ's proper subsets. Many of them are clearly unstable. Let's look at an example. What would have happened had Coulomb's law been violated sometime in the past? In that case, Coulomb's law would not have been in force (i.e., would not have been a law), and so it might also have been violated sometime in the future. Accordingly, consider a restriction of Coulomb's law to times *after* today, and take the set containing exactly this restricted generalization and its subnomic, broadly logical consequences. Our counterfactual antecedent (positing that Coulomb's law was violated sometime in the past) is logically consistent with this set, but as I just argued, the set is not invariant under that antecedent. Therefore, this proper subset of Λ is unstable.

However, some of Λ's proper subsets may be stable. We might start to build such a set by considering that it is widely thought that the fundamental dynamical law relating force to motion (which, in classical physics, may be Newton's second law together with its analogue relating applied torque to angular acceleration, or Hamilton's principle, or the Euler-Lagrange equations, etc.) would still have held, even if the force laws had been different. As I mentioned in chapter 1, when Ehrenfest (1917) famously showed that the planets would eventually have collided with the Sun or escaped from the Sun's gravity if gravity had been an inverse-cube force, he presupposed that Newton's second law would still have held, if gravity had been an inverse-cube force.[35] Of course, the mere fact that Newton's second law is preserved under this particular counterfactual antecedent in the context of Ehrenfest's argument does not show that in every conversational context, Newton's second law is preserved under a broad range of antecedents that violate the force laws. But the distinction between the laws of motion and the various force laws has long been recognized as important; Newton (1979, 401) in the *Opticks* distinguished between passive principles associated with the laws of motion and "certain active principles, such as that of Gravity, and that which causes Fermentation, and the Cohesion of Bodies." On my view, this is a modal distinction if the laws of motion "transcend" the force laws in belonging to a subnomically stable set that omits the force laws (and the closure law). The fundamental dynamical law then possesses (I will argue) a stronger variety of necessity than the force laws do and so can figure in the distinctively mathematical explanation (given in chapter 1) of the fact that every double pendulum has at least four equilibrium configurations.

I suggest that a law qualifies as a constraint if and only if it belongs to a non-maximal, subnomically stable set other than Λ (which, as I have shown, would have to be a proper subset of Λ). If the conservation laws are constraints, then (as I will show shortly) they join the fundamental dynamical law in a subnomically stable proper subset of Λ. In later chapters, I will look more closely at some other laws that have often reasonably been thought to transcend the force laws, such as the spacetime coordinate transformations (chapter 3) and the law of the parallelogram of forces (chapter 4). Each of these laws, I will argue, has been reasonably thought to belong to some subnomically stable proper subset of Λ that omits the various force laws and closure law. If energy conservation belongs to a stable proper subset of Λ that omits the force laws and closure law, then that set's stability requires the subjunctive fact that (I proposed earlier) distinguishes constraints from coincidences (namely, that energy would still have been conserved, had there been additional kinds of forces) since the supposition that there are additional kinds of forces is logically consistent with each of the stable proper subset's members. Energy conservation's status as a constraint is then associated with its invariance under a certain range of counterfactual antecedents, and that range consists of those antecedents that are logically consistent with every member of a stable proper subset of Λ to which energy conservation belongs. For instance, if the various particular force laws are all omitted from that subset, then by the subset's stability, energy conservation would still have held, had gravity not been an inverse-square force.

This approach provides a natural place for the distinction between constraints and coincidences by leaving room for various "strata" of natural law in the hierarchy of subnomically stable sets. Some of the sets that could reasonably have been taken as members of this hierarchy are depicted in figure 2.5. In fact, this approach leaves room for more than one level of constraints on the force laws, each level associated with a stable set that occupies a spot somewhere above Λ in the nested hierarchy of stable sets. Let's now see how this approach accounts for the conception of constraints as laws that are modally more exalted than the force laws they constrain and so as able to explain why all of the forces share certain features. In particular, let's see how it accounts for the way in which the constraints carve out a species of possibility that is broader than natural possibility (as I showed in the previous section in connection with "thermodynamic possibility," which includes some natural impossibilities).

By the definition of "subnomic stability," the members of a subnomically stable set would all still have held under any subnomic counterfactual antecedent with which they are all logically consistent—that is, under which they could (i.e., without contradiction) all still have held. In other words, a stable set's members are collectively as resilient under subnomic counterfactual antecedents as they could collectively be. They are *maximally* resilient. That is, I suggest, they are *necessary*. In other words, I propose that a subnomic truth has a species of necessity exactly when it belongs to a (nonmaximal) subnomically stable set, and that for each of these sets, there is a distinct species of necessity that is possessed by exactly its members.[36]

On this picture, there can be many species of natural necessity—many strata of natural laws (forming a nested hierarchy) that do not include all of the subnomic truths that are laws. A stable proper subset of Λ is associated with a stronger variety of necessity than Λ. That is, the range of antecedents under which the proper subset's members are all preserved, in connection with its stability, is wider than the range of antecedents under which Λ's members are all preserved, in connection with Λ's stability.[37] A greater breadth of stability-associated invariance corresponds to a stronger variety of necessity.

On this view, then, whereas constraints and coincidences are both necessary, a constraint also possesses a species of necessity that it would lack if it were instead a coincidence; it possesses a species of necessity that force laws lack. Thus, a constraint limits the kinds of forces *there could have been*, whereas a coincidence merely reflects the kinds of forces *there happen to be*. The actual inventory of forces is a matter of natural necessity and yet also a matter of happenstance in that it lacks the stronger necessity possessed by a constraint. The conservation laws as constraints would thereby *transcend* the force laws.

The same approach applies to the mathematical truths that serve as constraints in the distinctively mathematical explanations described in chapter 1. Mathematical truths belong to a stable set that lies even higher on figure 2.5's pyramidal hierarchy than any stable set containing the conservation laws that constrain the force laws. To appreciate the modal status of these mathematical truths, consider the subjunctive fact that if the electric force had been a bit stronger, the nuclear force would have been too weak to hold protons together in carbon nuclei, considering their mutual electric repulsion (Barrow and Tipler 1986, 326). In ascertaining that this is so, we appeal to the fact that various mathematical truths would still have held, even if the force laws had been different. Likewise, as Augustine (1982, 112) said, six would still have been a perfect number even if the works of God's creation had not existed—and, I would add, even if there had been different natural laws.[38] By the same token,

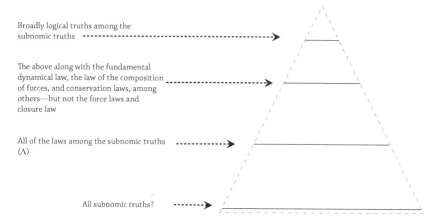

Broadly logical truths among the
subnomic truths ·····································>

The above along with the fundamental
dynamical law, the law of the composition
of forces, and conservation laws, among
others—but not the force laws and
closure law ··························>

All of the laws among the subnomic truths ·············>
(Λ)

All subnomic truths? ········>

Figure 2.5 Some (though not all) of the plausibly subnomically stable sets . At left are
specified the members of the sets on each rung of the hierarchy.

consider the way in which R. A. Fisher expressed the fact that most of his syn-
thesis of evolutionary theory and population genetics, *The Genetical Theory of
Natural Selection* (1930), is not an account of various particular events in the history of life, but rather concerns the mathematical theorems of population genetics. He said that most of his book would still have been true even if God had
created the world a few thousand years ago—and that this subjunctive conditional is associated with the especially strong kind of necessity possessed by such
mathematical theorems: "if I had had so large an aim as to write an important
book on Evolution, I should have had to attempt an account of very much work
about which I am not really qualified to give a useful opinion. As it is there is surprisingly little in the whole book that would not stand if the world had been created in 4004 B.C., and my primary job is to try to give an account of what Natural
Selection *must* be doing, even if it had never done anything of much account
until now" (Fisher 1930, 222). Mathematical theorems and other broadly logical truths would still have held, even if the laws of nature had been different; they
would still have held under any counterfactual antecedent that is logically consistent with the broadly logical truths. That is, the broadly logical truths form a
stable proper subset of Λ that omits even the conservation laws and other merely
natural laws that constitute constraints. The broadly logical truths transcend the
natural laws in that the varieties of necessity possessed by the laws are all weaker
than the variety characteristic of broadly logical truths.

This picture of necessity as associated with stability identifies what is common to broadly logical necessity and to the various grades of natural necessity
in virtue of which they are all species of the same genus. My account not only
teases apart the various grades of natural necessity among subnomic truths,
but also explains *why* there is a natural ordering among them: because for any

two subnomically stable sets, one must be a proper subset of the other. By capturing the sense in which one variety of necessity is stronger than another, this account identifies the way that some laws constrain others and thereby explain certain of their features. (I will further elaborate explanation by constraint in chapter 3.)

Finally, this view explains why any conservation law that follows from a symmetry principle within a Hamiltonian dynamical framework constitutes a constraint rather than a coincidence and so, as Wigner says (in the remark I quoted at the end of section 2.2), "transcends" the various force laws. It thereby identifies the way that symmetry principles non-causally explain conservation laws. I will devote the remainder of this section to elaborating this idea.

A symmetry principle expresses a regularity *among the laws*. (For instance, temporal symmetry says that *the laws* privilege no particular moment in the universe's history—that is, they are invariant under arbitrary temporal displacement.) Hence, a symmetry principle is not expressed by a *subnomic* claim. Rather, a symmetry principle is made true by which facts *are* laws. It is expressed by a "nomic" claim—that is, a claim that purports to describe which truths expressed by subnomic claims are (or are not) matters of law. (That all emeralds are green is a subnomic fact, whereas that it is a law that all emeralds are green is a nomic fact.)

Therefore, a symmetry principle cannot belong to a subnomically stable set. If a symmetry principle is a constraint rather than a coincidence, then it must be a "metalaw": a law that governs the laws that are expressed by subnomic claims (the "first-order" laws). For example, as a metalaw, temporal symmetry would explain why the first-order laws are all invariant under arbitrary temporal displacement by making it the case that they *must* be. To characterize the invariance under counterfactual antecedents that sets metalaws apart from other nomic and subnomic truths, we need an analogue of subnomic stability that applies to sets of claims that may contain both subnomic and nomic truths. Here it is (now allowing lowercase letters such as p to stand for claims that are either subnomic or nomic):

> Consider a nonempty set Γ of truths that are nomic or subnomic containing every nomic or subnomic logical consequence of its members. Γ possesses *nomic stability* if and only if for each member m of Γ (and in every conversational context), $\sim (p \diamond\!\!\rightarrow \sim m)$ for any p where $\Gamma \cup \{p\}$ is logically consistent.

For instance, Λ lacks nomic stability because energy might not have been conserved if there had been no *law* requiring its conservation. (The preceding was a nomic counterfactual antecedent logically consistent with Λ. Since this antecedent is nomic, Λ did not have to be preserved under it in order for Λ to be *sub*nomically stable.) Although Λ lacks nomic stability, perhaps the set spanned by all of the truths about which subnomic claims are laws and which are not (such as the fact that it is a law that all emeralds are green but not a law that all gold cubes are smaller than a cubic meter) possesses nomic stability, just as Λ possesses subnomic stability. There may, in addition, be more exclusive sets that possess nomic stability. (By the same kind of argument that I gave regarding the subnomically stable sets, the nomically stable sets form a nested hierarchy.) I suggest that the metalaws are exactly the members of any nomically stable set that is more exclusive than the set spanned by all of the truths about which subnomic claims are laws and which are not.

The members of a nomically stable set would all still have held under any nomic or subnomic counterfactual antecedent with which they are all logically consistent—that is, under which they could (i.e., without contradiction) all still have held. Therefore, the members of a nomically stable set possess a kind of *maximal* resilience in that they are collectively as resilient under nomic or subnomic counterfactual suppositions as they could collectively be. Accordingly, they possess a species of necessity. If they are metalaws, then the corresponding necessity is stronger than that possessed by coincidences concerning which subnomic claims are laws and which are not. (These coincidences belong to the set spanned by all of the truths about which subnomic claims are laws and which are not.)

Let's now see how it follows from this picture that if various conservation laws are logically entailed by symmetry metalaws within a Hamiltonian dynamical framework, then they are constraints: they belong to a subnomically stable set that is more exclusive than Λ. This result bears out Wigner's remark that conservation laws associated with symmetry principles "transcend" the various force laws. The key to this result is the connection between nomically stable sets and subnomically stable sets: for any nomically stable set Γ, its subnomic members must form a subnomically stable set Σ. Here is the proof:

1. If p (a subnomic claim) is logically inconsistent with a nomically stable set Γ, then Γ entails $\sim p$ (also subnomic) and so p is also logically inconsistent with the set Σ containing exactly Γ's subnomic logical consequences.
2. Conversely, if p is logically inconsistent with Σ, then obviously p is logically inconsistent with Γ.
3. Therefore (from 1 and 2), the subnomic claims that are logically consistent with Σ are exactly the subnomic claims that are logically consistent with Γ.
4. By Γ's nomic stability, Γ and hence its subset Σ are preserved under every subnomic antecedent p that is logically consistent with Γ—which (by 3) are exactly the subnomic antecedents that are logically consistent with Σ.
5. Hence, Σ is subnomically stable.

Thus, each nomically stable set Γ is associated with a subnomically stable "projection" Σ (see fig. 2.6.).

Suppose, then, that the symmetry metalaws (forming a nomically stable set) entail various subnomic facts, including the fact that a given conservation law holds under the Hamiltonian dynamical framework. The fact that the conservation law is true if the Hamiltonian fundamental dynamical law is true then belongs to the nomically stable set's subnomically stable projection. Presumably, that projection is more exclusive than Λ since not all of Λ's members belong to the symmetry metalaws' nomically stable set. Hence, there is a subnomically stable set possessing a strong variety of natural necessity that contains the fact that various conservation laws hold if the Hamiltonian dynamical law holds, but presumably does not contain the force laws or the Hamiltonian dynamical law (the Euler-Lagrange equations).

I suggested earlier that the fundamental dynamical law is also a constraint. Suppose that it does not belong to the subnomically stable projection of the symmetry metalaws' nomically stable set, but rather to some subnomically stable set that is lower in the hierarchy (though above Λ)—see figure 2.6. Then since the subnomically stable sets form a nested hierarchy, the fact that the conservation law holds under the Hamiltonian framework must also belong to that set, since it belongs to a set that is higher in the hierarchy (namely, the subnomic projection of the symmetry metalaws). Therefore, since a subnomically stable set contains every subnomic logical consequence of its members, the conservation law must also be a member of any subnomically stable set that includes the Hamiltonian dynamical law along with the fact that the conservation law

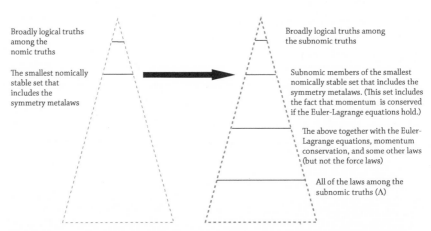

Figure 2.6 Some (though not all) of the plausibly nomically stable sets (on the left) and plausibly subnomically stable sets (on the right); they form separate hierarchies, but as the arrow shows, the subnomic proper subset of a nomically stable set forms a subnomically stable set (though not every subnomically stable set is such a subnomic "shadow" of a nomically stable set)

holds if the Hamiltonian dynamical law holds. Thus, the conservation law is a constraint.

In other words, the fact that a given conservation law would still have held, even if the force laws had been different, follows from the fact that not only the fundamental dynamical law, but also the symmetry metalaw would still have held, had the force laws been different. The explanation of conservation laws by symmetry metalaws and the fundamental dynamical law is a venerable proposed explanation by constraint, and the conservation laws so explained are themselves constraints. Moreover, I am now in a position to explain why it is that although (within the Hamiltonian dynamical framework) the entailment between the symmetry principle and conservation law runs in both directions, a conservation law that constitutes a constraint cannot help to explain (non-causally) why the corresponding symmetry metalaw holds. That is because the symmetry metalaw is modally stronger than the conservation law, since the range of counterfactual antecedents under which the symmetry metalaw is preserved, in connection with its necessity (i.e., its membership in nomically stable sets), is broader than the range of counterfactual antecedents under which the conservation law is preserved, in connection with its necessity (i.e., its membership in subnomically stable sets).

For instance, consider the counterfactual antecedent positing that the fundamental dynamical law is different. That is a nomic antecedent and so falls outside the range of invariance associated with the conservation law's natural necessity. But it falls within the range of invariance associated with the symmetry metalaw's natural necessity. Had the fundamental dynamical law been different, the symmetry metalaw would still have held (by the relevant set's nomic stability) but the conservation law might not still have held. (The same applies to the counterfactual antecedent positing that the conservation law is violated.)

Since the symmetry metalaw is modally stronger than the conservation law, it cannot be explained by the conservation law, since to explain the symmetry metalaw, a fact must be at least as modally strong as it is (but need not be modally stronger than it is). For an antecedent p under which the symmetry metalaw is preserved in connection with its characteristic necessity, but under which the conservation law is not preserved, it cannot be that in the "closest p-world," the symmetry metalaw holds because the conservation law holds—since the conservation law does not hold. Hence, the conservation law cannot explain why the symmetry metalaw is preserved in the closest p-world. Therefore, the conservation law cannot help to account for the symmetry principle's necessity and thus cannot help to explain why the symmetry principle holds. (In chapter 3, I will say more about the relation between explaining a constraint's necessity and explaining why the constraint holds.)

This argument that the conservation law cannot be partly responsible for the symmetry principle's holding is essentially the same as the argument I gave earlier that if energy conservation is a constraint, then the reason why fluids undergo no spontaneous circulation cannot be that electric forces fail to induce circulation (because of the electric-force law), gravitational forces fail to induce circulation (because of the gravitational-force law), and so forth for all of the actual kinds of forces actually experienced by fluid parcels. This account fails to explain why fluids do not circulate because it depicts the explanandum as depending on which particular possible kinds of forces are actually acting on fluid parcels and hence as more contingent than it is, since no force that would produce fluid circulation is even possible (where the *possible* kinds of force go beyond the kinds listed in the closure law). The fluid's noncirculation is modally too strong to be explained by the force laws when its necessity is connected with the fact that it would still have held even if the force laws had been different. Likewise, a given symmetry principle is modally too strong to be explained by the corresponding conservation law (together with the fundamental dynamical law) when the symmetry's necessity is connected with the fact that it would still have held even if the conservation law (or the fundamental dynamical law) had not held.[39]

I have merely tried to show how one account of natural lawhood incorporates the distinction between constraint and coincidence in a natural way and thereby accounts for explanations by constraint. I will conclude this chapter by looking at two alternative approaches to natural law that cannot make the same boast.

■ 2.7 ACCOUNTS THAT RULE OUT EXPLANATIONS BY CONSTRAINT

Some of the "explanations by constraint" that I have drawn from scientific practice are deemed to be explanatorily impotent by some accounts of scientific explanation. Consider, for instance, Woodward's manipulationist account of scientific explanation, according to which an explanans must provide information about how the explanandum would have been different under various counterfactual changes to the variables figuring in the explanans:

> It is built into the manipulationist account of explanation I have been defending that explanatory relationships must be change-relating: they must tell us how changes in some quantity or magnitude would change under changes in some other quantity. Thus, if there are generalizations that are laws but that are not change-relating, they cannot figure in explanations. (Woodward 2003, 208)

> If some putative explanandum cannot be changed or if some putative explanans for this explanandum does not invoke variables, changes in which would be associated with changes in the explanandum, then we cannot use that explanans to explain the explanandum. (233)

These criteria rule out many typical explanations by constraint. Unlike the charges and distances in Coulomb's law, there are no obvious variables to be changed in the law that every fundamental force acts by contact, or in the fact that 23 is not divided evenly into whole numbers by 3, or in the law that every kind of interaction conserves energy. Yet these constraints power explanations, on my view. Admittedly, we could insist on treating "act by contact" as the value of a variable in the law that all fundamental forces act by contact, and we might then ask what force laws would have been like had that variable's value instead been "act at a distance." But the answer is: any force law might have held. Hertz's argument from action by contact to the law that all fundamental forces must be inverse-square (or, more accurately, must obey Yukawa force laws) reveals nothing about how the forces' strength would have been a function of separation if the forces had operated instead by action at a distance: the argument does not show, for example, that all fundamental forces would then have been inverse-cube. Hertz's argument simply goes nowhere if "action by contact" is changed to "action at a distance," since under action at a distance, a force does not have to satisfy a uniqueness theorem.

Woodward (2003, 220–221) compares his account of scientific explanations to Steiner's (1978a, b) account of explanations in mathematics. In part III, I will look at explanations in mathematics; in section 8.5, I will look at Steiner's proposal and compare it to mine. For now, let me describe Steiner's proposal very briefly merely to highlight its similarity to Woodward's account of scientific explanation. According to Steiner, a proof of the mathematical theorem that all S_1's are P_1 explains why the theorem holds if and only if the proof reveals how the theorem depends on S_1's "characterizing property" in that if S_1's characterizing property is replaced in the proof by the characterizing property for another kind S_2 in the same "family" (while the original "proof idea" is maintained), then the resulting "deformation" of the original proof proves that all S_2's are P_2 for some property P_2 incompatible with being P_1. One of the problems with Steiner's approach is analogous to the problem with Woodward's approach that I have just mentioned. The problem (to be discussed in section 8.5) is that when some explanatory proofs in mathematics are deformed to fit a different class in what is presumably the same "family," the proofs simply go nowhere rather than yielding a parallel theorem regarding that other class. Thus, it is not always the case that "in an explanatory proof we see how the theorem changes in response to variations in other assumptions" (Woodward 2003, 220).

The failure of Woodward's account to allow for typical explanations by constraint is not very surprising. As I just mentioned, Woodward says that a putative explanandum must be capable of being changed, if certain other conditions were to change. In contrast, the facts being explained in many of the explanations by constraint that we have examined are themselves constraints. (After all, they follow entirely from constraints.) As constraints, they possess an especially strong variety of necessity and therefore have an especially strong resistance to being changed. Consider that Woodward takes the value of Newton's gravitational constant G as having no explanation in classical gravitational theory because "from the point of view of Newtonian gravitational theory, G is a constant, which cannot be changed by changing other variables. . . . To explain something, we must be able to think of it as (representable by) a *variable*, not as a constant or a fixed parameter" (2003, 234). What Woodward says about Newton's G applies even more strongly to constraints. Although Woodward leaves open the possibility of non-causal explanations in science, he insists that both causal and non-causal explanations "must answer what-if-things-had-been-different questions" (221). But consider an explanation by constraint such as "Every kind of force at work in this particular spacetime region conserves momentum because a force that fails to conserve momentum is impossible; momentum conservation constrains the kinds of forces there could have been." This explanation reveals nothing about the kinds of forces that would have existed in this region under various hypothetical conditions where momentum conservation is not a constraint. Even more strongly than G's value, momentum conservation is "fixed" in classical physics.

Of course, the explanation by constraint does reveal that even if there had been different kinds of forces, momentum would still have been conserved. It seems to me arbitrary for Woodward to regard information about the conditions under which the explanandum would have *remained the same* as irrelevant to explanation, while regarding information about the conditions under which it would have been *different* as explanatory.[40]

Woodward (2003) appears content with his account's failure to accommodate explanations by constraint.[41] For instance, he acknowledges that on his account, the "speed limit" fact that all physical processes must propagate at speeds less than or equal to that of light does not explain why a given physical process does so because the "speed limit" fact fails to specify the conditions under which a given physical process's speed would have been different and what its speed would then have been (208–209). But in failing to accommodate explanations by constraint, Woodward's account departs too far from scientific practice.[42] A proposed explanation like Hertz's should be disconfirmed (or confirmed) by empirical scientific investigation, rather than being ruled out a priori by an account of what scientific explanations are.[43]

Let's conclude by turning to another popular approach that fails to do justice to explanations by constraint. According to Bird (2007), every sparse fundamental property of physics is constituted by one or more dispositions. On Bird's view, the association between a fundamental property of physics and some disposition is a matter of metaphysical necessity. (Moreover, the identity of a given fundamental property of physics is exhausted by its dispositional character.)

Therefore (when the disposition is "surefire"), it is metaphysically necessary that any entity possessing a certain sparse fundamental property of physics exhibit certain further properties if suitably causally stimulated. These regularities, or the corresponding relations among properties, are the laws of nature. Although metaphysically necessary, the laws do not perform the explanatory heavy lifting. The motor and cement of the universe are the dispositional essences of the fundamental properties of physics. Views along roughly similar lines have been proposed by Ellis (2001, 2002) and Mumford (2004), among others. These views differ in some details from Bird's. For example, Ellis takes the dispositional essences responsible for laws to be the essences of the natural kinds rather than of the sparse fundamental properties of physics. Mumford holds that any fundamental property of physics is constituted by a cluster consisting of its causal roles and other connections to other properties (such as its excluding certain properties and being compatible with certain others); there are no laws because nothing governs property instances in the manner traditionally ascribed to laws. However, these differences among different versions of "dispositional essentialism" will make little difference here.

A conservation law does not say that any entity possessing a certain sparse fundamental property of physics exhibits certain further properties if suitably causally stimulated. Unlike (for instance) the occurrence of a certain force, energy's remaining conserved is not the characteristic manifestation of a particular body's disposition. Therefore, it is difficult for views like Bird's to accommodate conservation laws, as Bird (2007, 211) himself notes.

It is worth distinguishing three forms that this objection to dispositional essentialism can take. The first form is that energy's remaining conserved under any interaction of a given kind is simply not the manifestation of any of the dispositions constituting any of the sparse fundamental properties of physics manifested in such interactions. The dispositions associated with electric charge, for instance, may manifest themselves in various accelerations or various contributions to the electric field. Thus, the laws specifying that charges manifest themselves in certain ways under certain conditions do not include among these manifestations anything about energy being conserved. The law that electric interactions conserve energy therefore seems to have been left out of the account.

However, it seems to me that the law has not been omitted. From various laws concerning electric interactions, it follows logically that such interactions conserve energy. So on this account, energy's conservation in electric interactions is a metaphysical necessity arising from the dispositions essential to various fundamental properties of physics, including charge. There is no problem yet for Bird's view.

The second form of the objection is that the law of energy conservation does not follow simply from the law that energy is conserved in electric interactions, the law that energy is conserved in gravitational interactions, and so forth. There must be a further premise, since these force laws taken together do not preclude the existence of another kind of process that fails to conserve energy. One premise that would close the gap is a "closure law": that electric interactions, gravitational interactions, and so forth are all of the kinds of interactions there are—that is, that every fundamental natural process belongs to one of these kinds. The objection, then, is that this "closure law" does not reflect any property's dispositional essence. Hence, the overall conservation law is not the reflection of the dispositional essences of the fundamental properties of physics.

Ellis's view purports to be invulnerable to this form of the objection. Ellis takes the laws to be grounded not in the dispositional essences of various properties, but rather in the essences of the various natural kinds. He suggests (following Bigelow, Ellis, and Lierse 1992) that the world is the only member of a certain natural kind and that the essence of this kind includes various quantities being conserved (Ellis 2001, 205 and 250). Its essence also includes there being exactly certain sorts of particles and fields undergoing exactly certain sorts of interactions, thereby accounting for what I have called "closure laws." I have replied elsewhere that this move "seems like a desperate attempt to find *something* the essence of which could be responsible for various laws. Even if gravity and the electron have essences, it is not obvious that 'the world'—reality—does" (Lange 2009a, 83). Bird also finds this move "somewhat ad hoc" (2007, 213). However, I shall not pursue this concern here.

This form of the objection may turn out not to pose a terribly severe challenge for Bird's view. One option that Bird might explore is to say simply that although the energy conservation "law" is not a metaphysical necessity, the fact that energy is conserved is no accident either. Rather, it is grounded in the sparse fundamental properties of physics—that is, in the world's repertoire of fundamental causal powers. But this option would require Bird to allow different repertoires in different possible worlds, which Bird is reluctant to do (since in that case the actual laws, though still true in all worlds, are not laws in some of them). Another option for elaborating Bird's view accords metaphysical necessity to the conservation law and allows every world to have exactly the same laws. As I just explained, energy's conservation in electric interactions is (on Bird's view) a metaphysical necessity arising from the dispositions essential to various fundamental properties of physics. So likewise is energy's conservation in gravitational interactions, and similarly for any other actual type of interaction. On Bird's view, the various fundamental properties of physics would be different properties if they bestowed additional powers and susceptibilities—for instance, the power to exert and the susceptibility to feel some alien force that fails to conserve energy. Presumably, no metaphysical necessity precludes the instantiation of alien fundamental properties of physics. But "electric charge" (or any other nonalien property) would be a different property if it bestowed susceptibility not just to the influence of other electric charges, but also to some other alien influence. Suppose that all of the nonalien properties (or, at least, enough of them that all nonalien kinds of entities must possess one) have as part of their essences that their possession bestows immunity to being influenced by any other entity's alien property. Then one entity's possession of alien properties could not influence the behavior of other entities possessing the nonalien properties and so could not disturb the conservation of the quantities that are in fact conserved under each of the various actual types of interaction, as long as those quantities are possessed only by entities possessing the nonalien properties. In that case, although these quantities are not instantiated in every possible world, they are conserved in any world where they are instantiated, since the nonalien properties constituting these quantities bestow immunity to any other influences besides the various actual types of forces. Energy conservation is then metaphysically necessary even if the closure law is not and even though the conservation law is not the manifestation of any single fundamental property's dispositional essence.

However, let's now consider a third form of the original objection that views like Bird's cannot properly accommodate conservation laws. This form of the objection will prove more difficult for dispositional essentialism to address. On Bird's picture, even if energy conservation is metaphysically necessary, it is the product of the various particular types of interactions there are: that gravitational forces conserve energy, electric forces conserve energy, and so forth. The various dispositions essential to various fundamental natural properties are responsible for energy's conservation. So although energy conservation is metaphysically necessary, it is a coincidence rather than a constraint.

To appreciate this, recall the subjunctive fact that (I suggested earlier) is what it is for energy conservation to be a constraint: that energy would still have been conserved even if there had been an additional kind of interaction experienced by some of the entities undergoing some of the actual kinds of interaction. On Bird's view, there is no disposition (or collection of dispositions) essential to some sparse fundamental property of physics (or collection of such properties) that is available to underwrite this conditional's truth. The causal powers constituting those properties do the metaphysical heavy lifting, but these causal powers cannot underwrite this conditional's truth; no actual causal power has as its manifestation that certain alien fundamental natural properties are instantiated, and none has as the stimulus inducing its manifestation that some alien kind of interaction occurs. The conditional associated with being a constraint does not concern what the actual causal powers would produce under suitable stimulation, but rather concerns what causal powers there would be if there were more besides the actual ones. So the actual causal powers do not sustain this conditional's truth. The same applies to other subjunctive facts associated with a conservation law's membership in an elite stable proper subset of Λ. For example, the fact that energy would still have been conserved, had gravity not been an inverse-square force, is underwritten by no causal powers, on Bird's view.[44]

Ellis's view faces a similar problem: there is no natural kind whose essence can step in to sustain the subjunctive conditional needed to make energy conservation a constraint. Even the world's essence cannot do the job since the subjunctive conditional's antecedent (positing an additional, alien kind of interaction) is inconsistent with that essence. On Ellis's view, had there been additional kinds of interactions, there would have been a different kind of world. Presumably, it might have been a world where energy is conserved, but then again, it might not have been. Energy conservation is therefore a coincidence, not a constraint.

On a view like Bird's, a conservation law cannot be a constraint because a conservation law cannot be explanatorily prior to the force laws—or, rather, to the various dispositions responsible for the force laws and essential to the various sparse fundamental properties of physics. Gravitational interactions conserve energy not because the law of energy conservation requires them to, but rather because of the causal powers involved in gravitational interactions (which the gravitational-force law reflects). It is not the case that energy conservation explains (regardless of which of the actual kinds of fundamental forces are experienced by fluid parcels) why no fluid spontaneously circulates; rather, the explainers must be the particular powers involved. Even if a given power's conserving energy suffices to entail the explanandum, energy conservation as a comprehensive law covering all of the actual powers is explanatorily irrelevant. All that matters to explaining the outcome is the fact that the particular power operating in the given case conserves energy. This is how all scientific explanations must work, according to Ellis—causally: "Essentialists seek to expose the underlying causes of things, and to explain why things are as they are, or behave as they do, by reference to these underlying causal factors. Consequently, explanations of the sort that essentialists are seeking must always have two parts. They must contain hypotheses about the underlying structures or causal powers of things, and hypotheses about how things having these structures and powers must behave in the specific circumstances in which they exist" (Ellis 2002, 159–160). This approach to scientific explanation leaves no room for explanations by constraint. Why are two forces alike in conserving energy? Why do no kinds of interaction put fluids spontaneously into circulation? On Ellis's picture, the facts being explained are merely upshots of the various particular kinds of interaction built into the world's essence, all of which conserve energy.

Bird likewise seems to find explanations from constraining conservation laws to be problematic: "There is something mysterious about conservation laws. They seem to require explanation. . . . How does a system know that energy should be conserved? . . . It is not clear how these could be fundamental laws—they seem to stand in need of a deeper explanation" (Bird 2007, 213). The deeper explanation that Bird has in mind would be in terms of the particular causal powers at work in the system. It is these powers that allow a system to "know that energy should be conserved." But this is the order of explanatory priority that is characteristic of conservation laws as coincidences: the various force laws (or, for the essentialist, the various particular causal powers responsible for the force laws) come before the conservation laws. By contrast, as I showed earlier, conservation laws as constraints provide explanations that transcend the particular powers involved. By constituting common explainers, conservation laws as constraints unify the noncirculation of ropes and fluids, for example, and likewise unify various otherwise unrelated forces as all inverse-square (or as all subject to uniqueness theorems) or as all conserving energy for the same reason. These explanations reveal that the fact to be explained would still have held even if there had been different fundamental forces at work.

That conservation laws must be coincidences rather than constraints on Bird's account seems to be roughly what Bird has in mind when he acknowledges that his account cannot accommodate conservation laws: "Conservation and symmetry laws tell us that interactions are constrained by the requirement of preserving, e.g., mass-energy or momentum. . . . The dispositional essentialist holds that the laws are necessary. If that is correct there is no room for further constraints. Properties are already constrained by their own essences and so there is neither need nor opportunity for higher-order properties to direct which relations they can engage in" (2007, 211 and 214). Bird's thought seems to be that as constraints on (the causal powers responsible for) the various force laws, conservation laws would have to impose limitations on the possible manifestations of the powers associated with electric charge, mass, and so forth, limiting the interaction laws to those that conserve energy. But these interaction laws are already fully determined by the properties (charge, mass, . . .) involved in the interactions, since those properties are essentially constituted by various causal powers, which fix their own possible manifestations. So there is no further constraining for a conservation law to do. It seems to me that on the contrary, there is more that the conservation law could constrain: what powers there *would* be, if additional fundamental natural properties were instantiated. However, this view requires the conservation law to do some metaphysical heavy lifting—a job that, on Bird's picture, is reserved for the causal powers.[45]

In short, a conservation law as a constraint has greater necessity than any of the motley collection of various particular force laws (or the closure law) and thus explains why those laws are alike in all exhibiting certain features. But on views like Bird's and Ellis's, the particular force laws hold as matters of metaphysical necessity. No greater necessity is left for a constraint to possess; necessity has already been maxed out in the force laws. So there is no genuine "thermodynamic possibility" (as we saw Gibbs invoke in section 2.5)—no sense in which various actual properties could have been associated with certain alien powers but not with others (namely, with only those alien powers that, in being manifested, would conserve energy, momentum, and so forth). Therefore, conservation laws cannot be constraints; they can only be coincidences.

Bird seems content with this result: "The dispositional essentialist ought to regard symmetry principles as pseudo-laws. . . . So it may be that symmetry principles and conservation laws will be eliminated as being features of our form of representation rather than features of the world requiring to be accommodated within our metaphysics" (Bird 2007, 214). However, I have argued throughout this chapter that the price of adopting this view is too high. It precludes explanations of a kind that science has reasonably taken seriously—indeed, on which science has often placed great importance. Views like Bird's rule out scientifically respectable theories. Perhaps Bird's prognostication regarding future science will be proved right; perhaps symmetry principles and conservation laws, along with the alleged explanations they supply, will ultimately be eliminated from physics (without their place being taken by other constraints). Personally, I doubt it. But in any event, a metaphysics that cannot do justice to explanations by constraint is at a serious disadvantage even if as a matter of fact, there turn out to be no such explanations. Room should still be left for them; it should be up to science rather than metaphysics to foreclose them.

Consider, for instance, the conservation of baryon number in contemporary physics. By energy conservation, an isolated proton can decay only into particles that have less rest-mass than it does, and the proton is the lightest baryon (that is, the lightest particle with nonzero baryon number). The conservation of baryon number thus entails that the proton is stable (radioactively, I mean—not subnomically!). Does baryon-number conservation (together with energy conservation and the proton's being the lightest baryon) explain why the proton is stable? This remains controversial.

It is no explanation if the conservation of baryon number is an "accidental symmetry," a term that was introduced by Weinberg (1995, 529). An accidental symmetry reflects merely the particular forces in action at lower-energy regimes rather than some deeper "symmetry of the underlying theory" (529). Accordingly, if baryon-number conservation is an accidental symmetry, then it may not even hold at higher energies (and so the proton may turn out not to be stable, but rather to have an extremely long half-life). But even if an accidental symmetry is unbroken, it would still be a coincidence of the particular kinds of interactions written "by hand" into the underlying theory, and so it would fail to explain. The stability of the lightest baryon would then help to explain why baryon number turns out to be conserved, not vice versa.

On the other hand, baryon-number conservation may turn out to be a consequence of a more fundamental symmetry, in which case it would help to explain the proton's stability. For example, Wigner writes, "It is conceivable, for instance, that a conservation law for the number of heavy particles (protons and neutrons) is responsible for the stability of the protons in the same way as the conservation law for charges is responsible for the stability of the electron. Without the conservation law in question, the proton could disintegrate, under emission of a light quantum, into a positron, just as the electron could disintegrate, were it not for the conservation law for the electric charge, into a light quantum and a neutrino" (Wigner 1949, 525).[46] (Note the counterlegal that Wigner invokes: "Had there been no such conservation law, the proton would have been unstable"!) If the baryon conservation law is a constraint, then there is only one kind of explanation of the fact that any isolated system's baryon number after some lapse of time is the same as its initial baryon number: an explanation by constraint as supplied by the conservation law. Even if the various particular interaction laws together with the initial state determine the final state (and hence its baryon number), a description of the causal processes at work (including the interaction laws governing them) would fail to capture the fact that baryon number would still have been conserved even if different or additional kinds of interactions had occurred. The explanandum has no causal explanation.

Whereas some physicists cite baryon-number conservation as helping to explain why the proton is stable (e.g., Davies 1986, 159; Duffin 1980, 82), other physicists put scare-quotes around "explain" (Lederman and Teresi 1993, 303) or say that the jury is still out (Ne'eman and Kirsh 1996, 150–151). The uncertainty regarding the conservation law's explanatory power is matched by the uncertainty regarding the law's status as a constraint or a coincidence. But this live scientific controversy would be settled outright by views like Bird's. I do not think that metaphysics should prejudge the outcome.[47]

If the laws are the upshot of the inventory of powers and hence (according to dispositional essentialism) of the sparse fundamental properties of physics, then any regularity in these powers (even if metaphysically necessary) is coincidental; no law transcends the various actual powers, constraining the powers there could have been. However, metaphysics should permit Feynman's "great general principles which all the laws seem to follow" to be constraints. It should not oblige them to be coincidences.

3

The Lorentz Transformations and the Structure of Explanations by Constraint

The Lorentz transformations are central to Einstein's special theory of relativity, entailing such famous relativistic results as time dilation, length contraction, the relativity of simultaneity, and the velocity addition rule. The transformations specify how a pointlike event's spacetime coordinates (x',y',z',t') in one reference frame S' relate to its coordinates (x,y,z,t) in another frame S, where the two frames are "inertial." (If there were bodies feeling no external forces, then they would exhibit no acceleration in an "inertial" frame, thereby according with Newton's first law of motion there.) For S and S' in "standard configuration" (see fig. 3.1: the corresponding primed and unprimed axes are parallel, the origin of the spatial coordinates in S' is moving uniformly in S with speed v in the $+x$ direction, the spatial origins in S and S' coincide when the times at each are $t = 0$ and $t' = 0$, the frames are equivalent when $v = 0$), the Lorentz transformations are:

$$x' = (x - vt)/\left(1 - v^2/c^2\right)^{\frac{1}{2}}$$

$$y' = y$$

$$z' = z$$

$$t' = \left(t - vx/c^2\right)/\left(1 - v^2/c^2\right)^{\frac{1}{2}}$$

The Lorentz transformations replace the Galilean transformations from classical physics:

$$x' = x - vt$$

$$y' = y$$

$$z' = z$$

$$t' = t$$

Why do the Lorentz transformations hold?[1] My main concern in this chapter will be to understand what it would be for the Lorentz transformations to

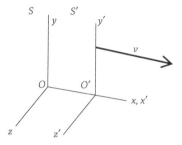

Figure 3.1 Reference frames *S* and *S'* in standard configuration

have one or another possible explanation. This question is a direct analogue of the question I examined in the previous chapter: what would it be for a conservation law to have one or another possible explanation? Just as a conservation law can be either a constraint or a coincidence, depending upon its explanatory role, so likewise the Lorentz transformations can be either constraints or coincidences, depending upon their explanatory role. A transformation law, just like a conservation law, may constrain the force laws, thereby transcending them. Alternatively, a transformation law may be explained by the force laws and so be a coincidence of them. As a constraint, a transformation law is explained only by non-causal explanations: explanations by constraint. As a coincidence, by contrast, a transformation law is explained only by causal explanations—that is, dynamically.

My aim, then, will be to identify the facts that determine whether the transformation laws have an explanation by constraint or a causal explanation. To do this, I will use the apparatus that I elaborated in chapter 2. Both views regarding the transformation laws' explanation represent genuine (broadly logical) possibilities—ways that a world could be. Accordingly, it is a scientific, empirical question as to whether the transformation laws "transcend" the force laws. My aim will not be to argue that they do, but rather to understand what it would be for them to do so—and how a non-causal explanation of them would work.

Some philosophers who have written recently about the status of the Lorentz transformations deliberately avoid discussing issues concerning scientific explanation. For instance, Norton (2008, 824) says that such discussions "seem only to lead to futile disputes over just what it means to explain, over which is the better explanation and, most opaquely, which is the 'real' explanation." In contrast, I see this case as affording us a valuable opportunity to understand what one kind of non-causal explanation (explanation by constraint) amounts to—as well as to appreciate the important role that such proposed explanations play in science.

For example, the Lorentz transformations offer a useful example of how Salmon's (1989, 180–182) distinction between "top-down" and "bottom-up" explanations figures in scientific practice. An explanation by constraint is an important kind of top-down scientific explanation whereas a dynamical, causal explanation of the Lorentz transformations would be a paradigm case of a bottom-up explanation. Salmon's distinction strikes me as very similar to Einstein's (1919) distinction between "principle" and "constructive" theories (though Salmon does not make this comparison); Einstein emphasizes that special relativity is a principle theory. Several philosophers have invoked Einstein's distinction (and Einstein's own remarks in drawing it) as supporting the view that the Lorentz transformations cannot be explained from the top down and, moreover, that what I have called an "explanation by constraint" is actually no explanation at all. In chapter 2, I began to elaborate how such explanations work. I will continue that task in this chapter by investigating the basis for the order of explanatory priority in explanations by constraint. The Lorentz transformations will be a useful example in this regard; we can ask, for example, why the Lorentz transformations are explained partly by the invariance of the spacetime interval rather than the other way around (or neither way). In laying out how explanations by constraint derive their power to explain, I will object to the view that principle theories are explanatorily impotent because all scientific explanations are causal. I will also argue that Einstein is not correctly interpreted as denying the explanatory power of principle theories.

In section 3.2, I will elaborate what it would be for the Lorentz transformations to be independent of light and the other inhabitants of spacetime. Part of what would make them independent is for the principle of relativity to be a metalaw. I will thus cash out the idea that Einstein's "great advance of 1905" was his taking symmetries not as mere "consequences of the dynamical laws of nature," but rather "as the primary feature of nature that constrains the allowable dynamical laws" (Gross 1996, 14256). In cashing out this idea, I will appeal to exactly the same notion of constraint that figured in my account (in chapter 2) of conservation laws as explaining by constraining the force laws. I will thereby account for the fact that scientists associate certain subjunctive facts with top-down explanations of the Lorentz transformations.

In section 3.3, I will argue that when Einstein's remarks about principle and constructive theories are properly interpreted, they help us to understand the different roles played by causal explanations and explanations by constraint in accounting for phenomena such as length contraction. Although we need a constructive theory in order to explain a given bar's length in a given reference frame, a principle theory rather than a constructive theory would explain the *relation* between the bar's lengths in the two frames if (and only if) the Lorentz transformations transcend the dynamics. I will contrast Einstein's picture with Salmon's account of the relation between top-down and bottom-up explanations.

In section 3.4, I will use this approach to understand the reason why (according to classical physics) there is a family of reference frames in which Newton's first law of motion holds. I will show what it would take for Newton's first law to transcend the dynamical laws. This explanation by constraint of Newton's first law would fill an explanatory gap for the relationalist regarding Newtonian space and time. More generally, my account of explanation by constraint will allow us to understand what it would be for certain features of space to constrain space's inhabitants and thereby explain why (for instance) all attempts to superimpose left and right human hands have failed. On this view, certain spatial necessities serve as a common reason why every kind of causal process is alike in failing to superimpose hands, making this similarity among the processes no coincidence. But this explanation requires that certain facts about the geometry of space have a kind of necessity that is stronger than that possessed by the dynamical laws.

In sections 3.5, 3.6, and 3.7, I will further develop my account of how explanations by constraint work. I will elaborate the idea that an explanation by constraint explains by supplying information about the source of the explanandum's especially strong necessity (just as a causal explanation works by supplying information about the explanandum's causal history or, more broadly, about the world's causal network). In other words, the idea that I will elaborate is that an explanation by constraint derives its power to explain by virtue of providing information about where the explanandum's especially strong necessity comes from. The context in which the why question is asked may influence what information about the origin of the explanandum's especially strong necessity is relevant. Context plays a similar role in connection with causal explanations: by influencing what information about the explanandum's causal history or the world's network of causal relations is relevant.

To understand what a "source" of the explanandum's especially strong necessity would be, I will distinguish "explanatorily fundamental" from "explanatorily derivative" laws among the constraints having the same especially strong variety of necessity. I will use this idea to understand why certain deductions of constraints exclusively from other constraints lack explanatory power. For example, every attempt to untie a trefoil knot while wearing a blue suit has met with failure (as I mentioned in chapter 1), but this fact is not explained by its being mathematically impossible to untie a trefoil knot while wearing a blue suit. The wardrobe doesn't enter into it.

I will also use the distinction between explanatorily fundamental and derivative constraints to understand why the spacetime interval's invariance is explanatorily prior to the Lorentz transformations rather than the other way around (or neither way)—and why the interval's invariance rather than (e.g.) the relativity of simultaneity helps to account for the Lorentz transformations. I will argue that there is no fully general ground for the distinction between explanatorily fundamental and derivative constraints. Rather, the order of explanatory priority among constraints that are on a modal par is grounded differently in different cases. I will identify how that order is grounded in relativity's explanation of the Lorentz transformations and—differently—in Hertz's proposed explanation of the inverse-square character of fundamental forces (from chapter 2).

▪ 3.2 THE LORENTZ TRANSFORMATIONS GIVEN AN EXPLANATION BY CONSTRAINT

Einstein (1905/1989) originally derived the Lorentz transformations from two premises:

1. The "principle of relativity," which entails that the laws of nature take the same form in all inertial frames
2. The "light postulate": that in one inertial frame, light's speed is independent of the motion of its source

Of course, not all deductions are explanations, and for various reasons, this derivation is not generally regarded as explaining why the Lorentz transformations hold. In particular, many commentators regard the light postulate as unable to help explain the Lorentz transformations. Rather, they say, the arrow of explanatory priority points in the opposite direction: the Lorentz transformations are responsible for some of light's features. For example, Stachel (1995, 270–272) sees the light postulate as "an unnecessary non-kinematical element" in Einstein's derivation:

> His presentation of the special theory bears distinct traces of its origins. Mesmerized by the problem of the nature of light, he ignored the discrepancy between the relativity principle, kinematical in nature and universal in scope, and the light principle . . . concerned with a particular type of electrodynamical phenomenon. [Stachel's footnote: The oddity of this reference to light would be even more apparent if one replaced it by a reference to some other massless field, basing the theory, for example, on the principle of the constancy of the speed of neutrinos.][2] Einstein later recognized such defects in his original arguments.

> "The special theory of relativity grew out of the Maxwell electromagnetic equations. So it came about that even in the derivation of the mechanical concepts and their relations the consideration of those of the electromagnetic field has played an essential role. The question as to the independence of those relations is a natural one because the Lorentz transformation, the real basis of the special relativity theory, in itself has nothing to do with the Maxwell theory." (Einstein 1935, 223, with minor corrections to Stachel's quote)

On Stachel's view, the Lorentz transformations are explanatorily prior to the laws describing the particular sorts of things (e.g., light, electromagnetic fields) that happen to populate spacetime.

I agree with Stachel that the older Einstein frequently emphasized the Lorentz transformations' priority over the properties of spacetime's inhabitants, as in remarks like this: "The new feature of [my work of 1905] was the realization of the fact that the bearing of the Lorentz transformation transcended its connection with Maxwell's equations and was concerned with the nature of space and time in general. A further new result was that the 'Lorentz invariance' is a general condition for any physical theory. This was for me of particular importance" (Einstein 1955/1956). Einstein's thought that the Lorentz transformations "transcend" Maxwell's electromagnetic theory is reminiscent of Wigner's view (quoted in chapter 2) that the conservation laws associated with spacetime symmetry principles transcend the various force laws. I will shortly interpret Einstein as characterizing the Lorentz transformations as "constraints" in the same sense as the conservation laws associated with spacetime symmetries according to Wigner. Indeed, just as (on my account) those conservation laws would acquire the modal status of constraints by being explained non-causally by symmetry principles serving as metalaws, so I will show shortly that the Lorentz transformation laws would acquire the modal status of constraints by being explained non-causally by the principle of relativity serving as a symmetry metalaw.

Many physicists and philosophers have interpreted the requirement that the dynamical laws be invariant under the Lorentz transformations (be "Lorentz covariant")[3] as constraining what dynamical laws there could have been and thereby explaining why all of the actual dynamical laws are Lorentz covariant. However, this notion of a "constraint" on the laws (and of symmetry principles as metalaws) is somewhat mysterious. Without my account of what a "constraint" and a "metalaw" would be, it is difficult to see how to make sense of a host of remarks common in discussions of the Lorentz transformations.

For instance, physicists commonly characterize the principle of relativity as "a sort of 'super law,'" as Lévy-Leblond (1976, 271) calls it (following Wigner 1985, 700), so that "all the laws of physics are constrained" by it. Philosophers follow suit. Earman (1989, 55), for example, says that the special theory of relativity "is not a theory in the usual sense but is better regarded as a second-level theory, or a theory of theories that constrains first-level theories." Despite the familiarity of such remarks, mysterious modal metaphysics lurks only slightly beneath their surface. Consider, for instance, Penrose's (1987, 24) characterization of Einstein's insight as "that one should take relativity as a *principle*, rather than as a seemingly accidental consequence of other laws" or this similar comment from Janssen (2009, 39): "Special relativity provid[ed] a new interpretation of Lorentz invariance. . . . In this new interpretation, the property of Lorentz invariance is no longer accidentally shared by all dynamical laws." What in the world could Penrose and Janssen mean? After all, a consequence of laws alone cannot really be *accidental*.[4] What could it be for the principle of relativity to be an accident or for it to be an accident that all dynamical laws are Lorentz covariant—and what is the alternative?

On my view, for it to be an "accident" that all dynamical laws are Lorentz covariant would be for it to be a *coincidence* in the sense I elaborated in the previous chapter: for there to be no common explanation of each law's Lorentz covariance. If it is instead no "accident," then each law is Lorentz covariant for the same reason: because the dynamical laws *must* be Lorentz covariant, as a result of certain laws constraining every dynamical law. In that event, the Lorentz transformations are explained entirely by certain laws possessing a stronger variety of natural necessity than the dynamical laws do. Some of the explainers (such as the principle of relativity) may do so by being metalaws in virtue of belonging to a nomically stable set. Other explainers (such as the spacetime interval's invariance) may possess a stronger variety of natural necessity than the dynamical laws do in that these explainers occupy a higher rung on the pyramidal hierarchy of subnomically stable sets (depicted in fig. 2.5) than the dynamical laws do. Such an explainer belongs to a subnomically stable set that is a proper subset of any subnomically stable set to which the dynamical laws belong. If the Lorentz transformations are explained entirely by laws possessing a stronger variety of natural necessity than the dynamical laws do, then the Lorentz transformations likewise transcend the dynamical laws and so cannot be explained dynamically (even if they can be deduced entirely from the facts about what the dynamical laws are). Any purported dynamical explanation would incorrectly characterize the transformation laws as coincidences when they are not (just as I showed in the previous chapter in connection with the conservation laws purportedly being explained by the various force laws).

In order to cash out "constraint" and "metalaw" in these modal terms, I must appeal to the hierarchy of natural necessities that I elaborated in chapter 2. That hierarchy specifies what it would be for the Lorentz transformations to "transcend" the force laws by being more necessary than they are. Some philosophers, despite recognizing that the Lorentz transformations transcend dynamics, try to cash out their transcendence without appealing to necessity, subjunctive facts, and the other heavy-duty metaphysics that I invoked in chapter 2. For instance, in taking a principle theory as supplying "criteria that any constructive theory must satisfy," Stachel (2002, 165) interprets this *must* epistemically rather than metaphysically: a principle theory will "serve to limit and guide the search for a constructive theory." Janssen (2009) takes a view similar to Stachel's. He emphasizes that relativity transcends the details of the particular force laws that obtain, constraining those laws and explaining why they are all invariant under the Lorentz transformations: "Special relativity does not decide which systems get to inhabit/carry Minkowski spacetime. All it has to say about such systems is that their spatio-temporal behavior must obey the rules encoded in Minkowski spacetime. This requirement is automatically met if the system is governed by

Lorentz-invariant laws. Special relativity thus imposes a kinematical constraint on all dynamical systems" (48). But then Janssen cashes out this constraint in terms of heuristics rather than modality: "So . . . special relativity plays the heuristic role of providing constraints on further theorizing. This heuristic role was the important feature of principle theories for Einstein" (48; see 27). I agree with Stachel and Janssen that Einstein saw the principle of relativity as having heuristic value: as giving him a way to avoid having to rely on any particular, dubious theory of the microstructure of matter.[5] But there has got to be a more modally robust sense in which relativity transcends and constrains the motley collection of force laws if (as Stachel and Janssen believe) relativity really explains why those laws are all Lorentz covariant. Relativity's utility as a heuristic is insufficient to supply it with explanatory power. One theory may be a useful guide to the discovery of another without helping to explain why what it guides us toward is true. Indeed, oftentimes theories are useful guides toward the discovery of their own explainers (as the extragalactic red-shift was a useful guide toward the discovery of the universe's expansion).

Stachel and Janssen regard the principle of relativity as helping to explain the Lorentz transformations; they deny that the facts about what the dynamical laws are explain why all of the dynamical laws are Lorentz covariant. Other philosophers instead deny that the principle of relativity can help to explain the Lorentz transformations and the dynamical laws' Lorentz covariance—or, at least, regard the transformations and covariance as having two explanations: one by the principle of relativity, and another by the facts about what the dynamical laws are. These philosophers argue that Einstein correctly believed that the Lorentz covariance of all dynamical laws is explained by the complete theory of the fundamental dynamical laws, since Einstein correctly believed that he could have inferred the Lorentz covariance of the dynamical laws from that complete theory, if only he had known it. (But since he didn't know it, he had to fall back on the indirect strategy of using the principle of relativity in arriving at his theory.)

However, this argument is mistaken: that the complete theory of the fundamental dynamical laws (whatever that theory turns out to be) *entails* that they are Lorentz covariant does not show that this theory *explains* why they are Lorentz covariant.

Consider, for example, the argument given by Dieks (2009, 237) that "the principle-theory approach should not lure us into the mistaken belief that no bottom-up, causal stories about the relativistic effect [such as time dilation and length contraction] are possible." Here is Dieks's argument that "relativistic dilations and contractions can surely also be understood in a constructive, bottom-up fashion" (233), namely, by being derived from the complete fundamental dynamics: "Einstein emphasizes that rods and clocks are ordinary bodies with a microscopic structure and therefore determined in their macroscopic features by what occurs at the microscopic level" (237). But (I say) that the macro-level facts are "determined" by the micro-level dynamics does not show that they are explained by the micro-level dynamics. I discussed a similar phenomenon in chapter 2. If energy conservation is a constraint, then the fact that gravitational and electrical forces both conserve energy is entailed ("determined") by the two force laws together with the fundamental dynamical law. But these laws do not explain why gravitational and electrical forces both conserve energy, since they would incorrectly portray this similarity as coincidental. Let's see this misstep from deduction to explanation again: "If we know what the fundamental building blocks of matter are, and know how the forces between them vary when the system is set into motion, it becomes possible in principle to calculate how the macroscopic features of these bodies will change when they start moving. Actually, it seems pretty obvious that bottom-up explanations of this type are possible for everything that happens according to relativity theory" (Dieks 2009, 242). But this argument is mistaken: That the various macroscopic phenomena to be explained (such as length contraction) can be *calculated* from the micro-level dynamics does not show that they can be *explained* by the dynamics.[6]

The idea (championed by the older Einstein) that Einstein in 1905 should not have depicted the Lorentz transformations as arising from the laws of electromagnetism, but rather as transcending all dynamical laws, has motivated a long tradition (dating from at least 1909) of trying to derive the Lorentz transformations without appealing to the light postulate.[7] For the sake of completeness (and because these derivations are omitted from most standard physics textbooks), I give such a purely kinematical derivation (drawn from the physics literature) in the appendix to this chapter, which I will now summarize. One premise of the derivation is the principle of relativity. But since the derivation aims to be free of dynamical considerations, it cannot presuppose that Newton's first law of motion holds in various reference frames and so cannot use the concept of an "inertial frame" (defined as a frame in which Newton's first law holds) in expressing the principle of relativity. Rather, the principle of relativity is given as follows:

> There is a frame S such that for any frame S' in any allowed uniform motion relative to S, the laws in S and S' take the same form.

The kinematical derivation then seeks the transformation laws

$$x' = X(t,v,x,y,z)$$

$$t' = T(t,v,x,y,z)$$

that relate the coordinates in any such frames S and S' when the coordinate axes are in the "standard configuration" (see fig. 3.1).[8] Along with the principle of relativity and the presuppositions implicit in the very possibility of such coordinate systems (such as that all events can be coordinatized in terms of a globally Euclidean geometry), the derivation also presupposes that the transformations X and T are differentiable and that the velocity of S in S' as a function of the velocity of S' in S is continuous and has a connected domain. Further premises are standardly entitled "spatial (and temporal) homogeneity" and "spatial isotropy":

> In any S' in the family of frames satisfying the principle of relativity, the laws treat all locations (and moments) and directions alike and so are unchanged under arbitrary spatial (and temporal) displacement—that is, under the replacement of every location r (time t) in the laws with $r + a$ $(t + a)$, for arbitrary a—and under arbitrary rotations.

From these premises, it follows (see the appendix) that the transformations take the form

$$x' = \left(1 - kv^2\right)^{-\frac{1}{2}} (x - vt)$$
$$t' = \left(1 - kv^2\right)^{-\frac{1}{2}} (-kvx + t)$$

for some constant k.

The final premise needed to derive the Lorentz transformations kinematically is the law that the "spacetime interval" $I = ([\Delta x]^2 + [\Delta y]^2 + [\Delta z]^2 - c^2[\Delta t]^2)^{\frac{1}{2}}$ between any two events is invariant (i.e., equal in S and in S'), where c is "as yet arbitrary, and need not be identified with the speed of light," as Lee and Kalotas (1975, 436) say in emphasizing that the transformation laws are not owing to the laws about any particular type of force or other spacetime inhabitant (such as light). Rather, c is merely a constant having the dimensions of speed without being identified as the speed of any particular thing. The spacetime interval's invariance together with the transformation laws' taking the above form entails[9] that

$$k = c^{-2}$$

Thus we have the Lorentz transformations. (Oftentimes instead of the spacetime interval's invariance, an explanation cites the existence of a finite invariant speed c. This is a trivial consequence of[10]—and is explained by—the interval's invariance.) If we replace the spacetime interval's invariance with the invariance of temporal intervals (i.e., $t = t'$), then the kinematical derivation yields the Galilean transformations instead.

What would it take for this kinematical derivation to explain why the Lorentz (or Galilean) transformations hold and thereby show that they do not depend on features of light or of any other inhabitants of spacetime? The Lorentz transformations would have to be independent of the various force laws in that they would have to possess a variety of necessity that is stronger than those force laws possess. In terms of the account given in chapter 2, the transformation laws would have to belong to a subnomically stable set that omits the force laws and so appears at a higher level than the force laws do on the pyramidal hierarchy of subnomically stable sets (see fig. 3.2). In that case, the range of counterfactual antecedents under which the transformation laws would still have held, in connection with their necessity, is broader than the range of counterfactual antecedents under which the dynamical laws would still have held, in connection with their necessity. For instance, the transformation laws would still have held even if the fundamental dynamical law and force laws had been different. Counterfactual conditionals like these are asserted by scientists and philosophers who regard such a derivation as explaining why the transformation laws hold. For instance, Lévy-Leblond (1976, 271) asserts that if the force laws had been different so that photons, gravitons, and other kinds of particles that actually possess zero mass instead possessed nonzero mass, then the Lorentz transformations would still have held (though these particles would not have moved with the speed c figuring in those transformations).

This is exactly the kind of subjunctive fact that, on my view, would help to make the transformation laws more necessary than the dynamical laws and hence subject to explanation by constraint. That such counterfactuals are asserted by scientists who regard the transformation laws as transcending dynamics supports

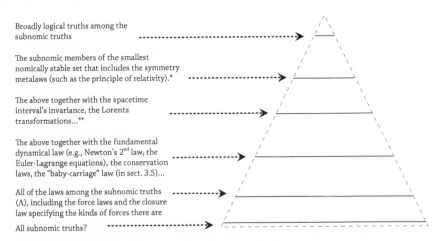

Broadly logical truths among the subnomic truths

The subnomic members of the smallest nomically stable set that includes the symmetry metalaws (such as the principle of relativity).*

The above together with the spacetime interval's invariance, the Lorentz transformations...**

The above together with the fundamental dynamical law (e.g., Newton's 2nd law, the Euler-Lagrange equations), the conservation laws, the "baby-carriage" law (in sect. 3.5)...

All of the laws among the subnomic truths (Λ), including the force laws and the closure law specifying the kinds of forces there are

All subnomic truths?

* This subnomically stable set includes (1) that momentum is conserved if the Euler-Lagrange equations hold, (2) that the Lorentz transformations hold if the spacetime interval is invariant, and (3) that the Galilean transformations hold if the temporal interval is invariant.

** In classical physics, this rung would instead include the temporal interval's invariance and the Galilean transformations. It would also include Newton's first law, if that law is explained by the explanation given in section 3.4.

Figure 3.2 Some (perhaps not all) of the plausibly subnomically stable sets

my account of their transcendence in terms of their having greater necessity than the dynamics, where having greater necessity is associated with having a broader range of invariance under counterfactual antecedents. In chapter 2, I argued that if scientists believed energy conservation to be a coincidental similarity among various kinds of fundamental interactions rather than a constraint on the kinds of interactions there could have been, then scientists could not consistently believe that if there were additional kinds of fundamental interaction, then they too would conserve energy. If energy conservation is a coincidence rather than a constraint, then if there had been additional kinds of fundamental interaction, they might also have all conserved energy, but they might just as well not have done so. Now I have made the analogous point regarding the transformation laws: if scientists believed that the Lorentz transformations arise from a coincidence of the fundamental force laws, then scientists could not consistently believe that if the fundamental force laws had been different, then the Lorentz transformations would still have held. Nor could scientists justly use Lorentz covariance as a heuristic for discovering further laws (as I have just shown some philosophers emphasizing that scientists do). As Penrose (1987, 21) says, if it is just "a 'fluke'" that certain dynamical laws exhibit a kind of invariance, then "there is no need to believe that this fluke should continue to hold when additional ingredients of physics are" discovered (see Barton 1999, 17).[11] On my approach, the covariance's being nonfluky would amount to its being a constraint rather than a coincidence if it is true. This approach captures the analogy between the conservation laws and Lorentz covariance in the eyes of those who see both as explaining why the force laws have certain features.

If the Lorentz transformation laws belong to some higher stratum on the pyramidal hierarchy than the dynamical laws do, then even if the facts about the dynamical laws entail the truth of the transformation laws (as Dieks emphasizes), the dynamical laws' necessity is too weak to account for the stronger necessity possessed by the transformation laws. The force laws' necessity fails to ensure their preservation under some counterfactual antecedents under which the transformation laws are preserved in connection with their necessity (i.e., in connection with their membership in the most elite subnomically stable set to which they belong). So the dynamical laws' necessity cannot explain why the transformation laws are preserved under those antecedents. Let p be an antecedent under which the transformation laws are preserved in connection with their membership in a stable set, but under which the dynamical laws are not preserved. It cannot be that in the "closest p-world," the transformation laws hold because the dynamical laws hold—since the dynamical laws do not hold there! So the dynamical laws' necessity cannot explain why the transformation laws are preserved in the closest p-world, and hence cannot explain the transformation laws' stronger necessity. Therefore, if the kinematical derivation constitutes an "explanation by constraint" of the transformation laws' characteristic necessity, then their possessing this necessity has no causal explanation. If the transformation laws' *characteristic necessity* has no causal explanation, then I am inclined to conclude that even the transformation laws' *truth* has no causal explanation, since presented as an explanation, a derivation of the transformation laws' truth from facts about the dynamical laws misrepresents the modal status of the transformation laws' truth. It misrepresents the transformation laws as depending on facts possessing less necessity than the transformation laws do.[12]

Roughly the same argument bears on the principle of relativity and the other premises to which the kinematical derivation appeals. If the derivation explains why the Lorentz transformations hold and thereby makes them independent of the force laws, then the necessity of the various laws m from which the Lorentz transformations n are derived must be responsible for making the transformations more necessary than the force laws. On my view, a law's necessity involves its belonging to a stable set—that is, involves its being invariant under a certain range of counterfactual antecedents. Hence, if m entails n, then for m's necessity to be responsible for making n so strongly necessary, the range of counterfactual antecedents under which m is invariant, in connection with its necessity, must include the range of counterfactual antecedents under which n is invariant, in connection with its strong necessity. Otherwise, there will be some antecedent p under which n would still have held, in connection with its necessity, but m's necessity fails to ensure that n would still have held under p, and therefore m's necessity cannot explain why n would still have held under p and so cannot explain n's necessity. If m entails n, then the only way for m's necessity to be responsible for n's holding under p is for m's necessity to require that m hold under p—so that m's holding in the "closest p-world" entails n's holding there. Hence, in order for the kinematical derivation to explain why the Lorentz transformations hold and thereby make the transformations independent of the force laws, the laws from which the transformations are derived must be at least as necessary as the transformations are.

The principle of relativity (and the homogeneity of space and time, the isotropy of space, and some of the derivation's other premises) are not subnomic facts; they concern which subnomic facts are (or are not) matters of law. Hence, they cannot belong to a subnomically stable set; they are not first-order laws. For them to possess the necessity requisite to explain the Lorentz transformations and thereby make the transformations independent of the force laws, they must be metalaws just like the symmetry principles that explain the conservation laws as constraints. On my account, then, they must belong to a nomically stable set that is more exclusive than the set spanned by all of the truths about which subnomic claims are laws and which are not.

As shown in chapter 2, the subnomic members of such a set (that is, the members' subnomic logical consequences) form a subnomically stable set. That set must appear high in the hierarchy of subnomically stable sets (see fig. 3.2);

it must be associated with a strong variety of necessity. One subnomic member of that set is the conclusion arrived at near the end of the kinematical derivation: that the transformations take the form

$$x' = (1 - kv^2)^{-\frac{1}{2}} (x - vt)$$
$$t' = (1 - kv^2)^{-\frac{1}{2}} (- kvx + t).$$

Therefore, this conclusion *must* hold, where this *must* involves a stronger variety of necessity than the force laws exhibit. As a metalaw, the principle of relativity would help to explain why the transformations would still have taken the above form even if the force laws had been different (as in the conditional endorsed by Lévy-Leblond). The force laws have insufficient necessity to explain that fact. This is the way that the metalaws constrain the first-order laws: any subnomic truth that follows from the metalaws is a constraint imposed by the metalaws on the first-order laws in that it belongs to a subnomically stable set located higher on the pyramid than Λ. By this means, "In Einstein's Special Theory of Relativity, the Poincaré global symmetry group rules over the kinematics" (Ne'eman 1999, 143).

There is another important consequence of the subnomic stability of the subnomic logical consequences of some nomically stable set that includes the principle of relativity and the other metalaws used in the derivation of the transformation laws. Its subnomic stability requires not only that the transformation laws would take the form given above if the spacetime interval were invariant (i.e., equal in S and in S'), but also that the transformation laws would take the above form if the temporal interval were invariant. In the former case, the Lorentz transformations would hold; in the latter case, the Galilean transformations would hold instead. Thus, the principle of relativity and the other metalaws limit what the transformation laws could have been.

Suppose the spacetime interval's invariance is a first-order law where the highest stratum of subnomically stable set in which it appears is located higher than Λ on the pyramid, but below the stratum consisting of the subnomic members of the principle of relativity's most exclusive nomically stable set (see fig. 3.2). Since the subnomically stable sets form a nested hierarchy, every member of a stratum above the most exclusive subnomically stable set that includes the spacetime interval's invariance must also belong to that set. Therefore, the fact that the transformations take the above form belongs to the most exclusive subnomically stable set that includes the spacetime interval's invariance. Since the set must contain every subnomic logical consequence of its members, the set must also contain the Lorentz transformations. In this way, the Lorentz transformations join the spacetime interval's invariance in transcending the dynamics.

On this picture, the principle of relativity transcends the force laws in that it would still have held even if there had been different fundamental forces; it belongs to a nomically stable set that omits the force laws and various other first-order laws. That set's members are then collectively as invariant under nomic or subnomic antecedents as they could collectively be. They possess a strong variety of necessity, and so it is not merely the case that the force laws *happen* to conform to the principle. They *must* do so—as a matter of metalaw. This is the conception of the principle of relativity's status that seems to be held by those who regard it as helping to explain why the Lorentz transformations hold. A good example is Minkowski (Corry 1997, 280, 286), who compares the principle of relativity to energy conservation in that both hold of whatever unknown forces there might be or might have been. He places the principle of relativity at the peak (*Spitze*) of mechanics, as in my pyramidal hierarchy. Similarly, my account is in a position to capture the thought expressed by Pars (1921, 249–250) in arguing that the principle of relativity explains the Lorentz transformations. He maintains that the principle of relativity "is altogether more deep-seated in the scheme of things than the consequent phenomena of" length contraction and light's having the same speed in all inertial frames. "Its inevitableness lies deeper," Pars says—a view that we need strata of natural necessity to cash out.

There is another way to appreciate the status of the principle of relativity according to those who advance the kinematical derivation as explaining why the Lorentz transformations hold. Although I have followed the usual custom of treating spatial and temporal homogeneity and spatial isotropy as separate premises in the derivation, they actually all follow from the principle of relativity (contrary to Balashov and Janssen 2003, 333), which was already a premise. To see this, suppose that S' results merely from an arbitrary spatiotemporal displacement or rotation of S. Then S' is forever at rest relative to S and so trivially in an allowed uniform motion relative to S. Therefore, by the principle of relativity, the laws in S cannot (e.g.) violate spatial homogeneity by privileging the spatial origin, since the laws in S' would then have to privilege a location other than the origin in S' and so would not take the same form as the laws in S. Accordingly, Minkowski (1908/1952, 75) emphasizes that the principle of relativity subsumes homogeneity and isotropy.

What is especially revealing is the way that Minkowski (and others who regard the kinematical derivation as accounting for the Lorentz transformations) characterize the status of the principle of relativity, considering that it subsumes homogeneity and isotropy. Minkowski contends that whereas homogeneity and isotropy (that is, the laws' invariance under arbitrary displacement in space or time and under arbitrary spatial rotation) had standardly been considered "fundamental," invariance under (nonzero uniform) velocity boosts had previously been treated "with disdain" or contempt at best:

Whereas the existence of the group [of invariances of the equations of mechanics] corresponding to the first invariance [i.e., associated with an arbitrary spatial or temporal displacement] had usually been seen as expressing a fundamental property of space, the existence of the second (i.e., the group of Galilean transformations [involving invariance under velocity boosts as well]) had never attracted any special interest as such. At best, Minkowski said, it had been accepted with disdain (Verachtung) in order to be able to make physical sense of the fact that observable phenomena do not enable one to decide whether space, which is assumed to be at rest, is not after all in a state of uniform translation. (Corry 2010, 23)

Before relativity, the two symmetries were widely believed to have different statuses. But in unifying them all under the principle of relativity, Einstein (or Minkowski) revealed that invariance under velocity boosts possesses the same exalted status as spacetime homogeneity and isotropy:

An observer in uniform motion can never determine anything concerning his speed and one is never in a position to indicate a point in the universe, of which it may be stated that it be in absolute rest. . . . This theorem is called the classical "principle of relativity" (to be well distinguished from the modern principle of relativity due to Einstein, which unifies the invariance of the equations of motion under a rotation of the coordinate system, discussed before, and the invariance with respect to a uniform motion of the origin of the coordinate system, from a higher point of view). (Planck quoted in Speiser 1987, 44; see Barton 1999, 18)

The different role played by the variable t in the Galileo-Newton group has had a decisively inhibiting effect on the historical development of mechanics. Although Lagrange had already called mechanics a 4-dimensional geometry, one has only recently made real use of this interpretation. All the older authors always considered only the Euclidean group and did not connect to it either time translation or the proper Galileo transformations [i.e., under velocity boosts] although they knew them. This also happened to me when I wrote the *Erlanger Programm*. I remember distinctly that I had not overlooked Lagrange's remark, but I believed that I could not find a place for it in my group principle. Only the appearance of the Lorentz group has led mathematicians to a correct appreciation of the Galileo-Newton group. (Klein quoted in Speiser 1987, 34)

But what, precisely, is the difference between the lowly status that invariance under velocity boosts was originally thought to possess and the more exalted status (on a par with homogeneity and isotropy) that it was later accorded under relativity when it was used to explain the Lorentz transformations? Cacciatori et al. (2008, 731) say that according to Minkowski, invariance under velocity boosts had formerly been regarded as "somewhat accidental." How can a consequence solely of the laws be accidental?

My answer, once again, is that this fact about what the laws are can nevertheless be a "coincidence." The various dynamical laws' invariance under velocity boosts could have no common explanation; it could fail to be the result of a metalaw. Before the advent of relativity, invariance under boosts was treated as coincidental (merely a fortuitous similarity among the dynamical laws) although homogeneity and isotropy were believed to be metalaws (and hence were used by Lagrange and Hamilton to explain by constraint why various conservation laws hold). In other words, before the advent of relativity, homogeneity and isotropy were regarded as constraints on the force laws imposed from above, whereas invariance under boosts was regarded as a coincidence of the force laws. Einstein, however, deemed it implausible that the laws of Maxwellian electromagnetism should just happen to work out so as to give the same net force under velocity boosts. This was the majestic opening argument in Einstein's 1905 paper introducing special relativity (Einstein 1905/1989, 140) and was (according to Einstein) his main motivation for the theory (Lange 2002, 175–204). After Einstein, the principle of relativity was recognized as a metalaw, and so invariance under boosts was regarded as constraining the dynamics just as homogeneity and isotropy do. We need the notion of a metalaw constraining first-order laws in order to understand the change in the status accorded to invariance under velocity boosts as a result of relativity theory.

▪ 3.3 PRINCIPLE VERSUS CONSTRUCTIVE THEORIES

There is a possible world where the first-order laws exhibit homogeneity, isotropy, and invariance under velocity boots, but these symmetries are not metalaws. Rather, they are coincidences; they hold because of what the first-order laws are, rather than the first-order laws exhibiting these spacetime symmetries because metalaws require them to do so. Brown (2005) argues that the actual world is such a possible world. On his view, facts about "spacetime structure," such as the principle of relativity, do not explain the Lorentz transformations. Rather, the principle of relativity and the Lorentz transformations have a common source in the Lorentz covariance of the fundamental equations of dynamics: "The appropriate structure is Minkowski geometry *precisely because* the laws of physics of the non-gravitational interactions are Lorentz covariant" (133).

If Brown is correct, then it is a coincidence ("a 'fluke,'" as Penrose put it) that every single member of the motley crew of fundamental interaction laws is Lorentz covariant. There is no common reason why they all have this feature, despite their diversity in other respects. They just do: "In the dynamical approach to length contraction and time dilation ... the Lorentz covariance of all the fundamental laws of physics is an unexplained brute fact. This, in and of itself, does not count against the approach: all explanation must stop somewhere" (Brown 2005, 143).[13] If the Lorentz covariance of the various force laws is a coincidence, then (contrary to Lévy-Leblond) it is not the case that the Lorentz transformations would still have held even if the force laws had been different so that photons, gravitons, and other kinds of particles that actually possess zero mass instead possessed nonzero mass. On Brown's view, the Lorentz transformations are explained "dynamically"; they arise from the way in which (in a given frame) the forces within a rod or clock depend upon its uniform speed: "a moving rod contracts, and a moving clock dilates, *because of how it is made up and not because of the nature of its spatio-temporal environment*" (8).

This view is inspired by the fact that the electric field of a point charge moving uniformly with speed v is diminished in the direction of its motion by a factor of $(1 - v^2/c^2)$. Although nowadays this result is standardly derived by taking the electric field of a stationary charge and using the Lorentz transformations to determine what it looks like in a frame where the charge is moving, Heaviside originally derived it in 1888 directly from Maxwell's electromagnetic-field theory—that is, entirely within a single reference frame. As Brown says (2005, 144), "Molecular forces inside chunks of matter might mimic electromagnetic forces in a specific sense"—in being Lorentz covariant—so that a bar's equilibrium length changes when it is moving. If every bar at rest in S' and extending from the origin to x' has a length equal to $L(1 - v^2/c^2)^{1/2}$, where L is its length in S, then since in S the x-coordinate of the origin in S' is vt, the x-coordinate of x' is $vt + x'(1 - v^2/c^2)^{1/2}$. Solving for x' yields

$$x' = (x - vt)/(1 - v^2/c^2)^{1/2}.$$

Thus, we would have a dynamical explanation of the x-component of the Lorentz transformation.[14]

On my view, there is a possible world with many rods, some held together by fundamentally different forces than others, yet every rod is shorter by the very same factor in an inertial frame where it is moving than in a frame where it is at rest, and the factor's ubiquity is coincidental.[15] Whether the Lorentz transformations transcend the force laws or are explained dynamically is a question for empirical science to answer. In contrast, Brown contends that it is impossible for the Lorentz transformations to be explained by the principle of relativity. He seems to find any non-causal explanation unintelligible. Like the dispositional essentialists I discussed at the close of chapter 2 (who are obliged to regard conservation laws as coincidences rather than constraints), Brown forecloses even the metaphysical possibility of the Lorentz transformations transcending the dynamical laws.

I agree that "talk of Lorentz covariance 'reflecting the structure of space-time posited by the theory' and of 'tracing the invariance to a common origin' needs to be fleshed out if we are to be given a genuine explanation here" (Brown 2005, 143). That is exactly what I have tried to do. Brown is correct that an explanation of the Lorentz transformations as transcending the dynamical laws cannot be an explanation that cites forces or any other causes of the Lorentz transformations. But Brown is incorrect if he believes that there are no such non-causal scientific explanations. On the contrary, I have argued that there are many explanations by constraint—not only supplied by revolutionary theories such as the theory of relativity, but also in the various humble cases that I mentioned in chapter 1 (such as Mother's failure to distribute strawberries evenly among her children). Brown (143) asks, "how is [spacetime structure']s influence on these laws supposed to work? How in turn are rods and clocks supposed to know which spacetime they are immersed in?" and Brown (24) then points out that rods and clocks cannot "know" because they "have no space-time feelers." These remarks suggest that in order for a constraint (such as a metalaw) to explain a feature of the dynamics, there would have to be a causal mechanism by which bodies could feel its influence. This seems to me a category mistake akin to requiring that laws be causes in order for them to explain.

Brown is inspired by Einstein's distinction between "constructive theories" and "theories of principle." Constructive theories, such as the kinetic-molecular theory of gases, entail phenomena by showing how they arise from the relatively simple behaviors of their constituents. Theories of principle, such as thermodynamics, entail phenomena by invoking general conditions, such as energy conservation, that all natural processes must satisfy. As Einstein (1919, 228) puts it, principle theories take as their basis "principles that give rise to mathematically formulated criteria which the separate processes or the theoretical representation of them have to satisfy." I take these principles to be "constraints" in the sense I have described: truths holding with stronger necessity than that possessed by ordinary laws of nature concerning particular kinds of "separate processes."[16] Einstein took the principle of relativity to be such a principle: "The principle of relativity is a principle that narrows the possibilities; it is not a model, just as the second law of thermodynamics is not a model" (1911, 357). Such talk of "narrowing the possibilities" fits well with my conception of constraints as limiting the kinds of forces there could have been.

It is widely believed that Einstein regarded only constructive theories as explanatorily potent, as suggested by remarks such as this: "When we say that we have succeeded in understanding a group of natural processes, we invariably mean that a constructive theory has been found which covers the processes in question" (Einstein 1919, 228). Accordingly, many philosophers (including Brown) take Einstein to have regarded the principle of relativity as unable to help explain the Lorentz transformations.[17] Many of these philosophers are thereby led to conclude that "principle theories fail to be explanatory" (Brown and Pooley 2006, 76) and to regard principle theories as constraints only in the sense that they allow us to dismiss certain constructive theories as not being viable hypotheses: "The 'principles' that make up a principle theory like special relativity or macroscopic thermodynamics are empirically well-grounded generalizations that serve a heuristic role by constraining the search for the deeper constructive theories that provide ultimate explanations of phenomena in terms of models constructed from an ontology of systems, states, and interactions" (Howard 2010, 349). For the principle of relativity to "constrain" the search for constructive theories that themselves do all of the explanatory work is a far cry from the principle's figuring in an explanation by constraint.

I believe that this is an incorrect interpretation of Einstein's view. I will now argue that the correct interpretation helps us to understand the different roles played by causal explanations and explanations by constraint in explaining phenomena such as length contraction.

Many scientists besides Einstein have distinguished constructive theories from theories of principle, placing the principle of relativity alongside various conservation laws, the laws of thermodynamics, and other laws that are often taken to be "constraints." But this conception of relativity as a theory of principle has not generally led scientists to deny relativity's explanatory power or to regard only constructive theories as able to explain: "Einstein's relativity principle 'explains' the failure of all the ether-drift experiments much as the principle of energy conservation explains a priori (that is, without the need for a detailed examination of the mechanism) the failure of all attempts to build a perpetual motion machine" (Rindler 2006, 12). To understand what Einstein was getting at in the remark I quoted earlier that appears to deprecate the explanatory power of principle theories, we should look to one of Einstein's contemporaries who wrote expansively about the distinction between principle and constructive theories in connection with relativity—namely, James Jeans. Very much like Einstein, Jeans appears at first glance to contend that relativity, as a theory of principle rather than a constructive theory, is explanatorily impotent. In this regard, he says that the principle of relativity is like the usual suspects, namely, energy conservation and the second law of thermodynamics:

> The three principles have in common that they do not explain how or why events happen; they merely limit the types of events which can happen. Thus the principle of the Conservation of Energy shows that water cannot flow uphill; the Second Law of Thermodynamics shows that heat cannot flow from a cold body to a hot; the principle of Relativity shows that a planet cannot describe a perfect ellipse about the sun as focus. But it would be as unreasonable to expect the principle of Relativity to explain why a planet describes an orbit or how a ray of light is propagated as it would be to propound the same questions to the principle of Conservation of Energy or the Second Law of Thermodynamics. All three principles deal with events, and not with the mechanism of events. . . .
>
> New and mysterious continents appear for science to explore, but it is not for the theory of Relativity to explore them. The methods of that theory are destructive rather than constructive, and, when the theory predicts a positive result, it is

invariably for the same reason, namely, that a process of exhaustion shows that any other result would be impossible. (Jeans 1920, 66)

This passage sounds so much like Einstein's remarks from about the same time!

Nevertheless, Jeans also characterizes relativity as explanatorily powerful. Regarding the Lorentz transformations, he says, "These equations explain and predict a great number of physical phenomena—e.g., the variation of mass with velocity" (1920, 67). Elsewhere he writes that relativity "at once explained the negative results of the Michelson-Morley and of all similar experiments" (1951, 294).

How can Jeans's various remarks be reconciled? The key to understanding his view (and Einstein's too, I believe) is contained in remarks like this:

> Thus the hypothesis of relativity predicts that a freely moving planet cannot describe a perfect ellipse around the sun as focus. This prediction is made on quite general grounds, just as the conservation of energy predicts that a stream of water cannot flow uphill. But the conservation of energy by itself is powerless to predict what will be the actual course of a stream of water, and in precisely the same way the hypothesis of relativity alone is powerless to predict what will be the orbit of a planet. Before this or any other positive gravitational predictions can be made, additional hypotheses must be introduced. (Jeans 1921, 793)

These "additional hypotheses" are constructive theories. Jeans's point is that although the principle of relativity and other constraints impose certain limitations on the kinds of phenomena that could occur, these constraints alone are not enough to entail the details of the particular events that do occur within the broad range allowed by the constraints. Rather, the particular outcomes are entailed by (initial conditions and) the dynamical laws supplied by constructive theories. The principle of relativity and its fellow constraints do not form a complete theory, and they cannot explain what they do not entail. They must be supplemented by constructive theories. But they can explain "a great number of physical phenomena," namely, those that they do suffice to entail.[18]

For instance, consider a bar of a certain length moving uniformly in a given inertial frame S. What accounts for the bar's length in S? Only a constructive theory giving the bar's internal constitution and the intermolecular forces within the bar can explain its length. Admittedly, the bar's length in another inertial frame S' where it is at rest, together with the Lorentz transformations (and the speed in one frame of the other frame's origin), entails its length in S. But these facts do not explain its length in S. Otherwise, the explanations would run in a circle, since its length in S together with the Lorentz transformations would by the same token explain its length in S'. There is no reason to privilege one of these frames as explanatorily prior to the other.

However, suppose we aim to explain not the bar's length in S or its length in S', but rather the *relation* between the two lengths. The Lorentz transformations explain that relation and thus explain "length contraction." This is an explanation by constraint, if the Lorentz transformations transcend the dynamics in the way that I described in the previous section. Just as energy conservation "is powerless to predict what will be the actual course of a stream of water," so relativity cannot predict the bar's actual length. But just as energy conservation as a constraint would help to explain why a stream of water does not flow uphill (because its doing so is impossible), so the principle of relativity as a constraint would help to explain why the bar's lengths in the two frames stand in a certain relation (because any other relation is impossible).

Suppose that the bar, having a certain length and moving uniformly in S, is accelerated to a new speed and then brought into uniform motion at that new speed in S. Once again, the principle of relativity together with other constraints does not suffice to entail (or to explain) the relation between the bar's new length in S and its former length in S. The process of acceleration could have changed the bar's internal constitution in a host of ways that only a constructive theory could entail. No theory of principle suffices to entail (or even to assign some chance to) its internal constitution remaining the same in various respects despite its having undergone acceleration. In contrast, the relation between the postacceleration bar's length in S and its length in another inertial frame S' is again entailed and explained by the principle of relativity together with other constraints. On my view, this relation has no causal explanation if the Lorentz transformations follow entirely from constraints, since this relation's necessity is then stronger than any dynamical laws possess.

Here I agree with Dieks. He considers an example from Bell (1987, 67) involving two rockets: "[they] undergo equal accelerations in such a way that their mutual distance remains the same. A rope connecting the rockets will tend to Lorentz contract during the process, because it acquires a velocity. As a consequence, the rope will become tighter and may eventually even break when the velocity becomes high enough" (Dieks 2009, 241). Dieks (244) contends that only a constructive theory of the intermolecular forces within the rope can explain the point during the process of acceleration at which the rope breaks. I agree; only a constructive theory entails (or could explain) how much acceleration the rope can withstand without being torn apart. In each frame in which the sequence of events may be described, there will be some causal explanation of the rope's breaking given by a constructive theory (and the preceding events in that frame). But if we ask instead why the rope's length in one frame stands in a certain relation to its length in another frame, then the Lorentz transformations as constraints would supply the explanation; this relation would then have no causal explanation.

The same applies to a force law more generally. The inventory of force laws explains why there are certain forces in nature rather than certain other, hypothetical forces that we might imagine. The constraints are not enough to entail the particular force laws there are. However, I maintain, certain *relations* between the force laws governing two distinct interactions (such as that they are both Lorentz covariant) are entailed by the two force laws but are not explained by them if Lorentz covariance is a constraint rather than a coincidence. Rather, these relations are explained by the principle of relativity and other constraints, which restrict the kinds of forces there could have been.

I believe that these limits on the explanatory power of principle theories, rather than the wholesale explanatory impotence of principle theories, was what Einstein was trying to express in his terse remarks about how we cannot understand a group of natural processes without having a constructive theory covering them. Some results of those processes are not entailed by principle theories alone, so Einstein is correct that without a constructive theory, we cannot explain all of the outcomes of those processes.[19] But it does not follow from Einstein's remarks that those phenomena that *are* entailed by principle theories alone are not explained by them. Indeed, Einstein's remarks are compatible with the phenomena entailed by principle theories having no explanation by constructive theories at all.

This reading of Einstein's remarks is confirmed by other comments he makes about the incompleteness of relativity theory:

> The principle of relativity . . . is not to be conceived as a "complete system," in fact, not as a system at all, but merely as a heuristic principle. . . . It is only by requiring relations between otherwise seemingly unrelated laws that the theory of relativity provides additional statements.
>
> For example, the theory of the motion of electrons arises in the following way. One postulates the Maxwell equations for vacuum for a system of space-time coordinates. By applying the space-time transformation derived by means of the system of relativity, one finds the transformation equations for the electric and magnetic forces. Using the latter, and applying the space-time transformation once again, one arrives at the law for the acceleration of an electron moving at arbitrary speed from the law for the acceleration of the slowly moving electron (which is assumed or obtained from experience). Thus, we are not dealing here at all with a "system" in which the individual laws are implicitly contained and from which they can be found by deduction alone, but only with a principle that (similar to the second law of the theory of heat) permits the reduction of certain laws to others. (Einstein 1907, 236–237)

In emphasizing that relativity is not "a system," Einstein is saying that the relation between the principle of relativity and various constructive theories concerning particular types of interactions is not the relation of axioms to theorems. In my terms, Einstein's point is that the members of a lower rung in the pyramid of subnomically stable sets do not all follow logically from the members of a higher rung. For example, the principle of relativity and other constraints cannot entail (or explain) the law for the acceleration of a slowly moving electron.[20] But they can entail and explain the relation between that law and the law for the acceleration of an electron moving at arbitrary speed. Although in this passage Einstein notes the heuristic value of the principle of relativity, he also emphasizes that it has the consequence of "requiring relations between otherwise seemingly unrelated laws." These relations (though not the individual relata) thereby have explanations by constraint.

My view of the relation between causal explanations and non-causal explanations by constraint is usefully contrasted with Salmon's. As I mentioned in chapter 1, Salmon at one time took all scientific explanation to be causal. However, he later argued (1989, 182–185) that the same fact can have both "top-down" and "bottom-up" explanations.[21] An explanation taking a bottom-up approach describes the causal processes, interactions, and (often hidden) mechanisms responsible for particular occurrences or general regularities, as when the kinetic-molecular theory of gases explains Boyle's law. In contrast, an explanation taking a top-down approach subsumes the explanandum under some extremely general principles, thereby unifying it with other facts.[22] In different contexts, one or the other of these kinds of explanation may be appropriate, according to Salmon. One of Salmon's favorite examples of a fact having both top-down and bottom-up explanations is the fact that a helium-filled balloon in the cabin of an airplane moves toward the front of the cabin as the airplane is accelerating for takeoff:

> Why did the balloon move toward the front of the cabin? Two explanations can be offered, both of which are correct. First, one can tell a story about the behavior of the molecules that made up the air in the cabin, explaining how the rear wall collided with nearby molecules when it began its forward motion, thus creating a pressure gradient from back to front of the cabin. This pressure gradient imposes an unbalanced force on the back side of the balloon, causing it to move forward with respect to the walls of the cabin. Second, one can cite an extremely general physical principle, Einstein's *principle of equivalence*, according to which an acceleration is physically equivalent to a gravitational field. Since helium-filled balloons tend to rise in the atmosphere in the earth's gravitational field, they will move forward when the airplane accelerates, reacting just as they would if a gravitational field were suddenly placed behind the rear wall. (Salmon 1989, 183; see Salmon 1998, 73; 2001, 67–68)

According to Salmon, these two explanations provide different kinds of understanding of the same fact: "It is my present conviction that both of these explanations are legitimate and each is illuminating in its own way" (Salmon 1989,

183–184; see Salmon 1998, 9–10; 2001, 67) Salmon's distinction between causal-mechanical, bottom-up explanations and top-down explanations from general overarching principles appears to be very similar to Einstein's distinction between the roles played by principle theories and constructive theories. (However, Salmon himself does not draw this comparison, perhaps because Einstein is widely regarded as contending that only constructive theories explain whereas Salmon's point is that both types of theories do.) Einstein and Salmon both give the kinetic-molecular theory of gases and relativity theory as representing the two approaches.

I believe that the same lessons I drew from Einstein's discussion apply to Salmon's example. According to Salmon, the principle of equivalence together with the behavior of helium-filled balloons in Earth's gravitational field explains their behavior in the accelerating airplane. ("Since helium-filled balloons tend to rise in the atmosphere in the earth's gravitational field, they will move forward when the airplane accelerates.") But I see no reason for the balloon's behavior in Earth's gravitational field to take explanatory priority over the balloon's behavior inside the accelerating airplane (even if the principle of equivalence is a constraint). With the principle of equivalence, we could just as well infer what balloons do in Earth's atmosphere from what they do inside the airplane. Neither fact explains the other—just as (I suggested earlier) a bar's length in an inertial frame where it is moving uniformly, together with the Lorentz transformations (and the speed in one frame of the other frame's origin), entails but does not explain the bar's length in another inertial frame where it is at rest, since its length in one frame does not take explanatory precedence over its length in another. To explain the bar's length in either frame, we would need a constructive theory. The same applies to explaining the balloon's behavior inside the accelerating airplane (or in Earth's gravitational field).

However, if the relevant principles are in fact constraints, then just as there is a top-down explanation of the *relation* between the bar's lengths in the two frames, so there is a top-down explanation (that is to say, an explanation by constraint) of the *relation* between what balloons do in Earth's gravitational field and what they do in the accelerating airplane. If the principle of equivalence is a constraint, then it is no coincidence that balloons behave the same way in the two cases. Contrary to Salmon, then, we do not have here two explanations of the same fact, one proceeding from the bottom up and the other working from the top down. Rather, we have two explanations of different facts.

The same lesson applies to the scientific explanation that Feynman (1987) gives in his lecture "The Reason for Antiparticles" as able to "explain why there must be antiparticles if you try to put quantum mechanics with relativity" (1987, 2–3). Suppose an electron leaves location x_1 at t_1, and then at (x_2, t_2) enters some field of force. In quantum mechanics, there are various probabilities of the electron's being accelerated to various locations. In particular, there is a nonzero (albeit small) probability that the later event of the electron's exiting from the field will be separated by a spacelike interval from the earlier event of its entering the field. In other words, there is a nonzero chance that the electron will exit the field somewhere outside of the entrance event's light cone.[23] Suppose this is what happens as the electron exits the field at (x_3, t_3) and that the electron subsequently moves subluminally to (x_4, t_4). At least, that is the sequence of events in one inertial reference frame. But because the entrance and exit events are separated by a spacelike interval, relativity ensures that there is an inertial reference frame in which their temporal order is reversed, though the other events retain their temporal order since they are separated by timelike intervals. What happens in such a frame? First, an electron leaves some location x_1' at t_1' (where the primes denote the spacetime locations in the second frame that correspond to the unprimed locations in the first frame). At t_4', an electron arrives at x_4'. But what happens between these events? In particular, how can the temporal order of the middle two events be reversed? How can an electron at (x_4', t_4') have previously arrived at x_3' before it left from x_2'?

Feynman suggests a solution. After an electron departs x_1' at t_1', the next thing that happens is that two particles appear spontaneously at x_3': an electron and a particle having the electron's mass but opposite quantum numbers (such as electric charge). Because the quantum numbers are additive inverses, this pair creation does not violate various conservation laws (such as charge conservation). Energy conservation is also not violated if the additional energy disappears quickly enough for the fluctuation to be within the limits set by the uncertainty principle. The created electron moves subluminally from x_3' to x_4'. Meanwhile, the created "positron" moves superluminally to x_2', where it meets and annihilates the electron that departed x_1'. Thus, Feynman proposes that when the first frame is transformed into the second, the electron traversing the force field from x_2 to x_3 is transformed into its antiparticle moving from x_3' to x_2'—that is, into a particle with the same mass but opposite quantum numbers.

On this view, then, a particle can be transformed into its antiparticle when one inertial frame is transformed into another. "The reason for antiparticles" is that antiparticles are just particles as seen from another inertial frame. Whether something is a particle or an antiparticle is frame-dependent, just as length is. Feynman (1987, 10) nicely summarizes his explanation: "In other words, *there must be antiparticles*. In fact, because of this frame-dependence of the sequence of events we can say that one man's virtual particle is another man's virtual antiparticle." Feynman's argument is commonly presented as successfully explaining why there are antiparticles:

Space and time must mix so that the time order of events in space-time is not immutable. Furthermore, quantum uncertainty allows a particle to spill over just a little into space-like no-man's-land. Because of these two facts, we find that to each particle there corresponds an antiparticle. (Icke 1995, 124)

[Feynman] explains why a relativistic theory of electrons . . . *requires* antiparticles. (Krauss 2011, 133–134)

Let's consider, then, how this scientific explanation is supposed to work.

The events in one reference frame do not stand in any *causal* relation to the events in another frame. Causal relations may hold among the events, but not between how they appear in one frame and how they appear in another. Furthermore, just as I said (in connection with Salmon's example) that a balloon's behavior in Earth's gravitational field takes no explanatory priority over a balloon's behavior inside the accelerating airplane, so the electron traversing the field in one frame is not explanatorily prior to the positron traversing the field in another frame. It is not the case that the electron is real whereas the positron is merely how the electron appears in another frame. Rather, that an electron crossed the field and that a positron crossed it are both frame-dependent facts. Accordingly, then, Feynman's argument does not use the existence of particles to explain the existence of antiparticles, since the former is not explanatorily prior to the latter (or vice versa).

Instead Feynman's argument explains why it is that to every kind of particle there corresponds a kind of antiparticle. It explains the *relation* between particles and antiparticles, just as relativity does not explain a bar's length in a given frame, but rather explains the *relation* between its lengths in various frames. For instance, regarding his example, Feynman's argument does not explain the positron's existence in a given frame; its existence has a causal explanation, just as a body's length in a given frame does. But Feynman's argument explains the relation between the events in the two frames: namely, that where there is a particle traversing the force field in one frame, there is its antiparticle in the other frame.

This explanation works only by the pairing of particles with antiparticles being necessitated by facts that transcend the details of the particular kinds of particles or forces there happen to be. That is, the spacetime transformations that turn particles into antiparticles must join the Lorentz transformations as among the constraints on any species of particle or interaction. That every particle species has a corresponding antiparticle species (and vice versa) is no coincidence of the particular kinds of things there are. The pairing is a constraint laid upon the various species so that if there had been an additional particle species, it too would have had an antiparticle. Icke (1995, 125) nicely captures the way that Feynman's explanation works: "The existence of antiparticles, pair creation and annihilation must be built into any description of the forces in our world, because it so happens that the space-time of which our Universe is built is Lorentz symmetric." The framework of coordinate transformations in which "one man's virtual particle is another man's virtual antiparticle" constrains any possible forces. Feynman's argument gives "the reason for antiparticles" in that it explains why there are particles and antiparticles rather than solely particles, but it does not use the existence of particles to explain the existence of antiparticles.[24]

Brown is correct that in a given reference frame, there is a causal explanation of a rod's length, a balloon's motion, a clock's behavior, a particle's annihilation, or a string's snapping. Indeed, as Mermin (2005, 185) says, "The mechanism that gives the real explanation for a phenomenon in one frame of reference, may be quite different from the mechanism that gives the real explanation in another." But this focus on a causal explanation as "the real explanation" tends to distract us from noticing that there are also facts to be explained concerning the relations among various frames. These facts do not have causal explanations (the relation is not explained by the conjunction of the two separate causal explanations of the two relata) if the principle of relativity and its colleagues have sufficient modal strength to constrain the dynamics. Mermin displays symptoms of being distracted by his focus on a causal explanation as "the real explanation": "One yearns for a mechanism. What *causes* moving clocks run slowly? What *causes* moving sticks to shrink? If the only available explanation is that moving clocks run slowly and moving sticks shrink in order to maintain the consistency of relativity, one cannot help wondering why clocks and sticks should know or care about the coherence of relativity" (Mermin 2009, 180). Such ridicule of an explanation by constraint is unwarranted. A rod does not have to "know or care" about the coherence of relativity in order for the relevant dynamical laws to be constrained by Feynman's "great general principles which all the laws seem to follow," just as Mother and her 23 strawberries (from chapter 1) do not have to "know or care" about the coherence of arithmetic in order for Mother's failure to distribute the strawberries evenly among her 3 children to be explained by the mathematical impossibility of her success.[25]

■ 3.4 HOW THIS NON-CAUSAL EXPLANATION COMES IN HANDY

In the previous sections, I have used various subjunctive conditionals to express what it would be for the Lorentz transformations to transcend the various force laws and therefore to have an explanation by constraint but not a causal explanation given by the dynamics. I will now argue that the same account applies nicely to another scientific explanation that poses some of the same philosophical questions as the explanation of the Lorentz transformations.

As I have argued, the explanation by constraint of the Lorentz transformations does not appeal to the fact that there is a family of "inertial frames," defined as reference frames in which Newton's first law holds. Rather, it appeals to the fact that there is a family of frames (in relative uniform motion) in each of which the same laws hold, from which it follows that there is a family of frames where spatial and temporal homogeneity and spatial isotropy hold. Why, then, is there a family of inertial frames—or even a single frame in which Newton's first law holds? Brown (2005, 142) poses this question by asking, "How do all the free particles in the world know how to behave in a mutually coordinated way" so that they are unaccelerated relative to the same family of reference frames? "Anyone who is not amazed by this conspiracy," Brown (15) says, "has not understood it." Brown may inadvertently mislead by putting the fact to be explained in terms of the motions of "all of the free particles in the world." That there are in fact no free bodies (at least classically, because every body is influenced gravitationally by others) does not eliminate the mystery because it really concerns the trajectories that any free bodies, if there were any, would take: why do all of these trajectories involve nonacceleration relative to the very same frames?[26] The explanandum is the law that would, in turn, explain the behavior of any free bodies, were there any.

Brown says that this law cannot be explained by spacetime's structure because "there is no *dynamic coupling*" between spacetime and matter (Brown 2005, 142; see 25)—no "mechanism" by which a body is "informed as to what this structure is" (8). But as I have just argued in connection with an explanation of the Lorentz transformations, an explanation does not require a mechanism or coupling: a force. A feature of spacetime structure can help to explain without spacetime being a cause—namely, through an explanation by constraint. Various laws may constrain the dynamics so that there must be a family of frames in which Newton's first law holds. No force is needed to explain how bodies "know" what the natural laws are.

In classical physics, an explanation by constraint of Newton's first law could appeal to:

(1) Metalaws: that there is a reference frame S where spatial homogeneity and isotropy hold and where a free body's subsequent trajectory is determined by its initial position and velocity (i.e., a metalaw of determinism for free bodies: the first-order laws must be strong enough to determine such a body's subsequent trajectory given its initial position and velocity), and

(2) Various first-order laws that transcend the dynamical laws: that the Galilean transformations hold between S (the frame posited by (1) above) and any other frame in arbitrary uniform motion relative to S. (Hence, the metalaws in (1) hold in · any such reference frame.)

Regarding (2), recall from section 3.2 that the Galilean transformations may transcend the dynamics in classical physics in precisely the same way as the Lorentz transformations may in special relativity.

From constraints (1) and (2), Newton's first law can be explained by an argument given by Wigner (1992, 340–341). Take a free body and a reference frame (in the family of frames in arbitrary uniform motion relative to S) where the body starts from rest at the origin. Since space is isotropic and the body's motion is determined by its initial position and velocity, it must stay put. Suppose instead that the body starts from rest at any other location r. By spatial homogeneity, the body must stay put at r, too. Now view this case from a frame moving uniformly at $-v$ relative to the first frame. The body begins there with velocity v. By the Galilean transformations, the body's position at t must be $x + vt$. Thus it is a law that in any of these frames, free bodies undergo no acceleration.

This argument does not appeal to any conspiracy or mysterious coordination among the free bodies in order to explain why they are all unaccelerated in the very same frames. Rather, the explanation is that these are the frames where various symmetries and other laws transcending the dynamics hold. Here we have another explanation by constraint that uses metalaws and first-order laws transcending the dynamics.

The fact that there is a frame where Newton's first law holds can be explained in this way only if the laws to which this derivation appeals are constraints rather than coincidences. Of course, that there is a frame where Newton's first law holds follows from the fact that there is a frame where Newton's second law holds. However, this derivation from Newton's second law portrays the first law as dependent on the dynamics. It thereby mischaracterizes the explanandum as more contingent than it is, if the laws to which Wigner's derivation appeals are constraints rather than coincidences. In that case, this derivation from Newton's second law is no explanation. The second law cannot be responsible for the first law's necessity if that necessity is associated with membership in a subnomically stable set with a characteristic range of invariance that extends beyond that of the second law. If the laws to which Wigner's derivation appeals are constraints rather than coincidences, then the fact that there are frames where Newton's first law holds must belong to a subnomically stable set (to which the coordinate transformations also belong) on a higher rung of the pyramidal hierarchy than the rung occupied by dynamical laws such as Newton's second law and the force laws (see fig. 3.2).

That Newton's first law is independent of the second is one instance of a more general idea: that a principle of statics does not depend on any principle of dynamics. That statics is an autonomous science, transcending dynamics, is an idea that I will discuss again in chapter 4. It motivates some objections to dynamical explanations of the law of the parallelogram of forces (a law that, like Newton's first law but unlike the second, makes no reference to mass). Of course, my aim will not be to argue for the autonomy of statics (just as I am not arguing for any particular explanation of the Lorentz transformations). Rather, my aim will be to understand what the autonomy of statics would amount to in order to understand the kinds of non-causal scientific explanations that various laws would have if statics were autonomous.

The above non-causal explanation of Newton's first law would come in very handy, filling an explanatory gap for the relationalist regarding space and time in classical physics. Spacetime substantivalism can explain why certain trajectories can be traversed only under the influence of a force: because those trajectories involve absolute acceleration (i.e., acceleration relative to absolute space). Relationalism can offer no such explanation. As Sklar (1977, 229–232) points out, a relationalist could posit a primitive property possessed by exactly those trajectories that the substantivalist characterizes as involving absolute acceleration, and she could then appeal to their possession of that property as responsible for making them able to be traversed only under the influence of forces (and hence for making them accompanied by "inertial effects"). However, as Teller notes, "Sklar's suggestion feels ad hoc": "For relationalists to say that inertial effects go with an unexplained primitive property . . . which we characterize only as that property which goes with inertial effects, is for them to say about inertial effects no more than that they go wherever they happen to go. This would not appear to be a very enlightening thing to say about inertial effects" (1991, 370). But relationalism can do better: by exploiting the explanation by constraint of Newton's first law. In place of the primitive property, the relationalist can appeal to the property of involving acceleration in a reference frame S where spatial homogeneity and isotropy hold and where a free body's subsequent trajectory is determined by its initial position and velocity. The metalaw in the explanation of Newton's first law posits that there is such a frame. By that explanation, for any frame S' in arbitrary uniform motion relative to S, if a body feels no forces then it undergoes no acceleration in S'. Hence, for any such S', a body undergoing acceleration in S' must be under the influence of forces. Relationalism can thereby explain why certain trajectories (but not others) require impressed forces: because they are exactly the trajectories involving acceleration in a(ny) reference frame where spatial homogeneity and isotropy hold and where a free body's subsequent trajectory is determined by its initial position and velocity.[27]

More generally, my account of explanation by constraint can help us to understand what it would be for certain features of space to constrain space's inhabitants and thereby explain some of their behaviors. Why is it, for example, that all attempts to superimpose left and right human hands (that are—to a sufficient approximation—perfect mirror-images) have failed? Not because no one has ever tried a certain technique for superimposing them (or because they are too massive for anyone to move, or are held fast by very strong forces, or . . .), but rather because it is impossible to superimpose them. In other words, the explanation of the failure of all such attempts (or similarly all attempts to place five point particles so that each pair is the same distance apart) takes the same form as the explanation of the failure of all attempts to untie trefoil knots or to cross the Königsberg bridges (two examples of explanations by constraint that I gave in chapter 1). Nerlich (1979, 69; see 1994, 67–68) calls this "a geometric style of explanation" that "does not reduce to a causal explanation," and I agree.

But in mathematics, there are nonorientable spaces in which left and right hands can be superimposed. So it is not conceptually or narrowly logically impossible to superimpose left and right hands. In what sense, then, is it impossible? It is certainly naturally impossible to superimpose them; the laws of nature describe no physical process that would produce superimposed left and right hands. But to regard this fact as explaining our failure to superimpose the hands would be to treat the explanandum as having a causal explanation. In other words, it would mischaracterize the fact that no kind of causal process could produce superimposed hands, mistakenly portraying that fact as a coincidence of the various kinds of causal processes there happen to be. Accordingly, Nerlich (1991, 166–170) emphasizes that for left and right hands to be superimposed is not merely inconsistent with the laws of nature, but inconsistent with the structure of space.

Again, I agree. But to use "spatial [or geometric] impossibility" as a label for inconsistency with certain facts about space is not to reveal what makes those facts necessary—that is, what makes inconsistency with them constitute a genuine species of impossibility.[28] We need a specification of which facts about space are such that inconsistency with them is associated with a distinct species of impossibility, together with an account of what sets those facts apart. After all, it is a fact about space that there is insufficient space on my bookshelf for another book, but for there to be another book on my shelf is not "spatially impossible" in the manner of superimposing left and right hands. By the same token, the size of the universe at a given moment is a fact about space, but its being about space would not seem to be enough to make it "spatially necessary" and hence able to supply explanations like the above.

To understand what makes "spatial necessity" a species of the same genus as (but stronger than) natural necessity (and weaker than narrowly logical necessity), it is helpful to appeal to the pyramidal hierarchy of subnomically stable sets. The spatial necessities are among the facts that form a certain subnomically stable set high in that hierarchy. They do not include the fact about my bookshelf, but they do include the fact that there are no superimposed bodies having certain shapes. In virtue of its stability, this set is associated with a species of necessity; as I showed in chapter 2, the facts that form a stable set are collectively as invariant under counterfactual suppositions as they could collectively be. The spatial necessities occupy a higher rung on the hierarchy than the dynamical laws. (Perhaps they occupy the same rung as the Galilean transformations in classical physics.) Their place in the hierarchy reflects the fact that even if the force laws had been different, it would still have been impossible to superimpose left and right hands.[29] The range of counterfactual antecedents under which the hands remain nonsuperimposable, in connection with spatial necessity, is broader than the range of counterfactual antecedents under which the dynamical laws would still have held, in connection with their natural necessity.

On this view, certain spatial necessities serve as a common reason why every kind of causal process is alike in being powerless to superimpose hands, making this similarity among them no coincidence. In order for the geometry of space to explain non-causally why all attempts to superimpose left and right hands fail, certain facts about the geometry of space must belong to a subnomically stable set that is a proper subset of the natural laws. Of course, these facts about the geometry of space tell us something about the kinds of causal processes there are (e.g., that no causal processes produce superimposed hands). But these geometrical facts explain not by telling us about (or by constraining) *causal* processes in particular. Rather, these geometrical facts explain by virtue of constraining facts of every kind, whether or not they concern the stages of causal processes. These geometrical explanations are non-causal.

■ 3.5 HOW EXPLANATIONS BY CONSTRAINT WORK

The non-causal explanation of the Lorentz transformations that I have extracted from the physics literature has two steps. First it appeals to the principle of relativity to explain why the coordinate transformations must take a certain form (consistent with both the Galilean and the Lorentz transformations). Then it appeals to the spacetime interval's invariance to explain why the Lorentz rather than the Galilean transformations hold. On my account, the principle of relativity's status as a metalaw would give it the power to constrain the coordinate transformations. Its metalegal status would be manifested in the existence of a subnomically stable set containing its subnomic logical consequences (along with those of other symmetry metalaws) located above the transformation laws on the pyramidal hierarchy of subnomically stable sets (see fig. 3.2).

But in contrast to the principle of relativity as a metalaw, the spacetime interval's invariance is *not* modally stronger than the coordinate transformations. The interval's invariance and the Lorentz transformations belong to exactly the same subnomically stable sets; the interval's invariance does not stand above the transformation laws in the hierarchy. On what grounds, then, does the interval's invariance take explanatory priority over the coordinate transformations?[30]

Any kinematic consequence of special relativity that departs from classical mechanics can combine with the result from the non-causal explanation's first step to entail the Lorentz transformations. The relativistic formula for adding parallel velocities[31] suffices, for instance, as does the relativity of simultaneity. Why, then, does the interval's invariance rather than either of these two other relativistic facts help to explain the Lorentz transformations? For that matter, why don't the Lorentz transformations instead explain the interval's invariance (which they entail)? Furthermore, as I mentioned earlier, an explanation of the Lorentz transformations may cite the existence of a finite invariant speed c in place of the spacetime interval's invariance. The existence of such a speed follows from the interval's invariance. Why do physicists appeal to the existence of such a speed (or the interval's invariance) in order to help explain the Lorentz transformations, whereas they do not appeal to the relativity of simultaneity, for example?

Analogous questions apply within classical physics to the corresponding explanation of the Galilean transformations. That explanation appeals to the invariance of the temporal interval. Why is its invariance explanatorily prior to the other Galilean transformations? For that matter, the same kind of question can be posed regarding other explanations by constraint that have been proposed. Recall from chapter 2 that Hertz believed it to be no coincidence that all fundamental forces that are functions of distance are proportional to the inverse-square of the separation. He saw this fact as explained by the three-dimensionality of space and the fact that all fundamental forces operate through fields (rather than as action at a distance). Even if Hertz's explanandum turns out to be false, we can ask what (if anything) would have made the three-dimensionality of space and the fact that all fundamental forces operate by contact action explanatorily prior to the fact that these forces are all inverse-square.

In previous sections, I emphasized that a constraint must be explained by other constraints rather than by modally weaker facts. But the deduction of the spacetime interval's invariance from the Lorentz transformations, for instance, fails to explain even though it involves the deduction of one constraint from another that is modally at least as strong. There are plenty of other kinds of examples where constraints are deduced exclusively from other constraints that are modally at least as strong, and yet the deductions fail to explain their conclusions. We need to understand why they fail.

For example, consider the explanation by constraint at the start of chapter 2: that the law of energy conservation explains why every interaction that is either electric or gravitational conserves energy. The conservation law entails the explanandum, and so the conservation law combined with any other, arbitrary constraint (e.g., momentum conservation) also entails the explanandum. But that deduction does not explain it since the momentum conservation law is explanatorily irrelevant.

An account of explanation by constraint should enable us to understand why the explanandum is not explained by being deduced in this way—even though the deduction proceeds entirely from constraints that are at least as modally strong as the explanandum. By way of comparison, let's look briefly at how the analogous puzzle regarding causal explanation is resolved. Consider the law that the electric force on any point charge Q exerted in the static case by any long, linear charge distribution with uniform charge density λ at a distance r is equal (in Gaussian CGS units) to $2Q\lambda/r$. As I described in chapter 1, this line-charge law follows from and is explained causally by Coulomb's law (together with the parallelogram of forces), since the force consists of the sum of the forces exerted by the line charge's pointlike elements, and the causes of each of these forces are identified by Coulomb's law. Thus, Coulomb's law explains the line-charge law by specifying the causes of the force in every possible instance of the line-charge law. Coulomb's law is explanatorily prior to the line-charge law because Coulomb's law governs the fundamental causal processes at work in every instance of the line-charge law (and in a wide range of other cases as well). Any such approach to causal explanation can account for the fact that the derivation of the line-charge law loses its power to explain if an arbitrary law, such as the simple pendulum law, is added to Coulomb's law in the explanans (or if Coulomb's law is simply replaced with "Anything that is either a pair of point charges or a simple pendulum is . . . if the former or . . . if the latter"). The deduction of the line-charge law from this enhanced premise remains valid, of course. But it lacks explanatory power because the pendulum law does not help to describe the causal processes at work in instances of the line-charge law.[32]

Notice that to account for this derivation's failure to explain the line-charge law, we cannot appeal to the fact that the combined Coulomb-pendulum premise is stronger than it needs to be in order to entail the explanandum. That appeal fails because even Coulomb's law by itself (which *does* explain the line-charge law) is stronger than it needs to be in order to entail the explanandum: the line-charge law still follows even if Coulomb's law is restricted just to the case of a line charge's pointlike elements interacting with a point charge. The reason why the unrestricted Coulomb's law explains the line-charge law, but the broader Coulomb-pendulum law does not, is that the additional pendulum content does not help to describe the causal processes at work in instances of the line-charge law. Coulomb's law does. Even when two point charges are interacting electrostatically and neither is an element of a line charge, the same kind of causal process is at work as in instances of the line-charge law.

In contrast, as I have argued in the previous two chapters, explanations by constraint do *not* work by virtue of describing causal processes. So we cannot appeal to those processes in order to account for the fact that if we add an arbitrary constraint (such as momentum conservation) to energy conservation, then we spoil the explanation of the fact that both gravitational and electric forces conserve energy. (Of course, the conjunction of energy conservation and momentum conservation is stronger than it needs to be in order to entail the explanandum. But even energy conservation alone is stronger than it needs to be in order to entail the explanandum.) We cannot resolve this puzzle in the same way as we do in understanding how causal explanations work. Whereas all instances of the line-charge law involve the same kind of fundamental causal interaction (the kind described by Coulomb's law), this is not the case for all instances of energy conservation. Indeed, as I argued in chapter 2, an explanation by constraint works precisely by providing information about the way that the explanandum is required by laws that "sweep across" physically diverse kinds of causal interactions. As constraints, those laws do not depend on the particular kinds of interactions there actually happen to be.

To better understand explanation by constraint, we need to distinguish three types, differing in the type of explanandum they target. The explanandum may be a constraint (that is, it may possess a stronger species of necessity than ordinary laws of nature do). For example, it could be the fact (in the example from chapter 1) that whenever Mother tries to distribute 23 strawberries evenly among her 3 children (without cutting any), she fails. If the explanandum is a constraint, then let's call the explanation a "type-(c)" ("c" for "constraint") explanation by constraint. The explanans in such an explanation consists entirely of constraints, since (as I have argued) the explanandum does not depend on any facts possessing less necessity than it does.

By contrast, in a "type-(n)" explanation by constraint, the explanandum is *not* a constraint. For example, one type-(n) explanation by constraint explains why it is that whenever Mother tries to distribute her strawberries evenly among her children (without cutting any), she fails. (Unlike the previous explanandum, this explanandum does not specify the numbers of children and strawberries, so it is not necessary enough to be a constraint.) The explanans in a type-(n) explanation does not consist entirely of constraints, since the explanandum is not a constraint and so must depend on some facts that are not as necessary as constraints are. In the example that I have just mentioned, the explanans includes the contingent facts that Mother has 23 strawberries and 3 children.

In contrast to both types-(c) and -(n), the explanandum may be the fact that a given fact is a constraint. Since this explanandum is a modal fact, let's call this variety of explanation by constraint "type-(m)." For example, the explanandum in one type-(c) explanation is the fact that no one has ever managed to cross the bridges in a certain arrangement K (namely, as they were in Königsberg in 1735); I gave the details of this explanandum in chapter 1. (If the explanandum referred expressly to Königsberg in 1735 rather than to "arrangement K," then the explanation would be type-(n) rather than type-(c).) By contrast, the explanandum in a type-(m) explanation is that *it is impossible* to cross bridges in arrangement K, where the relevant species of impossibility is understood to be stronger than the ordinary natural impossibility of (for example) violating Coulomb's law. The explanans in a type-(m) explanation is that certain other facts possess the same (or stronger) species of modality, entailing that the fact figuring in the explanandum does, too.

This threefold distinction allows us to ask further questions that should be answered by an account of explanations by constraint. The same constraint that helps to explain (in a type-(n) manner) why Mother fails whenever she tries to distribute her strawberries evenly among her children also helps to explain (type-(c)) why Mother fails whenever she tries to distribute 23 strawberries evenly among 3 children. Is there some general relation between type-(c) and type-(n) explanations? I will propose one below.

We might likewise ask about the relation between type-(c) and type-(m) explanations. That it is impossible (whatever forces may be at work) to divide 23 objects evenly (without cutting any) into 3 groups (or simply the mathematical fact that it is impossible to divide 23 by 3 evenly into whole numbers) explains (type-(m)) why it is similarly impossible for Mother to distribute 23 strawberries evenly (without cutting any) among 3 children. Now suppose the explanandum is not the modal fact that it is impossible for her to succeed, but merely the fact that she never succeeds. Having switched from a type-(m) to a type-(c) explanation, does the explanans remain that it is impossible to divide 23 objects evenly (without cutting any) into 3 groups?

To better appreciate this question, let's look at an example where the variety of necessity at issue is not as strong as mathematical necessity. Consider a baby carriage with the baby sleeping inside, securely seat-belted so that the baby cannot separate much from the carriage. (The baby's mass is considerably less than the carriage's.) Suppose that the carriage and baby are initially at rest, the ground fairly smooth and level, and the carriage's brakes disengaged so that there is negligible friction between the ground and the wheels. Now suppose that the baby tosses and turns, shaking the carriage vigorously in many different directions. Why, despite the baby's pushing back and forth on the carriage for some time, does the carriage end up very nearly where it began? Bondi (1970, 266; 1980, 11–14) gives an explanation that, he says (let's suppose correctly), transcends the details of the various particular forces exerted by the baby on the carriage. Since there are negligible horizontal external forces on the carriage-baby system, the system's horizontal momentum is conserved; since it was initially zero, it must remain zero. Therefore, whatever may occur within the system, its center of mass cannot begin to move horizontally. The only way for the carriage to move, while keeping the system's center of mass stationary, is for the baby to move in the opposite direction. But since the baby is strapped into the carriage, the baby cannot move far without the carriage moving in about the same way. So the carriage cannot move much.

The law that a system's momentum in a given direction is conserved, when the system feels no external force in that direction, can supply this top-down explanation because this law holds "irrespective of what goes on inside that system" (Bondi 1970, 266). It would still have held even if there had been kinds of forces inside the system other than those covered by the actual force laws. For this reason, Bondi calls momentum conservation a "super-principle," echoing

Wigner's remark (quoted in chapter 2) about its transcending the force laws.[33] It constrains the kinds of forces there could have been just as the fact that 23 cannot be divided evenly by 3 constrains the ways Mother could have distributed her strawberries among her children.

That it is impossible (whatever forces may be at work) for a system's momentum in a given direction to change, when the system feels no external force in that direction, explains (type-(m)) why it is similarly impossible for any baby-carriage system (of the specified kind) to move much. Now suppose the explanandum is not the modal fact that it is impossible for such a system to move much, but merely that no such system in fact moves much. In other words, let the "baby-carriage law" be that any system consisting of . . . (a baby carriage in the specified conditions) moves only a little; the explanandum is now that the "baby-carriage law" is true. Having switched from a type-(m) to a type-(c) explanation, does the explanans remain that momentum conservation is a constraint? Or is the explanans merely that momentum is conserved, with no modality included in the explanans—though in order for this explanation to succeed, momentum conservation must be a constraint?[34] This is the analogue of the question that I originally asked regarding the type-(c) and type-(m) explanations of Mother's failure to distribute the strawberries evenly. I will shortly investigate whether it makes any difference for momentum conservation's status as a constraint to be included in the explanans or merely to be required for the explanation to succeed.

We can ask some further questions about the explanatory power (or impotence) of various deductions of constraints exclusively from other constraints. For instance, suppose we ask, "Why has every attempt to cross bridges in arrangement K while wearing a blue suit met with failure?" Suppose we receive the reply "Because it is impossible to cross such an arrangement while wearing a blue suit." That no one succeeds in crossing that arrangement while wearing a blue suit is a constraint; it is no coincidence. But of course, it is equally impossible for someone to cross such an arrangement of bridges whatever clothing (if any) he or she may be wearing. So is the reply "Because it is impossible to cross such an arrangement while wearing a blue suit" no explanation or merely misleading?

To better understand explanation by constraint, I will be guided by the idea that type-(c) explanations by constraint work roughly by supplying information about the *source* of the explanandum's especially strong necessity. As a constraint, the explanandum in a type-(c) explanation has a stronger variety of necessity than ordinary laws of nature (such as force laws) do. A type-(c) explanation by constraint works by supplying some information about the kind of strong necessity possessed by the explanandum and how the explanandum comes to possess it. The explanans may be simply that the explanandum possesses some particular sort of necessity, as in: "Why has no one ever untied a trefoil knot? Not from lack of imagination or persistence, but because it is mathematically impossible to do so."[35] In many explanations by constraint, however, the explanans does not merely characterize the explanandum as a constraint. Rather, the explanans supplies further information about where the explanandum's necessity comes from.

For example, an explanation of the "baby-carriage law" may go beyond pointing out that the explanandum transcends the various laws for the particular forces at work in the baby-carriage system. An explanans may also show how the explanandum follows from the law that a system's horizontal momentum is conserved if the system feels no external horizontal forces, where this law also transcends the various force laws. The explanans thereby supplies considerable information about where the inevitability of the baby-carriage law comes from. It could supply even more information by pointing out that there is nothing special about the horizontal direction; the law about horizontal forces and momentum is necessary because the same law holds of any direction. This constraint, in turn, derives its necessity from that of two others (see fig. 3.2). The first is the fundamental dynamical law relating force to motion (in classical physics: the Euler-Lagrange equation), which possesses exactly the same strong necessity as the baby-carriage law since the general relation between motion and forces of any kind also transcends the particular kinds of forces there happen to be. The second is the constraint that if that fundamental dynamical law holds, then linear momentum is conserved. That constraint possesses greater necessity than the fundamental dynamical law since it, in turn, follows from a symmetry metalaw: that the first-order laws are invariant under arbitrary spatial translation.

Each of these various, increasingly informative, type-(c) explanations of the baby-carriage law supplies information about how the explanandum acquires its especially strong inevitability. One way for an explanation by constraint to work is simply by telling us that the explanandum possesses a particular kind of inevitability (strong enough to make it a constraint)—that is, by locating it on the highest rung to which it belongs in the pyramidal hierarchy (fig. 3.2). But an explanation by constraint can also tell us about how the explanandum comes to be inevitable. To elaborate this idea, I need only to add a bit more structure to the pyramidal hierarchy.

A given constraint can be explained only by constraints at least as strong; a constraint's necessity cannot arise from any facts that lack its necessity. But a constraint cannot be explained entirely by constraints possessing stronger necessity than it possesses, else it would follow logically from those constraints and so itself possess that stronger necessity. Accordingly, on a given rung of constraints on the pyramidal hierarchy, there are three mutually exclusive, collectively exhaustive classes of truths:

1. There are truths that also lie on the next higher rung—truths possessing some stronger necessity.

2. There are truths that are not on the next higher rung and that some other truths on the given rung help to explain. Let's call these the rung's "explanatorily derivative" laws (i.e., "EDLs" on that rung).
3. There are truths that are not on the next higher rung and that no other truths on the given rung help to explain. Let's call these the rung's "explanatorily fundamental" laws (i.e., "EFLs" on that rung). Notice that an EFL on a given rung will appear on every rung further below, but it will not be an EFL there. Rather, it will belong there to the first of these three categories.

I suggest that every EDL on a given rung follows logically from that rung's EFLs together (perhaps) with truths possessing stronger necessity.[36] A type-(c) explanation by constraint explains a given constraint either by simply identifying it as a constraint of a certain kind or by also supplying some information about how its necessity derives from that of certain EFLs. Any EDL can be explained entirely by some EFLs that together entail it: some on its own rung and perhaps also some on higher rungs.[37]

I have said that when the "baby-carriage law" is given an explanation by constraint, then it is explained by the fact that it transcends the various force laws, and this explanation can be enriched by further information about how its necessity derives from that of EFLs. I have thereby suggested that the explanans in a type-(c) explanation is not simply some constraint's truth, but the fact that it is a constraint, since the explanation works by supplying information about where the explanandum's necessity comes from. The explanans in a type-(c) explanation thus takes the same form as the explanans in a type-(m) explanation. These are my answers to some of the questions that I asked earlier about explanations by constraint. I will give another argument for these answers at the end of the next section. (When I say, then, that a given EFL helps to explain a given EDL, I mean that the EFL's *necessity* helps to explain the EDL.)

No truth on a given EFL's own rung—and, therefore, no truth on any higher rung of the hierarchy (since any truth on a higher rung is also on every rung below)—helps to explain that EFL. A truth in the given pyramidal hierarchy (e.g., the hierarchy of subnomically stable sets, which I identified in chapter 2 as the hierarchy of first-order laws) that is *not* on the rung for which a given truth is an EFL also cannot help to explain the EFL, since the EFL cannot depend on truths that lack its necessity. An EFL on some rung of the first-order (i.e., subnomic) hierarchy may be brute—that is, have no explanation (other than that it holds with a certain kind of necessity). This may be the case (according to classical physics) with the fundamental dynamical law (classically, the Euler-Lagrange equation). But an EFL on some rung of the hierarchy of subnomically stable sets may not be brute, but instead may be explained by one or more *nomic* facts (apart from the nomic fact that the given EFL is necessary) that are metalaws and so appear high in the hierarchy of *nomically* stable sets.

For example, the constraint that momentum is conserved if the Euler-Lagrange equation holds (which, as I mentioned a moment ago, figures in the explanation of momentum conservation) may have no explanation among subnomic truths, but it may be explained by a nomic truth (namely, by the symmetry principle that the first-order laws are invariant under arbitrary spatial translation). It is entailed by the symmetry metalaw, so although it may be an EFL on some rung of the pyramid of subnomically stable sets, it is an EDL on the rung of the pyramid of nomically stable sets that the symmetry principle occupies. As I have argued, an analogous relation holds between the principle of relativity as a metalaw and the constraint that the Lorentz transformations hold if the spacetime interval is invariant (as well as the constraint that the Galilean transformations hold if the temporal interval is invariant). This constraint, together with the spacetime interval's invariance (which may be an EFL), explains why the Lorentz transformations hold (as I argued in section 3.2) if those transformations are constraints rather than coincidences.

In the next section, I will argue that if we understand type-(c) explanations as working by virtue of supplying information about the source of a constraint's necessity, then we can understand why certain deductions of constraints exclusively from other constraints nevertheless fail to explain. In this way, we can answer some of the questions about explanation by constraint that I posed at the start of this section. But of course, this picture presupposes a distinction between EFLs and EDLs on a given rung of the hierarchy. In section 3.7 (the chapter's final section), I will examine what makes a constraint an EFL.

■ 3.6 SUPPLYING INFORMATION ABOUT THE SOURCE OF A CONSTRAINT'S NECESSITY

Although any EDL can be explained by being deduced from EFLs on its own rung (together, perhaps, with some on higher rungs), not every such deduction is an explanation. For example, the baby-carriage law is explained by the EFLs responsible for momentum conservation, but this argument loses its explanatory power (while retaining its validity) if its premises are supplemented with an arbitrary EFL possessing the explanandum's necessity (such as the spacetime interval's invariance). The added EFL keeps the deduction from correctly specifying exactly the EFLs from which the explanandum acquires its inevitability. Accordingly, I propose:

> If d (an EDL) is logically entailed by the conjunction of $f, g, \ldots$ (each conjunct an EFL on or above the highest rung on which d resides), but g (a logically contingent truth[38]) is dispensable (in that d is logically entailed by the conjunction of the other premises), then the argument from $f, g, \ldots$ does not explain d.

Of course, g may be dispensable to one such argument for d without being dispensable to every other.[39] But (I suggest) if g is dispensable to every such argument, then g is "explanatorily irrelevant" to d—that is, g is a premise in no explanation by constraint of d. In other words, if no other EFLs on d's rung (or above) combine with g to entail d, where g is indispensable to the argument, then no EDLs on d's rung (or above) render g explanatorily relevant to d. Any power that g may have to join with other constraints to explain d derives ultimately from its power to join with some other EFLs (or its power standing alone) to explain d. This idea is part of the picture (sketched in the previous section) of explanations by constraint as working by virtue of supplying information about how the explanandum's necessity derives from the necessity of some EFLs.[40]

If d is an EDL and g is an EFL on a given rung, then even if there are no deductions of d exclusively from EFLs (on or above that rung) to which g is indispensable, there are deductions of d from *EDLs* and EFLs on d's rung to which g is indispensable. For example, g is indispensable to d's deduction from g and $g \supset d$. But g's indispensability to such a deduction is insufficient to render g explanatorily relevant to d. To be explanatorily relevant to d, an EFL must be indispensable to a deduction of d from EFLs alone. If every logically contingent premise is indispensable to such an argument, then the argument qualifies (I suggest) as an explanation by constraint (of type-(c)):

> If d (an EDL) is logically entailed by the conjunction of $f,g, \ldots$ (each conjunct an EFL on or above the highest rung on which d resides) and the conjunction of no proper subset of $\{f,g, \ldots\}$ logically entails d, then the argument explains d.

If g (a logically contingent EFL on or above d's highest rung) is explanatorily irrelevant to d (an EDL), then in particular, g figures in no explanation of d exclusively from EFLs. So for any deduction of d exclusively from g and other EFLs on or above d's highest rung, some logically contingent premise must be dispensable (else that argument would explain d, contrary to g's explanatory irrelevance to d). If g is not the sole dispensable premise, then suppose one of the other ones is omitted. The resulting argument must still have a dispensable premise, else it would explain d and g would be explanatorily relevant. If there remain other dispensable premises besides g, suppose again that one of the others is omitted, and so on. Any argument that is the final result of this procedure must have g as its sole dispensable premise—in which case g must have been dispensable originally. Therefore, if g is explanatorily irrelevant to d, then g is dispensable to every deduction of d exclusively from EFLs on or above d's highest rung. (This is the converse of an earlier claim.)

I began this section by suggesting that an EDL fails to be explained by its deduction exclusively from EFLs on or above its highest rung if one of the deduction's logically contingent premises is dispensable. The distinction between EFLs and EDLs is crucial here; an EDL's deduction from *EDLs* on its own rung may be explanatory even if some of the deduction's logically contingent premises are dispensable. For example, the baby-carriage law is explained by the law that a system's horizontal momentum is conserved if the system feels no horizontal external forces. Validity does not require the additional premise that the same conservation law applies to any nonhorizontal direction. But the addition of this premise would not spoil the explanation. Rather, it would supply additional information regarding the source of the baby-carriage law's inevitability: that it arises from EFLs that in this regard treat all directions alike. The baby-carriage law is explained by the EDL that for any direction, a system's momentum in that direction is conserved if the system feels no external forces in that direction.

An EDL figures in an explanation by constraint in virtue of supplying information about the EFLs that explain the explanandum. It supplies this information because some of those EFLs explain it. Hence, d (an EDL) helps to explain e (another EDL) only if any EFL that helps to explain d also helps to explain e. For example, the spacetime interval's invariance does not help to explain the baby-carriage law, so the Lorentz transformations must not help to explain the baby-carriage law (because the interval's invariance helps to explain the Lorentz transformations).

If we remove the restriction to EFLs, then this idea becomes the transitivity of explanation by constraint: if c helps to explain d and d helps to explain e, then c helps to explain e. Although the philosophical literature contains several kinds of putative examples where *causal* relations are intransitive, none of those examples suggests that explanations by constraint can be intransitive. For example (see Lewis 2007, 480–682; Strevens 2008, 209–212), event c (the throwing of a spear) causes event d (the target's ducking), which causes event e (the target's surviving), but according to some philosophers, c does not cause e because c initiates a causal process that threatens to bring about $\neg e$ (though is prevented from doing so by d). Whether or not this kind of example shows that causal relations can be intransitive, it has no analogue among explanations by constraint, since they do not reflect causal processes such as threats and preventers. In other putative examples of intransitive causal relations (see Lewis 2007, 481–482; Strevens 2008, 212–215), c (a switch's being thrown) causes d (along some causal pathway), which causes outcome e, but according to some philosophers, c does not cause e if e would have happened (though in a different way) even if $\sim c$. Again, regardless of whether this kind of example demonstrates that token causal relations can be intransitive, explanations by constraint cannot reproduce this phenomenon since they do not aim to describe causal pathways. They involve no switches; if constraint d follows from one EFL on d's highest rung and follows separately from another, then each EFL suffices to explain d by constraint.[41]

I have just been discussing explanations by constraint where the explanandum is a constraint. Earlier I termed these "type-(c)" explanations by constraint. In contrast, a "type-(n)" explanation gives the reason why Mother fails whenever she tries to distribute her strawberries (without cutting any) evenly among her children. That reason involves not only constraints, but also the nonconstraint that Mother has exactly 23 strawberries and 3 children. This explanation works by supplying information about how Mother's failure at her task, given nonconstraints understood to be constitutive of that task (as I discussed in chapter 1), comes to possess an especially strong variety of necessity.

What about Mother's failure to distribute her strawberries evenly among her children *while wearing a blue suit*? Although that task consists partly of wearing a blue suit, Mother's failure has nothing to do with her attire. Its explanatory irrelevance can be captured by this principle:

> Suppose that s and w are nonconstraints specifying that the kind of task (or, more broadly, kind of event) in question has certain features. Let w be strictly weaker than s. Suppose that s and some EFLs logically entail that any attempt to perform the task fails (or, more broadly, that no event of the given kind ever occurs), and this failure is not entailed by s and any proper subset of these EFLs. But suppose that w suffices with exactly the same EFLs to logically entail that any attempt fails (or that no such event occurs). Then the argument from s and these EFLs (or EDLs that they entail) fails to explain by constraint why any such attempt fails (or why no such event occurs).

Roughly, if s is stronger than it needs to be, then it includes explanatorily superfluous content. That Mother is wearing a blue suit thus figures in no type-(n) explanations of her failure at her task.

This above principle says that for w to make s "stronger than it needs to be," w must be able to make do with exactly the same EFLs as s. But a nonconstraint s can explain even if it can be weakened without rendering the argument invalid—as long as that weakening must be balanced by the argument's EFLs being strengthened. Let's look at an example. The fact that Mother has exactly 23 strawberries and 3 children is not stronger than it needs to be to entail the explanandum when the other premise (let's suppose it to be an EFL) is that 3 fails to divide 23 evenly into whole numbers. However, it is stronger than it needs to be to entail the explanandum when the other premise is that 3 fails to divide 23 evenly *and* 2 fails to divide 23 evenly. With this stronger pair of EFLs, the nonconstraint premise s can be weakened to the fact w that Mother has exactly 23 strawberries and 2 or 3 children. Nevertheless, the original, stronger nonconstraint is explanatory. Notice that the EFL that 2 fails to divide 23 evenly is not a premise in the original deduction—and had it been, then it would have been dispensable there. Accordingly, the above principle specifying when s is stronger than it needs to be requires that the argument from w use exactly the same EFLs as the argument from s and that each of those EFLs be indispensable to the argument from s.[42] Hence, that Mother's task involves her having 23 strawberries and 3 children helps to explain why Mother always fails in her task; this fact about her task requires no weakening to eliminate explanatorily superfluous content, unlike any fact entailing that the task involves her wearing a blue suit.

Any constraint that joins with Mother's having 23 strawberries and 3 children to explain (type-(n)) why she fails to distribute her strawberries evenly among her children also explains (type-(c)) why she fails to distribute her strawberries evenly among her children if she has 23 strawberries and 3 children. Here is a way to capture this connection between type-(c) and type-(n) explanations by constraint:

> If there is a type-(n) explanation by constraint whereby non-constraint n and constraint c explain why events of kind e never occur, then there is a type-(c) explanation by constraint whereby c explains why it is that whenever n holds, e-events never occur.

The converse fails, as when c is that 3 fails to divide 23 evenly, n is that Mother's task involves her having 23 strawberries and 3 children and wearing a blue suit, and e is Mother's succeeding at distributing her strawberries evenly among her children; with regard to explaining why e-events never occur, n contains explanatorily superfluous content.

Suppose that constraint c explains (type-(c)) why all attempts to cross bridges in a certain arrangement K (instantiated by Königsberg's bridges) while wearing a blue suit fail. Why, then, do all attempts to cross Königsberg's bridges while wearing a blue suit fail? This explanandum is not a constraint. Accordingly, the explanans consists not only of c, but also of the fact that Königsberg's bridges are in arrangement K. But although the explanans in this type-(n) explanation includes that the task involves crossing bridges in arrangement K, it does not include that the task involves doing so while wearing a blue suit; any such content would be explanatorily superfluous. So the same explanans explains why no one ever succeeds in crossing Königsberg's bridges, blue suit or no. Since c and the fact that Königsberg's bridges are in arrangement K explains (type-(n)) why no one ever succeeds in crossing Königsberg's bridges, the above connection between type-(c) and type-(n) explanations entails that c explains (type-(c)) why it is that if Königsberg's bridges are in arrangement K, no one succeeds in crossing them. Presumably, the same applies to bridges anywhere else.

I have just argued that if a constraint explains why all attempts to cross bridges in arrangement K while wearing a blue suit fail, then the same constraint also explains why all attempts to cross bridges in arrangement K fail. By the same kind of argument, any constraint that explains why all *past* attempts to untie tre-foil knots failed also explains why all attempts to untie trefoil knots fail. There is no special reason why all past attempts fail.

It might be objected that the fact that every attempt to untie trefoil knots fails obviously does not explain itself but nevertheless explains (by constraint) why, in particular, every past attempt failed. But I do not agree that the fact that every attempt to untie trefoil knots fails explains (by constraint) why every past attempt failed. Rather, the *modal* fact that every attempt to untie trefoil knots *must* fail (as a matter of mathematical necessity) explains by constraint why every past attempt failed and likewise explains why every attempt fails. The explanans in a type-(c) explanation is not simply some constraint's truth, but the fact that it is a constraint. The explanans in a type-(c) explanation thus takes the same form as the explanans in a type-(m) explanation. Both are modal facts even though the explanandum in a type-(c) explanation is not.[43] Here, then, is one difference it makes that a certain law's status as a constraint is included in the explanans rather than merely required for the explanation to succeed.

■ 3.7 WHAT MAKES A CONSTRAINT "EXPLANATORILY FUNDAMENTAL"?

I have been elaborating the idea that an explanation by constraint works roughly by supplying information about the source of the explanandum's especially strong necessity. My approach depends upon a distinction between EFLs and EDLs among the constraints having the same rung as their highest on the pyra-midal hierarchy of subnomically stable sets (where each set is associated with its own variety of necessity). What, then, grounds this distinction among con-straints possessing the same characteristic variety of necessity? For example, what makes the spacetime interval's invariance an EFL (and so able to help account for the Lorentz transformations) whereas the formula for adding par-allel velocities, the relativity of simultaneity, and the Lorentz transformations themselves are not? Likewise, in connection with Hertz's proposed explanation, what would make the fact that all forces act by fields an EFL, whereas the fact that all forces are inverse-square is not?

I believe that there is no fully general reason why certain constraints rather than others on a given rung (but none higher) constitute EFLs. The order of explanatory priority is grounded differently in different cases. A principle sufficiently general to apply to any rung of the hierarchy, no matter what its content, and purporting to specify which constraints are "axioms" (EFLs) and which are "theorems" (EDLs) will find it very difficult to discriminate as scientific practice does between the Lorentz transformations, the interval's invariance, the velocity addition law, and the relativity of simultaneity. EFLs are set apart from EDLs on specific grounds that differ in different cases rather than on some uniform, wholesale basis.

As an example of how an attractive wholesale approach founders, consider Watkins's (1984, 204–210) criteria for distinguishing "natural" from "unnatural" axiomatizations having exactly the same deductive consequences. He contends that a natural axiomatization contains as (finitely) many axioms as possible provided that

(1) each axiom in the axiom set is logically independent of the conjunction of the others;

(2) no predicate or individual constant occurs inessentially in the axiom set;

(3) if axioms containing only nonobservational predicates can be separately stated, without violating any other rules, then they are separate; and

(4) no axiom contains a (proper) component that is a theorem of the axiom set (or becomes one when its variables are bound by the quantifiers that bind them in the axiom).[44]

These criteria deem certain axiomatizations to be unnatural. Rule 2, for example, ensures that a natural axiomatization not have as one axiom "A system's horizontal momentum is conserved if the system feels no horizontal external forces" and an analogous constraint for nonhorizontal momentum as another, separate axiom. However, Watkins's criteria cannot privilege the interval's invariance over the velocity-addition law, the relativity of simultaneity, or the Lorentz transformations. I see no way for wholesale rules like Watkins's to pick out which of these is an EFL.

What, then, grounds the order of explanatory priority among the Lorentz transformations and the other constraints on a modal par with it? What is the main difference between the interval's invariance and the invariance of some finite speed c (which can help to explain the Lorentz transformations), on the one hand, and the relativity of simultaneity, the Lorentz transformations, and the velocity-addition law, on the other hand? I suggest that the main difference between them is that both of the former identify certain quantities as invariant whereas each of the latter relates frame-dependent features in two frames or within in a given frame. The behavior of invariant quantities is explanatorily prior to the behavior of frame-dependent quantities because invariant quantities are features of the world, uncontaminated by the reference frame from which the world is being described, whereas frame-dependent quantities reflect not only the world, but also the chosen reference frame. How things *are* explains how they *appear* from a given vantage point. This view is often expressed by physicists and philosophers alike:

> Invariants—quantities that everybody agrees on regardless of their frame of reference—play a more important role in our understanding of the world than quantities that vary from one frame of reference to another. (Mermin 2009, 79)

The old and natural idea that what is objective should not depend upon the particular perspective under which it is taken into consideration is . . . reformulated into the following group-theoretical terms: what is objective is what is invariant with respect to the transformation group of reference frames, or, quoting Weyl (1952, 132), "objectivity means invariance with respect to the group of automorphisms [of space-time]." (Brading and Castellani 2003, 15)

In physics, the frame-dependent quantities . . . are taken to be non-fundamental. . . . Frame-*independent* quantities, on the other hand, . . . *do* correspond to fundamental, objective features of the world. The space-time interval *is* a fundamental, objective feature of the world, according to the theory of special relativity. . . . Reality is observer-independent. It does not depend on our arbitrary descriptions or conventions. (North 2009, 63, 67; see Salmon 1998, 259)

An observer on the earth sees and measures an oblong block; an observer on another star contemplating the same block finds it to be a cube. Shall we say that the oblong block is the real thing, and that the other observer must correct his measures to make allowance for his motion? All the appearances are accounted for if the real object is the four-dimensional, and the observers are merely measuring different three-dimensional appearances or sections; and it seems impossible to doubt that this is the true explanation. (Eddington 1920, 181)

Reality explains mere appearances (as philosophy has emphasized since Plato's Cave), and so the law that a certain quantity is invariant takes explanatory priority over the law specifying how a certain frame-dependent quantity transforms. For the same reason, the Galilean spatial transformations are not treated as EFLs in classical physics; explanations of why they hold (according to classical physics) finish by appealing not to (e.g.) the classical velocity addition law, but rather to the law that temporal intervals are invariant (i.e., $t = t'$). Time's absolute character is "fundamental" in Newtonian physics (see Barton 1999, 12).

But although reality's explanatory priority over appearances grounds the EFL/EDL distinction in this case, it cannot do so generally. In other cases, the distinction must be grounded in other ways. Return, once again, to Hertz's proposed explanation of the fact that all fundamental forces are inverse-square. What makes the three-dimensionality of space and the fact that all fundamental forces operate through fields explanatorily prior to the fact that those forces are all inverse-square, according to Hertz?[45] That reality explains mere appearances cannot account for the order of explanatory priority in this case.

I suggest that the distinction between EFLs and EDLs in this case arises instead from the common idea that features of the spatiotemporal theater are explanatorily prior to features of the actors who strut across that stage. For instance, if it were a law that space has a certain finite volume V, then the fact that no material object's volume exceeds V would be an EDL that is explained by a feature of space: only entities of a certain maximum size could fit within the theater. Space's three-dimensionality is likewise prior to the features of any of space's denizens, including forces.[46] Whereas the fact that all forces are inverse-square concerns a feature of space's occupants, the fact that all forces act by fields rather than at a distance is (for Hertz) more fundamental than that. Hertz sees it as bound up with the fact that causes must be local in space and time to their effects. Thus, that all forces are constrained to operate by mediated contact concerns in the first instance the nature of the spatiotemporal arena within which things act. That the arena imposes limits on the kinds of inhabitants it can accommodate is what makes the constraint that all fundamental forces act by mediated contact qualify as an EFL (according to Hertz) and so as explanatorily prior to the constraint that all fundamental forces are inverse-square.

Of course, my purpose here is not to endorse Hertz's implicit conception of space as an inert stage having dimensions and other features that constrain the kinds of physical interactions there could be. We may regard Hertz's conception as untenable in the wake of general relativity, according to which certain general features of spacetime are explained by the entities within it, as when the occurrence of a cosmological "Big Crunch" depends on how much mass there is, or the arrangement of matter is partly responsible for whether there are any closed timelike curves. On the other hand, we can also understand Gödel's (1949, 562) remark that a view according to which the existence of an objective time order "depends on the particular way in which matter and its motion are arranged in the world . . . can hardly be considered as satisfactory." My purpose, then, is not to endorse Hertz's explanation (or even its explanandum), but rather to use this example to help reveal the basis of the distinction between EFLs and EDLs. I think we can grant that the conception of space and time that I have ascribed to Hertz is the kind of fact that could ground that distinction in this case. But plainly it could not play this role in every case—or even in every case concerning spacetime geometry. For instance, it cannot ground the explanatory priority of the spacetime interval's invariance over the Lorentz transformations.

I therefore suggest that what makes one constraint an EFL rather than an EDL may have little to do with what makes another constraint an EFL rather than an EDL. This is not to say that the EFL/EDL distinction is groundless. On the contrary, I have just given two examples of the kinds of facts that might organize a given rung into EFLs and EDLs.

We have learned a good deal about explanations by constraint from studying the kinds of explanations that the Lorentz transformations might receive. The idea that the Lorentz transformations do not depend on dynamics is one manifestation of a more general view: that (as Whewell puts it) "the science of pure motion," kinematics (or, as Ampère dubbed it, *cinématique*), is "a separate science" from dynamics, "the science of motion viewed with reference to its causes" (Whewell 1840, 145).[47] It is common to find kinematics characterized in non-causal terms as "a branch of geometry" (Rankine 1872, 15) or "the purely geometrical science of motion in the abstract" (Thomson and Tait 1888, vi), thereby placing it between dynamics and mathematics. Its nearness to mathematics can be captured by the pyramidal hierarchy of subnomically stable sets. Likewise, Maxwell (1860/1990, 665) takes kinematics to be concerned with "the possible motions of a body apart from the causes of that motion"; I have shown what it would take for this species of possibility to be broader than dynamical possibility—to transcend the particular kinds of forces there happen to be.[48] In chapter 4, I will explain that Whewell also saw statics as a separate science transcending dynamics. Accordingly, he held that the law of the parallelogram of forces is not explained dynamically. Rather, it has a non-causal explanation by constraint.

■ APPENDIX: A PURELY KINEMATICAL DERIVATION OF THE LORENTZ TRANSFORMATIONS

We seek the transformation laws

$$x' = X(t,v,x,y,z)$$
$$t' = T(t,v,x,y,z).$$

The only privileged axis is x, along which the origin of S' is moving in S. By spatial isotropy, then, x' and t' are independent of y and z. By spatial homogeneity, the x'-separation of (x,y,z,t) and $(x + \Delta,y,z,t)$ depends only on Δ, not on x. Therefore

$$(\partial/\partial x)[X(t,v,x+\Delta)-X(t,v,x)]_{\Delta,t,v} = 0.$$

Dropping the reminder of what's being held fixed as we take the partial derivative with respect to x,

$$(\partial/\partial x)X(t,v,x+\Delta)=(\partial/\partial x)X(t,v,x).$$

Thus $(\partial X/\partial x)$ is equal for all x, so X is linear in x—and, by analogous reasoning, T is linear in x and (using temporal homogeneity) X and T are linear in t:

(1) $$x'=X(t,v,x)=A_v x+B_v t$$
(2) $$t'=T(t,v,x,y,z)=C_v x+D_v t$$

where the subscripts indicate that A–D are functions exclusively of v. (For simplicity, I omit the subscripts when the function is understood to be evaluated at v.)[49]

Let us derive "reciprocity": that the origin of S is moving in S' with velocity w = −v.[50] Since the frames are in "standard configuration" (recall fig. 3.1), the +x and +x' directions are the same: A = $(\partial x'/\partial x) > 0$. Without loss of generality, suppose that the +t and +t' directions are the same: D = $(\partial t'/\partial t) > 0$. From (1), the x and t coordinates of x' = 0 obey x = $(-B/A)t$, so v = $-B/A$. Take S (S') and invert the direction of the x (x') axis, yielding $\mathcal{S}(\mathcal{S}')$. By the principle of relativity, the laws transforming coordinates in S to coordinates in S' take the same form as the laws transforming $\mathcal{S}$ to $\mathcal{S}'$:

$$x' = \mathcal{A}_v x + \mathcal{B}_v t$$
$$t' = C_v x + \mathcal{D}_v t$$

where v is the velocity in $\mathcal{S}$ of the origin of $\mathcal{S}'$. Since $x = -x$, $t = t$, $x' = -x'$, and $t' = t'$, (1) and (2) yield

$$x' = A_v x - B_v t$$
$$t' = -C_v x + D_v t.$$

Hence

$$\mathcal{A}_v = A_v$$
$$\mathcal{B}_v = -B_v$$
$$C_v = -C_v$$
$$\mathcal{D}_v = D_v$$

and the x and t coordinates of $x' = 0$ obey $x = (B_v/A_v)\,t$, so $v = B/A = -v$. Therefore

(3)
$$\begin{cases} A_{-v} = A_v \\ B_{-v} = -B_v \\ C_{-v} = -C_v \\ D_{-v} = D_v. \end{cases}$$

For x = 0 and t' = 1, (1) and (2) yield

$$x' = B_v t$$
$$1 = D_v t$$

so at t' = 1, x' = B_v/D_v. That is, in S', the origin of S moves a distance of B_v/D_v in one unit of time, so its velocity w = B_v/D_v, which is some unknown function $\varphi(v)$. Since $B_{-v} = -B_v$ and $D_{-v} = D_v$, $\varphi(-v) = -\varphi(v)$. By the principle of relativity, the function φ that takes us from the velocity of S' in S to the velocity of S in S' also takes us from the velocity of S in S' to the velocity of S' in S: v = $\varphi(w)$. Therefore, v = $\varphi(\varphi(v))$. Because φ takes us from S to S' and vice versa, φ is one-to-one and (since, by the principle of relativity, the same range of relative velocities must be allowed in each frame) φ maps its domain onto itself—and (assuming any real number between two velocities that one frame may have relative to another is also an allowed velocity) it follows that $\varphi(v)$ is either strictly increasing (i.e., if $v_2 > v_1$, then $\varphi(v_2) > \varphi(v_1)$) or strictly decreasing. Take these two options in turn.

If φ is strictly increasing and $v < w$, then $\varphi(v) < \varphi(w)$. But $\varphi(w) = \varphi(\varphi(v)) = v$, so $w = \varphi(v) < v$, contradicting $v < w$. A contradiction likewise arises from $v > w$. So the only possibility is $v = w$, that is, $v = \varphi(v)$. Then since we found $\varphi(v) = B/D$, $D = B/v$, and since we found $B = -vA$, $D = -A$. By substitution into (1) and (2)

$$x' = Ax - vAt$$
$$t' = Cx - At$$

so $(\partial x'/\partial x) = A$ and $(\partial t'/\partial t) = -A$. These cannot both be greater than zero, contrary to our initial supposition.

If φ is strictly decreasing then if $\zeta = -\varphi$, then ζ is strictly increasing. We found $\varphi(\varphi(v)) = v$, so $\zeta(-\zeta(v)) = -v$. We found $\varphi(-v) = -\varphi(v)$, so $\zeta(-v) = -\zeta(v)$. Putting these together, we find $\zeta(\zeta(-v)) = -v$. So ζ is a strictly increasing function whose double application is the identity function. By the previous paragraph's argument, $\zeta(v) = v$, so $\varphi(v) = -v$, that is, reciprocity (!).

By the principle of relativity, the laws transforming coordinates from S to S' take the same form as the laws transforming S' to S (but, by reciprocity, with "$-v$" replacing "v"):[51]

$$x = A_{-v}x' + B_{-v}t'$$
$$t = C_{-v}x' + D_{-v}t'.$$

Substituting these into (1) and (2)

$$x' = A_v\left(A_{-v}x' + B_{-v}t'\right) + B_v\left(C_{-v}x' + D_{-v}t'\right)$$
$$t' = C_v\left(A_{-v}x' + B_{-v}t'\right) + D_v\left(C_{-v}x' + D_{-v}t'\right).$$

By (3)

$$x' = A_v\left(A_vx' - B_vt'\right) + B_v\left(-C_vx' + D_vt'\right) = \left(A^2 - BC\right)x' + \left(-AB + BD\right)t'$$
$$t' = C_v\left(A_vx' - B_vt'\right) + D_v\left(-C_vx' + D_vt'\right) = \left(AC - CD\right)x' + \left(-BC + D^2\right)t'.$$

So

$A^2 - BC = 1.$
$B(D - A) = 0.$
$C(A - D) = 0.$
$D^2 - BC = 1.$

The two middle equations have two solutions: (i) B = C = 0, yielding the identity coordinate transformations—the trivial result; not what we were seeking—and (ii)

$$D = A$$

$$C = (A^2 - 1)/B.$$

Since v = -B/A, the latter equation yields C = (1-A²)/vA. Thus

(4)

$$x' = A_v x - vA_v t$$

$$t' = \left[(1 - A_v^{\,2})/vA_v \right] x + A_v t.$$

Consider a frame S″ in standard configuration whose origin is moving uniformly with speed u relative to S′. By the principle of relativity, the laws transforming coordinates from S to S′ take the same form as the laws transforming S′ to S″. So

$$x'' = A_u x' - uA_u t'$$
$$= A_u \left[A_v x - vA_v t \right] - uA_u \left(\left[(1 - A_v^{\,2})/vA_v \right] x + A_v t \right)$$

$$t'' = \left[(1 - A_u^{\,2})/uA_u \right] x' + A_u t'$$
$$= \left[(1 - A_u^{\,2})/uA_u \right] \left[A_v x - vA_v t \right] + A_u \left(\left[(1 - A_v^{\,2})/vA_v \right] x + A_v t \right).$$

By the principle of relativity, the laws transforming coordinates from S to S″, given above, take the same form as the laws transforming S to S′, where we found D = A. Hence the coefficient of t in the equation for t″ must equal the coefficient of x in the equation for x″:

$$\left[(1 - A_u^{\,2})/uA_u \right] (-vA_v) + A_u A_v = A_u A_v - uA_u \left(\left[(1 - A_v^{\,2})/vA_v \right] \right).$$

Simplifying and rearranging:

$$(A_u^{\,2} - 1)/u^2 A_u^{\,2} = (A_v^{\,2} - 1)/v^2 A_v^{\,2}.$$

Since these quantities are equal for all u and v, they must be independent of u and v: For some constant k,

$$(A_v^{\,2} - 1)/v^2 A_v^{\,2} = k.$$

So $A = (1 - kv^2)^{-\frac{1}{2}}$. By (4)

$$x' = \left(1 - kv^2\right)^{-\frac{1}{2}} x - v\left(1 - kv^2\right)^{-\frac{1}{2}} t = \left(1 - kv^2\right)^{-\frac{1}{2}} \left(x - vt\right)$$

$$t' = -kv\left(1 - kv^2\right)^{-\frac{1}{2}} x + \left(1 - kv^2\right)^{-\frac{1}{2}} t = \left(1 - kv^2\right)^{-\frac{1}{2}} \left(-kvx + t\right).$$

The constant k is fixed by the invariance of the spacetime interval, as I explain in the main text.[52]

4 The Parallelogram of Forces and the Autonomy of Statics

In this final chapter of part I, I will conclude my study of "explanations by constraint." I will argue that one influential proposed scientific explanation of the parallelogram law for the composition of forces would be an explanation by constraint. I will examine the arguments that scientists have given for this proposal as well as the arguments for its rivals. Some of these arguments anticipate topics that I will investigate in later chapters, such as dimensional explanations (chapter 6), explanations in mathematics that reveal a pair of mathematical theorems to be no mathematical coincidence (chapter 8), and non-causal scientific explanations that account for similarities in derivative laws concerning physically unrelated phenomena (chapter 10). This chapter will thus launch us toward parts II, III, and IV of the book.

Today's classical physics textbooks tell us without ceremony that forces, as vectors (i.e., directed quantities), combine by "vector addition." A force applied at a point can be represented by an arrow starting from that point, pointing in the force's direction, and having a length proportional to the force's magnitude (see fig. 4.1a). The resultant of forces F and G acting together at a point is the force represented by the arrow extending from that point to form the diagonal of the parallelogram whose adjacent sides represent F and G (fig. 4.1b). Accordingly, this principle is frequently called "the parallelogram of forces."

Despite the routine treatment it generally receives today, the parallelogram of forces was the subject of considerable controversy throughout the nineteenth century. Its truth was unquestioned. The controversy concerned its explanation. In the words of a standard reference work from 1880: "The doctrine of the parallelogram of forces has given rise to much controversy, not as to its truth, but as to its derivation" (Anonymous 1880, 208–209). The main point in dispute was whether the parallelogram of forces is explained by statics or by dynamics. If it is explained statically, then statics (the study of systems in equilibrium) is *autonomous*; it has its own laws. In particular, it is independent of dynamics (the study of systems responding to forces); the laws of statics are separate from and *transcend* the laws of dynamics. The parallelogram law then has an explanation by constraint. On the other hand, if the parallelogram of forces is explained

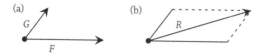

Figure 4.1 (a) Forces *F* and *G* are represented as acting at a single point; (b) their resultant *R* is represented by the diagonal of the parallelogram having *F*'s and *G*'s representations as adjacent sides

dynamically, then "statics thus becomes a special case of dynamics, when the forces concerned happen to be in equilibrium" (Cox 1904, 68). The laws of statics then become corollaries to the dynamical laws.

My concern is not to settle this controversy,[1] which concerns a matter of contingent fact that is for empirical science to investigate. My concern is to understand *what it would be* for one or the other of these rival views to be correct—to identify what facts would make it the case that the laws of statics transcend the laws of dynamics. I will show that the apparatus elaborated in chapters 2 and 3 identifies what the statical and dynamical interpretations are disagreeing about. In particular, I will suggest that various subjunctive facts constitute what it would take for the parallelogram law to be grounded either in statics or in dynamics. For the laws of statics to transcend the laws of dynamics would be for the range of counterfactual circumstances under which the statical laws would still have held, corresponding to the necessity they possess, to extend beyond the range of counterfactual circumstances under which the dynamical laws would still have held, corresponding to the (weaker) variety of necessity they possess. This account, I will argue, makes good sense of what is at stake in the controversy concerning the parallelogram law's metaphysical status and proper explanation.

I will also argue that various other accounts of natural law cannot make good sense of this dispute, whether they are Humean "Best System Accounts" (Lewis 1973, 1983, 1986b, 1999), accounts involving nomic necessitation relations among universals (Armstrong 1978, 1983, 1997; Dretske 1977; Tooley 1977), or dispositional essentialist accounts according to which laws reflect causal powers essential to possessing various properties (Bird 2007; Ellis 2001, 2002). On any of these accounts, it is not easy to see what it would be for the parallelogram of forces to belong to a higher stratum of natural law than the dynamical laws and so to have no dynamical explanation. These familiar philosophical accounts of natural law not only make it difficult to see what the point of this dispute could have been, but also foreclose some options in the dispute that were taken seriously in science.[2]

If some accounts of natural law and scientific explanation cannot make good sense of this dispute over the parallelogram law's explanation, then it may be tempting to dismiss their failures as not at all serious considering the dispute's obscurity, apparently narrow scope, and somewhat antique character. However,

I believe that this response would be mistaken. The dispute over the parallelo-gram law's explanation is not an isolated curiosity of merely mild antiquarian interest, but rather part of a much broader, longstanding controversy concern-ing the relation between statics and dynamics (see Duhem 1991, 184–186 and 418–422). I first mentioned this controversy in section 3.4, where I showed how Newton's first law might have a statical explanation and so be independent of Newton's second law. The dispute over the parallelogram law's explanation is a good example of the difference that a law's modal status makes to the kind of explanation it receives. In section 6.5, I will give another example where the sta-tus of statics as transcending dynamics would make a difference to a derivative law's explanation—namely, to whether a dimensional argument or a hydrody-namical derivation accounts for a feature of the law giving the terminal velocity of a small sphere falling through a viscous fluid.

The dispute over the parallelogram law's explanation (and, more broadly, over the autonomy of statics) should not be settled by philosophical accounts of scientific explanation or natural law. Rather, it should be settled empirically. I am not suggesting that some possible observation is logically consistent with a statical explanation of the parallelogram law but not with a dynamical expla-nation, or vice versa. Rather, I am suggesting that questions about why some natural law holds are the province of empirical science. Even if our most per-spicacious application of "inference to the best explanation" in this case fails to yield a decisive argument favoring one proposed explanation over its rivals, I would not conclude that metaphysics should settle the matter. I would still insist that metaphysics should leave room for possible worlds where either proposal is true. I see the dispute over the parallelogram law's explanation as like the dispute over the Lorentz transformations' explanation that I examined in chapter 3. Both ultimately come down to certain subjunctive facts that must hold if certain laws are to be "constraints." Although a fact expressed by a coun-terfactual conditional cannot be observed, we know many of these facts by confirming them empirically. I will present some of the *scientific* arguments by which rival proposed explanations of the parallelogram law have been evaluated.

I will examine closely the three chief approaches to explaining why the paral-lelogram law holds. In section 4.2, I will start with the dynamical explanation. Its advocates portrayed it as Newton's own approach and as demonstrating how the parallelogram of forces arises from Newton's second law of motion and the parallelogram of displacements. In this way, the dynamical argument depicts the parallelogram of forces as partly rooted in the same geometric principle as the par-allelograms of velocities and accelerations. However, the dynamical explanation was criticized for failing to reflect the independence of the parallelogram of forces from Newton's second law and any other dynamical principle.

In section 4.3, I will lay out the statical explanation that was most widely accepted in the mid-nineteenth century, which originated in an 1804 paper by the otherwise obscure French physicist Charles Dominique Marie Blanquet Duchayla. This explanation exploits the "principle of the transmissibility of force," which concerns rigid extended bodies rather than mass points. Critics of this argument's explanatory power objected that the parallelogram of forces is not confined to forces acting on extended bodies. Duchayla's proposed explanation was also criticized for failing to give a unified explanation of the resultant force's direction and magnitude. (My study of explanations in mathematics in part III will later shed some light on the kind of disunity that Duchayla's explanation exhibits.) Nevertheless, Duchayla's proposal had many advocates; they praised it for correctly capturing the parallelogram law's independence from dynamics.

In section 4.4, I will examine Poisson's statical explanation, which became increasingly popular in the late nineteenth century. Like Duchayla's proposal, Poisson's explanation belongs to statics. But it avoids the principle of the transmissibility of force to which Duchayla appealed, using instead various symmetries, dimensional considerations, and the fact that two forces have a unique resultant determined entirely by their magnitudes and directions. Advocates of Poisson's argument saw it not only as giving a unified treatment to direction and magnitude, but also as applicable to a wide range of quantities, explaining why they all compose vectorially despite their profound physical differences. On this view, the similarity in the composition laws for these physically diverse quantities is a physical coincidence but mathematically non-coincidental—a distinction that I will study more closely in chapter 10.

In section 4.5, I will examine whether various notable accounts of natural law can leave room for statical explanations of the parallelogram law. I will argue that their inability to do so is a serious strike against these proposals. In section 4.6, I will argue that the statical explanation proposed by Poisson would be an "explanation by constraint." To specify what would make the parallelogram law have such an explanation, I will appeal to the hierarchy of subnomically stable sets. This apparatus will allow me to clarify what this dispute over the parallelogram law's explanation is all about: whether the parallelogram law transcends Newton's second law and the transmissibility principle, or whether it depends on one of them. On my view, the dispute turns on whether or not the parallelogram law would still have held, even if Newton's second law of motion or the transmissibility principle had not. If it would then still have held, the parallelogram law is modally stronger than and so cannot depend on either of these principles. Finally, I will compare my account of statical explanations as "explanations by constraint" to philosophical proposals that characterize non-causal scientific explanations as "structural explanations."

■ 4.2 THE DYNAMICAL EXPLANATION OF THE PARALLELOGRAM OF FORCES

The parallelogram law for the composition of forces first appeared in 1586 in Simon Stevin's *Principles of the Art of Weighing* (Stevin 1955, 174–179). (The parallelogram law for the composition of velocities was known to the ancients. It was stated in *Mechanical Problems* (Aristotle 1980, 337–339), which is traditionally ascribed to Aristotle but may have been written by one of his early followers.) The parallelogram of forces seems to have been widely recognized by Newton's day, since both Pierre Varignon and Bernard Lamy stated it in the same year (1687) as Newton published the *Principia*.[3]

Physicists who endorse the dynamical explanation[4] typically characterize it as the explanation that Newton (1687/1999, 417–418) gave, at least loosely, in deriving the first two corollaries from his laws of motion. The dynamical explanation follows Newton's derivation in applying the second law of motion (force = mass x acceleration) not only to the resultant force R, but also individually to each of the two component forces F and G, thereby grounding the parallelogram law in the two forces' independence. The dynamical explanation also follows Newton's argument in appealing to the "parallelogram of accelerations": that if a body simultaneously undergoes two accelerations represented in magnitude and direction by the adjacent sides of a parallelogram, then its net acceleration is represented by the parallelogram's diagonal. The dynamical explanation of the parallelogram of forces begins by noting that the accelerations produced independently by two forces are in the directions of those forces, are proportional to their magnitudes, and compose parallelogram-wise. Because the resultant force is in the direction of and proportional to the resultant acceleration, the two forces must likewise compose parallelogram-wise.

More fully: Suppose a point particle of mass m is acted upon by two forces represented in magnitude and direction by line segments AB and AC having lengths b and c, respectively, and enclosing angle BAC measuring a radians (see fig. 4.2, which was often used to illustrate the dynamical explanation[5]). By Newton's second law, the two forces cause accelerations in their respective directions, represented by segments AB' and AC' having lengths b/m and c/m,

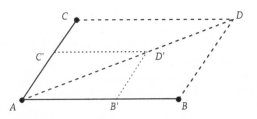

Figure 4.2 The dynamical explanation

respectively. The resultant acceleration is represented by the diagonal of parallelogram $AB'D'C'$, having length

$$\sqrt{(b/m)^2 + (c/m)^2 + 2(b/m)(c/m)\cos\alpha} \qquad (1)$$

By Newton's second law,[6] the resultant acceleration is associated with a resultant force directed along the diagonal with magnitude

$$m\sqrt{(b/m)^2 + (c/m)^2 + 2(b/m)(c/m)\cos\alpha} \qquad (2)$$

which simplifies to

$$\sqrt{b^2 + c^2 + 2bc\cos\alpha} \qquad (3)$$

Equation (3) is the length of the diagonal of the parallelogram having segments AB and AC as adjacent sides.

Advocates of one or another derivation of the parallelogram law tend to defend it over other derivations not primarily on the grounds of its being shortest, simplest, or easiest for students to grasp. Rather, the greatest emphasis is typically placed on whether a given derivation is "philosophically" (or "methodologically") correct—that is, whether it correctly identifies the principles that are responsible for the parallelogram law. For example, in arguing for the dynamical derivation, William Thomson (Lord Kelvin) and Peter Guthrie Tait (1888, 244–245) emphasized that "we believe it contains the most philosophical foundation" for physics. In contrast, the dynamical argument's critics generally charge it not with being unnecessarily complicated or difficult to follow, but rather with being "unnatural and a defect in method" (in the words of an American advocate of Poisson's derivation [Anonymous 1829, 314], which I will give in section 4.4). Although the statical derivations are arguably more complicated than the dynamical derivation, their advocates (as the following sections will illustrate) tend to advance them as reflecting the actual relations of explanatory dependence among various physical principles.

Objections to the dynamical derivation, then, tend to dispute not its cogency, but rather its explanatory power. A common objection is that the law determining the resultant of two forces is fundamentally nothing more than the law determining which forces combine to yield zero force, since forces F and G combine to yield force R if and only if F, G, and $-R$ (a force equal and opposite to R) combine to yield zero force.[7] Furthermore, the law determining which forces combine to yield zero force (i.e., which forces are in equilibrium) is independent of what would happen in case of nonequilibrium. That is, the law is not based on the precise connection between force and motion. Therefore, notions such as motion, change, time, and mass (the proportionality constant relating unbalanced force to motion) should not enter into an explanation of the parallelogram law.

Of course, all of these notions figure prominently in the dynamical derivation. It turns precisely on the relation between force and motion. But since in equilibrium there is no effect on motion, and since the law of the composition of forces is fundamentally just the law specifying the conditions of equilibrium, the particular motion that would ensue under nonequilibrium must (the objection runs) be irrelevant to the parallelogram law's explanation. Its irrelevance is manifested by the fact that as I just showed, mass m is introduced in the dynamical derivation only to cancel out in the step from equation (2) to equation (3). According to the objection, the fact that m ultimately cancels out in the dynamical derivation is not fortuitous. Rather, it reflects the fact that the parallelogram law is not dynamical and so m (as the constant of proportionality between a force and the motion it produces) plays no role in explaining it.

Critics of the parallelogram law's having a dynamical explanation often cite William Whewell as having pressed their case in the first half of the nineteenth century. For example, James Challis (the Plumian Professor of Astronomy at Cambridge, most famous today for having narrowly missed discovering Neptune in 1846) praised Whewell for having done "away with the illogical method of proving the parallelogram of forces by means of bodies in *motion*, which had previously been adopted in English works" (Challis 1875, 6, italics in the original). Whewell (1858, 225) contended that the parallelogram of forces is "independent of any observed laws of motion." He wrote:

> The composition of motion ... has constantly been confounded with the composition of force. But ... it is quite necessary for us to keep the two subjects distinct.... The conditions of equilibrium of two forces on a lever, or of three forces at a point, can be established without any reference whatever to any motions which the forces might, under *other* circumstances, produce.... To prove such propositions by any other course, would be to support truth by extraneous and inconclusive reasons. (1858, 226)

> The composition of forces cannot be deduced from the second law of motion. The conditions of magnitude and direction under which pressures balance each other, are not and cannot be dependent on the laws of the motions which take place when the forces do not balance. (1832, 88)

Note Whewell's remark that the parallelogram law "cannot be dependent" on the laws of dynamics; the issue here is clearly explanation. As Einstein came to regard the Lorentz transformations as purely kinematic and hence independent of dynamics (as I argued in chapter 3), so Whewell saw statics as transcending dynamics: "the purity and independence of Statics, as a mathematical science, were disregarded, by the mathematicians who were zealously following the rapid advance and rising fortunes of Dynamics." (Whewell 1832, ix; see Todhunter 1876, 19). Many physicists have agreed with Whewell that the dynamical argument cannot explain why the parallelogram of forces holds because the parallelogram law depends exclusively on statics. For instance, William H. Macaulay (the English mathematician and physicist after whom "Macaulay's method" for determining the deflection of beams is named) emphasized that this objection to the dynamical explanation is "philosophical" rather than pedagogical: "to make [the parallelogram of forces] ... dependent on a theory of mass, as appears to be usual in modern text-books, somewhat grates upon one's sense of logical order" (Macaulay 1900, 403). Other critics, such as the Edinburgh physicist John Robison and the Cambridge logician, mathematician, and economist W. E. Johnson, focus even more explicitly on the dynamical argument's explanatory impotence:

> We cannot help being of the opinion, that a separate demonstration [of the law of composition of forces—separate, that is, from the composition of motions] is indispensably necessary. ... The composition of motions will not explain the composition of pressures, unless we take it for granted that the pressures are proportional to the velocities [i.e., that a constant force experienced by a body beginning at rest, multiplied by the duration over which the body experiences it, is proportional to the body's resulting velocity—a special case of Newton's second law]; but this is perhaps a gratuitous assumption. (Robison 1822, 64; see Robison 1803, 599)

> The resultant ... depends upon the components alone, and not upon the mass ... of the body upon which the forces act. For this reason we find in many works upon mechanics the correctness of the parallelogram of forces demonstrated without reference to the mass. (Weisbach 1875, 178)

> [The dynamical argument] is open to ... serious objections ... for it introduces kinetic ideas which are really nowhere again used in statics. (Johnson 1889, 153)

> This cannot be considered perfectly satisfactory, as we are making the fundamental theorem of statics dependent upon a dynamical argument. (A.G.G. 1890, 413)

> Statics ... , in itself, does not involve the ideas of motion and time. In it the idea of mass may also be entirely eliminated. Newton's proof of the parallelogram of forces has been objected to on the grounds that it requires the introduction of the fundamental conceptions of a much more complicated science than the one in which it is employed. Among the demonstrations which avoid this objectionable feature is the one due to Poisson. (Moulton 1914, 6)

(I will examine Poisson's proposed explanation in section 4.4.)

In the view of these authors, it is no "algebraic miracle" that m cancels out in the parallelogram law's dynamical derivation. Rather, this cancellation is required by the autonomy of statics. By mischaracterizing the parallelogram law as dependent on Newton's second law, the dynamical argument gives an incorrect account of why m fails to appear in the law for the composition of forces.

The argument that mass's role in the dynamical derivation shows the derivation to be incapable of explaining why the parallelogram law holds is similar to an argument that might be made against a purported dynamical explanation of Newton's first law of motion—an explanation according to which the first law is merely a special case of Newton's second law. Unlike the second law, the first law does not require that all bodies have mass; in fact, it makes no reference to mass at all. On this basis, some physicists have reasonably suspected that the first law does not depend on the second law. As I showed in section 3.4, Newton's first law can be derived from symmetry principles alone, without any appeal to dynamical considerations. Presumably, that argument would be regarded as explanatory by those who see the parallelogram law as part of an autonomous statics.

That the parallelogram of forces is independent of Newton's second law is commonly put by saying that forces would still have combined parallelogram-wise even if Newton's second law had been false so that force connected differently to motion—for example, even if the resultant force on a body had been proportional to the body's net velocity rather than its net acceleration. Daniel Bernoulli (1726/1982, 121), who gave a pioneering statical explanation of the parallelogram of forces, suggested that a wide range of alternatives to Newton's second law might have held but didn't. Among these counterfactual alternatives are that the resultant force is proportional to the resultant acceleration's square root, or to its cube root, or to its square. But (Bernoulli held) even if one of these counterfactual alternatives had been the case, the parallelogram of forces would still have held.[8] On Bernoulli's view, the parallelogram law has greater necessity than Newton's second law, so the latter cannot be responsible for the former.

Although Bernoulli maintained that the parallelogram of forces was geometrically necessary and thus knowable a priori, Bernoulli's objection to the dynamical explanation (namely, that the parallelogram of forces would still have held even if dynamics had not been governed by Newton's second law) continued to be taken seriously long after the parallelogram of forces had been recognized as not belonging to geometry and as knowable only empirically.[9] That the parallelogram of forces would still have held, even if Newton's second law had not held, was identified by the English mathematician James Cockle, for instance, as the crucial respect in which the statical explanation developed by Bernoulli and Poisson contrasts with the dynamical explanation favored by Thomson and Tait: "we may seek to arrive at the composition of pressures, independently of the second law of motion, by processes which are valid whether that law be a law of nature or not, and which would be valid even if we had not any conception of motion, and which, indeed, do not render it necessary to consider whether pressure does or does not tend to produce motion" (Cockle 1879, 12–13). Robison emphasized the same counterlegal:

If the velocities produced by these forces are not in the proportion of those intensities, but in the subduplicate ratio of them [that is, if the velocity resulting from the application of a given force for unit time to a given body, beginning at rest, is proportional not to the force's strength, as Newton's second law demands, but to the square root of the force's strength] . . . [then] this composition [that is, the composition of these forces] follows precisely the same rule as the composition of the forces which are measured by the velocities . . . but it does not appear that it can be held as demonstrated by the arguments employed in the case of motions. . . . Accordingly, philosophers of the first eminence have turned their attention to this problem. It is by no means easy; being so nearly allied to first principles, that it must be difficult to find axioms of greater simplicity by which it may be proved. (1822, 54–55)

As earlier chapters will likely have suggested to you, I will appeal to precisely such counterlegals to specify the subjunctive facts that would make the parallelogram of forces have a statical explanation and so possess greater necessity than the second law of motion (albeit less necessity than mathematical truths).

In contrast, the dynamical explanation's defenders frequently praised it for unifying the parallelogram of forces with the parallelogram of accelerations (and velocities), giving them all a common origin in the parallelogram of displacements. For example, after characterizing Whewell's proposed statical explanation as "forced and unnatural," one proponent of the dynamical explanation wrote: "With regard to mechanics itself, the extended and comprehensive view of this subject would embrace what are usually termed the parallelogram of forces and the composition of motion (or the 'parallelogram of velocities,' as it is sometimes called) in the same fundamental idea. The separation of these two things—which are in reality but one—is justly censured by Lagrange, as depriving them of their 'evidence and simplicity' " (A.H. 1848, 107). Indeed, in a remark widely endorsed (e.g., by Cockle 1879, 13; Routh 1896, 18) as capturing an attractive feature of the dynamical explanation, Lagrange (1813/1881, 349–450) said that the dynamical explanation "has the advantage of demonstrating clearly why the composition of forces necessarily follows the same laws as the one of velocity." As I will discuss in section 4.4, a similar argument from unification is frequently used to defend Poisson's statical explanation of the parallelogram law.

4.3 DUCHAYLA'S STATICAL EXPLANATION

The statical explanation "usually given" (Browne 1883, 36; see Goodwin 1846, 272) in mid-nineteenth-century textbooks[10] originated with Duchayla (1804).[11] Although Duchayla's derivation is subtle and complex, nineteenth- and early twentieth-century textbooks commonly presented it in full. For example, an applied mechanics text intended for engineering students devoted three pages to giving it in detail (Church 1908, 4–6). To illustrate the argument's steps, I will use the same figures that many textbooks employed.

Duchayla's explanation proceeds like a proof by mathematical induction.[12] I will begin (as was customary) with the rule for the argument's inductive step, giving Duchayla's account of why the rule holds. Here Duchayla appealed to the "principle of the transmissibility of force." Then I will give Duchayla's argument by induction, whereby he explained why the parallelogram law gives the resultant force's direction. Finally (continuing to follow the standard order of presentation), I will show how Duchayla used the parallelogram law for the resultant's direction to explain why the parallelogram law also holds for the resultant's magnitude.

Let's begin with the rule for the derivation's inductive step:

> If forces P and Q, acting together at a point, result in a force directed along the diagonal of the parallelogram representing the two forces, and if the same applies to forces P and R acting together at the same point, with R acting in Q's direction, then the same applies to P acting together with the resultant of Q and R.

Here is Duchayla's account of why this rule holds:

> Let P be represented by segment AB (fig. 4.3) and be directed toward B. Grant that the resultant of Q and R (each directed toward E) is in their common direction and equal in magnitude to the sum of their magnitudes; let it be represented by segment AE, with Q represented by AC, so that segment CE is the proper length and direction to represent R—except that R is actually applied at A rather than at C. (Draw the rest of [fig. 4.3] to complete the two parallelograms.) Nevertheless, the "principle of the transmissibility of force" says that when a force acts on a body, the result is the same whatever the point, rigidly connected to the body, at which it is applied, provided that the line through that point and the force's actual point of application lies along the force's direction. So although R is applied at A, its effect is the same if it is applied at C, since AC is in the force's direction. With the

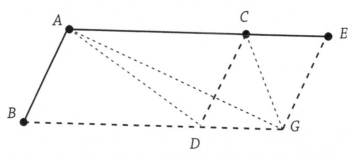

Figure 4.3 Duchayla's explanation of why the rule for the inductive step holds

parallelograms in fig. 4.3 forming a rigid body, the three forces can be applied to other points along their lines of action without changing their resultant. We cannot move P's point of application directly to C, since AC does not lie along P's direction. But by hypothesis, the resultant of P and Q acts along diagonal AD, so the resultant can be applied at D. It can then be resolved into P and Q, now acting at D. Q's direction lies along DG, so Q can be transferred to G. P's direction lies along CD, so P can be transferred to C, where it meets R. By hypotheses, their resultant acts along diagonal CG, so it can be transferred to G, where it meets Q. Now the converse of the principle of the transmissibility of force says that if a force's effect would be unaltered were its point of application changed to another point rigidly connected to its actual point of application, then the line through that other point and the force's actual point of application must lie along the force's direction. By that converse principle, AG must lie along the line of action of the force resulting from P composed with the resultant of Q and R.

Thus Duchayla used the transmissibility principle (and its converse) to explain why the rule for the inductive step holds. Duchayla then appealed to symmetry to explain why the resultant of two equal forces acting at the same point is represented by an arrow from that point in the same plane as the arrows representing the two forces and bisecting the angle between them.[13] This conclusion places us on the first "rung" of the "ladder" of Duchayla's mathematical induction; the inductive rule enables us to ascend the ladder to any height:

Start with a given force F, another force G with F's magnitude but in a different direction, and a third force H identical to G, all acting at the same point. Symmetry gives the resultant of F and G as lying along the corresponding parallelogram's diagonal, and likewise for F and H. The inductive rule then shows that the resultant of F composed with a force of twice F's magnitude—the resultant of G and H—points along the corresponding parallelogram's diagonal.

Now take F, this force of twice F's magnitude, and H. The inductive rule shows that the resultant of F together with a force of thrice F's magnitude points along the corresponding parallelogram's diagonal—and so forth for F composed with a force having n times F's magnitude (for any positive integer n).

Now take a force in F's direction but n times F's magnitude, another force G with F's magnitude but pointing in a different direction, and a third force H identical to G. By the inductive rule, the resultant of nF with a force of twice F's magnitude points along the corresponding parallelogram's diagonal—and so forth for nF composed with mF (for any positive integers n, m), i.e., for any two commensurable forces.

Any two incommensurable forces can be approximated to any desired degree by a pair of commensurable forces, so the explanation is thereby extended to any two forces.

Thus Duchayla explains why the parallelogram law holds regarding the resultant's direction. The final step of Duchayla's explanation shows why the parallelogram of forces also yields the resultant's magnitude:

Let AB and AC (fig. 4.4) represent two forces; their resultant (as we just explained) points in the direction of AD (the parallelogram's diagonal). Let AE extend AD in the opposite direction, its length representing the resultant force's magnitude. Duchayla shows that the parallelogram's diagonal represents the resultant's magnitude by showing AD's length to equal AE's. The forces represented by AB, AC, and AE balance. Construct parallelogram AEFB on AB and AE; we just showed why the resultant of the forces represented by AB and AE points along its diagonal AF. Hence AF must lie along the same straight line as AC. As opposite sides of parallelogram ACDB, AC and BD are parallel, and since AF and AC lie along the same line, AF is parallel to BD. As opposite sides of parallelogram AEFB, AE and BF are parallel, and since AE and AD lie along the same line, AD is parallel to BF. Since AF–BD and AD–BF are pairs of parallels, AFBD is a parallelogram. Its opposite sides AD and BF are equal in length. But as opposite sides of parallelogram AEFB, AE and BF are equal in length. Therefore, AD and AE (as both equal to BF) are equal, as Duchayla set out to show.[14]

So ends Duchayla's explanation of the parallelogram law. Despite its length, many praised Duchayla's explanation as "very simple and beautiful" (Mitchell, Young, and Imray 1860, 47; see Pratt 1836, 7; Galbraith and Haughton 1860, 7).[15] However, in the second half of the nineteenth century, Duchayla's argument came increasingly to be regarded as failing to explain why the parallelogram law holds. While admitting that the argument is sound, many considered it "forced and unnatural . . . a considerable waste of time" (Besant 1883, 581; see Lock 1888, 155); "the proof of our youth . . . now voted cumbrous and antiquated,

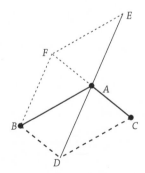

Figure 4.4 Duchayla's explanation of why the parallelogram law applies to the resultant force's magnitude

and only retained as a searching test of logical power" (A. G. G. 1890, 413); "brainwasting . . . elaborate and painstaking, though benumbing" (Heaviside 1893, 147); and (my favorite) "certainly convincing . . . but . . . essentially artificial . . . *cunning* rather than honest argument" (Goodwin 1849, 273).

Apart from name-calling, two specific deficiencies in Duchayla's proposed explanation are commonly cited. First, as Macaulay put it (echoing Whewell's characterization of Newton's second law as "extraneous" to the parallelogram law): "Duchayla's proof . . . held its own in text-books for many years . . . in spite of the extraneous feature which the appeal to the transmissibility of forces intrudes. Logically the best form of proof seems to be one on the lines adopted by Laplace." (Macaulay 1900, 403). (In the next section, I will turn to the kind of argument that Macaulay sees as "logically" best.) W. E. Johnson (after criticizing the dynamical explanation as introducing extraneous kinetic ideas) explains more fully why the transmissibility principle is "extraneous" to the parallelogram law: "To base the fundamental principle of the equilibrium of a *particle* on the 'transmissibility of force,' and thus to introduce the conception of a *rigid body*, is certainly the reverse of logical procedure" (1889, 153; see Anon. 1850, 378). The emphasis that Macaulay, Johnson, and others placed on correct "logical procedure" is similar to the "philosophical" grounds on which the dynamical argument was generally evaluated. Although Thomson and Tait differed from Macaulay and Johnson in favoring the dynamical explanation, they joined Macaulay and Johnson in criticizing Duchayla's argument for appealing to the transmissibility principle. With Duchayla's proposal in mind, they criticized derivations of the parallelogram law involving "the introduction of various unnecessary Dynamical axioms, more or less obvious, but in reality included in or dependent upon Newton's laws of motion" (Thomson and Tait 1888, 244). Thomson and Tait criticized these derivations not for being difficult to follow, but primarily for misrepresenting which principles really depend on which others. According to Thomson and Tait (244–245), the parallelogram law and the transmissibility of force do not reside in an autonomous statics, but arise together with dynamics from Newton's laws. Tait (1885, 356), for example, characterizes Newton's second law of motion as the law "upon which the *Parallelogram of Forces* depends."

As I have shown, the standard objection to the dynamical explanation was sometimes expressed in terms of a counterlegal: that the parallelogram of forces would still have held even if dynamics had not been governed by Newton's second law. Likewise, the standard objection to Duchayla's explanation (that the parallelogram of forces cannot depend on the principle of the transmissibility of force) was expressed in terms of a counterlegal: that the parallelogram law would still have held even if the transmissibility principle had not held. For example, in the preface to his 1845 textbook, the English physicist and mathematician Samuel Earnshaw (who first proved Earnshaw's theorem in electrostatics) wrote that although he had decided to introduce the parallelogram law in his book by proving it "after Duchayla's method, by reason of its simplicity" (1845, v), this proof fails to explain why the parallelogram law holds because of the same defect that Macaulay and Johnson would later emphasize: its appeal to the transmissibility principle. Like Macaulay and Johnson, Earnshaw regarded Poisson's argument rather than Duchayla's as explanatory: "I think it necessary here to inform the reader that, as [Duchayla's] method is inapplicable when the forces act upon a single [that is, separate, unattached] particle of matter (as a particle of a fluid medium on the hypothesis of finite intervals), on account of its assuming the transmissibility of the forces to other points than that on which they act, I have, in an Appendix, given [Poisson's proof]" (v). Earnshaw distinguished one proof's pedagogical advantages from another proof's philosophical virtues. He then clarified why the transmissibility principle cannot help to explain the parallelogram law. Here counterfactual considerations enter: "[Duchayla's] method . . . can never be exclusively adopted in a treatise which professes to take a more philosophical view of the subject; for, were the transmissibility of force *not* true in fact, the law of the composition of forces acting on a point would still be true; it is evident, therefore, that to make the truth of the former an essential step in the proof of the latter, is erroneous in principle" (v). According to Earnshaw, the key point is that the parallelogram law cannot be explained by the transmissibility principle because the parallelogram law would still have held even if the transmissibility principle had not been true. I will, of course, be exploiting exactly these purported subjunctive facts in order to understand what would make statics autonomous and thereby make dynamics too weak to explain the parallelogram law.

Whereas critics of Duchayla's explanation contend that the parallelogram law, as a fact about point particles, cannot rest on a fact about rigid extended bodies, proponents of Duchayla's explanation depict statics as concerned fundamentally with rigid extended bodies rather than material points. For example, according to Challis (1869, 98), "statics is restricted to the equilibrium of *rigid* bodies."

The second deficiency that critics identified in Duchayla's proposed explanation was that it incorrectly represents the way in which the parallelogram law's applicability for direction relates to its applicability for magnitude. Duchayla's argument depicts these two aspects of the parallelogram law as having different explanations. In fact, the final step of Duchayla's argument appeals to the parallelogram law for the resultant's direction to explain why the parallelogram law also holds for the resultant's magnitude. But rather than one depending on the other, these two aspects of the parallelogram law must (according to this objection) arise in the same way from the same, more fundamental principles.

This objection was pressed, for instance, by the Cambridge mathematician (and later bishop of Carlisle) Harvey Goodwin. Decrying Duchayla's proof as "artificial," he focused on its final step—where the parallelogram law for the resultant's direction is used to explain why the parallelogram law holds for the resultant's magnitude:

> The extreme simplicity of this part of the proof shews how intimate the connexion must be between the two parts of the proposition, a connexion which I think we should not have been led to expect from anything occurring in the proof itself. . . . [From the proof of the parallelogram law's holding with regard to direction] there is not a shadow of a hint that . . . the law will hold as respects magnitude: so that a very remarkable proposition is proved by a mere artifice without apparently the least reason in the nature of things why we should anticipate the result. (Goodwin 1849, 273)

As Goodwin sees it, Duchayla's proof, while sound, mistakenly depicts as *coincidental* the fact that the parallelogram's diagonal represents the resultant in *both* direction and magnitude. It fails to capture the actual "connexion" between these two components of the parallelogram law.[16]

Of course, since Duchayla's proof derives the parallelogram law's applicability for magnitude from its applicability for direction, the proof depicts its applicability for magnitude as deriving from exactly the same premises as its applicability for direction. As an explanation, Duchayla's proof would portray its applicability for magnitude and its applicability for direction as having the very same explainers—as both originating from the transmissibility of force, for instance. So as an explanation, Duchayla's proof does not depict the parallelogram law as a *physical* coincidence in the manner of a fact consisting of two components having no important common cause (such as Presidents Lincoln and Kennedy both having vice presidents named "Johnson"). In what sense, then, does Duchayla's derivation depict the parallelogram law as coincidental in applying to both magnitude and direction?

To answer this question, it will be helpful to anticipate an idea that I will study more fully in part III: the idea of a "*mathematical* coincidence." In chapter 8, for example, I will consider these two Diophantine equations (that is, equations where the variables can take only integer values):

$$2x^2\left(x^2-1\right)=3\left(y^2-1\right)$$

and

$$x(x-1)/2=2^n-1.$$

Each equation turns out to have exactly the same five positive solutions for x: 1, 2, 3, 6, and 91. This fact (as far as we know) is just a (mathematical) coincidence. What makes it coincidental is that there is no proof of the result that traces each equation's positive solutions for x in the same way to some respect in which the two equations are alike. Such a proof (according to the "big Lange theory" of explanation in mathematics) would explain why the two equations' solutions are exactly the same. But because it has no such "common proof," this similarity between the two equations has no explanation in mathematics and is therefore a mathematical coincidence.

Of course, we could simply cobble together two proofs, one for each equation, to make a single proof that covers both of the result's components (one component for each equation). However, to count as a "common proof" of the result's components, it would have to be the case that if we take any single component and make each step of the proof as logically weak as it can afford to be while still allowing the proof to prove that component, then the weakened proof remains able to prove each of the result's other components as well (once we remove any restrictions to that single component). If the result's components have a "common proof," then no further resources are needed to expand the proof's scope from any single component to cover every other component.

Duchayla's argument derives the parallelogram law for both direction and magnitude. But if we take Duchayla's derivation and make it as logically weak as it can afford to be while still allowing the argument to derive the parallelogram law for direction, then it fails to derive the parallelogram law for magnitude. As I described, further steps (depicted in fig. 4.4) are needed to expand the proof from direction to magnitude. Therefore, although Duchayla's argument does not depict the parallelogram law as a *physical* coincidence, it depicts the parallelogram law as a *mathematical* coincidence.

I will elaborate this distinction more fully in chapter 10. There I will give an example where the similarity between a pair of derivative thermodynamic and electrostatic laws is *physically* coincidental but no *mathematical* coincidence. It is physically coincidental because the two derivative laws have no important common explainer, since the more fundamental laws of thermodynamics are distinct from the more fundamental laws of electrostatics. But mathematically, the two derivative laws can be derived by a "common proof" from their respective more fundamental laws. Therefore, it is no mathematical coincidence that the two derivative laws have the same mathematical form, since they amount to the same mathematical solution to the same mathematical problem.

Critics of Duchayla's argument suspect that the parallelogram law's applicability to direction and its applicability to magnitude actually arise together: that they have a "common proof." If their suspicion is correct, then Duchayla's argument fails to explain why the parallelogram law holds since it mischaracterizes the law's holding for magnitude as well as for direction as a mathematical coincidence.

Later, I will be in a position to compare Duchayla's argument to an example of explanation in mathematics that I will present in section 8.3. I will argue there that when a mathematical theorem is proved by mathematical induction, the theorem's holding in the base case is used to prove its holding for all other cases, and so the proof fails to give *uniform* treatment to every case falling under the theorem. This deprives a proof by mathematical induction of the capacity to explain a mathematical result having as its salient feature that it identifies a respect in which various cases are all alike. Just as a proof by mathematical induction uses the base case to derive the rest of the cases, so Duchayla's derivation of the parallelogram law uses the law's holding for direction to derive its holding for magnitude. Therefore, Duchayla's argument fails to give *uniform* treatment to both of the parallelogram law's components.[17]

In this respect, Duchayla's derivation of the parallelogram law contrasts sharply with Poisson's. Furthermore, if Poisson's explanation goes through, then it is no mathematical coincidence (though it is physically coincidental) that a host of physically diverse directed quantities compose in the same way (parallelogramwise).

■ 4.4 POISSON'S STATICAL EXPLANATION

After Duchayla's, the next most commonly proposed statical explanation of the parallelogram law is Poisson's (1811, 11–19; 1833/1842, 36–42).[18] It is not vulnerable to either of the two major objections to Duchayla's proposed explanation. It avoids the first objection because instead of appealing to the transmissibility principle, the explanans includes symmetries, dimensional considerations, and the fact that two forces have a unique resultant determined entirely by their magnitudes and directions. (For example, their resultant is independent of what other forces are acting. Thus, if forces A and B have C as their resultant, then they still do so even if force D is also acting, so the resultant of A, B, and D is the resultant of C and D.) Poisson's argument avoids the second objection to Duchayla's proposal because it treats magnitude and direction together in a "common proof."

Textbooks of the period frequently devote several pages to Poisson's explanation, often illustrating it with the same figures that I will use.[19] The central step of Poisson's derivation explains why the parallelogram law gives the resultant of two forces P_1 and P_2, each of magnitude P, acting in directions subtending angle $2x$ (less than π). The explanation begins with the premise that the resultant of P_1 and P_2 must not only (by symmetry)[20] be coplanar with P_1 and P_2, but also be unchanged under an interchange of P_1 and P_2 and thus must bisect the angle between them.[21] Poisson then appeals to the premise that the resultant must reflect only the two forces' magnitudes and directions. Hence, the resultant's magnitude R must be some function f of P and x alone. Because $R = f(P,x)$ must hold in any system of units for R, P, and x (i.e., is "dimensionally homogeneous"—see chapter 6) and angle is dimensionless, $f(P,x)$ must equal $P^a g(x)$ for some dimensionless a and some dimensionless function g.[22] Since R and $P^a g(x)$ must both have dimensions of force, and P has dimensions of force, it follows that $a = 1$, and so $R = P\, g(x)$.

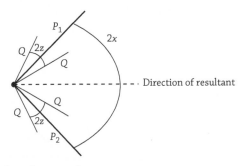

Figure 4.5 Poisson's explanation, first step

Poisson has now reduced the problem to explaining why g accords with the parallelogram law. To explain g, create another instance of the same problem (i.e., two equal forces acting in different directions): let P_1 be the resultant of two equal forces, each of some magnitude Q, subtending some angle $2z$ (fig. 4.5). Hence $P = Q g(z)$. Since $R = P g(x)$, it follows that $R = Q g(z)g(x)$. Poisson now appeals to the principle that the composition law must exhibit rotational symmetry: if we alter the direction of each component force by the same arbitrary angle, then their resultant alters by the same angle. It follows that if the two equal Q forces are rotated together through the appropriate angle, then the two new Q forces thereby produced have P_2 as their resultant. The resultant of these four Q forces is therefore the resultant of P_1 and P_2, with magnitude R.

The two inner Q forces in fig. 4.5 create yet another instance of the same problem: their resultant bisects the angle $2(x - z)$ between them, and so it points in the same direction as the resultant of P_1 and P_2 and has magnitude $Q g(x - z)$. Likewise, the resultant of the two outer Q forces is in that same direction, having magnitude $Q g(x + z)$.

Poisson then invokes the principle that if two forces point in the same direction, their resultant's magnitude is the arithmetic sum of their magnitudes. Therefore, as the magnitude of the four Q forces' resultant, R equals the sum of $Q g(x - z)$ and $Q g(x + z)$. Since $R = Q g(z)g(x)$,

$$Q g(z)g(x) = Q g(x - z) + Q g(x + z), \text{ so}$$
$$g(z)g(x) = g(x - z) + g(x + z).$$

The solution to this functional equation is

$$g(z) = 2 \cos az, \text{ for arbitrary } a.\text{[23]}$$

Therefore,

$$R = P g(x) = 2P \cos ax.$$

To determine a, let the explanans include that if two forces are equal and oppo-site, then they have zero resultant.[24] That is, $R = 0$ when $x = \pi/2$.

(Before continuing, note that although Poisson presents this premise as an independent assumption, it actually follows from the other premises that he has already included in the explanans. If equal and opposite forces are rotated by a half circle around an axis perpendicular to their common line of action, then by rotational symmetry, the resultant is rotated by the same amount. But since the forces have merely swapped places, the resultant must be unchanged, since the resultant depends only on the forces' magnitudes and directions. The only resul-tant unchanged under such rotation is a resultant of zero.)

By $R = 2P \cos ax$ and the fact that $R = 0$ when $x = \pi/2$ (remember that the angle subtended by the two forces is $2x$—see fig. 4.4), $\cos a\pi/2 = 0$, so a must be an odd integer. But if $a = 3$, for example, then $\cos ax = 0$ for $x = \pi/6$, and so by $R = 2P \cos ax$, $R = 0$. Indeed, if a is 3 or 5 or . . ., then $R = 0$ for $a \neq \pi/2$. This zero resultant is disallowed by Poisson's premise that if two forces have zero resultant, they must be equal and opposite. By this reasoning, a cannot be an odd integer greater than 1. Hence, $a = 1$, so $R = 2P \cos x$, which is the length of the diagonal of the rhombus with side P, angle $2x$. Thus, Poisson has explained why the paral-lelogram law works in the special case of two equal forces.

(Again, although the premise that two forces having zero resultant must be equal and opposite is presented by Poisson as an independent assumption, it actually follows from premises to which he has already appealed. If forces A and B have zero resultant, then the resultant of A, B, and some third force is the third force. But if the third force is equal and opposite to B, then by the previous result, it and B have zero resultant. Therefore, the three forces' resultant must be A, which contradicts the resultant's uniqueness unless A and the third force are the same, i.e., unless A is equal and opposite to B.)[25]

Poisson then extends the explanation to unequal, orthogonal forces. Suppose they are applied at P (fig. 4.6) and represented by PC and PC'. Complete rect-angle $CPC'R$. Use the previous result to decompose each of these two forces into

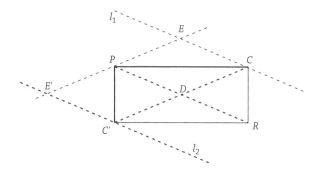

Figure 4.6 Poisson's explanation, second step

two equal forces: one along the rectangle's diagonal, the other canceling its partner from the other force's decomposition. Draw diagonals meeting at D. Draw
line l_1 (l_2) through C (C') parallel to PR. Draw a line through P parallel to CC';
let E (E') be its point of intersection with l_1 (l_2). Since the diagonal PR bisects
the diagonal CC', $C'D = DC$, and so (since l_1 and l_2 are parallel to PR) $PE' = PE$.
Treat PE' and PE as representing hypothetical equal and opposite forces acting
at P, directed toward E' and E respectively. Since they have no resultant, they
can be joined with the PC and PC' forces without changing the resultant. $EPDC$
$(E'PDC')$ is a rhombus, so (by the result just shown) PC (PC') represents the
resultant of the forces represented by PE (PE') and PD. Consequently, the resultant of the forces represented by PC and PC' is the force represented by the resultant of PD, PD (again), PE, and PE'. Hence it is twice the force represented by
PD, which is the force represented by the diagonal PR.

Finally, Poisson employs a similar strategy to extend this result to any two
forces, completing his proposed explanation of the parallelogram law. Suppose
the two forces are applied at P (fig. 4.7) and represented by PC and PC'. Complete
parallelogram $PCRC'$. Draw l_1 (l_2) through C (C') parallel to diagonal PR. Draw
another line through P perpendicular to PR, and let E (E') be its point of intersection with l_1 (l_2). Draw a line through C (C') perpendicular to PR, and let D
(D') be its point of intersection with PR. Triangles CRD and $C'PD'$ are congruent since they have two pairs of angles and a pair of corresponding nonincluded
sides congruent: angles CDR and $C'D'P$ are congruent (both are right angles),
$PC' = CR$ (they are opposite sides of a parallelogram), and angles CRD and $C'PD'$
are congruent (as alternate interior angles). Therefore, $CD = C'D'$, so $PE = PE'$.
Treat PE and PE' as representing hypothetical equal and opposite forces acting
at P, directed toward E and E'. Since they have no resultant, they can be joined
with the PC and PC' forces without changing the resultant. $CEPD$ $(C'E'PD')$ is a
rectangle, so (by the result just shown) PC (PC') represents the resultant of the
forces represented by PE (PE') and PD (PD'). Consequently, the resultant of the

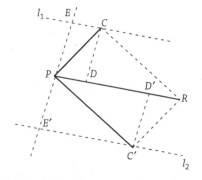

Figure 4.7 Poisson's explanation, final step

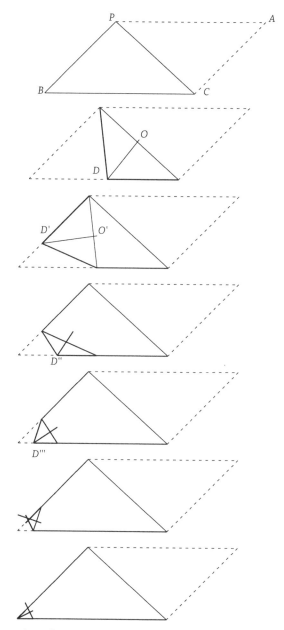

Figure 4.8 Poisson's explanation, alternative procedure

forces represented by PC and PC' is the force represented by the resultant of PD, PD', PE, and PE', and so is the resultant of the forces represented by PD and PD'. But since triangles CRD and C'PD' are congruent, DR = PD', and so the resultant of the forces represented by PD and PD' is the force represented by PR.

Thus the parallelogram law is explained. (Whew!)

An alternative to Poisson's procedure may clarify how the parallelogram law for two equal forces can explain the parallelogram law for any two forces.[26] Suppose PA and PB (fig. 4.8) represent any two forces. I will now show how PC represents the sum of pairs of equal forces that approximate the original two forces to any desired degree. Let O be PC's midpoint; draw OD perpendicular to PC. Triangles POD and COD are congruent (by Side-Angle-Side: OD is a shared side, the angles at O are right angles, PO and CO are equal by construction). Hence, PD and DC represent equal forces. Their resultant is represented by PC (by the result already shown for two equal forces). Now repeat this procedure: let O' be the midpoint of PD; draw O'D' perpendicular to PD. The forces represented by PD' and D'D are equal and compose to the force represented by PD, so those two forces with the force represented by DC result in the force represented by PC. By continuing this procedure as shown in fig. 4.8, the successors of D, D'. . . approach arbitrarily closely to B, and the accumulated equal and opposite forces approach arbitrarily closely to the original two forces.

Unlike Duchayla's explanation, Poisson's treatment unites the parallelogram law's holding for the resultant's magnitude with its holding for the resultant's direction. Except in the explanation's small first step, where the resultant's direction follows immediately from symmetry, the resultant's direction and magnitude are treated together throughout the argument. It is a "common proof" and so as an explanation, Poisson's argument would show it to be no "mathematical coincidence" that the parallelogram law holds both for direction and for magnitude.

Unlike the proposed dynamical explanation, Poisson's proposal portrays the parallelogram law as independent of the relation between force and motion. In Cockle's words, Poisson's explanation does "not render it necessary to consider whether pressure does or does not tend to produce motion" (1879, 12–13). Indeed, nothing much about force in particular figures anywhere in Poisson's explanans, suggesting an objection expressed, though significantly not endorsed, by the British mathematician Augustus De Morgan: "many have been puzzled by finding that the thing which, by its very definition, tends to produce motion, is reasoned on . . . under a compact that any introduction of the idea of motion would be out of place. The statical proofs . . . seem to be *all geometry and no physics* (1859, 299; italics in original)." Proponents of Poisson's explanation seize upon this feature as favoring this explanation over its rivals and as revealing one of its distinctive contributions. If it is an explanation, then it unifies the parallelogram of forces not only with the parallelograms of displacements, velocities, and accelerations, but also with the parallelograms of gravitational fields, bulk magnetizations, energy flux densities, water flux densities through soils, electric current densities through three-dimensional conductors,[27] sound and light flux densities through three-dimensional media, entropy fluxes, heat flows, temperature gradients, and so forth—all quantities that compose by vector addition. If each of these various parallelogram laws is explained by a Poisson-style argument, then it is no coincidence that these quantities, despite their physical differences, all compose in the same way.

Of course, that they all compose parallelogramwise remains *physically* coincidental since the premises of these various Poisson-style arguments are largely distinct and so fail to supply all of these parallelogram laws with an important common explainer. For example, the fact that the resultant of two forces depends only on their magnitudes and directions has no explanation in common with the fact that the resultant of two water flux densities through soils depends only on their magnitudes and directions; there is no common reason why equal-and-opposites cancel out for all of the physically diverse quantities that I have just mentioned. But that they all compose parallelogramwise is no *mathematical* coincidence, just as the similarity in mathematical form between certain derivative thermodynamic and electrostatic laws (to be discussed in chapter 10) arises from a similarity in mathematical form between the fundamental thermodynamic and electrostatic laws. If these Poisson-style explanations go through, then they show why *any* physical quantity with certain basic features (namely, the symmetries and other properties figuring in the premises in Poisson's explanans) composes by a parallelogram law. As Maxwell puts it: "the proof which Poisson gives of the 'parallelogram of forces' is applicable to the composition of any quantities such that turning them end for end is equivalent to a reversal of their sign" (1873, 10; see Anon. 1837, 43). Under Poisson-style explanations, two such quantities both compose parallelogramwise because they are alike in having equal-and-opposites cancel out (and in the other respects to which Poisson appeals).

■ 4.5 STATICAL EXPLANATION UNDER SOME FAMILIAR ACCOUNTS OF NATURAL LAW

I have presented some scientists who argue that the parallelogram law is explained dynamically and others who argue that it is explained statically. My aim is not to adjudicate this dispute, but rather to understand what the world would have to be like in order for one or another of these proposals to explain why the parallelogram law holds. Ultimately, I will argue that Poisson's explanation would be an explanation by constraint and that my account of what would make such an explanation work applies nicely to Poisson's proposal.

When (as in this case) there have been serious competing candidates for a given fact's scientific explanation, philosophical accounts of what is at stake should generally permit any of these candidates to have been correct. For example, there was once scientific controversy over whether the Copernican or Ptolemaic model of the heavens explains our observations of the night sky. A metaphysical account of natural law, cause, and scientific explanation should not have been enough to settle this controversy; any such account should permit Copernican possible worlds and Ptolemaic possible worlds (see Armstrong 1983, 26). Although there may be rare cases where a theory once taken seriously in science can safely be revealed by a philosophical account to have been a nonstarter, I see no reason to think that philosophy alone should suffice to foreclose any of the candidates that I have just presented for explaining the parallelogram law.[28] Accordingly, let's now consider whether several leading philosophical accounts of natural law could leave room for the possibility that the parallelogram law has a statical rather than a dynamical explanation.

According to Lewis's "Best System Account," natural laws are distinguished from accidents by virtue of belonging to the best deductive system of truths. Some deductive systems of truths are stronger (i.e., more informative); others are simpler (e.g., by having fewer or simpler axioms). Typically, less strength brings greater simplicity. If "nature is kind" (Lewis 1999, 232–233), then one system has the optimal combination of strength and simplicity by any reasonable standard of strength, simplicity, and their trade-off, and this system is far ahead of any other. The contingent generalizations belonging to that system are the laws.[29]

Advocates of a dynamical explanation see the parallelogram law and other laws of statics as corollaries to the dynamical laws—as all forming a single deductive system of laws. Advocates of a statical explanation acknowledge that the truth of the laws of statics can be deduced from the dynamical laws.[30] But these scientists regard the statical laws as *transcending* the dynamical laws and so as forming their own deductive system of laws that omits the dynamical laws. The Best System Account could apparently accommodate advocates of a statical explanation by interpreting them as suggesting that these two systems are tied for best. (The statical system has less strength but greater simplicity than the more comprehensive system that also includes the dynamical laws.) Admittedly, Lewis (1999, 233) says that "if two very different systems are tied for best . . . there would be no very good deservers of the name of laws." But the statical and dynamical systems are not so very different; the statical system's members all belong to the dynamical system. Accordingly, we could perhaps amend the Best System Account to permit exactly two systems of natural law just in case the two systems are tied for best (and are far better than any others) and the members of one of these systems are all members of the other. Statics could then apparently qualify as autonomous—as having its own laws—and the existence of two "best systems" would not keep either system's members from deserving to qualify as laws. So amended, the Best System Account would apparently offer an interpretation of the point at issue between advocates of the statical and dynamical explanations: they disagree about whether the statical system is tied for best with the dynamical system.

However, this interpretation fails to capture what advocates of the statical explanation believe. In the more comprehensive system, dynamical laws constitute the axioms; statical laws are their corollaries. So in that system, statical laws depend on dynamical laws. The order of explanation in this system remains unchanged by the existence of another, equally good system where statical laws do not rest on dynamical laws. Advocates of the statical explanation do not believe that the parallelogram law is *also* explained dynamically. Rather, as I have shown, they believe that the statical picture "gives a better view of its true position," whereas the dynamical picture "grates upon one's sense of logical order" (Macaulay 1900, 403). The Best System Account thus cannot easily be amended to reflect the parallelogram law's "true position" if it has a statical explanation.[31]

This argument presupposes that an explanation of the parallelogram law consists of a deduction of that law from more fundamental laws—ultimately, on Lewis's account, from the axioms of (one of) the best system(s). But the argument is unaffected if this presupposition is weakened (in the spirit of Lewis 1986b, 217–231) to acknowledge that an explanation of the parallelogram law might merely provide *some information* about how the law follows from the axioms—information that tells its recipient what he or she wanted to know about such a deduction.

If defenders of the statical explanation differed from defenders of the dynamical explanation in their interests and concerns, for example, then we might use that difference to account for their differences regarding the parallelogram law's explanation. A similar "pragmatic" account of the preference for a statical explanation might be available if they differed in the contrast classes they had in mind in posing their why questions, or in the kinds of information they lacked, or in their beliefs about which facts are laws and which are accidents. But advocates of the statical explanation differ from advocates of the dynamical explanation in none of these respects. They do not pose their why questions in different contexts. They both recognize the explanatory task as the deduction of the parallelogram law from more fundamental laws. That is why advocates of each view take themselves to be genuinely *disagreeing* with advocates of the other view (as I have shown) rather than as merely differing from them in their interests, priorities, or tastes in the style of explanation they prefer. Advocates of statical and dynamical explanations differ in their beliefs regarding the relation between statics and dynamics—roughly, in whether statics is just a special case of dynamics or "transcends" dynamics. This disagreement, rather than a more "pragmatic" difference, ultimately accounts for their disagreement regarding the parallelogram law's explanation.

The problem encountered by the Best System Account also arises on the accounts (proposed by Armstrong, Dretske, and Tooley) depicting laws as irreducible, contingent relations of "nomic necessitation" among universals. Such an account can distinguish between "underived" laws and derived laws: the underived laws (nomic necessitation relations among universals) metaphysically necessitate certain regularities among the particulars instantiating these universals, and these regularities, in turn, entail other regularities "that involve no new relations between universals" (Armstrong 1983, 145; and see 173). These others are the derived laws. This distinction between underived and derived laws would appear to allow for an interpretation of the issue at stake regarding the parallelogram law. Advocates of the dynamical explanation seem to be holding that the parallelogram law and the other laws of statics are all derived laws; they derive from fundamental dynamical laws so that statics becomes a special case of dynamics. Advocates of the statical explanation, on the other hand, seem to be holding that there are fundamental statical laws and that the parallelogram law is a derived law deriving from some of them. Thus the universals account seems to have identified the issue at stake.

However, advocates of the statical explanation acknowledge that certain dynamical laws are underived laws and that they entail the parallelogram law's truth. They regard the dynamical derivation as sound but nevertheless not explanatory. So on the picture of laws as relations among universals, there appears to be nothing that could possibly keep the fundamental dynamical laws from explaining the parallelogram law. Even if certain statical laws are underived and so lie alongside the fundamental dynamical laws, the parallelogram law could at best be explained by a statical route *and* by a dynamical route. Once again, this is not the view defended by advocates of the statical explanation. There is nothing in this picture to make a statical explanation of the parallelogram law give "a better view of its true position."[32]

Room for a statical explanation is also difficult to find within dispositional essentialism (as defended by Ellis and Bird), according to which laws reflect the causal roles essential to various properties and so are metaphysically necessary. For example, according to dispositional essentialism, part of the essence of being electrically charged is having the power to exert (and the liability to feel) forces in accordance with Coulomb's law. But if all of the laws are metaphysically necessary, what could it be for the laws of statics to *transcend*—to be *more* necessary than—the laws of dynamics? To put all natural laws on a modal par with metaphysical necessities such as that red is a color (or, according to some philosophers, that water is H_2O) is to put them all on a modal par with one another, which is inaccurate if the laws of statics have greater necessity than the laws of dynamics. (I made a similar point in section 2.7 in connection with essentialism having to treat all conservation laws as coincidences.)

There is a second reason why essentialism precludes the parallelogram law from having a statical explanation and thus takes sides in a controversy that should be left to science. Essentialism takes causal powers as fundamental and elaborates them in terms of the way in which something possessing a given power would respond to certain stimuli under certain conditions. For example, the property of being a point body, electrically charged to 1 statcoulomb, is elaborated in terms of subjunctive conditionals such as "If the body were exposed to an electric field of 300,000 volts per meter, then the body would feel 10 dynes of electric force." This conditional's antecedent specifies a stimulus: an initial condition, logically consistent with the laws, that activates the causal power. Now as I have shown, physicists defending the statical explanation of the parallelogram law elaborate the autonomy of statics in terms of conditionals such as "Had forces and motions not accorded with Newton's second law, then the composition of forces would still have accorded with the parallelogram law." This counterfactual is a counterlegal; its antecedent posits a violation of the laws. Essentialists must interpret its antecedent as positing a metaphysical impossibility. Its antecedent certainly does not posit a naturally possible initial condition that engages a causal power; its antecedent is not found in any of the stimulus-response conditionals elaborating the causal powers that essentialists believe fundamental. Hence, those causal powers cannot underlie the parallelogram law's capacity to withstand changes to the dynamical laws. There is nothing in the essentialist picture to make the parallelogram law so resilient. (Once again, I made a similar point in section 2.7 in connection with the subjunctive facts that would make conservation laws into constraints rather than coincidences.)

Here is another way to put this point. According to essentialism, laws are epiphenomenal; causal powers do all of the work that laws have traditionally been seen as doing. For example, causal powers figure in all scientific explanations (whereas laws, which describe regularities holding because of those powers, are explanatorily idle). A dynamical explanation of the parallelogram law fits this model well. Essentialists could characterize a force as essentially a power to cause masses to accelerate in accordance with Newton's second law.[33] The dynamical explanation uses force's causal role to explain why forces compose parallelogramwise.

However, Poisson's statical explanation of the parallelogram law (which, I will contend, purports to be a non-causal explanation—an explanation by constraint) does not fit this model. It does not exploit the causal power essential to force. Indeed, defenders of the statical explanation see its explanatory strength as deriving precisely from the fact that it *does not* exploit force's causal role. The statical explanation identifies certain symmetries and other features common to forces, electric currents, sound, light, heat, and many other, physically diverse quantities. According to the statical explanation, these quantities all compose parallelogramwise because of these common features (rather than because of their respective causal powers). Essentialism cannot recognize the statical argument as deriving its capacity to explain from its *failure* to exploit the essence of force.

Likewise, essentialism leaves no room for English mathematician Olinthus Gregory's critique of the dynamical explanation: "It may be proper to remark here that the Composition and Resolution of *forces*, and the similar Composition and Resolution of *motions*, are completely distinct objects of enquiry. . . . Some authors have inferred from their demonstrations of the latter problem, the truth of the former: but this cannot well be admissible, because wherever statical equilibrium obtains there can be no motion, and of course the principle on which the inference is grounded [namely, Newton's second law] is foreign to the nature of the thing to be proved" (1826, 14–15). Essentialism cannot accommodate Gregory's claim that Newton's second law is "foreign to the nature of the thing to be proved" (or Whewell's claim that it is "extraneous," as quoted earlier). On the contrary, according to essentialism, force's power to cause acceleration captures force's essence and is therefore precisely what *must* explain the parallelogram law. Essentialism cannot recognize force's causal role as "out of place" (as De Morgan said) in the explanation of the parallelogram law.

Of course, essentialism could allow force's causal role to explain the various symmetries and other facts figuring in Poisson's explanans, and then allow Poisson's explanation to proceed from there. But advocates of the statical explanation see the parallelogram law as deriving from a *deeper* source than force's causal role—so that the parallelogram law would still have held, even if that role had been different. Essentialism cannot embrace this view; according to essentialism, there is nowhere deeper than force's essence. Advocates of the statical explanation cannot believe that the facts figuring in Poisson's explanans hold only by virtue of force's causal role, since advocates of the statical explanation believe that those facts would still have held, had force's causal role been different. This subjunctive fact is crucial to the way I propose to cash out what it would take for Poisson's proposed statical explanation to hold—as an explanation by constraint.

▪ 4.6 MY ACCOUNT OF WHAT IS AT STAKE

The account that I elaborated in chapters 2 and 3 nicely captures what it would take for the laws of statics to *transcend* the dynamical laws by possessing a stronger variety of necessity than they do—and thus what it would be for the parallelogram law to have a statical explanation by constraint rather than a dynamical, causal explanation. If Poisson's explanation holds, then central to making it hold are the subjunctive facts (expressed by counterlegals) used by advocates of the statical explanation to express the parallelogram law's independence from dynamics, such as the fact that forces would still have composed in the same way even if force had stood in a different relation to motion.

Poisson's explanation invokes two metalaws: that there is a law by which the resultant of two forces is determined by the two components' magnitudes and directions, and the symmetry principle that the first-order laws are collectively invariant under spatial rotation. As metalaws, these belong to some nomically stable set. In chapter 2, I proved that there is a connection between nomically stable sets and subnomically stable sets: for any nomically stable set, its sub- nomic members must form a subnomically stable set. In this way, I argued, the conservation laws that follow from symmetry metalaws and the fundamental dynamical law "transcend" the various force laws by belonging to a subnomically stable set that is associated with a stronger variety of natural necessity than the force laws possess. Similarly, if the two metalaws in Poisson's explanation hold, then the law of the parallelogram of forces is a subnomic logical consequence of the metalaws in a certain nomically stable set. Therefore, the parallelogram law belongs to a subnomically stable set that contains all and only the subnomic con- sequences of these metalaws. Since that subnomically stable set does not include any dynamical laws, the parallelogram law has a stronger variety of necessity than the dynamical laws have. In particular, the set's subnomic stability (that is, its invariance under all subnomic counterfactual antecedents with which its members are all logically consistent) requires that the parallelogram law would still have held, had the force laws been different—or had the relation between force and motion been different. Each of these counterfactual antecedents is logically consistent with all of the set's members (since the set does not include the force laws or the fundamental dynamical law). The parallelogram law would then have an explanation by constraint (the metalaws serving as the constraints) and would transcend dynamics.

The various strata of natural law would then form a hierarchy of subnomically stable sets that includes the laws of statics as a distinct level (see fig. 4.9). On this picture, although there is a sound derivation of the parallelogram law from the dynamical laws, it cannot explain the parallelogram law because its premises lack the stronger variety of necessity that the parallelogram law possesses. The par- allelogram law cannot rest on the dynamical laws because the dynamical laws, lacking the parallelogram law's necessity, cannot be responsible for the parallelo- gram law's possessing it. In connection with its membership in an elite stable set, the parallelogram law is preserved under certain counterlegal antecedents, and its preservation there cannot be explained by its following from the dynamical laws since the dynamical laws are not preserved there. If Poisson is correct, then although the dynamical laws entail the parallelogram law's truth, their necessity is too weak to entail its characteristic necessity.[34]

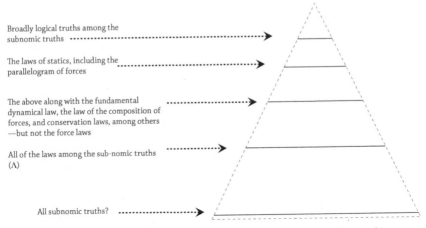

Figure 4.9 Some (though perhaps not all) plausibly subnomically stable sets (for simplicity, only sets arising in this chapter are included)

In elaborating what it would be for the statical laws to be independent of the dynamical laws, I have appealed to precisely the sort of counterlegals that (I have shown) advocates of the statical explanation frequently invoke. As a further example, consider the French mathematician and physicist Louis Poinsot, who offered a statical explanation of the parallelogram law that (like Duchayla's) appeals to the principle of the transmissibility of force. He maintained that the laws of statics would still have held even if Newton's second law had not held: "in Statics properly so called it is not necessary to know the actual effect of forces upon matter . . . to ascertain, for instance, if a double force produces upon the same body a double velocity, or if the same force applied to a body of double the mass produces but half the velocity, &c. [In statics,] whatever the action of forces upon bodies may be, be they [the forces] proportional or not to their sensible effects, still the truths which we are about to expound will remain no less the same" (1847, 2–3). The parallelogram law's invariance under certain counterlegal antecedents is not only the fundamental point in dispute between advocates of the dynamical and statical explanations, but also the main point over which defenders of Duchayla's and Poisson's explanations disagree. Advocates of Poisson's account hold that contrary to Duchayla's account, the parallelogram law would still have held even if the principle of the transmissibility of force had not been true. (Earlier I gave Earnshaw's appeal to this subjunctive fact.)

The symmetry metalaw that Poisson's explanation invokes (that the first-order laws are collectively invariant under rotation) is identical to one of the constraints ("spatial isotropy") in the non-causal explanation of the coordinate transformations, which I presented in chapter 3. It is also identical to one of the constraints in the non-causal explanation of the conservation of angular momentum (if that conservation law is itself a constraint rather than a coincidence), as I discussed in chapter 2. Poisson himself uses the first-order laws' symmetry under rotation to derive other first-order laws besides the parallelogram law, suggesting that he sees it as covering all first-order laws.[35]

The proposed statical explanations of the parallelogram law provide a good opportunity to compare explanations by constraint to "structural explanations." There is no single, widely accepted definition of what a "structural explanation" is. But the basic idea, according to its proponents (such as Railton 1980, Hughes 1989a and 1989b, Clifton 1998, Bokulich 2008, and Dorato and Felline 2010), is that a structural explanation is a non-causal explanation that works by showing the explanandum to follow solely from the explanatory theory's "structure."

One common way of elaborating this idea is to interpret the theory's "structure" as the formal (especially mathematical) equipment it uses to represent features of the world. Then a fact receives a "structural explanation" when it is shown to be built automatically into that bare equipment; the explanandum is required by the representational apparatus alone and so would still be present in the theory whatever further details the theory might incorporate in order to cover the full range of facts for which it is responsible. For instance, Bokulich says that in a structural explanation, "the explanandum is explained by showing how the (typically mathematical) structure of the theory itself limits what sorts of objects, properties, states, or behaviors are admissible within the framework of that theory, and then showing that the explanandum is in fact a consequence of that structure" (2008, 149). For example, Hughes (1989a, 198–199; see 1989b, 256–257) argues that special relativity gives a structural explanation of the fact that there exists a finite speed that is the same in all inertial reference frames:

> Suppose we were asked to explain why, according to the Special Theory of Relativity (STR), there is one velocity which is invariant across all inertial frames. (This velocity is actually the speed of light, and we often express the invariance by saying that the speed of light is the same for all observers; however, since I am here regarding STR just as a theory of space-time, that fact is irrelevant.) A structural explanation of the invariance would display the models of space-time that STR uses, and the admissible coordinate systems for space-time that STR allows; it would then show that there were pairs of events, e_1, e_2, such that, under all admissible transformations of coordinates, their spatial separation X bore a constant ratio to their temporal separation T, and hence the velocity X/T of anything moving from e_1 to e_2 would be the same in all coordinate systems. It would also show that only when this ratio had a particular value (call it "c") was it invariant under these transformations.

This "structural explanation" works by "show[ing] how the explanandum gets built into the models of space-time that STR postulates" and so is present in every admissible model of the theory (Hughes 1989a, 199).

182 ■ SCIENTIFIC EXPLANATIONS BY CONSTRAINT

However, there are problems with thinking about "structural explanations" in this way. The mere fact that every model of some theory incorporates the explanandum does not constitute the theory's explanation of why the explanandum holds. Rather, the theory's explanation involves the reason why every model incorporates the explanandum—that is, something about the way in which the explanandum follows from the theory. Indeed, in the passage just quoted, Hughes does not appeal merely to the fact that every model of Minkowski spacetime involves the explanandum. Rather, he appeals to various facts (according to the theory) and derives the explanandum from them. In particular, Hughes appeals to the Lorentz transformations ("all admissible transformations of coordinates"). But why are the Lorentz transformations explanatorily prior to the existence of an invariant finite speed? The conception of structural explanation as showing the explanandum to be present in every admissible model cannot say why certain features present in every model are explanatorily prior to certain others. In fact, I argued in chapter 3 that scientists and philosophers generally regard the order of explanatory priority as running in the opposite direction from the order that Hughes gives. That is, the invariance of some finite speed explains the Lorentz transformations, not the reverse.

For that matter, nothing in this conception of structural explanation would prevent the invariance of light's speed in particular (the "light postulate") from being used to account for the Lorentz transformations. As I discussed in chapter 3, the Lorentz transformations follow from the light postulate (together with the principle of relativity), and the light postulate holds in every admissible model of special relativity. But as I showed (and as Hughes mentions parenthetically), the main point of the long tradition of explaining the Lorentz transformations non-causally is to show that the transformations are independent of any particular kind of spacetime inhabitant, such as light.

In short, the order of explanatory priority among the facts that are built into every admissible model cannot be captured by an account of structural explanation as working simply by showing the explanandum to be required by the theory's formal apparatus. Such an account would allow us to give a "structural explanation" of the parallelogram of forces merely by pointing out that the theory represents forces as vectors and that vectors compose parallelogramwise. The parallelogram law would thereby be shown to follow from the theory's formal equipment alone. That would apparently be sufficient to explain the parallelogram law according to some philosophical characterizations of structural explanation, such as Clifton's: "We explain some feature B of the physical world by displaying a mathematical model of part of the world and demonstrating that there is a feature A of the model that *corresponds* to B" (1998, 7). If this is all that a structural explanation of the parallelogram law has got to do, then there is no point to the elaborate derivations that were given by Poisson and Duchayla and that many authors felt it necessary to include in their textbooks. But an adequate account of structural explanation should accord with scientific practice—and in practice, these explanations must do a good deal more than show merely in some way or other that the explanandum is built into the theory's representational apparatus.[36]

To take a theory's "structure" in structural explanation to be its representational machinery threatens to invert the actual order of explanatory priority. Vectors adequately represent forces partly because vectors add parallelogramwise and forces do, too. To say that forces add parallelogramwise because they are adequately represented by vectors, which (by stipulation) add parallelogramwise, is to get the order of explanatory priority backward.

The basic idea that advocates of "structural explanation" try to cash out is that such an explanation works by showing that the theory's structure alone suffices to entail the explanandum. This idea obviously presupposes a sharp distinction between a theory's structure and its content. To understand structural explanation, we need some general account of how to draw this distinction and of why it is that in deriving an explanandum from a theory's structure, we explain it (and, presumably, reveal to be non-explanatory any derivation of the explanandum that ineliminably involves the theory's content). I have just mentioned that one common way to elaborate the basic idea behind "structural explanation" is to identify a theory's "structure" with its representational equipment. The shortcomings of this approach can be avoided by thinking of a theory's structure as instead determining a variety of possibility: whatever fits within that structure qualifies as "structurally possible." The theory's content within its structure helps to mark out a narrower species of possibility. This conception of structural explanation, with an exalted stratum of structural possibility that is broader than ordinary natural possibility, obviously brings it much closer to "explanation by constraint."

Some philosophers who regard certain scientific explanations as "structural" characterize structural explanations as working "by limiting the possible states or possible transitions of systems, or by showing certain systems but not others to be structurally possible" (Railton 1980, 348, 350–351). On this conception of "structural explanation," the difference between a theory's "structure" and its content is a modal difference, not a difference that depends on privileging certain parts of a theory as merely specifying its representational apparatus.

Here is one of Railton's (1980, 35) purported examples of a structural explanation—as described by Lewis: "A star has been collapsing, but the collapse stops. Why? Because it's gone as far as it can go. Any more collapsed state would violate the Pauli Exclusion Principle. It's not that anything caused it to stop—there was no countervailing pressure, or anything like that. There was nothing to keep it out of a more collapsed state. Rather, there just was no state for it to get into. The state-space of physical possibilities gave out" (Lewis 1986b, 222). Whereas Railton interprets this explanation as structural and therefore non-causal, Lewis interprets it as causal: "I reply that information about the causal history of the stopping has indeed been provided, but it was information of an unexpectedly negative sort. It was the information that the stopping had no causes at all, except for all the causes of the collapse which was a precondition of the stopping. Negative information is still information. If you request information about arctic penguins, the best information I can give you is that there aren't any" (222–223). As I argued in chapter 1, a scientific explanation may be non-causal even if it provides information about the explanandum's causal history—as long as the explanans's power to explain does not arise by virtue of its supplying information about the explanandum's causal history per se. Suppose the explanation in Railton's example is roughly that the stopping has no causes—that the collapse stopped because its causes ceased and stopping is what happens to collapses when their causes go away (and no new causes take their place). In that case, the explanation is indeed causal. It is like a Newtonian explanation of why a certain body stopped accelerating: because the forces that caused its acceleration went away (and no new forces arrived) and bodies feeling no forces undergo no acceleration. That there are no longer any forces on the body (no causes of acceleration) explains causally why the body no longer accelerates, and the explanation (as I showed in chapter 1) works by describing the world's network of causal relations.

However, suppose we instead think of Railton's explanation in terms of an elite variety of "structural possibility" that figures in the fact that "there just was no state [of greater collapse] for it to get into. The state-space of physical possibilities [that is, of *structural* possibilities] gave out."[37] In that case, the fact that there is no state of greater collapse for it to get into is like the fact that there is no way to divide 23 strawberries evenly (without cutting any) among 3 children, no way to cross a certain arrangement of bridges, and no way to untie a trefoil knot (as I discussed in chapter 1). Accordingly, in Railton's example, the explanans's explanatory power does not derive from its supplying information about the explanandum's causal history ("information that the stopping had no causes at all"). Rather, the explanation works by showing that even if the world's network of causal relations had been different, with different force laws (or even different laws about what happens in the absence of forces or other causes), the explanandum would still have obtained, since the explanandum arises from constraints on all *possible* causal relations—where these possibilities range far beyond the causal relations allowed by the various particular force laws. Indeed, these constraints are not constraints on *causal* relations per se. They constrain *all* states and events, regardless of whether or not those states and events are caught up in causal relations or have causal explanations. Any information about causal relations that happens to be supplied in the course of an explanation by constraint is incidental to its explanatory significance. Even if the force laws dictate that there is "countervailing pressure" causing the star's collapse to stop (so that the stopping has causes), the stopping has no causal explanation since the collapse must have stopped whether or not there were those particular force laws. The stopping does not depend on the force laws just as the parallelogram law does not depend on the dynamical laws (and has no dynamical explanation) if it has a statical explanation.

Some other quantum-mechanical scientific explanations likewise involve natural laws that plausibly transcend the dynamical laws (underwriting various Hamiltonians) in that they specify the limits of "structural possibility"—the limits of the range of states allowed by laws possessing a stronger variety of natural necessity than typical dynamical laws do. Let's stick with Railton's example of stellar collapse and look at white dwarf stars (the products of one common kind of stellar collapse). Why do electrons in white dwarfs move so quickly (at nearly the speed of light)? Because the "uncertainty" in their positions is relatively small (since they are confined to a relatively small star), and so the Heisenberg uncertainty principle (which plausibly transcends the dynamical laws) requires that the "uncertainty" in their momenta be relatively great, thereby requiring the electrons' average speed to be relatively great. This argument is widely regarded as explaining why electrons in white dwarfs move so quickly (and hence why the electron degeneracy pressure exerted by the electrons is so great): "The consequence [of the uncertainty principle] is that any attempt to force the electrons in a star to occupy a precise location results in an increase in velocity. That is why electrons inside white dwarfs move at speeds close to that of light" (Miller 2005, 75).[38] Of course, this explanation uses the electrons' uncertainty in position to help explain their uncertainty in momentum. The position uncertainty is explanatorily prior to the momentum uncertainty because the explanandum (the fact that the electrons in white dwarfs move so quickly) specifies that we take for granted that the electrons in question are confined to a white dwarf, so the relatively small position uncertainty is (as I discussed in chapter 1) contextually understood to be constitutive of the arrangement or task at issue in the why question. (The electrons' confinement to a white dwarf is like the bridges' arrangement in Königsberg, for example.)

Of course, the parallelogram law is not an event and so cannot be a cause or an effect. Furthermore, the parallelogram law does not even link causes to their effects. Plausibly, component forces are *parts* of the resultant force and so are not distinct enough from it to be its causes. Nevertheless, the parallelogram law would have a causal explanation if the proposed dynamical explanation held, since as I have shown, that proposal tries to use force's causal role to explain why force composes parallelogramwise. Although the parallelogram law's explanation, whatever it may be, might automatically seem to merit being termed a "constitutive explanation" (in that it shows why the state of a whole bears a certain relation to the states of its parts), its explanation could nonetheless also merit being termed a "causal explanation" (if it works by virtue of supplying information about the world's causal network). That the parallelogram law concerns a part/whole relation rather than a causal relation does not suffice to ensure that the parallelogram law's explanation is non-causal.

I have not tried to argue that the parallelogram law has a statical explanation. I have tried merely to identify the contingent facts responsible for determining its explanation—that is, the facts that advocates of its proposed statical and dynamical explanations are at bottom disagreeing about. I have identified these as various subjunctive facts, expressed by certain counterfactual (indeed, counterlegal) conditionals.

These subjunctive facts are to be ascertained empirically, and I have presented some of the scientific arguments that have been offered to support various hypotheses about them. Subjunctive facts are routinely ascertained empirically. Our past observations of emeralds confirm not only that all of the actual emeralds lying forever undiscovered in some far-off land are green, but also that had there been an emerald in my pocket right now, then my pocket would have contained something green. (It is not self-evident which of these predictions is more "remote" from our observations.) When we confirm that my pocket would contain something green if there were emeralds in it, that confirmation is unaffected by whatever evidence we may have regarding whether there actually are any emeralds in my pocket. So in confirming that my pocket would contain something green if there were emeralds in it, we may be confirming both a prediction about the actual world and a counterfactual conditional. Facts about what *would have been* are confirmed right along with facts about what actually *is*.[39]

The same applies to the confirmation of counterlegals. For instance, scientists typically regard the spacetime symmetries of known force laws as confirming (to some degree) that the same symmetry principles hold of whatever unknown laws govern as yet undiscovered kinds of forces. As in the emerald example, this confirmation fails to discriminate between actual unexamined cases and counterfactual cases; the evidence confirms that had the laws of nature been different so that there had been an additional or different kind of force, its laws would have exhibited the same symmetry. Evidence bears on the forces there would have been for the same reason as it bears on the unknown forces there actually are.

Of course, without some background opinions regarding the relation between the way things would have been and the way things are observed to be, we cannot use our empirical evidence to confirm counterfactual conditionals. But this is no objection to my view that counterfactuals are confirmed empirically: the analogous point holds for the confirmation of claims regarding actual unexamined cases. Indeed, I have argued (Lange 2004) that even when our accepted background theory is highly impoverished, the fact that we can nevertheless make observations requires that we possess the sorts of background opinions that could underwrite the confirmatory power of those observations—including their power to confirm counterfactual conditionals. However, as van Fraassen (1980, 19) nicely puts it, "we cannot settle the major questions of epistemology *en passant* in philosophy of science"!

Two Other Varieties of Non-Causal Explanation in Science

5

Really Statistical Explanations and Genetic Drift

■ 5.1 INTRODUCTION TO PART II

In chapter 1, I carved out one conception of what it takes for a scientific explanation to be "causal." I then described one kind of "non-causal" scientific explanation, which I characterized as "distinctively mathematical." Having identified how distinctively mathematical scientific explanations work, I suggested that they would be our first examples of "explanations by constraint." In chapters 2, 3, and 4, I gave other examples of constraints besides the mathematical facts that play this role in distinctively mathematical explanations. These other constraints figure in various other putative explanations by constraint that I gave over the course of part I. I offered an account of how explanations by constraint operate.

Now, in part II (chapters 5 and 6), I will argue that there are other kinds of non-causal scientific explanation besides explanation by constraint. In the present chapter, I will describe RS ("Really Statistical") explanations, and in the following chapter, I will investigate dimensional explanations. I will propose accounts of how each of these kinds of explanations works. I will argue that each of them is non-causal in the sense given in chapter 1.

In section 5.2, I will introduce RS explanations and contrast them with causal explanations. I will supply several examples of important kinds of RS explanations. Although RS explanations are non-causal, that some fact has an RS explanation does not preclude its also having a causal explanation. But an RS explanation supplies a kind of understanding that a causal explanation of the same fact cannot supply. Roughly speaking, an RS explanation shows the fact to be mere statistical fallout—that is, just a statistical fact of life.

In section 5.3, I will argue that explanations in population biology appealing to drift (a.k.a. "genetic drift," "random drift") are RS explanations. I will contrast my conception of drift explanations with several rival conceptions. On my view, drift is not distinguished from natural selection by constituting a distinct kind of causal process. But explanations by drift are sharply distinguished from selectionist explanations: drift explanations are non-causal whereas selectionist explanations are causal. Selection and drift involve different kinds of explanations, not different kinds of causal processes.

■ 5.2 REALLY STATISTICAL (RS) EXPLANATIONS

Why in my class were the students with the very lowest scores on the first exam by and large not the students with the very lowest scores on the second exam? The explanation could have been that the worst performers on the first exam dropped the course before the second exam. The explanation could instead have been that the first exam's worst performers were all frightened into working harder and consequently did somewhat better on the second exam. But in many classes, neither of these is the case. Rather, "regression toward the mean" explains the outcome.

How does this explanation work? Suppose that there is a statistical relation rather than a perfect correlation between two variables—for example, the outcomes of two exams: insofar as one student has a lower score than another on the first exam, the former student is likely to have a lower score on the second exam but is not certain to do so. In any such case, extreme scores in one variable tend to be associated with less extreme scores in the other variable (so there tends to be "regression toward the mean" from the extremes). Accordingly, just as students who did the very worst on the first exam were by and large not the students who did the very worst on the second exam, so for the same reason students who did the very best on the first exam were by and large not the students who did the very best on the second exam. This explanation does not propose that the first exam's worst performers prepared more carefully for the second exam or that the first exam's best performers were complacent in preparing for the second exam. Rather, this explanation portrays the result being explained as just (in the words of one textbook) "a statistical fact of life" (Gravetter and Wallnau 2009, 536).

Of course, if a phenomenon is explained by regression toward the mean, then there may still be particular causes that were in fact responsible for moving various individuals toward the mean. Among the students who did the very worst on the first exam, perhaps one student happened to receive several questions on the second exam concerning the few topics she understood; another student may have gotten luckier on the second exam with her guesses on multiple-choice questions; perhaps a third was hampered by sickness during the first exam but not the second. The conjunction of such individual causal explanations explains the same fact as regression toward the mean explains: that the students who did the very worst on the first exam are by and large not the students who did the very worst on the second exam. This conjunctive explanation treats the students individually, whereas regression toward the mean proceeds at the level of the population as a whole.

Furthermore, regression toward the mean unites the best first-exam performers with the worst, supplying a common explanation for both groups' fates on the second exam—unlike an explanation that treats each student separately, describing in each case the causes at work. Similarly, regression toward the mean unites the case of the second exam with other cases that receive the same kind of explanation, such as the less exceptional heights of children who have exceptionally tall or short parents (Galton's original [1886] example of regression toward the mean). These cases plainly cannot all be given the same sort of explanation in terms of the separate causes at work on the individuals involved.

The explanations describing the separate causes acting on various individuals may themselves be statistical explanations. For instance, suppose a fair coin is tossed 100,000 times. Consider the various runs of 20 consecutive tosses beginning with toss numbers 1, 11, 21, . . .; neighboring runs share 10 tosses, so a run with more than 10 heads tends to be followed by another run with more than 10 heads. Nevertheless, a run with an exceptionally high number of heads (let's say, 18 or above) tends to be followed by a run with fewer heads. This result is explained by regression toward the mean. It is also explained by the coin's 50% chance of landing heads on any given toss (independently of the outcomes of other tosses): if we compute the chance that a run with an exceptionally high number of heads will be followed by a run with fewer heads, we will find the chance to be high. (For instance, the chance that a run of 20 heads will be followed by a run with fewer heads is just the chance of at least one tail's appearing in the next 10 tosses, which is $1 - (.5)^{10} = 1023/1024$.)

Both of these explanations are aptly termed "statistical." However, they are fundamentally dissimilar. The explanation that does not appeal to regression toward the mean is causal whereas the regression explanation is non-causal. I first drew this distinction in chapter 1. Let's revisit it.

The nonregression explanation appeals to the coin's fairness—that is, to the propensity of the coin (together with the coin-tossing mechanism and background conditions) to produce a "heads" outcome. This propensity is a (nonsurefire) disposition. Philosophers differ on whether dispositions themselves qualify as causes of their manifestations.[1] But whether or not a disposition is a cause of its manifestation, an explanation of some result that appeals to the underlying disposition manifested in the result is "causal" in the broad sense that I elaborated in chapter 1: the explanation derives its explanatory power from describing relevant features of the result's causal history or, more broadly, of the world's network of causal relations. For this reason, Lewis (1986b, 220) says that a causal explanation is given when the question "Why was the CIA agent there when His Excellency dropped dead?" is answered by "Just coincidence, believe it or not." Despite identifying no causes, this explanation is causal because it is explanatory by virtue of describing relevant features of the result's causal history. In this case, the relevant feature is that the causes of the CIA agent's presence in the country at that time have nothing relevant in common (such as planning for a coup d'état) with the causes of His Excellency's death.[2]

Likewise the above nonregression explanation of the coin-toss result is causal in that it works by describing the relevant features of the result's causal history: the chance of any toss's landing heads and the way that those chances combine to yield the chance that an extreme run will be followed by a less extreme run. Since this explanation is causal, it could be deepened by being supplemented with descriptions of the causal factors responsible for giving the setup a 50% chance of yielding heads, such as the coin's mass distribution and the details of the coin-tossing mechanism.

In contrast, the explanation by regression toward the mean is not causal. It depicts the result as fallout from the statistical character of the case: not from the 50% chance of a toss's landing heads, not even from the chances of a 10-toss run's having various numbers of heads, but rather from the mere fact that there is a statistical association between the outcomes of overlapping 20-toss runs. This explanation is not deepened by being supplemented with descriptions of the coin's mass-distribution or the tossing mechanism. These facts have no place in the explanation since the explanation does not derive its power to explain from its describing relevant features of the result's causal history. The point of the explanation is instead to exhibit the result as arising from the fact that successive runs have a statistical relation, regardless of that precise relation or its (perhaps probabilistic) causes—or, indeed, whether it has any causes at all.[3]

Accordingly, I will call explanations of this kind RS (Really Statistical) explanations. An RS explanation does not proceed from the particular chances of various results—or even from the fact that some result's chance is high (or low). It exploits merely the fact that some process is chancy, and so an RS explanation shows the result to be just "a statistical fact of life."[4]

As I discussed in chapter 1, that Mother has 23 strawberries and 3 children explains why she failed to distribute her strawberries evenly (without cutting any) among her children. What makes this explanation non-causal is not that it fails to cite causes; the numbers of children and strawberries happen to be causes of Mother's failure. What makes it non-causal is that it does not work by describing the outcome's causes (or the world's causal network). In this explanation, Mother's having 3 children helps to explain her failure not by being one of its causes, but by helping to make her success mathematically impossible.

This distinctively mathematical explanation is non-causal but is not RS. However, just as it is non-causal despite supplying information about causes, so an RS explanation may happen to supply information about causes. In the coin-toss case, what makes the regression explanation non-causal is neither its failure to exploit the coin's 50% chance of landing heads nor its invoking only something less specific (namely, that there is a statistical association between the outcomes of overlapping 20-toss runs). After all, as I argued in chapter 1, the explanation of the flask's cracking is causal despite appealing only to the water's boiling, not to a specific molecular collision. What makes the regression explanation non-causal is that the explainer (that there is a statistical association between the outcomes of overlapping 20-toss runs) acquires its power to give this explanation other than by virtue of supplying information about causes. The explanation succeeds whether or not any causal relations at all generate the statistical association.

Since the explanation of the coin-toss result by regression toward the mean is an RS explanation rather than a causal explanation, it unifies the coin-toss result with the result regarding my class's second exam, Galton's result regarding children's heights, and a host of other phenomena. These results arise from a statistical structure shared by all of these cases. No causal explanation could unify these results; their causes are dissimilar.[5]

Not all RS explanations exploit regression toward the mean. For example, in 1910 Rutherford and Geiger set out to explain why it is that "in counting the α particles emitted from radioactive substances . . . the average number of particles [emitted] from a steady source is nearly constant, when a large number is counted, [but] the number appearing in a given short interval is subject to wide fluctuations. . . . For example, during a considerable interval it may happen that no α particle appears; then follows a group of α particles in rapid succession; then an occasional α particle, and so on" (Rutherford and Geiger 1910, 698).[6] Rutherford and Geiger concluded that the departures from the mean in various intervals (and the fact that these departures tend to be smaller in longer intervals) are explained by "the laws of probability and that the α particles are emitted at random" (704) rather than, "for example, that the emission of an α particle [precipitates] the disintegration of neighboring atoms" (698). Once again, that this is an RS explanation rather than a causal explanation is reflected in the fact that the explanation would not have been deepened by being supplemented with an account of the causal factors responsible for the radioactive sample's rate of α-particle emission. For instance, the explanation given by Rutherford and Geiger does not appeal to whether or not each atom in the sample has the same chance of undergoing radioactive decay. (They do not; their sample was a mixture of many isotopes of polonium.) The explanation does not appeal to whether or not a given sample's chance of emitting a certain number of α-particles in a given period depends on the sample's latitude or temperature. (It does not.) The explanation does not even appeal to whether or not different polonium samples have the same chance of α-particle emission. Rutherford and Geiger appealed simply to a given sample's having a constant chance of emission during the experiment (however that fact was to be explained) and then used the "laws of probability" to explain the departures they observed from the mean number of decays (and those departures' tendency to be greater as the intervals became briefer).

Of course, to explain why a given sample has a constant chance of emission, we must appeal to various causal factors concerning the sample's physical constitution (as well as various natural laws). But the fact that an RS explanation appeals to a fact that itself has only a causal explanation does not make the RS explanation covertly causal. A scientific explanation is not responsible for explaining the facts in its own explanans (Hempel 2001, 329–344). Admittedly, the relevant "law of probability" applies to a radioactive sample only because of the sample's physical constitution, which accounts for its constant chance of emission. But the RS explanation does not appeal to that physical constitution, since the RS explanation does not explain why the law of probability applies. Rather, the RS explanation simply appeals to the law's applicability (in this case, the constant chance of radioactive emission) and applies the law.

In short, Rutherford and Geiger explained the departures from the mean as mere artifacts of the statistics—as simply due to chance.[7] A causal explanation that begins with the half-lives of various polonium isotopes and their proportions in the sample, and then deduces the likelihoods of various numbers of emissions over various intervals, would also explain the observed result.[8] But all of this information about the result's causal history is beside the point when the point is to show that the result reflects the fact that the emission process is statistical, whatever the specific half-lives, proportions, and other causal details may be. Once again, this RS explanation unifies the radioactive-decay case with other cases involving fundamentally dissimilar causal mechanisms. The reason why Rutherford and Geiger recorded different numbers of emissions during different 10-minute periods is the same kind as the reason why different runs of 20 consecutive tosses of a fair coin resulted in different numbers of heads—and in both cases, there is also the same kind of reason why longer runs tend to give results closer to the mean rate. Notice that an RS explanation does not have to show that the phenomenon to be explained is certain or even likely considering merely that it arises from some underlying statistics. An RS explanation can explain why a particular run of the experiment yielded a result extremely far from the mean value. The RS explanation is that "It's just statistics."[9]

However, an RS explanation says a good deal more about the explanandum than merely that "It's just statistics." An RS explanation identifies the explanandum as an instance of some particular kind of behavior that is characteristic of statistical systems in virtue of their being statistical. For instance, the RS explanation of the fact that the students with the very lowest scores on the first exam tend not to be the students with the very lowest scores on the second exam is that the explanandum is an instance of regression toward the mean. The fact that 10 of the 15 students admitted this year to a given graduate program decided to accept their offer of admission (a much higher rate than in previous years) might have an RS explanation as being a statistical fluke: when a statistical trial is run many times, an occasional run may have a result quite far from the mean value. An RS explanation does not have to deem the explanandum likely given the explanans, but it must identify some particular signature of statistical phenomena that the explanandum exemplifies.

Some signatures have well-known names, such as "regression toward the mean," but others do not. There is no familiar moniker for the fluctuations (observed by Rutherford and Geiger) in the frequencies of various outcomes in runs of repetitions of a given experiment, or for the considerable departures of some of these frequencies from their mean values, or for the tendency of departures from the mean value to diminish as the runs lengthen. Nevertheless, all of these familiar behaviors are characteristic of runs of independent, identically distributed trials; the runs exhibit these features solely by virtue of their statistical character. These behaviors can thus receive RS explanations.[10]

RS explanations are especially illuminating when the phenomenon being explained does not initially appear to be merely a matter of statistics. For example, suppose that daily for 20 successive days, two students are given a different problem to solve, where the first student to solve the day's problem will win one point. The student in the lead at the end of the 20-round contest will win a prize. Suppose we run this contest for many pairs of students and in more than half of the contests, there is one student who is either never in the lead or in the lead just once in the 20 rounds. It would be tempting to conclude that this is because students who fall behind early tend to lose heart and slacken off or because in every contest, one student is much more talented than the other. But the correct explanation may in fact be that the outcome of the contest is the product of a "random walk." Regardless of the difference between the two students' abilities (that is, between their chances of winning a point in any round)—even if there is no difference between their abilities—it is more likely than not that one student will be behind in the contest only once or never, when a given student's chance of winning a given round is the same in every round.[11] This "one-sidedness" is a characteristic feature of random walks.[12] To explain the result as the product of a random walk is like explaining some phenomenon as a case of regression toward the mean. Both explain the result as a characteristic kind of statistical fallout.

The RS explanation of the improvement on the second exam of the worst-performing students on the first exam does not say merely that this improvement was just "a statistical fact of life." It goes on to identify the result as a case of regression toward the mean in particular. Thus, the RS explanation does not say merely that the result has no causal explanation appealing to some cause common to many of the students. Rather, it supplies a genuine explanation by identifying the particular signature of statistical phenomena that the explanandum exemplifies. That is why RS explanations are characterized in science as answering certain why questions, not merely as rejecting why questions that ask for a common cause (see note 3).

An RS explanation may proceed without appealing to any laws of nature—unlike statistical explanations that require natural laws to associate a given setup with various chances of various possible outcomes. An RS explanation does not appeal to the particular propensities at work, merely to the fact that there are some. Consequently, instead of subsuming the result to be explained under a statistical law of nature, an RS explanation exploits a theorem of the probability calculus (what Rutherford and Geiger called "the laws of probability"). Although the probability calculus is broadly logically necessary, an RS explanation is not a "distinctively mathematical" explanation of the kind I examined in chapter 1. That is because it does not appeal solely to "constraints" such as mathematical necessities (together, perhaps, with various contingent facts that are presupposed by the why question that the explanandum answers—for example, in the Königsberg bridge example, that the arrangement of bridges and islands is fixed). Crucially, an RS explanation appeals to the contingent fact (that is not presupposed by the why question) that a given system is statistical—for instance, that the students' scores on the two exams are correlated statistically. Thus, an RS explanation is not an "explanation by constraint."

An RS explanation does not proceed by the brute-force approach of putting everything in and then calculating everything out—that is (in the coin-toss example), by calculating the explanandum's chance from more basic chances (the chance of a toss's landing "heads"), after perhaps inferring those chances from the setup conditions (the coin's mass distribution) and the natural laws by which those conditions are associated with some propensities. Rather, *an explanation is RS if and only if it works by identifying the explanandum as an instance of some characteristically statistical phenomenon* such as regression toward the mean, departure from the expectation value, or the one-sidedness of random walks. Whereas the brute-force approach can be applied to explain any result of statistical processes, a phenomenon has an RS explanation only when it arises from the mere fact that statistics is at work.

■ 5.3 DRIFT

Population biology calls upon drift to explain many kinds of phenomena. It explains why the frequencies of various traits (or genotypes or genes) in a given population experiencing no mutations, migration, or selection pressure nevertheless change over time. It explains why a population's frequencies depart from their expectation values (which reflect the selection pressure on the population) and why these departures tend to be greater for smaller populations. It explains why different populations of the same size, with the same initial frequencies, and experiencing the same selection pressures (and no mutations or migrations) nevertheless have different frequencies at the end of a given period—and why these differences tend to be greater for smaller populations. Drift explains all of these results as "just statistics"—that is, as "sampling error" (whether drift enters the picture when certain organisms but not others become parents, or certain gametes but not others from a given parent contribute to a zygote, or in some other way). Explanations by drift are RS explanations.[13]

To see how this characterization of drift explanations can help us to understand them better, I shall briefly contrast my view with some of the other ways that drift explanations have recently been characterized.

It might initially appear that "drift" refers to all and only departures of a population's frequencies from their expectation values. However, it is commonly noted (e.g., Beatty 1992, 36; Plutynski 2007) that if drift *consists* of such departures, then drift cannot *explain* these departures (as population biologists call upon it to do). Accordingly, some philosophers identify drift as the *propensities* of a population to have frequencies departing to various degrees from their expectation values: "in a finite series of trials, there is a spread of possible outcomes, each with its own probability. Drift is simply the uncertainty associated with this spread of possibilities" (Matthen 2009, 484). On this view, the ground (i.e., the "categorical base" or "causal basis") for the propensities associated with drift are no different from the ground for the propensities associated with natural selection. Indeed, drift and selection are not distinct causal processes and an explanation appealing to drift is no different from an explanation appealing to selection—except for the kind of outcome being explained:

> Drift explains what natural selection cannot in the sense that drift accounts for those differences between the actual outcome of a series of births, deaths, and reproductions and the outcome predicted by differences in trait fitness. (Walsh, Lewens, and Ariew 2002, 465)

> Natural selection and drift are not distinct processes working on a finite population, but mathematically connected aspects of the same accumulation. (Matthen 2009, 484)

On this view, neither drift nor selection for some trait is a causal process. Drift consists just of the chances for various frequencies to depart to various degrees from their expectation values through births and deaths resulting from various separate processes affecting individual organisms.

Many philosophers (e.g., Millstein 2006; Shapiro and Sober 2007) have criticized this view as failing to recognize selection for some trait as a unified causal process acting on a population as a whole—in other words, for failing to understand that "selection *for* is the causal concept par excellence" (Sober 1984, 100).[14] (As I will show, these critics generally regard drift and natural selection as *distinct causal* processes.) More relevant to my concern with drift is that the view expressed by Matthen, Walsh, and others fails to account for those cases where drift explains a phenomenon that does *not* consist of a departure from expectation values. For example, consider a population where some rare, widespread catastrophe (e.g., an epidemic) wipes out many individuals and "selects" without regard to their heritable traits, but leaves the population with the same frequencies as before—namely, with frequencies coinciding with their expectation values. Population biologists would attribute the outcome (including the population crash and the resulting frequencies) to drift. This explanation by drift is an RS explanation: the occurrence of such a catastrophe (like a period of exceptionally frequent α-particle emission from Rutherford's and Geiger's radioactive sample) is just a statistical fluke that is virtually bound to happen from time to time in the long run. Of course, the outcome also has a causal explanation—namely, that an epidemic struck the population—and there are even causal explanations of why certain individuals but not others were victims (though these causal explanations are not selectionist, since differences in heritable traits made no difference to which creatures survived the catastrophe).

Let me give another kind of example where drift explains a phenomenon that does not consist entirely of a population's departure from expectations. Consider two populations of the same (finite) size, with the same initial frequencies, and experiencing the same selection pressures (and no mutations or migrations). Suppose they have different frequencies at the end of a given period: one has frequencies coinciding with their expectation values and the other has frequencies departing from their expectation values. Population biologists would attribute this difference to drift; that is, they would hold drift responsible for explaining why the two populations' frequencies diverged despite their having the same initial conditions and their experiencing the same selection pressures (and no mutations or migrations). The same explanation would apply whether both populations' frequencies departed from their expectation values or only one population's did; drift explains their divergence.

The drift explanation is that such variation is characteristic of statistical phenomena (as Rutherford and Geiger also emphasized). It is an RS explanation. The two populations are subject to the same selection pressures. It is not the case that one population in the pair was acted upon by selection and the other by drift. Indeed, the outcome could be explained by drift or by the selection pressures operating (since those pressures, like a coin's propensity for landing heads, do not determine an outcome). But an RS explanation is non-causal whereas an explanation in terms of what is being selected for is causal. A selectionist explanation describes the ground of the propensities for various frequencies and so explains by virtue of supplying information regarding the sorts of causes at work. By contrast, the RS explanation in terms of drift identifies the result being explained as the same sort of typically chancy behavior as Rutherford and Geiger saw their radioactive source exhibit: considerable fluctuations in short periods. Thus, in interpreting drift explanations as not appealing to some sort of causal process, I agree with Matthen, Walsh, and others—but without agreeing with them that selection for some trait is likewise not a causal process. On my view, a selectionist explanation of the two populations' divergence is like a causal explanation of the fact that runs of 20 coin tosses with an exceptional frequency of heads tend to be followed by less exceptional runs—namely, an explanation that begins by describing the causal basis of the 50% chance of any toss's landing heads. In contrast, an explanation by drift is like an explanation of the coin-toss outcome as regression toward the mean.

Here is another example where (contrary to Matthen, Walsh, and others) drift is invoked to explain a result that does not consist just of a population's departure from expectation values. Consider a population under constant selection pressure with frequencies that in the short run depart from their expectation values but in the long run largely coincide with their expectation values. Again, drift explains this behavior—but not because drift explains only the short-run result (that is, only the departures from expectation). Rather, an RS explanation appealing to drift explains the difference between the short- and long-run results as characteristic of statistical phenomena. (Rutherford and Geiger observed this feature, too.) This drift explanation cannot be accommodated by the view that "a series of births, survivals, deaths, and reproductions manifests drift just if the outcome—measured as changes in trait frequencies—diverges from that predicted by differences in fitness" (Walsh, Lewens, and Ariew 2002, 459). Note the "just if."

Of course, this outcome can also be explained causally: in terms of the selection pressure. As I have argued, RS explanations and causal explanations work differently and respond to different interests that we may have in asking "Why?" As I understand it, a population biologist who wants to know whether the difference between the population's short-run and long-run frequencies is a matter of drift or a matter of selection is asking whether the selection pressure early in the period under study was different from the selection pressure during the rest of the period. She is asking about causes. But she is *not* presenting drift as a possible causal explanation—a rival to selection for some trait. Rather, in asking whether the difference between the short-run and long-run results is explained by drift or selection, she is asking whether this difference has an RS explanation by drift or whether some *difference* in selection pressure accounts for the difference in frequencies. These *are* rivals, whereas a causal explanation for the population's short- and long-run frequencies that appeals to various unchanging selection pressures is compatible with an RS explanation by drift for the difference between these frequencies.

The population biologist's question "Was it drift or selection?" is like a question that could be asked regarding Lewis's example (given in the previous section): "Was there any reason why the CIA agent was there when His Excellency dropped dead, or was there no reason why he was there then?" To answer "There was no reason" is not to say that the CIA agent was there for no reason at all—that his presence there then had no cause. Rather, to answer "There was no reason" is to say that his presence had no cause *of the sort that is salient in the given context*—that is, had no cause that is also an interesting cause of His Excellency's death (such as a meeting that planned a coup). Likewise, for the population biologist to respond to the question "Was it drift or selection?" by saying "It was drift, not selection" is not for the population biologist to say that there is no selectionist explanation at all of the population's short-run or long-run frequencies. Some selection pressure (itself having a causal explanation) causally explains the frequencies. But to answer "It was not selection; it was drift" is to say that the frequencies have no selectionist explanation *of the sort that is salient in the given context*—that is, have no selectionist explanation appealing to some important difference between the selection pressures during the short and long runs.

Likewise, if the population biologist is asked "What caused the short-run frequency to depart from its expectation value?" an appropriate answer is "Nothing; it was drift." Similarly, if I am asked (regarding my initial example) "What caused the students with the very lowest scores on the first exam not to have the very lowest scores on the second exam?" an appropriate answer is "Nothing; it was regression toward the mean." Of course, in each case, the explanandum has a causal explanation. But there is no causal explanation of the sort that we can reasonably presume the questioner to have had in mind. In the exam case, there is no common cause (or similar cause) of each student's improvement (such as their all having studied harder for the second exam); there are only separate, unrelated causal explanations for the individual students. In the population biology case, there is no difference between the short run and long run in the population-level causes at work.[15]

Suppose the answer to the population biologist's "Drift or selection?" question regarding the difference between the population's short- and long-run frequencies is "Drift, since the degree of selective advantage afforded by various traits was unchanged throughout the period." This answer plainly does not require that no trait has been selected for during the period. This drift explanation fails to accord with the idea championed by Millstein (2002; see Hodge 1987, 252–253) that drift always consists of a sampling process that is *indiscriminate* (in that heritable physical differences are causally irrelevant to differences in reproductive success). Of course, the distinction between discriminate and indiscriminate sampling is genuine, and some phenomena explained by drift result from indiscriminate sampling (as in the epidemic example). However, as many philosophers have noted (e.g., Brandon 2005; Matthen 2009, 467), a product of *discriminate* sampling can also be explained by drift. For example, as I mentioned, drift explains why two populations of the same size, with the same initial frequencies and experiencing the same selection pressures (and no mutations or migrations), have different frequencies at the end of some period.

Another example of drift with discriminate sampling is Beatty's (1984, 195) famous case where dark moths in a given period are eaten by predators disproportionately; although trees with dark bark are more common than trees with light bark (and consequently dark moths are fitter than light), "the dark moths chanced to land on light trees more frequently than on dark trees," whereas the light moths landed on a representative sample of trees. The sampling here is discriminate, since predators are more likely to eat moths that contrast with their backgrounds.[16] On my view, the outcome has an RS explanation in terms of drift because the outcome constitutes just the sort of fluctuation that is characteristic of statistical phenomena. It also has a causal explanation in terms of the selection pressure—or, more deeply, in terms of the setup's physical features that are responsible for the selection pressure (e.g., that 60% of the trees have dark bark).

Of course, some paradigm instances of drift involve indiscriminate sampling, as Millstein emphasizes. For example, Kimura's "neutral theory of molecular evolution" says that "the overwhelming majority of evolutionary changes at the molecular level [result from] random fixation (due to random sampling drift in finite populations) of selectively neutral (i.e., selectively equivalent) mutants" (Kimura 1991, 367). On my view, once again, when drift explains the fixation of some selectively neutral mutant, the explanation is RS because it identifies the result as just the sort of fluctuation that is characteristic of statistical phenomena. (The explanation thus characterizes the fluctuation as akin to a period where Rutherford's and Geiger's radioactive sample undergoes an extreme rate of α-particle emission. Recall that the explanans in an RS explanation need not make the explanandum likely.) The result would still involve this sort of fluctuation even if the mutant were very slightly deleterious, for example. However, on Millstein's view, the result would then not be the product of drift at all, since sampling would be discriminate rather than indiscriminate. I agree with Brandon (2005) that discriminate sampling does not differ *qualitatively* from indiscriminate sampling. Accordingly, drift explanations should be available in either case.

One motivation for Millstein's identification of drift with indiscriminate sampling (and selection with discriminate sampling) is that otherwise, it is difficult to see how drift and selection can be distinct kinds of population-level causal processes. Accordingly, Brandon (2005, 167) concludes that "there is a single process, sampling," and so "the outcome, deviation or lack thereof from expectation, is a necessary component of our concepts of drift and selection," respectively. But I have already argued that drift need not be associated with departure from expectation values. Shapiro and Sober (2007) suggest that drift and selection are distinct, population-level causal processes (just as Millstein says) but (contrary to Millstein) drift does not require indiscriminate sampling. Rather, drift occurs whenever a population has a finite effective size (Shapiro and Sober 2007, 255). What, then, sets drift apart from selection? "We view selection and drift as distinct processes whose magnitudes are represented by distinct population parameters (fitnesses on the one hand, effective population size on the other). Changes in each of these parameters will be associated with changes in the probabilities of different outcomes. If you intervene on fitness values while holding fixed population size, this will be associated with a change in the probability of different trait frequencies in the next generation. And the same is true if you intervene on population size and hold fixed the fitnesses" (256). In short, even if drift cannot be eliminated from a population undergoing selection, drift remains distinct from selection. Drift, unlike selection, is stronger insofar as population size is smaller. Abrams agrees: "drift and selection are distinct causal factors because they can be independently manipulated by changing, respectively, population size and fitness differences" (Abrams 2009, 667). Several other philosophers (e.g., Reisman and Forber 2005) have joined Shapiro and Sober in arguing that since population size can be manipulated to yield predictable differences in the chances of various frequencies, drift is a causal process. In addition to manipulability, some philosophers (e.g., Millstein 2006, 632) have also appealed to counterfactual dependence and probability raising as signs of causal relations. On all of these grounds, philosophers have argued that in drift, "the size of the population can be said to play a causal role" (631) and so that drift is a causal process distinct from selection.[17]

A fundamental problem with these arguments[18] is that the explanatory power of effective population size in drift explanations is mediated not by any laws of nature, but merely by the "laws of probability"—that is, by math. No causal law is responsible for making greater departures from expectation values more likely as population size diminishes. Given the chances of various possible outcomes on any particular independent trial, the relation between population size and the likelihoods of various population-wide outcomes is not contingent.[19] For all of its manipulationist, counterfactual-dependence, and probability-raising credentials, population size does not act as a population-level *cause* in drift explanations since these credentials are mathematically necessary, not beholden to any mere law of nature.[20] This feature of drift explanations fits well with their interpretation as RS explanations, since RS explanations employ theorems of the probability calculus in place of statistical laws of nature.

Sober (1984, 115) says that coin-tossing "affords the same distinction" as selection versus drift, revealing why they are distinct causal processes. Just as selection cannot occur without drift, so a coin flipped with some chance of landing heads must be flipped some definite number of times. Nevertheless, the distinction remains: "Two coins may have the same chance of landing heads but may be tossed a different number of times. Two other coins may be tossed the same number of times but may differ in their chances of landing heads. The first two coins have something in common, and so do the second" (Sober 1984, 115). Of course, this last remark is correct. But I do not think that the coin example shows drift and selection to be distinct *causal processes* any more than a series of coin tosses consists of several causal processes running simultaneously.

The coin-toss example also illustrates my claim that the number of coin tosses is not a *cause* of the resulting frequency of heads because no contingent law of nature gives it its alleged "causal role." Suppose we aim to explain why the coin's percentage departures from its expected frequency of heads have generally been greater in runs of 50 tosses than in runs of 50,000 tosses. We could explain this fact by the brute-force approach of using the coin's chance of landing heads on an individual toss to compute the chances of various great departures from the frequency's expectation value in runs of 50 and 50,000 tosses. We could deepen this causal explanation by replacing the propensity with its ground in the setup, including the coin's mass distribution and the tossing mechanism. Then the explanation would require laws of nature to associate this setup with a propensity for a head. These are causal explanations. But the role in these explanations played by the number of coin tosses in the run (which enters after a natural law has associated the setup with a toss's chance of a head outcome) is beholden not to any mere law of nature, but entirely to a theorem of the probability calculus. The run's length is thus not a cause.[21]

Suppose an explanation instead sets aside the coin's particular chance of landing heads on an individual toss as well as the fact that we are dealing with runs of 50 and 50,000 tosses—and even that we are dealing with coin-tossing in particular. The explanation then proceeds not by describing relevant features of the outcome's causal history, but rather by characterizing the fact being explained as an instance of a general, characteristic feature of statistical phenomena: outcomes are more likely to adhere more closely to expectation values in the longer run than in the shorter run. This explanation is non-causal. It computes no chances regarding the case at hand. It is mediated not by ordinary laws of nature, but rather by a theorem of probability. This is the kind of explanation that drift supplies.[22]

On my view, some instances of drift involve indiscriminate selection (one kind of causal process) whereas other instances involve discriminate selection (a causal process of another kind). Drift is not distinguished from selection by constituting a distinct kind of causal process. But explanations by drift are sharply distinguished from selectionist explanations, since drift explanations are non-causal. That in every case of drift, some population-level causal process is at work does not entail that a drift explanation is a causal explanation or that there is some distinct kind of population-level causal process that constitutes drift and so is present in every case of drift. (Watch the order of those quantifiers!) What is distinctive about drift, I have suggested, is not the outcome or the causal process, but rather the kind of non-causal explanation it supplies.[23]

6 Dimensional Explanations

■ 6.1 A SIMPLE DIMENSIONAL EXPLANATION

Dimensional analysis is well known in physics and engineering as a convenient shortcut and memory aid. Suppose you have identified all of the relevant quantities characterizing a given physical system, including the dimensional constants (such as the speed of light c and Newton's gravitational-force constant G). Suppose that you also know the dimensions of all of these quantities. Then by dimensional considerations alone, you may be able to figure out a great deal about the relations holding among those quantities.

However, some dimensional arguments are more than mnemonics; they possess explanatory power.[1] Scientists who give dimensional arguments are occasionally explicit about the arguments' explanatory power. For instance, in "Dimensional Analysis, Falling Bodies, and the Fine Art of *Not* Solving Differential Equations," an article in the *American Journal of Physics*, the physicist Craig Bohren writes: "The aim of physics is physical understanding, not solving differential equations. They are sometimes a means to an end, but not the end itself, and if that end can be reached by simpler means, especially more physically transparent and intuitive ones, all to the good" (2004, 534). Bohren has dimensional reasoning in mind as the "simpler means" to "physical understanding" (by which I take him to mean scientific explanation).

Dimensional explanations form the subject of this chapter. I will distinguish two varieties of scientific explanations that use dimensional arguments: one later in this section and the other in sections 6.2, 6.3, and 6.5. (I will describe a third, related kind in chapter 10.) All of these dimensional arguments exploit the notion of "dimensional homogeneity," which I will introduce later in this section and elaborate further in section 6.4. I will argue that all of these dimensional explanations are non-causal scientific explanations.

The kind of dimensional explanation that I will examine in this section is an "explanation by constraint." (In Poisson's explanation of the parallelogram law for the composition of forces, which I discussed in Chapter 4, dimensional considerations served as constraints in an explanation by constraint.) In contrast, the kind of dimensional explanation that I will examine in sections 6.2, 6.3, and 6.5 is not an explanation by constraint. I will contrast both of these varieties of dimensional explanation with causal explanations.

Furthermore, I will argue that although a causal explanation of a derivative law can explain certain features of the law that a dimensional explanation cannot explain, by the same token a dimensional explanation can sometimes explain certain features of the law that a causal explanation cannot explain. For instance, as I will argue in section 6.2, a dimensional explanation may reveal that one of the law's features results entirely from certain dimensional aspects of the more fundamental laws entailing it, and so the other aspects of those more fundamental laws are not responsible for that feature of the derivative law. Likewise, as I will argue in section 6.3, different features of the same derivative law may receive quite different dimensional explanations, whereas they are not traced to different sources in the law's derivation from the causal influences at work.

The notion of "dimensional homogeneity" raises several puzzles for any account of dimensional explanation. I will deal with some of these puzzles in sections 6.4 and 6.5. There I will show that if a derivative law is causally explained by being derived from various more fundamental laws, then a feature of the derivative law may be dimensionally explained partly by a fact about independence: that some relation is independent from some laws figuring in the derivative law's causal explanation. The relation's independence involves its "constraining" a stratum of natural law that it "transcends"—ideas that I elaborated in part I.

Let's begin our account of dimensional explanation by looking at what may well be the earliest dimensional argument in the history of science.[2] It exemplifies a kind of dimensional explanation that is similar to the distinctively mathematical scientific explanations in chapter 1. In virtue of these shared features, both constitute "explanations by constraint."

In 1638, Galileo (1974, 167) published his theory that if a body (near Earth's surface) falls freely to Earth from rest, then in successive equal intervals of time, the distances it traverses grow as the sequence of ascending odd numbers. In other words, Galileo proposed that if s is the distance that the body traverses in the first time interval, then in the succeeding intervals, it covers $3s, 5s, 7s, 9s, \ldots$. There were rival theories to Galileo's "odd-number rule." Honoré Fabri proposed that the distances traversed grow as the sequence of natural numbers (that is: $1s$, $2s, 3s, 4s, \ldots$), whereas Pierre Le Cazre proposed that the distances grow as the sequence of powers of 2 (that is: $1s, 2s, 4s, 8s, \ldots$). In October 1643, Marin Mersenne mentioned these rival proposals in a letter to Theodore Deschamps. In his reply, Deschamps argued that neither Fabri's nor Le Cazre's proposal is correct. He wrote: "if one chooses for the time of the first space another time than the one formerly chosen, for example its double or triple, the spaces traversed will follow no longer either the one or the other progression [i.e., will follow neither Fabri's nor Le Cazre's proposal], as they do, by contrast, in the progression of odd numbers" (Palmerino 1999, 295). That is, if Fabri's or Le Cazre's proposal holds for time intervals expressed in one unit (e.g., seconds), then it follows that the proposal will not hold for time intervals expressed in another unit (e.g., minutes). Let's see this explicitly.[3] If we take the distances given by these proposals for successive 1-unit intervals of time

Fabri: $1s, 2s, 3s, 4s, 5s, 6s, \ldots$
Le Cazre: $1s, 2s, 4s, 8s, 16s, 32s, \ldots$

and (following Deschamps) switch to a new unit of time that is twice as long as the original, we find the distances traversed in successive 1-new-unit intervals of time to be

Fabri: $3s \ (= 1s + 2s), 7s \ (= 3s + 4s), 11s \ (= 5s + 6s), \ldots$
Le Cazre: $3s \ (= 1s + 2s), 12s \ (= 4s + 8s), 48s \ (= 16s + 32s), \ldots$

These distances do not fit the proposals. For example, Fabri's proposal is that the distances traversed grow as the sequence of natural numbers. But the distances $3s, 7s,$ and $11s$ do not stand in the ratio of 1 to 2 to 3.

Expressed in today's terminology, Deschamps's point is that neither Fabri's nor Le Cazre's proposal is "dimensionally homogeneous." Omitting a few details that I will add later, we can define "dimensional homogeneity" as follows:

> Relation R is "dimensionally homogeneous" exactly when it is a broadly logi-
> cal truth that if R holds in one system of units, then R holds in any system of
> units for the various fundamental dimensions (e.g., length, mass, time) of the
> quantities so related.[4]

Of course, a relation can hold without being dimensionally homogeneous. For example, on a given date it may be that my son's weight equals my age—but this relation holds only if my son's weight is measured in pounds and my age is measured in years. The relation is therefore not between my son's weight and my age *themselves*, but rather between their measures in a particular system of units. In contrast, the relation at issue among the distances traversed in successive equal time intervals by a body falling freely from rest is supposed to be a relation among those quantities themselves, not among them as measured in some particular way. (Neither Fabri nor Le Cazre specified some particular units as having to be used to measure distance or time.) Thus, the relation at issue is supposed to be dimensionally homogeneous. Since neither Fabri's nor Le Cazre's proposal is dimensionally homogeneous, the relation in question could not possibly have been given by either of these proposals.

That is Deschamps's point—along with the fact that Galileo's proposal, by contrast, is dimensionally homogeneous. For example, if we take the distances it dictates $(1s, 3s, 5s, 7s, 9s, 11s, \ldots)$ and switch to a unit of time that is twice as large, we find that the distances covered in these longer intervals are $4s \ (= 1s + 3s),$

$12s (= 5s + 7s), 20s (= 9s + 11s), \ldots$. The ratio of 4 to 12 to 20 is the ratio of 1 to 3 to 5—the odd-number sequence that Galileo's rule demands.

The proposals from Fabri and Le Cazre, then, do not just turn out as a matter of fact to be false. Rather, their truth is impossible. There is no possible world where freely falling bodies fit Fabri's or Le Cazre's proposal. That is because there is no way for those bodies to be that would fit the proposal in every unit for measuring time, yet the proposal purports to specify a relation among the distances and times themselves (i.e., a dimensionally homogeneous relation). (Of course, there are possible worlds where either Fabri's or Le Cazre's proposal holds for distance and time measured in certain particular units.)

The dimensional argument shows that Fabri's and Le Cazre's proposals are necessarily false. I do not mean that it is *naturally* impossible for falling bodies to accord with one of them—though, of course, it *is* naturally impossible, since Galileo's rival hypothesis states a law of nature. Rather, I mean that there is a stronger species of modality in terms of which Fabri's and Le Cazre's proposals are impossible.

Deschamps was aiming simply to *show that* Fabri's and Le Cazre's proposals are false (and that Galileo's proposal is not likewise ruled out). But I suggest that Deschamps's dimensional argument also *explains why* these proposals are false. Consider the question: Why is it not the case that the distances traversed in successive equal time intervals by a body falling freely from rest are related according to Fabri's proposal—that is, why is it not the case that they stand in the ratios of the sequence of natural numbers? This question asks why it is not the case that the distances and times *themselves* conform to a certain relation. The answer is given by the fact (shown by a dimensional argument) that Fabri's proposal does not specify a dimensionally homogeneous relation.

This is not a causal explanation. It does not work by describing the world's network of causal relations; it does not supply any information about whatever causes bodies to fall. Indeed, as far as the explanation is concerned, the body's positions over time might not form a causal process at all, but instead form a pseudoprocess like a disk of light moving along a wall, projected by a rotating spotlight (Salmon 1998, 194–195). The dimensional explanation appeals only to the fact that any relation among these quantities themselves is dimensionally homogeneous and that Fabri's proposal does not give a dimensionally homogeneous relation. These facts possess a stronger variety of necessity than ordinary natural laws do. Therefore, these facts are "constraints" on any possible relation among the distances traversed in successive equal time intervals by a body falling freely from rest. These facts function in the dimensional explanation just as mathematical facts do in the distinctively mathematical scientific explanations in chapter 1. For the relation among the distances traversed in successive equal time intervals by a body falling freely from rest to accord with Fabri's proposal is just as impossible as for someone to untie a trefoil knot, to cross the Königsberg bridges, or to distribute 23 strawberries evenly among 3 children without cutting any (all examples from chapter 1).[5]

Therefore, although Newton's laws of motion and gravity (which explain why Galileo's law holds for falls near to Earth's surface) *entail that* Fabri's proposal is false, they cannot *explain why* Fabri's proposal is false. Its falsehood does not depend on the causal details given by Newton's laws. Its falsehood is more necessary than Newton's laws.[6]

Galileo's odd-number rule is not the only proposal regarding falling bodies that achieves dimensional homogeneity. Whereas the odd-number rule says that in the nth interval, the body covers $2n - 1$ times the distance covered in the first interval, consider the rule that in the nth interval, the body covers $3n^2 - 3n + 1$ times the distance covered in the first interval. On this proposal, the distances traversed in successive intervals are $1s, 7s, 19s, 37s, 61s, 91s, \ldots$. Like Galileo's rule, this proposal is dimensionally homogeneous. For example, in time intervals that are twice as long, the distances covered on this proposal are $8s (= 1s + 7s)$, $56s (= 19s + 37s)$, $152s (= 61s + 91s) \ldots$—and the ratio of 8 to 56 to 152 is the ratio of 1 to 7 to 19.

With this in mind, compare these two facts:

(1) It is not the case that the distances traversed in successive equal time intervals by bodies falling freely from rest are given by Fabri's proposal.

(2) The distances traversed in successive equal time intervals by bodies falling freely from rest are given by Galileo's proposal.

Fact (1) is broadly logically necessary (that is, its necessity belongs with narrowly logical necessity, metaphysical necessity, mathematical necessity, conceptual necessity, moral necessity, and so forth). By contrast, fact (2) is merely a natural necessity; in particular, there are other dimensionally homogeneous proposals besides Galileo's. Fact (1) has a dimensional explanation of the sort that we have been discussing; fact (2) does not.

Suppose we ask "Why is the relation among the distances traversed in successive equal time intervals by bodies falling freely from rest given by Galileo's proposal *rather than* Fabri's?" This question asks for the relevant difference between Galileo's and Fabri's proposals. Perhaps the dimensional argument suffices to answer this why question, at least in certain contexts. However, the dimensional argument cannot explain why Galileo's law holds rather than the $3n^2 - 3n + 1$ rule. In contrast, Newton's laws of motion and gravity entail and explain why the trajectory of any body that falls freely near Earth's surface accords with Galileo's odd-number rule rather than the $3n^2 - 3n + 1$ rule. This is a causal explanation. Moreover, the derivation of Galileo's law from Newton's laws explains why free bodies (near Earth) fall rather than rise. The dimensional argument cannot do that.

Thus, we have here two complementary explanations: the causal explanation of Galileo's law and the dimensional explanation of the fact that it is not the case that either Fabri's or Le Cazre's proposal holds. Neither explanation renders the other superfluous. The causal explanation of Galileo's law entails that but does not explain why neither of these proposals holds. Those proposals *could not have held*—their failure is *inevitable*—and the laws that explain why Galileo's law holds do not possess that same necessity. Thus, to regard those laws as explaining why these other proposals fail would be to mischaracterize their failure as more contingent than it is; they were never even possibilities (to put the matter picturesquely). On the other hand, the dimensional explanation of their failure does not explain why Galileo's law holds—for two reasons, each sufficient. First, Galileo's law is not the only possibility; there are other dimensionally homogeneous proposals for a relation between the distances traversed in successive equal time intervals and the times from the fall's start to those intervals. Second, the dimensional argument does not explain why free bodies near Earth fall, whereas the causal explanation explains this fact.

■ 6.2 A MORE COMPLICATED DIMENSIONAL EXPLANATION

Deschamps's dimensional argument may have been given even before he gave it in 1643. According to a 1627 letter from Gianbattista Baliani to Benedetto Castelli, Galileo himself argued that his proposal was unique in being dimensionally homogeneous (see Meli 2010, 32). As I have shown, this is not quite the case—though in a 1646 letter to Mersenne, the 17-year-old Christiaan Huygens showed that no distance rule involving a geometric progression $(a, ra, r^2a, r^3a, \ldots)$, such as Le Cazre's (which has $a = s$, $r = 2$), is dimensionally homogeneous, and in addition that no distance rule involving an arithmetic progression $(a, a + n, a + 2n, a + 3n, \ldots)$, such as Fabri's (which has $a = s$, $n = s$), is dimensionally homogeneous except one: Galileo's (which has $a = s$, $n = 2s$).[7]

Huygens's result can be extended by finding the general form of any dimensionally homogeneous relation. To arrive at this form, we must first recognize that the concept of dimensional homogeneity presupposes the concept of two units (e.g., grams and slugs) counting as different ways of specifying the same quantity (e.g., an object's mass). Two units so qualify only if necessarily whenever x is the numerical value in one unit and y is the corresponding numerical value in the other unit, $y = cx$ for some constant $c > 0$—the "conversion factor" between the units (Bridgman 1931, 18–21). This condition is motivated by the idea that two units are not means of specifying the same quantity if, by changing between the units, the ratio between two measurements is not preserved.[8]

For example, since grams and slugs are units for expressing the same quantity (mass), my measure in grams is twice my son's measure in grams if and only if my measure in slugs is twice my son's measure in slugs.[9]

Suppose $v = f(s, t, u, \ldots)$ is continuous and dimensionally homogeneous, where $s, t, u, v, \ldots$ are the (positive-valued) quantities expressed in one system of units. Suppose we now use a new system of units for these quantities, involving various positive-valued conversion factors $c, d, e, \ldots$, respectively; s when converted into the new units becomes cs, t becomes dt, u becomes eu, and so forth. Then since the equation is dimensionally homogeneous, $f(cs, dt, eu, \ldots)$ must equal whatever v becomes when converted into the new system of units, which must be v multiplied by some function φ of $c, d, e, \ldots$ (where φ gives the conversion factor for the quantity expressed by v). That is, $f(cs, dt, eu, \ldots) = \varphi(c, d, e, \ldots) f(s, t, u, \ldots)$. It can be shown[10] that this condition holds for any new system of units if and only if $f(s, t, u, \ldots)$ is proportional to $s^\alpha\, t^\beta\, u^\gamma, \ldots$, where the constant of proportionality and the exponents are "dimensionless" constants (that is, quantities expressed in no measurement units, i.e., "pure numbers")—as long as there is no dimensionless combination of $s, t, u, \ldots$ (e.g., the ratio of s to t is not dimensionless). If there is a dimensionless combination, then $f(s, t, u, \ldots)$ is proportional to $s^\alpha\, t^\beta\, u^\gamma, \ldots$, times some function of the dimensionless combination(s). Dimensional analysis alone is insufficient to identify the function.

Let's apply this result to the case of falling bodies. Le Cazre's proposal is that the total distance covered by the end of each successive unit-length time interval is $1s, 3s, 7s, \ldots$. Therefore, Le Cazre's proposal is that the total distance covered after t intervals have passed is proportional to $2^t - 1$. With t in the exponent, Le Cazre's proposal does not take the form that (I just asserted) is required for dimensional homogeneity. Fabri's proposal is that the total distance covered after t intervals is proportional to the sum of the first t natural numbers, which is $t(t+1)/2$, and so is proportional to $t^2 + t$, which again does not take the form required for dimensional homogeneity. In contrast, Galileo's rule is that the total distance covered after time t has passed is proportional to t^2, and the $3n^2 - 3n + 1$ rule is that the distance is proportional to t^3. Both of these proposals fit the form required for dimensional homogeneity.

That form plays an important part in another kind of dimensional explanation—a kind that is neither a causal explanation nor an "explanation by constraint." (This variety of dimensional explanation will be the subject of the rest of this chapter.) Let's begin with an example. Consider a planet of mass m orbiting with period T in a circular orbit of radius r around a star of mass M (with the planet and star otherwise isolated and each spherically symmetric). Let's focus solely on T's relation to r: that $T \propto r^{3/2}$. (The symbol $\propto$ means "is proportional to.") Suppose we ask: Why is $T \propto r^{3/2}$?

Here is a dimensional explanation that answers this why question.[11] In terms of the dimensions of length (L), mass (M), and time (T), T's dimension is T^{-1}, m's dimension is M, M's dimension is M, the gravitational constant G's dimensions are $L^3 M^{-1} T^{-2}$, and r's dimension is L. In tabular form:

	T	m	M	G	r
L	0	0	0	3	1
M	0	1	1	-1	0
T	1	0	0	-2	0

As I have just mentioned, if T stands in a dimensionally homogeneous relation to some subset of m, M, G, and r, then T must be proportional to $m^\alpha M^\beta G^\gamma r^\delta$ (times some unspecified function of the dimensionless combination M/m) for some dimensionless exponents α, β, γ, and δ. The table gives us three simultaneous equations (one from each horizontal line) with four unknowns:

From L: $0 = 3\gamma + \delta$
From M: $0 = \alpha + \beta - \gamma$
From T: $1 = -2\gamma$

The L equation entails that $\gamma = -\frac{1}{2}$, and so from the T equation, it follows that $\delta = 3/2$. Therefore, T is proportional to $r^{3/2}$, which is what we were trying to explain.

The explanans in this explanation is that T stands in a dimensionally homogeneous relation to some subset of m, M, G, and r. The mere fact that T stands in such a relation turns out to suffice to fix certain particular features of that relation, such as that $T \propto r^{3/2}$. In particular, $T \propto r^{3/2}$ arises from G's being the only source of T dimensions from among m, M, G, and r, and r's being the only remaining source of L dimensions to compensate for the L dimensions from G.

The explanans is not a "constraint"; it does not possess greater necessity than an ordinary law of nature.[12] Neither does $T \propto r^{3/2}$. The above dimensional explanation is not an "explanation by constraint"; it does not show the explanandum to have greater necessity than an ordinary law of nature. Furthermore, I will argue that this dimensional argument is not a *causal* explanation. Obviously, it does not work by tracing the various causal influences acting on the planet, describing the impacts of those influences taken individually, combining those impacts in some way, and from this net result extracting an equation for the planet's orbital period. In chapter 1, I gave such a causal explanation for the derivative law[13] concerning the strength of the electric field of an infinite uniform line charge. That explanation worked by describing an aspect of the world's network of causal relations (in particular, the contributions to the field that would be made by the various causes of a given infinite line charge's field, along with the way in which those contributions would combine). There is a derivation of this kind for the fact that $T \propto r^{3/2}$. It derives the explanandum from Newton's laws of motion and gravity (and some "closure law" specifying that no other forces are operating besides gravity):

> These laws tell us that that $F = ma$ and $F = GMm/r^2$, respectively, where F is the force on the planet and a is the planet's acceleration. A body undergoing circular motion at a constant speed v experiences an acceleration $a = v^2/r$ toward the center. Hence,
>
> $$GMm/r^2 = m\,v^2/r,$$
>
> and so
>
> $$GM/r^2 = v^2/r,$$
>
> and therefore
>
> $$GM/r = v^2.$$
>
> For a circular orbit with circumference $c = 2\pi r$, the period equals the distance c covered in one revolution divided by the speed v. That is,
>
> $$T = 2\pi r/v,$$
>
> and so
>
> $$T^2 = 4\pi^2 r^2/v^2.$$
>
> By inserting the expression for v^2 derived from Newton's laws, we find
>
> $$T^2 = 4\pi^2 r^2/(GM/r) = 4\pi^2 r^3/GM. \text{ Therefore,}$$
> $$T = 2\pi\sqrt{(r^3/GM)}, \text{ and so}$$
> $$T \propto r^{3/2}.$$

Certainly, this derivation is a causal explanation of the fact that $T = 2\pi\sqrt{(r^3/GM)}$.[14] But it does not follow that this derivation explains why $T \propto r^{3/2}$. After all, even some fundamental laws (or some facts about the fundamental laws) that suffice to entail this relation may fail to explain it. For example, since it is entailed by Newton's laws of motion and gravity (presumed fundamental), it is entailed by Coulomb's law together with Newton's laws of motion and gravity. But such a derivation is not explanatory since Coulomb's law is irrelevant; it does not help to describe the causes of a planet's orbital period.

Nevertheless, one might insist that the derivation from Newton's laws of motion and gravity causally explains why $T \propto r^{3/2}$ whereas the dimensional argument does not explain why $T \propto r^{3/2}$. One might hold that although (as I have shown) $T \propto r^{3/2}$ is *entailed* by the fact that T stands in a dimensionally homogeneous relation to (some subset of) m, M, G, and r, both of these facts are explained by $F = ma$ and $F = GMm/r^2$. The supposed explanans and explanandum of a dimensional "explanation" have a common origin; one is not responsible for the other.

But dimensional arguments appear explanatory. Why might one insist that nevertheless, they are not? Perhaps because a dimensional argument cannot yield more than various proportionalities (for instance, that $T \propto r^{3/2}$ and $T \propto G^{-1/2}$), whereas more fundamental laws entail the complete equation ($T = 2\pi\sqrt{(r^3/GM)}$), including the values of dimensionless constants of proportionality (2π) and that T is independent of the planet's mass (m).[15] This difference might seem to suggest that whereas the derivation from more fundamental laws is explanatory, the dimensional argument is not. However, I see no reason why the dimensional argument would have to explain the complete equation above in order to explain why $T \propto r^{3/2}$ and $T \propto G^{-1/2}$.

I will suggest that the dimensional argument *is* explanatory. Indeed, it reveals that as far as explaining $T \propto r^{3/2}$ is concerned, certain features of Newton's second law of motion and law of gravity are as idle as Coulomb's law. For example, $T \propto r^{3/2}$ does not depend on the features of $F = ma$ and $F = GMm/r^2$ that are captured by the M equation (extracted from the second row of the dimensional table above). Rather, $T \propto r^{3/2}$ arises from G's being the only source of T dimensions from among m, M, G, and r, and from r's being the only remaining source of L dimensions to compensate for the L dimensions from G. The M equation does not figure in the argument. The explanans is then merely that T stands in a relation to (some subset of) m, M, G, and r—a relation that is dimensionally homogeneous in terms of L and T. This explanans captures the only feature of T's standing in a relation to m, M, G, and r that is explanatorily relevant to $T \propto r^{3/2}$. Any further detail of the fundamental laws is explanatorily irrelevant.

On this view, $T \propto r^{3/2}$'s derivation from $F = ma$ and $F = GMm/r^2$ contains elements that are otiose as far as explaining $T \propto r^{3/2}$ is concerned. The derivation is in this respect like the famous counterexample from Kyburg (1965) to Hempel's and Oppenheim's D-N model of scientific explanation (Hempel 1965): we cannot explain why a given sample dissolved by saying that it was table salt, hexed (i.e., a person wearing a funny hat waved a "wand" and mumbled something over it), and placed in water, and that as a matter of natural necessity, all hexed samples of table salt dissolve when placed in water.[16] To illustrate the independence of $T \propto r^{3/2}$ from the features of $F = ma$ and $F = GMm/r^2$ expressed by the M equation, let us suppose that (contrary to natural law) the gravitational force had been proportional to M^2m^2 rather than to Mm but otherwise had been no different. Then although G's M dimension would have been different, its L and T dimensions would not. Thus, the L and T lines in the table would have been no different, and so $T \propto r^{3/2}$ would still have held.

The derivation from $F = ma$ and $F = GMm/r^2$ cannot reflect this independence, since there is no point in the course of that derivation after which the M dimensions of various quantities drop out or remain isolated from all of their other dimensions. The derivation begins with the actual, more fundamental laws, not some generalizations thereof, and it simply churns on like a bulldozer, deducing consequences of those laws until it generates the explanandum. In this respect, it is like a brute-force proof in mathematics, such as the brute-force proof (to be given in chapter 7) of d'Alembert's theorem that the complex-number solutions to polynomial equations with real coefficients come in complex-conjugate pairs. Each of these arguments simply calculates everything directly, plugging in everything and grinding out the result.

In contrast, the dimensional explanation of $T \propto r^{3/2}$ is like the *explanation* of d'Alembert's theorem—a proof (given in chapter 7) that invokes the fact that the axioms of complex arithmetic are symmetric under the replacement of i with $-i$. The explanation in mathematics and the dimensional argument are both *selective*; just as the explanation in mathematics reveals precisely which features of the axioms are responsible for and which details are irrelevant to d'Alembert's theorem, so the dimensional argument identifies which features of the fundamental laws are responsible for and which details are irrelevant to making $T \propto r^{3/2}$. The dimensional explanation begins by teasing apart various features of the fundamental laws, and then it keeps these strands apart, allowing each one's significance to be traced separately. Thus it can depict certain features as explanatorily relevant and others as making no contribution to the explanation.[17]

On this view, the dimensional argument explains why $T \propto r^{3/2}$ and the derivation from $F = ma$ and $F = GMm/r^2$ does not; it includes some facts that are explanatorily irrelevant to $T \propto r^{3/2}$. Another way to put this point involves turning to the putative explanans in the dimensional explanation and asking why *it* holds. The explanans is that T stands in a relation to (some subset of) m, M, G, and r that is dimensionally homogeneous in terms of L and T. Suppose that the explanans holds because of laws such as $F = ma$ and $F = GMm/r^2$. In that case, those details would presumably be explanatorily relevant to $T \propto r^{3/2}$.[18] But as I have just argued, certain features of those laws do not help to explain why $T \propto r^{3/2}$. Therefore, the explanans in the dimensional explanation is not *explained by* Newton's laws of motion and gravity (any more than Newton's gravitational-force law explains why gravity is an inverse-square force). Neither one is explanatorily prior to the other. Rather, the dimensional explanans captures exactly the explanatorily relevant aspects of the fundamental laws—those aspects that are responsible for $T \propto r^{3/2}$.

The explanans in the dimensional explanation is that T stands in a dimensionally homogeneous relation to some subset of m, M, G, and r. Now m, M, and r were defined in the case under discussion. However, G was not. Strictly speaking, then, the dimensional explanans does not identify G as the *gravitational* constant (any more than it specifies G's magnitude). Rather, all that matters to the explanans is that G is some quantity having dimensions $L^3 M^{-1} T^{-2}$. The explanans is that T stands in a dimensionally homogeneous relation to some subset of m, M, r, and some unspecified quantity with dimensions $L^3 M^{-1} T^{-2}$. That G's identity as the gravitational constant is irrelevant to the dimensional explanation emphasizes once again that the dimensional explanation does not work by describing the world's causal nexus. I argued for something similar regarding the kinematical explanation of the Lorentz transformations examined in section 3.2. In that explanation by constraint, the explanans does not identify c as the speed of light (or of any other particular entity). All that matters to the explanans is that c is a quantity having the dimensions of speed, just as all that matters to the above dimensional explanans is that G is a quantity having dimensions $L^3M^{-1}T^{-2}$.

▪ 6.3 DIFFERENT FEATURES OF A DERIVATIVE LAW MAY RECEIVE DIFFERENT DIMENSIONAL EXPLANATIONS

I have just argued that a dimensional explanation may reveal certain aspects of the more fundamental laws entailing a given derivative law to be explanatorily irrelevant to that law. That is because a dimensional explanation disregards certain aspects of the fundamental laws (by considering only their dimensional architecture) and treats certain other aspects separately from one another (by treating distinct dimensions separately). The way in which dimensional explanations tease apart the various dimensions has a further consequence: different aspects of a given derivative law may receive different dimensional explanations. This is another respect in which a law's dimensional explanation may differ from the law's deduction from fundamental laws. Just as a dimensional explanation may distinguish the explanatory contributions (if any) made to a derivative law by different aspects of the fundamental laws, so also it may reveal that different aspects of the derivative law have different explanations.

Here is an example. Consider a body with mass m lying on a smooth table and subject to the force of a spring (fig. 6.1). Suppose we grasp the body and pull, stretching out the spring to a distance x_m beyond its equilibrium length, and then let go. The body moves back and forth. Here are two why questions concerning this case:

(1) Why is the body's period of oscillation T proportional to $\sqrt{(m/k)}$, where each spring has a characteristic constant k?
(2) Why is T not a function of x_m?

We could identify the causal influences acting on the body, invoke the laws determining those influences and how they affect the body's motion, and

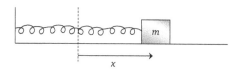

Figure 6.1 Body on a table attached to a spring

thereby derive an equation specifying its trajectory. This argument would constitute a causal explanation of the body's trajectory; it would also explain why the body's motion consists of an oscillation. From the derived equation for the body's motion, it follows that the oscillation's T is proportional to $\sqrt{(m/k)}$ and that T is not a function of x_m. However, as I have just argued, the more fundamental laws entailing these two results may contain elements that are not explanatorily relevant to these results. I will suggest that whereas the causal explanation of the body's motion supplies a single derivation for both the fact that T is proportional to $\sqrt{(m/k)}$ and the fact that T is not a function of x_m, actually these two properties of the body's period depend on different features of the more fundamental laws. Accordingly, they receive different dimensional explanations. The causal explanation of the body's motion does not explain the fact that T is proportional to $\sqrt{(m/k)}$ and the fact that T is not a function of x_m, despite "unifying" them under the equation of motion that it does explain.

The causal explanation of the body's motion appeals to Newton's second law of motion ($F = ma$) and Hooke's law (that the force F exerted by the spring on the body is toward the spring's equilibrium position and, to a sufficiently good approximation, is proportional to the body's displacement x from that position). From these laws, we can deduce and thereby explain $x(t)$, the body's displacement as a function of time:

$ma - F = 0$. Letting k be the constant of proportionality in Hooke's law, $F = -kx$.

So

$ma + kx = 0$, and so

$a + (k/m)\, x = 0$.

This differential equation (a is x's second-derivative with respect to time) is solved by

$x(t) = x_m \cos(\sqrt{(k/m)}\, t + \varphi)$, which has a period of $2\pi\sqrt{(m/k)}$.

Thus, the body's motion turns out to be an oscillation with a period $T = 2\pi\sqrt{(m/k)}$, so T is not a function of x_m and is proportional to $\sqrt{(m/k)}$.

Although this argument causally explains the body's motion, my concern is whether it explains certain features of its period. That the argument explains why the body has a given equation of motion, and that this equation entails that the body's period is independent of x_m, does not ensure that the argument explains why the body's period is independent of x_m. The dimensional explanation reveal that certain features of the more fundamental laws are irrelevant to explaining why T is independent of x_m and proportional to $\sqrt{(m/k)}$. In addition, the dimensional explanation reveals that certain of the more fundamental laws' features that help to explain one of these facts are irrelevant to explaining the other.

No dimensional argument explains why the body oscillates—that is, why it has a period at all. As I just showed, the body's oscillation has a causal explanation. However, to explain why the oscillation's period is independent of x_m rather than a function of x_m (note the contrast class), we do not have to explain why the body oscillates in the first place.[19] The explanans in the dimensional explanation presupposes that the body oscillates by presupposing that T exists. The explanans is that (to a sufficiently good approximation) x_m, k, and m suffice (and may even be more than enough) to form a quantity standing in a dimensionally homogeneous relation to T. So here is our table:

	T	x_m	k	m
L	0	1	0	0
M	0	0	1	1
T	1	0	-2	0

If T is proportional to $x_m{}^\alpha \, k^\beta \, m^\gamma$, then it follows from the table's first line that $\alpha = 0$. In other words, the reason why T is not a function of x_m is that x_m is the only quantity (among those figuring in the relation) that involves an L dimension, so there is nothing available to compensate for its L dimension in order to leave us with T (which has no L dimension).

This dimensional explanation of T's independence from x_m is distinct from the dimensional explanation of T's varying with $\sqrt{(m/k)}$. The latter explanation is given by the M and T equations:

From M: $0 = \beta + \gamma$
From T: $1 = -2\beta$

Solving, we find that $\beta = -\frac{1}{2}$ and $\gamma = \frac{1}{2}$, and so that T is proportional to $k^{-1/2} \, m^{1/2}$, that is, $\sqrt{(m/k)}$.

The first dimensional explanation identifies the specific feature of the more fundamental laws (whatever they may be) that is responsible for T's independence from x_m, and the second dimensional explanation distinguishes this feature from the one that is responsible for T's varying with $\sqrt{(m/k)}$. By contrast, these features of the fundamental laws are not distinguished in the brute-force derivation of $x(t) = x_m \cos(\sqrt{(k/m)} \, t + \varphi)$. Different dimensional arguments thus answer different why questions about the derivative law $T = 2\pi\sqrt{(m/k)}$, since dimensional arguments pull the various dimensions apart. The causal argument treats all of those dimensions together and thus cannot distinguish the reason why T varies with $\sqrt{(m/k)}$ from the reason why T is independent from x_m; these different aspects of the derivative law all arise together at the conclusion of the law's derivation from more fundamental laws. That derivation nevertheless explains causally why the body oscillates. It also explains causally why the proportionality constant between T and $\sqrt{(m/k)}$ equals 2π. The dimensional explanation cannot explain those facts.

Let's now see how a dimensional explanation accounts not for the above derivative law, but rather for a particular instance of that law. We can also then see how a dimensional explanation need not invoke the general form that (I mentioned in the previous section) any dimensionally homogeneous relation must take.

Suppose we have a small-scale working model of a machine involving the apparatus in fig. 6.1, where the model has properties m_1, k_1, x_{m1}, and T_1. Suppose we want to scale up this model so that the full-size machine has somewhat larger values for m, k, and x_m, but we want its T not to exceed a certain threshold. In particular, we want $m_2 > 10m_1$, $k_2 < 5k_1$, $x_{m2} > 10x_{m1}$, and $T_2 < \sqrt{2}\,T_1$. Suppose we construct a variety of full-scale systems similar to our model, but we never manage to achieve our goal. Why do we keep failing? Why do our scaled-up systems not work?

A dimensional explanation of our failure has as its explanans that in such a system, T stands in a dimensionally homogeneous relation to some subset of m, k, and x_m. Whatever this relation may be, it is evidently satisfied by m_1, k_1, x_{m1}, and T_1. The model and its scaled-up cousin are similar; they have exactly the same parts, merely at different scales. In fact, we can use the same numbers to represent the properties of the two systems if we are willing to measure the industrial-size system in larger units than we used for measuring the small-scale model. Suppose we change the units in which we measure m_2, k_2, x_{m2}, and T_2 so as to make the values of these properties numerically equal to those of m_1, k_1, x_{m1}, and T_1, respectively, as measured in the old units. Then since the relation satisfied by m_1, k_1, x_{m1}, and T_1 is dimensionally homogeneous, that relation must hold in all units and so, in particular, must be satisfied by the scaled-up machine's properties as measured in the new units. To convert m_2 from old units into new units so that its value is numerically equal to m_1's value in old units, we must multiply m_2's value in old units by m_1/m_2, and to make a similar conversion for k, we must multiply k_2's value in old units by k_1/k_2. However, since m_2 has dimension M and k_2 has dimension M/T^2, it follows that $\sqrt{(m_2/k_2)}$ has dimension T, so the conversion factors for the units in which we measure m_2 and k_2 determine the conversion factor for the units in which we measure T_2. That is, T_2 in old units multiplied by $\sqrt{[(m_1/m_2)/(k_1/k_2)]}$ yields T_2 in new units— which is numerically equal to T_1 in old units. So $T_2\sqrt{[(m_1/m_2)/(k_1/k_2)]} = T_1$, that is, $T_2 = T_1\sqrt{(k_1m_2/m_1k_2)}$. Hence, if $m_2 > 10\,m_1$ and $k_2 < 5\,k_1$, then necessarily $T_2 > \sqrt{2}\,T_1$. Therefore, the reason we failed in our efforts to scale up the prototype is because it was impossible for us to succeed in view of the dimensional homogeneity of the relation in which T stands to some subset of m, k, and x_m (whatever the particular relation turns out to be).

This explanation has as its explanans that T stands in a dimensionally homogeneous relation to some subset of m, k, and x_m. But the explanation does *not* presume that T is an *effect* of some subset of these other properties. As far as this explanation is concerned, causal priority might just as well run in the opposite direction or all of these properties might be effects of some unmentioned common cause. The explanation does not work by supplying information about the world's network of causal relations. It is not a causal explanation. We could instead explain why a given industrial-scale system has a period $T_2 > \sqrt{2}\, T_1$ by tracing the causes of the given system's period. But the dimensional argument explains without doing so. According to the dimensional explanation, m and k are explanatorily relevant because they are among the properties in a set having a subset of properties that stand in a dimensionally homogeneous relation to T and because the unit conversions for m and k suffice to fix T's unit conversion. Those are the roles played by m and k in the dimensional explanation. They do not play the roles of T's causes.

In this way, a dimensional argument can explain why a model fails to scale up in a certain way: because its so scaling up would violate the dimensional homogeneity of some relation among the system's properties. According to Price (1862, 120), such a dimensional argument answers the following question: "A model succeeds; a machine made after the model breaks into pieces: what is the cause of this?" I would say "explanation" ("because"), not "cause." Price is correct in regarding the dimensional argument as explanatory. But it explains other than by virtue of supplying information about causes.

■ 6.4 DIMENSIONAL HOMOGENEITY

In a dimensional explanation of the kind that I examined in sections 6.2 and 6.3, the explanans is the fact that there exists a dimensionally homogeneous relation between a given quantity and a subset of certain other quantities—a relation involving no other quantities besides (some of) those. A relation is "dimensionally homogeneous" exactly when it is a broadly logical truth that if the relation holds in one system of units, then it holds in any other system of units for the fundamental dimensions of the quantities so related. As I mentioned earlier, not all relations are dimensionally homogeneous. For example, that (right now) my son's weight equals my age is not dimensionally homogeneous; this relation holds only if my son's weight is measured in pounds and my age is measured in years.

This example illustrates the falsehood of remarks like this, from a standard physics textbook: "Any equation must be *dimensionally consistent*; that is, the dimensions on both sides must be the same." (Resnick, Halliday, and Krane 1992, 9).[20] On the contrary, the numerical value of one quantity, measured in one unit, can be equal to the numerical value of another quantity, measured in another unit. It might be suggested that "equation" in the above remark refers only to laws of nature, not mere accidents, and that (as Luce (1971, 157) declares) any law of nature must be dimensionally consistent. But that is not so; for example, it is a natural law (by courtesy, since it has more than natural necessity; it is a broadly logical truth) that if a body starting at rest at $t = 0$ moves by time t a distance s under uniform acceleration a, then (where v is its speed at t) $v^2 - 2as = v - at$. The two sides have different dimensions but are numerically equal, as a matter of natural law. Both sides equal zero—as does $(F - ma)$, in yet other dimensions. Furthermore, it is a broadly logical truth that this equation holds no matter what units are used throughout for distance and time.[21] Dimensional consistency is not necessary for dimensional homogeneity.[22]

Although not every relation is dimensionally homogeneous, every relation can be transformed into a dimensionally homogeneous relation by the addition of further relata. For example, that my son's weight in pounds equals my age in years entails that my son's weight in any unit, times the reciprocal of the number of those units in 1 pound, equals my age in any unit, times the reciprocal of the number of those units in 1 year. This relation is dimensionally homogeneous, but it involves not only my son's weight and my age, but also two "dimensional constants." (They could be combined into one.) Familiar dimensional constants appearing in natural laws include the speed of light c and Newton's gravitational-force constant G. The explanans in a dimensional explanation specifies all of the quantities (including dimensional constants) that are eligible to participate in some relation. So the explanans (that there is a dimensionally homogeneous relation between quantity Q and *no other quantities besides* a subset of the following quantities . . .) is not a trivial truth. But it is a trivial fact that among the relations that obtain, some are dimensionally homogeneous.

The fact that any relation can be transformed into a dimensionally homogeneous relation by the addition of relata undermines any remark along these lines: "The fact that practically every law of physics is dimensionally invariant is certainly no accident. We need an explanation of this invariance" (Causey 1967, 30; for similar remarks, see Causey 1969, 256; Luce 1971, 151; Krantz, Luce, Suppes, and Tversky 1971, 504–506). We need neither to appeal to some metaphysical analysis of natural lawhood nor to posit some metalaw of nature (e.g., that it is a law that all laws are dimensionally homogeneous)[23] in order to explain why all actual laws involve dimensionally homogeneous relations. Rather, we need note only that any law expressed in terms of a relation that is not dimensionally homogeneous can also be expressed in terms of a relation that is dimensionally homogeneous.[24] For instance, in middle school I was taught that it is a law of nature that the distance s in feet traversed in t seconds by a body falling freely to Earth from rest at a low altitude is equal to $16t^2$. This law is plainly not dimensionally homogeneous. But if we replace the pure number 16 with the dimensional constant 16 feet per second^2, then we will have a dimensionally homogeneous relation.[25]

That all laws of nature are dimensionally homogeneous is neither part of the metaphysics of what it is to be a law of nature nor "a constraint imposed by our mind . . . a condition imposed by our mind on the possible or reasonable form experimental results can take" (Meli 2010, 32). Rather, that any law can be expressed in dimensionally homogeneous terms, once sufficient dimensional constants are included in it, is a logical truth. This is worth remembering when we read Deschamps and Huygens being charged with making an unjustified presupposition: that there is a distance rule for falling bodies that is dimensionally homogeneous: "Huygens behaves as if this property [dimensional homogeneity] was some *conditio sine qua non* for any true law of free fall and which only Galileo's can satisfy. Given that he does not try to justify in any way whatsoever why this property was essential, his argument has—not unjustly—been accused of circularity" (Palmerino 1999, 324). But if there is a relation among the distances traversed in equal time intervals by bodies falling freely from rest that holds only for a certain particular set of units, then there is a dimensionally homogeneous relation with additional relata. So the presupposition that a dimensionally homogeneous relation exists, over and above the presupposition that a relation exists, is no presupposition at all. It is impossible for either Fabri's or Le Cazre's proposal to give a dimensionally homogeneous relation as these proposals stand—that is, without some particular dimensional constant being added to them. That neither proposal *can* state a relation that actually holds of the free-fall distances themselves explains why neither proposal *does* state such a relation—and there must be such a relation if there is a relation among those distances when they are expressed in a specific system of units.

In any event, a particular dimensional explanation does not presuppose some general principle that all laws involve dimensionally homogeneous relations. Rather, the explanans in a given dimensional explanation is much narrower. In dimensional explanations of the simple kind that I examined in section 6.1, the explanans is that any relation among certain quantities *themselves* is dimensionally homogeneous and that a given proposal does not specify a dimensionally homogeneous relation. In the more complicated dimensional explanations that I examined in sections 6.2 and 6.3, the explanans is that there obtains a relation between a given quantity and a subset of several other quantities that is dimensionally homogeneous for a certain set of fundamental dimensions. This reference to certain dimensions is the final topic that I will discuss.

6.5 INDEPENDENCE FROM SOME OTHER QUANTITIES AS PART OF A DIMENSIONAL EXPLANANS

In a dimensional explanation of the kind that I examined in sections 6.2 and 6.3, the explanans is that certain quantities $s, t, \ldots, u$ suffice to form a quantity that stands in a dimensionally homogeneous relation to another quantity v. The explanans, then, entails that no other dimensional quantities need to be added to

$s, t, \ldots, u$ to form a quantity standing in a dimensionally homogeneous relation to v. Thus, the explanans entails that even if certain other quantities independent of $s, t, \ldots, u$ do in fact characterize the system at hand, v is not a function of them once $s, t, \ldots$, and u are given.

For instance, I argued in section 6.2 that $T \propto r^{3/2}$ (in connection with a planet orbiting a star) is explained by the fact that T stands in a dimensionally homogeneous relation to some subset of m, M, G, and r. The explanans entails that even if the planet is also characterized by some volume, color, chemical composition, or dimensional astrological quantity, nevertheless T is not a function of the value of that additional quantity once the values of m, M, G, and r are given. This fact is part of what explains why $T \propto r^{3/2}$, since the premise that m, M, G, and r are *enough* to form a relatum standing in a dimensionally homogeneous relation to T is what underwrites the fact that T is proportional to $m^\alpha M^\beta G^\gamma r^\delta$ (times some unspecified function of M/m) for some dimensionless exponents α, β, γ, and δ. So the explanans in the dimensional explanation includes that m, M, G, and r do not need to be supplemented by any other dimensional quantity in order to form a quantity that stands in a dimensionally homogeneous relation to T.

As I will now explain, whether some quantity is in fact a dimensional quantity depends on what the fundamental dimensions are. Therefore, by taking a particular combination of dimensions as fundamental, a dimensional explanation is able to make its explanans include the fact that even if there is a certain kind of dimensional quantity, a certain sort of relation can achieve dimensional homogeneity without it. Sometimes a dimensional explanation requires an explanans where the fundamental dimensions have been selected carefully.

Consider, for instance, a small sphere of radius r falling slowly through a fluid of viscosity η. It quickly reaches a steady speed, its "terminal velocity," which turns out to be proportional to gr^2/η. This fact may be derived hydrodynamically or dimensionally. (I use the neutral term "derived" to avoid presupposing which of these arguments is explanatory. If the dimensional argument is explanatory, then although the hydrodynamic argument causally explains the specific equation for the sphere's terminal velocity, certain hydrodynamic laws to which that argument appeals are idle as far as explaining merely why the terminal velocity is proportional to gr^2/η, and so the hydrodynamic argument does not explain this proportionality.)

The hydrodynamic derivation begins with Newton's second law of motion: the net force on the sphere equals its ma. When terminal velocity is reached, $a = 0$. The net force on the sphere is the sum of the downward gravitational force F_g, the upward buoyant force F_b, and the upward drag force F_d that increases with the sphere's speed. By Archimedes's principle, F_b equals the weight of a fluid volume equal to the body's volume. Furthermore, F_d is given by Stokes's law when the fluid flow around the body is not turbulent (roughly, for a small body at low speed). If the fluid's density is ρ_f and the sphere's density is ρ_s, then

$$F_g = mg = \rho_s (4/3)\pi r^3 g$$

$$F_b = -\rho_f (4/3)\pi r^3 g$$

$$F_d = -6\pi rv\eta.$$

So at terminal velocity v, $a = 0$, so $F = ma = 0$, and therefore $F_g + F_b + F_d = 0$. Thus,

$$(4/3)\pi g r^3 (\rho_s - \rho_f) = 6\pi rv\eta.$$

Hence

$$v = (2/9)g r^2 (\rho_s - \rho_f)/\eta.$$

Thus, we have derived that v is proportional to gr^2/η.

Now consider a dimensional derivation of this law. Let the premise be roughly that ρ_s, ρ_f, r, g, and η suffice to characterize the system physically. Hence (since ρ_f/ρ_s is dimensionless, and so its contribution is inaccessible from exclusively dimensional considerations), there is a dimensionally homogeneous relation $v = r^\alpha \rho_s^\beta \eta^\gamma g^\delta$ f(ρ_f /ρ_s) for some function f.[26] If this relation is dimensionally homogeneous in terms of three dimensions (such as L, T, and M), then unhappily, a table yields three simultaneous equations in four variables (α, β, γ, and δ). However, suppose (as Bridgman 1931, 66, suggests) that this relation is dimensionally homogeneous in terms of four dimensions: L, T, M, and force (F). With these four dimensions instead of three, the constant of proportionality k between force and mass x acceleration ($F = kma$) is a *dimensional* constant. However, if the dimensional argument's premise is that v stands in a relation to ρ_s, ρ_f, r, g, and η that is dimensionally homogeneous in terms of L, T, M, and F, then the premise includes that if there is a dimensional constant of proportionality k between force and mass x acceleration, it is *not* among the quantities standing in the dimensionally homogeneous relation. Then we have four simultaneous equations in four variables. Our table is

	v	r	ρ_s	η	g
L	1	1	-3	-2	0
M	0	0	1	0	-1
T	-1	0	0	1	0
F	0	0	0	1	1

Our four equations are then

From L: $1 = \alpha - 3\beta - 2\gamma$
From M: $0 = \beta - \delta$
From T: $-1 = \gamma$
From F: $0 = \gamma + \delta.$

Hence: $\alpha = 2$, $\beta = 1$, $\gamma = -1$, $\delta = 1$, yielding $v = (r^2 \rho_s g / \eta) \, f(\rho_f / \rho_s)$.[27] Thus, we have derived that v is proportional to gr^2/η.

If this dimensional argument explains this proportionality, then the proportionality is explained by the fact that v stands in a relation to some subset of ρ_s, ρ_f, r, g, and η that is dimensionally homogeneous *using these four dimensions*. That is, the proportionality is explained partly by the fact that even if there is a dimensional constant k, it does not need to supplement ρ_s, ρ_f, r, g, and η in forming a quantity that stands in a dimensionally homogeneous relation to v. Whereas the putative hydrodynamic explanation says that $F = ma$ helps to explain why v is proportional to gr^2/η, the putative dimensional explanation not only fails to appeal to $F = ma$, but actually appeals to the fact that no dimensional constant k such that $F = kma$ needs to be added to ρ_s, ρ_f, r, g, and η in order to form a quantity that stands in a dimensionally homogeneous relation to v. The point of using four dimensions instead of three is to strengthen the explanans to include this fact by allowing for there to be such a dimensional constant. According to the putative dimensional explanation, part of the reason why v is proportional to gr^2/η is that v's relation to these other quantities is independent from a certain law that is used to derive it hydrodynamically.

What would it take for the dimensional rather than the hydrodynamic derivation to explain why v is proportional to gr^2/η? Here we can draw upon a notion that I used to understand "explanation by constraint" in part I: that one stratum of natural laws may "transcend" another. A law of the higher stratum is explanatorily independent of the laws belonging to the lower even if it can be deduced from them alone. For the dimensional argument to explain why v is proportional to gr^2/η, the fact that k does not need to join ρ_s, ρ_f, r, g, and η in forming a quantity that stands in a dimensionally homogeneous relation to v must help to explain why v is proportional to gr^2/η. How could this be? Notice that whatever the value of k such that $F = kma$, its value is the same for all three component forces acting on the sphere. Hence, its value does not affect the conditions under which those forces are balanced (i.e., add vectorially to zero), which is the condition with which the explanandum is concerned. In that condition, no force is unbalanced, so no force is producing acceleration, so the rate of exchange between force and ma does not matter. Thus, the explanandum is a matter of *statics*, not of *dynamics*. The fact that k does not need to join ρ_s, ρ_f, r, g, and η in forming a quantity that stands in a dimensionally homogeneous relation to v is one aspect of such a relation's also being a matter of statics, not dynamics. Now if statics *transcends* dynamics, then any law of statics must be explained exclusively in statical terms, not as a special case of a dynamical law. A dynamical quantity (such as k) and a dynamical law (such as Newton's second law) can have no place in the explanation of a law of statics; it is independent of them. If statics transcends dynamics, then since v's proportionality to gr^2/η is a matter of statics, its explainers' modal status as also transcending dynamics helps to explain it; to appeal to any modally weaker premises would mischaracterize the explanandum's status, treating it as more contingent than it is. Part of what explains it, then, is that some other relation not only obtains, but also is a matter of statics.

In chapter 1, I suggested that a "constraint" is a law that transcends the ordinary laws of nature by having greater necessity than they. I suggested that mathematical truths constrain the laws of nature and that Newton's second law of motion constrains the force laws. For the dimensional argument to explain why v is proportional to gr^2/η, the laws of statics must constrain such dynamical laws as Newton's second law of motion. In chapter 2, I tried to unpack this notion of one stratum of law's "transcending" or "constraining" another. In chapter 4, I discussed another example of a law that has sometimes been regarded as statical and therefore transcending dynamics: the law of the parallelogram of forces. If the parallelogram law is a law of statics, then if statics transcends dynamics, the parallelogram law cannot have a dynamical explanation; Newton's second law of motion cannot help to explain it. My aim in chapter 4 was not to argue that statics does in fact transcend dynamics—and my aim here is not to argue that the dimensional argument explains why v is proportional to gr^2/η. Rather, my concern has been to understand what it would be for statics to transcend dynamics and what difference its transcendence would make to scientific explanations. My point in connection with the dimensional derivation of v's proportionality to gr^2/η is merely that in taking four dimensions (L, T, M, and F) rather than three as fundamental, the dimensional derivation acquires a stronger premise (namely, a premise entailing that k does not need to join ρ_s, ρ_f, r, g, and η in forming a quantity that stands in a dimensionally homogeneous relation to v). This premise helps (when statics transcends dynamics) to explain why v is proportional to gr^2/η.

This strengthening of a dimensional argument's premise by adding dimensions is crucial to resolving a venerable dispute. In an early discussion of dimensional methods, Rayleigh (1915a) considered the rate at which heat passes from a hot wire to a cooler stream of air passing across it—or, idealizing and generalizing, the rate h of heat loss by a rigid body of infinite conductivity that presents a linear dimension a to an ideal (i.e., incompressible, inviscid) fluid flowing at speed v around it, where the body's temperature is kept constant and exceeds the fluid's initial temperature (i.e., far upstream from the body) by θ. Let c be the fluid's specific heat per unit volume (i.e., the heat needed to raise the temperature of a unit volume of fluid by one degree) and let κ be the fluid's thermal conductivity (i.e., the rate of heat flow through a unit thickness of the fluid per unit area and unit temperature difference). Rayleigh used dimensional analysis to derive an expression for h, though I suggest that we view him as giving a dimensional explanation of that expression. His proposed explanans is that h stands in a dimensionally homogeneous relation to some subset of a, v, θ, c, and κ, where the fundamental dimensions are L, T, Θ (temperature), and Q (heat). If h is to have the same dimensions as $a^{\alpha} v^{\beta} \theta^{\gamma} c^{\delta} \kappa^{\varepsilon}$, then our table is

	h	a	v	θ	c	κ
L	0	1	1	0	-3	-1
T	-1	0	-1	0	0	-1
Θ	0	0	0	1	-1	-1
Q	1	0	0	0	1	1

Thus (Rayleigh argued) we have these four simultaneous equations with five unknowns:

From L: $0 = \alpha + \beta - 3\delta - \varepsilon$

From T: $-1 = -\beta - \varepsilon$

From Θ: $0 = \gamma - \delta - \varepsilon$

From Q: $1 = \delta + \varepsilon$

yielding $\alpha = \beta + 1$, $\gamma = 1$, $\delta = \beta$, and $\varepsilon = 1 - \beta$. Therefore, h has the same dimensions as $a^{\beta+1} v^{\beta} \theta c^{\beta} \kappa^{1-\beta}$, that is, as $(avc/\kappa)^{\beta} a\theta\kappa$, and so $h = a\theta\kappa \, f(avc/\kappa)$ for some unknown function f. Apparently, we have thereby explained why the rate of heat loss is proportional to the temperature difference, why it is the same in cases involving different values of v and c but where vc is the same, and so forth.

However, in an economical three-sentence reply, Riabouchinsky (1915) noted that temperature and heat have the same dimensions as energy, so that we really have here only three fundamental dimensions, not four. (The average kinetic energy of random motion per molecule is related to temperature by Boltzmann's constant, equal to about 1.38×10^{-16} ergs/degree Kelvin, and the rate of exchange between heat and energy units is given by the mechanical equivalent of heat, equal to 4.184 Joules/calorie.) We thus have one fewer equation, but the same number of unknowns, so dimensional analysis yields less information—merely that $h = a\theta\kappa \, F(v/\kappa a^2, ca^3)$, for some unknown function F. This dimensional argument cannot explain why heat loss is the same in cases where vc is the same, for instance. Rayleigh (1915b) replied uncertainly:

> The question raised by Dr. Riabouchinsky belongs rather to the logic than to the use of the principle of similitude, with which I was mainly concerned. It would be well worthy of further discussion. The conclusion that I gave follows on the basis of the usual Fourier equations for conduction of heat, in which heat and temperature are regarded as *sui generis*. It would indeed be a paradox if the further knowledge of the nature of heat afforded by molecular theory put us in a worse position than before in dealing with a particular problem. The solution would seem to be

that the Fourier equations embody something as to the nature of heat and temperature which is ignored in the alternative argument of Dr. Riabouchinsky.

Commentators have generally been hard on Rayleigh. (Bridgman 1931, 11, for example, says that Rayleigh's reply "is, I think, likely to leave us cold.") However, Rayleigh is essentially correct. His dimensional argument (whether used as prediction or explanation) takes as a premise that the target equation for h is dimensionally homogeneous *using L, T, Θ, and Q as fundamental dimensions*, just as in the case of the sphere falling through the viscous fluid, the explanans was that v stands in a relation to ρ_s, ρ_f, r, g, and η that is dimensionally homogeneous using L, M, T, and F as fundamental dimensions. This is indeed further information beyond the fact that the target equation for h is dimensionally homogeneous using L, M, and T (or equivalently L, T, and energy). This is not a case where more information puts us in a worse position than before. Rather, more information puts us in a better position than before.

In the putative dimensional explanation of the derivative law governing the falling sphere's terminal velocity, the explanans includes the fact that if there is a dimensional constant k, it does not need to supplement ρ_s, ρ_f, r, g, and η in forming a quantity that stands in a dimensionally homogeneous relation to v. In other words, the explanans includes the fact that v's relation to these other quantities is independent of the constant of proportionality between force and ma. Likewise, in Rayleigh's dimensional explanation of the heat-flow equation, the explanans includes the fact that h's relation to a, v, θ, c, and κ is independent of Boltzmann's constant and the mechanical equivalent of heat. In the falling-sphere case, the dimensional argument is explanatory if statics transcends dynamics, since in that event, the fact that no constant of proportionality between force and acceleration appears in a given relation helps to make that relation statical and hence a constraint on dynamics, and its status as a constraint can help to explain why another law of statics holds. The law governing the sphere's terminal velocity is a law of statics since no force is producing an acceleration when the sphere has reached its terminal velocity. Likewise, in the heat-flow case, if Rayleigh's dimensional argument is explanatory, then the rate of exchange between heat and energy, or between temperature and random molecular kinetic energy, is explanatorily irrelevant to the law regarding the hot wire's heat loss because no thermal energy is being converted into mechanical energy (or any other sort of energy) or vice versa. For example, the fluid is not being called upon to do work (e.g., by pushing against a piston) and no internal molecular energy is being transformed into thermal energy. The thermal energy of the rigid wire is simply contributing to the fluid's thermal energy.[28] Suppose thermodynamics transcends any laws concerning the other forms of energy into which heat can be transformed (so that as far as thermodynamics is concerned, heat might just as well be a subtle fluid as random molecular motion). Then the fact that nothing like Boltzmann's constant or the mechanical equivalent of heat figures in a given relation helps to make that relation thermodynamical and hence a constraint. Its status as a constraint can help to explain why there obtains another thermodynamical law, such as the law regarding the hot wire's heat loss. Insofar as the wire's heat loss is a purely thermodynamic process, the laws governing it must be ·explained purely thermodynamically (if thermodynamics transcends the laws governing the behavior of the molecules whose motion constitutes heat), since otherwise the putative explanation will mischaracterize the explanandum as more contingent than it actually is.

In chapter 3, I discussed the sense in which thermodynamics has sometimes been regarded as a "principle theory" imposing top-down constraints on other laws, as well as the difference that this status would make to thermodynamics' explanatory role. I argued that explanations that proceed from the top down are non-causal explanations.

In what I believe he intends to be an allusion to the Rayleigh-Riabouchinsky exchange, Bridgman writes regarding dimensional reasoning: "how [shall we] choose the list of physical quantities between which we are to search for a relation[?] We have seen that it does not do to merely ask ourselves 'Does the result depend on this or that physical quantity?' for we have seen in one problem that although the result certainly does 'depend' on the action of the atomic forces, yet we do not have to consider the atomic forces in our analysis, and they do not enter the functional relation" (1931, 49–50). Here Bridgman appears to distinguish dimensional analysis from scientific explanation (which traces what a result "depends" on). By contrast, I regard dimensional analysis as sometimes supplying explanations of derivative laws. A derivation of the complete heat-flow equation invokes the molecular nature of heat. However, the heat-flow equation (up to the unspecified function $f(avc/\kappa)$) can be derived dimensionally. The equation considers heat flow purely at a phenomenological level (e.g., in employing c and κ, which are properties of bulk matter), and (as Sedov 1959, 42, emphasizes) no thermal energy is converted into other forms of energy or vice versa (since the fluid is ideal). Therefore, it is not evident that all aspects of the equation actually "depend" (as Bridgman puts it) on the molecular nature of heat. In fact, its independence from the molecular nature of heat is part of what explains some aspects of the equation, if the dimensional argument is explanatory.

Explanation in Mathematics

7

Aspects of Mathematical Explanation
Symmetry, Salience, and Simplicity

7.1 INTRODUCTION TO PROOFS THAT EXPLAIN WHY MATHEMATICAL THEOREMS HOLD

We now enter part III (chapters 7, 8, and 9), where our attention turns from non-causal explanation in science to explanation in mathematics ("mathematical explanations").

Compared to scientific explanation, with which philosophy has been seriously engaged since at least 1948, mathematical explanation has been little explored by philosophers. Its neglect is remarkable. Mathematical proofs that explain why some theorem holds were distinguished by ancient Greek mathematicians from proofs that merely show that some theorem holds (Harari 2008), and this distinction has been invoked in various ways throughout the history of mathematics. Fortunately, mathematical explanation has now begun to receive greater philosophical attention. I agree with Mancosu (2008, 134) that the topic's "recent revival in the analytic literature is a welcome addition to the philosophy of mathematics."[1]

One reason that mathematical explanation has received relatively scant philosophical attention may be the temptation among philosophers to believe that when mathematicians apparently characterize some proof as explanatory, they are merely gesturing toward an aesthetically attractive quality that the proof possesses (such as elegance or beauty)—a quality that seems to be very much in the eye of the beholder (like a proof's being interesting, understandable, surprising, pleasing, or witty). However, no such suspicion is seriously entertained with regard to *scientific* explanation, and we should demand some reason why mathematical explanation deserves to be regarded differently. Of course, some aspects of explanation (whether in science or math) may well depend on the audience. Philosophers have generally come to accept that in science, one fact may explain another only in a given context—that is, only in light of the audience's interests, which help to make certain facts salient and certain styles of argument relevant. But the interest-relativity of scientific explanation does not mean that "anything goes": that an explanation in a given context is whatever strikes the given audience as explanatory or just whatever facts or arguments are of interest to them.[2] Presumably, the same applies to explanation in mathematics.

A key issue in the philosophical study of scientific explanation is the source of explanatory asymmetry: why does one fact explain another rather than vice versa? Many philosophers have argued that in science, explanatory priority is often grounded in causal priority: causes explain their effects, not the reverse. By contrast, in mathematical explanations consisting of proofs, the source of explanatory priority cannot be causal priority. Rather, at least part of its source would seem to be that axioms explain theorems, not vice versa. Of course, there may be several different ways to axiomatize a given branch of mathematics. Perhaps only some of these axiomatizations are correct for explanatory purposes. Or perhaps any axiomatization is equally good for explanatory purposes, but a proof's status as explanatory is relative to a given axiomatization.

I will be concerned with a logically prior issue. By means of many examples drawn from mathematical practice, I will argue that two mathematical proofs may prove the same theorem from the same axioms, yet only one of these proofs is explanatory. My goal in this chapter and the two that follow will be to identify the ground of this distinction. Accordingly, my focus will be on the course that a given proof takes *between* its premises and its conclusion. The distinction between explanatory and non-explanatory proofs from the same premises must rest on differences in *the way* they extract the theorem from the axioms.

In addition, for a theorem of the form "All *F*'s are *G*," I will argue that the distinction between explanatory and non-explanatory proofs rests on differences between proofs in their ways of extracting the property of being *G* from the property of being *F*. A proof's explanatory power depends on the theorem being expressed in terms of a "setup" or "problem" (involving *F*'s instantiation)—such as the "problem" of Zeitz's coin (discussed in the following section)—and in terms of a "result" or "answer" (*G*'s instantiation). Furthermore, as I will also argue, the manner in which a theorem is expressed may call attention to a particular feature of the theorem, where that feature's salience helps to determine what a proof must do in order to explain why the theorem holds.

In section 7.2, I will focus on two proofs of the same theorem: one explanatory and the other not (as judged by a working mathematician). In section 7.3, I will try to spell out the difference between these proofs that is responsible for their difference in explanatory power. I will suggest that one proof is explanatory because it exploits a symmetry in the problem—a symmetry of the same kind as the symmetry that we initially found striking in the result being explained. In sections 7.4 and 7.5, I will present several other, diverse examples where different proofs of the same theorem have been recognized as differing in explanatory power. I will suggest that in each case, this difference arises from a difference in whether or not the proofs exploit a symmetry in the problem that is like a salient symmetry in the result being explained. In addition, these cases will illustrate how "brute-force" proofs fail to explain, when the theorem being explained exhibits a striking symmetry, and also why some auxiliary constructions but not others are "artificial." In section 7.6, I will generalize my proposal to explanations that do not exploit symmetries. (Many additional examples of this kind will be given in chapters 8 and 9.) I will argue that in many cases, what it means in mathematics to ask for a proof that explains is to ask for a proof that exploits a certain kind of feature in the problem: the same kind of feature that is outstanding in the result. The distinction between proofs that *explain why* some theorem is true and proofs that merely *show that* the theorem is true arises only when some feature of the result is salient. A proof explains by revealing just where in the setup the result's salient feature comes from. I will devote chapters 8 and 9 to elaborating this account.

Although my concern throughout part III will be the distinction between explanatory and non-explanatory *proofs* in mathematics, I do not contend that *all* mathematical explanations consist of proofs. Indeed, in section 7.4, I will give some examples of mathematical explanations that are not proofs. (I will return to one of these varieties of explanation in section 9.6.) In addition, although my main concern will be the explanation of mathematical theorems, I do not contend that theorems are the only targets of mathematical explanations. In section 7.7, I will give some examples of what else besides a theorem might be explained in mathematics.[3]

I will be paying close attention to various examples of explanatory and non-explanatory proofs. Proposed accounts of *scientific* explanation have long been tested against certain canonical examples. Various arguments from the history of science are paradigmatically explanatory, such as Darwin's explanations of various facts of biogeography and comparative anatomy, Wegener's explanation of the correspondence between the South American and African coastlines, and Einstein's explanation of the equality of inertial and gravitational mass. Any promising comprehensive theory of scientific explanation must deem these arguments to be genuinely explanatory (as far as science now knows). By the same token, there is widespread agreement that various other arguments are not explanatory—examples so standard that I need only give their familiar monikers, such as "the flagpole," "the eclipse," "the barometer," and "the hexed salt" (Salmon 1989, 46–50). Although there are some controversial cases, of course (such as "explanations" of the dormitive-virtue variety), philosophers who defend rival accounts of scientific explanation nevertheless largely agree on the phenomena that they are trying to save.

Alas, the same cannot be said when it comes to philosophical work on explanation in mathematics. The philosophical literature contains few, if any, canonical examples of mathematical explanation (or non-explanation) drawn from mathematical practice. Accordingly, I will try to supply some promising candidates—especially examples where the mathematics is very simple and the explanatory power (or impotence) of the proofs is easily appreciated. I will be particularly interested in examples that mathematicians themselves have characterized as explanatory (or not). In this way, I will be joining others (such as Hafner and Mancosu 2005 and Tappenden 2005) who have recently offered examples to show that explanation is an important element of mathematical practice.[4]

As I will show, mathematicians have often distinguished proofs that explain why some theorem holds from proofs that merely show that it holds. For instance, in the *Port-Royal Logic* of 1662, Pierre Nicole and Antoine Arnauld characterized indirect proof (that is, proof of p by showing that $\sim p$ implies a contradiction) as "useful" but non-explanatory: "such Demonstrations constrain us indeed to give our Consent, but no way clear our Understandings, which ought to be the principal End of Sciences: For our Understanding is not satisfied if it does not know not only that a thing is, but why it is? which cannot be obtain'd by a Demonstration reducing to Impossibility" (Nicole and Arnauld 1717, 422; pt. 4, chap. 9). Nicole and Arnauld obviously took explanation—"diving into the true reason of things" (427)—to be as important in mathematics as it is in science. I will argue that they are correct (though I do not agree with them, and perhaps Lipton, 2009a, 49, that indirect proofs cannot ever explain). More recently, the mathematician William Byers (2007, 337) has characterized a "good" proof as "one that brings out clearly the reason why the result is valid." Likewise, empirical researchers on mathematics education have recently argued that students who have proved and are convinced of a mathematical result often still want to know why the result is true (Mudaly and de Villiers 2000), that students assess alternative proofs for their "explanatory power" (Healy and Hoyles 2000, 399), and that students expect a "good" proof "to convey an insight into *why* the proposition is true" even though explanatory power "does not affect the *validity* of a proof" (Bell 1976, 24).[5] However, none of this work investigates what it is that *makes* certain proofs but not others explanatory. This question will be my focus in part III.

■ 7.2 ZEITZ'S BIASED COIN: A SUGGESTIVE EXAMPLE OF MATHEMATICAL EXPLANATION

Consider this problem:[6]

> A number p between 0 and 1 is generated randomly so that there is an equal chance of the generated number's falling within any two intervals of the same size inside $[0,1]$. Next a biased coin is built so that p is its chance of landing heads. The coin is then flipped 2000 times. What is the chance of getting exactly 1000 heads?

As you consider this problem, your thoughts might run along the following lines. If p turns out to be very close to 1, then a sequence with a vast majority of heads is likely—and analogously for a tails-rich sequence if p is very close to 0. If p takes on any of these extreme values, the chance of getting exactly 1000 heads on 2000 tosses will be very small indeed. But an extreme p is not the only possibility; p is being generated at random—and the same value of p is operating for all 2000 tosses. So p may well take on some middling value, in which case the resulting sequence is likely to be at least roughly evenly balanced between heads and tails—and perhaps it will even be perfectly balanced, with 1000 heads out of 2000 tosses. How do the various chances of getting 1000 heads, for various possible biases p, together with the chances of the coin's having various sorts of possible biases p, all combine so as to yield the overall chance of getting exactly 1000 heads? There are 2001 possible outcomes: from 0 heads to 2000 heads. Does 1000 heads being right in the middle of this range end up counting in its favor or against it? Paul Zeitz (a mathematician at the University of San Francisco) gives the answer: "The amazing answer is that the probability [of 1000 heads in 2000 tosses] is 1/2001. Indeed, it doesn't matter how many heads we wish to see—for any [integer r] between 0 and 2000, the probability that r heads occur [in 2000 tosses] is 1/2001" (Zeitz 2000, 2). That is, each of the 2001 possible outcomes has the same probability (which must then be 1/2001). That is remarkable. It prompts us to ask, "Why is that?" (There is nothing special about 2000 tosses; the analogous result holds for any number n of tosses.)

Here is an elaboration of one proof that Zeitz sketches. (I give all of the gory details, but you may safely skim over them, if you wish.)

If you flip a coin n times, where p is the chance of getting a head on any single flip, then the chance of getting a *particular* sequence of r heads and $(n-r)$ tails is $p^r(1-p)^{n-r}$. Now let's consider all of the sequences with exactly r heads. There are

$$\binom{n}{r} = \frac{n!}{r!(n-r)!}$$

different ways of arranging r heads and $(n-r)$ tails. So the chance of getting exactly r heads is $\binom{n}{r}p^r(1-p)^{n-r}$. This is the chance for a given value p of the coin's bias. But the coin's bias can assume any value from 0 to 1, so to arrive at the total chance of getting exactly r heads, we must take into account the chance of getting exactly r heads for each possible value of the coin's bias. The total chance of getting exactly r heads is the sum, taken over all possible biases p for the coin (ranging from 0 to 1), of the chance of getting r heads if the coin's bias is p, multiplied by the chance dp that p is the coin's bias. This sum is an integral:

$$\int_0^1 \binom{n}{r}p^r(1-p)^{n-r}\,dp = \binom{n}{r}\int_0^1 p^r(1-p)^{n-r}\,dp.$$

The easiest way to tackle this integral is to use the textbook technique of "integration by parts," according to which $\int u\,dv = uv - \int v\,du$. To apply this formula, we express $\int p^r(1-p)^{n-r}\,dp$ in the form $\int u\,dv$ by letting $u = (1-p)^{n-r}$ and $dv = p^r\,dp$. It follows by routine differentiation of u that $du = -(n-r)(1-p)^{n-r-1}\,dp$, and it likewise follows from routine antidifferentiation of dv that $v = \dfrac{p^{r+1}}{r+1}$. Plugging all of this into the formula for integration by parts, we find

$$\int_0^1 p^r (1-p)^{n-r}\, dp = (1-p)^{n-r}\, \frac{p^{r+1}}{r+1}\Bigg|_0^1 + \frac{n-r}{r+1}\int_0^1 p^{r+1}(1-p)^{n-r-1}\, dp.$$

The first term on the right side equals zero at both $p = 0$ and $p = 1$, so that term disappears. We can leave behind to be gathered later the coefficient $\dfrac{n-r}{r+1}$ preceding the integral in the second term on the right side. As for that integral, it takes the same form as the integral on the left side—merely with the first exponent increased by 1 and the second exponent decreased by 1. So we can apply integration by parts in the same way to this integral, yielding the same increase and decrease (respectively) by 1 in the two exponents:

$$\int_0^1 p^{r+1}(1-p)^{n-r-1}\, dp = \frac{n-r-1}{r+2}\int_0^1 p^{r+2}(1-p)^{n-r-2}\, dp.$$

Again leaving behind the coefficient $\dfrac{n-r-1}{r+2}$ on the right side to be gathered later, we can repeatedly integrate by parts until $(1-p)$'s exponent eventually decreases to 0. The remaining integral is much simpler to solve than its predecessors:

$$\int_0^1 p^n (1-p)^0\, dp = \int_0^1 p^n dp = \frac{p^{n+1}}{n+1}\Bigg|_0^1 = \frac{1}{n+1}.$$

Having finally gotten rid of all of the integrals, we can go back and gather the various coefficients we left behind that were produced by each of the preceding integrations by parts:

$$\int_0^1 p^r (1-p)^{n-r}\, dp = \left(\frac{n-r}{r+1}\right)\left(\frac{n-r-1}{r+2}\right)\ldots\left(\frac{1}{n}\right)\left(\frac{1}{n+1}\right)$$

$$= \left(\frac{1}{n+1}\right)\frac{1}{\dfrac{n(n-1)(n-2)\ldots(r+2)(r+1)}{(n-r)(n-r-1)\ldots(2)}} = \left(\frac{1}{n+1}\right)\frac{1}{\dbinom{n}{n-r}}.$$

This result times $\dbinom{n}{r}$—the coefficient of the first integral that we tackled by parts—is the total chance of getting exactly r heads in our problem. But $\dbinom{n}{n-r} = \dbinom{n}{r}$ since the number of different arrangements of exactly $(n - r)$ tails in n coin tosses equals the number of different arrangements of exactly r heads in n tosses. So the total chance of getting exactly r heads in our problem (with

$$n = 2000) \text{ is } \binom{n}{r}\left(\frac{1}{n+1}\right)\frac{1}{\binom{n}{n-r}} = \left(\frac{1}{n+1}\right) \text{—the result we sought.}[7]$$

Although this proof succeeds, Zeitz (2000, 2–4) says that it "shed[s] no real light on *why* the answer is what it is. . . . [It] magically produced the value $\left(\frac{1}{n+1}\right)$." Although Zeitz does not spell out this reaction any further, I think we can readily sympathize with it. This proof makes it seem like an accident of algebra, as it were, that everything cancels out so nicely in the end, leaving us with just $\frac{1}{n+1}$.

Of course, nothing in math is genuinely accidental; the result is mathematically necessary. Nevertheless, until the very end, nothing in the proof suggested that every possible outcome (for a given n) would receive the same chance.[8] The result simply turns out to be independent of r, and this fact remains at least as remarkable after we have seen the above proof as it was before. (Indeed, it becomes even more remarkable when we observe that the independence from r seems to come out of nowhere in this proof.) I think that many of us would be inclined to suspect that there is some *reason why* the chance is the same for every possible outcome (given n)—a reason that eludes the above proof. (Notice how natural it becomes in this context to talk of a "reason why" the result holds.)

Zeitz (2000, 5) says that in contrast to the foregoing argument, the following argument allows us to "understand *why* the coin problem had the answer that it did":

> Think of the outcomes of the n coin tosses as dictated by n further numbers generated by the *same* random-number generator that generated the coin's chance p of landing heads: a number less than p corresponds to a head, and a number greater than p corresponds to a tail. (The chance that the number will be less than p is obviously p—the chance of a head.) Thus, the same generator generates $n + 1$ numbers in total. The outcomes are all heads if the first number generated (p) is larger than each of the n subsequent numbers, all but one of the outcomes are heads if the first number generated is larger than all but one of the n subsequent numbers, and so forth. Obviously, if we were to rank the $n + 1$ generated numbers from smallest to largest, then the first generated number (p) has the same chance of being ranked first as it has of being ranked second, and likewise for any other position. Hence, every possibility (from 0 heads to n heads) is equally likely, so each has chance $\frac{1}{n+1}$.

In light of this proof, Zeitz (2000, 5) concludes that the result "is not unexpected, magical algebra. It is just simple, almost inevitable symmetry." I agree: this proof explains why every possible outcome has the same chance (and, therefore, why each possible outcome's chance is $\frac{1}{n+1}$). The proof explains this symmetry in the possible outcomes (namely, that each has the same chance) by showing how it arises not from an algebraic miracle, but rather from a symmetry in the setup, namely, that when the $n + 1$ generated numbers (from the same random-number generator) are listed from smallest to largest, each possible position on the list is equally likely to be occupied by the first number that was generated.[9] A symmetry in the setup accounts for the same symmetry in the possible outcomes.

The argument that the first proof is non-explanatory is worth comparing to an objection I presented (in section 4.2) to the power of a dynamical argument to explain the law of the parallelogram of forces. The objection was that because the dynamical argument derives the parallelogram law from Newton's second law of motion, the dynamical argument must portray it as an "algebraic miracle" that the mass m cancels out in the course of the derivation—which seems implausible. (On Poisson's view, by contrast, the reason why mass is absent from the force composition law is because the law is actually explained purely by statics and so mass does not figure anywhere in its explanation.) In the case of Zeitz's coin as well as in the dynamical derivation of the parallelogram law, the fact that a given property of the setup (the number of heads r and the mass m, respectively) fails to figure in the explanandum (the outcome's likelihood and the composition law, respectively) may reasonably make us suspect that a derivation in which the property plays a large role, only to disappear fortuitously in the end, must be missing something important about why the explanandum holds. A derivation that explains why it holds would then dig into the setup, uncovering there the origin of the result's independence from the given property, rather than portraying its independence as arising "miraculously" in the course of the theorem's derivation.

In short, our curiosity was initially aroused by the symmetry of the result: that, remarkably, every possible outcome has the same chance. The first proof did not satisfy us because it failed to exploit any such symmetry in the set up; it derived the result "magically." We suspected that there was a reason for the result—a hidden "evenness" in the setup that is responsible for the same "evenness" in the result. The second proof revealed the setup's hidden symmetry and thereby explained the result.

The difference in explanatory power between these two proofs is a nice example of the phenomenon that I will be examining in this chapter and the rest of part III.

■ 7.3 EXPLANATION BY SYMMETRY

The example of Zeitz's biased coin is instructive in several ways. To begin with, it involves a mathematician explicitly distinguishing a proof that explains from a proof that does not. Moreover, because this case is relatively simple and vivid, we nonmathematicians can readily feel the motivation behind his distinction. Finally, this case suggests the following proposal, for which I will argue.

Oftentimes, a mathematical result that exhibits some striking symmetry is explained by a proof showing how it follows from a similar symmetry in the problem. Each of these symmetries consists of some sort of invariance under a given transformation; the same transformation is involved in both symmetries. For instance, in the above example, both symmetries involve invariance under a switch from one possible outcome (e.g., 1000 heads and 1000 tails) to any other (e.g., 999 heads and 1001 tails). In such a case, what makes a proof that appeals to an underlying symmetry in the setup count as "explanatory"—in contrast to other proofs of the same result? Nothing beyond the fact that the result's symmetry was what drew our attention in the first place.

For instance, in the example of Zeitz's coin, had the result been some complicated, unremarkable function of n and r, then the question "Why is *that* the chance?" would probably have amounted to nothing more than a request for a proof. One proof might have been shorter, less technical, more pleasing or accessible to some audience, more elegant in some respect, or more fully spelled out than some other proof. But any proof would have counted as answering the question. There would have been no distinction between a proof that explains the result and a proof that merely proves it.

However, the result's symmetry immediately struck us, and it was made even more salient by the first proof that I gave, since in that proof, the solution's symmetry emerged "magically" from out of the fog of algebra. Its origin was now especially puzzling. The symmetry, once having become salient, prompts the demand for an explanation: a proof that traces the result back to a similar symmetry in the problem. In light of the symmetry's salience, there is a point in asking for an explanation over and above a proof. A proof that exploits the setup's symmetry is privileged as explanatory because the result's symmetry is especially striking. Zeitz's second proof explains by revealing where in the setup the result's symmetry comes from.

My proposal predicts that mathematical practice contains many other examples where an explanation of some result is distinguished from a mere proof of it only in view of the result's exhibiting a puzzling symmetry—and where only a proof exploiting such a symmetry in the problem is recognized as explaining why the solution holds. I will present several further examples of this phenomenon in the next two sections.

■ 7.4 A THEOREM EXPLAINED BY A SYMMETRY IN THE UNIT IMAGINARY NUMBER

Consider this theorem (first proved by d'Alembert in 1746):

If the complex number $z = a + bi$ (where a and b are real) is a solution to $z^n + a_{n-1}z^{n-1} + \cdots + a_0 = 0$ (where the a_i are real), then z's "complex conjugate" $\bar{z} = a - bi$ is also a solution.

Why is that? Why do the solutions come in these complex-conjugate pairs?

We can prove this theorem directly by evaluating $\overline{z}^n + a_{n-1}\overline{z}^{n-1} + \cdots + a_0$. First, we show by calculation that $\overline{z}\,\overline{w} = \overline{zw}$:

Let $z = a+bi$ and $w = c+di$. Then $\overline{z}\,\overline{w} = (a-bi)(c-di) = ac-bd+i(-bc-ad) =$

$ac-bd-i(bc+ad) = \overline{ac-bd+i(bc+ad)} = \overline{(a+bi)(c+di)} = \overline{zw}.$

Hence, $\overline{z}^2 = \overline{z}\,\overline{z} = \overline{zz} = \overline{z^2}$, and likewise for all other powers. Therefore, $\overline{z}^n + a_{n-1}\overline{z}^{n-1} + \cdots + a_0 = \overline{z^n + a_{n-1}z^{n-1} + \cdots + a_0}$. Now we show by calculation that $\overline{z} + \overline{w} = \overline{z+w}$:

Let $z = a+bi$ and $w = c+di$. Then $\overline{z} + \overline{w} = (a-bi) + (c-di) = a+c+i(-b-d)$

$= a+c-i(b+d) = \overline{a+bi+c+di} = \overline{z+w}.$

Thus, $\overline{z}^n + a_{n-1}\overline{z}^{n-1} + \cdots + a_0 = \overline{z^n + a_{n-1}z^{n-1} + \cdots + a_0}$, which equals $\overline{0}$ and hence 0 if z is a solution to the original equation.

Although this proof shows d'Alembert's theorem to be true, it pursues what mathematicians call a "brute-force" approach. That is, it doggedly calculates everything directly, plugging in everything we know and then grinding out the result. The striking feature of d'Alembert's theorem is that the equation's nonreal solutions all come in pairs where one member of the pair can be transformed into the other by the replacement of i with $-i$. Why does exchanging i for $-i$ in a solution still leave us with a solution? This symmetry just works out that way ("magically") in the above proof. But we are inclined to suspect that there is some reason for it. In other words, the symmetry in d'Alembert's theorem puzzles us, and in asking for the theorem's "explanation," we are seeking a proof of the theorem from some similar symmetry in the original problem—that is, a proof that exploits the setup's invariance under the replacement of i with $-i$.

The sought-after explanation is that $-i$ could play exactly the same roles in the axioms of complex arithmetic as i plays. Each has the same definition: each is exhaustively captured as being such that its square equals -1. There is nothing more to i (and to $-i$) than that characterization. Of course, i and $-i$ are not equal; each is the negative of the other. But neither is intrinsically "positive," for instance, since neither is greater than (or less than) zero. They are distinct, but they are no different in their relations to the real numbers. Whatever the axioms of complex arithmetic say about one can also be truly said about the other. Since the axioms remain true under the replacement of i with $-i$, so must the theorems—for example, any fact about the roots of a polynomial with real coefficients. (The coefficients must be real so that the transformation of i into $-i$ leaves the polynomial unchanged.) The symmetry expressed by d'Alembert's theorem is thus grounded in the same symmetry in the axioms. Feynman captures the explanation in his characteristically pungent style:

> Let us suppose that a specific solution of $x^2 = -1$ is called something, we shall call it i; i has the property, by definition, that its square is -1. That is about all we are going to say about it; of course, there is more than one root of the equation $x^2 = -1$. Someone could write i, but another could say, "No, I prefer $-i$. My i is minus your i." It *is* just as good a solution, and since the only definition that i has is that $i^2 = -1$, it must be true that any equation we can write is equally true if the sign of i is changed everywhere. This is called taking the *complex conjugate*. (Feynman et al. 1963, vol. 1, 22-7)

Here we have another example where a proof is privileged as explanatory because it exploits a symmetry in the problem—a symmetry of the same kind as initially struck us in the fact being explained. Furthermore, this is a good example with which to combat the impression that a proof's being explanatory is no more objective (no less "in the eye of the beholder") than a proof's being understandable, being of interest, or being sufficiently spelled out. Mathematicians largely agree on whether or not a proof is aptly characterized as "brute force," and I suggest that in cases where there is a striking symmetry in the fact being explained, no "brute-force" proof is explanatory. A brute-force approach is not selective; it sets aside no features of the problem as irrelevant. Rather, it just "ploughs ahead" like a "bulldozer" (Atiyah 1988, 215), plugging everything in and calculating everything out. (The entire polynomial, not just some piece or feature of it, was used in the first proof above.) In contrast, an explanation must be selective; it must pick out a particular feature of the setup and deem it responsible for (and other features irrelevant to) the result being explained. (Shortly I will give another example in which a brute-force proof is explanatorily impotent. I presented a similar idea in sections 6.2 and 6.3, where a dimensional argument that selects the relevant features of the fundamental laws is contrasted with a brute-force derivation of the derivative law being explained.) Mathematicians commonly say that a brute-force solution supplies "little understanding" and fails to show "what's going on" (e.g., Levi 2009, 29–30).

Suppose I had begun not with d'Alembert's theorem, but instead merely with some particular instances of it (as d'Alembert might have done). The solutions of $z^3 + 6z - 20 = 0$ are 2, $-1+3i$, and $-1-3i$. The solutions of $z^2 - 2z + 2 = 0$ are $1 - i$ and $1 + i$. In both examples, the solutions that are not real numbers are pairs of complex conjugates. Having found many examples like these, one might ask: Why is it that in all of the cases I have examined of polynomials with real coefficients, their nonreal roots all fall into complex-conjugate pairs? Is it a coincidence, or are they all like that? One possible answer to this why question is that they are not all like that; I have simply gotten lucky by having examined an unrepresentative sample of cases. Another possible answer is that my examples were unrepresentative in some systematic way: not all polynomials (with exclusively real coefficients) have their nonreal solutions coming in complex-conjugate pairs, but all polynomials of a certain kind (e.g., with powers less than 4) are like that, and as it happened, all of the polynomials I examined were of that kind. In fact, as I have shown, d'Alembert's theorem is the explanation; any polynomial with exclusively real coefficients has all of its nonreal roots coming in complex-conjugate pairs. Here we have a mathematical explanation that consists not of a proof, but merely of a theorem.

However, it is not the case that just any broader mathematical theorem at all that subsumes the examples to be explained would suffice to account for them. After all, I could have subsumed my two examples under this gerrymandered theorem: For any equilateral triangle or equation that is either $z^3 + 6z - 20 = 0$ or $z^2 - 2z + 2 = 0$ (the two examples above), either the triangle is equiangular or the equation's nonreal solutions all form complex-conjugate pairs. This theorem does not explain why the two equations have the given feature. (Neither does a theorem covering only these two equations.) Plausibly, whether a theorem can be used to explain its instances depends on whether that theorem itself has a certain kind of explanation. I will pursue this thought in section 9.6. For now, my concern is with *proofs* that explain why theorems hold, not with *theorems* that explains why their instances hold.[10]

Here is another example of a proof that is widely respected as possessing explanatory power because it derives a result exhibiting a salient symmetry from a similar symmetry in the setup.[11] It had been well known before Lagrange that a cubic equation of the form $x^3 + nx + p = 0$, once transformed by $x = y - n/3y$, becomes a sixth-degree equation $y^6 + py^3 + n^3/27 = 0$ (the "resolvent") that, miraculously, is quadratic in y^3. Lagrange aimed to determine why: "I gave reasons why [raison pourquoi] this equation, which is always of a degree greater than that of the given equation, can be reduced" (1826, 242). Lagrange showed that exactly the resolvent's solutions y can be generated by taking $1/3\,(a_1 + \omega a_2 + \omega^2 a_3)$ and replacing a_1, a_2, and a_3 with the cubic's three solutions x_1, x_2, and x_3 in every possible order—where $\omega = (-1 + \sqrt{3}i)/2$, one of the cube roots of unity. But the three solutions generated by even permutations of x_1, x_2, and x_3—namely $1/3\,(x_1 + \omega x_2 + \omega^2 x_3)$, $1/3\,(x_2 + \omega x_3 + \omega^2 x_1)$, and $1/3\,(x_3 + \omega x_1 + \omega^2 x_2)$—all have the same cubes (since $1 = \omega^3 = (\omega^2)^3$)—and likewise for the three solutions generated by odd permutations. Since y^3 takes on only two values, y^3 must satisfy a quadratic equation. So "this is why the equation that y satisfies proves to be a quadratic in y^3" (Kline 1972, 602). The symmetry of $1/3\,(a_1 + \omega a_2 + \omega^2 a_3)$ under permutations of the three x_i explains the symmetry that initially strikes us regarding the sixth-degree equation (that three of its six roots are the same, and the remaining three are, too). As mathematicians commonly remark, y^3 "assumes two values under the six permutations of the x. It is for this reason that the equation of degree six which [y] satisfies is in fact a quadratic in [y]^3" (Kiernan 1971, 51).

For a proof to explain a result that displays a striking symmetry, the proof may have to dig deeply beneath superficial features of the setup in order to uncover a similar symmetry in the setup. Here is a good example. The finite continued fraction

$$3+\cfrac{1}{7+\cfrac{1}{15+\cfrac{1}{1+\cfrac{1}{292}}}},$$

represented as $[3, 7, 15, 1, 292]$, and its "reversal" $[292, 1, 15, 7, 3]$,

$$292+\cfrac{1}{1+\cfrac{1}{15+\cfrac{1}{7+\cfrac{1}{3}}}},$$

have the same numerator (in lowest terms): 103933. (In lowest terms, the former equals 103933/33102, whereas the latter equals 103933/355.) This is true generally:

For any positive integers a_i, if $[a_0, a_1, \ldots, a_{n-1}, a_n] = p/a$ in lowest terms, then for some b, $[a_n, a_{n-1}, \ldots, a_1, a_0] = p/b$ in lowest terms.

Why is that? Obviously, this theorem identifies a striking invariance (unchanging numerator) under a transformation (reversal). On my view, to ask why this theorem holds is to demand a proof that traces this result to the setup's exhibiting another invariance under the same transformation. Benjamin and Quinn (2003, 53) say that this theorem "is typically proved using [a mathematical] induction argument which we feel yields little insight."[12] Benjamin and Quinn present a combinatorial proof as an "explanation" (143) of the reversal theorem. The setup's invariance under reversal that Benjamin and Quinn hold responsible for this result is rather subtle:

Let $p(a_0, a_1, \ldots, a_{n-1}, a_n)$ and $q(a_0, a_1, \ldots, a_{n-1}, a_n)$ be functions giving the numerator and denominator in lowest terms of $[a_0, a_1, \ldots, a_{n-1}, a_n]$. Then since $[a] = a/1, = p(a) = a$. We will use this fact in a moment. Furthermore,

$$\frac{p(a_0, \ldots, a_n)}{q(a_0, \ldots, a_n)} = [a_0, a_1, \ldots, a_{n-1}, a_n] = a_0 + 1/[a_1, \ldots, a_n]$$

$$= a_0 + \frac{q(a_1, \ldots, a_n)}{p(a_1, \ldots, a_n)} = \frac{a_0 p(a_1, \ldots, a_n) + q(a_1, \ldots, a_n)}{p(a_1, \ldots, a_n)},$$

which is in lowest terms since otherwise, $p(a_1,\ldots,a_n)$ and $q(a_1,\ldots,a_n)$ would have to have a common factor, which they cannot have since $p(a_1,\ldots,a_n)/q(a_1,\ldots,a_n)$ expresses $[a_1,\ldots,a_n]$ in lowest terms. So by equating the two numerators and the two denominators, we find

$$p(a_0,\ldots,a_n)=a_0 p(a_1,\ldots,a_n)+q(a_1,\ldots,a_n)$$
$$q(a_0,\ldots,a_n)=p(a_1,\ldots,a_n),$$

respectively. The second equation entails that

$$q(a_1,\ldots,a_n)=p(a_2,\ldots,a_n).$$

Substituting for $q(a_1,\ldots,a_n)$ in the first equation, we find

$$p(a_0,\ldots,a_n)=a_0 p(a_1,\ldots,a_n)+p(a_2,\ldots,a_n),$$

a nice recursive formula that I will use in a moment.

Now consider a row of $n+1$ squares (such as a row on a checkerboard), numbered 0 (on the left) through n (on the right). Suppose that on each square, we can either pile one or more checkers or place a domino that occupies that square and a neighboring square. Nothing can be put on top of or underneath a domino and every square in the row must be occupied by something. I will refer to the checkers and dominos as "tiles." For each square in the row, suppose that there is a height limit to the pile of tiles that can be stacked there. For instance, "$(7, 2, \ldots, 5)$" means that square 0 can have a pile of 7 tiles or fewer, square 1 can have a pile of 2 tiles or fewer, and ... and square n can have a pile of 5 tiles or fewer. Let the suggestively named $P(a_0,\ldots,a_n)$ be the number of ways of tiling the row in accordance with the height limit $(a_0,\ldots,a_n)$. Clearly, $P(a)=a$. Now $P(a_0,\ldots,a_n)$ can be computed by considering two cases: (1) if a domino covers the first square, then it also covers the second, so there are $P(a_2,\ldots,a_n)$ ways of tiling the rest of the row in accordance with the height conditions; (2) if no domino covers the first square, then there are a_0 options for the first square and $P(a_1,\ldots,a_n)$ for the rest, so $P(a_0,\ldots,a_n)=a_0 P(a_1,\ldots,a_n)+P(a_2,\ldots,a_n)$.

Drawing these strands together, we have

$$p(a)=a \text{ and } p(a_0,\ldots,a_n)=a_0 p(a_1,\ldots,a_n)+p(a_2,\ldots,a_n),$$
$$P(a)=a \text{ and } P(a_0,\ldots,a_n)=a_0 P(a_1,\ldots,a_n)+P(a_2,\ldots,a_n).$$

So p and P have the same initial and recurrence conditions. Therefore, $p(a_0,\ldots,a_n)=P(a_0,\ldots,a_n)$. In other words, the numerator of $[a_0,\ldots,a_n]$ in lowest terms equals the number of ways of tiling an $(n+1)$-length row in accord with height conditions $(a_0, \ldots, a_n)$. The setup for the theorem can be interpreted as concerning such tiling.

Now to explain why the reversal theorem holds. Clearly, the number of ways of tiling an $(n + 1)$-length row in accord with height conditions $(a_0, \ldots, a_n)$ equals the number of ways of tiling an $(n + 1)$-length row in accord with height conditions $(a_n, \ldots, a_0)$. Any tiling scheme that satisfies one of these height conditions will satisfy the other after being rotated 180 degrees. Here we have a symmetry in the setup under the "reversal" transformation. We can exploit this symmetry to prove the theorem: since $P(a_0, \ldots, a_n) = P(a_n, \ldots, a_0)$, it follows that $p(a_0, \ldots, a_n) = p(a_n, \ldots, a_0)$.

According to Benjamin and Quinn (2003), a finite continued fraction and its "reverse" have the same numerator—the numerator is invariant under the fraction's "reversal"—because the task of tiling the row is invariant under the height conditions' "reversal."

Tiling considerations might well seem extraneous to the theorem being explained. Yet their apparently exogenous character evidently does not prevent mathematicians from regarding this proof as explanatory. In section 9.2, I will look carefully at another explanatory proof that invokes considerations exogenous to the defining features of the elements figuring in the theorem being proved.

▪ 7.5 GEOMETRIC EXPLANATIONS THAT EXPLOIT SYMMETRY

Proofs in geometry can also explain by exploiting symmetries. Consider the theorem: If ABCD is an isosceles trapezoid as shown in figure 7.1 (AB parallel to CD, AD = BC) such that AM = BK and ND = LC, then ML = KN. A proof could proceed by brute-force coordinate geometry: first let D's coordinates be $(0,0)$, C's be $(0,c)$, A's be (a,s), and B's be (b,s), and then solve algebraically for the two distances ML and KN, showing that they are equal. A more inventive, Euclid-style option would be first to draw some auxiliary lines and then to exploit the properties of triangles:

Draw the line from N perpendicular to CD; call their intersection P (see fig. 7.2); likewise draw line LS. Consider triangles DNP and CLS: angles D and C are congruent (since the trapezoid is isosceles), ND = LC (given), and the two right angles are congruent. Hence, by having two angles and the nonincluded side congruent, $\Delta DNP = \Delta CLS$, so their corresponding sides NP and LS are congruent. They are also parallel (being perpendicular to the same line). That these two opposite sides are both congruent and parallel shows PNLS to be a parallelogram. Hence, NL is parallel to DC. By the same argument with two new auxiliary lines, AB is parallel to MK. Therefore, MK and NL are parallel (since they are parallel to lines that are

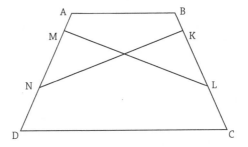

Figure 7.1 An isosceles trapezoid

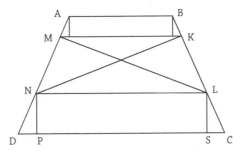

Figure 7.2 A Euclid-style proof of the theorem regarding isosceles trapezoids

parallel to each other), so MKLN is a trapezoid. Since MN = AD – AM – ND, KL = BC – BK – LC, AM = BK, AD = BC, and ND = LC, it follows that MN = KL. As corresponding angles, ∡KLN = ∡LCS; since ∆CLS = ∆DNP, ∡LCS = ∡NDP; as corresponding angles, ∡NDP = ∡MNL. Therefore, ∡KLN = ∡MNL. From this last (and that NL = NL, MN = KL), it follows (by having two sides and their included angle congruent) that ∆MNL = ∆KLN, and so their corresponding sides ML and KN are the same length.

This proof succeeds, but only by using a construction that many mathematicians would regard as artificial or "clever." (See, for instance, Vinner and Kopelman 1998, from whom I have taken this example; Nicole and Arnauld (1717, 423) disparage a similar construction as "Cunning.") The construction is artificial because the proof using it seems obliged to go to elaborate lengths—all because it fails to exploit the figure's striking feature: its symmetry with respect to the line between the midpoints of the bases (the dotted line in fig. 7.3).

The theorem (that ML = KN) "makes sense" in view of the figure's overall symmetry. Intuitively, a proof that fails to proceed from the figure's symmetry strikes us as failing to focus on "what is really going on": that we have here the same figure twice, once on each side of the line of symmetry. Folding the figure along

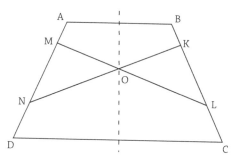

Figure 7.3 The line of symmetry

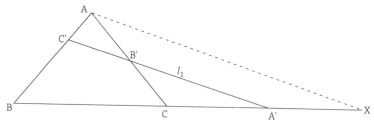

Figure 7.4 First proof of Menelaus's theorem

the line of symmetry, we find that NO coincides with LO and that MO coincides with KO, so that MO + OL = KO + ON, and hence ML = KN. Of course, to make this proof complete, we must first show that the point at which ML intersects KN lies on the line of symmetry. But that is also required by the figure's overall symmetry: if they intersect off of the line of symmetry, then the setup will be symmetrical only if there is another point of intersection at the mirror-image location on the other side of the line of symmetry, but two lines (ML and KN) cannot intersect at more than one point.

Of course, this proof exploits a very simple symmetry: mirror reflection across a line. A proof in geometry can explain by virtue of exploiting a more intricate symmetry in the setup. For instance, consider one direction of Menelaus's theorem: if the three sides of triangle ABC are intersected by a line l_1 (fig. 7.4), where C′ (A′, B′) is the point where l_1 intersects line AB (BC, CA), then (letting "AC′," for instance, be the distance between points A and C′)

$$\frac{AC'}{BC'} \frac{BA'}{CA'} \frac{CB'}{AB'} = 1$$

We are immediately struck by the symmetry on the left side of this equation. (Indeed, we inevitably use the symmetry to get a grip on what the left side is all about.) The left side consists of a framework of primed points, $\dfrac{\square C' \ \square A' \ \square B'}{\square C' \ \square A' \ \square B'},$

exhibiting an obvious symmetry: "A," "B," and "C" all play the same role around the primes (modulo the order from left to right, which makes no difference to the product of the three terms). Within this framework, the three unprimed points are arranged so that "A," "B," and "C" all again play the same role: each appears once on the top and once on the bottom, and each is paired once with each of the other two letters primed. (For example, "A" appears once with "B'" and once with "C'," once on the top and once on the bottom.) These constraints suffice to fix the expression modulo the left-right order, which does not matter to their product, and modulo the inversion of top and bottom, which does not matter since the equation sets the top and bottom equal. In short, the left-hand expression is invariant (modulo features irrelevant to the equation) under any systematic interchange of "A," "B," and "C" around the other symbols. In the literature, the primed points are almost always named as I have named them here (e.g., with C' as the point where l_1 intersects line AB) in order to better display the expression's symmetry.

Having recognized this symmetry in the theorem, we regard any proof of the theorem that ignores the symmetry as failing to explain why the theorem holds. For instance, consider this proof:

> Draw the line through A parallel to l_1 (dotted line in fig. 7.4); let X be its point of intersection with line BC. As corresponding angles, $\angle BA'C' = \angle BXA$. Therefore (since they also share $\angle B$), $\triangle BC'A'$ is similar to $\triangle BAX$, so their corresponding lengths are in a constant proportion. In particular, $\dfrac{AC'}{BC'} = \dfrac{XA'}{BA'}$. Likewise, as corresponding angles, $\angle CB'A' = \angle CAX$. Therefore (since they also share $\angle B'CA'$), $\triangle ACX$ is similar to $\triangle B'CA'$, so their corresponding lengths are in a constant proportion. In particular, $\dfrac{AB'}{CB'} = \dfrac{XA'}{CA'}$. Solving this for $XA' = (AB')(CA')/CB'$ and substituting the resulting expression for XA' into the earlier equation yields $\dfrac{AC'}{BC'} = \dfrac{AB'}{BA'}\dfrac{CA'}{CB'}$. The theorem follows by algebra.

Einstein (Luchins and Luchins 1990, 38) says that this proof is "not satisfying" and Bogomolny (2009) agrees. Both cite the fact that (in Einstein's words) "the proof favors, for no reason, the vertex A [since the auxiliary line is drawn from that vertex], although the proposition [to be proved] is symmetrical in relation to A, B, and C." The point here is that although the proof could have been carried out with an auxiliary line parallel to l_1 drawn through vertex B or C rather than through A, the choice of any one vertex through which to draw the line breaks the symmetry between A, B, and C in what had been an entirely symmetric arrangement.[13] That symmetry is then restored in the resulting equation. Consequently, this proof depicts the symmetric result as arising "magically," whereas to explain why the theorem holds, we must proceed entirely from the figure's symmetries over A-B-C.

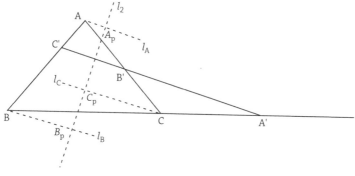

Figure 7.5 Second proof of Menelaus's theorem

Following Brunhes (1991, 84), Bogomolny (2009) offers such a proof, which I now elaborate (fig. 7.5):

Add a line l_2 perpendicular to l_1. Project A onto l_2 by a line l_A from A parallel to l_1; let A_p be the point on l_2 to which A is projected. Perform the same operation on B and C, adding lines l_B and l_C, and points B_p and C_p. Of course, A', B', and C' all project to the same point on l_2 (since l_1 is their common line of projection), which can equally well be called "A'$_p$," "B'$_p$," or "C'$_p$." Now the following equation exhibits the same symmetry as the theorem:

$$\frac{A_p C'_p}{B_p C'_p} \frac{B_p A'_p}{C_p A'_p} \frac{C_p B'_p}{A_p B'_p} = 1.$$

This equation is true (considering that A'$_p$, B'$_p$, and C'$_p$ are the same point, allowing a massive cancellation) and is strikingly invariant (modulo features irrelevant to the equation: left-right order and inversion of top and bottom) under systematic interchange of "A," "B," and "C" around the primes and subscript p's—the same symmetry that the theorem possesses. To arrive at the theorem, all we need to do is to find a way to remove the subscript p's from this equation, which is easily done. For any side of the triangle, l_1 and the two lines projecting its endpoints onto l_2 are three parallel lines, and all three are crossed by the triangle's side and by l_2. Now for a lemma: Whenever two transversals cross three parallel lines, the two segments into which the three parallels cut one transversal stand in the same ratio as the two segments into which the three parallels cut the other transversal. That is, the ratio of one transversal's segments is preserved in the ratio of their projections onto the other transversal.[14] By projecting each side onto l_2, we find

$$\frac{A_p C'_p}{B_p C'_p} = \frac{AC'}{BC'}$$

$$\frac{B_p A_p'}{C_p A_p'} = \frac{BA'}{CA'}$$

$$\frac{C_p B_p'}{A_p B_p'} = \frac{CB'}{AB'}.$$

Thus the theorem is proved by an argument that begins with an equation that treats A, B, and C identically and in each further step treats them identically. This proof reveals how features of the setup that are A-B-C symmetric are responsible for the theorem's symmetry. The result's symmetry does not just come out of nowhere. Indeed, the proof's general strategy is to project A', B', and C' onto the very same point (thereby treating them identically) by projecting the triangle's three sides onto the same line.

This explanation also illustrates that a proof's auxiliary lines need not be "artificial"; that is, the use of auxiliary lines does not suffice to make the proof non-explanatory. Although the auxiliary lines in the Euclid-style proof of the trapezoid theorem were mere devices to get the theorem proved, and likewise for line AX in the first proof of Menelaus's theorem (fig. 7.4), the scheme of auxiliary lines in the second proof of Menelaus's theorem is A-B-C symmetric (Bogomolny 2009).

A result's striking symmetry may involve its invariance under certain changes in the setup that we would have expected to affect the result. For example, take a sphere of radius r and drill through it from top to bottom (fig.7.6), removing from it the two "polar caps" and the drilled-out right circular cylinder of radius R. (The cylinder's axis coincides with the sphere's vertical diameter.) The volume of the resulting figure (shaped like a wedding band or napkin ring, with curved outer sides and straight inner sides) is $\frac{4}{3}\pi h^3$, where h is the figure's half-height.

The result is independent from r and R. For example, a cylinder 6 inches long cut through an Earth-sized sphere (necessitating very large "polar caps" and large R) leaves the same residue as a 6-inch cylinder cut through a bowling ball (so with much smaller "polar caps" and smaller R). The result's independence from r and R appears "incredible" (Gardner 1988, 133) and "extremely paradoxical" (Polya 1954, 191). Its shock value is frequently exploited by calculus texts that pose this problem (e.g., Stewart 2009, 369). Levi (2009, 102) remarks that after proving it by standard textbook methods, "I could not explain *why* it is true—a formal calculation did not seem satisfying." Here is such a proof:

> Let's start by computing the sphere's volume from h above to h below its midline (set at $y = 0$), since the rest of the sphere's volume will not contribute to the napkin ring's volume because the two polar "caps" will come off when we drill the cylinder. A horizontal volume element of the sphere is a circle with radius

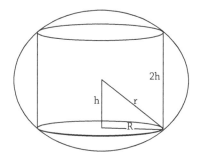

Figure 7.6 The napkin ring

$\sqrt{(r^2 - y^2)}$, so the cross-sectional area is $\pi(r^2 - y^2)$. By adding these elements from $y = -h$ to $y = h$, we find

$$\pi \int_{-h}^{h} (r^2 - y^2)\,dy = \pi r^2 \int_{-h}^{h} dy - \pi \int_{-h}^{h} y^2\,dy = 2h\pi r^2 - \frac{2\pi}{3}h^3.$$

The napkin ring's volume V is the above minus the cylinder's volume $\pi R^2(2h)$:

$$V = 2h\pi r^2 - \frac{2\pi}{3}h^3 - 2\pi R^2 h = 2\pi\left(r^2 h - \frac{h^3}{3} - R^2 h\right).$$

Now by the Pythagorean theorem (see fig. 7.6),

$$h^2 + R^2 = r^2.$$

So let's replace r^2:

$$V = 2\pi\left(h^3 + hR^2 - \frac{h^3}{3} - R^2 h\right).$$

A fortuitous cancellation removes all dependence on R, leaving $V = \frac{4}{3}\pi h^3$.

As Gardner (1988, 121) puts it, "all terms obligingly cancel out except" those solely involving h. This algebraic miracle makes the result's independence from r and R even more striking than it was before—and more suspicious. We suspect it is no coincidence that all terms involving R go away. (I will discuss "mathematical coincidence" in chapter 8.)

In contrast to this proof, an explanation of the result is a proof showing how the result arises not from an algebraic miracle, but rather from a symmetry in the setup that involves invariance under the same transformation as the symmetry that caught our attention in the result. Here is such a symmetry in the setup: a cross-section taken at any "latitude" (i.e., any distance y above or below the mid-line, from 0 to h) of any napkin ring of half-height h, *regardless of its r and R*, has the same area as the cross-section at the same latitude of a sphere with radius h.

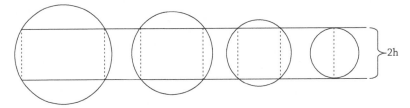

Figure 7.7 The napkin ring's symmetry (after Graham 1959, 146)

To put it more picturesquely (fig. 7.7), if we start with a sphere of radius h, we can pull it apart into any napkin ring of half-height h, no matter its r or R. Here is the proof:

> A cross-section of the napkin ring is an annulus of inner radius R, outer radius $\sqrt{(r^2 - y^2)}$, so its cross-sectional area is $\pi(r^2 - y^2 - R^2)$. The cross-section of a sphere with radius h is a circle with radius $\sqrt{(h^2 - y^2)}$, so its cross-sectional area is $\pi(h^2 - y^2)$, but since (by the Pythagorean theorem) $h^2 + R^2 = r^2$, we can substitute for h^2 and find the sphere's cross-sectional area to be $\pi(r^2 - R^2 - y^2)$, which equals the napkin ring's.

The proof of the napkin ring's volume then concludes quickly: since the ring and a sphere of radius h have equal cross-sectional areas at all latitudes, they have the same volumes, so the napkin ring's volume must be $\frac{4}{3}\pi h^3$. Though this proof is only slightly different from the standard one, it is explanatory because it exploits a symmetry in the problem of the very same kind as the symmetry that initially stood out in the result: an invariance under variation in R and r.

Any proof of the napkin-ring theorem that begins with this cross-section of the napkin ring will reveal *from the outset* that the volume depends only on h: since $h^2 + R^2 = r^2$, the cross-sectional area equals $\pi(r^2 - y^2 - R^2) = \pi(h^2 - y^2)$. (Integration then yields as the volume $\int_{-h}^{h} \pi(h^2 - y^2)\,dy = \frac{4}{3}\pi h^3$.) By beginning with a feature of the setup that is independent of R and r, any such proof constitutes an "explanation," Graham (1959: 147) says, because it "adroitly . . . shows that r and R appear [in the cross-sectional area] only as $r^2 - R^2$, which is equal to the square of half the depth of hole, regardless of the value of r and R" (using our notation). Such a proof explains the theorem by revealing just where the result's independence from r and R comes from.[15]

When a geometric result exhibits a striking symmetry, but no known proof of the theorem works by uncovering and exploiting a similar symmetry in the setup, then the theorem is typically regarded as mysterious; further proofs are sought to explain why it holds. A nice example is afforded by Morley's theorem (fig. 7.8): that for any Euclidean triangle, an equilateral triangle is formed by the three intersection points of adjacent interior angle trisectors. This result

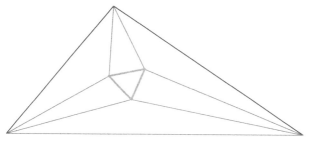

Figure 7.8 Morley's theorem

is commonly characterized as "spectacular" (Dunham 1999, 148), "amazing" (Isaacs 2001, 82), or "the marvel of marvels" (Newman 1996, 31) at least partly in virtue of the striking symmetry it reveals to be buried within even the most ungainly triangle: "the symmetry of an equilateral triangle arises miraculously from an arbitrary triangle" (Connes 2004, 11).[16] Proofs of the theorem often proceed "backward": by starting with an equilateral triangle and generating the larger triangle from it. Other, direct proofs are commonly deprecated as operating by "ingenious" (Connes 2004, 14), "brute force" (Bollobás 2006, 126) trigonometry or instead by "elephantine" (Francis 2002) geometrical constructions; none is characterized as explanatory. Although some relatively simple proofs have been found, one still frequently encounters sentiments like these: "even when I read the much simpler proof based on trigonometry, or the fairly simple geometric proof due to Navansiengar, there was still too much complexity and lack of motivation. (A series of lucky breaks!) Were we to give up, forever, understanding the Morley Miracle?" (Newman 1996, 31). That common epithet (along with "Morley's Mystery") reflects the idea that until the theorem has been derived from some similar symmetry in the setup, its truth will remain unexplained; it will still seem to arise from a series of "lucky" (though mathematically necessary) breaks. That Morley's theorem has not yet been explained seems to be behind the ongoing search for new proofs of it. (As far as I can see, there is no guarantee that Morley's theorem can be proved in a manner that explains why the theorem holds; the theorem may simply have no explanation.)

Morley's theorem is usefully compared to Varignon's theorem (fig. 7.9): that for any quadrilateral, if segments are drawn connecting the midpoints of adjacent sides, then the "midpoint quadrilateral" so formed is a parallelogram. Just as Morley's theorem reveals a symmetry buried within even the most ungainly triangle, so likewise the feature of Varignon's theorem that is often remarked upon is that it uncovers a symmetry buried within even the most ungainly quadrilateral. For instance, Keyton (2004, 3) says that Varignon's theorem "takes an unordered object and creates a very structured one." Some authors make

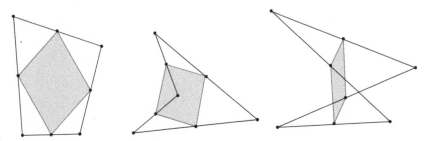

Figure 7.9 Varignon's theorem

the symmetry of the resulting parallelogram even more salient by illustrating Varignon's theorem with highly asymmetric (e.g., concave and crossed) quadrilaterals (as in fig. 7.9).

Varignon's theorem can be proved by using coordinate geometry: we can label the vertices of the original quadrilateral as $(0,0)$, $(a,0)$, (b,c), and (d,e), and then show algebraically that opposite sides of the midpoint parallelogram are parallel. However, this proof works by brute force. By contrast, the proof often described as explanatory (e.g., by de Villiers 2003, 60–61, 169; Gravina 2008; Keyton 2004, 3) exploits the "midpoint theorem": that for any triangle, the segment connecting the midpoints of two sides is parallel to the third side. Consider the triangle formed by a diagonal and two sides of the original quadrilateral. By the midpoint theorem, the diagonal is parallel to the segment connecting the midpoints of those sides. By the same reasoning applied to the triangle formed from the same diagonal and the other two sides of the original quadrilateral, the diagonal is also parallel to the segment connecting the midpoints of those sides. Since those two segments are parallel to the same line, they are parallel—and the same reasoning applied to the original quadrilateral's other diagonal shows that the other two sides of the midpoint parallelogram are also parallel.

In sum, Varignon's theorem exhibits a striking symmetry: that the slope remains invariant from one side of the midpoint quadrilateral to the opposite side. The proof shows how the result arises from a similar symmetry in the setup: that the slope remains invariant from the quadrilateral's diagonal to a segment connecting the midpoints of the quadrilateral's sides. In other words, the proof works by tracing the parallelism in the midpoint quadrilateral back to a parallelism in the original figure's triangles. Accordingly, the proof is explanatory, on my account. An analogous proof, if it existed, would explain Morley's theorem.

■ 7.6 GENERALIZING THE PROPOSAL

I have now given several examples of mathematical explanations consisting of proofs that exploit symmetries. However, I do not mean to suggest that only a proof that appeals to some symmetry can explain why a mathematical theorem holds. Rather, I am using proofs by symmetry to illustrate the way in which certain proofs manage to become privileged as explanatory. Symmetries are not somehow intrinsically explanatory in mathematics. Rather, some symmetry in a mathematical result is often salient to us, and consequently, in those cases, a proof that traces the result to a similar symmetry in the problem counts as explaining why the result holds. A mathematical result exhibiting no symmetry at all could likewise have a salient feature, prompting a why question answerable by a proof deriving the result from a similar feature of the given. At least in many cases, what it *means* to ask for a proof that explains is to ask for a proof that exploits a certain kind of feature in the setup—the same kind of feature that is outstanding (i.e., salient) in the result. The distinction between proofs that explain *why* some theorem is true and proofs that merely show *that* the theorem is true exists only when some feature of the result being proved is salient. The feature's salience makes certain proofs explanatory. A proof is accurately characterized as an explanation (or not) only in a context where some feature of the result being proved is salient.[17]

My proposal predicts that if the result exhibits no noteworthy feature, then to demand an explanation of why it holds, not merely a proof that it holds, makes no sense. There is nothing that its explanation over and above its proof would amount to until some feature of the result becomes salient. Of course, a new proof of the result could reveal a remarkable feature of the result that was not evident before, thereby grounding the distinction between an explanation and a mere proof. But not every new proof has this effect.[18] Another important prediction made by my proposal is that a mathematical result may have no explanation at all, despite having a proof from the relevant axioms. As I will show in chapter 8, this prediction distinguishes my proposal from certain rival accounts of mathematical explanation.

My proposal's predictions are borne out. Mathematicians themselves sometimes point out that not all mathematical theorems have explanations, so in searching for some theorem's explanation, we may be searching for something that does not exist. For example, after asking *why* a given Taylor series fails to converge, Spivak says, "Asking this sort of question is always dangerous, since we may have to settle for an unsympathetic answer: it happens because it happens—that's the way things are! In this case there does happen to be an explanation" (1980, 482). (I will discuss this explanation in section 8.3, and I will return to it once more and quote the remainder of Spivak's remark in chapter 9.) Furthermore, whereas the theorem in Spivak's example has a salient feature (as I will show) and so there is something that it would be for a proof to explain why that theorem holds, some theorems have no noteworthy feature and so (on my proposal) no explanation. For example, as far as I know, there is nothing that it would be for some proof to explain why, not merely to prove that,

$$\int_1^3 \left(x^3 - 5x + 2 \right) dx = 4.$$

Consider another example. If (a,b) is a solution to $x^2 + y^2 = 1$, then so is (b,a). Why is that? The relation between the two solutions, (a,b) and (b,a), immediately captures our attention, and consequently, there is a point to the demand for an explanation (over and above a proof) of this result. We can explain this result immediately by noting that the equation exhibits the same x-y symmetry as the result—in other words, that x and y play the same roles in the equation. By contrast, merely to insert b for x and a for y in the equation, and to show by (very simple) algebra that the equation is then solved if (a,b) was a solution, would be to prove the result, but to miss the reason why it holds. Now it is also true that if (a,b) is a solution to $x^2 + y^2 = 1$, then so is $\left(\frac{3}{5}a + \frac{4}{5}b, \frac{4}{5}a - \frac{3}{5}b \right)$. Insofar as this result exhibits no striking symmetry or other outstanding feature, there is no sense in which some proof could explain why this result holds. We can still derive the result algebraically, of course:

$$\text{For } x = \frac{3}{5}a + \frac{4}{5}b, y = \frac{4}{5}a - \frac{3}{5}b:$$

$$x^2 + y^2 = \left(\frac{3}{5}a + \frac{4}{5}b \right)^2 + \left(\frac{4}{5}a - \frac{3}{5}b \right)^2$$

$$= \frac{9}{25}a^2 + \frac{24}{25}ab + \frac{16}{25}b^2 + \frac{16}{25}a^2 - \frac{24}{25}ab + \frac{9}{25}b^2 = a^2 + b^2,$$

which equals 1 if (a,b) was a solution.

But this brute-force proof does not make salient some feature of the result that had formerly gone unnoticed. The algebra shows that $\left(\frac{3}{5}a + \frac{4}{5}b, \frac{4}{5}a - \frac{3}{5}b \right)$ must be a solution if (a,b) is a solution, but as yet there is no point to asking *why* this is so.

However, we might later be struck by a noteworthy feature of the result: that it incorporates a Pythagorean triple $(3,4,5)$. In a context where this feature is salient, a proof of the result that exploits this feature (by showing that from any Pythagorean triple, another solution to the equation could be constructed in the same way) explains the result by revealing what the triple is doing there. (For more on how shifts in context can influence a proof's explanatory significance, see section 8.4.)[19]

My proposal also predicts that if a result exhibits some noteworthy feature, but no proof traces the result to a similar feature in the setup, then the result has no explanation. This prediction is also borne out. Take the following example of a "mathematical coincidence" given by the mathematician Timothy Gowers: "Consider the decimal expansion of e, which begins 2.718281828. . . . It is quite striking that a pattern of four digits should repeat itself so soon—if you choose a random sequence of digits then the chances of such a pattern appearing would be one in several thousand—and yet this phenomenon is universally regarded as an amusing coincidence, a fact that does not demand an explanation" (2007, 34; see Baker 2009a, 140). Mathematicians regard this fact about e's decimal expansion as having no explanation. Of course, there are many ways to derive e's value and thus to derive that the third-through-sixth digits of its base-ten representation are repeated in the seventh-through-tenth digits. For example, we could derive this result from the fact that e equals the sum of $(1/n!)$ for $n = 0$, 1, 2, 3 . . . . However, such a proof does not *explain why* the seventh-through-tenth digits repeat the third-through-sixth digits. It merely proves that they do. On my view, that is because the expression $(1/0!) + (1/1!) + (1/2!) + \ldots$ from which the proof begins does not exhibit any feature similar to the repeated sequence of digits in e's decimal expansion. (None of the familiar expressions for calculating e makes any particular reference to base 10.) There is, I suggest, no reason why that pattern of digits repeats. It just does. (I will return to the topic of "mathematical coincidences" in chapter 8.)

Besides some symmetry, what other outstanding feature might a mathematical result exhibit, where a proof of the result qualifies as explanatory by virtue of exploiting the same kind of feature in the setup? Simplicity is another feature that generally stands out when a mathematical result possesses it. An especially simple result typically cries out for a proof that exploits some similar, simple feature of the setup. In contrast, a proof where the result, in all of its simplicity, appears suddenly out of a welter of complexity—through some fortuitous cancellation or clever manipulation—tends merely to heighten our curiosity about why the result holds. Such a proof leaves us wanting to know where such a simple result came from. After such a proof is given, there often appears a sentence like the following: "The resulting answer is extremely simple despite the contortions involved to obtain it, and it cries out for a better understanding" (Stanley 2012, 14). Then another proof that traces the simple result to a similar, simple feature of the problem counts as explaining why the result holds. As Sawyer (1955, 129) says regarding some results involving determinants: "The results . . . are very simple. But the method I have suggested for verifying them involves long and formless calculations. Seeing the results are so simple, should there not be a correspondingly simple way of proving them? If I really understood why these results came, ought I not to be able to prove them by an argument containing little or no calculation?"

Examples of this kind often arise in proofs of "partition identities." The number $P(n)$ of "partitions of n" is the number of ways that the nonnegative integer n can be expressed as the sum of one or more positive integers (irrespective of their order in the sum). For instance, $P(5) = 7$, since 5 can be expressed in 7 ways: as $5, 4 + 1, 3 + 2, 3 + 1 + 1, 2 + 2 + 1, 2 + 1 + 1 + 1$, and $1 + 1 + 1 + 1$. (By convention, $P(0) = 1$.) Consider this "partition identity" (proved by Euler in 1748): The number $O(n)$ of partitions of n into exclusively odd numbers ("O-partitions") equals the number $D(n)$ of partitions of n into parts that are distinct, that is, that are all unequal ("D-partitions"). For instance, $O(5) = 3$ since $5, 3 + 1 + 1$, and $1 + 1 + 1 + 1 + 1$ are the O-partitions of 5, and $D(5) = 3$ since $5, 4 + 1$, and $3 + 2$ are the D-partitions of 5.

There are two standard ways of proving partition identities: either with "generating functions" or with "bijections." By definition, the "generating function" $f(q)$ for a sequence $a_0, a_1, a_2 \ldots$ is $a_0 q^0 + a_1 q^1 + a_2 q^2 + \ldots = a_0 + a_1 q + a_2 q^2 + \ldots$. It does not matter whether the sum in the generating function converges because the generating function is merely a device for putting the sequence on display; "q^n" does not stand for some unknown quantity, but just marks the place in the generating function where a_n appears (as this term's coefficient). For example, the generating function for the sequence $1, -1, 1, -1, 1 \ldots$ is $1 - q + q^2 - q^3 + q^4 - \ldots$. This series results from "long division" of $1 + q$ into 1, that is, the expansion of $1/(1 + q)$. (Again, it does not matter whether this sum converges.) Such a "formal power series" can generally be manipulated in precisely the same way as a genuine power series. For example, we can multiply $1/(1 + q)$ by 2 to yield $2/(1 + q) = 2 - 2q + 2q^2 - 2q^3 + 2q^4 - \ldots$, the generating function for the sequence $2, -2, 2, -2, 2 \ldots$.

To prove Euler's partition identity, let's first find a generating function for the sequence of partitions of n: $P(0), P(1), P(2), \ldots$. Let's "consider (or as that word often implies, 'look out, here comes something from left field'" [Wilf 2000, 6]) this formidable-looking generating function:

$$\left(1+q+q^2+q^3+\ldots\right)\left(1+q^2+q^4+q^6+\ldots\right)$$
$$\left(1+q^3+q^6+q^9+\ldots\right)\left(1+q^4+q^8+q^{12}+\ldots\right)\ldots$$

The product of the factors in this expression is a long polynomial $a_0 + a_1 q + a_2 q^2 + a_3 q^3 + \ldots$ —the generating function for the sequence $a_0, a_1, a_2 \ldots$. What sequence is this? As an example, let's compute a_3. Since multiplying q^m by q^n involves adding their exponents ($q^m q^n = q^{m+n}$), the coefficient of q^3 will be increased by 1 for every combination of terms where the exponents add to 3, with exactly one term in the combination drawn from each factor in the above formidable expression. For instance, q^3 from the first factor $(1+q+q^2+q^3+\ldots)$ multiplied by 1's from each other factor ($1 = q^0$) will increase a_3 by 1. Another 1 is contributed to a_3 by q from the first factor multiplied by

q^2 from the second factor and 1's from each of the other factors. Another, final 1 comes from q^3 drawn from the third factor multiplied by 1's from each other factor. Those three 1's make $a_3 = 3$; each combination of exponents adding to 3 contributes 1 to a_3. Now the exponents in the first factor $(1 + q + q^2 + q^3 + \ldots)$ increase by 1, those in the second factor $(1 + q^2 + q^4 + \ldots)$ increase by 2, and so forth. So we can think of the first factor's exponents as counting by 1's, the second factor's exponents as counting by 2's, and so forth. Therefore, when we add the exponents from a combination of terms where exactly one term q^f was drawn from the first factor, one term q^s from the second factor, and so forth, we can think of this sum as representing the sum of f 1's plus the sum of $(s/2)$ 2's and so forth. Each combination that sums to n contributes 1 to q^n's coefficient a_n. For instance, as I just mentioned in the case of q^3, the product of q^3 from the first factor (representing three 1's) with 1's from every other factor (zero 2's, zero 3's, $\ldots$) contributes 1 to a_3; another 1 comes from the product of q from the first factor (one 1) by q^2 from the second factor (one 2) and 1's from every other factor (zero 3's, zero 4's, $\ldots$); and the final 1 comes from the product of q^3 from the third factor (one 3) with 1's from each of the other factors (zero 1's, zero 2's, zero 4's, $\ldots$). Thus, each of these combinations contributing 1 to a_3 represents one of the three partitions of 3: its partitions are $1 + 1 + 1$, $1 + 2$, and 3. That is, a_3 equals the number of partitions of 3. The same thing happens for every coefficient a_n. Thus, the above formidable expression is $P(n)$'s generating function: $P(0) + P(1)q + P(2)q^2 + \ldots$. Since by "long division" $1 = (1 + q + q^2 + q^3 + \ldots)(1 - q) = (1 + q^2 + q^4 + \ldots)(1 - q^2) = (1 + q^3 + q^6 + \ldots)(1 - q^3)$, the same function can be expressed as

$$\left(\frac{1}{1-q}\right)\left(\frac{1}{1-q^2}\right)\left(\frac{1}{1-q^3}\right)\cdots$$

Now let's derive the generating functions for the numbers of n's odd-partitions and distinct-partitions. In the generating function for $P(n)$

$$\left(1+q+q^2+q^3+\ldots\right)\left(1+q^2+q^4+q^6+\ldots\right)$$
$$\left(1+q^3+q^6+q^9+\ldots\right)\left(1+q^4+q^8+q^{12}+\ldots\right)\ldots$$

the first factor (in counting by 1's) represents the number of 1's in the partition, the second factor (counting by 2's) the number of 2's, and so on. Therefore, by including only the factors corresponding to the number of 1's, number of 3's, number of 5's, and so on, we produce

$$\left(1+q+q^2+q^3+\ldots\right)\left(1+q^3+q^6+q^9\ldots\right)$$
$$\left(1+q^5+q^{10}+q^{15}\ldots\right)\ldots=\left(\frac{1}{1-q}\right)\left(\frac{1}{1-q^3}\right)\left(\frac{1}{1-q^5}\right)\cdots$$

—the generating function for $O(n)$. Returning to the mth factor $(1 + q^m + q^{2m} + q^{3m} \ldots)$ of $P(n)$'s generating function, we see that the terms beyond q^m allowed m to appear more than once in the partition. Their removal yields $D(n)$'s generating function

$$(1+q)(1+q^2)(1+q^3)\ldots$$

By manipulating these generating functions in various ways (justified for infinite products by taking to the limit various manipulations for finite products), we can show (as Euler first did) that the two generating functions are the same, and hence that $O(n) = D(n)$:

$$\left(\frac{1}{1-q}\right)\left(\frac{1}{1-q^3}\right)\left(\frac{1}{1-q^5}\right)\ldots$$

$$=\left(\frac{1}{1-q}\right)\left(\frac{1-q^2}{1-q^2}\right)\left(\frac{1}{1-q^3}\right)\left(\frac{1-q^4}{1-q^4}\right)\left(\frac{1}{1-q^5}\right)\left(\frac{1-q^6}{1-q^6}\right)\ldots$$

$$=\left(\frac{1-q^2}{1-q}\right)\left(\frac{1-q^4}{1-q^2}\right)\left(\frac{1-q^6}{1-q^3}\right)\left(\frac{1-q^8}{1-q^4}\right)\ldots$$

$$=\left(\frac{(1-q)(1+q)}{1-q}\right)\left(\frac{(1-q^2)(1+q^2)}{1-q^2}\right)\left(\frac{(1-q^3)(1+q^3)}{1-q^3}\right)\left(\frac{(1-q^4)(1+q^4)}{1-q^4}\right)\ldots$$

$$=(1+q)(1+q^2)(1+q^3)\ldots$$

Wilf (2000, 10) terms this "a very slick proof," which is to say that it involves not only an initial generating function "from left field," but also a sequence of substitutions, manipulations, and cancellations having no motivation other than that miraculously, it works out to produce the simple result in the end. Proofs of partition identities by generating functions, although sound and useful, in many cases "begin to obscure the simple patterns and relationships that the proof is intended to illuminate" (Bressoud 1999, 46).[20]

In contrast, "A common feeling among combinatorial mathematicians is that a simple bijective proof of an identity conveys the deepest *understanding* of why it is true" (Andrews and Eriksson 2004, 9, italics in the original). A "bijection" is a one-to-one correspondence. A bijective proof that $O(n) = D(n)$ finds a way to pair each O-partition with one and only one D-partition. Let us look at a bijective proof (from Sylvester 1882) that $O(n) = D(n)$. Display each O-partition as an array of dots, as in figure 7.10's representation of the partition $7 + 7 + 5 + 5 + 3 + 1 + 1 + 1$ of 30. Each row has the number of dots in a part of the partition, with the rows weakly decreasing in length and their centers aligned. (Each row has a center dot since each part is odd.) Here is a simple way to transform this O-partition into a D-partition. The first part of the new partition is given by the dots on a line running from the bottom up along the center column and

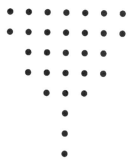

Figure 7.10 A partition of 30

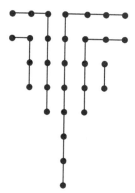

Figure 7.11 A fishhook depiction of the bijection

turning right at the top—11 dots. The next part is given by the dots on a line running from the bottom, up along a column one dot left of center, turning left at the top—7 dots. The next part runs from the bottom up along a column one dot right of center, turning right at the last available row (the second row from the top)—6 dots. This pattern leaves us with figure 7.11's fishhook diagram. The result is a D-partition $(11 + 7 + 6 + 4 + 2)$, and the reverse procedure on that partition returns the original O-partition. With this bijection between O-partitions and D-partitions, there must be the same number of each. The key to the proof is that by "straightening the fishhooks," we can see the same diagram as depicting both an O-partition and a D-partition.

Because the bijection is so simple, this proof traces the simple relation between $O(n)$ and $D(n)$ to a simple relation between the O-partitions and the D-partitions. Moreover, the simple feature of the setup that the proof exploits is similar to the result's strikingly simple feature: the result is that $O(n)$ and $D(n)$ are the same, and the simple bijection reveals that n's O-partitions are essentially the same objects as n's D-partitions, since one can easily be transformed into the other. It is then no wonder that $O(n) = D(n)$, since effectively the same objects are being counted twice. This is the source of the explanatory power of a simple

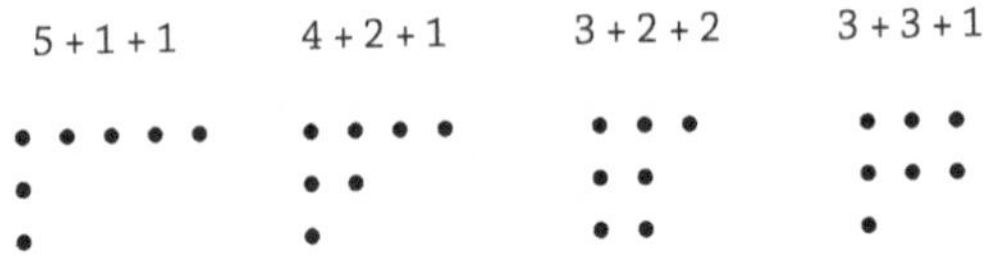

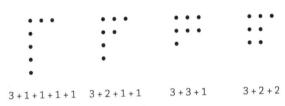

$$5 + 1 + 1 \qquad 4 + 2 + 1 \qquad 3 + 2 + 2 \qquad 3 + 3 + 1$$

Figure 7.12 Partitions of 7 with exactly three parts

$$3 + 1 + 1 + 1 + 1 \qquad 3 + 2 + 1 + 1 \qquad 3 + 3 + 1 \qquad 3 + 2 + 2$$

Figure 7.13 Partitions of 7 having 3 as their largest part

bijective proof. As Wilf (personal communication, September 2009) puts it, a simple bijective proof reveals that "in a sense the elements [of the two sets of partitions] are the same, but have simply been encoded differently."

That is, the bijective proof shows that in counting O-partitions or D-partitions, we are effectively counting the same set of abstract objects. Each of these objects can be represented by a dot diagram; the same diagram can be viewed as representing an O-partition and a D-partition. As another example (Andrews and Eriksson 2004, 16–17), consider this partition identity: the number of partitions of n with exactly m parts equals the number of partitions of n having m as their largest part. For instance, figure 7.12 represents the partitions of 7 with exactly three parts.[21] Figure 7.13 depicts each of these representations seen from a different vantage point—namely, after being rotated one-quarter turn clockwise and then reflected across a horizontal line above it. These represent the partitions of 7 with 3 as their largest part. Clearly, then, both sets of partitions are represented by essentially the same set of 4 arrays. A partition of one kind, seen from another vantage point, is a partition of the other kind. The number of partitions of one kind is the same as the number of partitions of the other kind because the same abstract object can be represented as either kind of partition, and the number of those abstract objects is the same no matter how we represent them.

Whereas the generatingfunctionology "seems like something external to the combinatorics" (Andrews, personal communication, September 2009) that just miraculously manages to yield the simple result, a simple bijective proof shows that there is the same number of partitions of two kinds because partitions of those two kinds, looked at abstractly, are the same things seen from different perspectives. Such a proof "makes the reason for the simple answer completely transparent" (Stanley 2012, 15); "it provides a 'natural' explanation . . . unlike the generating function proof which depended on a miraculous trick" (Stanley and Björner 2010, 24).[22]

When one mathematical result is compared to (or contrasted with) another, certain similarities or differences between them may be rendered salient. In this way, there may arise a difference between explaining why the result holds and merely proving that it holds. For example, consider the Fourier series

$$F(x)=(4/\pi)\begin{bmatrix}\cos(\pi x/2)-(1/3)\cos(3\pi x/2)\\+(1/5)\cos(5\pi x/2)-(1/7)\cos(7\pi x/2)+...\end{bmatrix}.$$

For $-1 < x < 1$, $F(x) = 1$, and so its derivative $F'(x) = 0$. However, differentiating $F(x)$ term by term, we obtain

$$G(x)=-2\left[\sin(\pi x/2)-\sin(3\pi x/2)+\sin(5\pi x/2)-\sin(7\pi x/2)+...\right]$$

and so, for instance,

$$G(.5)=-\sqrt{2}\left[1-1-1+1+1-1-1+1+...\right],$$

which fails to converge. Therefore, $G(x) \neq F'(x)$; we have proved by example that the derivative at $x = a$ of a sum of infinitely many terms, each differentiable at $x = a$, need not equal the sum of the terms' derivatives at $x = a$. This result does not have a salient feature until we contrast it with another result: the derivative at $x = a$ of a sum of *finitely* many terms, each differentiable at $x = a$, equals the sum of the terms' derivatives at $x = a$. We are now readily struck by the difference between these results and so it now means something to ask: *Why* is the derivative of an infinite sum not always the sum of the derivatives? The result concerning finite sums introduces a distinction between an explanation and a mere proof of the result concerning infinite sums: an explanation is a proof that reveals the difference it makes that the sum is infinite rather than finite. (This is like the role that contrasts sometimes play in scientific explanations, as in "Why did Jones die of lung cancer when Smith did not?" which calls for the difference in their fates to be traced to some other relevant difference between them.)

My example (that $G(.5) \neq F'(.5)$) suffices to prove the result concerning infinite sums (i.e., that it is not true of every infinite sum that its derivative is the sum of the derivatives of its terms). But obviously this proof fails to trace the result to a particular respect in which infinite sums differ from finite ones. Therefore, it fails (in this context) to explain why the result holds. An explanation would consist of a proof of the result regarding finite sums and a demonstration that this proof cannot be extended to infinite sums because of some particular difference between infinite and finite sums. Here is such an explanation:

Let's take a sum of two functions (f and g) and show that $(f+g)'(a) =f'(a) + g'(a)$. By definition, $f'(a)=\lim\limits_{h\to 0}\dfrac{f(a+h)-f(a)}{h}$ and $g'(a)=\lim\limits_{h\to 0}\dfrac{g(a+h)-g(a)}{h}$. Let's unpack these limits: for every $\varepsilon/2 > 0$, there are $\delta_1, \delta_2 > 0$ such that if $|h| < \delta_1$, then $\left| f'(a) - \dfrac{f(a+h)-f(a)}{h} \right| < \varepsilon/2$, and if $|h| < \delta_2$, then $\left| g'(a) - \dfrac{g(a+h)-g(a)}{h} \right| <$

$\varepsilon/2$. Let δ be the smaller of δ_1 and δ_2 (or their common value if they are equal).

Then for any $\varepsilon/2 > 0$, if $|h| < \delta$, then $\left| f'(a) + g'(a) - \dfrac{(f+g)(a+h)-(f+g)(a)}{h} \right| =$

$\left| f'(a) - \dfrac{f(a+h)-f(a)}{h} + g'(a) - \dfrac{g(a+h)-g(a)}{h} \right| \leq \left| f'(a) - \dfrac{f(a+h)-f(a)}{h} \right| +$

$\left| g'(a) - \dfrac{g(a+h)-g(a)}{h} \right| < \varepsilon/2 + \varepsilon/2 = \varepsilon$. So $f'(a)+g'(a) = \lim\limits_{h\to 0} \dfrac{(f+g)(a+h)-(f+g)(a)}{h}$,

which (by definition) equals $(f+g)'(a)$.

To prove the analogous result for the sum of n functions, we replace $\varepsilon/2$ with ε/n and let δ be the smallest of $\delta_1, \ldots, \delta_n$; out of any finite number of positive numbers, there is certain to be one that is smaller than (or as small as) each of the others. But not so for an infinite number of positive numbers; with infinitely many functions and hence infinitely many δ_i, there is no guarantee that some positive number is less than or equal to every δ_i. Rather, the δ_i may approach arbitrarily near to 0.

This difference between finite and infinite sums is responsible for the difference between the two results. Thus we can "explain why it is that sometimes you can differentiate an infinite series by differentiating each term, and sometimes you cannot" (Bressoud 1994, 69).[23]

Symmetry and simplicity are two of the features that are most commonly salient in mathematical results and thus often inform the distinction between proofs that explain and proofs that do not.[24] As I have shown, some mathematical results have no notable features at all. Still other results have outstanding features that are particular to them or, at least, are not nearly as common as symmetry and simplicity. Nevertheless, such striking features can also establish what would make a proof explanatory. Let's look briefly at an example.

Figure 7.14 displays the first few triangular numbers and the first few square numbers. Consider the fact that for any triangular number T, $8T + 1$ is a square number. (For example, 8 x 6 + 1 = 49 = 7^2.) The striking thing about this result, of course, is its "geometric" or "polygonal" character (as evoked by the terms "triangular numbers" and "square number"). Therefore, to explain why this result holds, a proof must exploit some other geometric relation between triangular and square numbers.

Here is such a proof. As figure 7.15 depicts, two of the triangles corresponding to the nth triangular number T_n form a rectangle of sides n and $n +$ 1. As figure 7.16 depicts, four of these rectangles (formed from eight of the T_n

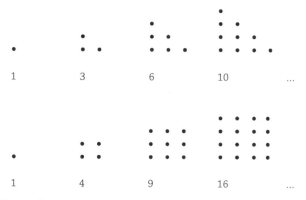

Figure 7.14 Triangular numbers and square numbers

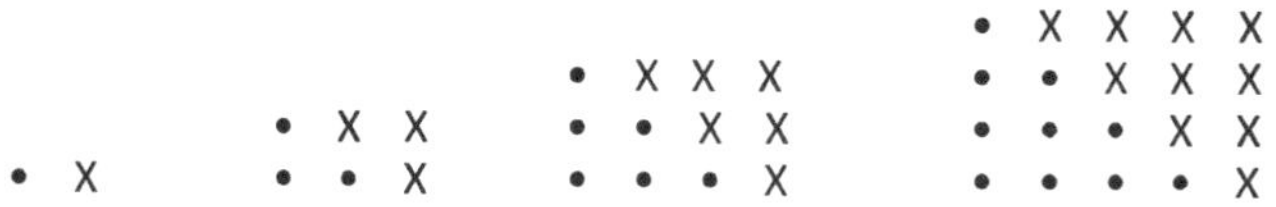

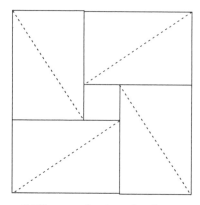

Figure 7.15 Two triangles form a rectangle

Figure 7.16 Four of Figure 7.15's rectangles, joined with a 1x1 square, form a square

triangles) can be arranged to form a square of side $2n + 1$ with a 1 x 1 hole in the middle. Thus, eight of the T_n triangles + 1 yield a square—namely, $(2n + 1)^2$.[25]

Throughout this proof, the triangular and square numbers are treated exclusively geometrically. The same result can be proved algebraically:

$$T_n = n(n+1)/2.$$

$$8T_n + 1 = 8n(n+1)/2 + 1 = 4n(n+1) + 1 = 4n^2 + 4n + 1 = (2n+1)(2n+1).$$

This proof exploits what triangular and square numbers *are* in algebraic terms; it does not treat these numbers geometrically. In the geometric proof, each T_n's triangle functions as a unit, an elemental building block of rectangles and, ultimately, of a square. By contrast, in the algebraic proof, the $n(n + 1)/2$ expression for T_n is not treated as a unit. Rather, it is broken down into its algebraic components, which are then recombined and massaged into a perfect square. The algebraic proof is therefore not explanatory in the context that I initially set up.

The geometric character of the result to be proved was made salient by the result's having initially been expressed in terms of "triangular" and "square" numbers. The same result might have been presented in purely algebraic terms:

For every natural number n, there is a natural number m where $8\left(\sum_{k=1}^{n}k\right)+1=m^2$.

This algebraic way of putting the result fails to bring out its geometric character. As far as I can tell, the result as expressed algebraically has no outstanding features; it fails to establish any distinction between a proof that explains the result and a proof that merely proves it. There is a general lesson here: we can make a feature of some result more or less salient by the way we express it. What's salient is a feature of the result *under a certain representation*.

In the mathematical explanations that I have been examining, the explanandum consists of a given theorem and the theorem's having some salient feature grounds the distinction between explaining it and merely proving it. It might then seem that the explanandum could just as well be characterized instead as the fact that the result has that salient feature. Indeed, I see no difference between asking (with regard to Zeitz's biased coin) "Why, for any natural number n, is the chance that Zeitz's coin yields r heads in n tosses the same for any integer r (where $0 \le r \le n$)?" and asking "Why, for any natural number n and any integer r (where $0 \le r \le n$), is the chance that Zeitz's coin yields r heads in n tosses equal to $1/(n + 1)$?"[26] However, in other examples, the explanandum cannot be understood as the theorem's possessing the salient feature; the explanandum is the theorem. For example, in explaining why it is that for any triangular number T, $8T + 1$ is a square number, we are not explaining why the theorem is a relation between two types of polygonal numbers (that's too trivial) or why there is any relation at all (rather than none) between triangular and square numbers (that's too unspecific).

Figures 7.15 and 7.16 are sometimes described as a "proof without words" (Wells 1991, 198; see Nelson 1993). Unlike the algebraic proof, it enables the result to be visualized, thereby allowing it to be proved "on sight." However, on my view, visualizability does not automatically contribute to a proof's explanatory power. Visualizability matters to explanatory power in this case only because the result's salient feature (in the given context) is its geometric character.[27]

Likewise, my proposal entails that if an explanatory proof appeals to a symmetry in the setup, but the result being explained fails to exhibit any similar striking symmetry, then the proof's explanatory power does not arise from its appeal to symmetry. Let's look at an example.[28] Suppose you write down all of the whole numbers from 1 to 99,999. How many times would you write down the digit 7? The answer turns out to be 50,000 times. This is a striking result: 50,000 is almost exactly ½ of 99,999. Here is one proof of this result:

> The digit 7 appears once between 1 and 10, once between 11 and 20, in fact once in every "regular" 10-plet of numbers; here "regular" means that there are no digits 7 in the tens or higher decimal places. Between 61 and 70, there are two digits 7; between 71 and 80, there are 10; collecting all of these, one concludes that the digit 7 appears 20 times between 1 and 100, and thus 20 times in every "regular" 100-plet. In the 100-plet from 601 to 700, there is an additional 7, i.e., the digit 7 occurs 21 times, and in the following 100-plet there are 99 additional 7's, yielding all together 300 7's between 1 and 1000. Proceeding in a similar way, one finds that the digit 7 appears 4,000 times between 1 and 10,000, and it appears 50,000 times between 1 and 100,000. (Dreyfus and Eisenberg 1986, 3)

This methodical (or, if you prefer, plodding!) proof tallies every appearance of 7 but has no explanatory power. That is because (on my view) it does not reveal something in the setup corresponding to the salient ½ in the result and generating that feature of the result. Rather, it portrays the number of 7's as just turning out in fact to be very nearly half of 99,999. We still want to know why that is. Compare this proof:

> Include 0 among the numbers under consideration—this will not change the number of times that the digit 7 appears. Suppose all of the whole numbers from 0 to 99,999 (100,000 of them) are written down with five digits each, e.g., 1306 is written as 01306. All possible five-digit combinations are now written down, once each. Because every digit will take every position equally often, every digit must occur the same number of times overall. Since there are 100,000 numbers with five digits each—that is, 500,000 digits—each of the 10 digits appears 50,000 times. That is, 100,000 x 5/10 = 50,000. (Dreyfus and Eisenberg 1986, 3)

This proof is more illuminating than the first one. In particular, it explains why the number of 7's is almost exactly ½ of 99,999. It reveals where the ½ comes from: There are 5 digits in each number being written down (if 1306 is being written as 01306), there are 10 digits in base 10 (0 through 9), and 5/10 = 1/2. This proof explains, then, by virtue of tracing the result's striking feature to a similar feature of the setup. Of course, the proof "recognizes and uses the fact that the digit 7 is in no way different from the other digits, and thus appeals to the symmetric role played by all nonzero digits in the list of numbers" (Dreyfus and Eisenberg 1986, 3). Indeed, the proof makes the digit 0 play the very same role as the others do, augmenting the symmetry. But this appeal to symmetry is not responsible for the proof's explanatory power. That is because the result's striking feature lies elsewhere.

■ 7.7 CONCLUSION

As I have shown, symmetry and simplicity are frequently salient in mathematical results. One or the other often informs the distinction between a proof that explains and a proof that does not. In chapter 8, I will examine another feature that many mathematical results strikingly exhibit, where a proof qualifies as explanatory by virtue of exploiting the same feature in the setup.

Some mathematical results are striking for *both* their symmetry *and* their simplicity. For instance, consider the fact that for any real m, $\int_0^{\pi/2} \frac{dx}{1+\tan^m x} = \pi/4$.

The simplicity of this result strikes us at once. Part of what makes it so strikingly simple is that over the domain of integration (from $x = 0$ to $x = \pi/2$), the function $f(x) = \frac{1}{1+\tan^m x}$ ranges between 0 and 1, so (as fig. 7.17 illustrates for two values of m) the $f(x)$ curve marks out a rectangle of area $\pi/2$, and the integral (the area under the curve) turns out to equal exactly half of this rectangle's area. That is a remarkably simple relation between the $f(x)$ curve and the rectangle. The result remains mysterious in the absence of a proof that exploits some similar, simple feature of the setup; any demand for the reason why the result holds is informed by this salient feature of it. But in addition, the why question is also informed by the result's notable invariance under change in m. Nahin (2009, 319) nicely captures the strikingness of the result's symmetry: "This holds for *any* real value of m, for example, $m = -\pi$, 0 (this special case should be obvious!) and 11,073,642.07. How in the world, you may fairly ask, can such a wonderful result be established?" Its invariance under change in m is indeed "wonderful." In view of these two salient features, my view dictates that to explain this result, a proof must trace it to some other simple relation of the $f(x)$ curve to the rectangle it marks out, a relation that displays the same symmetry (namely, invariance under change in m) as the result itself does.

Just such a feature is identified by the fact that for any real m, $f(x) = \frac{1}{1+\tan^m x}$ is symmetric about the point $(\pi/4, 0.5)$—the point located

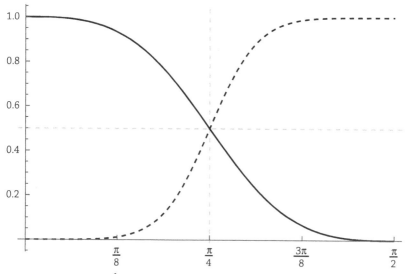

Figure 7.17 $f(x) = \dfrac{1}{1+\tan^{m}x}$ for two values of m (after Nahin 2009, 319): $m = 3$ (———) and $m = -5$ (-------).

exactly in the middle of the rectangle that the $f(x)$ curve marks out. Figure 7.17 illustrates this symmetry for two values of m: if the figure is folded lengthwise over the midline $x = \pi/4$ (the vertical dotted line) and then folded again width-wise over the midline $y = 0.5$ (the horizontal dotted line), then for any m, the two segments of the $f(x)$ curve superimpose. That is to say, however far above the x axis ($y = 0$) the curve lies when it is x to the right of the origin (for x between 0 and $\pi/2$ inclusive), that is how far below the line $y = 1$ the curve lies when it is x to the left of the line $x = \pi/2$. In other words, $f(x) = 1 - f(\pi/2 - x)$ for any x in $[0, \pi/2]$. This relation is easily proved:

Let's use the trigonometric identity $\tan(\pi/2 - x) = \sin(\pi/2 - x)/\cos(\pi/2 - x) =$

$$\cos x/\sin x = \cot x;\ f(x) + f(\pi/2 - x) = \frac{1}{1+\tan^{m}x} + \frac{1}{1+\tan^{m}(\pi/2-x)} = \frac{1}{1+\tan^{m}x} +$$

$$\frac{1}{1+\cot^{m}x} = \frac{1}{1+\tan^{m}x} + \frac{1}{1+\dfrac{1}{\tan^{m}x}} = \frac{1}{1+\tan^{m}x} + \frac{\tan^{m}x}{1+\tan^{m}x} = 1.$$

Although (as fig. 7.17 illustrates) changing m's value obviously changes the shape of the $f(x)$ curve in many important respects, it leaves unchanged the curve's symmetry about the rectangle's midpoint—an invariance in the setup over change in m. We have here a simple relation of the $f(x)$ curve to the rect-angle it marks out, a relation with the same symmetry as the result exhibits.

From this feature of the setup, it is easy to prove the result. Since the $f(x)$ curve is symmetric about the rectangle's midpoint, the curve must divide that rectangle in half by area. The rectangle's area is $\pi/2$. Hence, the integral (the area under the curve) equals $\pi/4$—which was the result to be explained. This proof works by exploiting the same kinds of features in the setup as were salient in the result. My proposal thus accounts for the proof's explanatory power.

To appreciate this proof's explanatory power, it is helpful to contrast it with another proof of the same result. Oftentimes a pesky integral like this one, which cannot be solved by any of the standard methods, succumbs to a trick—a clever substitution. Such an approach works in this case:

Let $t = \pi/2 - x$, so $x = \pi/2 - t$ and $dx = -dt$. For the bounds of integration, $x = 0$ becomes $t = \pi/2$ and $x = \pi/2$ becomes $t = 0$. So the desired integral S becomes

$$\int_{\pi/2}^{0} \frac{-dt}{1+tan^m\left(\frac{\pi}{2}-t\right)} = \int_{\pi/2}^{0} \frac{-dt}{1+cot^m t} = \int_{0}^{\pi/2} \frac{dt}{1+cot^m t} = \int_{0}^{\pi/2} \frac{tan^m(t)\,dt}{1+tan^m t}$$

$$= \int_{0}^{\pi/2} \frac{\left[1+tan^m(t)-1\right]dt}{1+tan^m t} = \int_{0}^{\pi/2} dt - \int_{0}^{\pi/2} \frac{dt}{1+tan^m t} = \frac{\pi}{2} - S.$$

We have thus regenerated the original integral. So $S = \pi/2 - S$, and so $S = \pi/4$.

This clever proof solves the integral without explaining why it equals $\pi/4$.

Yet for all its tricky appearance (why in the world would anyone have ever thought that this particular change of variable would turn out to be useful?), this proof is in certain respects not much different from the proof that explains why the result holds. The two proofs use the same trigonometric identities, and the clever substitution flips the function left-to-right within the rectangle and so allows the curve's symmetry over the rectangle's midpoint to work its magic without ever having been made explicit. What the explanatory proof accomplishes by explicit appeal to the curve's symmetry about the rectangle's midpoint (i.e., by appeal to $f(x) = 1 - f(\pi/2 - x)$) is allowed to emerge by the tricky proof's clever change of variables from x to $\pi/2 - x$. The tricky proof's failure to explain derives not from its overall strategy (after all, it does not proceed by brute force!), but rather from its failure fully to bring out features of the setup that are exploited explicitly by the explanatory proof—features of the setup that are similar to the result's salient features.

Though the tricky substitution is pulled seemingly "out of nowhere" and so has no explanatory virtues, its success could easily lead someone to recognize the very feature of the setup that the explanatory proof exploits. When we find that the trick works, we may well ask why it works, and the reason turns out to be that for any m, the $f(x)$ curve is symmetric about the rectangle's midpoint. Here we have an account that explains why some problem yields to a certain sort of strategy, rather than an explanation of the kind that I have been investigating (namely, a proof that explains why some theorem is true).[29] In this case, the trick works because the change of variable allows us to exploit the same feature of the setup that explains why the result holds. I suspect that in many other cases as well, to demand an explanation of why some trick works in a given case is to ask for a connection between the trick's success in "cracking the case" and the reason why the result thereby arrived at holds. There needn't be a reason why some trick works—just as there needn't be a reason why some result holds. But I suspect that in many cases, an explanation of why some trick works is parasitic on an explanation of why the result arrived at by the trick holds.

In other cases, the "tricky" method of solution has some salient feature itself—something unconventional that puts the method's validity in doubt. To explain why the method nevertheless manages to arrive at the right answer, it is not enough to prove in some other, rigorous way that the answer it yields is correct. Rather, an explanation must use a method of proof that has the same salient feature as the "tricky" method, but reveals the method's mathematically rigorous basis. An "independent" proof of the answer originally arrived at through the tricky method (that is, a proof that does not share that method's salient feature) fails to explain why that method worked. An independent proof makes it look like an "accident" or "coincidence" that a method with the salient, problematic feature happened to arrive at the right answer.[30]

For example, consider the following method of showing that the area (in square units) enclosed by a circle of unit radius is numerically equal to half of its circumference (measured in that unit):

> The circle consists of infinitely many, equal, infinitesimally short line segments, so the area it encloses is the area of infinitely many triangles, each triangle with height equal to the circle's radius and with one of the infinitesimal segments as its base. The area of each triangle is half its (infinitesimal) base times its (unit) height. The circle's area is the sum of the triangles' areas, which is ½ times the sum of the infinitesimal segments, and their sum is the circumference.

This method's salient feature is obviously its use of infinitesimals, which is problematic: if each of the equal, infinitesimal segments is finite, then infinite total area is covered by infinitely many triangles having these segments as their bases, and if each segment is zero, then no area is covered. Nevertheless, the method somehow manages to give the right answer, as can be proved independently (that is, without the use of infinitesimals) in various ways, including this one:

> Suppose (for the sake of *reductio*) that the circle's area differs from half of its circumference by some nonzero quantity *d*. Then if about the circle we circumscribe

a regular polygon with enough sides (each finitely long), we can bring the polygon's perimeter to within $d/2$ of the circle's circumference and also bring their areas to within $d/2$. The circumscribed n-gon can be decomposed into n triangles each having one of the n-gon's sides (of length s) as its base and having unit height. Now we follow the earlier argument, only without infinitesimals: the area of each triangle is $s/2$, and the polygon's total area is the sum of these triangles' areas ($ns/2$), which is ½ of the polygon's perimeter. So the polygon's area differs by zero from half of its perimeter, the polygon's area differs from the circle's by less than $d/2$, and the polygon's perimeter differs from the circle's circumference by less than $d/2$. It follows that the circle's area differs from half of its circumference by less than d, contradicting the initial supposition.

This independent proof shows that the original, problematic method gives the correct answer. But the independent proof fails to explain *why* that method works. Indeed, the independent proof moves mathematicians to seek an explanation of why the original, problematic method works. (For example, regarding the problematic method, Stewart, 1996, 74, asks, "If it's nonsense, why does it give the right answer?") Of course, the independent proof is similar in one respect to the problematic method: both make use of the decomposition of a shape into triangles of unit height. But this similarity is not enough to enable the independent proof to explain why the original method works. That is because the independent proof does not share the original method's salient feature: its use of infinitesimals. A proof that makes do without infinitesimals cannot explain the success of a method whose salient feature is precisely its use of infinitesimals.

In contrast, the last 50 years have revealed several ways to put the use of infinitesimals on a mathematically rigorous footing. The best known is Abraham Robinson's "nonstandard analysis," which uses mathematical logic to prove the existence of a nonstandard model of the theory of real numbers consisting of the "hyperreal numbers." These numbers include not only the reals, but also infinitesimals and their infinite reciprocals. If a theorem's hypothesis and conclusion are stated over the reals, then the theorem can be proved by transforming its hypothesis into its hyperreal analogue, using nonstandard methods (featuring infinitesimals) to derive the corresponding conclusion, and then restricting that conclusion back to the reals. Because nonstandard analysis uses infinitesimals, which are the salient feature of the original, problematic method for deriving the relation between a circle's area and circumference, nonstandard analysis may explain why that method gets the right answer. Of course, Robinson's infinitesimals differ in some respects from the infinitesimals used by Newton, Leibniz, Euler, and others before Weierstrass defined the concept of a limit entirely in terms of finite numbers. But Robinson's infinitesimals function seamlessly in proofs like the one that I have been examining. Thus, nonstandard analysis is able to explain why some of the Newton/Leibniz-style arguments exploiting infinitesimals work. The explanatory power of nonstandard analysis is frequently acknowledged:

> A preliminary explanation of why the calculus could develop on the insecure foundation of the acceptance of infinitely small and infinitely large quantities is provided by the recently developed nonstandard analysis. (Bos 1974–75, 13)

> Nonstandard analysis makes it possible to answer a delicate question bound up with earlier approaches to the history of classical analysis. If infinitely small and infinitely large magnitudes are regarded as inconsistent notions, how could they serve as a basis for the construction of so grandiose an edifice as one of the most important mathematical disciplines? (Medvedev 1998, 664)

> Nonstandard analysis showed *why* infinitesimals were safe for consumption in mathematics. (Dauben 1988, 184, his emphasis)

There are many other, originally problematic mathematical methods (such as the use of the Dirac delta function and Heaviside's operational calculus) where mathematicians have gone on to develop other methods that establish the same results as the problematic methods first reached. But mathematicians distinguish proofs of those results by independent methods from proofs that also explain *why* the problematic methods arrived at correct results. The explanatory proofs differ from the original, problematic methods by virtue of their rigor. In this respect, they are like the proofs using independent methods. But even rigorous proofs of the same results as the original, problematic methods reached need not explain why those methods worked.[31] The explanatory proofs differ from the proofs using independent methods by exhibiting the same salient features as the original methods, thereby explaining why those methods worked.[32]

When a trick works in a given case, it is sometimes natural not only to ask why it works there, but also to try out the same trick in other cases—and, if it works there as well, to try to prove a theorem specifying the range of cases where it works. An explanation of why such a theorem holds is just another instance of the kind of explanation that I have been examining throughout this chapter. In section 7.4, I presented one example of such an explanation: Lagrange's explanation of why any cubic equation of the form $x^3 + nx + p = 0$ can be solved by making the "tricky" change of variables $x = y - n/3y$, thereby turning it into a sixth-degree equation $y^6 + py^3 + n^3/27 = 0$ (the "resolvent") that, miraculously, is quadratic in y^3. Lagrange's investigation into such tricks did not stop there. Mathematicians such as Cardano, Euler, Hudde, Bezout, and Tschirnhaus had already developed various other tricks for solving cubic and quartic equations. One of Lagrange's tasks in his monumental 1770–1771 "Reflections on the Solution of Algebraic Equations" was to explain why his predecessors' various methods all worked ("pourquoi ces méthods réussissent" (Lagrange 1869, 206; see Kline 1972, 601, Wussing 1984, 71–74)). By showing that these different procedures all amounted fundamentally to the same method, Lagrange showed that it was·no coincidence that they all worked. In other words, faced with the fact that Cardano's method works, Euler's method works, Tschirnhaus's method works, and so forth, one feature of this fact is obviously salient: that it identifies something common to each of these methods (namely, that each works). Lagrange's explanation succeeds by tracing this common feature to other features that these methods have in common—in sum, that they are all fundamentally Lagrange's own method: "These methods all come down to the same general principle" (Lagrange 1869, 355; quoted in Kiernan 1971, 45). Part of the point in asking why these methods all work is to ask whether their success can be traced to a feature that is common to them all or is merely a coincidence. (In chapter 8, I will investigate the notion of a "mathematical coincidence.")

Closely related to questions about why a given trick works are question of the form "Why is this result so hard to prove?" "Why is this problem so much harder to solve than that one, when they appear so much alike?" "Why does this strategy succeed in proving this theorem but not that theorem?" and "Why does this technique fail here despite working there?"[33] Questions of the form "Why is this result so hard to prove when that one isn't?" have long been a focus of mathematical research. Here is one such famous question with which mathematicians remain engaged today. Standard techniques allow all of the following results to be derived:

$$1-1/3+1/5-1/7+...=\pi/4$$

$$1/1^2+1/2^2+1/3^2+...=\pi^2/6$$

$$1/1^2-1/2^2+1/3^2-1/4^2+...=\pi^2/12$$

$$1/1^3-1/3^3+1/5^3-1/7^3+...=\pi^3/32$$

But despite its similarity to all of these examples, no one has found such an expression to complete the equation

$$1/1^3+1/2^3+1/3^3+...=?$$

Why is this sum[34] so much more difficult than the others, from which it differs only slightly? This is a notorious why question: "Why the problem goes from 'not hard' to 'stupendously hard' just by making what appears to be such minor changes remains an immensely deep mystery" (Nahin 2009, 99). Philosophers have a different mystery on their hands: To identify what it would take for mathematicians to resolve their mystery. Philosophers should devote some attention to understanding how mathematical explanations answer questions like "Why is this problem so difficult?"[35]

8

Mathematical Coincidences and Mathematical Explanations That Unify

In this chapter, I will continue to elaborate my account (introduced in chapter 7) of how mathematical proofs that explain why some result holds differ from mathematical proofs that prove the result without explaining why it holds. Besides its symmetry or simplicity, what else about a mathematical result might stand out where a proof of the result would qualify as explanatory insofar as the proof exploits the same kind of feature in the setup? Here is an example from the mathematics literature that was called to my attention in a lovely unpublished essay by Roy Sorensen. Take an ordinary calculator keyboard (though without the zero):

7	8	9
4	5	6
1	2	3

We can form a six-digit number by taking the three digits on any row, column, or main diagonal on the keyboard in forward and then in reverse order. For instance, the bottom row taken from left to right, and then right to left, yields 123321. There are 16 such "calculator numbers": 123321, 321123, 456654, 654456, 789987, 987789, 147741, 741147, 258852, 852258, 369963, 963369, 159951, 951159, 357753, and 753357. As you can easily verify (with a calculator!), every one of these numbers is divisible by 37. Is this (as the title of a recent *Mathematical Gazette* article asks) a coincidence?[1]

The striking thing about this result is that it applies to every single calculator number. A proof that simply takes each calculator number in turn, showing it to be divisible by 37, treats the result as if it were a coincidence. That is, it fails to explain why all of the calculator numbers are divisible by 37. Indeed, such a case-by-case proof merely serves to highlight the fact that the result applies to every single calculator number. Especially in light of this proof, an explanation would be a proof that proceeds from some property that is common to each of these numbers by virtue of their all being calculator numbers. This property must be a genuine respect in which these numbers are similar, that is, a mathematically

natural property—unlike the property of being either 123321 or 321123 or . . .
Here is such a proof (from a later *Mathematical Gazette* article pithily entitled
"No Coincidence"): "This is *no* coincidence. For let a, $a + d$, $a + 2d$ be any three
integers in arithmetic progression. Then

$$a.10^5 + (a+d).10^4 + (a+2d).10^3 + (a+2d).10^2 + (a+d).10 + a.1$$
$$= a(10^5 + 10^4 + 10^3 + 10^2 + 10 + 1) + d(10^4 + 2.10^3 + 2.10^2 + 10)$$
$$= 111111a + 12210d = 1221(91a + 10d).$$

So not only is the number divisible by 37, but by 1221 $(= 3 \times 11 \times 37)$" (Nummela
1987, 147).

This proof exploits the fact that every calculator number can be expressed
as $10^5 a + 10^4(a+d) + 10^3(a+2d) + 10^2(a+2d) + 10(a+d) + a$ where
a, $a + d$, $a + 2d$ are three integers in arithmetic progression. These three integers, of course, are the three digits on the calculator keypads that, taken forward
and backward, generate the given calculator number. Hence, this proof traces
the fact that every calculator number is divisible by 37 to a property that they
have in common by virtue of being calculator numbers (namely, that each can
be expressed in the form given above).[2]

In short, an explanation of this result consists of a proof that treats every
calculator number in the same way. This unified treatment makes the proof
explanatory because what strikes us as remarkable about the result, especially
in light of the case-by-case proof, is that it identifies a property that is common
to every calculator number. In other words, the result's unity is salient. The
point of asking for an explanation is then to ask for a proof that exploits some
other property that is common to them by virtue of their all being calculator
numbers.[3]

I have just put on the table several important notions, including a mathematical coincidence, a natural property in mathematics, and a proof that treats
various cases in the same way and thereby unifies them. Each of these notions
will receive closer scrutiny in this chapter and its successor. But before turning
first to mathematical coincidence, let me pause to emphasize the relations that
(I will propose) obtain among these notions. Suppose that a given result's salient
feature is that it identifies a property that is common to every case of a certain
sort.[4] Suppose it is a natural property in mathematics (that is, a sparse property
in mathematics rather than a mere shadow of a predicate), else it does not constitute a respect in which those cases are genuinely alike. A proof of the result
then explains why it holds exactly when the proof exploits some other respect in
which all of these cases are alike and from there arrives at the result by treating
all of the cases in the same way. Such a unifying proof shows the result to be no
mathematical coincidence, where a mathematical coincidence has such a salient
feature but no explanation. For a mathematical coincidence, then, there is no

"common proof"—roughly speaking, no deduction from the axioms that in the same way proves each of the result's components by exploiting a natural property that is common to the various cases dealt with by those components. Thus, a mathematical coincidence is similar in some respects to a physical coincidence (such as the fact that Presidents Lincoln and Kennedy both had vice presidents named "Johnson"): just as the components of a mathematical coincidence have no "common proof," the components of a physical coincidence have no common explainer (or, at least, none of any interest).

For instance, I argued in chapter 1 that it is no coincidence that all double pendulums are alike in having at least four equilibrium configurations. What makes it no coincidence is that every double pendulum has this property for the same reason, namely, because of the kind of configuration space they all have in virtue of being double pendulums. This explanation does not reveal that the same kind of *causes* are responsible for every double pendulum's having at least four equilibrium configurations. Instead, this explanation is a "distinctively mathematical" scientific explanation; it is a non-causal explanation (in particular, an "explanation by constraint"). Analogously, what makes it no coincidence that every "calculator number" is divisible by 37 is a unifying explanation appealing to the fact that all calculator numbers can be expressed in the same way in virtue of being calculator numbers. In each example, an explanation that unifies different cases makes their resemblance non-coincidental. (In the final part of this book, I will say more about this similarity between explanations in science and mathematics.)

Although it is a coincidence that every calculator number is divisible by 37, there are plenty of mathematical coincidences. For example, Davis (1981, 312) points out that it is coincidental that 9 is both the thirteenth digit in the decimal representation of π (= 3.14 159 265 358 979 3 ...) and the thirteenth digit in the decimal representation of e (= 2.71 828 182 845 904 5 ...). (That the same digit appears in the same place in both expansions is clearly the striking feature of the fact that 9 is the thirteenth digit of π and the thirteenth digit of e.) Likewise, consider these two Diophantine equations (that is, equations where the variables can take only integer values):

$$2x^2\left(x^2-1\right)=3\left(y^2-1\right)$$

and

$$x(x-1)/2=2^n-1.$$

As it happens, each equation has exactly the same five positive solutions for x: 1, 2, 3, 6, and 91 (Guy 1988, 704). As far as I know, this is just a coincidence. If it is in fact a coincidence, then that is because there is no proof that in a uniform way traces this similarity in the equations to some other respect in which they are alike. Such a proof would have explained why the two equations' positive solutions are exactly the same. In the absence of such a "common proof," this similarity has no explanation; it is coincidental.[5] Notice that the question "*Why* does $x(x - 1)/2 = 2^n - 1$ have exactly $x = 1, 2, 3, 6$, and 91 as its positive solutions?" is pointless; there is no distinction between an explanation of why these results hold and a mere proof that they hold. However, once this result is combined with the fact that the other equation has exactly the same positive solutions, there is a distinction between an explanation and a mere proof. The question "*Why* do they have exactly the same positive solutions?" is asking for something. My account explains this phenomenon. Taken in isolation from the second equation's positive solutions, there is nothing striking about the fact that the first equation has exactly $x = 1, 2, 3, 6$, and 91 as its positive solutions. But there is obviously something striking about this fact as juxtaposed with the second equation's positive solutions.

The same applies in the case of a non-coincidence, such as the theorem regarding calculator numbers. The question "Why is 123321 divisible by 37?" makes no demand over and above a proof of this fact. But not just any proof of the explanandum would answer the question "*Why* are 123321, 654456, and 789987 all divisible by 37? Is it a coincidence?" I have suggested that this fact is no coincidence because its three components have not only a salient similarity, but also a "common proof": each of its components can be proved in the same way from a feature that these three calculator numbers share (namely, that each is expressible as $10^5 a + 10^4 (a+d) + 10^3 (a+2d) + 10^2 (a+2d) + 10(a+d) + a$ where $a, a + d, a + 2d$ are three integers in arithmetic progression). This proof therefore explains why they are all divisible by 37. But as I just argued, it would be misleading to say that this proof explains why 123321 is divisible by 37—as if the question "Why is 123321 divisible by 37?" makes sense in a context where this fact is taken in isolation (rather than juxtaposed with, say, the fact that 789987 is divisible by 37). Taken by itself, there is nothing striking about the fact that 123321 is divisible by 37, and so in such a context, it has no explanation over and above a proof. It is likewise somewhat misleading to say that the fact that 123321 is divisible by 37 and the fact that 789987 is divisible by 37 have a common mathematical explanation—as if there is an explanation of the former taken in isolation and an explanation of the latter taken in isolation, where these two explanations are largely the same. Rather, the fact that both 123321 and 789987 are divisible by 37 has an explanation—roughly, a uniform proof that exploits a property that 123321 and 789987 share. The proof's power to explain why both are divisible by 37 does not derive from its somehow having the power to explain why 123321 is divisible by 37, and independently the power to explain why 789987 is divisible by 37. Only in a context where 123321's divisibility by 37 has some outstanding feature (as when it is juxtaposed with 789987's divisibility by 37) is there any distinction between its explanation and its mere proof.

In this respect, the components of a mathematical coincidence differ from the components of a physical coincidence. It makes sense to ask why Lincoln had a vice president named "Johnson" even in isolation from the fact that Kennedy did, too. Whether a certain event qualifies as a cause of Andrew Johnson's joining the Republican ticket in 1864 is not relative to whether Kennedy's vice president is under consideration. In contrast, it does not make sense to ask why 123321 is divisible by 37 (over and above asking for a proof of this fact) outside of a context where this result exhibits some noteworthy feature, and arguably it exhibits a noteworthy feature only in juxtaposition with some other result (as I also showed occurring in the Fourier series example in section 7.6). In the case of a pair of physical facts that is no coincidence, each component taken in isolation has an explanation, and their explanations are prior to the explanation of their combination. That combination is no coincidence because the components' explanations have something of interest in common. Such is not the case, on my view, for a pair of mathematical facts that constitute no mathematical coincidence; it is not the case that the joint result is no mathematical coincidence by virtue of *each component having an explanation* that exploits some feature of its setup, where these features turn out all to be alike. Rather, the joint result is no coincidence because *the joint result has an explanation* that treats each component alike, deriving each component in the same way from a feature it shares with the others. Nevertheless, a mathematical coincidence resembles a physical coincidence in that just as the components of a physical coincidence have no (interesting) common explainer (such as a common cause), the components of a mathematical coincidence have no "common proof."[6]

In section 4.3, I showed that one prominent objection to Duchayla's proposed explanation of the parallelogram law was that his proposal incorrectly portrays as coincidental the fact that the parallelogram law holds for both magnitude and direction. I suggested that this objection be cashed out in terms of mathematical (rather than physical) "coincidence"—in particular, in terms of Duchayla's proposal offering no "common proof" of the parallelogram law's holding for both magnitude and direction. Duchayla's explanation does not treat magnitude and direction in a uniform way. In this chapter, I will redeem the promissory notes issued in chapter 4.

The question "Is that mathematical result a coincidence?" sometimes sounds more natural than the question "Why is that mathematical result true?" Both questions, on my view, demand mathematical explanations. But the former question is appropriate only when a salient feature of the result is its identifying some property common to cases that otherwise seem unrelated. In the calculator-keyboard example, the question of whether the result is coincidental is provoked not only by the result, but also by the proof that treats each of the calculator numbers separately, showing each to be divisible by 37. The proof's plodding, case-by-case approach contrasts sharply with and thereby highlights the fact that the result being proved identifies a respect in which all of the calculator numbers are alike. It thus provokes the question "Is that similarity really a coincidence?"

Sometimes it requires a proof by cases to make salient the fact that the result being proved identifies a respect in which certain cases are alike. Without the proof dividing the result into certain cases, no one would not have focused on them as separate cases at all. For instance, take one standard proof of the formula for the sum $S = n(n + 1)/2$ of the first n nonzero natural numbers $(1 + 2 + \ldots + (n - 1) + n)$.

> There are two cases.
>
> When n is even, we can pair the first and last numbers in the sequence, the second and second-to-last, and so forth. The members of each pair sum to $n + 1$. No number is left unpaired, since n is even. The number of pairs is $n/2$ (which is an integer, since n is even). Hence, $S = (n + 1)n/2$.
>
> When n is odd, we can pair the numbers as before, except that the middle number in the sequence is left unpaired. Again, the members of each pair sum to $n + 1$. But now there are $(n - 1)/2$ pairs, since the middle number $(n + 1)/2$ is unpaired. The total sum is the sum of the paired numbers plus the middle number: $S = (n + 1)$ $(n - 1)/2 + (n + 1)/2$. This simplifies to $(n + 1)n/2$—remarkably, the same as the expression that we just derived for even n.

Before seeing this proof, one would probably have found it unremarkable that the theorem gives the same formula for both even n and odd n. However, this feature of the result strikes one forcibly in light of the proof, which treats the two cases differently. One might then well wonder: Is it a coincidence that the same formula emerges in both cases? This proof depicts it as an algebraic miracle. Accordingly, in this context, to ask for the reason why the formula holds, not merely for a proof that it holds, is to ask (roughly) for a feature common to both of these kinds of cases from which the common result follows in the same way.

Indeed there is such a feature; the result is no coincidence. Whether n is even or odd, the sequence's midpoint is half of the sum of the first and last numbers: $(1 + n)/2$. Furthermore, all sequences of both kinds consist of numbers balanced evenly around that midpoint. In other words, for every number in the sequence exceeding the midpoint by some amount, the sequence contains a number less than the midpoint by the same amount. Allowing the excesses to cancel the deficiencies, we have each sequence containing n numbers of $(1 + n)/2$ each, yielding the formula. This is essentially what happens in the standard proof of the formula, where each sequence member having an excess is paired with a member having an equal deficiency, and vice versa:

$$S = 1 + 2 + \ldots + (n - 1) + n$$
$$S = n + (n - 1) + \ldots + 2 + 1$$

If we pair the first terms, the second terms, and so forth in each sum, then each pair adds to $(n + 1)$, and there are n pairs. So $2S = n(n + 1)$, and hence $S = n(n + 1)/2$.

This proof is just slightly different from the proof that deals separately with even n and odd n. The use of the same sequence twice, in forward and reverse order, could be considered nothing but a trick for collapsing the even n and odd n cases. But it is more than that. It brings out something that the earlier proof by cases obscures: that the common result for even n and odd n arises from a common feature of the two cases. For this reason, the earlier proof fails to reveal it to be no coincidence that the same formula works for both even n and odd n. What allows the second proof to show that this is no coincidence?[7] My answer is that it traces the result to a property common to the two cases: that the terms in the sum are balanced around $(1 + n)/2$. (Whether or not a term in the sequence actually occupies that midpoint is irrelevant to this balance; there is such a term for odd n but not for even n.) The earlier proof does not exploit this common feature; it simply works its way through the two cases individually and then magically finds itself with the same formula for both. Moreover, that the same formula applies both to even n and odd n is not a feature of the result that strikes us forcibly simply upon being given the result. It is a salient feature of the result only in light of a proof that treats the even and odd cases differently.

That a proof treating separate cases differently is not explanatory (when the theorem's salient feature is its identifying a similarity among those cases) is an idea that I believe has often been expressed (at least roughly) by mathematicians. For instance, writing about the computer-aided proof of the four-color theorem that Kenneth Appel and Wolfgang Haken found in 1976, Douglas Woodall and Robin J. Wilson write:

> a disadvantage of a long proof is that it tends not to give very much understanding of why the result is true. This is particularly true of a proof that involves looking at a large number of separate cases, whether or not it uses the computer. Many mathematicians would consider that proving theorems is only a means to the true end of pure mathematics, which is to understand what is going on. Sometimes a proof is so illuminating that one feels immediately that it explains the real reason for the result being true. It may be unreasonable to expect every theorem to have a proof of this sort, but it seems nonetheless to be a goal worth aiming for. (Woodall and Wilson 1978, 100; see Baker 2009a, 148)

In section 8.2, I will continue my argument that the concept of a mathematical coincidence plays an important role in mathematical reasoning. I will look at whether this concept can be understood without appealing to the idea of mathematical explanation—for instance, whether it can be understood in terms of a result's being surprising or unforeseen or misleading or unfruitful. In section 8.3, I will elaborate my proposal that a mathematical coincidence has a certain sort of salient feature but no explanation. Roughly speaking, the components of a mathematical coincidence have no "common proof." In section 8.4, I will examine closely a case that illustrates one important feature of my account: that a proof's explanatory power depends on which feature of the result is salient, which may shift with the context. In section 8.5, I will take my account of proofs that explain and briefly contrast it with rival proposals that have been offered by Steiner (1978a, 1978c), Kitcher (1984b, 1989), and Resnik and Kushner (1987). Finally, in section 8.6, I will suggest that some non-causal *scientific* explanations operate in the same way as the explanations in mathematics that I have examined.

■ 8.2 CAN MATHEMATICAL COINCIDENCE BE UNDERSTOOD WITHOUT APPEALING TO MATHEMATICAL EXPLANATION?

Examples like those in section 8.1 suffice to show that mathematics is interested in determining whether or not certain facts constitute "mathematical coincidences." Having already sketched my account of what a mathematical coincidence is, I will now look at some rival approaches—in particular, approaches that differ from mine in not appealing to mathematical explanation. I will argue that none of these approaches succeeds. Their failure suggests that mathematical coincidence can be understood only in terms of mathematical explanation. Accordingly, I see this section as constituting another argument for the importance of mathematical explanation in mathematical practice.

After giving the calculator-number example, Sorensen (in his unpublished essay) proposed that the distinction between mathematical coincidences and non-coincidences is epistemic, so that from a mathematically omniscient viewpoint, there are no mathematical coincidences. One way to elaborate this idea is to define a "mathematical coincidence" simply as an unforeseen or surprising mathematical result. In this light, let's return to some of the examples given in the previous section: that every calculator number is divisible by 37; that the sum of the first n nonzero natural numbers, whether n is odd or even, equals $n(n + 1)/2$; that 9 is the thirteenth digit of π as well as the thirteenth digit of e; and that the two Diophantine equations I mentioned are solved by exactly $x = 1, 2, 3, 6$, and 91. Each of these results is surprising and difficult to foresee in advance of being proved. Moreover, suppose we are given one part of any one of these results (for example, that the sum of the first n numbers, when n is even, equals $n(n + 1)/2$; that one of the calculator numbers is divisible by 37; that $2x^2(x^2 - 1) = 3(y^2 - 1)$ is solved by exactly $x = 1, 2, 3, 6$, and 91; that 9 is the thirteenth digit of e). Even given that one part, the rest of the result remains unexpected. However, as I suggested, two of these results (concerning the thirteenth digit and the Diophantine equations) are mathematical coincidences, whereas the other two (concerning the calculator numbers and the sum of the first n nonzero natural numbers) are not coincidental. Therefore, the "unforeseen or surprising fact" proposal does not immediately capture the phenomenon of mathematical coincidence. (However, there is a grain of truth in this proposal, as I will explain in the next section.)

A suggestion more like Sorensen's own is that a mathematical coincidence is a mathematical fact that misleads us, provoking expectations that turn out to be false. Some of the mathematical coincidences that Sorensen mentions certainly provoke false expectations, such as the coincidence that $3^2 + 4^2 = 5^2$ and $3^3 + 4^3 + 5^3 = 6^3$. (Contrary to the expectations thus provoked, $3^4 + 4^4 + 5^4 + 6^4 = 2258 \neq 2401 = 7^4$.) Likewise, when a mathematical fact provokes expectations that turn out to be true, we might then be inclined to say that the fact is no coincidence. For instance, is it a coincidence that 25 has at least as many divisors of the form $4k + 1$ (1, 5, and 25) as of the form $4k - 1$ (none), and that the same goes for 21 (1 and 21; 3 and 7)? No, it is no coincidence—these two examples have not misled us—since what they have led us to expect is true: every positive integer possesses this property (Guy 1988, 706).

One way to understand the suggestion that a mathematical coincidence involves a "misleading fact" is that a mathematical fact is coincidental exactly when it misleads us. (Sorensen says that from a mathematically omniscient viewpoint, there are no mathematical coincidences, presumably because someone who is mathematically omniscient is not misled about mathematics.) But this suggestion entails that once we know that $3^4 + 4^4 + 5^4 + 6^4 \neq 7^4$, it is no longer coincidental that $3^2 + 4^2 = 5^2$ and $3^3 + 4^3 + 5^3 = 6^3$ since we are no longer misled into thinking that $3^4 + 4^4 + 5^4 + 6^4 = 7^4$. Yet in mathematical practice, certain facts are still deemed to be mathematical coincidences even after we have stopped being misled by them.

Accordingly, a more promising way to understand the "misleading fact" suggestion is that a mathematical fact is coincidental insofar as it has the power to mislead those who do not already know that the expectations it tends to provoke (in those who do not already know better) turn out to be false. However, a mathematical fact may still be no coincidence even though it has tremendous capacity to mislead anyone who lacks any better information. For example, consider this sequence of definite integrals (each running from 0 to ∞):

$$\int (1/x) \sin 4x \cos x \, dx$$

$$\int (1/x) \sin 4x \cos x \cos (x/2) \, dx$$

$$\int (1/x) \sin 4x \cos x \cos (x/2) \cos (x/3) \, dx$$

$$\int (1/x) \sin 4x \cos x \cos (x/2) \cos (x/3) \cos (x/4) \, dx$$

$$\vdots$$

Suppose we check each of these through

$$\int (1/x) \sin 4x \cos x \cos (x/2) \cos (x/3) \ldots \cos(x/30)\, dx$$

and find that, remarkably, each equals $\pi/2$. This result strongly suggests that

$$\int (1/x) \sin 4x \cos x \cos (x/2) \cos (x/3) \ldots \cos(x/31)\, dx = \pi/2.$$

This turns out not to be the case; the sequence is misleading. Yet it is no coincidence that each of the first 30 integrals equals $\pi/2$. We can prove the following theorem:

> Let $a_1, \ldots, a_n, b$ be positive real numbers. Then $\int (1/x) \sin bx \cos a_1 x \cos a_2 x \ldots$ $\cos a_n x\, dx = \pi/2$ if $a_1 + \ldots + a_n < b$. (Lord 2007, 283)

Therefore, since $1 + 1/2 + 1/3 + \cdots + 1/30 < 4$, it is no coincidence that each of the first 30 members of the sequence equals $\pi/2$. ($1 + 1/2 + 1/3 + \cdots + 1/31 \approx 4.027244 > 4$.)

Thus, a combination of mathematical facts that has great power to mislead those who do not already know better need not be a mathematical coincidence. Conversely, a mathematical coincidence may not be misleading at all. That the thirteenth digits of π and e are both 9 does not mislead anyone into thinking that all of the subsequent digits of π and e are 9 (or, at least, are the same) or that anything else remarkable is going on. That the thirteenth digits of π and e are the same leads Davis (1981, 313) to propose (and might lead us to think) that on average, every tenth digit of π and e is the same. But even if this turns out to be true—and so we are not *misled*—the fact that the thirteenth digits of π and e are the same is still a coincidence. Furthermore, that the formula for the sum of the first n nonzero natural numbers is the same, whether n is even or odd, does not immediately suggest any broader result and so could not have misled us—but for all we initially knew, that the same formula works for both evens and odds might have been coincidental.

Likewise, consider the start of the sequence of numbers n such that n^4 contains exactly four copies of each digit in n:

5702631489, 7264103985, 7602314895, 7824061395, 8105793624, 8174035962, 8304269175, 8904623175, 8923670541, 9451360827, 9785261403, 9804753612, 9846032571, . . .

For instance, 5702631489 is in the sequence since its fourth power

1057550783692741389295697108242363408641

contains exactly four 5's, four 7's, four 0's and so on. All of the terms in the sequence that are 10-digit numbers are pandigital: each contains all of the digits 0 through 9 exactly once. Sloane (2007, sequence A114260) terms this fact "probably accidental, but quite curious," and I am inclined to agree. But whether or not this fact turns out to be coincidental, it does not readily lead us to formulate any broader hypotheses. For instance, this fact would not lead us to think that every number in this sequence is pandigital, since numbers longer than 10 digits cannot possibly be. (A number n longer than 10 digits can belong to the sequence; if such an n contains exactly two 7's, for instance, then n^4 contains exactly eight 7's. See Sloan 2007, sequence A114258.)

Furthermore, suppose I had presented only the first five numbers n such that n^4 contains exactly four copies of each digit in n. That these are all pandigital might naturally have led us to expect that any other *10-digit* number n such that n^4 contains exactly four copies of each digit in n is likewise pandigital. In forming this expectation, we would not have been *misled*, since as I have indicated, it turns out to be true that all of these 10-digit numbers are pandigital. However, this fact may well nevertheless be just a coincidence.

To identify a mathematical coincidence as a misleading fact is to suggest that if a particular mathematical truth leads exclusively to truths when it is generalized in various natural ways, then it must have been no coincidence. But as I have just shown, a natural generalization of one coincidence could be a broader coincidence. That a particular mathematical truth leads to truths when it is broadened in a natural way may sometimes be some *evidence* that the initial mathematical truth is no coincidence. But it fails to *ensure* that this is so. (In the next section, I will explain why the fact that a particular mathematical truth leads to truths upon being generalized sometimes counts as evidence that the initial truth is no coincidence.)

Rather than taking a mathematical coincidence to be a fact suggesting further mathematical claims that turn out to be false, we might instead take a mathematical coincidence to be a fact that is misleading in a broader (and vaguer) sense: it does not repay further study, it is not fruitful, it leads to no further interesting mathematics. (This seems to me closest to Sorensen's own proposal in the essay I have cited.) The calculator-keyboard fact is then no coincidence because it leads to Nummela's general result regarding numbers having digits extracted from arithmetic sequences, and the fact that the summation formula applies to both even n and odd n is no coincidence because the two separate proofs for the two cases lead us to an interesting common proof of the same formula for all n.

I think that these further results are indeed involved in making the calculator-keyboard fact no coincidence and in making the summation formulas for even n and odd n no coincidence. But it is not the case that they are non-coincidences *because* they suggest further interesting mathematics. Rather, they suggest further interesting mathematics because they are non-coincidences. It is fruitful to think further about a non-coincidence because we may thereby uncover the facts that make it no coincidence. On my account, the reason why a genuine mathematical coincidence leads nowhere is that there is nowhere interesting for it to lead. In particular, a coincidence has no mathematical explanation; its components lack a common proof. The reason that a coincidence is not mathematically fruitful is that there is no explanation of it to be found.[8]

To sum up this section: epistemic and psychological considerations seem insufficient to reveal what makes certain combinations of facts qualify as mathematical coincidences. Even from a mathematically omniscient perspective, there are mathematical coincidences. Indeed, mathematical omniscience would require knowledge that a given pair of facts forms a mathematical coincidence— that they bear to each other none of the mathematical relations that would make them non-coincidental.

■ 8.3 A MATHEMATICAL COINCIDENCE'S COMPONENTS HAVE NO COMMON PROOF

Suppose that a given result's salient feature is that it identifies a property common to various cases (e.g., to each of two Diophantine equations, or to π and e, or to sums of the first n nonzero natural numbers for both odd n and even n, or to each calculator number). In the given context, the result presents itself as the conjunction of various components, each of which ascribes the same property to a distinct case or class of cases. (For example, the two components might be that the sum of the first n nonzero natural numbers is $n(n + 1)/2$ when n is even and that the sum of the first n nonzero natural numbers is $n(n + 1)/2$ when n is odd.) I have proposed that a proof of the result explains why it holds only if the proof is a "common proof" of these various components. That is, the proof must exploit some other, similar respect in which those cases are alike and must proceed from there to arrive at the result by treating all of the (classes of) cases in exactly the same way. (This proposal fits within the previous chapter's conception of a proof that explains why some result holds—namely, as a proof that exploits a feature in the setup that is similar to the result's salient feature.) A mathematical coincidence, on this proposal, has such a salient feature but no explanation.

This proposal has the virtue of focusing on the *relation* between the result's various components, a feature that was not emphasized by most of the epistemic proposals in the previous section (having to do with a single, undecomposed fact's being surprising or leading to no further interesting mathematics, for instance). Of course, that the sum of the first n nonzero natural numbers is $n(n + 1)/2$ could be decomposed into many different pairs of facts—for example: (1) that $n(n + 1)/2$ gives the sum on Mondays and also on other days of the week, (2) that $n(n + 1)/2$ applies when $n < 100$ and also when $n \geq 100$, and (3) that $n(n + 1)/2$ applies when n is odd and also when n is even. We are never inclined to wonder whether the first pair of facts might actually be a coincidence, even after this decomposition has been rendered salient. The same presumably applies to the second pair of facts. But after having seen the separate proofs for even n and odd n, we might well have found ourselves wondering whether the third pair of facts is a coincidence. That is because (on my account) it is obvious that the components of the first decomposition have a "common proof" and likewise for the second decomposition. However, the separate proofs for even n and odd n might well have made us wonder whether the components of the third decomposition have a "common proof."

Even if it is coincidental that F and G are both true, and $F\&G$ is logically equivalent to $H\&J$, it can be no coincidence that H and J are both true. (It is coincidental that the thirteenth digits of π and e are both 9, but it is no coincidence that they are both 9 not only on Mondays, but also on every other day of the week.) Something about the relation between the components, then, must determine whether or not it is coincidental that both are true. On my view, the components' having no "common proof" makes the result coincidental. Unless some particular decomposition of a given mathematical result is made salient (by, for instance, a proof that proceeds by cases), there is nothing that its being coincidental (or no coincidence) would amount to. Thus, my proposal captures the idea that a given mathematical fact is coincidental (or not) only relative to a particular way of decomposing it.

To cash out my proposal, we must be more explicit about what it takes to give a "common proof" of a mathematical result's components—that is, a proof that exploits some respect in which all of the cases dealt with by the various components are alike, and that proceeds from there to arrive at the result by treating all of the cases in exactly the same way. For now, I will set aside the question of what it is for those cases to be alike—that is, to have in common some natural property in mathematics. I will take up the subject of natural mathematical properties in section 9.5. For now let's take for granted the notion of a natural property in mathematics and consider what it would be for a proof to treat all of the cases in exactly the same way. For instance, take the second proof I gave that the $n(n + 1)/2$ summation formula works for all n. Why does that proof count as giving a *uniform* treatment of the formula's holding for both odd n and even n? Alternatively, take the separate proofs for even n and odd n. Together they prove that the summation formula holds for all n. Why does this conjunction of proofs nevertheless fail to treat the two cases in the same way?

Consider the conjunction of the separate proofs for even n and odd n. This conjunction has more than is needed to prove that the formula holds for even n. When we omit what is not needed, what remains does not suffice to prove that the formula holds for odd n. In contrast, take the second proof I gave, which covers all n together. Suppose we insert from the outset the requirement that n be even, so that the argument proves only that the formula holds for even n. Apart from this added restriction, no part of the argument is dispensable for proving that result. Furthermore, nothing needs to be added to that argument in order to prove that the formula holds for odd n as well. We need only omit the initial restriction to even n; no part of the argument depends on that restriction, so once it is omitted, nothing needs to be added to yield the result for all n, odd and even.

The same approach accounts for the way that Nummela's demonstration makes the calculator-number result qualify as no coincidence. We can prove that result by taking each of the 16 calculator numbers in turn, individually showing each number to be divisible by 37, and then conjoining the 16 proofs. If we omit from this proof whatever is unnecessary for showing that (for instance) 123321 is divisible by 37, then we omit the treatment of the other 15 numbers. What remains cannot show that (say) 321123 is divisible by 37. On the other hand, suppose that we take Nummela's argument and use it to show that 123321 is divisible by 37. That argument begins by noting that 123321 takes the form

$$10^5 a + 10^4 (a+d) + 10^3 (a+2d) + 10^2 (a+2d) + 10(a+d) + a$$

where a, $a + d$, and $a + 2d$ are three integers in arithmetic progression. To extend this argument to show that every calculator number is divisible by 37, we need only omit the initial restriction to 123321. Nothing needs to be added to the argument's other steps in order to cover the other 15 calculator numbers since all of them take the above form.

No such common proof exists of the fact that the Diophantine equations $2x^2(x^2 - 1) = 3(y^2 - 1)$ and $x(x - 1)/2 = 2^n - 1$ have exactly the same five positive solutions. (Or, at least, so I presume, in presuming this combination of facts to be coincidental.) We could take separate procedures for solving the two equations and cobble them together into one proof. But the steps of the procedure for solving the first equation could then be omitted without impeding the proof from solving the second equation—though the stripped-down proof would be unable to solve the first equation.

In short, a "common proof" of a mathematical result's various components treats all of those components alike in that it possesses the following feature. Suppose we take any single component and make each step of the proof as logically weak as it can afford to be while still allowing the proof to prove that component. Then the weakened proof remains able to prove each of the other components as well (once we remove any restrictions to that single component, such as "Let n be even" for the summation formula). No further resources are needed to expand the proof's scope from any single component to cover each other component.[9]

Admittedly, this notion of a proof that treats all of a result's components alike may be vague at the margins—for instance, in whether a given proof of one component can be expanded to cover another component merely by removing an otiose restriction or adding some slight resource. But our notion of a "mathematical coincidence" will, I suspect, be correspondingly vague in marginal cases. What count as further resources may also be context sensitive. That F and G both hold qualifies in a given context as no coincidence only if there is at least one proof of F that can be expanded also to prove G in the same way by adding resources regarded in that context as negligible.

Here is an example. Consider the fraction $1/(1 + x^2)$. By long division,

$$
\begin{array}{r}
1-x^2+x^4-\ldots \\
\hline
(1+x^2)\overline{\smash{\big)}\,1} \\
-\left(1+x^2\right) \\
\hline
-x^2 \\
-\left(-x^2-x^4\right) \\
\hline
x^4 \\
-\left(x^4+x^6\right) \\
\hline
\vdots
\end{array}
$$

it yields the Taylor series

$$1-x^2+x^4-x^6+\ldots.$$

Plainly, for real number x, this series will converge only if $|x| < 1$. (When $|x| > 1$, each successive term's absolute value is greater than its predecessor's, so the sum will oscillate in an ever widening manner.) Now is it a coincidence that the two Taylor series

$$1/\left(1-x^2\right)=1+x^2+x^4+x^6+\ldots$$

$$1/\left(1+x^2\right)=1-x^2+x^4-x^6+\ldots$$

are alike in that for real x, each converges when $|x| < 1$ but diverges when $|x| > 1$? The salient feature of this result is that it identifies a respect in which the two functions behave alike. This likeness in their convergence behavior stands out especially strongly against the obvious difference between the two functions regarding $x = 1$: although $1/(1 - x^2)$ goes undefined there, $1/(1 + x^2)$ behaves quite soberly there. That each converges when $|x| < 1$ but diverges when $|x| > 1$ might therefore appear to be utterly coincidental (like the fact that the two Diophantine equations have exactly the same positive solutions). The two

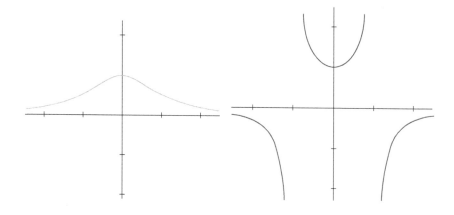

Figure 8.1 At left is $f(x) = 1/(1 + x^2)$, at right is $f(x) = 1/(1 - x^2)$

functions appear to be quite dissimilar in other respects (fig. 8.1). However, when we look at matters in terms of the complex plane, the result is revealed to be no coincidence. Rather, any of the usual proofs of the following theorem constitutes a "common proof" of the result's two components (one component for each series):

> for any power series $\sum a_n z^n$ (from $n = 0$ to ∞), either it converges for all complex numbers z, or it converges only for $z = 0$, or there is a number $R > 0$ such that it converges if $|z| < R$ and diverges if $|z| > R$ (Spivak 1980, 524).

This theorem's proof "helps explain the behavior of certain Taylor series obtained for real functions" (528), such as these two. It is no coincidence that both of them have the same convergence behavior because both functions go undefined at some point on the unit circle centered at the origin of the complex plane (the first function at $z = 1$, the second at $z = i$). Here we have a respect in which the functions are alike (despite differing in their behavior at $x = 1$) from which the proof traces the result—a result having as its salient feature that it identifies another respect in which the two functions are alike. Any standard proof of the theorem (which involves no division into cases) then makes the similarity in the two functions' convergence behavior no coincidence. Now admittedly, to arrive at the behavior of the $1/(1 + x^2)$ series, the theorem's proof must be supplemented by the fact that $1/(1 + z^2)$ goes undefined at $z = i$. This fact, in turn, plays no role in arriving at the behavior of the $1/(1 - x^2)$ series; besides the theorem's proof, that deduction must also appeal to the fact that $1/(1 - z^2)$ goes undefined at $z = 1$, a fact playing no role in arriving at the behavior of the former series. However, in a context where infinite series and the like are being placed on the table, we ordinarily would regard these humble further resources as quite negligible. In such a context, any of the usual proofs of the theorem constitutes a common proof of the convergence behaviors of both series, making their similarity no coincidence.[10] (This is the mathematical explanation of the Taylor series' behavior that Spivak was anticipating in his remark quoted in section 7.6.) As Sawyer (1943, 232) says, complex numbers reveal "the reasons for results which had previously seemed quite accidental."

This example nicely illustrates the fact that a proof's explanatory power is distinct from its "purity" in the rough sense of its making use of no concepts foreign to the concepts in the theorem being proved (or in their definitions). Imaginary numbers do not figure in the two functions exhibiting similar convergence behavior, so an appeal to them is a violation of purity. Despite its foreign elements, the proof involving imaginary numbers is explanatory. (In chapter 9, I will give another example where the introduction of foreign elements enables a proof to explain: a third dimension and points at infinity in projective geometry help to account for Desargues's theorem, a two-dimensional theorem of Euclidean geometry.) Explanatory power is just one of the many respects in which one proof can be evaluated by comparison with another proof of the same theorem; purity is another respect, and beauty, brevity, and fruitfulness are still others. Explanatory power is distinct from these other features. Even after mathematicians have found a proof of some theorem and are entirely satisfied that the theorem is true, they may well seek other proofs having virtues absent from the proof that they have already found. Explanatory power is just one of these virtues. Like science, mathematics values explanatory power as an end in itself, not merely as a means for discovering techniques that might prove as yet unproved theorems (or suggest new theorems) and not as a means for finding proofs that exhibit other virtues.

Here is another example given by a mathematician (Ian Stewart) where the salient feature of a theorem (from elementary set theory) is its unity (i.e., that it reveals a respect in which the various cases it covers are alike). The theorem (i.e., the similarity among these cases) turns out to be no coincidence because the theorem has an explanation that consists of a "common proof" of its various components. Stewart (1975, 53–55) begins by giving several examples of "laws" of set theory, putting them suggestively (where it is understood that they apply to any sets A, B, and C):

$$A \cup B = B \cup A$$
$$A \cap B = B \cap A$$

$$(A \cup B) \cup C = A \cup (B \cup C)$$
$$(A \cap B) \cap C = A \cap (B \cap C)$$

$$(A \cup B) \cap C = (A \cap C) \cup (B \cap C)$$

$$(A \cap B) \cup C = (A \cup C) \cap (B \cup C)$$

A few pages later, Stewart gives a mathematical explanation:

We can explain a phenomenon which you may have noticed already. The various set-theoretic identities, or "laws," seem to come in *pairs*. If I take a law involving the signs $\cup$ and $\cap$, and turn all the $\cup$s into $\cap$s and all the $\cap$s into $\cup$s, the result is another law. The laws mentioned in the section on unions and intersections [the six laws just above] were in fact written down in such pairs.

This is no accident. It is a consequence of two more identities, known as *De Morgan's Laws*; for any sets A and B, we have [where A' is the complement of A]

$$(A \cup B)' = A' \cap B'$$

$$(A \cap B)' = A' \cup B'$$

Even these come in pairs. Now anything not not in a set S is in S, and conversely; so S" = S. So we can rewrite these as

$$(A \cup B) = (A' \cap B')'$$

$$(A \cap B) = (A' \cup B')'. \qquad (+)$$

Take any set-theoretic law, such as

$$(A \cup B) \cap C = (A \cap C) \cup (B \cap C).$$

Change all the As, Bs, and Cs to their complements, obtaining

$$(A' \cup B') \cap C' = (A' \cap C') \cup (B' \cap C').$$

This is also a law, because the first equation is true for *any* sets A, B, and C. Now take complements of both sides:

$$((A' \cup B') \cap C')' = ((A' \cap C') \cup (B' \cap C'))'$$

and use De Morgan's laws, as rewritten in (+), to simplify. The left-hand side becomes

$$\left(A'\cup B'\right)'\cup C$$

which on further application of (+) is

$$(A\cap B)\cup C.$$

(You must remember that $A''=A, B''=B, C''=C$.) Similarly the right-hand side is

$$\left(A'\cap C'\right)'\cap\left(B'\cap C'\right)'$$

or

$$(A\cup C)\cap(B\cup C).$$

So we have shown that

$$(A\cap B)\cup C=(A\cup C)\cap(B\cup C),$$

which is the original law, with $\cup$s and $\cap$s interchanged. The same method works for any law which involves only unions and intersections. (58–59)

Take the theorem that each of the six "laws" above remains true under interchange of $\cup$s and $\cap$s. By calling this theorem "no accident," Stewart plainly does not mean that it is mathematically necessary. (It is mathematically necessary, of course, but that is not Stewart's point.) Rather, by calling it "no accident," Stewart means (I believe) that the theorem is no mathematical coincidence. According to my proposal, part of what makes it no coincidence is that in the way that Stewart presents the theorem (by encouraging the reader to notice the common thread running through all three pairs of "laws"), the theorem's salient feature is that it identifies a respect in which its six instances are alike (in that each remains true under interchange of $\cup$s and $\cap$s). The other part of what makes it no coincidence, on my proposal, is that there is a proof of the theorem that begins from another respect in which the six "laws" are alike (namely, that each involves only unions and intersections) and then shows, from their possessing this property, that they also all possess the property ascribed to them by the theorem. This proof thus reveals a common reason why they all behave alike under interchange of $\cup$s and $\cap$s. This is a "common proof" of each of the theorem's components in that the recipe Stewart specifies for taking a given "law" and deducing its partner under interchange of $\cup$s and $\cap$s is the same for all of the theorem's six cases (rather than treating some of them separately from the others). Intuitively, the recipe's generality is crucial to its giving a common reason why all six "laws" behave alike under the interchange—and so is crucial to the proof's power to make the theorem no coincidence.[11]

I have proposed that a mathematical coincidence is a result having as its salient feature that its various components ascribe a common property to the cases they cover, but having no explanation (i.e., its components having no "common proof"). A common proof would have to treat those various cases alike in deriving each component in the same way from something else that those cases have in common. It follows from my proposal that if it is a coincidence that F and G are both true, then any proof of F must not proceed from something that F and G have in common or must not, in so proceeding, treat F and G alike. A proof of F cannot in like manner also give us a proof of G. In this way, my proposal finds a grain of truth in the idea that if it is a coincidence that F and G are both true, then G's truth remains surprising even in light of F's truth. This idea was one version of the "unforeseen or surprising fact" conception of mathematical coincidence—a conception that was rejected in the previous section.

I also suggested there that when some mathematical truth leads to further truths upon being generalized, then sometimes we may reasonably consider its fruitfulness as some evidence that the initial truth is no coincidence—and that if instead its generalization leads to a falsehood, then sometimes we may reasonably consider its failure to bear fruit as some evidence that the initial truth was coincidental. Here is another example of this phenomenon. Consider the fact (mentioned by Sorensen) that 31, 331, 3 331, . . . , and 33 333 331 are all prime numbers. Is this a coincidence? Note that the next member of this sequence, 333 333 331, is composite (i.e. not prime; it is the product of 17 and 19 607 843). This fact, though insufficient to make it just a coincidence that 31, 331, 3 331, . . . , and 33 333 331 are all prime, is nevertheless some evidence that it is coincidental. My account explains why it is some evidence. That 333 333 331 is not prime precludes a general theorem (with a common proof of all of its components) that any number is prime if every digit in its decimal representation is "3" except for a final "1"—which would have made it no coincidence that 31, 331, 3 331, . . . , and 33 333 331 are all prime.[12] Likewise, before you knew that 333 333 331 is not prime, you might well have taken the fact that 33 331, 333 331, 3 333 331, and 33 333 331 are all prime as some grounds for suspecting it to be no coincidence that 31, 331, and 3 331 are all prime, since the primality of the larger numbers would presumably have been some evidence that there is a general theorem (with a common proof of all of its components) that all numbers of this form are prime—which would have made the primality of the smaller numbers no coincidence.

Here is another example where further cases displaying the same salient feature reasonably lead us to doubt that a given pattern is coincidental. An irrational number $a.bcdef \ldots$ (in base 10) is obviously approximated by $ab/10$ to within $1/10$, by $abc/100$ to within $1/100$, and so forth. Thus, it is easy to approximate a given irrational number to within $1/10^{k-1}$ by using a fraction having integers as its numerator and denominator—namely, by using a denominator equal to 10^{k-1} and so having k digits. But 22/7, with its denominator of only 1 digit, manages to approximate π to within $1/10^2$:

$\pi = 3.1415\ldots$
$22/7 = 3.1428\ldots.$

That is, 22/7 (with $k = 1$) approximates π to within $1/10^{2k}$. It is a much better approximation than it has any right to be. But that is not all:

$\pi = 3.1415926\ldots$
$355/113 = 3.1415929\ldots.$

So 355/113 (with $k = 3$) also approximates π to within $1/10^{2k}$. Is it just a coincidence that π has *two* such unreasonably good approximations?

Our suspicions might justly be further aroused by another irrational number exhibiting the same behavior. The most obvious candidates do not disappoint us:

$\sqrt{2} = 1.41421356\ldots$
$99/70 = 1.4142857\ldots$ ($k = 2$, approximates $\sqrt{2}$ to within $1/10^{2k}$)
$8119/5741 = 1.41421355\ldots$ ($k = 4$, approximates $\sqrt{2}$ to within $1/10^{2k-1}$)

$\log 2 = 0.30102999566\ldots$
$87/289 = 0.3010380\ldots$ ($k = 3$, approximates $\log 2$ to within $1/10^{2k-1}$)
$21306/70777 = 0.30102999562\ldots$ ($k = 5$, approximates $\log 2$ to within $1/10^{2k}$).

These further examples of irrational numbers having two unreasonably good approximations justly lead us to suspect that π's having this property was no coincidence. Of course, separate proofs of the accuracy of two such approximations for π do nothing to show it to be no coincidence that π has two such approximations. Likewise, a proof that π has one such approximation (e.g., showing 22/7 to be so good) coupled with a separate proof that $\sqrt{2}$ has one such approximation (showing 99/70 to be so good) fails to reveal it to be no coincidence that both of these irrational numbers have such unreasonably good approximations.

In contrast, Apostol and Mnatsakanian (2002) have proved that for *any* irrational number n, there are *infinitely* many fractions p/q (in lowest terms) that approximate n to within $1/10^{2k-1}$ where q has k digits (in base 10). Their proof of this theorem constitutes a "common proof" that (for example) π and $\sqrt{2}$ both have many unreasonably good approximations. Apostol and Mnatsakanian (307) conclude that it "is not merely a coincidence" that there are two such approximations

(22/7 and 355/113) for π and likewise that it is no coincidence that both π and $\sqrt{2}$ have many such approximations. Their conclusion fits nicely with my account of what mathematical coincidences are. The salient feature of the fact that both π and $\sqrt{2}$ have such approximations is obviously that this fact identifies a respect in which these two numbers are alike. This fact is no coincidence, on my account, because its two components have a "common proof" such as the proof given by Apostol and Mnatsakanian. That proof treats every irrational number alike and thereby makes it no coincidence that both of these numbers have so many such approximations. To suspect that this fact about π and $\sqrt{2}$ is no coincidence is to suspect that there is such a theorem with such a proof.[13]

As I have mentioned, my account of mathematical coincidence presupposes that there is a well-defined sense in which a given result's components ascribe (or fail to ascribe) a *common property* to each of the cases it covers. That the result's various components identify a genuine similarity among these cases must somehow be sharply distinguished from their ascribing the same unnatural (i.e., gerrymandered, gruesome, wildly disjunctive) "property" to them. By the same token, my account presupposes that there is a well-defined sense in which a given proof derives the result's various components *in the same way*. If we take proofs of two arbitrary theorems (e.g., one about triangles and the other about prime numbers) and combine their steps by using gerrymandered, wildly disjunctive predicates, then the resulting proof (of "All triaprimes are . . .") does not count as giving uniform treatment to the two cases (triangles and primes). The predicates used in this derivation create only a specious unity; they paper over different treatments with a linguistic veneer of uniform treatment. That is because these predicates do not refer to natural properties in mathematics. Thus, my proposal must appeal to the distinction between natural and unnatural properties in mathematics. In the next chapter, I will try to redeem this promissory note by supplying an account of this distinction.

A proof does not have to give separate treatment to each and every one of a given result's components in order for the proof to fail to treat them all alike.[14] Consider this proof by mathematical induction that the product of any three consecutive nonzero natural numbers is divisible by 6:

> First the base case: The product of 1, 2, and 3 is 6, which is divisible by 6.
> Now the inductive step: Suppose that the product of $(n-1)$, n, and $(n+1)$ is divisible by 6. Let's show that the product of n, $(n+1)$, and $(n+2)$ is divisible by 6. By algebra, that product equals $n^3 + 3n^2 + 2n = (n^3 - n) + 3n(n+1)$. Now $(n^3 - n) = (n-1)n(n+1)$, so by hypothesis, it is divisible by 6. And $n(n+1)$ is even, so $3n(n+1)$ is divisible by 3 and by 2, and therefore by 6. Hence, the original product is the sum of two terms, each divisible by 6. Hence, that product is divisible by 6.

This proof fails to treat every product of three consecutive nonzero natural numbers alike. Instead, it divides them into two classes: the product of 1, 2, and 3; and all of the others. This proof, then, does not identify a feature common to every triplet of consecutive nonzero natural numbers and then derive divisibility by 6 from this feature. Rather, it treats the first triplet as a special case, using it to derive the others (just as in Duchayla's proof of the parallelogram law from section 4.3, the law's holding of the resultant's direction is used to show that it also holds of the resultant's magnitude). Insofar as we found the theorem remarkable for identifying a property common to every triplet, our point in asking for an explanation was to ask for a proof that treats all of the triplets alike. This feature of the theorem is thrown into especially sharp relief by a proof that (unlike the proof by mathematical induction) *does* treat all of the triplets alike:

> Of any three consecutive nonzero natural numbers, at least one is even (i.e., divisible by 2) and exactly one is divisible by 3. Therefore, their product is divisible by $3 \times 2 = 6$.[15]

Like the explanation of the fact that every calculator number is divisible by 37, this proof traces the result to a property common to every triplet. Hence (when the result's unity is salient), this proof explains why the result holds.[16] It follows that in a context where the result's unity is salient, a proof by mathematical induction cannot explain what it proves, since a proof by mathematical induction always treats the base case as a special case.[17]

However, the inductive proof of the triplet theorem is a far cry from the proof of the calculator-number theorem that treats each of the 16 calculator numbers separately.[18] The inductive proof *nearly* treats every triplet alike. It gives special treatment only to the base case; all of the others receive the same treatment. Therefore, although this inductive proof is not an explanation (when the result's unity is salient), it falls somewhere *between* an explanation and a proof utterly lacking in explanatory power. A result (displaying unity as its striking feature) having such a proof by induction,[19] but (unlike the triplet theorem) having no proof that treats every case alike, has no fully qualified explanation, but is not utterly mathematically coincidental either, since the inductive proof ties all but one of its cases together. My account's nuanced verdict seems to me to strike the right note: the triplet theorem's inductive proof is inferior in explanatory power to the fully unifying proof, but nevertheless retains some measure of explanatory significance.[20]

■ 8.4 A SHIFT OF CONTEXT MAY CHANGE A PROOF'S EXPLANATORY POWER

On my account (the "big Lange theory"), whether a proof qualifies as an explanation of the theorem being proved depends on what feature of the theorem is salient. In different contexts, different features may be salient. Therefore, a proof that qualifies as an explanation in one context may fail to do so in another.

I have also suggested that sometimes, a particular *proof* renders some feature of the theorem salient—but not necessarily in a way that makes the given proof qualify as an explanation. For example, consider the proof of the summation formula for the first n nonzero natural numbers that treats the case of even n separately (and differently) from the case of odd n. That proof makes salient a feature of the theorem that would otherwise have received no notice: that the same summation formula applies to both even n and odd n. In that context, the proof fails to explain why the summation formula holds since the proof fails to treat the even n and odd n cases alike. In fact, even a proof that *explains* a theorem in one context may call attention to some previously ignored feature of the theorem. Under the proof's influence, the context may shift so that the proof no longer qualifies as explanatory since a different feature of the theorem has become salient. Let's look at an example.

Here is a way to amaze and amuse your friends. Tell them that you can add numbers much more rapidly than they can—even if they use a calculator. Demonstrate your addition wizardry by asking them to select any two numbers and to insert one in the first row and one in the second row of the table in figure 8.2. Then ask them to complete the table by inserting the sum of those two rows in row 3, the sum of rows 2 and 3 in row 4, the sum of rows 3 and 4 in row 5, and so forth through row 10—and finally by computing the grand total by summing all of the numbers in rows 1 through 10. While your friends are furiously filling in the table, you look over their shoulders and wait until they fill in row 7. Then when they fill in row 7, you simply take that entry, multiply it by 11 in your head, and boldly announce the grand total long before they can reach it. They will be

1.	
2.	
3.	
4.	
5.	
6.	
7.	
8.	
9.	
10.	
total	

Figure 8.2 The empty table

1.	4
2.	7
3.	11
4.	18
5.	29
6.	47
7.	76
8.	123
9.	199
10.	322
total	836

Figure 8.3 One way to fill in the table

astonished. (Fig. 8.3 shows the completed table for the case where the initial numbers are 4 and 7; note that 76 × 11 = 836.)

Your friends may well want to see if your success was just a fluke; they may ask you to perform your feat again beginning with different numbers. They may try having you begin with fractions, negative numbers, and so forth. Eventually, they will ask you to divulge your secret—or you will reveal it to them anyway: that for any initial two numbers, the grand total equals 11 times the entry in row 7. Your audience will then probably want to know *why* this technique works—that is, why this "11 times row 7" theorem holds. In this sort of context ("Here's some mathemagic to astonish you . . ."), the theorem's salient feature is obviously that it allows your trick to work on every occasion. In other words, the theorem's salient feature is that it identifies a property that is common to every one of the cases: that in each case, the grand total equals 11 times row 7. Your audience wants to know whether this similarity among the various cases covered by the theorem is a coincidence or not. In other words, your audience is interested in a proof that deduces this common feature (the success of your trick) from some other feature that is common to every setup of this kind. That is their point in asking *why* the theorem holds. Such a proof would reveal the theorem to be no coincidence.

In asking why the theorem holds, the members of your amazed audience are demanding exactly the kind of proof that books of mathematical "magic," parlor games, and wonders—such as Martin Gardner's *Mathematical Circus* (1979, 101–104, 167–168)—standardly present as explaining why the trick works. Start with the Fibonacci sequence (1, 1, 2, 3, 5, 8, 13 . . .), which is the sequence that begins with two 1's and then generates each further term as the sum of the two previous terms. The trick's explanation is that in any table of the kind in

1.	x
2.	y
3.	x + y
4.	x + 2y
5.	2x + 3y
6.	3x + 5y
7.	5x + 8y
8.	8x + 13y
9.	13x + 21y
10.	21x + 34y
total	55x + 88y

Figure 8.4 The table completed in general

figure 8.2, the two initial numbers x and y generate a "Gibonacci" (a.k.a. "generalized Fibonacci") sequence $x, y, x + y, x + 2y, 2x + 3y, \ldots$, where the sequence's first 10 members occupy the table's first 10 rows. As the algebra in figure 8.4 proves, the sum of the first 10 members in any Gibonacci sequence $(55x + 88y)$ is 11 times the seventh member $(5x + 8y)$. This "common proof" covering all cases alike makes it no mathematical coincidence that the theorem holds, that is, that the trick works in any possible case. The proof unifies all of the cases falling under the theorem.

Looking at figure 8.4, we cannot help but think of the x's and y's as forming two separate sequences. We then recognize that the coefficients of the x terms in lines 3–10 are the first 8 members of the Fibonacci sequence and the coefficients of the y terms in lines 2–10 are the first 9 members of the Fibonacci sequence. This proof, then, reveals that the result's holding on the x side consists of the fact that the sum of the first 8 Fibonacci numbers (the x-coefficients for lines 3–10) plus 1 (the x-coefficient from line 1) equals 11 times the fifth Fibonacci number (line 7's x-coefficient), and that the result's holding on the y side consists of the fact that the sum of the first 9 Fibonacci numbers equals 11 times the sixth Fibonacci number (line 7's y-coefficient). In other words, the result consists of these two components (where F_i is the ith Fibonacci number):

$$F_1 + F_2 + \ldots + F_8 + 1 = 11 F_5$$
$$F_1 + F_2 + \ldots + F_9 = 11 F_6.$$

My point is that having proved the theorem by using the table filled in with x's and y's, we now find ourselves looking at the original result as having two components: an x-result and a y-result. The result's salient feature is now that the x-sum works out so that the coefficient in the grand total is 11 times the coefficient on the seventh line and that the y-sum turns out to have the very same property. In other words, the result's salient feature is now that the x-sum and y-sum are alike in this respect. In this new context, an account of *why* the theorem holds would have to be a proof that treats the result's two components alike, deducing each component in the same way from a feature that it has in common with the other component. The proof would thereby show that the above two features of the Fibonacci sequence are no coincidence—that they have a "common proof."

In this new context, the proof (using fig. 8.4) that made salient this feature of the result is no longer accurately characterized as explaining why the result holds, since that proof treats the x side separately from the y side. Indeed, it is precisely because this proof treats the two sides separately that we distinguished the two sides in the first place and so noticed their similarity. In answering the question that we originally asked—"Why does this theorem hold?"—this proof provoked another question (which we might also express as "Why does this theorem hold?") that this proof cannot answer.

This shift of context and salience is sometimes visible in math textbooks. For instance, one textbook (Benjamin and Quinn 2003, 30–31) begins in the familiar sort of mathemagical context by presenting "A Gibonacci Magic Trick," a title that indicates the kind of proof that would be correctly characterized as explanatory: one that reveals the trick's success in all possible cases to be no coincidence. The textbook then gives exactly the proof I have given, using figure 8.4: "the explanation of this trick involves nothing more than high school algebra." However, once figure 8.4 decomposes the result into the x side and the y side, the context shifts; a previously unrecognized feature of the result becomes salient. The textbook records that the explanation being given raises why questions that it cannot answer (though answers do exist): "the total of Rows 1 through 10 will sum to $55x + 88y$. As luck would have it, (actually by the next identity), the number in Row 7 is $5x + 8y$" (30–31). The result's x-side and y-side components (that is to say, the two facts given above regarding the sums of the first eight and the first nine Fibonacci numbers) are depicted by the proof in figure 8.4 as if their holding together were a matter of "luck": a mathematical coincidence. But in fact, it is not—as the teaser "by the next identity" hints. (Again, of course, all of the facts involved here are mathematically necessary. The only kind of "luck" that might be present is mathematical coincidence.)

That "next identity" concerns Fibonacci numbers. To explain why the sums of the first eight and first nine Fibonacci numbers stand in the above two relations, think of the Fibonacci sequence as *doubly* infinite: with $F_1 = 1$ and $F_2 = 1$, F_0 must equal $F_2 - F_1 = 0$, F_{-1} must equal $F_1 - F_0 = 1$, and so forth. (Here again—as with complex numbers and projective points at infinity—we have an example where a result is explained only when placed in a broader context.) Notice that F_0 and F_{-1} are the x-coefficients in lines 1 and 2 of the table in figure 8.4. So instead of using the relation $F_1 + F_2 + \ldots + F_8 + 1 = 11F_5$ to capture the x side, we can use

$$F_{-1} + F_0 + \ldots + F_8 = 11F_5$$

Likewise (since $F_0 = 0$), instead of using the relation $F_1 + F_2 + \ldots + F_9 = 11 F_6$ to capture the y side, we can use

$$F_0 + F_1 + \ldots + F_9 = 11F_6.$$

One is inclined to suspect that this pair of facts is no coincidence! In fact, the x side and y side are both cases of the fact that the sum of any 10 consecutive members of the doubly infinite Fibonacci sequence equals 11 times the seventh member, and there is a proof of this fact that treats all of its cases alike:

For any integer n,

$$F_{n+1} + F_{n+2} + F_{n+3} + F_{n+4} + F_{n+5} + F_{n+6} + F_{n+7} + F_{n+8} + F_{n+9} + F_{n+10}$$

$$= 2F_{n+3} + 2F_{n+4} + 2F_{n+5} + 0F_{n+6} + F_{n+7} + 2F_{n+8} + 2F_{n+9}$$

$$= 4F_{n+5} + 0F_{n+6} + 3F_{n+7} + 4F_{n+8}$$

$$= 4F_{n+5} + 4F_{n+6} + 7F_{n+7}$$

$$= 11F_{n+7}.$$

In virtue of this proof, then, it is no coincidence that the x side and the y side of the sum in figure 8.4 both allow the trick to work. The two sides work in the same way because of another feature that they have in common: that each involves the sum of 10 consecutive Fibonacci numbers.

This example shows how a proof's explanatory power may shift in association with shifts in the salience of particular features of the theorem being explained. However (as I will discuss further in section 8.6), the context-sensitivity of a proof's explanatory power in no way undercuts the idea that in explaining, an explanatory proof reveals how things *really* are. If mathematicians knew no proof of the "mathemagic" theorem besides the table filled in with x's and y's, then mathematicians would presumably not yet know that it is in fact no coincidence that the x-sum and y-sum both work out so that the grand total is 11 times the seventh line's coefficient. That this theorem is no coincidence (by my lights: that such a "common proof" exists) is a fact about mathematics no less than that the theorem holds. Admittedly, it is only in a certain context that we are in a position to ask whether this similarity between the x-sum and y-sum is a coincidence. Moreover, it is only in such a context that a proof has got to address that question in order for it to explain why the theorem holds. But none of this makes the light shed by an explanatory proof any less real—or makes what it illuminates any less real.[21]

■ 8.5 COMPARISON TO OTHER PROPOSALS

According to Steiner (1978a, 1978c), a proof that all S_1's are P_1 explains why this theorem holds if and only if the proof reveals how the theorem depends on S_1's "characterizing property"—that is, on the property essential to being S_1 that is just sufficient to distinguish S_1's from other entities in the same "family" (for example, to distinguish triangles from other kinds of polygons). To reveal the theorem's dependence on the characterizing property, the proof must be "generalizable." That is, if S_1's characterizing property is replaced in the proof by the characterizing property for another kind S_2 in the same family (but the original "proof idea" is maintained), then the resulting "deformation" of the original proof proves that all S_2's are P_2 for some property P_2. (Steiner may be inconsistent about whether P_2 must be incompatible with P_1; he appears to say so at 1978a, 143.) Thus, the theorem's explanation helps to show that there are different, but analogous, theorems for different classes in the same family.

Steiner's proposal nicely accommodates some of the explanatory proofs that I have examined (at least under a natural reading of the relevant "family" and "proof idea"). For instance, the proof I presented as explaining why the product of any three consecutive nonzero natural numbers is divisible by 6 ($= 1 \times 2 \times 3$) could be deformed to prove that the product of any four consecutive nonzero natural numbers is divisible by 24 ($= 1 \times 2 \times 3 \times 4$). However, this four-number result could also be proved by mathematical induction—by a "deformation" of the inductive proof of the three-number result. Yet (I have argued) the inductive proof of the three-number result is not fully explanatory (in a context where the result's unity is salient), and the inductive proof's "generalizability" in Steiner's sense does not at all incline me to reconsider that verdict.[22] The proof treats the first triplet of nonzero natural numbers differently from every other triplet, rather than identifying a property common to every triplet that in the same way renders each triplet divisible by 6.

Here is another theorem for which an inductive proof "generalizes" (at least in the sense that by using the same strategy, we can prove analogous theorems concerning other members of the same family), yet this inductive proof is regarded as unable to explain why the theorem holds. The theorem's subject is the Somos-4 sequence, which is defined by the following recursion formula:

$$a_0 = a_1 = a_2 = a_3 = 1$$
$$\text{for } n > 3, a_n = \left(a_{n-3}a_{n-1} + a_{n-2}{}^2\right)/a_{n-4}.$$

As successive values of the sequence were first computed (to beyond a_{100}), there was widespread surprise as each was discovered to be an integer. It was striking that all were alike in this respect. Ultimately, a general proof was sought that all a_i are integers. The earliest proofs were by mathematical induction. The base case was that the sequence's first 8 members $(1, 1, 1, 1, 2, 3, 7, 23)$ are all integers. The inductive step aims to show that if 8 successive members $B(0), \ldots, B(7)$ are integers, then $B(8) = \left[B(5)B(7) + B(6)^2\right]/B(4)$ is an integer, too—that

is, that $B(5)B(7) + B(6)^2 \equiv 0 \pmod{B(4)}$. A typical approach (Malouf 1992, 258) to proving the inductive step is first to show that

$$B(5)B(7) + B(6)^2 \equiv_{B(4)} B(1)B(2)\left[B(5)B(7) + B(6)^2\right]$$
$$= B(1)B(2)B(5)B(7) + B(1)B(2)B(6)^2$$

and then to substitute $B(2)B(4) + B(3)^2$ for $B(1)B(5)$ in the first term by appealing to the recursion formula for $B(5)$:

$$B(5) = \left[B(2)B(4) + B(3)^2\right]/B(1).$$

The substitution yields

$$\equiv_{B(4)} B(2)^2 B(4)B(7) + B(2)B(3)^2 B(7) + B(1)B(2)B(6)^2.$$

But since $B(2)$ and $B(7)$ are integers (by the inductive supposition that $B(0), \ldots, B(7)$ are integers), the first term is a multiple of $B(4)$ and so is equivalent $\pmod{B(4)}$ to 0, contributing nothing to the sum:

$$\equiv_{B(4)} B(2)B(3)^2 B(7) + B(1)B(2)B(6)^2.$$

In the same way, we then use the recursion formula for $B(7)$ to replace $B(3)B(7)$ in the first term

$$\equiv_{B(4)} B(2)B(3)B(5)^2 + B(1)B(2)B(6)^2$$

and the recursion formula for $B(6)$ to replace $B(2)B(6)$ in the second term

$$\equiv_{B(4)} B(2)B(3)B(5)^2 + B(1)B(3)B(5)B(6)$$

and the recursion formula for $B(6)$ again to replace $B(3)B(5)$ in the first term

$$\equiv_{B(4)} B(2)^2 B(5)B(6) + B(1)B(3)B(5)B(6)$$

$$\equiv_{B(4)} B(5)B(6)\left[B(2)^2 + B(1)B(3)\right].$$

Fortuitously, the bracketed expression is just the numerator of the recursion formula for $B(4)$, so

$$\equiv_{B(4)} B(0)B(5)B(6)B(4),$$

which (since $B(0)$, $B(5)$, and $B(6)$ are supposed integral) is just a multiple of $B(4)$, yielding

$$\equiv_{B(4)} 0.$$

As Gale (1991, 41) says, "although the proof is very simple, it depends on the fortuitous fact that the factor [in brackets above] turns up." It was later found that the same strategy works for the Somos-5 sequence

$$a_0 = a_1 = a_2 = a_3 = a_4 = 1$$
$$\text{for } n > 4, a_n = \left(a_{n-4}a_{n-1} + a_{n-3}a_{n-2}\right)/a_{n-5}$$

using the first 10 members of the sequence as the base case. Hickerson then used the same strategy (with the first 12 members as the base case) for the Somos-6 sequence

$$a_0 = a_1 = a_2 = a_3 = a_4 = a_5 = 1$$
$$\text{for } n > 5, a_n = \left(a_{n-5}a_{n-1} + a_{n-4}a_{n-2} + a_{n-3}^2\right)/a_{n-6}$$

and any generalization thereof for arbitrary $a_0, \ldots, a_5$. Thus, we have parallel results for different members of the same family, proved by the same "proof idea." But each of these proofs is widely regarded as exploiting a "fortuitous fact" here or there that deprives the proof of explanatory power. Gale (41) writes:

> But what have we learned? As Hickerson puts it, "The thing I dislike about my proof is that it doesn't explain why the result is true. It depends primarily on the fact that when you compute a_{12}, there's an unexpected cancellation. But why does this happen?" Indeed, the proof, rather than illuminating the phenomenon, makes it if anything more mysterious. I report this with some embarrassment since I have earlier asserted that a proof in mathematics is in some sense equivalent to an explanation.[23] We now see that this clearly need not be the case. Perhaps, if and when we find the "right" proof, the situation will become clarified, but must there necessarily be a right proof? One is reminded of the proof of the four-color theorem.

The four-color proof is an apt comparison. It notoriously divides all possible maps into a plethora of special cases that then receive individual treatment so that it "does not give a satisfactory explanation of why the theorem is true. . . . The answer appears as a kind of monstrous coincidence" (Stewart 1975, 304; see Sorensen n.d.). Likewise, each of the inductive proofs of Somos-sequence theorems divides up the given sequence's members and then exploits a lucky "accident" of algebra either in connection with some base case or in proving the inductive rule. These isolated lucky accidents, one here and another there, highlight the way that a given proof treats various cases separately, depriving the proof of explanatory power—considering that the theorem being proved strikingly reveals a respect in which every member of a given sequence is alike (namely, in being an integer). Despite "generalizing" when they are deformed to fit a different class in the same family, these inductive proofs of Somos-sequence theorems are not explanatory.

Another deficiency in Steiner's account of mathematical explanation is that some of the explanatory proofs that I have identified simply collapse rather than yield new theorems when they are deformed to fit a different class in what is presumably the same "family." For instance, the proof from the isosceles trapezoid's symmetry (in section 7.5) does not go anywhere when we shift to a nonisosceles trapezoid, since the symmetry then vanishes.[24] (I first made this objection to Steiner's account in section 2.7, where I compared this problem for Steiner's account of mathematical explanation to a deficiency in Woodward's account of scientific explanation that impedes it from recognizing "explanations by constraint.") For some of the other explanatory proofs I have presented, it is unclear what the relevant "family" includes. What, for instance, are the other classes in the family associated with d'Alembert's theorem (in section 7.4) that roots come in complex-conjugate pairs? Even if we could ultimately discover such a family,[25] we do not need to find it in order to recognize the explanatory power of the proof exploiting the setup's invariance under the replacement of i with $-i$. (I will return to this point momentarily.)

I turn now to Kitcher (1984b, esp. 208–209, 227; 1989, esp. 423–426, 437), who offers a unified account of mathematical and scientific explanation. In fact, he sees explanations of all kinds as involving unification. Roughly speaking, Kitcher says that an explanation unifies the fact being explained with other facts by virtue of their all being derivable by arguments of the same form. Explanations instantiate argument patterns in the optimal collection ("the explanatory store")—optimal in that arguments instantiating these schemes manage to cover the most facts with the fewest different argument schemes placing the most stringent constraints upon arguments. An argument instantiating an argument scheme excluded from the explanatory store fails to explain.

Thus, Kitcher sees a given mathematical proof's explanatory power as arising from the proof's relationship to other proofs (such as their all instantiating the same scheme or their covering different facts). My account contrasts with

Kitcher's (and with Steiner's) in doing justice to the fact that (as I have shown in various examples) we can appreciate a proof's explanatory power (or impotence) just from examining the details of that proof itself, without considering what else could be proved by instantiating the same scheme (or "proof idea") or how much coverage the given proof adds to what's covered by proofs instantiating other schemes.[26] In addition, Kitcher regards all mathematical explanations as deriving their explanatory power from their possessing the same virtue: the scheme's membership in the "explanatory store." It seems to me more plausible (especially given the diversity of our examples) to expect different mathematical explanations to derive their explanatory power from their displaying different traits. On my approach, different traits are called for in different conversational contexts—where different features of the result being explained are salient. On Kitcher's view (and Steiner's), by contrast, a proof's explanatory power is independent of the interests of any audience.

Of course, Kitcher and I both have a place for unification in our accounts. I agree with Kitcher that in some explanations in mathematics, "one adopts a new language which allows for the replacement of a disparate set of questions and accepted solutions with a single form of question and a single pattern of reasoning, which subsume the prior questions and solutions. . . . The new language enables us to perceive the common thread which runs through our old problem solutions, thereby increasing our insight into why those solutions worked" (Kitcher 1984b, 221). Kitcher's description applies beautifully to the example that I will examine in chapter 9—where projective geometry treats uniformly various disparate results from Euclidean geometry. But whereas Kitcher sees all explanations in mathematics as involving this sort of unification, I see such unification as a source of explanatory power only in a context where a salient feature of the result being explained involves unification (as in the calculator-number example and others that I have presented in this chapter).

Not every case of "unification" in Kitcher's sense is going to be accompanied by explanatory power. A typical proof by "brute force" uses a "plug and chug" technique that is perforce applicable to a very wide range of problems. Presumably, then, its proof scheme is likely to earn its way into Kitcher's "explanatory store." Not every brute-force proof instantiates the same scheme; there are many brute-force schemes. But a given brute-force proof instantiates a very widely applicable scheme—a particular plug-and-chug approach that can be used to prove a great many theorems. For example, as I mentioned in section 7.5, we could prove the theorem regarding isosceles trapezoids by first expressing the setup in terms of coordinate geometry and then algebraically grinding out the result. The same strategy could be used to prove a great many other geometric theorems (e.g., that the midpoints of any quadrilateral are the vertices of a parallelogram). Nevertheless, these proofs lack explanatory power.[27] The brute-force proof of the theorem regarding isosceles trapezoids is unilluminating because it begins by expressing the entire setup in terms of coordinate geometry and then never characterizes any features of the setup as irrelevant. Consequently, it fails to identify any particular feature of isosceles trapezoids (such as their symmetry) as the feature responsible for the theorem.[28] On my view, a brute-force proof is never explanatory when the salient feature of the theorem being explained is its symmetry or simplicity or some other such feature, since a brute-force proof does not exploit any such feature. However, if the theorem's salient feature is its unity, then a brute-force proof can explain, since it may well treat all cases alike—as in the initial context where I presented the mathemagic example from section 8.4. On that occasion, a brute-force proof (which placed x and y on the first two lines of figure 8.4 and simply calculated out everything else from there) was explanatory.

A new proof technique can explain why some theorem holds even if that technique allows no new theorems to be proved and would not cover all of the theorems proved by several (equally stringent) proof schemes that would otherwise be part of the "explanatory store" (and so would not enable a smaller collection of proof schemes to cover the same theorems without sacrificing stringency). My approach can account for this feature of mathematical explanation. It is more difficult to accommodate on Kitcher's proposal, since any explanatory argument scheme must earn its way into the "explanatory store" either by adding coverage (without unduly increasing the number of schemes or decreasing the stringency of their constraints) or by decreasing the number of proof schemes (without unduly decreasing coverage or stringency).[29]

One natural approach to explanation in mathematics that has remained relatively unexplored by philosophers is to construe mathematical reductions as explanations. If the objects in one mathematical domain can be reduced to the objects in another, then (according to this approach) a theorem concerning the reduced domain is explained by being proved in the reducing domain—in much the same way as a law of nature about light is explained by being derived from the account of light as a wave in the electromagnetic field.

I am inclined to resist this approach to mathematical explanation. If mathematical reduction sufficed for explanation, then pedestrian mathematical facts in the reduced domain—facts having no salient features at all—would nevertheless have mathematical explanations in terms of the reducing domain. That such proofs explain seems at odds with mathematical practice. In section 7.6, I argued that if a result exhibits no noteworthy feature, then there is nothing that its explanation over and above its proof would amount to. I quoted the mathematician Michael Spivak remarking that many mathematical theorems, despite having proofs, have no explanations at all. Gale echoes this thought in the passage I quoted earlier in this section ("Must there necessarily be a right proof?"). My proposal accounts for this feature of mathematical practice.

310 EXPLANATION IN MATHEMATICS

Furthermore, there appear to be plenty of examples where a theorem in a reduced domain can be proved in terms of a reducing domain, yet that proof is too "brute force" to explain the theorem, whereas it is explained by a proof in the reduced domain. Consider, once again, the theorem regarding isosceles trapezoids from section 7.5. Though this geometric theorem can be reduced to algebra and then proved by brute-force manipulation, this proof does not explain it. Rather, it is explained by a proof that remains geometrical and exploits the figure's striking symmetry. (Similar considerations apply to the reduction of complex numbers to ordered pairs of real numbers, for example; this reduction could be used to give a brute-force but non-explanatory proof of d'Alembert's theorem from the previous chapter.) In addition, I showed in section 8.4 that a proof's explanatory power shifts with the context, as new features of the theorem become salient. But mathematical reduction does not shift with the context.

Perhaps, though, I should leave room for contexts where a given result's salient feature has something to do with its relation to a potential reducing domain— and where a mathematical reduction accordingly explains. Nevertheless, such a view would not regard brute-force reductions as explanatory in every context. It would also not regard a mathematical result bereft of salient features in a given context as having an explanation there merely because it has a proof that reveals its "ground" in a reducing domain.[30]

Another natural-sounding approach to explanation in mathematics is to regard certain mathematical facts as explaining others by virtue of involving mathematical objects and properties that are more abstract than those figuring in the fact being explained.[31] Of course, it is difficult to evaluate this thought without an account of degrees of mathematical abstractness (or concreteness). Nevertheless, I worry that an account along these lines will depart from mathematical practice in according explanatory power to various brute-force proofs exploiting "turn the crank" reductions of more concrete domains to more abstract ones. In fact, I may have already given some examples of explanatory proofs where more concrete mathematical objects and properties are used to explain facts about more abstract ones. For instance, in section 7.4, I gave a number-theoretic result about finite continued fractions that is explained by a proof involving the tiling of a checkerboard with checkers and dominos. Arguably, these tiles have geometric properties that render them more concrete than the more austere, structural entities figuring in the theorem. (Of course, these tiles remain ideal, mathematical objects rather than physical ones governed by natural laws.) Despite their greater concreteness, the tiles reveal a symmetry in the setup that is like the salient symmetry in the theorem being explained.

Finally I turn briefly to Resnik and Kushner (1987), who doubt that any proofs explain *simpliciter*. They contend that a proof's being "explanatory" to a given audience is nothing more than its being the kind of proof that the audience wants—perhaps in view of the proof's premises, its strategy, its perspicuity, or the collateral information it supplies (or simply in view of its being a proof). I agree with Resnik and Kushner that a proof's explanatory power depends on its audience's interests. However, I do not think that whenever someone wants a certain kind of proof, for whatever reason, then such a proof qualifies for that person as explaining why the theorem holds. Explanatory power is just one of many properties that might make a proof desirable. Having already proved a given theorem, mathematicians might then want a proof that is pure, for instance. But such a proof would not thereby become explanatory.[32] Likewise, we might want to see a proof of the "calculator number" theorem that proceeds by checking each of the 16 calculator numbers individually. But this proof might then merely heighten our curiosity, motivating us to seek in addition the reason why all of the calculator numbers are divisible by 37. It is not the case that any kind of proof that we happen to want counts as an explanation when we want it.

▪ 8.6 CONCLUSION

I have tried to identify what makes some mathematical proofs explanatory while others are not. I have given no argument that every explanatory proof in mathematics works in the manner that I have identified. But many seem to do so.

Admittedly, several fairly elastic notions figure in my idea of a proof's exploiting the same kind of feature in the problem as was salient in the result. This elasticity allows my proposal to encompass a wide range of cases. Insofar as the notions figuring in my proposal have borderline cases, there will correspondingly be room for mathematical proofs that are borderline explanatory. But their existence would not make a proof's explanatory power rest merely "in the eye of the beholder."

As I mentioned at the start of chapter 7, it is challenging to find a source of explanatory asymmetry for mathematical explanation, since the usual suspects in scientific explanation (such as causal priority) are unavailable. In response, I have gestured toward the priority that axioms in mathematics have over theorems. I have also emphasized mathematical explanations that operate in connection with "problems," each problem having a "setup" and a "result." This structure supplies an asymmetry that enables mathematical explanation to get started by allowing why questions to be posed (as in my first example in chapter 7, where Zeitz (2000, 5) wants to "understand *why* the coin problem had the answer that it did"). When we consider a proof extracting the property of being G from the property of being F, the proof's explanatory status may depend on whether we take the setup and result as being F and being G, respectively, or as being non-G and being non-F—as well as on which of the theorem's features are salient to us. Nevertheless, it does not follow that a proof is explanatory merely by virtue of striking its audience as explanatory.

Of course, if some extraterrestrials differ from us in the theorem's features they find salient, then (on my account) the extraterrestrials also differ from us in the proofs they ought to regard as explanatory. I embrace this conclusion. As I have already shown, even *we* in different contexts properly regard different proofs of the same theorem as explanatory—namely, in contexts where different features of the theorem are salient. Furthermore, if extraterrestrials differ from us so much that they *never* regard symmetry, unity, simplicity, and so forth as salient, then even if we and they agree on the truth of various theorems, our practices in seeking and refining proofs of these theorems differ so much that it would be a strain to characterize the extraterrestrials as doing mathematics. (Similarly, Kuhn, 1977, 331–332, famously argues that a practice of developing empirical theories would be unrecognizable as science if its norms of theory choice valued social utility or permitted a theory to be rejected only after it was found to make a wildly inaccurate empirical prediction.) I have argued by example (and will argue further in chapter 9) that the search for mathematical explanations often drives mathematical discovery and innovation. Extraterrestrials with sensibilities radically different from ours would not seek the same things we seek.

Such extraterrestrials, judged as mathematicians, would be deficient in an important respect. Although the salience of a given feature exhibited by some theorem may depend partly on the context and the way in which the theorem is expressed, a salient feature is not merely a feature that happens to be attended to. A salient feature is one that, given the norms of mathematical practice, ought to be attended to. Even if no mathematician actually attends to a certain feature, it may still be salient; mathematicians may be mistaken in failing to deem it noteworthy.

The roles that setups and salience play in my account do not make mathematical explanations differ sharply from *all* scientific explanations. Some scientific explanations operate in much the same way as the mathematical explanations that I have examined. For instance, consider the notorious—or, if you prefer, "mildly famous" (Bennett 1970, 181; see Block 1974; Denyer 1994)—puzzle, "Why are mirror images reversed sideways but not up and down?"[33] This problem involves a setup: typically (as in Martin 2002, 176), you are standing before a full-length mirror, wearing a ring on your left hand. It also involves a result: your mirror image. The result's ring is on its right hand but it is not standing on its head. The why question is asking for a derivation in which the result, with its salient asymmetry between left-right and up-down, is traced to a similar asymmetry in the setup. The demand is not for a causal explanation. (In causal scientific explanations, the explanandum need not have a salient feature and even when it does, the explanans need not have a similar feature.) Indeed, a causal account of the reflection as given by geometrical optics will not suffice to answer this why question: "Where does the asymmetry come from? . . . To explain horizontal but not vertical reversal with optical ray diagrams is doomed to failure, for they are symmetrical and equally valid when held in any orientation" (Gregory 1987, 492; see Block 1974, 267). That is, a mirror reflects light rays symmetrically about the normal to the surface at the point of incidence. No asymmetry lurks here. The why question requires an answer that uncovers an asymmetry in the setup that is similar to the salient asymmetry in the result.

Here is one common way of trying to answer the why question by doing exactly that: "Why do you count that mirror image as right/left reversed? Because you imagine turning yourself so that you would face in the same direction as your mirror-image now faces ... and moving in back of the mirror to the place where it appears your image now stands. Having turned and moved, your hand with the ring on it is in the place where the un-ringed hand of your mirror-image is. . . .In other words, when you turn this way ... [your mirror-image is] reversed left-to-right, compared to you" (Martin 2002, 176–177; see Pears 1952; Block 1974; Gregory 1987). The setup's asymmetry, responsible for the asymmetrical privileging of one dimension (left-right) over the others, lies in a hidden feature of the setup: how you imagine moving from facing the mirror to facing out from behind it, namely, by rotating yourself around the vertical axis. This feature of the setup privileges that axis over the others. It answers the why question by tracing the result, with its salient asymmetry, back to a similar asymmetry in the setup. After all, we could imagine a different operation by which you could go from facing the mirror to facing out from behind it: by rotating yourself around a horizontal axis. Then you would be on your head behind the mirror and so reversed vertically (but not left-right) relative to your mirror-image. Compared to you after you have gotten behind the mirror in that way, your mirror-image is reversed vertically but not left-right. So mirrors reverse left-right rather than up-down only given one particular way that we imagine getting behind them—that is, only by virtue of the salience of one axis for turning ourselves behind a mirror.[34]

Mathematicians do occasionally reflect upon explanation in mathematics. For instance, Timothy Gowers writes: "[Some] branches of mathematics derive their appeal from an abundance of mysterious phenomena that demand explanation. These might be striking numerical coincidences suggesting a deep relationship between areas that appear on the surface to have nothing to do with each other, arguments which prove interesting results by brute force and therefore do not satisfactorily explain them, proofs that apparently depend on a series of happy accidents" (2000, 73). I hope that this chapter has managed to unpack some of these provocative remarks.

9

Desargues's Theorem as a Case Study of Mathematical Explanation, Existence, and Natural Properties

■ 9.1 A CASE STUDY

As I have shown in the previous two chapters, mathematicians distinguish proofs that explain why a given theorem holds from proofs that merely demonstrate that it holds. This chapter presents a case study of mathematical explanation that is attentive to the details of mathematical research. From this case study, I will extract some morals regarding mathematical explanation, unification, coincidence, existence, and mathematically natural properties. These morals will help me to elaborate my account of proofs that explain.

My case study will concern Desargues's theorem, which I will introduce in section 9.2. There I will present three proofs of Desargues's theorem in Euclidean geometry, only one of which mathematicians regard as explaining why the theorem holds. In section 9.3, I will argue that this proof explains Desargues's theorem only because a certain feature of the theorem strikes us as remarkable. In this context, what it means to ask for an explanation over and above a proof of Desargues's theorem is to ask for a proof that exploits some other, similar feature of the theorem's setup. Outside of such a context, there is no sense in which one proof is privileged over another as explanatory. The proof that explains Desargues's theorem in Euclidean geometry reveals it to be no mathematical coincidence even though the proof introduces a spatial dimension that is absent from the theorem. In all of these ways, this example fits nicely with the proposals I set out in the preceding two chapters.

However, mathematicians usually say that Desargues's theorem naturally belongs to *projective* geometry rather than to Euclidean geometry. A standard definition of "projective geometry" is that it concerns only those features of a geometrical figure that are preserved in all of its projections—for example, all of its possible shadows. For instance, three points' collinearity is preserved, whereas a segment's length is not; that some figure is a conic section is preserved, but that it is a circle is not. That projective geometry concerns only certain features of a figure can be compared to the way that dimensional analysis (which underwrites the scientific explanations that I examined in chapter 6) concerns only a case's dimensional architecture. An explanation in projective geometry, like a dimensional explanation, shows that the explanandum depends only on certain select features of the case.

In generalizing over cases that are alike in their projective properties, Desargues's theorem in projective geometry goes beyond Desargues's theorem in Euclidean geometry. In section 9.4, I will show how an explanation of Desargues's theorem in projective geometry unifies what Euclidean geometry portrays as a motley collection of special cases. Accordingly, Euclidean geometry is *mistaken* in portraying as coincidental at best certain results about Euclidean points, lines, and planes that in fact have a common, unified explanation given in projective geometry. Furthermore, projective geometry's talk of "points at infinity" is not a mere *façon de parler*. Rather, features of those points explain facts about Euclidean points, lines, and planes. Points at infinity exist even in *Euclidean* geometry by virtue of their playing such an explanatory role.[1]

This common, unified explanation of Desargues's theorem in projective geometry presupposes that various properties (such as the property of being a point, whether a Euclidean point or a "point at infinity") are natural properties in mathematics rather than wildly disjunctive, gerrymandered shadows of predicates. Here we seem to be caught in a vicious circle: the proof's explanatory power (indeed, even the why question concerning Desargues's theorem in projective geometry) presupposes that certain properties are mathematically natural, but presumably, they are natural purely in virtue of their roles in mathematical explanations of this kind. In section 9.5, I will argue that the naturalness of these properties and the explanatory power of these proofs arise together; neither is prior to the other. The case of Desargues's theorem also illustrates how mathematicians discover that certain properties are natural by finding them in many, diverse proofs that (mathematicians recognize) would be explanatory, if those properties were natural. In section 9.6, I will go on to use the notion of a natural property in mathematics to understand mathematical explanations in which facts are explained by being subsumed under a theorem that is no coincidence.

I hope that this case study suggests some of the roles that notions like explanation, existence, coincidence, unification, and naturalness have actually played in driving mathematical thought.

■ 9.2 THREE PROOFS—BUT ONLY ONE EXPLANATION—OF DESARGUES'S THEOREM IN TWO-DIMENSIONAL EUCLIDEAN GEOMETRY

Here is Desargues's theorem in two-dimensional Euclidean geometry:

If two triangles are so situated that the three lines joining their corresponding vertices all meet at a single point, then the points of intersection of the two triangles' corresponding sides—if those intersection points exist—all lie on one line.

Figure 9.1 should make this easier to understand. Disregard the shading in figure 9.1, which suggests a third dimension. I will come to that shortly, but for now, you must view the entire figure as lying on a plane. Triangles ABC and A'B'C' lie on the same Euclidean plane and their corresponding vertices (point A corresponding to point A', B to B', and C to C') are connected by lines that all meet at a single point (O). The two triangles are said to be "in perspective from O." Desargues's theorem concerns pairs of corresponding sides of the two triangles, where side CA corresponds to C'A', for example. Line CA may intersect line C'A' (remembering that each of these lines extends infinitely far beyond the segment forming a side of one of the two triangles in perspective); unless CA and C'A' are parallel, they will intersect somewhere on the plane. In the figure, M is their point of intersection. Likewise, N lies at the intersection of AB and A'B', and L lies at the intersection of CB and C'B'. The theorem says that these three points of intersection, if they exist, are collinear. (In fig. 9.1, they all lie on the dashed line.)

There are various ways of proving Desargues's theorem. For example, Girard Desargues (who discovered the theorem in the early 1600s) used Menelaus's theorem (discovered by Menelaus of Alexandria, c. 100 AD), which says:

Consider triangle RST, and let R', S', and T' be points on lines ST, TR, and RS, respectively (see fig. 7.4). Then R', S', and T' are collinear iff (RT'/ST')(SR'/ TR')(TS'/RS') = 1.

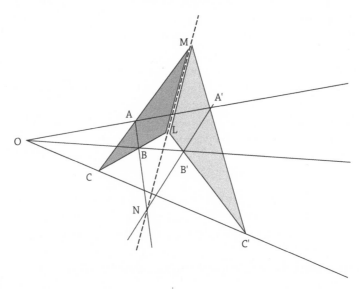

Figure 9.1 Desargues's theorem

Here is Desargues's proof of his theorem, first published in 1648 (Field and Gray 1987, 161–164):

> Consider triangle OBC (from fig. 9.1): L lies on BC, B' lies on OB, and C' lies on OC. From the collinearity of L, B', and C', Menelaus's theorem in the left-to-right direction entails that
>
> $$(CL/BL)(BB'/OB')(OC'/CC')=1.$$
>
> Likewise, from triangle OAB and line NA'B', Menelaus's theorem entails that
>
> $$(BN/AN)(AA'/OA')(OB'/BB')=1.$$
>
> Similarly, from triangle OAC and line MA'C', Menelaus's theorem entails that
>
> $$\left(AM/CM\right)(CC'/OC')(OA'/AA')=1.$$
>
> By multiplying all of the left sides together and all of the right sides together, we find
>
> $$(CL/BL)(BB'/OB')(OC'/CC')\ (BN/AN)(AA'/OA')(OB'/BB')$$
> $$(AM/CM)(CC'/OC')(OA'/AA')=1.$$
>
> Three fortuitous cancellations (e.g., BB'/OB' with OB'/BB') produce
>
> $$(CL/BL)(BN/AN)(AM/CM)=1.$$
>
> By the right-to-left direction of Menelaus's theorem applied to triangle ABC, it follows that L, N, and M are collinear.

This argument, though proving Desargues's theorem, is typically characterized by mathematicians as failing to explain why it is true. For example, according to Stankova (2004, 175), "A serious drawback of this solution is that it doesn't give us a clue *really why* Desargues's Theorem works." What is missing from the proof, depriving it of explanatory power?

One clue is that mathematicians typically describe this proof (and others like it) "as ingenious exercises in Euclidean geometry" (Gray 2007, 28), where "ingenious" here means "clever" (in a pejorative sense). What is clever about the proof is the way that the three equations "magically" cancel out one another's inconvenient terms. This cancellation appears out of nowhere, and the theorem arises from it. The proof thus makes it seem like an accident of algebra that everything cancels out so nicely, leaving us with just the terms needed for Menelaus's theorem to yield the collinearity of L, M, and N. The way that BB'/OB' and other ratios ultimately cancel out is similar to the way that mass m eventually cancels out in the dynamical derivation of the parallelogram law in section 2.2.

In each case, the "fortuitous" cancellation suggests that the argument in which these terms are introduced, only to cancel out later, is not the result's genuine explanation—where the term never appears in the first place.

I think that many of us, after working through Desargues's proof, are inclined to suspect that there is some *reason* why everything works out so neatly in the end—that is, a reason why all of the terms with primes ultimately disappear from the calculation. This reason eludes the above proof and must somehow explain why Desargues's theorem holds. (In these respects, the example is like several that I have given in preceding chapters, such as Zeitz's coin in chapter 7 and the "calculator number" theorem in chapter 8.)

To try to understand why this proof fails to explain, let's compare it to another proof of Desargues's theorem. This proof introduces a third dimension above and below the Euclidean plane on which the two triangles lie in perspective. One way to picture this third dimension is to imagine grabbing hold of line OCC' and pulling it below the plane of the page. Then the two shaded regions in figure 9.1 slice up through the paper's plane at AB and A'B', respectively, and from there rise above the plane of the page to meet along a peak at line LM. The dotted line is then envisioned as slanting from N in the paper's plane up through L above the paper's plane, ultimately rising further to M. (Picture the dotted line as like the line along which the two sides of a pitched roof meet.) Suitably positioned light sources below the paper's plane would project the shadows of triangles CAB and C'A'B' onto the corresponding triangles lying on the page.

For any arrangement of coplanar triangles in perspective from O, there are many arrangements of corresponding triangles jutting into the third dimension. Figure 9.2 (which includes fig. 9.1 on a plane seen nearly edge-on) shows how to construct one. Select any point S outside the plane of the two triangles in perspective from O. (S in fig. 9.2 is drawn below that plane.) Draw lines SC and SC'. Choose any line from O that intersects SC; let D be their point of intersection. Likewise, choose any line from O that intersects SC'; let D' be their point of intersection. Now triangle BAD (outlined in bold in fig. 9.2), extending below the original plane, projects onto triangle BAC lying on that plane, and likewise B'A'D' projects onto B'A'C'.

Any such projection preserves collinearity, so to show that L, M, and N are collinear, it suffices to show that the corresponding points in the three-dimensional figure are collinear. This is easily done. Let's return to figure 9.1, thinking of the two shaded triangles as jutting into the third dimension above and below the plane of the page. Each of those triangles lies on its own plane slanting through the plane of the page. These two planes meet, and any two planes that intersect meet at exactly one line. Since L, M, and N (in fig. 9.1—after we have pulled the figure into the third dimension) lie on this line, they are collinear. Here is the same point in terms of figure 9.2 (where the two shaded triangles from fig. 9.1

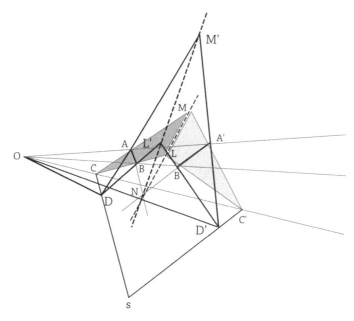

Figure 9.2 Desargues's theorem proved by using three dimensions

are lying on the original plane). M' (floating above the original plane, at the intersection of DA and D'A') is common to the plane containing triangle DAB and the plane containing triangle D'A'B' (since DA lies on the former plane, D'A' lies on the latter, and any point on one of these lines is on that line's plane). Likewise, L' (at the intersection of DB and D'B') is common to the two triangles' planes, and the same for N (on the original plane—where BA and B'A' intersect). Since the same pair of planes is involved in all three cases, and since any two planes that intersect meet at exactly one line, the three points (L', M', and N) are collinear—and hence so are their projections onto the original plane (L, M, and once again N). In case my busy figure 9.2 does not manage to make pellucid this strategy of exiting to the third dimension, figure 9.3 reproduces the illustrations of it given by two classic textbooks.

This proof is generally recognized by mathematicians as explaining why Desargues's theorem holds. The theorem holds in Euclidean geometry because the two triangles in perspective from O are projections of triangles jutting into the third dimension, and since the planes of those triangles must meet at a line, their projections must, too. Of course, we can appreciate this proof's explanatory power (especially by contrasting it with the proof using Menelaus's theorem) without seeing *precisely* what *makes* this proof explanatory. For instance, Gray (2007, 29) says, "How do we feel about this proof? We've changed the subject, of course, from two dimensions to three. We need to convince ourselves that any

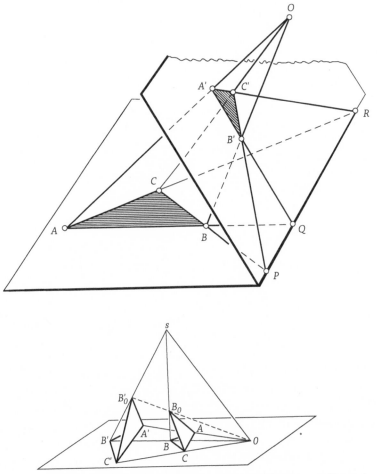

Figure 9.3 Two illustrations of the proof exiting to the third dimension: Courant, Robbins, and Stewart (1996, 171); and Hilbert and Cohn-Vössen (1952, 122)

two-dimensional figure can be drawn in three dimensions. That's easy enough if the triangles don't cross, but what if they do? Still, this ability to see the figure and see the truth of the theorem is a very powerful guide to understanding it. It conveys what a lengthy calculation may not always manage, a sense of the inevitability of the result." The proof using Menelaus's theorem employs just such a "lengthy calculation," where the three crucial cancellations seem fortuitous—coincidental rather than "inevitable." Yet Gray's attempt to contrast these proofs obviously remains unsatisfactory since, of course, everything here (including these cancellations) is inevitable in being mathematically necessary.

In the next section, I will return to Gray's remark.[2] But for now, let's try to improve our grip on the contrast between the two preceding proofs of

Desargues's theorem by looking briefly at another route to proving it—namely, by using coordinate geometry. The textbook technique (e.g., McLeod and Baart 1998, 149–150) is to use "homogeneous coordinates."[3] That is (briefly), three coordinates (x,y,z) rather than the usual two are used to represent each point on a plane figure; the third coordinate supplies some redundancy so that (x,y,z) and (nx,ny,nz) are the same point. Then for two arbitrary distinct points H (x_1,y_1,z_1) and J (x_2,y_2,z_2), line HJ consists of all points (x,y,z) such that for some real numbers a and b that are not both zero

$$x = ax_1 + bx_2, y = ay_1 + by_2, z = az_1 + bz_2$$

and so the equation for the line HJ is

$$\left(y_1 z_2 - y_2 z_1\right)x + \left(z_1 x_2 - z_2 x_1\right)y + \left(x_1 y_2 - x_2 y_1\right)z = 0.$$

In figure 9.1, we can let

A be $(1,0,0)$
B be $(0,1,0)$
C be $(0,0,1)$
O be (α,β,γ)

By the above, line OA consists of all points (x,y,z) such that for some real numbers a and b that are not both zero,

$$x = a\alpha + b1, y = a\beta + b0, z = a\gamma + b0.$$

If $a = 0$, then $y = z = 0$ and so any point A′ on line OA is $(b,0,0)$, which (by the redundancy in representing points) is the same point as A. Since A and A′ in the configuration with which Desargues's theorem is concerned (fig. 9.1) are distinct points, $a \neq 0$ and A′ is $(a\alpha + b,a\beta,a\gamma)$, which (by the redundancy) is the same point as $(\alpha + d,\beta,\gamma)$ for some real number d. By analogous reasoning, B′ is $(\alpha,\beta + e,\gamma)$ and C′ is $(\alpha,\beta,\gamma + f)$ for some real numbers e and f. The above equation for line HJ yields

For line BC: $(1 \cdot 1 - 0 \cdot 0)x + (0 \cdot 0 - 1 \cdot 0)y + (0 \cdot 0 - 0 \cdot 1)z = 0$, that is, $x = 0$.
For line B′C′: $[(\beta + e)(\gamma + f) - \beta\gamma]x + [\gamma\alpha - (\gamma + f)\alpha]y + [\alpha\beta - \alpha(\beta + e)]z = 0$, that is, $[ef + \beta f + e\gamma]x - f\alpha y - \alpha ez = 0$.

These two lines meet at $x = 0$ and

$$-f\alpha y - \alpha ez = 0, \text{ i.e.,} \alpha\left(fy + ez\right) = 0.$$

If $a = 0$, then BC and B′C′ are the same line, but they are distinct in the configuration with which Desargues's theorem is concerned (fig. 9.1). So $\alpha \neq 0$ and hence the intersection L of BC and B′C′ is where $x = 0$ and $fy + ez = 0$, that is, the point $(0,e,-f)$. By analogous reasoning, lines CA and C′A′ meet at M = $(-d,0,f)$ and lines AB and A'B' meet at N = $(d, -e, 0)$. Again using the above equation for line HJ, we find

For line NM: $(-ef - 0 \cdot 0)x + [0(-d) - fd]y + [d \cdot 0 - (-d)(-e)]z = 0$, that is,
$$efx + fdy + dez = 0.$$
For line NL: $[(-e)(-f) - e \cdot 0] \, x + [0 \cdot 0 - (-f)d]y + [de - 0(-e)]z = 0$, that is,
$$efx + fdy + dez = 0.$$

So NM and NL are the same line; L, M, and N are collinear.

This proof is widely regarded as failing to explain why Desargues's theorem holds. For example, the mathematicians Robin McLeod and Louisa Baart (1998, 125), in contrasting the proof exiting to the third dimension with a proof using homogeneous coordinates, say that "synthetic proofs [such as the former] tend to give more insight than algebraic ones [such as the latter]."[4] The coordinate-geometry proof seems to depend on another "algebraic miracle" at the end, where everything fortuitously turns out so nicely.

The coordinate-geometry proof employs a brute-force approach, simply calculating everything directly, plugging in everything we know and then grinding out the result.[5] Here we have another illustration of the claims that I made in sections 7.4 and 8.5 about brute-force proofs: that mathematicians generally agree on whether or not a proof is appropriately characterized as "brute force" and that a brute-force proof is never explanatory when the salient feature of the theorem being explained is its symmetry or simplicity or some other such feature, since a brute-force proof does not exploit any such feature. Whereas a brute-force approach is not selective in its focus, an explanation must pick out particular features of the setup as responsible for the result. The proof of Desargues's theorem that proceeds by exiting to the third dimension identifies the key feature as the fact that the two coplanar triangles in perspective are the projections of triangles on different planes (which perforce intersect in a line).

Nevertheless, the proof using coordinate geometry proceeds directly from the essential features of the setup. That the two triangles are in perspective is encoded directly into the coordinates of the various points, and the rest is mere algebra. One might have supposed that to explain why a given geometric theorem holds, it suffices to deduce the theorem directly from the "natures" or "essences" of the elements in the figure, as the proof using coordinate geometry does (with the assistance of the one-to-one correspondence between real numbers and points on a line). This idea (as I showed in section 8.5) is the core of Steiner's account of the difference between proofs that explain and proofs that fail to explain what they prove. Yet the proof using coordinate geometry is not respected as explaining why Desargues's theorem holds, despite merely unpacking the definitions of the elements in the theorem's setup. By contrast, the explanatory proof invokes considerations exogenous to the defining features of those elements. It introduces a third dimension that is not mentioned by the two-dimensional theorem. Here we have a potentially important and perhaps surprising lesson about mathematical explanation.

The great practical advantage of a brute-force proof (such as the coordinate-geometry proof of Desargues's theorem) is that the same reliable, mechanical, plug-and-chug argument scheme can be used to prove an enormously wide range of theorems. As I described in section 8.5, Kitcher proposes that arguments in mathematics or science are explanatory if and only if they instantiate argument schemes in the "explanatory store," which consists of the collection of schemes with the optimal combination of various virtues: the broadest coverage of facts, the fewest different argument schemes, and the most stringent constraints imposed by schemes upon arguments. But although a brute-force proof-scheme is a promising candidate for membership in Kitcher's "explanatory store," proofs instantiating it tend to lack explanatory power. The coordinate-geometry proof of Desargues's theorem is unilluminating because it never privileges certain features of triangles in perspective (such as their being projections of triangles on different planes) as responsible for the theorem. The meat-grinder of a brute-force approach is incapable of drawing that distinction.

But what makes Desargues's theorem in two-dimensional Euclidean geometry explained by the fact that two coplanar triangles in perspective are projections of two triangles in perspective on different planes jutting into the third dimension? Why is the proof that exits to the third dimension explanatory—despite introducing auxiliary lines and, for that matter, an entire dimension extraneous to a statement of Desargues's theorem in two-dimensional Euclidean geometry? Here we can appeal to my account of proofs that explain.

■ 9.3 WHY DESARGUES'S THEOREM IN TWO-DIMENSIONAL EUCLIDEAN GEOMETRY IS EXPLAINED BY AN EXIT TO THE THIRD DIMENSION

Desargues's theorem strikes us as remarkable because it identifies something common to the three points L, M, and N—namely, that they lie on the same line. (Of course, any *two* points are collinear, but here we have *three* points on the same line.) This commonality is salient; it prompts us to ask why the theorem holds. Accordingly, an explanation of the theorem must reveal something *else* given as common to these three points from which their collinearity follows. Now each of the three points is specified in the theorem's setup as the intersection of two lines that form corresponding sides of the two triangles in perspective. (For instance, L is where CB and C'B' intersect.) So to reveal a feature common to each of the three points is to reveal a feature common to each of the three pairs of lines (CB and C'B', BA and B'A', AC and A'C') joining corresponding vertices.

Of course, each *is* a pair of lines that form corresponding sides of two triangles in perspective; that is obviously a feature common to each of these pairs of lines. But this feature is the entire setup of the theorem. To explain why the theorem holds, a proof must at least select some feature but not others of the setup and exploit it in deriving the result. As I have shown, a brute-force proof fails to do that. Our task now is to understand the explanatory power of the feature privileged by the proof exiting to the third dimension, namely, that the two triangles in perspective are projections of triangles on different planes.

As I said, the striking feature of Desargues's theorem is that it reveals a property common to each of the three pairs of lines that form corresponding sides of two triangles in perspective. Hence, in order for a proof to explain why Desargues's theorem holds, it must trace the result to some other property common to each of these pairs of lines. Otherwise the proof treats it as *coincidental* that the three pairs of lines share the feature identified by Desargues's theorem (as I understood "mathematical coincidence" in chapter 8). By contrast, a mathematical explanation of Desargues's theorem would show it to be no coincidence. Thus, Gray's remark (from the previous section) was onto something: there is a sense in which an explanation of Desargues's theorem conveys the result's "inevitability." In contrast, a proof that first deduces the equation of NM and then separately deduces the equation of NL, "miraculously" finding them to be the same, portrays this fact as coincidental (albeit mathematically necessary).[6]

In the proof exiting to the third dimension, each of the three pairs of lines forming corresponding sides of the two triangles in perspective is the projection onto the original plane of a pair of lines, one line joining a pair of points on one plane jutting into the third dimension, and the other line joining another pair of points on another such plane. Crucially, *it is the same two planes for all three pairs*. By this proof, points L, M, and N have a line in common because the three pairs of lines that give rise to them have two planes in common. That the proof traces the salient commonality to another commonality is, I suggest, the source of its explanatory power. The proof explains by revealing where the result's salient feature comes from.

This proof explains Desargues's theorem only because a certain feature of the theorem strikes us as remarkable: its identifying a property common to each of the three points at which lines forming corresponding sides of the triangles intersect.[7] (This commonality seems even more remarkable in light of the "magical" way it emerges from the proof using Menelaus's theorem and the brute-force proof using coordinate geometry.) In this context, what it means to ask for an explanation over and above a proof of Desargues's theorem is to ask for a proof that exploits some other feature common to the three points (or, equivalently, to the three pairs of lines from which they arise). Outside of such a context, there is no sense in which one proof of Desargues's theorem is privileged over another as explanatory.

This account helps us to see why Desargues's theorem in *two*-dimensional Euclidean geometry is explained by a proof that proceeds by first proving Desargues's theorem in *three*-dimensional Euclidean geometry—a theorem concerning two triangles that are *not* coplanar (but are in perspective from O). The explanation of Desargues's two-dimensional theorem works by tracing that result to another feature common to these three pairs of lines—but requiring three dimensions: that if the two triangles are *pulled out* of their original plane as in figure 9.2, then each pair of lines forming corresponding sides of the two triangles involves the same two planes. These planes must meet along a line. The proof thus explains not only why Desargues's *two*-dimensional theorem holds, but also why Desargues's *three*-dimensional theorem holds.

We can now better appreciate why it is helpful to introduce the third dimension: because it supplies a second way to pick out the line LMN. If we stick to two dimensions, then the only way to pick out this line is as the line that runs through a given pair of points. (Through any two points, there is exactly one line.) But with the third dimension, we can also identify the line as where two given planes intersect. The two planes, in turn, are picked out as those containing one or the other of the two triangles in perspective, once those triangles have been pulled out of their original plane. (Any plane is individuated by three noncollinear points on it.) The two planes, then, *unite* the three pairs of lines forming corresponding sides, since the same two planes are common to each pair. Without the third dimension, there is no such unity and so (considering the salient feature of Desargues's result) no explanation.

Thus, the third dimension is not actually artificial to Desargues's theorem in two-dimensional Euclidean geometry.[8] Rather, because the third dimension provides an alternate means of picking out a line, it supplies the resources for specifying another feature common to points L, M, and N. A proof that proceeds entirely in two dimensions can compare lines NM and NL only by computing their equations (whether by coordinate geometry, as I have shown, or by using vectors or in some other way) and concluding that they are identical. More broadly, a proof confined to two dimensions must use *metrical considerations* (such as the ratios in Menelaus's theorem). As I have shown, these considerations end up depriving the proof of explanatory power (since the cancellations in the derivation of Desargues's theorem from Menelaus's theorem are fortuitous). In contrast, when the third dimension is introduced, Desargues's theorem regarding noncoplanar triangles in perspective follows without any appeal to metrical considerations—that is, entirely from axioms of incidence (that two points determine a line, three noncollinear points determine a plane, two intersecting planes determine a line, two intersecting lines determine a point, a line lies entirely in a given plane if two points on that line do). The three-dimensional theorem's projection onto a plane yields the two-dimensional theorem. By appealing only to the axioms of incidence, the proof that exits to the third dimension avoids the "algebraic coincidences" on which metrical proofs depend and explains why Desargues's theorem holds in two-dimensional Euclidean geometry.[9]

The proofs of Desargues's theorem that incorrectly depict it as coincidental are like the proofs that I have given of genuine mathematical coincidences. For instance, recall from chapter 8 that it is coincidental that these two Diophantine equations (that is, equations where the variables can take only integer values)

$$2x^2(x^2-1)=3(y^2-1)$$

and

$$x(x-1)/2=2^n-1$$

have exactly the same five positive solutions for x (namely, $x = 1, 2, 3, 6$, and 91). The two equations have nothing to do with each other. Of course, we could take separate procedures for solving the two equations and cobble them together into one proof. But the steps of the procedure for solving one equation could always be omitted without keeping the proof from solving the other equation. Compare the proof of Desargues's theorem using coordinate geometry. It shows that lines NM and NL are the same by ascertaining NM's equation, separately ascertaining NL's equation, and then finding these equations to be identical. This proof is similar to a proof regarding the above two Diophantine equations that proceeds by solving one equation, separately solving the other, and finally noting that the two sets of solutions are exactly the same. Likewise, in the derivation of Desargues's theorem from Menelaus's theorem, the cancellations (e.g., of BB′/OB′ by OB′/BB′) are fortuitous in that the appearance of a given term in one application of Menelaus's theorem, and of its reciprocal in a separate application of Menelaus's theorem, is coincidental. They arise independently.

The proof of Desargues's two-dimensional theorem that exits to the third dimension reveals the collinearity of L, M, and N to be no mathematical coincidence. In the next section, I will give another mathematical explanation of Desargues's theorem—but this time for the theorem's version in projective geometry. That explanation likewise reveals its target to be no coincidence. This example will lead us to a better understanding of mathematical coincidence. Moreover, just as I have shown that the third dimension is not artificial to Desargues's theorem in two-dimensional Euclidean geometry, so I will show that elements of projective geometry generally considered foreign to Euclidean geometry actually play a role in explaining a theorem in Euclidean geometry.[10]

■ 9.4 DESARGUES'S THEOREM IN PROJECTIVE GEOMETRY: UNIFICATION AND EXISTENCE IN MATHEMATICS

Here again is Desargues's theorem in two-dimensional Euclidean geometry:

> If two triangles are so situated that the three lines joining their corresponding vertices all meet at a single point, then the points of intersection of the two triangles' corresponding sides—if those intersection points exist—all lie on one line.

The qualification "if those intersection points exist" is included to acknowledge that there need not be three points of intersection (one for each pair of corresponding sides); if two corresponding sides are parallel, then in Euclidean geometry, they do not intersect. It may even be that *each* pair of corresponding sides consists of parallel lines, so there are *no* points of intersection at all (fig. 9.4). Hence, in Euclidean geometry, we cannot refer to "the points of intersection" without giving the qualification "if they exist" (as given, for instance, by Whitehead 1907/1971, 16; Stankova 2004, 173). Of course, if there are only two points of intersection, then they are necessarily collinear (since a line runs through any two points), and if there are none or exactly one, then collinearity among the points of intersection is trivially achieved.[11] These are "special cases" of Desargues's theorem; the above proofs of Desargues's two-dimensional theorem in Euclidean geometry covered only the nontrivial case: where there are three intersection points.

However, Desargues's theorem is usually understood as a theorem of *projective* rather than Euclidean geometry; projective geometry is its natural setting. In projective geometry, any two coplanar lines meet. Parallel lines meet at a point infinitely far away in the lines' direction (that is, at a single point, which is infinitely far away in *either* direction, one and the same point being reachable "either way"). This "point at infinity" is not located on the Euclidean plane (since for

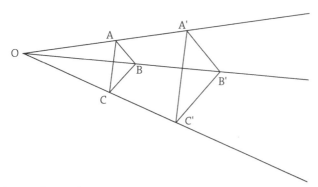

Figure 9.4 A special case of Desargues's theorem in Euclidean geometry

any two Euclidean points, there is some finite distance between them). All of the members of a set of mutually parallel, coplanar lines have the same single point at infinity in common, and for each different orientation that coplanar parallel lines can take, there is a distinct point at infinity. All (and only) the points at infinity on the lines on a given plane lie on a given "line at infinity." A "projective plane" thus consists of a "finite plane" (i.e., a Euclidean plane) plus a line at infinity.

One way to think about a point at infinity is as the point where endless straight railroad tracks on a Euclidean plane, viewed in perspective, are seen to meet (fig. 9.5). Admittedly, this way of thinking merely heightens our inclination to pose the question: "Of course, we can choose to speak in terms of 'points (and lines) at infinity,' if we wish, but do they really exist? After all, straight railroad tracks never really meet, no matter how long they run. Do parallel lines really meet, or do they only 'meet' inside inverted commas— that is, in the projective-geometry sense?" But as soon as we ask this question, we begin to worry that it is ill-posed. After all, mathematics is not concerned with whether *Euclidean* points (much less points at infinity) exist *physically*, and clearly (a familiar thought runs) they exist *mathematically*—in Euclidean geometry (as when a Euclidean geometer says "There exists a point at which the diagonals of a square meet"). In the same internal sense, then, "points at infinity" exist in projective geometry.[12] When doing mathematics, we can choose to study Euclidean geometry or to study projective geometry without any fear that our selection might be erroneous, since both are true; the former accurately describes Euclidean planes and the latter accurately describes projective planes. Considering the straightforward way that I just introduced the notion of "points at infinity," we might well doubt whether it could possibly make any difference (other than to our convenience) whether we choose to say "Two coplanar parallel lines meet at a point at infinity" or "Two coplanar parallel lines never meet," since anything expressed in one way can be translated into the other.

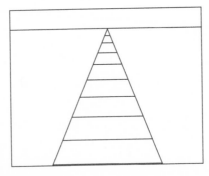

Figure 9.5 Rails meeting at infinity

This last thought suggests that it is merely for the sake of simplicity or convenience that Desargues's theorem is generally expressed in terms of projective geometry rather than Euclidean geometry. Yet mathematicians generally say that projective geometry is where Desargues's theorem really resides. This does not sound like a mere matter of convenience. But then what does it mean?

Since any two coplanar lines intersect in projective geometry, Desargues's theorem in two-dimensional projective geometry does not need the qualification "if those intersection points exist." It says simply

If two triangles are so situated that the three lines joining their corresponding vertices all meet at a single point, then the three points of intersection of the two triangles' corresponding sides are collinear.

Let's see how Desargues's theorem in two-dimensional projective geometry applies to the case depicted in figure 9.4, where each of the three pairs of corresponding sides consists of a pair of parallel lines, so none of the intersection points L, M, or N exists on the Euclidean plane. The lines of each pair intersect on the projective plane: at infinity. Since the three points of intersection are all on the same line at infinity, they are collinear, as demanded by Desargues's theorem in projective geometry.[13] In projective geometry, this is not a "special case" of Desargues's theorem, requiring separate treatment. Rather, it is proved automatically by the proof that exits to the third dimension and explains why Desargues's theorem holds in projective geometry. Whether the intersection points are at infinity or on the Euclidean plane, there are three intersection points, and so the case is covered by the proof in projective geometry. The proof that exits to the third dimension proves Desargues's theorem in two-dimensional projective geometry without having to treat any cases separately; there are no special cases.

Now suppose that two of the three pairs of corresponding sides are pairs of parallel lines. It follows that the third pair must also be a pair of parallel lines, so none of L, M, or N exists on the Euclidean plane. Here is a proof in Euclidean geometry (using the labels in fig. 9.4):

Suppose lines BC and B'C' are parallel and that lines AB and A'B' are parallel. Show that lines AC and A'C' are parallel:

Consider triangles OBC and OB'C'. They have the same angle O. Since BC and B'C' are parallel lines cut by the transversal OB', angles B and B' are corresponding angles, and so are equal. Thus, two angles of triangle OBC are equal to two angles of triangle OB'C'. Therefore, the triangles must be similar. For analogous reasons, triangles OAB and OA'B' are similar. Similar triangles have all of their corresponding sides in the same ratio. From the similarity of OAB and OA'B', OA/OA' = OB/OB', and from the similarity of OBC and OB'C', OB/OB' = OC/OC'. Hence, OA/OA' = OC/OC'. Hence, two sides of triangle OAC are in the same ratio as two sides of triangle OA'C', and the included angle O is the same. Hence, OAC and OA'C' are similar, so their corresponding angles A and A' must be equal. That is, lines AC and A'C' make equal angles with transversal OA', so AC and A'C' must be parallel.

Desargues's theorem in two-dimensional Euclidean geometry does *not* entail the result that we just proved: that it is impossible for exactly one of the three pairs of corresponding sides to have a point of intersection on the Euclidean plane. As far as that theorem is concerned, it could be that exactly one of the three pairs of lines has an intersection point; in that case, it is trivial that all of the intersection points are collinear. This is a "special case" of Desargues's theorem in Euclidean geometry.

By contrast, Desargues's theorem in two-dimensional *projective* geometry *does* entail the result that we just proved. Suppose two of the three pairs of corresponding sides are pairs of parallel lines. Then in each of those two pairs, the two lines intersect at infinity. The unique line through those two intersection points is the line at infinity associated with the given plane. By Desargues's theorem in projective geometry, all three points of intersection must be collinear. The only way for the third point of intersection to lie on the same line as the other two intersection points—namely, on the line at infinity—is for the third point also to lie at infinity, and hence for the third pair of corresponding sides to consist of two parallel lines.

Thus, Desargues's theorem in projective geometry has an implication regarding the Euclidean plane that fails to follow from Desargues's theorem in Euclidean geometry. Furthermore, this additional implication is not arbitrarily tacked on to the rest of the theorem, requiring a separate proof from the rest. Rather, in proving Desargues's theorem in projective geometry by exiting to the third dimension, one does not treat this case separately. Cases where one or more of the points of intersection are at infinity are not "special cases" of Desargues's theorem in projective geometry. All of this stands in stark contrast to Euclidean geometry: a proof of Desargues's theorem in Euclidean geometry does not thereby prove the further result that we just discovered. Rather, a Euclidean proof of that result (which I gave above) is entirely separate from any proof of Desargues's theorem in Euclidean geometry.[14]

We could, of course, supplement Desargues's theorem in Euclidean geometry so that the strengthened theorem does imply that it is impossible for exactly one of the three pairs of corresponding sides to have a point of intersection on the Euclidean plane. Here is the strengthened theorem:

> If two triangles are so situated that the three lines joining their corresponding vertices all meet at a single point, then the three points of intersection of the two triangles' corresponding sides—if those intersection points exist—all lie on one line, and if two pairs of corresponding sides are such that the two sides in each pair fail to intersect, then the two sides in the third pair also fail to intersect.

However, in Euclidean geometry, this strengthened theorem is merely two theorems cobbled together in that they have no "common proof." Of course, we could cobble together proofs of each into a single proof. But it would be no "common proof" since some of the steps needed to prove one could be weakened or omitted from the proof without compromising the derivation of the other—just like solutions to the two Diophantine equations mentioned in the previous section. At best, the strengthened theorem constitutes a mathematical coincidence according to Euclidean geometry.[15] But Euclidean geometry is mistaken in so depicting it. Projective geometry reveals the theorem to be in fact no coincidence; the two components of the strengthened Euclidean theorem have a common proof in an explanation of Desargues's theorem in projective geometry.

It is not merely the case that Euclidean geometry and projective geometry *differ* in whether or not they treat the strengthened Desargues's theorem as at best a coincidence. Rather, Euclidean geometry is *mistaken*; projective geometry reveals that these various "special cases" are actually no coincidence—just as the complex numbers reveal certain results involving real numbers alone to be no coincidence (though they appear to be coincidental when considered in the context of the real numbers alone). For instance, as I argued in section 8.3, it is no coincidence that the two Taylor series

$$1/(1-x^2)=1+x^2+x^4+x^6+\ldots$$
$$1/(1+x^2)=1-x^2+x^4-x^6+\ldots$$

are alike in that, for real x, each converges when $|x| < 1$ but diverges when $|x| > 1$. The reason why these functions both exhibit this convergence behavior is that both of them (considered as functions of complex numbers) are undefined for some z on the unit circle of the complex plane and because all of these cases can be treated together in a proof of the "radius of convergence" theorem:

> For any power series $\Sigma\, a_n z^n$ (from $n = 0$ to ∞), either it converges for all complex numbers z, or it converges only for $z = 0$, or there is a number $R > 0$ such that it converges if $|z| < R$ and diverges if $|z| > R$.

Just as considerations from the real numbers alone mischaracterize as coincidental the common convergence behavior of the two Taylor series, so considerations from Euclidean geometry alone fail to recognize that the various components of the strengthened Desargues's theorem are no coincidence.[16]

There are further respects in which Desargues's theorem in projective geometry unifies what Euclidean geometry treats as special cases, thereby revealing to be no coincidence various results that Euclidean geometry depicts as coincidental at best. Consider the case where exactly two of the three pairs of corresponding sides are pairs of lines that intersect on the Euclidean plane. As I have shown, a proof of Desargues's theorem in Euclidean geometry must treat this as a special case; the proofs in section 9.2 all concern only the case where there exist three points of intersection. (For example, we cannot make all of the requisite fortuitous cancellations with only two applications of Menelaus's theorem.) To treat it as a special case is no problem, of course, since when there are exactly two points of intersection, their collinearity is trivial. In projective geometry, by contrast, points at infinity are just points like any other. The case of two intersection points on the finite plane, but one at infinity, requires no special treatment; a proof does not have to proceed by cases at all.

Furthermore, if exactly two of the intersection points lie on the Euclidean plane (i.e., exactly one of the three pairs of corresponding sides consists of two parallel lines), then the line through those two intersection points is parallel to the two parallel sides. (See fig. 9.6, where line NL is parallel to lines AC and A'C'.) Once again, this result in Euclidean geometry does not follow from Desargues's theorem in Euclidean geometry. It can be proved in Euclidean geometry, but this proof is separate from a proof of Desargues's theorem. Once again, we could strengthen Desargues's theorem in Euclidean geometry by conjoining it with this result. But the strengthened theorem would have no common, unified proof in Euclidean geometry. Its various cases would have to be proved separately. Accordingly, mathematicians commonly refer to the strengthened theorem in Euclidean geometry as a mere collection of special cases. (See, for example, Gray 2007, 29; Jones 1986, 556; Sylvester 2001, 251.) In contrast, this result follows from Desargues's theorem in projective geometry by negligible additional steps and without having to be treated separately as concerning a special case: the intersection point M at infinity is collinear with the two intersection points L and N on the finite plane,[17] as demanded by Desargues's theorem in projective geometry, only if M lies at the intersection of line LN and the line at infinity, so lines LN, AC, and A'C' meet at a point at infinity and therefore must be parallel. It is no coincidence, then, that this result holds together with Desargues's

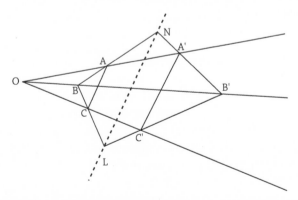

Figure 9.6 Another special case of Desargues's theorem in Euclidean geometry

theorem in Euclidean geometry; they receive a common proof in an explanation of Desargues's theorem in projective geometry.

The phenomenon that I have just described is not a peculiarity of Desargues's theorem. Projective geometry characteristically unifies what Euclidean geometry treats as separate theorems and special cases. This unification has long been recognized as among projective geometry's great achievements (Chasles 1837, 75–76, 87; Dieudonné 1985, 8; Lord 2013, 11). As Descartes wrote to Desargues on June 19, 1639: "Pour votre façon de considérer les lignes parallèles, comme si elles s'assemblaient à un but à distance infinie, afin de les comprendre sous le même genre que celles qui tendent à un point, elle est fort bonne" (Descartes 1639, 555).[18] Indeed, the search for such unified explanations—the suspicion that Euclidean geometry proves but fails to explain certain geometrical facts, that it incorrectly characterizes them as coincidences at best—was one of the original motivations for developing projective geometry in the first place. Consider Jean-Victor Poncelet, whose 1822 work made the first contribution to projective geometry after Desargues: "The lesson Poncelet set about drawing . . . was that there should be a better way of reasoning geometrically, one that did not pursue the argument down a maze of bifurcating cases: one when there are four points, another when there are two, a third when there are none, a fourth when two points coincide; one when this segment is less than that one, another when it is greater" (Gray 2007, 46). We have here a nice example of the role that concepts such as mathematical explanation, unification, and coincidence play in mathematical practice.

This role is not merely heuristic and pragmatic. Projective geometry is not merely a convenient way of proving theorems in Euclidean geometry—shortening the proofs, making them more efficient, allowing more to be proved at once. Rather, I have suggested that Euclidean geometry is *mistaken* in portraying certain results as at best coincidental and certain theorems as mere collections of special cases. Projective geometry reveals facts about Euclidean points, lines, and planes that escape Euclidean geometry—not because they are too difficult to prove in Euclidean geometry, but because Euclidean geometry gets them wrong. These facts concern whether certain results in Euclidean geometry have a common, unified explanation. As Dieudonné (1985, 9) puts it: "the projective view exposes properties that appear accidental" to be otherwise.

That Euclidean geometry can (in this respect) be *incorrect* regarding Euclidean points, lines, and planes runs contrary to the familiar thought that I mentioned near the start of this section: that when doing mathematics, we can choose to study Euclidean geometry or to study projective geometry without any fear that our selection might be erroneous, since both are true; the former accurately describes Euclidean planes and the latter accurately describes projective planes. Although the theorems of Euclidean geometry are true of Euclidean points, lines, and planes, Euclidean geometry taken more broadly (to include the proofs—and hence the explanations—that may be given of these theorems) may nevertheless mischaracterize those objects.

Earlier I also mentioned the familiar thought that to ask whether points at infinity *really* exist is to make a fundamental mistake. Trivially (this familiar thought runs), they exist in projective geometry but do not exist in Euclidean geometry. However, our case study of Desargues's theorem suggests that points at infinity are not a mere *façon de parler*. Rather, their features genuinely explain facts about Euclidean points, lines, and planes. In other words, points and lines at infinity exist in *Euclidean* geometry; mathematicians discovered that they do (via "inference to the best mathematical explanation") by working in projective geometry.

My argument can be put roughly as follows:

P1: Certain facts about points at infinity explain certain facts about Euclidean points, lines, and planes. (I have argued for this claim in the preceding sections.)

P2: What explains a fact about some entities must be on an ontological par with those entities. (Roughly: only facts about what exists can explain facts about what exists.)

C: Points at infinity exist in Euclidean geometry.

In arguing for P1, I have argued against the view that certain facts about Euclidean points, lines, and planes have an explanation *in projective geometry* but have no explanation *in Euclidean geometry*. Rather, they have an explanation, period; whether they have an explanation is not relative to some mathematical field. Of course, their explanation requires the resources of projective geometry, but it does not follow that their explanation is relative to the geometry in question— any more than whether a given empirical fact has an explanation is relative to the scientific theory in question. For example, certain facts about the observed motions of the planets in Earth's night sky have an explanation, which is supplied by the Copernican theory of the heavens. The Ptolemaic theory says that these astronomical facts have no explanation. It is the case, of course, that these astronomical facts have an explanation according to the Copernican theory and no explanation according to the Ptolemaic theory. But what the two theories say is not all there is to the matter; whether these astronomical facts do indeed possess an explanation is not relative to the theory in question. Rather, it turns out that the astronomical facts have an explanation, as the Copernican theory correctly says; the Ptolemaic theory is mistaken in portraying them as brute. Likewise, Euclidean geometry is mistaken in some of what it says about the explanation of certain facts about Euclidean points, lines and planes. Perhaps what it is for points at infinity to exist in Euclidean geometry is for them to play an explanatory role there.

I conclude that it is not merely for the sake of simplicity or convenience that Desargues's theorem is generally expressed in terms of projective geometry rather than Euclidean geometry. As mathematicians say, projective geometry is where Desargues's theorem naturally belongs.[19]

■ 9.5 DESARGUES'S THEOREM IN PROJECTIVE GEOMETRY: EXPLANATION AND NATURAL PROPERTIES IN MATHEMATICS

I have suggested that in projective geometry, the proof exiting to the third dimension explains Desargues's theorem because it exploits a feature common to the three points at which pairs of corresponding sides of the two triangles intersect. This feature gives the proof explanatory power, on my view, because a certain feature of Desargues's theorem strikes us as remarkable: its identification of a property common to each of the three intersection points—or (equivalently) each of the three pairs of corresponding sides of the two triangles. The salience of this feature makes meaningful the why question demanding the theorem's explanation over and above its proof. But the content of Desargues's theorem *in projective geometry* strikes us in this way (as identifying a property common to each of the three intersection points) only if *we already recognize points at infinity as just like other points*—as all "le même genre" (as Descartes said in the letter to Desargues that I quoted in the previous section). Otherwise, Desargues's theorem in projective geometry consists of Desargues's theorem in Euclidean geometry plus various other theorems (two of which I gave in the previous section). So understood, the theorem is a motley collection of results. It does not identify a property common to each of the three points of intersection. Therefore, only in projective geometry does it make sense even to ask *why* Desargues's theorem in projective geometry holds.

I have just presumed that a genuine resemblance among the three intersection points is distinguished from a difference among them—even though we could paper over that difference by using the same specious term to describe them all. I am thus invoking a familiar philosophical distinction between what Armstrong (1978, 38–41) and Lewis (1983, 345–350) call "natural" (i.e., "sparse") properties—that is, respects in which things may genuinely resemble each other—on the one hand, and mere shadows of predicates (i.e., "abundant" properties), on the other hand. Consider some of the properties figuring in projective geometry. For example, take the property of being a point, which is instantiated by both points on the finite plane and points at infinity. Or take the property of being a line, which is instantiated by both Euclidean lines and lines at infinity. These are natural properties according to projective geometry. In fact, according to projective geometry, they mark off natural kinds. In projective geometry "all lines are 'created' equal, regardless of whether they are usual lines or the 'lines at infinity'" (Stankova 2004, 176; see Courant 1996, 181). Explanatory proofs in projective geometry treat all lines in the same way; lines at infinity are not "special cases." For instance, in the proof explaining Desargues's theorem in projective geometry, the case where points L, M, and N all lie on the line at infinity does not require special treatment. Rather, that case is treated together with the others as all constituting instances of collinearity.

But any of these properties that is natural, according to projective geometry, is instead a gerrymandered, artificial, wildly disjunctive, unnatural "property" (all of these pejorative terms being roughly synonymous) according to Euclidean geometry—akin to Goodman's (1983) famous example of being "grue": of being green and observed before the year 3000 (to update Goodman's example) or blue and unobserved before the year 3000. For instance, the projective property of being collinear, as applying to the three intersection points according to Desargues's theorem in projective geometry, is understood in Euclidean geometry as the property of being collinear, if the three intersection points are on the Euclidean plane, *or* of the third intersection point's "existing at infinity" (i.e., the two corresponding sides of the triangles being parallel), if the other two intersection points "exist at infinity," *or* . . . (with each disjunct corresponding to a separate theorem in Euclidean geometry).

On my account, a mathematical coincidence is a result having as its salient feature that it reveals a respect in which the various cases covered by its components are alike (i.e., that the same natural property is ascribed by its various components to the cases they cover), but it has no explanation (i.e., those components have no "common proof"). For instance, it is a mathematical coincidence that the two Diophantine equations at the end of section 9.3 have the same positive solutions. In having the same positive solutions, the two equations genuinely resemble each other. But consider a result with components that do not saliently ascribe the same natural property to the cases they cover, such as the wild conjunction that there are exactly five perfect solids and that the two Diophantine equations have the same solutions. Because no resemblance among its cases is being highlighted, this result is not even a mathematical coincidence (although its components have no "common proof"). Euclidean geometry mistakenly depicts the components of Desargues's theorem in projective geometry as having no common proof, but it does not depict the theorem as coincidental because in Euclidean geometry, its components fail to reveal that various cases have something in common. Only if projective concepts denote natural properties do the components of Desargues's theorem in projective geometry show that these cases have something in common. Therefore, only in projective geometry does it make sense even to ask whether or not this combination of results is coincidental.

Thus, it is misleading to say simply that in Euclidean geometry, there is no explanation of the theorem called "Desargues's theorem" in projective geometry, since this formulation suggests that the lack of any such explanation is felt in Euclidean geometry. Rather, in Euclidean geometry, we cannot even properly ask the why question that the explanation answers; there is thus no call for any such explanation. Projective geometry is the natural habitat for Desargues's theorem in Euclidean geometry because only there does the theorem have a common explanation with various other Euclidean results, unifying them all (as Desargues's theorem in projective geometry)—even though in Euclidean geometry, the lack of any such explanation is not felt because it would not make sense even to ask for such an explanation.

Now according to my account, the proof exiting to the third dimension possesses the power to explain why Desargues's theorem in projective geometry holds. As I have argued, the proof's explanatory power depends on Desargues's theorem in projective geometry strikingly revealing a respect in which the three pairs of lines joining corresponding vertices are alike: each pair's point of intersection (whether a Euclidean point or a point at infinity) falls on the same line (whether a Euclidean line plus a point at infinity or a line at infinity). The proof exiting to the third dimension explains by tracing this respect in which the three pairs are alike to another respect in which they are alike: the three pairs have a line in common because they have a pair of planes in common. Thus, the proof's explanatory power depends on various properties being respects in which things are alike—that is, being mathematically natural properties. But these are all projective properties, such as the property of being a projective point—that is, being either a Euclidean point *or* a point at infinity. Is this a natural property or a wild disjunction? Likewise, whether the proof exiting to the third dimension unifies various theorems that Euclidean geometry must treat separately depends on whether projective properties are natural. If they are wildly disjunctive, then the "unity" they create is specious. Whether the concept of a projective point picks out a natural class, on the one hand, or is an artificial device for shortening proofs without genuinely unifying them, on the other hand, makes a big difference to projective geometry's explanatory power.[20]

In sum, the why question regarding Desargues's theorem in projective geometry functions only in a context where the theorem is already appreciated as identifying something common to the three pairs of corresponding sides, and the proof exiting to the third dimension succeeds in answering the why question only by virtue of exploiting another feature that these pairs share.[21] But here we seem to be caught in a vicious circle: the proof's explanatory power (indeed, even the request for an explanation) presupposes that certain properties are natural, but presumably, they are natural purely in virtue of their roles in such explanations. What makes the points at infinity just more points is that they function in explanations no differently from points on the finite plane; explanatory proofs do not treat them as special cases. Two projective points behave in the same way for the same reasons, and this is what makes the projective points form a natural class.[22] A single term covering not only pairs of lines intersecting at Euclidean points, but also pairs of parallel lines (intersecting "at infinity"), could be stipulated within Euclidean geometry and used to present proofs more compactly. But only by discovering projective geometry's explanatory power do mathematicians discover that this term is not a mere *façon de parler*, but rather denotes a natural kind in mathematics.

How do mathematicians discover the explanatory power of some proof in projective geometry if they must already know that projective concepts denote natural properties in mathematics, yet this knowledge, in turn, arises from their discovering projective geometry's explanatory power? Here we have the epistemic version of the ontological circularity I just mentioned. My suggestion is that (knowledge of) the naturalness of projective properties and (knowledge of) the explanatory power of proofs using those properties arise together; neither is prior to the other.

What makes a given proof in projective geometry explanatory is, in part, that it uses natural properties, and what makes those properties natural, in turn, is that they figure in other explanatory proofs. For each explanation, the existence of others secures the naturalness of the properties it uses. Of course, each of those others is beholden to others for the naturalness of the properties it uses. This holism does not involve vicious circularity because a given proof's status as an explanation *presupposes* the naturalness of the properties it exploits but does not also *make* those properties natural. An entire constellation of proofs that would be explanatory, were certain properties natural, is needed to make those properties natural. Insofar as those proofs are many and diverse (in that, e.g., one of these proofs is not contained in each one of the others, so that we are not getting a multiplicity of proofs on the cheap), the properties qualify as natural and the proofs as explanatory.[23] This ontology is mirrored in epistemology. Mathematicians discover that the properties in a given family are natural by finding them in many, diverse proofs that (mathematicians recognize) would be explanatory, if those properties were natural.

A wildly disjunctive property fails to figure in such a wide constellation of proofs. We could, of course, take two arbitrary theorems involving natural properties and make them into a single combined theorem by using disjunctive properties. We could likewise form a proof of the single combined theorem by taking a proof explaining why one of the original theorems holds and combining it with a proof explaining why the other holds—using further disjunctive properties to combine the first steps of the two proofs, the second steps, and so forth. The disjunctive properties figuring in the single combined theorem must appear in many other theorems: since the original two theorems involve natural properties, those properties figure in many other theorems as well, and so a given disjunctive property in the single combined theorem will appear in various combinations of these other theorems. However, although the disjunctive properties in the single combined theorem are guaranteed to appear in other theorems, no such guarantee applies to the other disjunctive properties in the steps of the combined proof of the single combined theorem. Rather, those properties are not apt to figure in proofs of any other theorems (apart from proofs of theorems logically related to the given theorem). The two original proofs have little in common; the disjunctive combinations created by the two proofs' combination are too idiosyncratic to be likely to arise in other proofs.

Now consider what happens when such seemingly disjunctive properties as "Euclidean point or point at infinity" are used to combine various Euclidean theorems into a theorem equivalent to Desargues's theorem in projective geometry.[24] We could take various proofs of these components individually (that exit to the third dimension) and combine them by using disjunctive properties. Lo and behold, the same few disjunctive properties (e.g., the properties in projective geometry of being a point, being a line, being a plane) arise in all of the combined steps—and exactly the same allegedly disjunctive properties appear in many other combinations of Euclidean theorems dealing with other allegedly special cases. Being collinear (whether the line is a Euclidean line plus a point at infinity or is a line at infinity), being coplanar, and other projective properties that would be ways of being alike, if these properties were natural, arise in many (otherwise diverse) theorems and proofs that would be explanatory, if these properties were natural. Thus, the projective properties become natural. The epistemology mirrors the ontology: By discovering that the same few projective properties recur in all of these proofs, mathematicians discovered that they are natural and that these proofs explain those projective-geometry theorems.

In contrast, the unnatural properties needed to combine two arbitrary proofs are ad hoc. The combination of (e.g.) "All triangles have interior angles adding to a straight angle" and "All isosceles trapezoids have base angles that are congruent" involves the property of being a triangle or an isosceles trapezoid, for instance, which is guaranteed to figure in other theorems produced by similar combinations (since there are many other theorems concerning triangles and many others concerning isosceles trapezoids). But the combination of a step in a proof of the triangle theorem with a step in a proof of the trapezoid theorem will involve properties such as being alternate interior angles where the transversal and one of the parallel lines are two sides of a triangle or being the foot of a perpendicular from a vertex to an isosceles trapezoid's base. There is no reason to expect this idiosyncratic property to recur in other such proofs (of theorems logically unrelated to the given theorem)—and if, remarkably, it does appear in some other proof, then the other disjunctive properties appearing there likely do not recur. Thus, it and those other properties are not natural and the proofs are not explanatory.

Among the few recent philosophical discussions of natural properties and kinds in mathematics are Tappenden's (2008a, 2008b).[25] Both Tappenden and I take a property's naturalness as not determined by its contribution toward simplifying theorems or making proofs more efficient. Rather, Tappenden says, natural properties are "fruitful" and one kind of fruitfulness, perhaps more easily understood than other kinds, involves how a concept "contributes to addressing salient 'why?' questions" (2008a, 259). Though Tappenden offers no general account of mathematical explanation, I agree with him that explanatoriness and naturalness "interact in ways that make them hard to surgically separate" (259). Discussing the function denoted by the Legendre symbol in number theory, he gives nice examples where unification is closely related to explanation.

Tappenden recognizes that unification and explanation are not achieved when gerrymandered properties are used. Therefore, Tappenden faces the task of specifying how the Legendre symbol creates genuine rather than spurious unification of what would otherwise constitute separate cases. Tappenden says that the unification results from the fact that the concept is "fruitful"; its use leads to lots of good mathematical theorems. But of course, unification is not supposed to be merely a heuristic matter and (as in the case of Desargues's theorem in projective geometry) many of these further theorems could be expressed (in more cumbersome ways) without the Legendre symbol. Moreover, if natural properties figure in lots of good mathematical results, then as I just pointed out, a disjunction of natural properties is guaranteed to figure in "grue"-some combinations of those results. (For example, Euclidean geometry might use the concept of "points at infinity" to combine several theorems without purporting to unify them.) So an appeal to "fruitfulness" has got to go on to specify the particular kinds of fruitfulness that contribute to a mathematical property's naturalness. I agree with Tappenden that we should be guided here by the features that mathematicians themselves treat as significant in making a property natural (such as, he says, the way that the function expressed by the Legendre symbol turns out to be a special case of a function central to the study of quadratic reciprocity, which itself turns out to connect to a wide variety of other mathematical domains). By getting a better grip on the kinds of fruitfulness that contribute to a mathematical property's naturalness, I hope to better understand how the fact that arbitrarily disjunctive properties figure in many mathematical results nevertheless fails to make those properties "fruitful" in a way that produces unification.

I have approached this issue by focusing on fruitfulness in connection with explanatory proofs. In particular, I have suggested that a given arbitrarily disjunctive property fails to belong to a family of properties any given member of which figures in proofs that would be explanatory, if the properties in the family were all natural, where these proofs are sufficiently numerous and diverse to make the given family member natural, if the proofs were all explanatory. But such service in explanatory proofs may well turn out to be only one of the possible contributors to a mathematical property's naturalness.

■ 9.6 EXPLANATION BY SUBSUMPTION UNDER A THEOREM

I have been concentrating on mathematical *proofs* that explain why some theorem holds and how they differ from mathematical proofs that merely prove some theorem without explaining why it holds. However, not all mathematical explanations involve proofs. In section 7.4, I gave several examples where a mathematical fact is explained merely by being subsumed under a theorem without the explanation including any proof of the theorem. For instance, I considered the fact that the solutions of $z^3 + 6z - 20 = 0$ are 2, $-1 + 3i$, and $-1 - 3i$, and that the solutions of $z^2 - 2z + 2 = 0$ are $1 - i$ and $1 + i$. In both cases, the solutions that are not real numbers are pairs of complex conjugates. Why is it that in the case of both of these polynomials, their nonreal roots all fall into complex-conjugate pairs? Is it a coincidence or what? One possible answer is that we have simply gotten lucky: we have examined an unrepresentative set of cases. Another possible explanation is that all polynomials in a certain natural class have nonreal roots all forming complex-conjugate pairs. In fact, as I have mentioned, all polynomials with real coefficients have all of their nonreal roots in complex-conjugate pairs. This theorem (from d'Alembert) explains why the two polynomials I looked at both have this property. Here we have a mathematical explanation that consists not of a proof, but merely of a theorem.

As I pointed out in section 7.4, it is not the case that just any broader mathematical theorem at all that subsumes the examples to be explained would suffice to account for them. After all, we could have subsumed those two cases under this gerrymandered theorem: for any equilateral triangle or equation that is either $z^3 + 6z - 20 = 0$ or $z^2 - 2z + 2 = 0$, either the triangle is equiangular or the equation's nonreal solutions form complex-conjugate pairs. This theorem does not explain why the two equations have the given feature. On my view, that is because this theorem lacks a "common proof" explaining why it holds and thereby making it no coincidence (as I described in chapter 8). Indeed, the theorem is not even a coincidence since it does not identify a property common to every case in its scope. Being equiangular or having nonreal solutions all forming complex-conjugate pairs is not a natural property in mathematics and so does not constitute a respect in which the theorem's cases are all alike.

I conjecture that in asking why these two polynomial equations both have their nonreal solutions coming in complex-conjugate pairs, we are recognizing that this result strikingly identifies a genuine similarity between these two equations, and so our why question asks what other natural property these two equations (and perhaps others) have in common where it is no coincidence that all equations with this property are also alike in having their nonreal solutions form complex-conjugate pairs. A theorem explains why these two equations' nonreal solutions all come in complex-conjugate pairs exactly when it has the two components of this result as two of its instances, the theorem refers to a natural property that these two equations share, the theorem says that all equations with this property have nonreal solutions coming in complex-conjugate pairs, and (in the context at hand) the theorem is no coincidence: its salient features include its revealing some respect in which all of the cases it covers are alike, and it has a proof that exploits some other respect in which all of the cases are alike and from there arrives at the theorem by treating all of the cases in the same way.

Unlike the gerrymandered theorem covering any equilateral triangle and these two equations, the theorem that the nonreal solutions of $z^3 + 6z - 20 = 0$ all belong to complex-conjugate pairs and so do the nonreal solutions of $z^2 - 2z + 2 = 0$ *does* have as a salient feature that it identifies a respect in which these two polynomial equations are alike. Moreover, although this theorem has a proof that proceeds by solving one of these equations and then separately solving the other, the theorem also has a "common proof"—a proof that begins by characterizing both cases as polynomial equations with real coefficients and then proceeds by proving d'Alembert's theorem. Nevertheless, the theorem whose scope is restricted to these two polynomial equations does not explain why they both have nonreal roots forming complex-conjugate pairs. That is because although this theorem is no coincidence, it does not identify a natural property that these equations have in common where it is no coincidence that all cases with this property are also alike in that their nonreal solutions form complex-conjugate pairs. The property of being one or the other of these two equations is not a natural property in mathematics. Rather, d'Alembert's theorem identifies such a property: being a polynomial equation with real coefficients.

On my proposal, to ask "Why do both of these equations' nonreal roots come in complex-conjugate pairs—is it a coincidence?" is to ask whether or not all cases like the two I have examined exhibit non-coincidentally the same feature as I have just noted in those two cases—where "all cases like the two I have examined" is understood to cover exactly the cases possessing some (perhaps as yet unidentified) mathematically natural property. By identifying such a property (namely, being a polynomial equation with real coefficients), d'Alembert's theorem answers this why question.

I might instead have considered only one of these two polynomials and wondered whether there is some reason why its nonreal roots come in complex-conjugate pairs. Even if there is nothing especially striking about this fact taken in isolation, we understand that it could be one instance of a theorem having as its salient feature that it identifies a property common to this and every other case possessing some mathematically natural property. In asking "Why do this polynomial's nonreal roots come in complex-conjugate pairs?" we are asking for such a theorem with a "common proof," so that for the given equation and any other one in the natural class, it is no coincidence that both instantiate the theorem.

There are many such examples in mathematical practice. For instance, Reese (1987a, 96) notes that 987,654,321 divided by 123,456,789 is 8.000 000 072 900 000 663 ...—remarkably close to a whole number. Reese asks, "Is the answer so close to 8 for some identifiable reason, or is it just a fluke?" Reese does not regard the fact that the long division yields a quotient so close to 8 as "some identifiable reason" why it yields a quotient so close to a whole number—or vice versa. Furthermore, that the result is so close to a whole number may still be "just a fluke" despite being mathematically necessary. What, then, would it be for there to be some reason why this quotient is so nearly a whole number?

On my view, it would be for this case to be similar to some (as yet unspecified) others, all of which form a single, mathematically natural class, where it is no coincidence that they are all alike—in other words, where the given case is one instance of a theorem not only having as its salient feature that it identifies a property common to this case and the other cases it subsumes, and also having a proof that is a "common proof" for all of these cases. In fact, just such a theorem leads Reese to entitle his follow-up article "Result of Really Long Division Is Not a Fluke" (Reese 1987b, 88). The theorem to which Reese appeals identifies a natural class to which the fraction $\dfrac{987,654,321}{123,456,789}$ belongs and that has a proof treating all of the cases in this class alike. The key to finding a natural class is to avoid focusing on base 10 by generalizing the example to an arbitrary base. Here is the theorem:

Consider the quotient n/d where n is the number represented in base b by all of the digits from $(b-1)$ to 1 inclusive, taken in descending order, and d is the number represented in base b by all of those digits taken in ascending order. (For example, where m_b is the number represented by "m" in base b, the quotient for $b = 3$ is $21_3/12_3 = 7/5$, for $b = 4$ is $321_4/123_4 = 57/27$, and for $b = 10$ is $\dfrac{987,654,321}{123,456,789}$.) Then $n/d = (b-2) + (b-1)/d$.

For example, by this theorem

when $b=4$, $321_4/123_4 = 57/27 = 2\dfrac{1}{9} = (4-2) + \dfrac{3}{27} = (b-2)+(b-1)/d$;

when $b=8$, $7654321_8/1234567_8 = \dfrac{2,054,353}{342,391} = 6.00\ 002\ 04 = (8-2) + \dfrac{7}{342,391}$
$= (b-2)+(b-1)/d$.

In the original case, $b = 10$ and so the quotient differs from 8 $(= 10-2)$ by only $\dfrac{9}{123,456,789}$.

According to Reese, this theorem makes it "not a fluke" that 987,654,321 divided by 123,456,789 is so close to 8. Likewise, Fermilab director Mike Witherell is reported (Castelvecchi 2004/2005) to have cited this theorem as able to "explain this riddle," namely, "Why does the result differ" from 8 by so little? My account agrees that this theorem answers this why question, considering that the theorem has a proof that treats all of the theorem's cases alike.

This approach to mathematical explanation by subsumption under a theorem is suggested by many other examples. In section 8.3, I showed that it is no coincidence that the two Taylor series

$$1/(1-x^2)=1+x^2+x^4+x^6+\dots$$
$$1/(1+x^2)=1-x^2+x^4-x^6+\dots$$

are alike in that, for real x, each converges when $|x| < 1$ but diverges when $|x| >$ 1. The reason why these functions both exhibit this convergence behavior is that both of them (considered as functions of complex numbers) are undefined for some z on the unit circle of the complex plane and that this theorem concerning the radius of convergence has a "common proof":

> For any power series $\Sigma\, a_n z^n$ (from $n = 0$ to ∞), either it converges for all complex numbers z, or it converges only for $z = 0$, or there is a number $R > 0$ such that it converges if $|z| < R$ and diverges if $|z| > R$.

From this idea, it is not much of a step to say that this theorem (and the fact $1/(1 + z^2)$ is undefined for some z on the unit circle) explains why the Taylor series $1/(1 + x^2) = 1 - x^2 + x^4 - x^6 + \dots$ diverges when $|x| > 1$. The theorem reveals that all cases like this one exhibit the same kind of behavior as this one. It does so by identifying a natural property that these cases share (being a power series for a function that goes undefined somewhere on the unit circle centered at the origin of the complex plane) where it is no coincidence that every case possessing this property is also like the case we are explaining. That the theorem explains an individual case by subsumption is borne out by many textbook discussions, such as this one (part of which I quoted in section 7.6, in connection with the fact that not all mathematical theorems have explanations):

> A careful assessment of our situation will reveal some unexplained facts. . . . Mysterious behavior is exemplified . . . strikingly by the function $f(x) = 1/(1 + x^2)$, an infinitely differentiable function which is the next best thing to a polynomial function. . . . If $|x| \geq 1$, the Taylor series does not converge at all. Why? What unseen obstacle prevents the Taylor series from extending past 1 and −1? Asking this sort of question is always dangerous, since we may have to settle for an unsympathetic answer: it happens because it happens—that's the way things are! In this case there does happen to be an explanation, but this explanation is impossible to give [here

at the end of chapter 23]; although the question is about real numbers, it can be answered intelligently only when placed in a broader context. (Spivak 1980, 482)

In his textbook's later chapter on complex power series, Spivak uses the radius-of-convergence theorem to answer the why question he asked earlier (as I discussed in section 8.3). My view entails that the theorem can explain the case only if the theorem is no coincidence and hence only if it has a certain kind of proof.[26] Moreover, this explanation presupposes that the property of going undefined somewhere on the unit circle centered at the origin of the complex plane is a natural property in mathematics and so a respect in which these two functions are alike—rather than a gerrymandered, wildly disjunctive shadow of a predicate. Why does this property qualify as natural? Because of the role it plays in other explanatory proofs (as I described in the previous section).

Another nice example of explanation by subsumption under a theorem is connected with the "mathemagical" addition trick in section 8.4. After you have amazed them once, your friends will want to know whether your success was a coincidence or not. After you have beaten them at the addition game several times, your friends will find it less plausible that your success was just a fluke—for instance, that it reflected an unrepresentative choice of initial numbers or other initial conditions. Let's suppose that you then reveal your secret technique. The theorem you disclose (that for any two initial numbers, the grand total is 11 times the entry in row 7 of the table) explains why your secret technique worked in each of the cases that your friends gave you. It reveals that your success was not a coincidence of the particular initial pairs of numbers that your friends chose.[27]

■ .9.7 CONCLUSION

On my account, certain mathematical properties are natural because they figure in proofs that (if these properties are natural) constitute explanations of various results that otherwise describe a miscellany of special cases, where these proofs are sufficiently numerous and diverse to make these properties natural. Poincaré nicely characterizes the unification achieved by mathematical proofs using natural properties, citing a host of examples including points at infinity: "mathematics is the art of giving the same name to different things. . . . When the language has been well chosen, we are astonished to see that all the proofs made for a certain object apply immediately to many new objects; there is nothing to change, not even the words, since the names have become the same. A well-chosen word usually suffices to do away with the exceptions from which the rules stated in the old way suffer; this is why we have created negative quantities, imaginaries, points at infinity, and what not" (Poincaré 1913, 375). This is exactly what we found in the case of the proof explaining why Desargues's theorem holds in projective geometry;

concerning Euclidean points and points at infinity, "the names have become the same." Poincaré regards these unifying proofs as explaining why various previous results had been so alike. Regarding "groups" and "invariants" as unifying concepts, he writes: "[These concepts] have made us see the essence of many mathematical reasonings; they have shown us in how many cases the old mathematicians considered groups without knowing it, and how, believing themselves far from one another, they suddenly found themselves near without knowing why. Today we should say that they had dealt with isomorphic groups" (375). When we discover that the same natural property is instantiated in various, apparently disparate cases (e.g., that they are all isomorphic groups), we may thereby finally understand why those cases are alike in so many ways. Their similarity turned out to be no mathematical coincidence.

Our study of the explanatory contributions made by projective geometry allows us to appreciate one important role that explanation plays in mathematics. It has often been suggested (e.g., by Kitcher 2011) that mathematics consists of various interrelated "games" of symbolic manipulation and that pure mathematicians have frequently extended their language and thereby begun to play new games that appeared to them to be worthwhile on purely mathematical grounds. A given game may be worth playing at least partly by virtue of its relations to other mathematical games that are independently worthwhile. One of the features that can make a game mathematically worthwhile, I suggest, is that it enables mathematical explanations to be given (or demanded) that could not be given (or demanded) before. These new opportunities are especially worthwhile when the new explanations unify results that have already been arrived at (but are unrelated) in games that are already recognized as worthwhile. Projective geometry is a good example: part of what makes it worthwhile is that it allows us to answer (and to ask) many why questions that could not be answered (or asked) in Euclidean geometry. It gives common, unified explanations in cases where Euclidean geometry supplies none. Mathematical entities (such as points at infinity) are discovered when mathematical practices involving them are discovered to be worthwhile, and the explanations made possible by those practices often help to make them worthwhile. This is one of the most important roles played by explanations in mathematics.

Explanations in Mathematics and Non-Causal Scientific Explanations—Together

10 Mathematical Coincidence and Scientific Explanation

■ 10.1 PHYSICAL COINCIDENCES THAT ARE NO MATHEMATICAL COINCIDENCE

This chapter begins part IV (the final part) of this book, which concerns several topics that bring together non-causal scientific explanations and explanations in mathematics.

In parts I and II, I described several ways that scientific explanations can work other than by describing aspects of the world's nexus of causal relations: as explanations by constraint (chapters 1, 2, 3, and 4), RS explanations (chapter 5), and dimensional explanations (chapter 6). In this chapter, I will look at a fourth variety of non-causal scientific explanation. An explanation of this kind aims to explain a pair of derivative laws concerning physically dissimilar cases. The two laws exhibit some striking similarity (or difference); the explanandum might equally well be taken to be the similarity (or difference) between them. Some analogous similarity (or difference) between the more fundamental laws relevant to each of these cases turns out to be responsible for the similarity (or difference) between the derivative laws covering them. The similarity (or difference) that does the explaining does not expressly concern the nexus of causal relations. Rather, it is a similarity (or difference) in the mathematical form or the dimensional architecture of the more fundamental laws that apply to these cases. In virtue of this similarity (or difference), the two derivative laws can be derived by the same mathematical or dimensional arguments. That is why the two physical problems have mathematically or dimensionally similar (or different) answers, as I will argue in sections 10.2 and 10.3, respectively.

To characterize these scientific explanations, I will draw on not only the account of dimensional explanations from chapter 6, but also the account of explanation in mathematics from part III—especially the notion of "mathematical coincidence" that I elaborated in chapter 8. Suppose we have two derivative laws that cover physically unrelated phenomena, yet are striking in having the same mathematical form. Is this a coincidence? It may be, but it may instead not be. A derivation of the first derivative law from the relevant more fundamental laws, together with a separate derivation of the second derivative law from some other more fundamental laws, treats the similarity in the two derivative laws as utterly coincidental. It is indeed *physically* coincidental, since the more fundamental laws relevant to the first derivative law have little or nothing to do with those relevant to the second. But although the similarity is *physically* coincidental, the two separate derivations nevertheless fail to explain the pair of derivative laws if the similarity in those laws is no *mathematical* coincidence. In that event, the more fundamental laws leave us with exactly the same mathematical problem in each case, and therefore it is no mathematical coincidence that the two problems have analogous answers. An explanation of the two derivative laws works by revealing them to be essentially the same solution to the same mathematical problem. The explanation works by unifying the two derivative laws in a way that has nothing to do with describing some common cause, law, process, or mechanism behind them. This is a non-causal scientific explanation.

Finally, in section 10.4, I will argue that dimensional thinking not only yields new explanations of antecedently appreciated similarities among the derivative laws governing causally diverse phenomena, but also identifies new respects in which these derivative laws can be similar—respects that are entirely dimensional. These similarities among the cases are explained by being shown to arise from a dimensional architecture that is common to the cases. By giving the physically diverse derivative laws a common dimensional treatment, the dimensional explanation works by revealing the derivative laws' dimensional similarity to be no mathematical coincidence, despite being physically coincidental. I argued in chapter 9 that projective geometry identifies mathematically natural properties; it reveals respects in which cases that are dissimilar in Euclidean geometry qualify as similar, allowing new why questions to be asked. Derivations in projective geometry explain these similarities. Likewise, dimensional thinking identifies natural properties; it reveals respects in which physically diverse cases qualify as similar, allowing new why questions to be asked. Dimensional derivations explain these similarities. This connection between explanations and natural properties, in mathematics as well as in science, will be pursued in chapter 11.

■ 10.2 EXPLANATIONS FROM COMMON MATHEMATICAL FORM

Consider the following two laws of nature. They are derivative rather than fundamental laws; each has a causal explanation from more fundamental laws. But I will deny that the conjunction of these explanations explains the laws' conjunction. Here are the two laws:

> Consider a cylinder (fig. 10.1) of length L, radius a, generating heat that keeps it at constant temperature T_1. (It might be a current-carrying wire or a steam-conveying airduct, for example.) The cylinder is surrounded by a uniform layer of thermal insulation, thickness $(b - a)$, the outside of which is kept at temperature T_2. We find experimentally that in all such cases, the rate Q at which heat

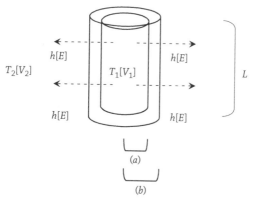

Figure 10.1 A thermodynamic [electrostatic] example

is generated inside the cylinder, thence to pass through the cylinder's surface, is proportional to $L(T_1 - T_2)/\log(b/a)$, where "$\log(x)$" stands throughout for x's natural logarithm. (Arrows in fig. 10.1 depict the direction of heat flow **h**.)

Consider a cylinder (once again, see fig. 10.1, but now using the labels in square brackets where applicable) of electrically conductive material of length L, radius a, held at a constant voltage (electrical potential) V_1. The cylinder is surrounded by a uniform layer of electrical insulation (dielectric), thickness $(b-a)$, the outside of which is kept at voltage V_2. We find experimentally that in all such cases, the charge q on the cylinder is proportional to $L(V_1 - V_2)/\log(b/a)$. (Arrows in fig. 10.1 depict the direction of the electric field **E**.)

The two derivative laws are remarkably alike. We might well wonder why. We might express our question by asking directly "Why are these two derivative laws so similar?" or we might just as well ask simply (where $\propto$ means "is proportional to") "Why is it that thermodynamically $Q \propto L(T_1 - T_2)/\log(b/a)$ and electrostatically $q \propto L(V_1 - V_2)/\log(b/a)$?" in a context where the salient feature of this combination of facts is the similarity between the two components.[1] The answer would allow us to answer this yes-or-no question: "Is it a coincidence that these two results are so analogous?"

There is one respect in which it *is* a coincidence: the two physical processes involved are distinct. They cannot be reduced to a common underlying physical process in the way that the tides, planetary motion, and falling bodies can. After all, the electric field is not heat. The laws of electrostatics do not govern thermodynamics.

But in another respect, it is *no* coincidence that the two results are analogous. The analogy would have been coincidental if the more fundamental laws of thermodynamics and electrostatics had been utterly unlike. It would then have been an "algebraic miracle" that in this example, these two dissimilar sets of more fundamental laws turn out to yield such similar derivative laws. But in fact, the more fundamental laws of thermodynamics and electrostatics take exactly the same form, and that is why these two results end up taking the same form. Of course, if we gerrymander or are excessively liberal about what counts as a "form," then any two laws take the "same form." But the more fundamental laws of thermodynamics and electrostatics take the same *mathematical* form. Their similarity allows each of the derivative laws I just mentioned to be derived from the respective more fundamental laws by exactly the same sequence of mathematical steps.

Let's look at the details of this common form and common mathematical proof. There is what Maxwell (1856/1890, 156) called a "physical analogy" between electrostatics and heat flow: a positively (negatively) charged body plays the nomic role of a heat source (sink), an electric field plays the nomic role of an unequally heated body, potential difference plays the nomic role of temperature difference, and so forth. That is, the relevant fundamental equations of electrostatics can be turned into the relevant fundamental equations of heat flow by exchanging electrostatic for thermodynamic quantities in a consistent way, and vice versa. Here are the relevant more fundamental equations of electrostatics [thermodynamics]:

(1) that the rate of heat flow h [the electric field E] at a given point is proportional to the negation of the temperature T [electrical potential V] gradient there, and

(2) that the heat flux $\int h \cdot ds$ [electric field flux $\int E \cdot ds$] through an enclosing surface is proportional to the heat Q generated [electric charge q] within.

Symbolically:

(1) $h \propto -\mathrm{grad}\, T$ $E \propto -\mathrm{grad}\, V$

(2) $\int h \cdot ds \propto Q$ $\int E \cdot ds \propto q$.

That these fundamental thermodynamic and electrostatic equations correspond to one another in this way explains why there is the same correspondence between a thermodynamic law deriving exclusively from the former and some electrostatic law deriving exclusively from the latter. For example, suppose we take the steps by which $Q \propto L(T_1 - T_2)/\log(b/a)$ is derived from the fundamental thermodynamic laws. Suppose we replace the thermodynamic quantities systematically by the corresponding electrostatic quantities. Then we have a derivation of the corresponding electrostatic law $q \propto L(V_1 - V_2)/\log(b/a)$ from the fundamental electrostatic laws. Here is the derivation using variables representing thermodynamic quantities; mathematically the same steps using variables representing the corresponding electrostatic quantities leads to the corresponding electrostatic result:

From symmetry, h is independent of the direction, so it depends only on the distance from the apparatus's center line. Consider a cylinder concentric with the apparatus, with radius r. Its surface area is $2\pi rL$. For this surface, that $\int h \cdot ds \propto Q$ entails that $2\pi rLh \propto Q$, and so $h \propto Q / 2\pi rL$. Since $h \propto -\text{grad } T$, it follows that $h \propto -dT/dr$, or $dT/dr \propto -h$. Substituting for h, $dT/dr \propto -Q/2\pi rL$. Integrating from $r = a$ to $r = b$, we find $\int(dT/dr)dr = (T_2 - T_1) \propto -(Q/2\pi L)\log(b/a)$. Thus, $Q \propto L(T_1 - T_2)/\log(b/a)$.

Since analogous quantities play analogous nomic roles, "any result we may have obtained either about electricity or about the conduction of heat may be at once translated out of the language of the one science into that of the other without fear of error" (Maxwell 1881, 52).

This "physical analogy" has the practical advantage of giving us two results for the price of one derivation. More important for my purposes, the "physical analogy" makes it no *mathematical* coincidence that these two derivative laws are so similar. In putting matters in this way, I am drawing upon my account of "mathematical coincidence" in chapter 8. There I suggested that (for example) the fact that every "calculator number" is divisible by 37 is no mathematical coincidence, whereas it is coincidental that 9 is the thirteenth digit in the decimal expansion of π and also the thirteenth digit in the decimal expansion of e. The feature of the "calculator number" theorem that immediately strikes us is that the theorem identifies some (mathematically natural) property as common to every calculator number. The π-e theorem also has such a salient feature: whereas the calculator-number theorem characterizes every calculator number as alike in being divisible by 37, the π-e theorem characterizes π and e as alike in the thirteenth digits of their decimal expansions. On my account, a theorem counts as a mathematical coincidence or as non-coincidental only if its salient feature is that the same property is ascribed by each of its components to the range of cases covered by that component. Such a theorem is no mathematical coincidence if and only if its various components all have a "common proof": each can be proved from the axioms in the same way, by a proof that exploits another property that is shared by all of the cases covered by the various components. For example, as I showed in chapter 8, the various calculator numbers can all be proved by the same argument to be divisible by 37. That proof appeals to the fact that by virtue of being calculator numbers, they are all expressible in the same mathematical form: as $10^5 a + 10^4(a+d) + 10^3(a+2d) + 10^2(a+2d) + 10(a+d) + a$ where $a, a+d, a+2d$ are three integers in arithmetic progression. Their divisibility by 37 follows from their taking that form by a proof that treats them all alike at each step (rather than as special cases requiring separate treatment).

In contrast, a mathematical coincidence is a result having as its outstanding feature that it ascribes the same property to each of its various cases, but where the components covering different cases have no common proof. The π-e

theorem is a mathematical coincidence because if we take any proof of it and make each step of the proof as logically weak as it can afford to be while still allowing the proof to prove that 9 is the thirteenth digit of π's decimal expansion, then the weakened proof is no longer able to prove that 9 is the thirteenth digit of e's decimal expansion. There is thus no common proof of the theorem's two components; any proof of the theorem is effectively a proof of one component stapled to a proof of the other.

It follows (I argued) that a mathematical coincidence has no explanation in mathematics, since (on my general account of explanation in mathematics) a proof that explains why some mathematical result holds is just a proof that exploits a feature in the setup that is similar to the result's salient feature. A theorem is a mathematical coincidence only if its salient feature is that it identifies some property as common to various different cases. Hence, for a proof to explain why such a theorem holds, the proof would have to proceed from some other property that all of the theorem's cases have in common and then arrive at the theorem by treating each of these cases alike. A mathematical coincidence has no such proof.

Let's apply these ideas about mathematical coincidence to the fact that thermodynamically $Q \propto L(T_1 - T_2)/\log(b/a)$ and electrostatically $q \propto L(V_1 - V_2)/\log(b/a)$. Of course, this fact is not a mathematical theorem. However, the derivation of one of these derivative laws from the relevant more fundamental laws is a purely mathematical exercise. As I have shown, the very same derivation (with an exchange of variables) yields each of the two derivative laws. The fundamental laws are mathematically the same; they merely employ variables for different quantities. Mathematically speaking, then, the two derivative laws are proved from the same axioms by the same steps. They have a "common proof." In other words: When juxtaposed, what is striking about the thermodynamic and electrostatic results is that they possess the same mathematical form.[2] The relevant fundamental laws of thermodynamics and electrostatics also have the same mathematical form. It turns out to be by virtue of this similarity between the setups that the two derivative laws are so similar, since they can be derived in the same way from the relevant more fundamental laws. It is therefore no mathematical coincidence that the two results are so similar. The common derivation that exploits only the common mathematical form of the fundamental laws thus explains why the two results take the same mathematical form. It answers the question "Why is it that thermodynamically $Q \propto L(T_1 - T_2)/\log(b/a)$ and electrostatically $q \propto L(V_1 - V_2)/\log(b/a)$?" as asked in a context where the salient feature of this combination of facts is the similarity between the two components.[3]

Of course, this explanation does not explain why the *fundamental* thermodynamic laws and electrostatic laws take the same mathematical form. But it does not have to do so; the why question that this explanation answers concerns the derivative laws, not the fundamental laws. Our having recognized a similarity in mathematical form between the derivative thermodynamic and electrostatic laws is what gives content to our question "Why is it that thermodynamically $Q \propto L(T_1 - T_2)/\log(b/a)$ and electrostatically $q \propto (V_1 - V_2)/\log(b/a)$?" Therefore, this question can be answered by an account of the facts making it no mathematical coincidence that thermodynamically $Q \propto L(T_1 - T_2)/\log(b/a)$ and electrostatically $q \propto L(V_1 - V_2)/\log(b/a)$.

That this pair of laws is mathematically no coincidence is usefully compared to the fact that it is no mathematical coincidence that 2 is the only real-number solution of $x^3 + 6x - 20 = 0$ and also the only real-number solution of $y^3 + 6y - 20 = 0$ (unsurprisingly!). The salient feature of this explanandum's two components is that they ascribe the same real-number solution—though this similarity between them will not surprise us in the least, once we notice that the two components concern exactly the same mathematical problem. Obviously, a mathematical proof that is no stronger than it needs to be in order to show that 2 is the only real-number solution of $x^3 + 6x - 20 = 0$ also suffices to show that 2 is the only real-number solution of $y^3 + 6y - 20 = 0$. That the derivative thermodynamic and electrostatic laws likewise have a "common proof" from their respective more fundamental laws is not obvious before we have seen the more fundamental thermodynamic and electrostatic laws. But by virtue of those more fundamental laws, the derivation of the thermodynamic result poses the same mathematical problem as the derivation of the electrostatic result.

In chapter 7, I gave several examples where a proof in mathematics counts as explaining why some theorem holds by virtue of the proof's exploiting a symmetry in the setup that is similar to the symmetry that is a salient feature of the theorem being explained. For example, d'Alembert proved that the solutions (that are not real numbers) to any polynomial equation with real coefficients come in complex-conjugate pairs ($a + bi$ and $a + b(-i)$). Being a solution is invariant under the replacement of i with $-i$ because the axioms of complex arithmetic are also invariant under the replacement of i with $-i$. The symmetry expressed by d'Alembert's theorem is thus grounded in the same symmetry in the axioms. In chapter 8, I mentioned that we may also use these ideas to understand the kind of mathematical explanation that sets mathematical non-coincidences apart from mathematical coincidences.[4] If a given theorem's salient feature is that it identifies a property as common to every case in the theorem's scope, then we may equally well think of the theorem's salient feature as a symmetry: that the possession of the property remains invariant under switches from one case covered by the theorem to another. For instance, divisibility by 37 remains invariant under switches from one calculator number to another. A proof of the theorem makes the theorem non-coincidental exactly when the proof exploits a similar symmetry in the setup—for example, that in switching from one calculator number to another, we preserve the number's having a given mathematical form (namely, being $10^5 a + 10^4(a+d) + 10^3(a+2d) + 10^2(a+2d) + 10(a+d) + a$ where $a, a+d, a+2d$ are three integers in arithmetic progression). Hence, once again, this proof (unlike a case-by-case proof) makes the theorem non-coincidental by explaining why it holds.

These ideas apply to the explanation of the pair of thermodynamic and electrostatic results that works by showing the two results to be *mathematically no coincidence* (despite being *physically* coincidental). The salient feature of two results, when they are juxtaposed, is that they exhibit a certain symmetry: when we replace the thermodynamic setup with an electrostatic setup by a certain scheme for systematically replacing thermodynamic quantities with electrostatic ones (or vice versa), the mathematical form of the relevant derivative law remains invariant. This symmetry in the two results prompts us to ask whether their joint truth amounts to a coincidence. Physically speaking, it does, since there is no common cause (or law, process, or mechanism) of the electric charge and the heat generation. But as I have shown, we can derive both results by a common proof from the fundamental laws relevant to each. We thereby exploit the fact that the thermodynamic and electrostatic "axioms" exhibit the same symmetry as is salient in the theorems: under the same scheme for exchanging thermodynamic and electrostatic quantities as we used for switching from the thermodynamic theorem to the electrostatic one, the relevant fundamental laws of thermodynamics are transformed into the relevant fundamental laws of electrostatics (just as the axioms of complex arithmetic are invariant under the replacement of i with $-i$). This symmetry explains why it is that for any result that follows from the thermodynamic axioms, a corresponding result follows from the electrostatic axioms, and vice versa (just as the $i/-i$ symmetry in the axioms of complex arithmetic explains why the replacement of i with $-i$ in one solution to a polynomial equation with real coefficients generates another solution).[5]

In other words, the two physical theories leave us with exactly the same *mathematical* problem, and therefore it is no *mathematical* coincidence that the two problems have analogous answers. William Thomson (later Lord Kelvin), who discovered this analogy between electrostatics and thermodynamics, put the point nicely:

> Corresponding to every problem relative to the distribution of electricity on conductors, or to forces of attraction or repulsion exercised by electrified bodies, there is a problem in the uniform motion of heat which presents the same analytical conditions, and *which, therefore, considered mathematically, is the same problem.* (Thomson 1845, 27, my emphasis)

The symmetry in the fundamental equations accounts for the symmetry in the derivative laws just as the symmetry between i and $-i$ in the axioms of complex arithmetic accounts for d'Alembert's result, which strikingly exhibits the same symmetry. Thus, an explanation in mathematics is used to give a scientific explanation—to explain why the two derivative laws are so similar.[6]

This scientific explanation is "mathematical" in a different way from ordinary scientific explanations where the explanans and explanandum involve mathematics. As I argued in chapter 1, those ordinary scientific explanations are causal explanations. In contrast, the explanation that we have just been examining does not work by describing the world's nexus of causal relations. It does not trace lines of causal influence. Presumably, the derivation of $Q \propto L(T_1 - T_2)/\log(b/a)$ from the relevant fundamental thermodynamic laws explains that derivative law causally; the same goes for the electrostatic law's derivation. But the explanation that I have just been examining is not the conjunction of those two derivations. Rather, it involves a single mathematical derivation employing variables that can be given either a thermodynamic or an electrostatic interpretation. It makes no difference to this explanation whether the fundamental electrostatic and thermodynamic laws describe causal processes—or, if so, how they do so. For instance, it does not matter whether electrical potential difference plays a *causal* role in electrostatics that is analogous to the *causal* role played by temperature difference in thermodynamics. (For instance, it could be that temperature differences are genuine causes whereas electrical potential difference is merely a useful theoretical device.) All that matters is that the two quantities play analogous *mathematical* roles in these two pairs of more fundamental laws. The explanation that I have been examining works not by describing causal relations (even in terms that abstract from many of their details), but rather by looking at the two derivative laws as the answer to a mathematics problem—that is, as if they were mathematical theorems, with the fundamental laws as the axioms. That those fundamental laws describe causal relations is incidental.

Although the scientific explanation that I have been examining is mathematical in a different way from ordinary scientific explanations where the explanans and explanandum involve mathematics, it is also unlike the "distinctively mathematical" scientific explanations that were the subject of chapter 1.[7] Those explanations, I suggested, work by deriving the explanandum from "constraints": facts possessing greater necessity than ordinary laws of nature do. No ordinary laws figure in those explanations; any law figuring in them possesses greater necessity than ordinary laws do. In contrast, various fundamental laws of thermodynamics and electrostatics figure in the explanation that I have been examining. They are not functioning as "constraints." In addition, although the fundamental thermodynamic and electrostatic laws' having a common mathematical form is revealed to be the only feature of those laws that is responsible for the similarity between the two derivative laws, there is presumably no "constraint" that compels the fundamental thermodynamic and electrostatic laws to possess this feature. Their doing so is not as necessary as the fact that, for instance, the trefoil knot is distinct from the unknot (the "constraint" that explains why no one has ever actually managed to untie a trefoil knot). That a certain mathematical form is exhibited by both the fundamental thermodynamic and fundamental electrostatic laws is not a constraint like the requirement that certain quantities be conserved in all kinds of fundamental interactions (a constraint that I examined in chapter 2).

Furthermore, I argued (contrary to Steiner) that explanations in mathematics play no role in the distinctively mathematical explanations in science under examination in chapter 1. Even if it has no explanation, the fact that the trefoil knot is distinct from the unknot has sufficient necessity to explain non-causally why no one has ever managed to untie a trefoil knot. No proof of this mathematical fact figures in or matters to the distinctively mathematical explanation of the failure of every attempt to untie a trefoil knot. All that matters to this distinctively mathematical explanation is that it is indeed a *mathematical* fact that the trefoil knot is distinct form the unknot. In contrast, an explanation in mathematics is crucial to the scientific explanation of the analogy between the thermodynamic and electrostatic results. The scientific explanation is that the problem of solving the more fundamental thermodynamic equations for the thermodynamic case in figure 10.1 turns out to be the same mathematically as the problem of solving the more fundamental electrostatic equations for the electrostatic case in figure 10.1. What makes them mathematically the same problem is that a single proof can solve both by exploiting solely certain features that they have in common. This proof is (in a certain context) an explanation in mathematics of the fact that they have solutions of the same mathematical form.

This explanation unifies the thermodynamic result with the electrostatic result in making it no mathematical coincidence that they have the same mathematical form, since they arise from more fundamental laws having the same mathematical form. Likewise, I showed in chapter 4 that on Poisson's proposed explanation of the parallelogram of forces, arguments of the same mathematical form apply to a wide range of quantities, explaining why each of them composes vectorially despite their profound physical differences. The similarity in their composition laws is then no mathematical coincidence, despite being physically coincidental. In 1822, Fourier recognized how physically diverse phenomena can be unified by such explanations: "the same expression whose abstract properties geometers had considered, and which in this respect belongs to general analysis, represents as well the motion of light in the atmosphere, as it determines the laws of diffusion of heat in solid matter. . . . Considered from this point of view, mathematical analysis is as extensive as nature itself. . . . It brings together phenomena the most diverse, and discovers the hidden analogies which unite them" (Fourier 1878, 7–8). These "hidden analogies" are mathematical.

Without the notion of a *mathematical* coincidence, we would be unable to specify why a scientific explanation of the similarity between the derivative thermodynamic and electrostatic laws cannot be simply a scientific explanation of the first result conjoined to a scientific explanation of the second. Such a conjunction might seem perfectly appropriate as an explanation considering that their similarity is a *physical* coincidence. But it incorrectly characterizes their similarity as a *mathematical* coincidence—as just a kind of algebraic miracle. Our earlier account of mathematical coincidence has thus paid dividends in helping us to recognize the way that certain scientific explanations work. The concept of a mathematical coincidence plays an important role in scientific practice.

Scientific explanations of the kind that I have been examining have a great deal in common with certain explanations in mathematics. To better appreciate their affinity, let's briefly compare the explanation unifying these thermodynamic and electrostatic results to an explanation in mathematics that unifies a result concerning exponentiation with a result concerning differentiation. Here are the two results that jointly constitute the explanandum:

Regarding powers: If f and g are numbers and n is a natural number, then the binomial theorem says that

$$(f+g)^n = f^n + \binom{n}{1}f^{n-1}g + \binom{n}{2}f^{n-2}g^2 + \ldots + \binom{n}{n-1}fg^{n-1} + g^n = \sum_{k=0}^{n}\binom{n}{k}f^{n-k}g^k$$

where $\binom{n}{k} = n!/k!(n-k)!$.

Regarding derivatives: If $f(x)$ and $g(x)$ are n-times differentiable functions of real numbers x, and if $f^{(n)} = \dfrac{d^n f}{dx^n}$ is the nth derivative of f (and the 0th derivative of f is f), then a generalization of the product rule ("general Leibniz rule") says that

$$(fg)^{(n)}(x) = g\frac{d^n f}{dx^n} + n\frac{dg}{dx}\frac{d^{n-1}f}{dx^{n-1}} + \frac{n(n-1)}{(1)(2)}\frac{d^2 g}{dx^2}\frac{d^{n-2}f}{dx^{n-2}} + \ldots + f\frac{d^n g}{dx^n}$$

$$= \sum_{k=0}^{n}\binom{n}{k}f^{(n-k)}(x)g^{(k)}(x)$$

Leibniz noticed the striking analogy between these two results as early as 1695; he even argued in a 1697 letter to Wallis that his notation was better than Newton's because it made this analogy more salient (Koppelman 1971, 157–158). The similarity "certainly calls for an explanation" (171). As Johann Bernoulli wrote to Leibniz in 1695: "Nothing is more elegant than the agreement you have observed . . . doubtless there is some underlying secret" (Leibniz 2004, 398).[8]

In fact, the similarity is no coincidence; it is not "founded on accidental analogy" (Gregory 1841, iv). Nor is the similarity explained by the fact that one of these operations is at bottom the other. Rather, the two operations (exponentiation and differentiation) are alike in this respect because they are alike in obeying the same three "laws of combination":

	Regarding exponentiation $a, f,$ and g are numbers	Regarding differentiation $f(x,y)$ and $g(x)$ are functions
Commutative law:	$fg = gf$	$\dfrac{\partial}{\partial x}\dfrac{\partial}{\partial y}f = \dfrac{\partial}{\partial y}\dfrac{\partial}{\partial x}f$
Distributive law:	$a(f+g) = af + ag$	$\dfrac{d}{dx}(f+g) = \dfrac{d}{dx}f + \dfrac{d}{dx}g.$
Law of repetition:	$f^n f^m = f^{n+m}$	$\dfrac{d^n}{dx^n}\dfrac{d^m}{dx^m}f = \dfrac{d^{n+m}}{dx^{n+m}}f$

From the fact that exponentiation obeys these three laws, the binomial theorem follows, and from the fact that differentiation obeys these three laws, the product rule follows in mathematically the same way. Thus, both of these results "depend only on the laws of combination to which the symbols are subject, and are therefore true of all symbols, whatever their nature may be, which are subject to the same laws of combination" (Gregory 1841, 237).[9] The symmetry in the result—the invariance it reveals under the exchange of powers and derivatives—arises from the symmetry in the given: that the laws of combination still hold under the interchange of powers and derivatives. (Today we would put the point in terms of the binomial theorem holding of any commutative ring.) As François-Joseph Servois (1814–15, 142) said regarding the analogy, "it is necessary to find the cause, and everything is very happily explained."[10] (Of course, there is "because" here without cause.) That the two operations obey the same laws of combination is, he said, "la véritable origine" (151) of the analogy between the two results. Separate, unrelated derivations of the two results would prove them but would not explain why they hold. As Boole said of the analogy deployed to solve a linear differential equation by solving an algebraic equation and then exchanging powers for derivatives: "The analogy . . . is very remarkable, and unless we employed a method of solution common to both problems, it would not be easy to see the reason for so close a resemblance in the solution of two different kinds of equations. But the process which I have here exhibited shows, that the form of the solution depends solely on . . . processes which are common to the two operations under consideration, being founded only on the common laws of the combination of the symbols" (Boole 1841, 119). Exponentiation and differentiation obey the same laws of expansion because they obey the same three laws of combination.

This mathematical explanation clearly has a great deal in common with the explanation that unifies the derivative laws from thermodynamics and electrostatics. Each explanation takes as its target a result consisting of two components that display some striking analogy—or, equivalently, that exhibit a striking symmetry in that they are invariant under some transformation. Each explanation then accounts for the result by showing that each of the components can be derived in mathematically the same way from the relevant set of more fundamental facts, where these separate sets display the same analogy as the components of the result being explained (i.e., display invariance under the same transformation). Each explanation thereby reveals the analogy between the two components to be no mathematical coincidence.[11] The two explanations achieve much the same kind of unification—whereas a pair of separate derivations of the two components, following routes that are not identified as mathematically similar, would fail to show the analogy's "véritable origine." It would incorrectly depict the analogy as coincidental.

The many respects in which these two explanations are alike, though one is from science and the other is from math, show that it is no coincidence (ahem!) that both are termed "explanations." I do not hold that there is an illuminating core essence of explanation—a single overarching explanatory schema with a variable that takes on different values (corresponding, perhaps, to what van Fraassen (1980) calls different "relevance relations") depending on whether we are dealing with one or another variety of mathematical, non-causal scientific, or causal scientific explanation. Nevertheless, it is no mystery why various important elements of scientific and mathematical practice are all alike termed "explanations." These varieties of explanation are knit together by a host of connections and similarities. I will identify some of these common threads at the close of chapter 11.

▪ 10.3 EXPLANATIONS FROM COMMON DIMENSIONAL ARCHITECTURE

The scientific explanation that I have just examined answers the question "Why is it that thermodynamically $Q \propto L(T_1 - T_2)/\log(b/a)$ and electrostatically $q \propto L(V_1 - V_2)/\log(b/a)$? " as asked in a context where this fact's salient feature is the similarity in mathematical form between the two derivative laws. The explanation works by showing the two results to be *mathematically* no coincidence (despite being *physically* coincidental). Whereas this example concerns two results having the same *mathematical* form, two results regarding physically dissimilar cases could instead have some other similarity. When the two results are juxtaposed, their similarity could be the combination's salient feature and thus inform a why question.

An explanation that answers this question works by showing that the two results' similarity is no coincidence considering that the two results concern setups with the same dimensional architecture. Each of the two results has a dimensional explanation of the sort that I examined in chapter 6. The two results' explanations may involve physically dissimilar quantities, but in the two explanations there are corresponding quantities playing dimensionally analogous roles. Hence, there is a common dimensional derivation of the two derivative laws just as there is a common mathematical derivation of the derivative thermodynamic and electrostatic laws. The similarity of the two derivative laws is thereby explained by the common dimensional architecture of the two setups. The explanation unifies physically dissimilar cases just as the thermodynamic and electrostatic results are unified by an explanation that reveals their common mathematical form to be no coincidence.

Let's look at an example. Consider a wave of pressure propagating in a fluid (or elastic solid) surrounded by rigid walls, such as water in a rigid pipe. A compression moves through the fluid so that at a given moment, there are alternating regions of compression and rarefaction along the pipe. Over time, a small region of the fluid alternately undergoes compression and rarefaction as the elements of the fluid in that region are pushed together or spread apart. Each element of the fluid oscillates back and forth along the same line as the wave propagates. That is, a pressure wave (such as a sound wave) is "longitudinal." Contrast this wave to the wave propagating down a stretched string, such as a guitar string held taut at both ends by tuning pegs and then plucked near one end. That wave is "transverse" in that the elements of the string oscillate back and forth in a direction perpendicular to the direction of the wave's propagation. (Assume that the amplitude of the wave is small compared to the length of the string.) Despite the differences between these two cases, the wave's speed v in the two cases is given by remarkably similar equations:

Longitudinal	Transverse
$v = \sqrt{(B/\rho)}$	$v = \sqrt{(F/\mu)}$
where ρ is the medium's density	where μ is the string's linear density
and B is its bulk modulus	and F is its tension

The analogy between ρ and μ is evident; the only difference between them reflects the fact that the medium in the longitudinal case occupies a volume, whereas the medium in the transverse case is a string (one-dimensional). The analogy between B and F may be less evident. A medium's bulk modulus B (also known as its "volume elasticity") reflects how much additional pressure must be exerted on the medium to reduce its volume by a certain fraction.[12] If, by changing the pressure the medium feels by dP, one changes its volume by dV in total, or by (dV/V) per unit of its volume V, then its bulk modulus is given by $B = -dP/(dV/V)$. (The minus sign makes B a positive quantity, since if $dP > 0$, then $dV < 0$; increased pressure brings decreased volume.) If the fluid's bulk modulus is larger, then greater additional pressure is needed to compress the fluid by a certain fraction. In this respect, the bulk modulus is like the string's tension: if the string is tighter, then greater force is needed to pluck it—that is, to make it bend (which requires lengthening it). In short, B and F both concern the medium's "springiness," and so $\sqrt{(B/\rho)}$ and $\sqrt{(F/\mu)}$ are alike in that each takes the form $\sqrt{(\text{medium's elasticity}/\text{medium's density})}$.

Why is there such a similarity between the expressions for the speeds of these physically dissimilar kinds of waves? A derivation of the stretched string's transverse-wave behavior from more fundamental laws causally explains why the string undergoes this behavior, and this derivation finds the wave's speed to equal $\sqrt{(F/\mu)}$. An unrelated derivation of the fluid's longitudinal-wave behavior causally explains why the fluid undergoes this behavior, and this derivation finds the wave's speed to equal $\sqrt{(B/\rho)}$. However, as I showed in chapter 6, these explanations may include material that is irrelevant to explaining the waves' speeds. Even if they do not, it does not follow that these separate causal explanations for each wave's v together explain why the two waves' velocities are each proportional to $\sqrt{(\text{medium's elasticity}/\text{density})}$. They do so only if this similarity in the waves' v is coincidental. But in fact, it is not coincidental. Rather, as the dimensional explanation reveals, their similarity actually arises from a feature that is common to the two kinds of waves.

Let's unpack all of that by starting with the causal explanation of the fluid's longitudinal-wave behavior (fig. 10.2). Take a fluid element thin enough in the direction of the wave's propagation that it has uniform density and internal pressure (though its density and pressure change as it becomes part of a compression or rarefaction). Let ρ be the fluid's density when not disturbed by a wave passing through, and let the element's original width be dz. Each fluid element

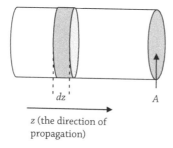

Figure 10.2 The longitudinal wave propagating down the pipe

has an initial location z along the length of the pipe, and an element's displacement $s(z,t)$ at time t from its original location z varies periodically in z and in t. That is the wave. The pipe has cross-sectional area A. The fluid element's front and back walls will be shifted from their equilibrium positions as a wave passes through it. The change in the element's length will be the change in its front wall's position minus the change in the rear wall's position: $s(z+dz)-s(z)$. The change dV in its volume will therefore be $A[s(z+dz)-s(z)]$, and since $B=-dP/(dV/V)$, we have

$$dP=-BdV/V=-BA[s(z+dz)-s(z)]/Adz=-B\partial s/\partial z,$$

and so

$$\partial P/\partial z=-B\partial^2 s/\partial z^2.$$

The force pressing inward on the element's front wall is $A\,P(z+dz)$ in the $-z$ direction, and the force pressing inward on the element's rear wall is $A\,P(z)$ in the $+z$ direction, so the net force F on the element is $A[P(z)-P(z+dz)]$, and so $dF/dz=-A\,\partial P/\partial z$. Hence,

$$dF/dz=AB\partial^2 s/\partial z^2.$$

By Newton's second law, the force dF on an element is given by its acceleration $\partial^2 s/\partial t^2$ times its mass $dm=\rho Adz$, and so

$$dF/dz=\rho A\partial^2 s/\partial t^2.$$

Equating our two expressions for dF/dz, we find $\rho A\partial^2 s/\partial t^2=AB\partial^2 s/\partial z^2$,

and so

$$\partial^2 s/\partial t^2=(B/\rho)\partial^2 s/\partial z^2.$$

This is a form of the wave equation, relating the way $s(z,t)$ changes over time at a given place to the way $s(z,t)$ changes over place at a given time. It is solved by a wave propagating in the $+z$ direction at speed $v=\sqrt{(B/\rho)}$.

Now let's causally explain the string's transverse-wave behavior. Take a small segment AB of the plucked string that makes an angle θ (fig. 10.3). Approximate AB as the arc of a circle of radius R, so that AB's length is $R\theta$ and mass is $\mu R\theta$. Since angles α, β, and γ are congruent and α is half of θ, the vertical component of the tension F at each end of the arc is $F\sin(\theta/2)$, so the two ends' contributions sum to $2F\sin(\theta/2)$, which can be approximated as $2F(\theta/2)=F\theta$ since θ is small. From the wave's viewpoint, the string is moving at speed v, and since

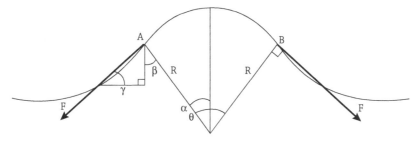

Figure 10.3 The transverse wave in the string

the centripetal force for segment AB moving in a circle of radius R at speed v is $mv^2/R = \mu R\theta\, v^2/R = \mu\theta v^2$, we have $F\theta = \mu\theta v^2$, and so

$$v = \surd(F/\mu).$$

Thus, each wave's v is proportional to its $\surd$(medium's elasticity/density). If this similarity in the two v equations were explained by the conjunction of these two derivations, then that similarity would amount to a coincidence. However, it is not, since a dimensional explanation reveals that the similarity arises from a common feature of the two waves. In so doing, the dimensional explanation unifies v's proportionality to $\surd(B/\rho)$ for the longitudinal wave with v's proportionality to $\surd(F/\mu)$ for the transverse wave. Take the explanans in the dimensional explanation to be that (to a sufficiently good approximation) for each wave, density, elasticity, and wavelength suffice (and may even be more than enough) to form a quantity standing in a dimensionally homogeneous relation to v. In other words, B, ρ, and the wavelength λ completely physically characterize the longitudinal-wave system, and F, μ, and λ completely physically characterize the transverse-wave system. Hence, v is proportional to $\rho^\alpha B^\beta \lambda^\gamma$ or to $\mu^\alpha F^\beta \lambda^\gamma$. Then the dimensional tables (of the kind I gave in chapter 6) are as follows:

	v	ρ	B	λ			v	μ	F	λ
L	1	−3	−1	1		L	1	−1	1	1
M	0	1	1	0		M	0	1	1	0
T	−1	0	−2	0		T	−1	0	−2	0

The M and T lines are identical in the two tables, and they give us two equations in two variables ($0 = \alpha + \beta$, $-1 = -2\beta$), from which it follows that v is proportional to $\surd(B/\rho)$ and $\surd(F/\mu)$, respectively. Although the L line in the table is different in the two cases, that difference makes no difference to α and β.[13]

Thus, unlike the derivations from more fundamental laws, the dimensional explanation traces the similarity (that each wave's v is proportional to its $\surd$(medium's elasticity/density)) to a dimensional feature that is common to the two systems.[14]

The explanandum is revealed to be independent of the physical differences between longitudinal and transverse waves. The common derivation of the derivative laws for longitudinal and transverse waves that exploits only the common dimensional architecture of the two cases is like the "common proof" of the thermodynamic and electrostatic results in the previous section that exploits only the common mathematical form of the fundamental laws, thereby explaining why the two results take the same mathematical form. The dimensional architecture's invariance under the switch from the quantities sufficient to characterize one case to the quantities sufficient to characterize the other is like the symmetry of the two pairs of fundamental laws in the earlier example under the exchange of thermodynamic and electrostatic quantities. The invariant features in each example (the dimensional architecture or the mathematical form of the fundamental laws) suffice to determine the salient features shared by the two derivative laws in each example.

Of course, this explanation from common dimensional architecture does not derive the two v equations from the very same facts. In each case, v is explained by the dimensional architecture of that particular case. The fact that there is a dimensionally homogeneous relation between v, B, ρ, and λ regarding longitudinal waves is plainly distinct from the fact that there is a dimensionally homogeneous relation between v, F, μ, and λ regarding transverse waves. The unification forged by dimensional explanations is not like the unification produced by a common cause.

Nor is it like the unification underwritten by Newton's theory of gravity in revealing that the Moon is just a falling body—or that the tides, lunar and planetary motions, and falling bodies are all governed by the same equations. Moreover, the unification forged by dimensional explanations is not like the unification produced by Darwin's theory of natural selection, which consists (according to Kitcher 1993) in showing various facts to be derivable through the same argument schemes. Although all dimensional explanations employ dimensional arguments, not all of the facts explained dimensionally are thereby unified with one another—unlike all of the facts about anatomy, physiology, biochemistry, biogeography, embryology, and so forth that are unified with one another in virtue of fitting into Darwinian selectionist histories.

Rather, an explanation from common dimensional architecture unifies the derivative laws concerning v for longitudinal and transverse waves by identifying dimensional features common to both systems that account for the similarities between the two v laws. Even if separate derivations of the two v laws from more fundamental laws causally explain the two v laws, the mere combination of the two derivations fails to explain why the two v laws are so similar, since that combination inaccurately depicts the laws' similarity as coincidental.[15] Instead, their similarity arises from features common to the fundamental laws as they apply to the two systems—features captured by the dimensional explanans.

The dimensional explanation that I have just been examining identifies certain dimensional features *shared* by physically disparate cases as responsible for their *similarity* in other respects. But a dimensional explanation might instead identify certain dimensional *differences* between cases as responsible for various other *differences* between them.[16] For example, consider a simple pendulum (a small, heavy body of mass m suspended near Earth's surface by a cord of invariable length l and negligible mass and cross-section, where every freely falling body experiences the same downward acceleration g from gravity) in a vacuum. The period T of its swing, when it has been released from a small angle, is (to a good approximation) proportional to $\sqrt{(l/g)}$. Compare the simple pendulum to the system depicted in figure 10.4: a spring of negligible mass hangs vertically near Earth's surface, and we suddenly attach a body of mass m to the spring. The spring stretches, and then the body moves up and down (assuming negligible internal friction and air resistance), where this oscillation's period T is proportional to $\sqrt{(m/k)}$. We might contrast these two cases and ask: Why is the pendulum's T a function of g whereas T in figure 10.4's system is independent of g?

One way to try to answer this question is to derive the two T's from more fundamental laws. Each derivation then constitutes a causal explanation of that system's complete motion. But as I have argued, such a derivation may contain some elements that are irrelevant to explaining a particular feature of that motion, such as its period. Moreover, even if each derivation constitutes a causal explanation of the motion's period, the combination of the two derivations may fail to explain why the two systems differ in their period's dependence on g, because the combination fails to trace this difference to some other difference between the two cases. Let's look at the two derivations in the combination. Regarding figure 10.4's system, we find from Newton's and Hooke's laws that $ma + kx - mg = 0$, and so the governing differential equation is $a + (k/m)\,x - g = 0$, which is simple harmonic motion with period $2\pi\sqrt{(m/k)}$. Regarding the simple pendulum, we find that $ma + [mg/l]x = 0$, and so the governing differential equation is $a + (g/l)\,x = 0$, which is simple harmonic motion with period $2\pi\sqrt{(l/g)}$. According to this putative explanation, the pendulum's period depends on

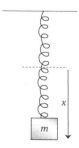

Figure 10.4 A body suspended from a spring

g, whereas the period of figure 10.4's system does not, simply because that is how it turns out in the two cases. No more specific points of difference are held responsible.

However, in dimensional terms, the two cases are more precisely contrasted. On the left is the table for the pendulum[17] and on the right is the table for figure 10.4's system:

	T	g	l	m			T	g	k	m
L	0	1	1	0		L	0	1	0	0
M	0	0	0	1		M	0	0	1	1
T	1	-2	0	0		T	1	-2	-2	0

The differences are confined to the third column. However, that is enough to make a considerable difference. In figure 10.4's system, T cannot depend on g because g is the only characteristic of the situation with an L dimension, so nothing is available to compensate for g's L dimension to leave us with pure T (for the period). In contrast, the pendulum has its characteristic l to compensate for g's contribution to the L dimension. Here we have an answer to the why question I asked about the contrast between the two cases in T's dependence on g; separate derivations from more fundamental laws cannot answer it.

Likewise, why does T depend on m in figure 10.4's system, but not for a pendulum? Because m is the only parameter characterizing the pendulum that has an M dimension, whereas in figure 10.4's system, k has an M dimension that can compensate for m's contribution. Separate derivations of T in the two cases from more fundamental laws fail to point out that as long as m remains the only characteristic with an M dimension, m cannot take any responsibility for T. As I showed in connection with the $T \propto r^{3/2}$ law in section 6.2, derivations from the more fundamental laws may fail to identify the specific features of those laws that are responsible for a given derivative law.

■ 10.4 TARGETING NEW EXPLANANDA

Consider the respects of similarity and difference that (I have just shown) dimensional explanations do a nice job of explaining—for example, that v is proportional to $\sqrt{\text{(medium's elasticity/density)}}$ for both longitudinal and transverse waves, or that T depends on m for figure 10.4's system but not for a pendulum. It is easy to recognize these as respects of similarity and difference and hence as suitable targets for scientific explanation. To do so, we do not need to think about the systems in dimensional terms. However, along with giving us new answers to why questions that present themselves independently of dimensional considerations, dimensional reasoning also suggests new why questions to ask. That is because dimensional considerations pick out new respects of similarity and difference for us to ask about.[18]

For example, consider a body at rest that begins to fall freely. In time t, it covers a distance $s = \frac{1}{2}gt^2$. That is, $t = \sqrt{(2s/g)}$, so t is proportional to $\sqrt{(s/g)}$. A freely falling body is physically not much like a pendulum. For instance, the falling body's motion is one-way, whereas the pendulum moves periodically; t in the above equation is not the period of any repeated motion. Yet dimensionally, t is like the pendulum's period T. Indeed, there is a dimensional similarity between the two systems: just as for a freely falling body, t is proportional to $\sqrt{(s/g)}$, so for a pendulum, T is proportional to $\sqrt{(l/g)}$.

Dimensional reasoning reveals this similarity to be no coincidence; it has an explanation from common dimensional architecture. Suppose that t for falling bodies stands in a dimensionally homogeneous relation to g, s, and m, and suppose also that T for pendulums stands in a dimensionally homogeneous relation to g, l, and m. Then the two systems have the same dimensional architecture, so dimensionally similar relations must hold among their parameters. In tabular form: the pendulum is on the left and the freely falling body is on the right:

	T	g	l	m
L	0	1	1	0
M	0	0	0	1
T	1	-2	0	0

	t	g	s	m
L	0	1	1	0
M	0	0	0	1
T	1	-2	0	0

Because the two systems have the same dimensional architecture, the derivative laws for the falling body's t and the pendulum's T must be dimensionally analogous.

A water wave having wavelength λ (traversing deep water, taking water to be incompressible and nonviscous) is physically neither like a falling body nor like a pendulum. Yet its period T is proportional to $\sqrt{(\lambda/g)}$.[19] We could ask why the derivative law for the water wave's period is so similar to the laws for the pendulum's T and the falling body's t, despite the physical differences among these phenomena. Once again, this similarity among the three derivative laws can be appreciated only in dimensional terms.

The dimensional explanation of the water wave's period starts by taking the gravitational acceleration (reflecting the restoring force on the water displaced in the wave), the water's density ρ, and the wavelength as sufficient to form a quantity standing in a dimensionally homogeneous relation to the wave's period. In tabular form:

	T	g	λ	ρ
L	0	1	1	-3
M	0	0	0	1
T	1	-2	0	0

Although this table is not perfectly dimensionally identical to the previous two, its single difference from them (in the L dimension of the only characteristic with an M dimension) makes no difference: Because that characteristic is the only one with an M dimension, it cannot figure in the dimensionally homogeneous relation. Since the three tables are otherwise identical, the resulting relations must be dimensionally analogous.

In view of the dimensional similarity among the three systems, it is inevitable that the expressions for the freely falling body's t, the pendulum's T, and the water wave's T are analogous. But that analogy can be appreciated only in dimensional terms; s, l, and λ are not otherwise analogous. This stands in contrast to the longitudinal and transverse wave example (in section 10.3), where the analogy between ρ and μ, and between B and F, could be appreciated without invoking dimensional considerations. (Indeed, the analogs do not have the same dimensions.)

Since the similarities among the expressions for the freely falling body's t, the pendulum's T, and the water wave's T are entirely dimensional, we can ask the why question that is answered by appealing to the common dimensional architecture of these three cases only *after* we have already recognized that quantities having the same dimensions thereby qualify as alike in a certain respect. I observed a similar phenomenon in chapter 9: that the why question regarding Desargues's theorem in projective geometry functions only in a context where properties in projective geometry (such as being collinear, whether the line is a Euclidean line plus a point at infinity *or* a line at infinity) are already recognized as genuine respects of similarity. Only in such a context is Desargues's theorem in projective geometry appreciated as identifying something common to each of the three intersection points (whether Euclidean points *or* points at infinity). In chapter 11, I will return to the relation between the naturalness of various properties and their roles in explanations.

11   What Makes Some Reducible Physical Properties Explanatory?

▪ 11.1 SOME REDUCIBLE PROPERTIES ARE NATURAL

In this book, I have identified several kinds of non-causal explanations in mathematics and science. I have not argued that every example of explanation in math or every example of non-causal scientific explanation falls into one of the kinds of non-causal explanation that I have identified. I have also not tried to force all of the explanations that I have examined into a single narrow mold. (Indeed I see no good reason to award any greater degree of plausibility to a proposed "model" of explanation in math and science—or even a "model" aiming merely to cover the scientific explanation of events—just because it purports to offer the same account of all examples.) However, I have tried to group the examples that I have studied into various kinds based on how the explanations work, and I have also tried to highlight some of the affinities among these kinds of explanation.

In this final chapter, I will argue that despite their diversity, all of these different kinds deserve to be grouped with one another and with causal explanations, too, as species of the same genus: explanations. There is an important respect in which they are all doing the same thing. It does not make any difference which kind of non-causal explanation is in play, nor does it matter whether the explanation is causal or non-causal—or whether it is scientific or mathematical. Regardless of these differences, there is a close connection (I will argue) between a reducible property's figuring in an explanation in a certain way and its being a natural property (that is, a respect in which things are genuinely alike). The distinction between natural and non-natural properties is drawn in both mathematics and science, and explanatory relations of all kinds in math and science are closely intertwined with the naturalness of some but not other reducible properties. This is an important respect in which explanations of all kinds in math and science (and presumably beyond) deserve to be grouped together.

I will devote much of this chapter to getting a grip on the distinction between properties that are natural and properties that are not—and on the roles that this distinction plays in explanation. In particular, I will be interested in this distinction as it pertains to *reducible* (i.e., nonfundamental) properties. To see this distinction in action, let's momentarily put aside the concept of "natural properties." Let's instead focus on a phenomenon involving scientific explanation that we would be inclined to understand in terms of the distinction among reducible properties between those that are natural and those that are not. We will thereby motivate the question of what, in turn, grounds this distinction.

Let's look at an example. Suppose that a seesaw on earth has two point bodies sitting on it: one on the right, with mass $m_R = 150$ kg, sitting $x_R = 2$ m to the right of the fulcrum, and one on the left, with mass $m_L = 200$ kg, sitting $x_L = 1$ m to the left of the fulcrum. Why does the seesaw tip to the right? This question asks for an event's scientific explanation. According to classical physics (a qualification that applies to all of my examples), one explanation of the event is that it is a natural law that any such seesaw[1] tips to the right if $m_R x_R - m_L x_L > 0$, and for the given seesaw, $m_R x_R - m_L x_L = 100$ kg-m. In this explanation, the crucial feature of the seesaw system is that its $m_R x_R - m_L x_L = 100$ kg-m. Of course, this property is simply certain of the system's more basic properties standing in a certain relation; the system's having $m_R x_R - m_L x_L = 100$ kg-m is not a fundamental property, but rather is reducible to its having $m_R = 150$ kg, $x_R = 2$ m, $m_L = 200$ kg, and $x_L = 1$ m. Despite this property's reducibility, the system's having $m_R x_R - m_L x_L$ equal to 100 kg-m can help to explain the seesaw's tipping to the right. We are not inclined to say that since $m_R x_R - m_L x_L = 100$ kg-m is nothing more than a relation among m_R, x_R, m_L, and x_L, the outcome is not explained by the system's $m_R x_R - m_L x_L$ (but instead by its having those more basic properties).

Some philosophers may insist that the seesaw tips to the right not because its $m_R x_R - m_L x_L = 100$ kg-m, but rather because its $m_R x_R - m_L x_L > 0$. For my purposes, it does not matter which of these views is correct. Perhaps each of these properties of the seesaw system explains why it tips to the right. The important point is that at least one of them has explanatory power despite being reducible. I will refer to such a property as "the seesaw's $m_R x_R - m_L x_L$." There is perhaps yet another way to explain the same event: the seesaw tips to the right because its $m_R x_R = 300$ kg-m, its $m_L x_L = 200$ kg-m, and it is a natural law that any such seesaw tips to the right if its $m_R x_R > m_L x_L$. Once again, the seesaw's having $m_R x_R = 300$ kg-m is reducible to its having $m_R = 150$ kg and $x_R = 2$ m, and its having $m_L x_L = 200$ kg-m is likewise reducible. But their reducibility does not deprive them of explanatory power.

Not every reducible physical property is like these properties in possessing explanatory power. Suppose two point bodies have long been held at rest, 1 cm apart. The magnitude of each body's electrostatic force (F_e) on the other is (causally) explained by the bodies' charges (q_1, q_2) and separation (r), together with Coulomb's law $(F_e = q_1 q_2 / r^2)$. Likewise, the magnitude of the bodies' mutual gravitational attraction (F_g) is explained by the bodies' masses (m_1, m_2) and separation (r), together with Newton's gravitational-force law $(F_g = G m_1 m_2 / r^2)$ and the value of the gravitational constant (G). Suppose that the pair of bodies possesses the property of having $m_1 m_2 / r^2 = 30{,}000$ kg^2/m^2. This property does not help to explain the mutual gravitational force, though it combines with Newton's gravitational-force law and G's value to entail that force. Similarly, the pair's q_1/r and q_2/r do not join Coulomb's law in explaining the electrostatic force (though they suffice to entail that force). The same applies to other arbitrary combinations, such as the pair's q_1r/q_2 and q_2^2/r^3 (the product of which is again q_1q_2/r^2). These two properties are manufactured clusters of quantities—mere conglomerates of certain properties that can actually do the explaining.

There is a distinction here. That q_1q_2 (measured in esu^2) exceeds r^2 (in cm^2) does not join with Coulomb's law to explain why the electrostatic force exceeds 1 dyne, whereas that $m_R\, x_R$ exceeds $m_L\, x_L$ joins with the relevant law to explain why the seesaw tips to the left. The pair's having $m_1m_2/r^2 = 30{,}000$ kg^2/m^2 has no explanatory significance whereas the seesaw's $m_R\, x_R - m_L\, x_L$ has explanatory power. What is responsible for this distinction among the reducible physical properties, making some but not others explanatorily powerful? In this chapter, I examine this question and try to answer it. The answer I propose applies not only to the various kinds of non-causal scientific explanations that I have considered in previous chapters, but also to causal explanations. The answer also highlights affinities between scientific explanations and explanations in mathematics—affinities that I have identified repeatedly over the course of this book.

Of course, the seesaw's having $m_R\, x_R - m_L\, x_L > 0$ is logically equivalent to its having $x_R - m_L\, x_L/m_R > 0$. Yet its $x_R - m_L\, x_L/m_R$ is just another arbitrary combination having no explanatory significance. How can $m_R\, x_R - m_L\, x_L > 0$ help to explain the outcome when it is logically equivalent to $x_R - m_L\, x_L/m_R > 0$, which is explanatorily powerless?

This challenge is based on the mistaken presupposition that if p and q are logically equivalent, then they must be equivalent in their explanatory power. As a simple counterexample, consider that Coulomb's law (l) together with various initial conditions (c) explains why the two point bodies in my earlier example feel their mutual electrostatic force (f). Since l&c logically entails f, l&c is logically equivalent to l&c&f. Yet l&c&f fails to explain f. There are obviously many such tricks: l&(c or $\sim f$)&f is also logically equivalent to l&c but lacks its explanatory power. Two bodies of liquid fit exactly into the same glass because they have the same volume V, not because they have the same V^2 or because they have the same $(1/V)$.[2]

In asking what makes the seesaw's $m_R\, x_R - m_L\, x_L$ differ in explanatory power from its $x_R - m_L\, x_L/m_R$, I am asking about a contrast between two reducible physical properties. Neither is a multiply realizable property that is irreducible to more basic properties in view of being the property of playing a certain functional or causal role, such as the property of being a predator, being a gene (Kitcher 1984a), or being money (Fodor 1974). Of course, to say that the properties with which I am concerned are reducible is not to say that they are eliminable; among the seesaw's properties is its having $x_R - m_L\, x_L/m_R > 0$.

The seesaw would still have tipped to the right even if m_R, x_R, m_L, and x_L had been different, as long as $m_R x_R - m_L x_L > 0$ had still held. But this is not enough to distinguish $m_R x_R - m_L x_L$ from $x_R - m_L x_L / m_R$ since the seesaw would still have tipped to the right even if m_R, x_R, m_L, and x_L had been different, as long as $x_R - m_L x_L / m_R > 0$ had still held—or, equivalently, as long as $m_R / x_L > m_L / x_R$ had still held. Yet all of these reducible properties are arbitrary combinations having no explanatory significance.

In asking what makes the seesaw's $m_R x_R - m_L x_L$ differ in explanatory power from its $x_R - m_L x_L / m_R$, I am not asking what makes one rather than the other a *cause* of the seesaw's tipping to the right. For one thing, causes are events and it is not obvious that the seesaw's being $m_R x_R - m_L x_L > 0$ is an event at all (even if, e.g., its having $m_R = 150$ kg is an event). It seems more like a mathematical relation's holding among events. For another thing, as I suggested in chapter 1, many non-causes (such as absences and omissions) figure in causal explanations, and (of course!) some scientific explanations are non-causal. I am concerned directly with scientific explanations, not with causal relations.

Let's look at another example. Consider two simple pendulums on earth, having lengths $l_1 = 1$ m and $l_2 = 0.5$ m and periods $T_1 = 2.0$ s and $T_2 = 1.4$ s. That $l_1 > l_2$ (together with various laws and background conditions) explains why $T_1 > T_2$. Though this is a causal explanation, there may well be no event consisting of l_1 exceeding l_2; there may merely be separate events involving each of the two pendulums. (The view that the difference between l_1 and l_2 is metaphysically ineligible to be a cause is like Strevens's 2008, 173–174, view regarding the difference in metabolic efficiency between two strains of bacteria, living in separate petri dishes: "Metaphysically, this difference is incapable of supplying causal oomph in the case at hand, being as it is an abstract relation between two states of affairs that act independently.")

In virtue of what, then, does the relation $l_1 > l_2$ (together with various laws and background conditions) causally explain why $T_1 > T_2$? Plausibly, the *l*-relation causally explains the *T*-relation because by law, the *l*-relation entails the *T*-relation, and because each *l*-relatum (together with laws and background conditions) causally explains the corresponding *T*-relatum. That is:

(1) $l_1 = 1$ m (together with background conditions) and the law that $T = 2\pi\sqrt{(l/g)}$ causally explains why $T_1 = 2.0$ s.
(2) $l_2 = 0.5$ m (together with background conditions) and the law that $T = 2\pi\sqrt{(l/g)}$ causally explains why $T_2 = 1.4$ s.
(3) By law (under the background conditions), if $l_1 > l_2$, then $T_1 > T_2$.

Thus, $l_1 > l_2$ (together with various laws and background conditions) causally explains why $T_1 > T_2$ even if $l_1 > l_2$ is, strictly speaking, not a cause.

Does an analogous account reveal what makes the seesaw's $m_R\, x_R - m_L\, x_L$ (together with various laws and background conditions) able to explain its tipping to the right? The torque τ_R on the right (tending to rotate the seesaw clockwise) is causally explained by x_R, the downward force F_R on the right, and the law $\tau_R = x_R \times F_R$. The force F_R, in turn, is causally explained by m_R, g, and the law $F_R = m_R\, g$. The seesaw's left side receives similar treatment. From the law $\tau = I\, a$ relating net torque, the seesaw's moment of inertia I, and its angular acceleration a, it follows that if $\tau_R > \tau_L$, then the seesaw tips to the right. Thus, by analogy to the way that the pendulum's $l_1 > l_2$ helps to causally explain why $T_1 > T_2$, we have

(1') $m_R = 150$ kg and $x_R = 2$ m (together with background conditions and laws) causally explains why $\tau_R = 2940$ N-m.

(2') $m_L = 200$ kg and $x_L = 1$ m (together with background conditions and laws) causally explains why $\tau_L = 1960$ N-m.

(3') By law (under the background conditions), if $m_R\, x_R > m_L\, x_L$, then $\tau_R > \tau_L$ and so the seesaw tips to the right.

Do we have here an account of why the seesaw's $m_R\, x_R - m_L\, x_L$, despite being reducible, manages (together with various laws and background conditions) to explain why the seesaw tips to the right?

No. The explanans in the pendulum example is that $l_1 > l_2$ (together with various laws and background conditions), and this relation accordingly appears in (3) with its two relata figuring in (1) and (2), respectively. However, (3') includes $m_R\, x_R > m_L\, x_L$ whereas our aim was to account for the explanatory power of $m_R\, x_R - m_L\, x_L > 0$. Of course, these two inequalities are logically equivalent. But we cannot thereby argue that they are equivalent in explanatory power, on pain of taking the seesaw's $x_R - m_L\, x_L / m_R > 0$ as also having the power to help explain the outcome. We were trying to identify what makes the seesaw's $m_R\, x_R - m_L\, x_L$ differ in explanatory power from its $x_R - m_L\, x_L / m_R$.

Although we were trying to account for the explanatory power of $m_R\, x_R - m_L\, x_L > 0$, (3') instead includes $m_R\, x_R > m_L\, x_L$. Do we have here, then, at least an account of how the seesaw's $m_R\, x_R > m_L\, x_L$ (together with various laws and background conditions) explains why the seesaw tips to the right? That would still be some progress since we are also trying to understand why the seesaw's $m_R\, x_R$ and $m_L\, x_L$ have explanatory power whereas the seesaw's $m_L\, x_L / m_R$, for instance, does not. However, we have not gotten even that far. In the pendulum example, the relation $l_1 > l_2$ doing the explaining appears in (3) and the two relata (l_1 and l_2) figure in (1) and (2), respectively. But although $m_R\, x_R > m_L\, x_L$ appears in (3'), $m_R\, x_R$ and $m_L\, x_L$ do not figure in (1') and (2'), respectively. Rather, m_R and x_R figure individually in (1') and m_L and x_L figure individually in (2'). We should not underestimate the difference that this makes. To replace

($1'$) $m_R = 150$ kg and $x_R = 2$ m (together with background conditions and laws) causally explains why $\tau_R = 2940$ N-m

with

($1''$) $m_R x_R = 300$ kg-m (together with background conditions and laws) causally explains why $\tau_R = 2940$ N-m

would be to *presuppose* that $m_R x_R$ is explanatorily powerful despite being reducible. What makes $m_R x_R$ explanatorily powerful, unlike arbitrary reducible properties such as $m_L x_L/m_R$, is exactly what we are trying to understand.

Notice, by the way, that the seesaw's $m_R x_R - m_L x_L$ does not derive its explanatory power from its being equal to the magnitude of some mechanical cause of the outcome, whether that cause be a force or torque, component or net. The various forces are $m_R g$ downward on the right and $m_L g$ downward on the left (along with an upward force exerted by the fulcrum), and the net torque is equal to $g (m_R x_R - m_L x_L)$. Of course, it follows that $(m_R x_R - m_L x_L)$'s sign determines the net torque's sign and hence the angular acceleration's direction. But the same is true of $(x_R - m_L x_L/m_R)$'s sign, for example.

In taking the seesaw's $m_L x_L/m_R$ and other arbitrary combinations as constituting properties, I am employing an "abundant" view of properties (in the sense of Lewis 1986a, 59), according to which every class of possible entities is associated with a property and every class of n-tuples of possibilia is associated with a relation.[3] We might be inclined to say that what privileges the explanatorily powerful properties over the arbitrary combinations is that they alone are natural (a.k.a. "sparse") properties. (I first set out this distinction in section 9.5.) Plausibly (as emphasized by Fodor 1974 and Loewer 2007, 316), the natural properties alone figure in laws of nature, whereas an unnatural property may figure in a logical consequence of laws that, though naturally necessary, is not a law (such as that under certain specified conditions, a seesaw tips to the right if $x_R - m_L x_L/m_R > 0$).[4] If natural laws are crucial to scientific explanations, then a difference in naturalness between the seesaw's $m_R x_R - m_L x_L$ and its $x_R - m_L x_L/m_R$ might seem a promising way to account for their difference in explanatory power.

To refine this response, we would have to consider whether naturalness comes in degrees, as Lewis (1986a, 61) believes. The difference in explanatory power between the seesaw's $m_R x_R - m_L x_L$ and its $x_R - m_L x_L/m_R$ does not seem to be a matter of degree; the latter seems explanatorily powerless. (I will return to naturalness as a matter of degree in section 6.) We would also have to consider whether any reducible properties could be (perfectly) natural. Lewis thinks not, since regarding (perfectly) natural properties, he says that "there are only just enough of them to characterise things completely and without redundancy"

(60). But if no reducible property is natural, then naturalness cannot be used to privilege the reducible properties that possess explanatory power.

I will set aside both of these concerns, since an appeal to naturalness faces a more fundamental obstacle: it does little to *account for* the differences in explanatory power among various reducible properties. If the seesaw's $m_R x_R - m_L x_L$ and its $x_R - m_L x_L/m_R$ differ in explanatory power because they differ in naturalness, then in virtue of what do they differ in naturalness? Lewis (1983) is prepared to take a property's naturalness as a metaphysical primitive, a brute fact. I am not— or, at least, I am considerably less willing to do so for reducible properties than for fundamental properties such as (perhaps) mass and electric charge.

Though an appeal to naturalness does little to explain why the seesaw's $m_R x_R - m_L x_L$ differs in explanatory power from its $x_R - m_L x_L/m_R$, I am happy to use naturalness to express our original puzzle in a new way: We want to know what makes certain reducible physical properties but not others natural. Two seesaws being alike in their $m_R x_R - m_L x_L$ "makes for qualitative similarity" (Lewis 1986a, 60) and so can explain why they are alike in both tilting to the right. It is no coincidence that they both tilt to the right; the two seesaws have something in common (namely, having $m_R x_R - m_L x_L > 0$) that explains the common tilt. In contrast, although the same two seesaws also have the same value for $x_R - m_L x_L/m_R$, this is not a genuine respect of similarity, just as two pairs of charged bodies' having the same value for $q_1 r/q_2$ does not amount to their resembling each other.

That two systems having a given reducible property in common are genuinely similar in a certain respect is often emphasized by scientists when they introduce a single term for that reducible property or appeal to that property in explanations. For example, when Whewell introduced into English a single term ("labouring force"—later supplanted by the term "work") for the product of a force and the distance through which it acts, he emphasized that two cases of equal laboring force constitute "the same thing" whatever the particular values of force and distance underwriting them—whether they involve "one pound raised twelve feet; two pounds raised six feet; three pounds raised four feet; six pounds raised two feet; and so on" (1841, viii).

One advantage of formulating our question in terms of the difference in naturalness between, say, $m_R x_R - m_L x_L$ and $x_R - m_L x_L/m_R$ is that it emphasizes that to answer our question, we do not have to give necessary and sufficient conditions for one fact or event to explain another. Rather, our question is confined to what makes one property natural enough (that is, far enough from being an arbitrary conglomerate of more fundamental properties) to be eligible to figure in explanations.[5] Whether or not the possession of a certain property that is natural enough to explain actually does help to explain a given fact is another question.

In section 11.2, I will try to motivate further the distinction in which I am interested by contrasting center of mass with reduced mass. I will also refine the question that I am addressing by contrasting it with other questions that philosophers have asked regarding center of mass. In section 11.3, I will underline the importance of the distinction among reducible physical properties between those that are and those that are not sufficiently natural to be explanatorily powerful. I will show how the failure to respect this distinction causes trouble for a recent account of scientific explanation given by Strevens (2008). In section 11.4, I will argue that in scientific practice, many important dimensionless quantities, despite being reducible, are treated as sufficiently natural to be explanatorily powerful. In section 11.5, I will offer my own account of why certain reducible physical properties but not others are sufficiently natural to be explanatorily powerful, and I will apply this account to all of the previous examples along with several others. Roughly speaking, I will propose that the possession of some reducible property P is natural enough to explain some fact, once P is joined in the explanans by a law L in which P figures (and perhaps further conditions), exactly when there is an explanation of L that the expression for P enters as a unit. The alternative to its entering as a unit in some explanation of L is its emerging somewhere in the course of every explanation of L by a fortuitous combination of the various properties to which P reduces. In section 11.6, I will use my account of what makes certain reducible properties natural to argue that all of the various kinds of non-causal explanations that I have presented—together with causal explanations—work in the same way to make certain reducible properties natural. Hence, these various kinds of explanations are all species of the same genus.

■ 11.2 CENTERS OF MASS AND REDUCED MASS

As I have shown, the seesaw's tipping to the right can be explained in terms of the forces on it and the torques they produce. The expression $m_R x_R - m_L x_L$ appears late in this explanation: in the sum of the torques from the left and right sides. This expression appears much earlier in a different (but equally correct) explanation of the seesaw's behavior, namely, as an instance of the "tipping law":

> (Tipping law) A rigid, initially stationary body of mass M (small enough that Earth's gravity varies negligibly over the body) under no external forces besides Earth's gravity and some support
> – tips over so as to lower its center of mass, if its center of mass is not located directly above or below a point of support, and
> – is at equilibrium otherwise

where the body's having its center of mass at location r is identical to the body's having $(\sum m_i r_i)/M$ (or, in the case of a continuous mass distribution, $(\int \rho(r) r \, dV)/M$ equal to r).

The expression $m_R x_R - m_L x_L$ appears as the numerator in the location of the seesaw's center of mass. If $m_R x_R - m_L x_L > 0$, the seesaw's center of mass is located to the right of the fulcrum (the point of support), and so by the tipping law, the seesaw tips to the right (thereby lowering its center of mass). Thus, the tipping law explains the seesaw's behavior.

In the seesaw's having its center of mass at $(m_R x_R - m_L x_L)/M$, we have a reducible property possessing explanatory power. Our challenge is to understand why such a reducible property is natural enough to explain.

The center of mass's role in the tipping law might seem to account somehow for its explanatory power. However, not every mathematical combination of various factors is natural enough to help explain the effect of those factors even if that combination figures in a law determining that effect. Let's look at a reducible property that is like center of mass in many ways but is not explanatorily relevant. The tipping law says roughly that a rigid, extended body moves in the manner of a single point body located at the extended body's center of mass. Here is a similar law concerning any classical two-body problem (i.e., any case where two point masses, feeling no external forces, move under their mutual influence): the first body moves relative to the second in the manner of a point body feeling the same force as the first body feels but with mass equal to the pair's "reduced mass" $\mu = m_1 m_2/(m_1 + m_2)$. For example, suppose that each of two mass points feels only the other's gravity. The above law can be used to predict their relative acceleration a:

> Treat one body as if it had mass μ and felt the force (given by Newton's gravitational-force law $F_g = G\, m_1 m_2/r^2$) it actually feels. By Newton's second law of motion (force = mass x acceleration)
>
> $G\, m_1 m_2/r^2 = \mu\, a.$
>
> Inserting some initial conditions—let's say: $m_1 m_2 = 3$ g^2, $r = 1$ cm, and $\mu = \frac{3}{4}$ g—we find $a = 2.67 \times 10^{-7}$ cm/s^2.

This argument is computationally very efficient and the law it uses is very concise. The concept of reduced mass thus promotes expressive economy and calculational ease, just like the concept of center of mass. But unlike the location of a system's center of mass, the magnitude of a pair's reduced mass does not help to explain its behavior. The pair's μ and $m_1 m_2$ are merely arithmetic combinations of some of the properties actually responsible for the bodies' relative acceleration: let's say, $m_1 = 3$ g and $m_2 = 1$ g (which join r, G, and the laws to explain a). Despite its utility, reduced mass is just a convenient conglomerate of some explanatorily powerful properties; in this respect, it differs from center of mass. My aim is to understand the grounds of this difference.

Although we can predict the relative acceleration in a two-body problem by imagining a body of mass μ feeling a given force, obviously the actual system contains no such body. But this fact is not what makes reduced mass explanatorily idle (despite its predictive utility). After all, a body's center of mass may lie entirely outside of that body, where there is nothing. Yet this fact does not keep the center of mass from helping to explain the outcome. A body has the property of having its center of mass at a given location, and a pair of bodies has the property of having a given reduced mass. The question is why these properties differ in their explanatory power, not which of them refers to the location or mass of some additional body existing alongside the bodies in question.

Azzouni (1997, 200) distinguishes "physically significant items which are not physically real (such as centers of mass)" from "mere mathematical objects (such as various functions of physical quantities that we could define)." Though Azzouni does not define "physically significant," his distinction appears not to be the same as the one I am examining. Azzouni (200) characterizes reduced mass as "physically significant," whereas his example of a quantity that does "not correspond to anything physically significant" is the product m_1m_2 of the masses of two gravitationally interacting bodies. But as I have just shown, reduced mass and m_1m_2 both figure in the argument for predicting relative acceleration in a classical two-body problem. If μ's "physical significance" were associated with the explanatory power of arguments like this, then Azzouni would have to regard m_1m_2 as likewise physically significant, which he does not.

Azzouni treats a pair's center of mass as a hypothetical body that "has mass $m_1 + m_2$" (1997, 199) and so as a useful fiction. By contrast, I see a pair's having its center of mass at a given location as a property just as real as any other that the pair possesses, though as distinguished in explanatory power even from such scientifically useful properties as having a given reduced mass. Haugeland (1993, 55) also considers the ontological status of a system's center of mass, but unlike Azzouni, he says that a center of mass "is nothing other than a spatial point at a time, or a point trajectory through time. Hence, its ontological status is exactly on a par with that of any other spatial point or trajectory," even a scientifically insignificant one (55). My concern, by contrast, is with the property rather than the point (or trajectory); as a property of a given system, its center of mass differs from many of its other (abundant) properties in being natural enough to play an explanatory role.

Haugeland's remarks are directed against Dennett. Yet unlike Haugeland (but like me), Dennett emphasizes the explanatory role played by centers of mass,[6] despite being reducible:

> *Explanations* may refer to centers of gravity. Why didn't the doll tip over? Because its center of gravity was so low. (Dennett 1983, 380, his emphasis)

> What did [America's Cup skipper] Connor do overnight to *cause* his boat to be so much faster? He lowered its center of gravity. Of course he did this by moving

gear, or adding lead ingots to the bilge, or replacing the mast with a lighter mast, or something—but what *caused* the boat's improvement was lowering its center of gravity. This is not just casual shorthand; it is the generalization that *explains* why any of these various changes (and a zillion others one could describe) would *likewise* cause an improvement in performance. (Dennett 2000, 357–358, his emphasis)

That all of these zillion changes would enhance the boat's speed is no coincidental similarity among them. Rather, they all have this property because they share the property of lowering the center of mass. Properties involving the center of mass must thus be natural enough to explain.

However, Dennett says little about what makes the center of mass natural enough to play this explanatory role. He says only that it is "implicated in important *causal* generalizations" (2000, 357). But as I have shown, precisely the same can be said of reduced mass—and, for that matter, of $m_1 m_2$ (since it appears in Newton's gravitational force law, for example). To account for the differences in explanatory power among various reducible physical properties, it will not suffice to appeal to remarks like Dennett's: that centers of mass "deserve to be taken seriously, learned about, used. If we go so far as to distinguish them as *real* (contrasting them, perhaps, with those abstract objects which are *bogus*), that is because we think they serve in perspicuous representations of real forces, 'natural' properties, and the like" (1991, 29, his emphasis). That there are "plenty of true, valuable, empirically testable things one can say with the help of the term" (Dennett 1983, 380) may account for the predictive utility and convenience of the concept of center of mass, but cannot account for its explanatory power or differentiate it from plenty of reducible properties that lack explanatory power.

■ 11.3 REDUCIBLE PROPERTIES ON STREVENS'S ACCOUNT OF SCIENTIFIC EXPLANATION

On the strength of several examples, I have suggested the importance in scientific practice of the distinction between reducible physical properties that are sufficiently natural to have explanatory power and those that are too unnatural to explain. Before looking further into science, let me give a different argument for this distinction's importance. I will give an example of a recently proposed philosophical account of scientific explanation that fails to attend to this distinction and suffers for it. I have in mind Strevens's proposal in his admirably ambitious book *Depth: An Account of Scientific Explanation* (2008). On Strevens's account, scientific explanations trace the operation of fundamental causal mechanisms, but an explanation must typically abstract from the explanandum's specific causes. That is because these details turn out not to "make a difference" to the explanandum and hence to be explanatorily irrelevant. However, Strevens's account of abstraction ends up treating all manner of conglomerate physical properties as explanatorily powerful when in fact, as I have suggested, only a select few are.

In the simplest case, Strevens says, an explanandum arises from various causes, laws, and conditions that logically entail it through a deductive argument that "mirrors" the causal process that produces it. An explanandum can have many such "causal models," and when a model is optimally pruned, according to Strevens, it is transformed into an explanation. Strevens's basic rationale for excising part of a model is that without it, the model still manages to entail the explanandum.

However, as Strevens fully recognizes, this approach encounters two obvious obstacles. Suppose that c explains e. (1) If the model contained $(c\&a)$ in place of c, for some arbitrary truth a, then e would still follow by an argument that mirrors the causal process that actually produced e, and generally the new model would no longer entail e if $(c\&a)$ were removed from it. But we do not regard $c\&a$ as explanatorily relevant. Rather, c is relevant and a is irrelevant. Even if a specifies further details of the events given in c, e happens because of c and not because of a. (2) Suppose that if a given falsehood b replaced c in the model, then e would still follow by an argument that traces a nomologically possible causal process. (Perhaps c and b are entirely dissimilar schemes for generating the same net force.) Then if $(c \text{ or } b)$ replaced c in the model, then e would still follow by an argument that mirrors the causal process that actually produced e, and generally the new model would no longer entail e if $(c \text{ or } b)$ were removed from it. But we do not regard $(c \text{ or } b)$ as explanatorily relevant. Rather, c is relevant. It might be suggested that the reason why c rather than $(c\&a)$ explains e is that c is weaker than $(c\&a)$ and still entails e. But this suggestion cannot be correct: $(c \text{ or } b)$ is weaker than c and still entails e, yet c rather than $(c \text{ or } b)$ explains e.

Strevens's solution to these problems, in brief, is to require that an explanation arise from "optimizing" a causal model. Part of optimizing it involves abstracting: $(c\&a)$ must be abstracted to c, since c says less than $(c\&a)$ does. (We cannot abstract to a, since the resulting model does not entail e.) However, Strevens says, abstraction must not be allowed to go too far: if c is abstracted to $(c \text{ or } b)$, then the model's metaphysically possible realizers may well be "incohesive" in that they fail to form a "contiguous set" in "causal similarity space." An explanation optimizes gain of abstraction against loss of cohesion.

Something like Strevens's strategy seems like a natural way to face the two obstacles. It deals nicely with Strevens's example of a cannonball that breaks a window exactly when its momentum (mass x velocity) exceeds 20 kg m/s. Intuitively, neither the ball's mass of 10 kg nor its speed of 5 m/s qualifies as an explainer, since the threshold involves momentum rather than either mass or velocity by itself. The condition that the ball's momentum exceeds 20 kg m/s is generated from the model's undergoing as much abstraction as it can withstand

(and involves no incohesion); further abstraction to the ball's momentum exceeding 10 kg m/s would prevent the model's entailing the window's breaking, and further abstraction to more than one projectile would produce incohesion. Strevens's approach thereby correctly identifies the explanatorily relevant feature. By abstracting mass or velocity separately, we would have gotten the wrong answer. The window would still have broken as long as the speed had exceeded 2 m/s (since the mass would still have been 10 kg, and so the momentum would have exceeded 20 kg m/s). But by treating velocity separately from mass, this approach fails to abstract far enough.

However, another case shows that Strevens's approach cannot pick out the reducible properties that are explanatorily powerful. Suppose that two point bodies charged to +5 statcoulombs and −6 statcoulombs, respectively, and long held at rest, 1 centimeter apart, are suddenly released in an otherwise empty universe (where other forces between them are negligible). By Coulomb's law $(F_e = q_1q_2/r^2)$, their mutual attraction measures 30 dynes. What explains this 30-dyne force? Just as Strevens's approach applied to the cannonball yields an explanation in terms of momentum mv, rather than in terms of mass m or velocity v separately, so the approach applied to this electrostatic case yields an explanation in terms of q_1q_2/r^2, rather than in terms of the individual charges or their separation. That the algebraic quantity q_1q_2/r^2 equals 30 dynes is as abstract as the model can become without incohesion; a serious loss of cohesion would result from abstracting further to, say, the fact that either q_1q_2/r^2 equals 30 dynes or q_1q_2/r^2 equals 15 dynes and the bodies also exert 15 dynes of some other kind of mutually attractive force. (Presumably, to introduce another species of non-negligible force would require crossing a gap in "causal similarity space"; the two disjuncts involve two quite different kinds of causal processes.) In contrast, small adjustments to q_1, q_2, and r that keep q_1q_2/r^2 equal to 30 dynes is as contiguous in causal similarity space as small adjustments to the cannonball's m and v that keep its momentum exceeding 20 kg m/s.

The point is that presumably, the force's magnitude is not in fact explained by the value of q_1q_2/r^2. Rather, it is explained by the values of q_1, q_2, and r, along with Coulomb's law and the absence of further influences. Strevens's requirement that an explanation abstract as far as possible (without undue sacrifice of cohesion) effaces the distinction between property combinations that are explanatorily significant in their own right (such as a system's having a given center of mass) and combinations that are mere conglomerates of the properties actually doing the explaining.

As another example, take one of Fick's laws of diffusion, namely, that the volume (V) of gas flowing across a tissue or membrane per unit time is directly proportional to the area (A) of the sheet, the difference $(P_1 - P_2)$ in the gas's partial pressures across the sheet, and the gas's solubility (S), and inversely proportional to the sheet's thickness (T) and to square root of the gas's molecular weight (m):

$$V \propto A\left(P_1 - P_2\right)S/T\sqrt{m}$$

Now $(P_1 - P_2)$ may well function as a unit in this explanation; pressure *differences*, not absolute values, are responsible for propelling the gas. But it is more doubtful that the entire right side of the above expression functions as a unit in an explanation. Yet as far as I can tell, maximal abstraction would drive us to this conclusion. There is a difference between a hodgepodge, ramshackle quantity such as reduced mass or $A(P_1 - P_2)S/T\sqrt{m}$, on the one hand, and momentum, density, work, and kinetic energy, on the other hand.

■ 11.4 DIMENSIONLESS QUANTITIES AS EXPLANATORILY POWERFUL REDUCIBLE PROPERTIES

Various dimensionless quantities are well-known examples of reducible properties that explain. Many are designated by the names of the scientists who discovered their explanatory significance, such as the Reynolds number, Prandtl number, Biot number, and Grashof number. For example, for a fluid flowing down a pipe where

ρ = fluid's density
v = fluid's mean speed of flow
d = pipe's linear dimension (e.g., its diameter, for a pipe with circular cross-section), and
η = fluid's viscosity,

the fluid's having a "Reynolds number" (Re) of n is identical to its having the above properties standing in a certain relation, namely, $n = \rho v d/\eta$. A fluid's Reynolds number is plainly a reducible property. Nevertheless, it is commonly said to "govern" or to "control" many features of the flow, such as whether it is laminar or turbulent—that is, whether the streamlines are parallel to the pipe's long axis and hold constant, or whether they change drastically and irregularly as eddies and vortices form and dissipate. There is no simple function from the Reynolds number to the flow's character. But two fluid systems that are alike in their background conditions (e.g., the pipe's geometry and smoothness, the external disturbances it feels) are alike in whether the flow is laminar or turbulent if they have the same Reynolds number.

The Reynolds number is not merely correlated with the flow's character; it helps to explain the flow's character: "In addition to geometry and pressure gradient, several other parameters influence separation. These include the Reynolds number as a very important parameter, with the wall's roughness . . . and the wall temperature having less but occasionally significant influence" (Potter, Wiggert, and Ramadan 2012, 351). Indeed, in fluid mechanics it is commonly said that the flow's character is explained by Re (along with various background conditions) *rather than* by ρ, v, d, or η taken individually—in other words, is explained by the more basic quantities only through their *relations* to one another in forming Re. Reynolds himself expressed his discovery in these terms, and modern textbooks agree:

> What appears to be the dependence of the character of the motion on the absolute size of the tube, and on the absolute velocity of the immersed liquid, must in reality be a dependence on the size of the tube as compared with the size of some other object, and on the velocity of the body as compared with some "other velocity." (Reynolds 1901, 53–54)

> Reynolds realized that the transition from laminar to turbulent flow did not depend on the pipe diameter, the flow velocity, or the fluid viscosity individually, but on the nondimensional grouping of those three parameters that we now call the Reynolds number. (Post 2011, 454)

Dimensionless quantities such as Re are especially useful in the construction of physical models for predicting the behavior of systems to which it is difficult in practice to apply the relevant fundamental equations. For instance, suppose we want to predict the force F that a large industrial stirrer of length d will experience while stirring (with speed v) a fluid of density ρ. By law, $F = \rho v^2 d^2\, \Phi(Re)$ for some function Φ of Re. Since in practice Φ cannot be predicted, the best way to predict F is to construct a smaller scale model of the stirrer with the same shape (and background conditions) so that Φ remains the same. If the model's d is one-tenth of the industrial stirrer's, for example, but the model's v is 10 times the industrial stirrer's, then (if the same fluid is used) they have the same Re. Then by using the model, the industrial stirrer's F can be discovered empirically.

So much for prediction; let's turn to explanation. Why does the model work— why do it and the industrial stirrer experience the same force? An explanation is that they have the same ρ, the model's v is 10 times the industrial stirrer's, the model's d is one-tenth the industrial stirrer's, they have the same Re, and by law $F = \rho v^2 d^2\, \Phi(Re)$ for some unspecified function Φ. Notice that Re is an explainer on a par with ρ, v, and d despite being a reducible property. In contrast, though the law could be expressed in terms of two reducible properties, $\rho v^2 d^2$ and Re, the former property is insufficiently natural to have explanatory power. I aim to account for this distinction.

Here is another way to appreciate it. Just as two seesaws both tip to the right because they are alike in having $(m_R x_R - m_L x_L) > 0$, so it is no coincidence that the modeled stirrer and the model experience the same force. They do so because they share certain other properties, notably Re. Likewise it is no coincidence that two instances of fluid flow are both turbulent; they are alike in that respect because they are alike in their pipe geometry (and other background conditions) and have the same Re. Thus, having the same Re must be a respect of similarity, so Re must be natural enough to explain. An account of the difference between natural and unnatural reducible properties should account for the naturalness of all dimensionless quantities that function in the same way as Re.

■ 11.5 MY PROPOSAL

In each of the cases that I have examined, a law L involving some reducible property P, together with some initial conditions that include P's instantiation, entail some outcome. When is P natural enough for its instantiation to be eligible to join with L and other initial conditions in explaining the outcome? I propose that P is natural enough to explain if and only if there is an explanation of L in which P (that is to say, the combination of properties to which it reduces) enters as a unit. For example, L must have an explanation (which need not be its only explanation) in which it is *not* the case that some of the properties to which P reduces enter under separate auspices from others so that it is only somewhere in the course of the derivation explaining L that these various properties happen to find themselves grouped together so as to form P. Intuitively, P is natural enough exactly when P figures in L as a result of entering an explanation of L as a unit rather than as a result of precipitating out over the course of any explanation of L by a kind of "algebraic miracle."

Let's apply this proposal to the seesaw example. The seesaw's $m_R x_R - m_L x_L$ is sufficiently natural to join the tipping law in explaining the seesaw's tipping to the right because it appears in the expression for the seesaw's center of mass, which figures in the tipping law, and the tipping law (in turn) has an explanation in which the system's center of mass (and hence its $m_R x_R - m_L x_L$) enters as a unit rather than emerging from factors that have entered separately. One such explanation proceeds from energy conservation. The only external forces on a system in the tipping law's scope are gravity and the force exerted by the support. Since the system is attached to its support, the supporting force cannot act through a distance and so only gravity can perform work on the system. Any change in the system's gravitational potential energy as a result of gravity's doing work on the system must be balanced by an equal and opposite change in the system's kinetic energy. The gravitational potential energy of a system in the tipping law's scope (i.e., under uniform gravity) is equal to the gravitational potential energy U of a hypothetical point particle having the system's mass M and located at its center of mass: $U = Mgh$, where h is the height of the center of mass. Here, then, is where the center of mass enters as a unit. A system initially at rest cannot begin to move, gaining kinetic energy, unless it thereby loses potential energy, and so if it begins to move, it must move so as to lower h. Moreover, it can begin to move exactly when there is a net force or a net torque on it, that is, exactly when $\partial U/\partial x \neq 0$ in some direction x in which it is free to move. This condition is met if and only if its center of mass is not located directly above or below a point of support. (For example, if its center of mass is directly above a point of support, then if the system moves a little while remaining attached rigidly to its support, its center of mass does not change its height, so U remains unchanged: $\partial U/\partial x = 0$.)

In this way, the tipping law is explained—and the center of mass's location (for the seesaw: $(m_R x_R - m_L x_L)/M$) enters this explanation as a unit. (In so doing, the seesaw's $m_R x_R$ and $m_L x_L$ also enter as units and so are also natural enough to help explain.) Of course, there are other ways to explain the tipping law in which the center of mass arises fortuitously in that the various, more basic properties figuring in the expression for the center of mass's location enter by playing different roles and come together to form that expression only in the course of the tipping law's derivation. For example, we could explain the tipping law by first finding the net torque $\tau = \Sigma (r_i \times F_i)$ produced by gravity to be $\tau = \Sigma (r_i \times m_i g)$ and then massaging this sum to isolate an expression for the center of mass's location. (From there, the explanation would take the internal torques' sum to vanish, by Newton's third law, and would then set the total torque equal to $I\alpha$.) The various properties to which the center of mass's location reduces enter this explanation under separate auspices: the r_i's as the lever arms in the component torques, the m_i's as factors in the forces creating each of those component torques. They do not all enter together, arriving prepackaged in the expression for the center of mass's location—as they do in the above explanation from energy conservation.[7] On my proposal, the existence of a single explanation of the tipping law in which the center of mass's location enters as a unit suffices to make that property natural enough to explain.

One does not need to know every detail of some explanation of the tipping law in which the center of mass's location enters as a unit in order to have good reason to believe that there is such an explanation, and hence that the seesaw's $(m_R x_R - m_L x_L)$ is natural enough to explain. Likewise, one who has not examined all possible explanations of the tipping law may justly believe that there is no explanation into which $(x_R - m_L x_L/m_R)$ enters as a unit, on the grounds that this combination of quantities seems quite arbitrary. Of course, further investigation might reveal that an arbitrary-looking quantity is not actually arbitrary after all. Nevertheless, one who has examined some but not all possible explanations of the tipping law, and also has some background knowledge of physics, may be warranted in being very confident that a given arbitrary-looking quantity fails to enter as a unit into any explanation of the tipping law.

In order for a derivation of the tipping law from energy conservation to explain why the tipping law holds, energy conservation does not have to be a "constraint" in the sense that I elaborated in part I. The derivation can proceed simply from the fact that *gravitational* interactions conserve energy (and that gravity alone is at work in this case) rather than from the general principle that all kinds of fundamental interactions conserve energy. The derivation would then be a causal explanation, not an explanation by constraint.

Let's look at another case where my proposal applies regardless of whether the explanation is causal or non-causal. In chapter 2, I gave another example where a conglomerate enters as a unit in an explanation from a conservation law, though not in an explanation that specifies the particular forces involved. The weight of the fluid displaced by a submerged body is a reducible property that helps to explain the buoyant force on the body. The covering law in this explanation is Archimedes's principle: that the buoyant force on a body surrounded by an ideally incompressible, nonviscous fluid in a container at rest in a uniform downward gravitational field equals the weight of the fluid displaced by the body. Let's review the two explanations of Archimedes's principle that I contrasted in chapter 2.

It is explained hydrostatically by the difference in pressure on the upper and lower surfaces of the submerged body. The weight of the displaced fluid does not enter this explanation as a unit. Rather, in the course of the derivation, there arise separately various factors that eventually coalesce to form an expression that turns out to equal to the weight of the displaced fluid: $A\rho gh$ for fluid density ρ, taking the submerged body for simplicity as a cylinder of height h with horizontal top and bottom surfaces, each of area A. (Any body can be taken as consisting of cylindrical elements.) The various factors in this expression enter the derivation separately: ρg as the rate at which the pressure changes with height, h as the difference in height between the body's upper and lower surfaces, and A as the factor by which the pressure on an upper or lower surface must be multiplied to yield the force downward or upward on that surface.

Archimedes's principle can also be explained by energy conservation, according to which the work done by the force just sufficient to raise the submerged body by some arbitrary distance d is equal to the energy thereby added to the system. With the body's rise, its gravitational potential energy rises by $W_b d$, where W_b is the body's weight. As the body rises, fluid flows downward to fill the space it vacates. As a result of its journey, the body effectively trades places with a fluid parcel of the body's size and shape that was initially located at a distance d above the body's initial position. That parcel thus descends by d, so its gravitational potential energy diminishes by $W_p d$, where W_p is the parcel's weight. Setting the work done equal to the net increase in the system's potential energy, we find $Fd = W_b d - W_p d$. Therefore, $F = W_b - W_p$. By contrast, had there been no fluid, then the force just sufficient to raise the body would have been simply W_b—just enough to balance the body's weight. But with the fluid present, we need less force by W_p: the weight of the fluid displaced by the body. That upward force supplementing F is the buoyant force.

In this explanation, W_p enters as a unit—in contrast to the hydrodynamic explanation. The explanation from energy conservation, then, reveals it to be no coincidence that each of the various factors to which W_p reduces figures in the expression for the buoyant force. In other words, this explanation reveals that each of these factors appears in that expression *for the very same reason*. They appear there together because they enter the derivation together rather than from different places. They have a common origin. On my proposal, this explanation thus makes W_p natural enough (despite being reducible) to join Archimedes's principle in explaining the magnitude of the buoyant force on a given body.[8]

As I argued in chapter 2, this explanation may appeal to the general principle of energy conservation. That principle must then be a constraint. Alternatively, this explanation may appeal merely to the fact that *gravitational* interactions conserve energy (and that only gravity is at work in this case). Then we have here a causal explanation. Whether it is causal or non-causal, an explanation from energy conservation makes W_p natural enough to join Archimedes's principle in explaining the magnitude of a given buoyant force.

Of course, even on the hydrodynamic explanation, it is no accident (in the manner of all gold cubes being smaller than a cubic meter) that the various factors in the weight $A\rho g h$ of the displaced fluid all manage to find their way into the expression for the buoyant force. It is a matter of natural necessity. But the explanation from energy conservation (whether causal or non-causal), unlike the hydrodynamical explanation, reveals it to be no coincidence that there come together just the factors that give the weight of the displaced fluid. Only that explanation reveals the common source of all of these factors. That the *submerged body's* size and shape should combine with the *fluid's* density in an expression for the buoyant force is no coincidence considering that they all characterize the displaced parcel of fluid, which itself figures in the derivation from energy conservation. All of these factors thus enter that derivation together.

That the derivation from energy conservation treats the parcel of fluid (and its weight $A\rho g h$) as a unit throughout is reminiscent of an example of explanation in mathematics from section 7.6. There I compared two proofs of the fact that for any triangular number T, $8T + 1$ is a square number. One proof proceeded geometrically, treating a given triangular number's triangle as a unit and assembling eight of these units (plus a 1 x 1 square) into a large square. The other proof proceeded algebraically, breaking apart the expression for a given triangular number into its components and then rearranging and reassembling them until a perfect square arose from out of the welter of algebra. I argued that in a context where the theorem's striking feature is its geometric or "polygonal" character (made especially salient by the theorem's being expressed in terms of "polygonal numbers"), only the geometric proof explains why the theorem holds. Just as this theorem's salient feature in a given context may be its involving polygonal numbers, so too in a given context the salient feature of Archimedes's principle may be that it involves the weight of the displaced fluid parcel. In such a context, the question "Why does Archimedes's principle hold?" may not be asking why there is some buoyant force rather than more, less, or none at all. Instead it may be asking why the weight of the displaced fluid figures in the expression for the buoyant force—what one has got to do with the other. Just as a proof of the theorem about triangular and square numbers may in a certain context acquire explanatory power by virtue of operating on the polygons as units, so in a certain context the derivation of Archimedes's principle from energy conservation may (by treating the displaced fluid parcel as a unit) be able to explain what that parcel's weight is doing in the expression for the buoyant force. Of course, just as even the algebraic proof of the theorem about triangular and square numbers shows the theorem to be a mathematical necessity, so even the hydrodynamic derivation of Archimedes's principle shows it to be a natural necessity that the weight of the displaced fluid parcel figures in the expression for the buoyant force. But the hydrodynamic derivation does not *explain why* the weight of the displaced fluid parcel appears in the expression for the buoyant force, since its presence there turns out to be no coincidence (by virtue of the derivation from energy conservation).

By this, I mean that it is no "physical coincidence" (rather than that it is no "mathematical coincidence"). For each of the various factors A, ρ, g, and h to which the weight of the displaced fluid parcel reduces, there is a common scientific explainer of its presence in the buoyant-force expression, so their all being present together in that expression is no physical coincidence. Nevertheless, the notion of salience that I first mentioned in connection with explanation in mathematics plays a role here, too. If the result's notable feature is its involving the weight of the displaced fluid, then to reveal the result to be no coincidence, an explanation must trace it back to a similar notable feature of the setup. The explanation from energy conservation does this by deriving the buoyant-force expression from the role played in the setup by the parcel of displaced fluid.

Even if the various properties to which a given reducible property reduces enter the explanation together, it does not follow that the reducible property enters as a unit. Those properties may all enter together, but not in an expression of the relation among them that is identical to the reducible property. For instance, take the explanation of the tipping law that I gave earlier in which the location of the center of mass (for the seesaw: $(m_R x_R - m_L x_L)/M$) enters as a unit. Suppose we add a step to the end of this explanation: having derived the law that the seesaw tips to the right if $(m_R x_R - m_L x_L) > 0$, we draw the conclusion that the seesaw tips to the right if $(x_R - m_L x_L/m_R) > 0$, thereby explaining why this derivative law holds. The various properties to which the seesaw's $x_R - m_L x_L/m_R$ reduces all enter the derivation together. But they do not enter as the unit $x_R - m_L x_L/m_R$; rather, they enter in the expression $(m_R x_R - m_L x_L)$ in the numerator of the seesaw's center of mass. Thus, the reducible property $x_R - m_L x_L/m_R$ does not enter as a unit, and so on my proposal, this explanation does not make the seesaw's $x_R - m_L x_L/m_R$ sufficiently natural to explain.

Let's look at another seesaw example: a seesaw on each arm of which is placed the same number N of bodies of negligible size having various masses, all piled up at the same distance $x = x_R = x_L$ from the fulcrum. Consider the covering law that under these circumstances, the seesaw tips to the right if the average mass of a body on the right is greater than the average mass of a body on the left. Plainly, though this derivative law predicts the outcome, it does not explain the outcome; the *average* masses on the right and left are *not* the explanatorily relevant features. The two averages $(m_{avR} = m_R/N_R$ and $m_{avL} = m_L/N_L)$ are merely artifacts of properties that can explain the outcome: the *total* masses m_R and m_L on the two wings (along with the seesaw's other conditions, including $x_R = x_L$). (An explanation could just as well proceed from the masses of the individual bodies.) The seesaw tips to the right because there is more mass on the right (and various other conditions hold, crucially $x_R = x_L$), not because there are equal numbers of bodies on the two arms and the average mass of a body on the right is greater than the average mass of a body on the left. Talk of averages here is just an unnecessarily roundabout way of getting at the explanatorily relevant fact that there is more mass on the right.

My proposal accounts for the averages being too unnatural to explain. Take the explanation of the tipping law that I gave earlier. Having explained the law that the seesaw tips to the right if $(m_R x_R - m_L x_L) > 0$, we now add some further steps at the end to derive the law covering this special case:

since $x_R = x_L$, the seesaw tips to the right if $(m_R - m_L) > 0$, which is to say (since $N > 0$) if $(m_R - m_L)/N > 0$, that is (since $N = N_R = N_L$), if $(m_R/N_R - m_L/N_L) > 0$, that is, if $m_{avR} > m_{avL}$.

Plainly, m_{avR} and m_{avL} do not enter as units; m_R (m_L) enters under different auspices from N_R (N_L) and they coalesce into the average only at the end. Intuitively, whereas m_R and m_L enter naturally (back in the tipping law's derivation), N_R and N_L enter artificially—merely to generate averages—and that is why the average masses fail to explain. My account captures this intuition.

My proposal likewise deems reduced mass explanatorily idle. In my earlier examples, the explanandum in a two-body problem was entailed by premises including the pair's reduced mass $\mu = m_1 m_2 / (m_1 + m_2)$ and the law that the first body moves relative to the second in the manner of a point body feeling the same force as the first body feels but with mass equal to the pair's μ. On my proposal, whether μ is natural enough to explain depends on whether this law has an explanation in which μ enters as a unit. Here is a standard explanation of this law:

By Newton's second law,

$$m_1 a_1 = F_{12}$$
$$m_2 a_2 = F_{21}$$

where F_{ij} is the force on body i exerted by body j, m_i is the ith body's mass, and a_i is the ith body's total acceleration (since in a two-body problem, the only forces are their mutual interactions). By Newton's third law,

$$F_{12} = -F_{21}.$$

Hence,

$$m_1 a_1 = -m_2 a_2,$$

so

$$a_2 = (-m_1 / m_2) a_1.$$

The first body's acceleration relative to the second is then

$$a_1 - a_2 = a_1 + (m_1/m_2)a_1 = (1 + m_1/m_2)a_1 = ((m_1 + m_2)/m_2)a_1 =$$
$$((m_1 + m_2)/m_1 m_2)m_1 a_1 = F_{12}/\mu.$$

Obviously, μ does not enter this explanation as a unit. Rather, m_1 and m_2 enter playing different roles and μ emerges fortuitously. Thus, on my view, μ and $(m_1 + m_2)$ and $m_1 m_2$ are all too unnatural to explain here.[9] The reduced mass figures in the two-body result as a matter of coincidence (though its appearance there is naturally necessary, of course). There is no common source of the various factors to which it reduces.

The explanation from energy conservation makes W_p natural enough to join Archimedes's principle in explaining the magnitude of the buoyant force whether that conservation-law explanation is causal or non-causal. Nevertheless, the existence of various non-causal explanations makes certain quantities natural enough to explain that would otherwise not be. Dimensional explanations of the kind that occupied the bulk of chapter 6 are a good example. In the previous section, I suggested that an account of why certain reducible properties but not others are natural enough to possess explanatory power should account for the naturalness of various dimensionless quantities, such as the Reynolds number Re. On my account, these quantities acquire their explanatory power by virtue of entering as units (that is, as wholes) into the dimensional explanations of various derivative laws. In one important kind of dimensional explanation (as I argued in chapter 6), the explanans is that some property v stands in a "dimensionally homogeneous" relation to some subset of other properties $s, t, u \ldots$—that is, a relation that holds for any system of units (e.g., meters and feet) for the various dimensions (e.g., length) of the quantities so related. From this premise, various features of the law $v = f(s, t, u \ldots)$ can be deduced and thereby explained as required by the dimensional architecture. If there is some dimensionless combination of $s, t, u \ldots$, then the dimensional argument can explain the law only up to an unspecified function of that combination; dimensional analysis alone is unable to specify the function. That is how a dimensionless combination enters as a unit into a dimensional explanation and thus becomes natural enough to possess explanatory power.

For instance, let's look at a dimensional explanation of the law appearing in the example from the previous section: that the force F that a large industrial stirrer of length d will experience while stirring (with speed v) a fluid of density ρ is equal to $\rho v^2 d^2 \, \Phi(Re)$ for some function Φ. The explanans is that F stands in a dimensionally homogeneous relation to $d, \rho, \eta,$ and v. It follows that the law takes the form $F = d^a \rho^b \eta^c v^e \Psi(\rho v d / \eta)$ for some unspecified function Ψ, since $\rho v d / \eta$ is dimensionless. Thus, the combination $\rho v d / \eta$ forming Re enters as a unit; it does not coalesce in the course of the derivation. The rest of the explanation involves giving the dimensions of each quantity and then solving for a, b, c, and e:

	F	d	ρ	η	v	
Mass	1	0	1	1	0	so $1 = b + c$
Length	1	1	-3	-1	1	so $1 = a - 3b - c - e$
Time	-2	0	0	-1	-1	so $-2 = -c - e$

Hence, $e = 2 - c$

$\qquad b = 1 - c$

$\qquad a = 2 - c.$

So $F = d^{2-c} \rho^{1-c} \eta^c v^{2-c} \Psi(\rho v d / \eta) = \rho v^2 d^2 (\rho v d / \eta)^{-c} \Psi(\rho v d / \eta) = \rho v^2 d^2 \Phi(\rho v d / \eta)$ for some unspecified function Φ.

By entering into and then behaving in this explanation as a unit, Re acquires explanatory significance.[10]

Other dimensionless quantities likewise possess explanatory power in virtue of functioning as units in dimensional explanations. For example, from a dimensional explanation of the law $P = W \, \Phi(h/l)$ [for some unspecified function Φ] concerning the tension P of a length l of cable having weight W and sag h between two points at the same height and a fixed distance apart, Douglas

(1969, 37) concludes that "the ratio h/l is a determining factor in the relationship rather than the separate quantities h and l." I do not interpret Douglas as claiming that h and l have no explanatory power themselves, merely that they do not explain except relative to each other—that is, except by way of h/l explaining.[11]

■ 11.6 CONCLUSION: ALL VARIETIES OF EXPLANATION AS SPECIES OF THE SAME GENUS

I have just looked at the seesaw's center of mass $(m_R x_R - m_L x_L)$ and $x_R - m_L x_L/m_R$ (and its m_{avR} and m_{avL}), a two-body problem's reduced mass, a submerged body's W_p, and a fluid's Reynolds number. In each case, the proposal I have offered gives the correct verdict regarding which reducible properties are natural enough to be explanatorily powerful. My proposal captures the intuition that a reducible property fails to explain when it is an arbitrary conglomerate of properties. A reducible property that enters the covering law's explanation as a prepackaged unit, rather than emerging fortuitously out of an algebraic fog, is no arbitrary combination.

For instance, the various factors A, ρ, g, and h to which the weight of the displaced fluid parcel reduces do not coalesce gradually as Archimedes's principle is derived from energy conservation. Rather, they all enter the derivation together as W_p and then remain together so that W_p ends up in the final expression for the buoyant force. On my view, this feature of the derivation's route allows the explanation of Archimedes's principle to endow W_p with the power to help explain a particular buoyant force. This proposal marks a further instance of a theme that has run through the entire course of this book: that a given argument's significance for explanation, whether in mathematics or in science, may depend not just on the argument's premises and conclusion, but also on the particular route that the argument takes from its premises to its conclusion.

I have declared this theme repeatedly. For instance, I showed in chapter 4 that Poisson's derivation of the parallelogram of forces (unlike Duchayla's) uses the same steps to derive the parallelogram law's holding for direction as it does to derive the law's holding for magnitude. This feature of the explanation's route allows the explanation to make it no coincidence that the parallelogram law holds for both magnitude and direction. In the same way, I showed in chapter 10 that analogous derivative laws in thermodynamics and electrostatics are explained by analogous derivations from distinct, more fundamental laws, making it no mathematical coincidence that the two derivative laws are alike. Likewise, in various mathematical explanations that I examined in chapters 8 and 9, some theorem (such that all "calculator numbers" are divisible by 37) turns out to be no coincidence not just because each of its components follows from the same premises in the setup, but crucially because the steps by which each follows are precisely the same.

My proposal thus has an important affinity with Kitcher's (1989) unification-ist account of scientific explanation. That account, unlike covering-law accounts, focuses not merely on the existence of some inferential relation between the explanans and explanandum, but also (and primarily) on the route by which that inference proceeds—the structure of the argument connecting them (Kitcher 1989, 430–431). Kitcher's account recognizes something that I have repeatedly shown: the explanatory importance of the same argument pattern being instan-tiated in different cases. Unlike Kitcher, I have not suggested that an argument's explanatory power arises from its pattern earning admission into the set of argu-ment patterns possessing an optimal combination of various properties (such as breadth of coverage, stringency of filling instructions, and economy). But I have highlighted several ways in which it can make a difference to explanation whether two arguments involve the same steps or different ones.

So far in this chapter, I have proceeded as if the distinction between explana-torily powerful and powerless reducible physical properties were a sharp dis-tinction. But this seems to me an oversimplification. The distinction appears to be more plausibly a matter of degree; some properties may be sufficiently natu-ral to have some explanatory power, but insufficiently natural to have much of it. My proposal leaves opportunities for such intermediate cases.[12] For instance, a property P might enter a given explanation of L as a unit, but only because this explanation of L is not much of an explanation; it derives L so trivially from facts standing so close to L that it supplies little information about where L ultimately comes from. If this is the only explanation of L that P enters as a unit, then P has little naturalness but it is not an utterly arbitrary combination of quantities.

Let's look briefly at a possible example. In section 11.3, I showed that accord-ing to Strevens's account of scientific explanation, the force between a pair of point charges suddenly released at rest in an otherwise empty universe (feel-ing negligible nonelectrostatic forces) is explained by Coulomb's law (concern-ing the electric force between two point charges that have long been at rest) together with the pair's q_1q_2/r^2. I suggested that in fact, this reducible property is too unnatural to explain. But perhaps this quantity does not quite fall at the extreme "unnatural" end of the spectrum. On my proposal, this property is natural enough to explain exactly when it appears as a unit in an explanation of Coulomb's law. Does it? According to some authors (e.g., Serway and Jewett 2008, 642), Coulomb's law is fundamental; that is, has no explanation. In that case, trivially q_1q_2/r^2 does not enter as a unit into an explanation of Coulomb's law. Other authors regard Coulomb's law as explained by being derived from Maxwell's equations.[13] In that case, my account again deems q_1q_2/r^2 to be explan-atorily powerless since q_1q_2/r^2 does not enter this explanation as a unit. However,

Coulomb's law is a special case of the general formula[14] for the electric force F_e between two point bodies with unchanging charges (q_1 and q_2) that have been in arbitrary relative motion:

$$F_e = q_1 q_2 \left[u/R^2 + (R/c)\left(u/R^2\right)' + \left(u''/c^2\right) \right]$$

where
   R is the distance between the body feeling the force and the position of the body exerting the force at the "retarded time" (that is, the moment when an electromagnetic wave (traveling at speed c) arriving at the body feeling the force would have left the body exerting the force),
   a prime (') denotes the rate of change of the preceding quantity,
   a double-prime (") denotes the rate of change of the rate of change of the preceding quantity,
   and u is the unit vector pointing from the body feeling the force directly away from the other body's position at the retarded time.

Coulomb's law follows trivially from this formula for the case where the bodies have not been moving: all rates of change are zero (so the second and third terms vanish) and R in the static case is equal to the bodies' current separation. If this quick derivation is an explanation of Coulomb's law, then it is a rather slight one; Coulomb's law just falls trivially out of the more general formula. So although $q_1 q_2/r^2$ enters this derivation as a unit (in the formula's first term), it does not thereby merit a place far along toward the explanatorily powerful end of the spectrum.[15]

On my proposal, a reducible property is natural by virtue of entering a scientific explanation as a unit. In some important ways, this view is similar to chapter 9's account of what makes a mathematical property natural. For example, I argued there that the property of being a point in projective geometry (that is, a Euclidean point *or* a point at infinity) is natural (rather than wildly disjunctive) by virtue of figuring in various mathematical explanations that succeed in explaining by treating all of these points alike. In the same way, two systems with the same Reynolds number are thereby alike (that is, having the same Re constitutes a genuine respect of similarity) by virtue of certain scientific explanations in which Re functions as a unit—explanations that thereby give uniform treatment to systems with equal Re's. Two projective points (or two systems with the same Reynolds number) may behave in the same way for the same reasons, and this is what makes the projective points (or the systems with a given Reynolds number) form a natural class. In both cases, there is an intimate connection between naturalness and explanatory role.[16] It makes no difference to this connection whether the explanation is mathematical or scientific, just as it does not matter to this connection whether the scientific explanation at hand is causal or non-causal.

The basis of this connection between naturalness and explanatory role can be appreciated more readily when all varieties of explanation are recognized as alike in being able to show various similarities to be no coincidence. The notion of a "coincidence" has arisen many times in the course of this book. Here is a brief reminder of some of those occasions. That we are both in Chicago at the same time is no coincidence when our similarity in this respect derives from some other similarity between us: an interesting common cause of our each being there. That all "calculator numbers" are divisible by 37 is no coincidence by virtue of this similarity's having an explanation in deriving (in the same way for each calculator number) from each calculator number's being expressible as the same kind of sum. That two Diophantine equations have exactly the same positive solutions is a coincidence since this result has no proof that uniformly traces each equation's having these solutions to some other respect in which the two equations are alike. That two double pendulums are alike in having at least four equilibrium configurations is no coincidence by virtue of their doing so for the same reason (namely, because they have similar configuration spaces from being double pendulums). That every kind of fundamental interaction conserves energy is no coincidence if energy conservation is a constraint and so serves as a common explainer of energy's conservation by each kind of fundamental interaction. That all force laws are Lorentz covariant is coincidental if it is explained separately for each force rather than from a common set of symmetry metalaws and other constraints on every possible kind of force. That the parallelogram of forces holds for both magnitude and direction is a coincidence on Duchayla's proposed explanation; although that proposal derives these two results from common premises, it does not derive them in the same way. Instead, it uses one to arrive at the other. That various derivative thermodynamic and electrostatic laws are mathematically alike is no coincidence since the fundamental laws from which they arise have the same mathematical structure. The more fundamental laws leave us with exactly the same mathematical problem in each case, and that is why the two problems have analogous answers; their doing so is therefore no mathematical coincidence (though it remains physically coincidental). That the expressions for the speeds of various physically dissimilar waves are so much alike is no coincidence considering that the two cases have the same dimensional architecture and so the expressions for the speeds receive the same kind of dimensional explanation. That the rate of emission from radioactive samples as well as the rate of heads outcomes from a coin's tosses are both more consistent over long periods than over short periods is no coincidence considering that both phenomena are statistical and so receive the same kind of RS explanation. That various physically diverse quantities all compose parallelogramwise is no coincidence considering that the reason they share the same composition law is because they share certain symmetries. That the various factors in the weight $A\rho gh$ of the displaced fluid all manage to find their way into the expression for the buoyant force, appearing there as *Aρgh,* is no coincidence considering that the weight of the displaced fluid parcel enters as a unit into the explanation of Archimedes's principle from energy conservation. Two seesaws' having similar $m_R x_R - m_L x_L$ makes it no coincidence that they both tilt to the right; they behave alike because there is another property they have in common (namely, having $m_R x_R - m_L x_L > 0$).

As I have shown over the preceding chapters, these ways of being a coincidence (or no coincidence) are not exactly the same. Some involve having no important common cause. Others involve having no important common explainer that is not a cause, such as common mathematical or dimensional structure. Others involve having no common derivation explaining them (even if they have important common explainers). Yet others involve having no common *kind* of derivation (from distinct explainers).[17] Nevertheless, there is a common thread running through these various ways of being a coincidence. This common thread not only ties together the different varieties of explanation (causal and non-causal, mathematical and scientific), but also relates them all to a property's status as natural.

The thread running through all of these varieties of coincidence in science and mathematics is roughly that a similarity is coincidental when it is not explained by another similarity, whereas a similarity is no coincidence when it turns out to be explained by another similarity. This common thread entails that explanations in science and mathematics, despite their diversity, are alike in their capacity to render similarities non-coincidental. Furthermore, an explanation's power to render some similarity non-coincidental depends upon its appealing to another similarity. Since a natural property is a respect in which things can be similar, there is automatically a connection between explanations and the naturalness of properties. Once again, this connection does not depend on whether we are dealing with causal or non-causal explanation. For instance, as I just argued, when an explanation of Archimedes's principle makes W_p natural enough to join Archimedes's principle in explaining the magnitude of some buoyant force, the explanation of Archimedes's principle may be causal (appealing to the fact that gravitational interactions in particular conserve energy) or non-causal (appealing to the constraint that all kinds of fundamental interactions must conserve energy).

I have suggested in this chapter that a reducible property is natural by virtue of its playing certain roles in explanations (and to the degree that it plays those roles). For example, having a given Reynolds number is a natural property (and so two systems' having the same Reynolds number explains their shared turbulent behavior) by virtue of the Reynolds number entering and functioning as a unit in dimensional explanations. A dimensional explanation can make it no coincidence that physically diverse systems share some property by tracing that similarity to the systems' shared dimensional architecture. But what, in turn, makes two systems' having the same dimensional architecture amount to a respect in which they are similar (that is, a natural property)? Plausibly, its status as a respect of similarity arises together with its role in dimensional explanations—in the same way as properties in projective geometry constitute respects of similarity (i.e., mathematically natural properties) by virtue of their roles in explanations in mathematics (as I argued in chapter 9). These explanations (e.g., of Desargues's theorem in projective geometry) treat all projective points alike (whether they are Euclidean points or points at infinity) rather than having to treat several special cases separately. These explanations thereby reveal it to be no coincidence that these cases are alike in various respects.

In both mathematics and science—and for both causal and non-causal explanations—there are tight connections between being an explanation, being able to render similarities non-coincidental, and being a natural property (that is, a respect of similarity). These common features contribute toward making all of these varieties of explanation, both mathematical and scientific, into species of the same genus.[18] To this extent, the property of being an explanation is a natural property, too.

◼ NOTES

◼ **Preface**

1. My title thus stands in counterpoint to Salmon's remark: "The time has come, it seems to me, to put the 'cause' back into 'because'" (Salmon 1984, 96). My title also evokes the "switch from 'cause' to 'because'" in Harman's (1973, 130) suggestion that our observations confirm hypotheses concerning not merely what *causes* observed facts, but also what *explains* them, such as laws of nature.

2. See, for instance, Salmon (1984), Lewis (1986b), Woodward (2003), and Strevens (2009).

3. "Nobody believes now that science *explains* anything; we all look upon it as a shorthand description, as an economy of thought" (Pearson 1911, v; see 111).

4. As I have mentioned, I will invoke various examples of explanations in mathematics and science. Perhaps some of these examples are not in fact explanations after all—perhaps because the "fact" purportedly being explained turns out not to obtain, or perhaps because it is a fact but some of the "facts" that are being called on to explain it turn out not to obtain. (Whether and, if so, how an explanation can appeal to idealizations, approximations, and claims that are implicitly hedged or qualified is a difficult question; we often regard classical physics as explanatory even though, interpreted "strictly," it is false.) Even if for these reasons some of my examples are not genuine explanations, they can still help us to understand how explanations work. Presumably, there are genuine explanations that work in the same ways as these examples were once thought to work.

◼ **Chapter 1**

1. Salmon (1984, 278) leaves perhaps a bit of room for non-causal scientific explanation, but not much: "It is my hope that the causal theory of scientific explanation outlined in this book is reasonably adequate for the characterization of explanation in most scientific contexts—in the physical, biological, and social sciences—as long as we do not become involved in quantum mechanics."

2. Though Lewis confines his remark to the explanation of a particular event, he also says (1986b, 225) that to explain a general kind of event (e.g., why struck matches light) is to describe similarities in the causal histories of the events of that kind. Furthermore, the passage from Lewis that I quoted in the third paragraph of the preface ("an explanation, I think, is an account of etiology"; 1986a, 73–74) explicitly covers all kinds of explanation, whether the fact being explained is singular, general, or existential.

3. Sober carefully limits himself to explanations of single events; he recognizes that there are explanations of natural laws and of mathematical truths, and he does not declare all of those explanations to be causal (though he does not discuss those kinds of explanations further in Sober 1984).

4. The example from Colyvan (1998, 2001) is somewhat more complicated: it concerns the fact that there are antipodal points at the same temperature *and pressure*, and so requires the Borsuk-Ulam theorem in place of the intermediate value theorem. The example from Colyvan (2007) is isomorphic to mine, which frequently appears in introductory calculus texts (e.g., Brannan 2006, 145–146).

402 ■ NOTES TO CHAPTER 1

As another example, consider the fact that in every layer of air extending over the entire globe, there is a point at which there is no wind tangential to that layer. This fact is explained (when the vectors giving tangential wind direction and speed at all points in the layer are taken to form a continuous vector field) by the "hairy ball theorem" (a.k.a. the "Poincaré-Hopf fixed-point theorem") of algebraic topology: that every continuous tangent vector field on an n-sphere with even n must vanish somewhere. (An ordinary sphere has $n = 2$.) Around the zero-wind point the winds will form a cyclone.

As yet another example (suggested by Luke Elson), consider the fact that no one has ever made a planar map of the Earth that does not exhibit some distortion. This fact is famously explained by Gauss's theorema egregium, a corollary of which is that an undistorted planar map of a curved surface is impossible.

5. Kitcher (1989, 426) mentions a different knot case as an example of non-causal explanation.

6. Mancosu's definition is endorsed by Baker (2012, 244).

7. No one believes that a causal explanation must appeal *exclusively* to causes of the explanandum, since a causal explanation can appeal to laws, and laws are not causes; they are not events occurring at some spatiotemporal location. The issue is whether a causal explanation could appeal to *no* causes at all.

8. Unlike the uniform motion of a body feeling nonzero forces that sum to zero. Such a body's uniform motion has causes (namely, the component forces).

Of course, the philosophical views that all causes are events, that absences are not events, and (as I will mention shortly) that dispositions are not causes have not gone unchallenged. My main point is not to endorse these views, but to emphasize that even if these views are correct, explanations that appeal to absences or to dispositions derive their explanatory power in fundamentally the same way as more familiar causal explanations. (If these views are incorrect because absences or dispositions are causes, then it is even more evident that explanations appealing to them are causal.)

9. Sober (personal communication, June 2012) now regards equilibrium explanations as causal explanations on the grounds that an equilibrium explanation specifies how the explanandum would (or would not) have been different had the explanans been different in various respects. On the same grounds, Sober also takes Mother's having 3 children and 23 strawberries as causally explaining why she failed a moment ago when she tried to distribute her strawberries evenly among her children; the explanandum can be manipulated by manipulating the numbers of children and strawberries. As I will shortly explain, I agree that the numbers of children and strawberries are causes of the outcome. But on my view, it does not follow that the explanation is causal. The numbers of children and strawberries are not functioning as causes in the explanation.

10. Thus, Sober (1984) can consistently maintain that the equilibrium explanation of some event is not a causal explanation while holding that "the explanation of an event describes the 'causal structure' in which it is embedded" (Sober 1984, 96)—but only by defining "causal explanation" more narrowly than as explanation that works by describing the "causal structure" in which the explanandum is embedded. On that broader conception (mine), an equilibrium explanation is a causal explanation.

11. Likewise, Achinstein (1983, 231–233) contends that since Roger Cotes believed that the power to exert gravitational forces is an ultimate and simple disposition of bodies, Cotes believed that nothing causes the Moon to exert forces on the waters of the Earth, so although Cotes took Newton's gravitational-force law as explaining why the Moon exerts forces on the

Earth's waters, Cotes did not regard this explanation as causal. Achinstein uses this example to argue that any explanation is non-causal if the explanandum is a regularity and the explanation works by revealing the explanandum to be a special case of a law. By contrast, I believe that Cotes should have regarded the Newtonian explanation as working by virtue of supplying information about the world's causal structure, including that gravitational forces are caused by distant masses, that the Moon's disposition to attract the Earth's waters is the composition of the dispositions of its constituent bodies to exert gravitational forces, and that these causal powers, in turn, are primitive. The key to Achinstein's argument is his contention that "the existence of a regularity is not caused by the existence of a law of which that regularity is a special case" (Achinstein 1983, 232). Of course, I agree. But as the Coulombic line-charge example illustrates, the explanation of a regularity as a special case of a law can still work by virtue of supplying information about causal relations.

12. I will make a similar point in section 5.2; see especially note 2 (and the surrounding text).

13. Suppose that a cloud of dust particles changes its shape because each dust particle feels negligible forces, so (by an analogue of Newton's first law) each is moving inertially, but the cloud is moving through space that is curved in such a way that the geodesics bring the dust particles closer together or farther apart. Nerlich (1979, 74) regards this explanation as non-causal because the curvature of space is not a force; space's geometry is not a cause. Admitting that this explanation cites no causes, I nevertheless regard it as a causal explanation since it works by specifying the causes (forces) that are acting on the dust particles (namely, none) as well as the laws and conditions determining how things in the particles' locations would behave were they under the influence of no causes. All of these facts are made explanatorily relevant by their significance for the network of causal relations. (Skow (2014) also regards this explanation as causal.) However, in section 3.4, I will look at a non-causal explanation of Newton's first law as well as another explanation (also involving the geometry of space) that Nerlich rightly considers non-causal.

14. See also my remarks about "constitutive explanations" in the preface.

15. A philosopher who adopts a narrower conception of "causal explanation" than mine will obviously find it easier to argue that some scientific explanations are "non-causal." But she will do so by characterizing as "non-causal" some explanations that seem to me to have great affinities with explanations that are uncontroversially causal. For example, suppose we explain why a body moves uniformly by appealing to the fact that it feels no forces (and hence to the absence of any causes of the body's motion). By my lights, we are giving a causal explanation. But it is not the case that "The reason the body moves uniformly is that it feels no forces" is true exactly when "The cause of the body's moving uniformly is that it feels no forces" (since the former is true but the latter is false, if omissions are not causes). Because these are not equivalent, Achinstein (1983, 230–231) concludes that the explanation is non-causal. But this explanation seems to me very similar to explanations of accelerated motion that appeal to forces, as well as to explanations of uniform motion that appeal to nonzero forces that sum to zero. By the same token, Achinstein (231–233) says that when a derivative law is explained by a more fundamental law that entails it, this explanation is non-causal because the following two claims regarding (for example) the derivative law for the electric field of a static, long, linear, uniform charge distribution are not equivalent: "The reason that the derivative law holds is that Coulomb's law holds" and "The cause of the derivative law's holding is that Coulomb's law holds." (The latter is false since—Achinstein and I agree—laws are not causes.) I think that an explanation of the line-charge law by Coulomb's law is very much like an explanation of a particular electric field by Coulomb's law together with the fact

that the nearby charge has a static, long, linear, uniform distribution; both work by describing causal relations. Achinstein deems the latter explanation to be causal. So I think that he should also regard the former explanation as causal.

16. Let me say a bit more about this notion of what a scientific explanation derives its power to explain from—the source of its explanatory power. Every philosophical account of scientific explanation identifies from where certain scientific explanations derive their explanatory power. On the D-N model, for instance, a given explanation derives its power from being a deductive argument for the explanandum from true premises, at least one of which is a law and indispensable, and so forth. I do not presume that there are conditions whose satisfaction, in any context, would bestow explanatory power. But I presume that in at least some contexts, there are conditions whose satisfaction would bestow explanatory power—even if those conditions differ in different contexts.

Whether a given explanation gets its explanatory power from supplying information about the world's causal network or in some other way cannot be determined simply by identifying what information is included in the explanation. A philosophical account of how the explanation works is required. (See the next note.)

The source of a scientific explanation's explanatory power is distinct from what an agent has to be told in order for her to know that something is an explanation. An agent who knows Coulomb's law may require only some additional information about mathematical truths (that $\int_{-\pi/2}^{\pi/2} \cos\theta \, d\theta = 2$) in order to learn that a given argument from Coulomb's law explains why the electric field strength at a distance r from a long, linear charge distribution with static uniform charge density λ is equal (in Gaussian CGS units) to $2\lambda/r$. But this does not make the explanation distinctively mathematical; what the agent thereby ascertains to be explanatory derives its explanatory power by virtue of supplying information about causes, and the mathematical fact that the agent learns may figure in this explanation by virtue of contributing to its description of the world's causal nexus.

17. It may be helpful to contrast my use of "causal explanation" with Skow (2014). According to Skow's principle (T3), a body of fact partially causally explains E if it is a body of fact about what causes, if any, E had. As I have just shown, the numbers of strawberries and children are causes of E. On Skow's view, then, they supply a causal explanation of E. The mere fact that an explanation conveys information that concerns E's causes suffices, according to Skow, to make the explanation causal. On my view, by contrast, an explanation's status as "causal" depends on how the explanation works. I will argue that the explanation in this example works by identifying constraints in virtue of which a different outcome was impossible—not just could not have been *caused*, but could not have *been*. The explanation does not work by showing that under these constraints, no potential *cause* sufficient to bring about a different outcome is allowed by the laws of nature. Rather, a different outcome is impossible, where this variety of impossibility transcends the range of potential causes allowed by the laws of nature.

18. If this is correct, then the scientific explanation of why there is (at that moment) a pair of antipodal equatorial points at the same temperature does not work by appealing to the fact that—or by explaining why it is the case that—those two particular antipodal equatorial points have the same temperature (at that moment). The scientific explanation of the existence fact then does not go through the facts that provide the "ground" (i.e., the "metaphysical explanation" or "in-virtue-of explanation") of the existence fact. Scientific explanation and grounding are then quite different in such a case. Lewis then incorrectly implies that

we explain why there exists such a pair of points by identifying such a pair: "Why is it that something is *F*? Because *A* is *F*. An existential quantification is explained by providing an instance" (Lewis 1986b, 223).

19. Kitcher makes a similar claim regarding the regularity (discovered by Arbuthnot) that in 82 successive years from 1623, more boys than girls were born in London. Suppose we took each birth during those years and described its causes (where one birth's causes have little in common with another's). By aggregating these, would we have thereby explained the regularity? "Even if we had this 'explanation' to hand, and could assimilate the details, it would still not advance our understanding. For it would not show that Arbuthnot's regularity was anything more than a gigantic coincidence" (Kitcher 2003, 69), whereas in fact, it is no coincidence (as Fisher's natural-selection explanation reveals). However, I am not sure if Kitcher is claiming that the description of all of the causes is not an explanation of the regularity (as I believe, since it inaccurately depicts the regularity as coincidental) or instead that it is a genuine causal explanation, albeit an unilluminating one.

20. I am presuming that the necessity possessed by ordinary laws of nature (which has been termed "natural," "nomic," or "physical" necessity) is weaker than mathematical necessity. This is the received view. Some philosophers (e.g., Ellis 2001; Bird 2007) argue that natural laws are metaphysically necessary and so are modally on a par with mathematical facts (as well as with the fact that Mark Twain and Samuel Clemens are identical). I shall not pause to examine this view here, though I have done so elsewhere (Lange 2009a) and will return to it in chapter 2.

There need not be a sharp distinction between mathematical necessity and certain other kinds of broadly logical necessity. For instance, suppose a male barber (the only barber in town, where every man keeps himself clean-shaven by either going to the barber or shaving himself) asked why he repeatedly fails in trying to carry out his intention to shave all and only those townsmen who do not shave themselves. The reason for the barber's failure is that his success is broadly logically impossible.

21. Presumably, we would be prompted to ask for an explanation of this fact (that in connection with predators having periodic life-cycles, cicadas with prime periods tend to suffer less from predation than cicadas with composite periods do) only as a result of our having already used this fact to help explain why cicada life-cycle periods are prime, an explanation that (I have just suggested) is causal. However, it is not generally the case that the facts having distinctively mathematical explanations arise in science only by figuring in causal explanations. Some facts having distinctively mathematical explanations (such as the repeated, frustrating failure to untie trefoil knots) might be recognized and prompt a why question without any motivation from some broader causal explanatory project. Other facts having distinctively mathematical explanations (such as that there are always antipodal equatorial points at the same temperature) would presumably have gone entirely unnoticed had they not been recognized as having distinctively mathematical explanations.

22. This explanation also seems to require that it be selectively advantageous for honeybees to divide their combs into regions of *equal* area. Lyon and Colyvan do not say why this might be. Moreover (as Alan Baker kindly pointed out to me), honeycomb cells in three dimensions are not quite the most economical shape, though they apparently come very close to optimality (see Hildebrandt and Tromba 1985, 156). Perhaps no honeybees ever actually possessed the neural architecture for producing the optimal shape, or perhaps that architecture was too costly in other ways and so it was overall most advantageous for honeybees to produce a cell shape that uses slightly more wax than necessary, or perhaps random drift is partly responsible for the outcome.

23. I presume throughout that classical physics is correct and so that this is a genuine explanation, that "Newton's second law" is a genuine natural law, etc. See the preface, note 4.

24. That is, the force points in the direction in which the potential energy would diminish most steeply; the force's magnitude equals the rate of the potential energy's decrease in that direction (a partial derivative).

25. This equation for $g = 0$ (topologically equivalent to a sphere) is sometimes called the "mountaineer's equation" and was proposed by Maxwell in "On Hills and Dales" in 1870, expanding on work by Cayley. The general equation was proved by Morse in 1925 and derives from Möbius's work "The Theory of Elementary Relationships" in 1863.

26. In chapter 4, I will show that other philosophers use the term "structural explanation" to characterize a kind of non-causal explanation. I will compare their conception of "structural explanation" to my conception of "explanation by constraint."

27. Its initial distribution is standardly given by a Dirac delta function localized at the origin.

28. Here is a simple proof. We have $f(a + b) = f(a)f(b)/f(0)$. So $f'(a) = \lim_{b \to 0} \dfrac{f(a+b)-f(a)}{b}$

$$= \lim_{b \to 0} \frac{\dfrac{f(a)f(b)}{f(0)} - f(a)}{b} = \lim_{b \to 0} \frac{\dfrac{f(a)f(b)}{f(0)} - \dfrac{f(a)f(0)}{f(0)}}{b} = \frac{-f(a)}{f(0)} \lim_{b \to 0} \frac{f(0)-f(b)}{b} =$$

$\dfrac{-f(a)f'(0)}{f(0)}$. Therefore, $f'(a) = k\, f(a)$ for some constant k. Therefore $f(a) = Ae^{ka+d}$ for some constants A and k.

29. The diffusion equation is that $\dfrac{\partial}{\partial t} \Phi = D\nabla^2 \Phi$ for the diffusion constant D. This equation, in turn, follows from and is explained by the continuity equation (that changes in concentration reflect the inflow and outflow of the diffusing substance, since that substance is conserved and moves only in continuous paths) and the fact that the flow of the diffusing substance at any point is proportional to the concentration gradient there.

30. Leading to the quip about the Gaussian distribution of errors that Poincaré (1908, v) attributes to an unspecified eminent physicist: "Everybody firmly believes in it because the mathematicians imagine it is a fact of observation and observers that it is a theorem of mathematics."

31. By contrast, Nickel (2010, 322) maintains that "After we entered '2 + 2 = ', the calculator showed '4' (rather than some other number) because 2 + 2 = 4" is not a causal explanation. That is, Nickel says that it does not work by "giving causal information."

32. Thanks to John Roberts for suggesting this example, though the moral I draw from it may not be his.

33. In particular, since the tidal force depends on the *difference* between the gravitational force on the solid earth and the gravitational force on the ocean, the tidal force varies with the *derivative* (the gradient) of the force, not with the force's magnitude, and so with the inverse-cube of the distance rather than with its inverse-square. In other words, the solid earth's acceleration caused by a distant gravitating body (of mass M at a distance R from the Earth's center) minus the ocean's acceleration caused by that body, for the ocean at the point on the Earth's surface nearest to the gravitating body (where the Earth's radius is r, and ignoring the Earth's rotation), equals $GM[1/R^2 - 1/(R-r)^2]$, which is approximately $2GMr/R^3$. This value is greater for the Moon than for the Sun; M is smaller but R is smaller, too, and the latter difference ends up dominating. Although the Moon's gravitational influence is less than the Sun's, the tidal force varies with inverse-cube of the distance rather than the inverse-square

(as the gravitational force does), thereby magnifying the causal significance of the Moon's being nearer than the Sun enough to outweigh the Sun's having greater mass than the Moon.

34. Let me emphasize (as I said in connection with Herschel's argument) that a mathematical ingredient in a *causal* explanation, no matter how prominent in a given context, does not make that explanation distinctively mathematical. For example, according to Lyon and Colyvan (2008, 238), "the theory of phase spaces, Poincaré maps, and differential equations explain why high-energy Hénon-Heiles systems [each system consisting of a point particle moving in a particular kind of potential] exhibit chaotic . . . motion and why low-energy ones exhibit regular . . . motion." I disagree; I do not think that this explanation works in the same way as the distinctively mathematical explanations given earlier. The dynamical equations (the solutions to which are displayed elegantly by a Poincaré map) do the explaining. This causal explanation is no more distinctively mathematical than any other derivation of equations of motion from force, potential, or energy functions. The phase space apparatus is a useful tool for displaying large classes of solutions to the dynamical equations. But it does not explain why those solutions tend to possess various properties.

35. Baker (2009b, 623–624; 2012, 261–264) makes the same point—though in terms of the cicada and honeycomb examples that I have argued do not straightforwardly qualify as distinctively mathematical explanations (and not in terms of my account of how distinctively mathematical explanations work). Presumably, there are also some scientific explanations that are not distinctively mathematical but (contrary to Steiner) incorporate explanations in mathematics.

■ Chapter 2

1. Feynman (1965, 46–55) emphasizes the value to physics in sometimes taking a given law as fundamental but on other occasions treating it as derivative. In this way, new laws can be discovered and a given law can sometimes be retained even after physics has discovered that another "law," from which the first law had sometimes been derived, is actually false. Feynman says that it is therefore not very "efficient" (47) to insist on certain laws as definitely more basic than others. However, Feynman emphasizes (49–50) that this "Babylonian" view (as he calls it) is exclusively an epistemic matter; physics should adopt it only as long as not all of the laws have been discovered. He emphasizes that the conservation laws' status as "wide principles which sweep across the different laws" (49) is not an artifact of the incompleteness of our knowledge or merely one of several equally accurate ways in which the laws of physics might be axiomatized. For instance, if we regard angular momentum conservation as holding merely because it can be derived from the various force laws, then "we take the derivation too seriously, and feel that [the conservation law] is only valid because [a given force law] is valid, [and] then we cannot understand the interconnections of the different branches of physics" (49). That is (I interpret Feynman as saying), we could not then accurately explain (with an "explanation by constraint") why each of these kinds of interaction conserves angular momentum.

2. And not just by scientists. For example, Steiner (1978b, 22) remarks (in passing): "Laws of conservation are simply not causal laws. They provide constraints on what is allowed to happen." I believe that Salmon senses the temptation to regard conservation laws as constraining the laws describing particular types of causal processes and interactions, and to combat this temptation, he offers a very minimal conception of what it takes for a law to be a "causal law": "Such laws as conservation of energy and momentum are causal laws in the

sense that they are regularities exhibited by causal processes and interactions" (Salmon 1998, 138). On my view, both constraints and coincidences are regularities exhibited by causal processes and interactions. (For that matter, so are accidental generalizations.) But a conservation law can figure in a non-causal explanation (an "explanation by constraint") only if it is a regularity that all causal processes not only do exhibit, but must exhibit—with a necessity stronger than the natural necessity that the various interaction laws possess.

3. What does "the law of energy conservation" say? It could be understood as (A) the law that each individual interaction conserves energy. Alternatively, it could be interpreted as (B) the law that every isolated system conserves energy, or, more weakly, as (C) the law that the universe's total energy remains constant. As (B) or (C), the energy conservation law does not follow from the various force laws (together with the "closure law" specifying that every force is covered by one of these force laws) along with the fundamental dynamical law (such as Newton's second law of motion). Additional premises are required to entail (B) or (C), such as that there are no point particles and that every isolated system has only a finite number of components. (See, for instance, Alper et al. 2000; Lee 2011, and references therein.) The distinction between energy conservation as constraint and energy conservation as coincidence can be drawn for each version of the energy conservation law.

4. Throughout I speak interchangeably of an argument explaining and of certain facts explaining. Certain facts explain if and only if they are expressed by the premises of some argument that explains.

5. Neither force law alone is enough to entail that the interaction will conserve energy. The explanation must also appeal to the fundamental dynamical law: the law relating forces to the motions they cause (in classical physics: Newton's second law of motion together with its analogue relating applied torque to angular acceleration, Hamilton's principle, the Euler-Lagrange equations, etc.).

6. I say "important" and "substantially" in order to acknowledge that two components of a coincidence may have some explainers in common—as long as they are beside the point in the context in which an explanation of the two components is being demanded. (I mentioned this at the end of section 1.2.) For instance, suppose that the two friends both happened to travel to Chicago on the same airplane flight. Then there would be some common explainers of their both being there (e.g., the flight, the natural laws governing jet engines, the composition of the atmosphere). But these are not the sorts of explainers that we would (ordinarily) be asking for in asking "What brings you to Chicago?" (The laws and the composition of the atmosphere would be common explainers even if they took separate flights.) Likewise, even if the fundamental dynamical law (see note 5) is common to the reason that gravitational interactions conserve energy and to the reason that electric interactions conserve energy, the fact that they both conserve energy is nonetheless coincidental in the context that I am stipulating to be relevant since the dynamical law is incidental there; the force laws involved are the focus of our explanatory demand.

7. The two possible explanations I just gave (labeled 1 and 2) do not exhaust the conservation law's possible explanations. But the distinction between constraints and coincidences arises for other possible explanations as well. For instance, a possible explanation is that each of the fundamental forces conserves energy because they have some other feature in common: each of the corresponding force laws exhibits the same symmetry (namely, invariance under arbitrary temporal displacement). Although this fact could serve in a given context as an adequate explanation, it also raises an obvious question: Why are all of the forces alike in this respect? This regularity is either a matter of constraint or a coincidence, and its

explanation would differ in the two cases. If this similarity in the forces is a coincidence, then so is energy conservation. (That a similarity among "interactions of totally different kinds" is no "coincidence" if it is explained in each case by the same overarching common principle seems to be what Steiner (1983b, 125–126) has in mind in a different example.)

8. They are not collectively exhaustive. Rather, they are the extremes; there are intermediate cases. For instance, suppose that some fundamental kinds of interactions have a certain feature (e.g., are capable of both attraction and repulsion) whereas others (namely, interactions A, B, and C) do not have this feature. Suppose it is a law that every kind of interaction with that feature conserves energy, and suppose that this law is a constraint. Then the fact that every kind of interaction conserves energy might be explained by this constraint together with A's force law, B's force law, and C's force law (along with the fundamental dynamical law). In that case, energy conservation is neither a complete coincidence nor a constraint. As another kind of intermediate case, the law of energy conservation might follow from exactly two separate constraints (e.g., that all of the forces capable of both attraction and repulsion must conserve energy, and that all of the forces capable only of attraction or only of repulsion must conserve energy). In another kind of intermediate case, the fact that gravitational interactions conserve energy has some important explainers in common with the fact that electric interactions conserve energy—but these common explainers do not suffice to explain either fact. For the sake of simplicity, I will not return to these intermediate possibilities, but I believe that it is clear how my remarks apply to them.

9. Accordingly, I shall speak interchangeably of the *fact* that energy is conserved (or that electric and gravitational interactions both conserve energy) as a coincidence and of the *law* of energy conservation as a coincidence (or as a constraint).

10. It is logically equivalent to (roughly speaking) an infinite conjunction, each conjunct specifying that any interactions that occur belonging to a given kind conserve energy, with one conjunct for each broadly logically possible kind of interaction. But as a coincidence, it is explained by the force laws and closure law and fundamental dynamical law (that relates force to motion; see note 5). Some of its conjuncts are explained by the fact that no interaction belonging to the given kind could occur (considering the kinds of forces represented by force laws and listed in the closure law). The conservation law behaves like a conjunction of the remaining conjuncts, one for each actual kind of force.

11. That a coincidence is explanatorily relevant only if all of its components are, too, applies to explanations in mathematics as well. For example, in chapter 8 note 3, I will show that the coincidence that each of two theorems involves exactly the positive integers n where $\varphi(n) \leq 2$ explains why both theorems involve $\{1,2,3,4,6\}$. One coincidence explains another—but only because both conjuncts of the former coincidence are explanatorily relevant.

12. It is a familiar point from the literature on scientific explanation that a deductive scientific explanation is spoiled when an arbitrary premise is added to it, even though the argument for the explanandum remains deductively valid. See, for instance, Lipton (2004, 150).

13. Explaining why a fluid *begins* to circulate is not the same as explaining why it is circulating. I do not think we can explain why a given closed system has total energy E at an earlier moment on the grounds that its energy at a later moment is E and energy is conserved. That is because the later moment's energy is not explanatorily prior to the earlier moment's; the order of causal priority is from past to future. (Compare Achinstein 1983, 243.) But the order of causal priority may not matter if the explanandum is instead the fluid's *beginning* to circulate (or failing to do so), since then the why question (e.g., "Why does the fluid begin to circulate rather than remain at rest?") presupposes the fluid's earlier behavior.

14. That such a loop does not turn is a key step in Stevin's famous 1586 *clootcrans* ("wreath of spheres") argument for the law of the inclined plane. He appealed to the impossibility of perpetual motion rather than to energy conservation. Nevertheless, it seems to me that what he gave purported to be an explanation (by constraint) of the loop's remaining still, not merely an argument for believing that it does. Some commentators have agreed; for example, Crombie (1952, 287–288) writes, "With the impossibility of perpetual motion . . . he showed why a loop of cord . . . would not move when hung over a triangular prism." Although I see energy conservation (if a constraint) as able to explain why (and not merely entail that) such a loop does not turn, I do not go as far as Halonen and Hintikka (1999, 32) do: they regard Stevin's entire argument for the law of the inclined plane as explanatory (if we appeal to energy conservation in place of his appeal to the impossibility of perpetual motion). Stevin's argument uses the behavior of a rope loop to figure out the behavior of a nonlooped length of rope laid across (but not hanging down beyond) the block's top surfaces, and then uses the behavior of that length of rope to figure out the behavior of two weights sitting on the block's surfaces. I do not see why the behavior of the looped rope is explanatorily prior to the behavior of the nonlooped rope or why the latter, in turn, is explanatorily prior to the behavior of the weights. Presumably, all of these behaviors have many explainers in common.

15. Another body's appearing out of nowhere, having the same mass as the body that vanishes, will not allow mass conservation to hold by compensating for the accelerating body's disappearance. There is no last moment at which the accelerated body has a definite position, only a first moment t at which it is gone. If there is no first moment at which another body appears, only a last moment t before it has appeared, then the total mass at t is less than it was before t. On the other hand, if the new body first appears at t, then although the universe's total mass at t is the same as it was before, the new body must have some particular location at t, and so the total mass in some finite isolated region surrounding that location must change at t, violating mass conservation. For the calculation of the accelerating body's trajectory, see Nahin (2009, 2–5).

16. It also makes a difference to the way that hypotheses are confirmed in science. If we believe that energy conservation is a constraint if it is true, then we are prepared to regard the hypothesis that energy is conserved as confirmed very differently than if we believe it to be a coincidence if it is true. Roughly speaking, if we believe energy conservation to be a coincidence if it is true, then typically we regard the fact that one fundamental kind of interaction conserves energy as no evidence that another kind does as well (just as typically we take my being in Chicago now as no evidence that you are there now, too, if we believe that our both being there now would be coincidental). However, if we believe that energy conservation might be a constraint, then we may well take the fact that one fundamental kind of interaction conserves energy as some evidence that another kind does as well. Feynman (1967, 76) acknowledges such confirmation when he says that we are "confident that, because we have checked the energy conservation here [i.e., that the known phenomena all conserve energy], when we get a new phenomenon we can say it has to satisfy the law of conservation of energy." A good example of such a new phenomenon was radioactive decay, which most physicists strongly believed to conserve energy before they had any significant confidence in any theories regarding the particular force(s) involved. (See note 24 and accompanying text, and in chapter 3 note 25 and the text accompanying note 11.) Although the distinction between constraints and coincidences has epistemological significance, I insist that it is not fundamentally an epistemic distinction. Rather, it is fundamentally concerned with metaphysics, modality, and explanation. See section 3.2 for more on a constraint's role as a heuristic and how this role derives from a constraint's modal significance.

17. For an arbitrarily shaped object, the calculation yields the same result: the body is decomposed into thin cylindrical elements, and although their top and bottom surfaces may tilt arbitrarily relative to the horizontal, the horizontal components of the pressure forces perpendicular to the body's variously tilted surface elements at any given level z add to zero.

18. For similar remarks characterizing this derivation as explanatory, see also Rudiak (1964); Tarasov and Tarasova (1973, 121); and Keeports (2002).

19. Of course, this argument does not reveal *how* the buoyant force acts. Admittedly, the earlier, thoroughly causal explanation also fails to identify the *fundamental* force at work in molecular collisions. But it does at least reveal that the buoyant force is exerted through these collisions. The derivation from energy conservation shows that the buoyant force must be present but fails to uncover the causal mechanism by which it acts. Thus, a distinctive explanatory contribution is made by the hydrostatic derivation.

20. For an elementary derivation, see Hanca et al. (2004). Being explained by symmetry principles is not the only way for conservation laws to have explanations and yet to be constraints rather than coincidences. Newton's third law of motion and that all forces are caused by bodies could be constraints that account for linear momentum conservation's status as a constraint. For more details, see Lange (2009a, 224).

21. For more on the ontological status and causal role of fields in classical physics, with particular attention to the notion of "action by contact," see Lange (2002).

22. A "central force" is a force directed along the line joining the body exerting it and the body feeling it.

23. I will return to the relation of statics to dynamics in chapter 4.

24. Whewell emphasizes that the PVW "was established as a general principle by being proved in each particular case" (1832, viii), that is, separately for each kind of simple machine—in the manner of a coincidence. To confirm it as if it would be a constraint, if it were true, would be to regard its holding for one kind of simple machine as inductive evidence that it holds of another (see note 16). Likewise, Whewell (22) characterizes a corollary of the PVW as "proved by shewing its truth in the case of each of the mechanical powers [i.e., simple machines] separately."

25. Many textbooks dance lightly over the fact that these membranes are generally naturally impossible, characterizing the two gases as separated "conceptually" (Yourgrau, Van der Merwe, and Raw 2002, 235) or "hypothetically" (Annamalai and Puri 2002, 145) without elaborating any further. Fermi (1956, 101) is admirably forthright: "We should notice . . . that in reality no ideal semipermeable membranes exist. The best approximation of such a membrane is a hot palladium foil, which behaves like a semipermeable membrane for hydrogen."

26. In order for this subjunctive conditional's truth-value to distinguish between constraints and coincidences, its antecedent must not specify anything about what the posited additional kind of force is like. The antecedent must simply be "Had there been an additional species of force," not "Had there been an additional species of force obeying the equation . . ." For instance, if the subjunctive conditional's antecedent specified the particular force law involved, then that energy conservation would (or would not) have been upheld by this additional force (as long as the fundamental dynamical law would still have held) might be trivial. This subjunctive fact would then fail to get at energy conservation's status as constraint or coincidence.

27. Even if there is in fact only a single kind of fundamental force (a "grand unified field"), it will either be the case or not be the case that energy would still have been conserved, had

there been another kind of fundamental force. Since the distinction between constraints and coincidences is drawn in terms of such subjunctive facts, this distinction applies even if there is only a single kind of fundamental force.

28. See Bergmann (1962, 144); Feynman (1967, 59, and 76, 83, 94); Planck quoted in Pais (1986, 107–108).

29. Recall notes 16 and 24.

30. The constraint/coincidence distinction is modal. As a coincidence, energy conservation would be no *more* necessary than the particular force laws there actually happen to be, since those laws would be partly responsible for it. In contrast, as a constraint on the forces there could have been, energy conservation would be *more* necessary than the actual force laws; it would still have held even if the force laws had been different.

31. These convenient simplifications could be dropped, however, by making compensating changes elsewhere.

32. A more sophisticated account would replace this appeal to "all conversational contexts" with a narrower range of contexts, thereby giving an account of the laws of some particular scientific field. But none of this would play any part in our discussion of non-causal explanation, so I will omit these complexities and continue referring to laws *simpliciter* rather than to laws of, say, aerodynamics or island biogeography or traffic science or human medicine.

33. For the sake of simplicity, this definition of "subnomic stability" omits some details from my (2009a) that will not make any difference here.

34. According to many proposed logics of counterfactuals, $p \mathbin{\square\!\!\rightarrow} q$ is true trivially whenever $p\&q$ is true (a principle known as "Centering"). If Centering is correct, then each member of the set of all subnomic truths is trivially preserved under every subnomic supposition p that is true. Of course, there are no subnomic suppositions p that are false and logically consistent with the set. (If p is a false subnomic supposition, then $\sim p$ is a member of the set.) In that case, the set of all subnomic truths trivially possesses subnomic stability. Accordingly, Λ is the largest *nonmaximal* set that is subnomically stable.

35. One might insist that Ehrenfest was actually concerned with what would have happened, had gravity been an inverse-cube force *and the other laws remained the same*. However, there is no more reason to suppose that Ehrenfest's counterfactual antecedent contained this further proviso than to suppose that in an ordinary conversation. "Had I struck the match, it would have lit" is really "Had I struck the match and the match remained dry and oxygenated, it would have lit." Just as the match would have remained dry and oxygenated, had it been struck, so (according to Ehrenfest) the fundamental dynamical law would still have held, had gravity been inverse-cube.

36. The laws' natural necessity is therefore not a "cheap and trivial" matter of self-entailment (Fine 2005, 246). They earn their status as necessary by virtue of forming a subnomically stable set. Natural necessity is not on a par with "feline necessity" (where something is "felinely necessary" if and only if it is true in all possible worlds containing cats). As Bird (2007, 48) remarks, feline necessity does not name a genuine variety of necessity. Natural necessity does.

37. This does not mean that if some conservation law constrains the force laws, there is no antecedent (and context) under which a force law is preserved but the conservation law is not. Obviously, "had the force law held but the conservation law not held" is such an antecedent. Nevertheless, the range of antecedents under which the constraints are all preserved *in connection with their stability* (that is, the range logically consistent with the constraints) is wider than the range under which Λ's members are all preserved *in connection with Λ's stability*

(that is, the range logically consistent with Λ). The above antecedent falls outside of both of these ranges since it is logically inconsistent with Λ.

38. Six is a "perfect" number because it is the sum of its divisors (1, 2, and 3) excepting itself.

39. I have not aimed to argue that a given conservation law is indeed a constraint or that a given symmetry principle is indeed a metalaw. I have not aimed to argue that conservation laws are explained by symmetry principles. Rather, I have tried to identify what sort of explanation this would be (an explanation by constraint) and what facts (expressed by subjunctive conditionals) would enable there to be such an explanation. Whether these facts obtain is an empirical, scientific question. Some philosophers have denied that symmetry principles explain conservation laws. For instance: "We have now established a *correlation* between certain dynamical symmetries and certain conservation principles. Neither of these two kinds of thing is conceptually more fundamental than, or used to explain the existence of, the other. . . . After all, the real physics is in the Euler-Lagrange equations of motion for the fields, from which the existence of dynamical symmetries and conservation principles, if any, jointly spring" (Brown and Holland 2004, 1138). It may be true that symmetries fail to explain conservation laws, but if it is, then (I maintain) that is because the sorts of subjunctive facts that I have identified as required to underwrite the status of conservation laws as constraints (and to underwrite their noncausal explanation by symmetry principles) fail to obtain. I see no argument from Brown and Holland that the requisite facts fail to obtain. At least some of Brown's and Holland's motivation may be the view that all scientific explanations are causal (see my discussion of Brown's view in chapter 3).

40. Here I am agreeing with Skow (2014, 456–457).

41. But he may not always have been so content. See chapter 3, note 6.

42. Woodward's account allows for an explanation of a given physical process's particular speed by some generalization that specifies how its speed would have been different under various counterfactual circumstances. Such a generalization explains why the process has a given (subluminal or luminal) speed *rather than some other speed that is subluminal or luminal*, since the generalization identifies the conditions under which these various speeds would have resulted. But by Woodward's lights, such a generalization fails to explain why the process's speed is subluminal or luminal *rather than superluminal*, since it does not specify conditions under which its speed would have been superluminal). Therefore, I do not agree with Woodward (2003, 209) that we have here some "mitigation" of the problem afflicting his account.

43. Explanations by constraint fit well within what Salmon terms the "modal conception" of scientific explanation, according to which "scientific explanations do their jobs by showing that what did happen had to happen" (1998, 320). Salmon (1998, 64 and 322–323, 397) rejects the modal conception on the grounds that it is inapplicable to statistical explanation. But Salmon's objection shows only that some explanations fall outside the modal conception; it does not show that the modal conception has no application. Lipton (2004a, 8; 2004b, 29) argues that a "causal conception" of explanation passes the "why regress test": it can account for the fact that we can explain E by citing H even if we have not explained H (since "we can know that C caused E without knowing what caused C"). However, Lipton says, the modal conception fails the "why regress test." I disagree. We can know that the energy conservation law requires a given fundamental force to conserve energy, explaining why it does, without knowing why, in turn, energy must be conserved.

44. Of course, Bird could accommodate conservation laws as constraints by modifying the heart of his view: he could hold that although some laws are underwritten by the dispositions constituting the sparse fundamental properties of physics, other laws are not.

45. Bird recognizes that least-action principles pose the same difficulties for his account as conservation laws do.

46. Likewise, Wigner (1952, 450) refers to using "the heavy particle conservation law . . . to explain the stability of the proton" and Goldhaber et al. (1980, 851) discuss "the hypothesis of a conservation law to explain proton stability."

47. Kosso (2000) also investigates the distinction between fundamental and accidental symmetries (though not in connection with the explanatory power of conservation laws). He says that a symmetry is accidental in virtue of having no relations to other features of nature; whether a symmetry is fundamental or accidental, according to Kosso, is a "holistic" matter, not a matter of the symmetry's modal status or its capacity to play a particular explanatory role. In contrast, I understand accidental symmetries as symmetries that impose no constraints on the allowable interactions in that the symmetries might not still have held, had there been different kinds of interactions.

■ Chapter 3

1. This formulation is ambiguous: Are we aiming to explain the truth of the Lorentz transformations, or are we aiming to explain the Lorentz transformation laws, or are we aiming to explain why they are laws of nature rather than accidental truths? The proposed explanations that I will be discussing would do all of these things, if they succeeded at doing any of them. We could take the explanandum to be simply that the transformations are true. But perhaps that the transformations are laws explains why they are true. (All parties to the dispute concerning their explanation agree that the Lorentz transformations are not accidents, but rather hold as a matter of law.) I am interested in rival proposed explanations of their truth that aim to go deeper than "Because they are laws" by also explaining why they are laws. As I will show, the dispute concerning their explanation is also a dispute about what sort of laws they are.

2. Today it is believed that neutrinos have small rest masses. But physicists have posited the photino (the photon's supersymmetric partner) and the graviton as massless.

3. That the laws are "Lorentz covariant" means that they remain unchanged under the Lorentz transformations (i.e., when "x" in the laws is replaced by "$(x - vt)/(1 - v^2/c^2)^{1/2}$," etc.) so phenomena in S' conform to the laws (expressed in primed coordinates) if and only if phenomena in S conform to the laws (in unprimed coordinates). It means, then, that the result of taking any possible world that accords with the laws and putting it through Lorentz transformations is always another such world.

4. Penrose's remark seems to presuppose that the fact that all of the dynamical laws possess the same form is a consequence of the dynamical laws. Of course, it is not a consequence of the truths L where it is a dynamical law that L, or even of the truths of the form "It is a dynamical law that L." It is a consequence of all of the truths about which facts are dynamical laws and which are not—that is, a consequence of the truths of the form "It is a dynamical law that L" together with the fact that there are no additional dynamical laws. Now in what sense could a consequence of the facts about what the dynamical laws are be "accidental," and what is the alternative? (Thanks to John Carroll for discussion of this point.)

5. "By and by I despaired of the possibility of discovering the true laws by means of constructive efforts based on known facts. The longer and more desperately I tried, the more I came to the conviction that only the discovery of a universal formal principle could lead

us to assured results" (Einstein 1949, 53). In the next section, I will examine the distinction to which Einstein alludes here: between "theories of principle" and "constructive theories."

6. At one time, Woodward emphasized this point (although as I showed at the end of chapter 2, explanations by constraint are alien to Woodward's 2003 account of scientific explanation): ". . . with respect to the explanations of length contraction and time dilation in a moving inertial frame provided by Special Relativity. A rapidly moving clock is a continuous causal process, but the time dilation and length contraction it will exhibit have their explanation in the structure of Minkowski spacetime and are geometrical effects rather than causal effects whose origin is to be sought in causal processes and their interactions. Indeed the contrast between the explanation of such phenomena in Special Relativity and their explanation in a theory like Lorentz's, in which these effects are regarded as a consequence of the operation of electromagnetic forces, seems to be precisely the contrast between a non-causal, geometrical explanation and a causal one" (Woodward 1989, 360).

7. Whittaker (1953, 42–43) writes, "When relativity had become recognized as a doctrine covering the whole operation of physical nature, efforts were made to present it in a form free from any special association with electromagnetic theory"; he gives references to much of the early literature. For more of these references, see Berzi and Gorini (1969, 1518); for more recent references, see Pal (2003).

8. This is a substantive premise of the explanatory argument: that there are coordinate transformation laws and that they involve only these various kinematic quantities. (This premise might be compared to a dimensional explanation's premise that certain quantities suffice to form a dimensionally homogeneous relation—see chapter 6.)

9. Here is the argument. In S', if I is the spacetime interval between one event at the spacetime origin and another at $(x',0,0,t')$, then $I^2 = x'^2 - c^2 t'^2$. By using the previous result in the main text to transform x' and t' in this expression into x and t, and then (by virtue of the interval's invariance) equating this result to I^2 between these events in S, we find:

$$\left(1-kv^2\right)^{-1}\left(x-vt\right)^2 - c^2\left(1-kv^2\right)^{-1}\left(-kvx+t\right)^2 = x^2 - c^2 t^2.$$

By boring algebra, this is

$$x^2 + v^2 t^2 - 2xvt - c^2 t^2 - k^2 v^2 x^2 c^2 + 2tkvxc^2 = \left(x^2 - c^2 t^2\right)\left(1-kv^2\right),$$

which is

$$\left(x^2 v^2 k + t^2 v^2 - 2xvt\right)\left(1-kc^2\right) = 0,$$

which is true for all x,v,t if and only if $k = c^{-2}$.

10. Here is the argument. Suppose that in frame S, a process moving at speed c links two events. Since distance is speed times time, $([\Delta x]^2 + [\Delta y]^2 + [\Delta z]^2)^{\frac{1}{2}} = c\Delta t$, and so the interval I between these events is 0. By I's invariance, the two events are separated by $I = 0$ in S', so $([\Delta x']^2 + [\Delta y']^2 + [\Delta z']^2 - c^2[\Delta t']^2)^{\frac{1}{2}} = 0$, so the speed in S' of the process linking these events is $([\Delta x']^2 + [\Delta y']^2 + [\Delta z']^2)^{\frac{1}{2}}/\Delta t' = c$. Hence the speed c is invariant.

11. See note 16 to chapter 2 and note 25 below.

12. In chapter 4, I will use historical evidence from the controversy regarding the parallelogram law's explanation to support my claim that such an explanation by constraint precludes such a causal explanation. As I will show, advocates of the statical explanation of the parallelogram law (a purported explanation by constraint) deny that the parallelogram law is *also* explained dynamically (that is, causally).

Just as the truth of modally weaker dynamical laws can entail the truth of modally stronger transformation laws (without explaining why they are true), so p can entail q even if p is contingent and q possesses some grade of necessity. For example, q can be $(p$ or $r)$ where it is a natural law that r—or even a logical truth that r. Once again, though, I am inclined to insist that p cannot explain why $(p$ or $r)$ obtains, since presented as an explanation, p misrepresents $(p$ or $r)$'s modal status. At least, p does not give a *scientific* explanation of $(p$ or $r)$. Some philosophers (see Kment 2015: 532) say that p "grounds" $(p$ or $r)$, specifying what it is in virtue of which $(p$ or $r)$ holds—and that r does likewise—and that such grounding is a kind of explanation. But I do not see p as thereby explaining why $(p$ or $r)$ holds. That is not because r also holds; by the same token I do not see p as explaining why $(p$ or $\sim p)$ holds. That is not a scientific explanation.

13. This remark (together with many of the others I cite from Brown) also appears in Brown and Pooley (2006, 84).

14. To explain the t-component, suppose every clock in uniform motion is such that the laws governing its operation make it tick slower by a factor of $(1-v^2/c^2)^{1/2}$ than it does at rest:

$$\Delta t' = \Delta t(1-v^2/c^2)^{1/2}.$$

Suppose the dynamics also makes a clock measure light's speed to be the same regardless of the light's direction or the clock's uniform motion. Then the previous equation requires that clocks resting at different locations in S' be set so that (again taking the transformations to be linear)

$$t' + Fx' = t(1-v^2/c^2)^{1/2},$$

where F is whatever quantity is needed for a momentary flash of light emitted at the frames' origins at $t = t' = 0$ to be accorded the same speed in the $+x'$ direction as in the $-x'$ direction. Hence

$$t = (t' + Fx')(1-v^2/c^2)^{-1/2}.$$

The flash's x-coordinate is $x = \pm ct$, and since we found $x' = (x - vt)/(1 - v^2/c^2)^{1/2}$,

$$x' = (\pm ct - vt)/(1-v^2/c^2)^{1/2}.$$

Substituting for t:

$$x' = (t' + Fx')(\pm c - v)/(1-v^2/c^2).$$

Rearranging:

$$x'/t' = [-F + (1-v^2/c^2)/(\pm c - v)]^{-1}$$

Since light's speed x'/t' in the $\pm x'$ directions must be equal in magnitude and opposite in sign,

$$-F + (1-v^2/c^2)/(c-v) = F + (1-v^2/c^2)/(c+v).$$

Solving

$$F = v/c^2,$$

so

$$t' = t(1 - v^2/c^2)^{1/2} - Fx' = t(1 - v^2/c^2)^{1/2} - (v/c^2)(x - vt)/(1 - v^2/c^2)^{1/2}$$
$$= (t - vx/c^2)(1 - v^2/c^2)^{1/2}.$$

15. As I understand them, Balashov and Janssen (2003, 340–342) and Nerlich (2006, 635) regard such a similarity among the forces as too suspicious to be plausibly a coincidence. (Presumably, then, they recognize that there is a possible world where this similarity among the forces holds as a matter of coincidence. See Brown 2005, 143.)

16. I discussed "thermodynamic necessity" in chapter 2. In section 6.5, I will explore thermodynamics' explanatory role as a "principle theory."

17. See, for instance, DiSalle (2006, 115–118). Even Janssen, who rejects Brown's dynamical explanation of the Lorentz transformations in favor of the view that the transformations are independent of all dynamical laws, now agrees with Brown that "principle theories are not explanatory" (Janssen 2009, 38). Accordingly, he believes Einstein was incorrect to regard special relativity as a principle theory. I shall argue that Janssen is incorrect.

18. Indeed, Jeans (1921, 793) even comments: "The main trunk of the tree is the relativity hypothesis already mentioned; these additional hypotheses form the branches. The trunk can exist without its branches, but not the branches without the trunk." Perhaps we have here a dark expression of relativity's transcending the various force laws.

19. Einstein (1919, 228) says, "The advantages of the constructive theory are completeness. . . ."

20. By the same token, the laws of thermodynamics (Einstein's paradigm of a theory of principle) cannot entail the molecular constitution of matter (where statistical mechanics is the constructive theory constrained by thermodynamics).

21. Salmon credits this terminology to Kitcher (1985, 638).

22. On Salmon's view, top-down explanations derive their explanatory power by virtue of the unification they create (in accordance with the account of scientific explanation defended by Kitcher 1989). They do not work (according to Salmon) in the manner that I have characterized as "explanation by constraint." I will set aside this point in identifying top-down explanations, explanations by constraint, and explanations given by principle theories.

23. For a calculation of this chance, see Peskin and Schroeder (1995, 14).

24. Likewise, when magnetism is explained as a relativistic phenomenon, Coulomb's law does not explain why there are magnetic forces. Electric and magnetic forces are both frame-dependent. Rather, what relativity (together with the invariance of electric charge) explains is why there are both electric and magnetic forces in the world rather than solely electric forces (namely, because a frame with solely electric forces transforms to a frame with both electric and magnetic forces). That is, it explains why there is a certain relation between the electric and magnetic forces in one frame and those forces in another frame. It is therefore misleading to say that "the magnetic field appears . . . as a result of the Lorentz transformation for electric force. In this respect, the magnetic field is not an independent entity, but rather a transformed aspect of the electric field" (Fayngold 2008, 204). The electric field is not explanatorily prior to the magnetic field.

25. Furthermore, Mermin (2005, 185) emphasizes that scientists were justified in expecting that the laws for newly discovered forces (such as the strong and weak nuclear forces) would turn out to be Lorentz covariant on the strength of their evidence for the principle of relativity. As I have noted, scientists could not be justified in such a belief unless they held

that it is (plausibly) a constraint rather than a coincidence if all first-order laws turn out to be Lorentz covariant. This is closely related to the evidence supporting Lévy-Leblond's conditional that various symmetries would still have held, even if the forces were different. Moreover, Mermin is eager to emphasize that relativity is not dependent on the particular kinds of forces that happen to exist: "It is the same for the principle of relativity and for the principle of the constancy of the velocity of light, which is better described, in this general context, as the principle of the existence of an invariant velocity, or, if you prefer, the principle of the invariance of the interval" (Mermin 2009, 184–185). "The first statement of the special theory of relativity was intimately tied to the first unambiguous assertion that the velocity of light in empty space has the value c, independent of frame of reference. Reflecting this historical circumstance, light has almost always had a central role in subsequent expositions of relativity. . . Relativity, however, is not a branch of electromagnetism and the subject can be developed without any reference whatever to light" (Mermin 1990, 247). Since he accepts the principle of relativity as a constraint transcending the laws of electromagnetism and the laws governing other particular kinds of interactions, Mermin should not deprecate explanations by constraint.

26. Brown suggests that we have a mystery on our hands because free particles are not in mutual causal contact and so cannot be coordinating their behavior so as all to be unaccelerated relative to the same frames: he calls it a "miracle" that "force-free . . . bodies conspire to move in straight lines at uniform speeds while being unable, by *fiat*, to communicate with each other" (2005, 14–15). Of course, even such coordination by causal contact among the particles would require an explanation of how they manage to "communicate."

27. As Teller (1991, 373) argues, one who employs neo-Newtonian (a.k.a. Galilean) spacetime faces the same explanatory problem as the relationalist. She, too, can avoid this problem by appealing to the non-causal explanation of Newton's first law.

28. For much more on how "geometric possibility" might be unpacked, see Belot (2011).

29. Of course, if the force laws had been different in a certain way, the attempt to superimpose left and right hands would have changed the hands' shapes so that they could then have been superimposed. But this is akin to changing the arrangement of Königsberg's bridges and so does not involve the accomplishment of the superposition task originally intended. See section 1.3.

30. Colyvan (1998, 322–323; 2001, 50–51) also says that the spacetime interval's invariance helps to explain non-causally why the Lorentz transformations hold. But he does not identify the origin of its explanatory priority.

31. In special relativity, the sum of parallel velocities v_1 and v_2 is $(v_1 + v_2)/(1 + v_1 v_2/c^2)$, whereas in classical physics it is $v_1 + v_2$.

32. For an account of causal explanation along these lines, see Strevens (2008), especially his discussion of "causal homogeneity." For a related discussion of the way that irrelevant premises can spoil an explanation, see Lipton (2004, 50). That the addition of arbitrary true premises deprives the argument of its explanatory power (without undermining its soundness) was originally posed (by Kyburg's example of the hexed salt or Salmon's example of Mr. Jones taking his wife's birth-control pills) as a problem for the D-N model of scientific explanation.

33. Without citing Bondi, Salmon (1998, 73 and 359) presents this example as an explanation that contrasts with the bottom-up explanation given by the particular forces exerted by the baby.

34. Compare Hempel's (1965) D-N model: for the expansion of a given gas to be explained by the fact that the gas was heated under constant pressure and that all gases expand when

heated under constant pressure, this last regularity must be a law. But according to Hempel, the explanans officially includes "All gases expand when heated," not "It is a law that all gases expand when heated."

35. This means that if we have a scientific explanation in which the explanandum E follows from the explanans C by some mathematical proof, then (in an appropriate context) an answer to "Why is it the case that if C, then E?" can be "Because this conditional fact is mathematically necessary." This would be a "distinctively mathematical" explanation. It would not, however, be an explanation in mathematics (as described in part III). For instance, suppose one learns that C (Newton's laws of motion and gravity together with certain other facts, such as that the Sun contains nearly all of the solar system's mass and that there are no disturbing factors) explains why it is the case that E (that planets move nearly in ellipses with the Sun at one focus—Kepler's first "law"). One might then ask "Why is E the case, given C?" An answer might be "Because E follows mathematically from C." Of course, one could then give the proof. Such a proof would supply additional information about where the conditional's necessity comes from. But this proof need not be an explanation in mathematics (as described in part III).

36. The EFLs on a given rung may be stronger than the minimum needed to supplement the necessities on a higher rung in order to entail all of the EDLs on the given rung. A proper subset of the EFLs may suffice (together with the stronger necessities) to entail not only all of the EDLs but also the remaining EFLs. But not all entailments are explanations (of course). Some EFLs may entail others without explaining them. Likewise, perhaps a given EDL can be explained by any of several combinations of EFLs. Of course, a textbook writer might choose as a matter of convenience to regard some of the EFLs as axioms and others as theorems. But that choice would be made on pedagogic grounds; the "axioms" among the EFLs would still not be explanatorily prior to all of the "theorems."

37. My view here might be compared to Lewis's (1983, 368); he takes the axioms of the "best system" to be the fundamental laws and the theorems to be the derivative laws. I amend this idea so that it applies to a hierarchy of systems of laws.

38. By "logically contingent" truths, I mean all but the *narrowly* logical truths. A mathematical truth then qualifies as "*logically* contingent" because its truth is not ensured by its logical form alone. All and only narrowly logical truths can be omitted from any valid argument's premises without loss of validity.

39. Even if g is dispensable to one such argument, g may nevertheless entail d. In that case, d would have two explanations by constraint exclusively from EFLs.

40. This paragraph addresses Pincock's objection to an article of mine: "The second problem is that Lange is working with the idea that an explanation need only cite some sufficient conditions for the phenomenon being explained. . . . There is a risk that redundant conditions will be included. These conditions will not undermine the modal strength of the entailment, so it is not clear why Lange would say they undermine the goodness of the explanation" (Pincock 2015b, 875).

41. In addition, explanation may sometimes be intransitive because although c explains and entails d, and d explains e, d does not suffice to entail e. Rather, e follows from d only when d is supplemented by premises supplied by the context put in place by the mention of d. In that case, c may neither entail nor explain e (Hempel 1965, 447–453; Owens 1992, 16). But explanations by constraint are all deductively valid.

42. Of course, there is a constraint that entails the explanandum when the other premise is that the task involves Mother's having 23 strawberries and 3 children and wearing a blue suit, and where the argument is rendered invalid if the same constraint is used but the other

premise is weakened so as not to entail wearing a blue suit. But such a constraint is an EDL, not an EFL as the criterion mandates. Thus, the criterion does not thereby render Mother's attire explanatorily relevant.

43. In section 6.5, I will give examples (in connection with dimensional explanation) where a given law's having a certain modal status, transcending certain other kinds of laws, helps to explain why that law has certain other features. Those examples are like the cases we have just been examining in that a modal fact helps to explain the truth of some law.

44. Watkins intends these criteria for a "natural axiomatization" to determine what counts as a "unified scientific theory" (rather than a "rag-bag 'theory'"); Watkins thereby uses these criteria to elaborate the idea that more fundamental explanations involve more unified theories. Salmon (1998, 401) also tentatively suggests that Watkins's criteria be used to understand scientific explanation.

45. Hertz's purported explanation also appeals to the existence of "uniqueness theorems" for some but not all functions. This is a mathematical fact and so occupies a higher rung on the hierarchy than the explanandum; its explanatory priority is thereby secured.

46. Callender (2005, 128) offers another case where the dimensionality of space seems to be recognized as taking explanatory priority over a feature of space's inhabitants, namely, that some forces are such as to permit stable orbits: "There is a strong feeling—which I think Russell, van Fraassen and Abramenko were all expressing—that stability is just the wrong kind of feature to use to explain why space is three dimensional. . . . The feeling is that stability . . . is simply not a deep enough feature to explain dimensionality; if anything these facts are symptoms of the dimensionality."

47. Contrast Brown (2005, 40): "kinematics and dynamics are not independent departments of physics."

48. Of course, I am not arguing that kinematics does, in fact, transcend dynamics—that it belongs on a higher rung of the pyramidal hierarchy of stability and thereby possesses a stronger variety of natural necessity. This is an open empirical, scientific question. My concern is rather to understand what sorts of facts would settle the answer to this question. It may be that under string theory, the distinction between kinematics and dynamics will break down. But even if that turns out to be the case, we will want to understand precisely what breaks down—what view of the hierarchy of natural laws turns out to be untrue and what facts make it untrue. While suspecting that the distinction between kinematics and dynamics may become "blurred," Gross (2004) recognizes that "traditional physics distinguishes between kinematics (the framework for physics and its interpretation) and dynamics (the specific laws of nature and the forms of matter)." This distinction between the "framework" and the "specific laws" is the distinction for which I am offering an account. This distinction does not automatically cease to play an important role in science—the laws do not automatically turn out all to be on a modal par—even if kinematics turns out *not* to be the framework for dynamics. (String theory may even turn out to deploy this distinction, even if does not treat kinematics as the framework for dynamics.)

49. Einstein (1905/1989, 146) says, without elaboration, that spatiotemporal homogeneity implies linearity. The argument that I have given is roughly from Terletskii (1968, 18–19). Gannett (2007) replaces the assumption of X's differentiability with the assumption of its boundedness on a compact set (i.e., that X takes all of the spatiotemporal points within a given finite R from the origin to points that, for some finite R^*, are within R^* from the origin).

50. This argument is adapted from Berzi and Gorini 1969.

51. The following argument is taken directly from Pal 2003.

NOTES TO CHAPTER 4 ■ 421

52. We could instead follow Pal (2003) in using the fact that light's speed c is the same in S and S' to derive $k = c^{-2}$ and hence the Lorentz transformations. But this would be to invoke a peculiarity of a particular force and so the derivation would not be purely kinematical.

■ Chapter 4

1. The issue seems to have passed out of general discussion early in the twentieth century. Philosophers and textbook writers became less concerned with the foundations of classical mechanics (having relativity and quantum mechanics to worry about). They also became less concerned with scientific explanation, tending to regard description rather than explanation as the aim of science. Typically, textbooks today simply stipulate that forces can be represented as vectors (e.g., Kibble and Berkshire 1996, 5).

2. Of course, a distinguished minority of natural philosophers rejects the standard interpretation of forces in classical physics as entities produced by various actors (such as fields or distant charges) and producing accelerations. I will presuppose the standard interpretation since the scientists whom I will discuss evidently do so in examining why the parallelogram law holds. This controversy's broader lessons apply whether or not forces should remain in our ontology.

3. See Dugas (1988), Duhem (1991).

4. Such as Horsley (1743, 14); Rutherford (1748, 16–17); Bartlett (1850, 109); Tait (1885, 356); Thomson and Tait (1888, 244–245); Lock (1891, 104–105); Lodge (1890, 96); Loney (1891, 60); Pearson (1911, 345–346); Routh (1896, 14); and Cox (1904, 158). Blaikie (1879, 39–40) not only gives the dynamical explanation but also includes questions from the BA examination at Oxford (142) and the Oxford and Cambridge School Examination Board (147) asking for the parallelogram law to be proved and specifying the dynamical explanation as the correct answer. Such exam questions about the parallelogram law seem to have been quite common (see note 15).

5. See, for instance, Bartlett (1850, 109), and Loney (1891, 60). The following version of the dynamical explanation generally follows the version appearing in many texts but makes more explicit the roles played by mass and by geometry.

6. Newton's second law is *not* interpreted by the dynamical explanation's advocates as relating the resultant acceleration to the resultant force *as defined by the parallelogram of forces*. Doing so would defeat the point of giving a dynamical explanation of the parallelogram of forces. Rather, Newton's second law is interpreted as applicable to each component force separately, as well as to the resultant force *however forces turn out to compose*. The derivation demonstrates how the resultant force must therefore relate to the forces from which it results.

7. This equivalence presupposes that equal and opposite forces have zero resultant and that the resultant of two forces is independent of which other forces may also be acting.

8. Of course, forces and accelerations cannot both combine parallelogramwise if any force is proportional to (say) the square of the acceleration for which it is responsible. Nevertheless, with forces and accelerations each combining parallelogramwise, the fundamental dynamical law could have been that force is proportional to acceleration squared as long as this law applies not to each component separately, but only to the *resultant* acceleration produced by the *resultant* force.

9. De Morgan (1859) influentially argued that statical explanations of the parallelogram law are compatible with that law's being knowable only empirically. Others argued that the parallelogram law's explanation can be investigated independent of whether the law is knowable a priori or only empirically (e.g., Anonymous 1850, 378).

10. Such as Tate (1853, 72–74); Galbraith and Haughton (1860, 7–13); Skertchly (1873, 23–25); Goodeve (1874, 65–68); and Todhunter (1878, 19–22).

11. Duchayla was a student at the Ecole Polytechnique in 1795–1796 (three years before Poisson). In 1806 he assisted Arago in his experiments on the velocity of light. He became a naval engineer and later taught at the academies in Turin, Montpelier, and Aix. His 1804 paper was apparently his only scientific publication (De Morgan 1864, 527–528; Wilkinson 1864, 39; Grattan-Guinness 1990, 310).

12. For an interesting variant, see Dobbs (1901, 27–29).

13. This step will be discussed further in the next section.

14. Whewell's (1847, 30–32) explanation of the parallelogram law is similar, though it does not proceed inductively and, in place of the transmissibility principle, uses the principle that on any lever (a rigid rod, bent at a fulcrum), two forces tending to turn it oppositely balance exactly when they have equal "moments" about the fulcrum. (A force's "moment" equals its magnitude times the length of the line from the fulcrum to the line in the force's direction through the force's point of application.) An earlier edition of Whewell's book gives Poisson's derivation, which Whewell says he arrived at independently (Todhunter 1876, 15–16).

15. Cambridge BA exams frequently requested proofs of the parallelogram of forces. Common questions asked students to prove that it holds for magnitude given that it holds for direction (e.g., in Cambridge 1856, 46) and to "prove that the parallelogram of forces is true as regards the *direction* of two *commensurable* forces" (in Cambridge 1884, 39), which seem designated specifically to elicit parts of Duchayla's proof.

16. Goodwin's remark that Duchayla's proof reveals no reason why the parallelogram law should have been anticipated is very much like remarks that we will encounter in part III in connection with certain mathematical proofs that fail to explain why the theorems they prove hold because they fail to capture the theorem's "inevitability." For instance, Goodwin's remark is very similar to Zeitz's remarks (quoted in section 7.2) about the punchline of a non-explanatory mathematical proof as creeping up on us without warning, there being no hint until the end of the proof that we will arrive at a result that displays the same striking symmetry as the theorem being proved. See also Poincaré's remark (quoted in chapter 7, note 19) about an explanatory proof in mathematics allowing us to foresee the characteristic traits of the theorem being explained.

17. That the parallelogram law holds for both magnitude and direction may strike us forcibly only in view of Duchayla's argument, just as I will suggest in chapter 8 that the fact that the formula for the first n natural numbers applies to both even n and odd n may strike us forcibly only in the context of proofs that treat even n and odd n differently. However, whereas (I will argue in part III) the power of a mathematical proof to explain the theorem proved may shift as context shifts to bring different features of the theorem into prominence, I do not see the explanatory status of Duchayla's argument as depending on whether it is a salient feature of the parallelogram law that it holds for both magnitude and direction. Scientific explanation differs in this respect from explanation in mathematics.

18. Among texts endorsing Poisson's explanation are Anonymous (1829, 314); Young (1834, 250–252); Earnshaw (1845, v and 214–220); Barlow (1848, 10–11); Price (1868, 19–21); Johnson (1889, 153); Macaulay (1900, 403); and Moulton (1914, 6). Poisson develops a strategy pursued earlier by Foncenex and d'Alembert. Another strategy in the same spirit, but different in the details, was pursued by Daniel Bernoulli, Laplace, and Cauchy. Robison (1822, 57–64) presents a hybrid.

19. For example, Young (1834, 250 [for my fig. 4.5], 20 [fig. 4.6], 21 [fig. 4.7]).

20. Van Fraassen (1989, 268–270) briefly emphasizes symmetry's role in "dictating" the parallelogram law.

21. Strictly speaking, Poisson is entitled to conclude only that the resultant lies along the bisector of the larger angle or along the bisector of the smaller angle between P_1 and P_2. To explain why it lies along the smaller angle's bisector, Poisson could have appealed to two further premises: that the resultant of two equal forces depends continuously on their angle and that the resultant of two forces in the same direction points in that direction, too, and thus bisects the smaller angle (measuring zero radians) between them. Suppose that for some angle measure $\beta > 0$, the resultant of two equal forces subtending an angle of measure β bisects the larger angle between them. By continuity, for some angle γ, where $0 < \gamma < \beta$, the resultant of two equal forces subtending an angle of measure γ has zero resultant. By Poisson's further premise that two forces have zero resultant only if they are equal and opposite, it follows that P_1 and P_2 are opposite—a contradiction. Hence, the resultant of two equal forces must bisect the smaller angle between them.

22. Poisson, following Foncenex and d'Alembert, appeals explicitly to dimensional homogeneity but does not specify that this step presupposes f's continuity, i.e., that R varies continuously with P and x. (See chapter 6.)

23. Poisson (1811, 14–16) solves the equation roughly as follows. (Poisson 1833/1842 takes a different approach; Perkins 1842 uses a third approach.) Let the explanans include that for all x, g is infinitely differentiable on some open interval containing x; that for all positive integers n, there are positive numbers r, M such that $|g^{(n)}(x+z)| \leq M$ for all $(x+z)$ in $<x-r, x+r>$; and that likewise for $(x-z)$. Then expanding by Taylor series, $g(x+z)=\sum_{k=0}^{\infty} z^k g^{(k)}(x)/k!; g(x-z)=\sum_{k=0}^{\infty}(-z)^k g^{(k)}(x)/k!$. Hence, $g(z)g(x)=g(x-z)+g(x+z)$ yields

$$g(z)g(x) = 2\left[g(x) + \left[g^{(2)}(x)\right]z^2/2! + \left[g^{(4)}(x)\right]z^4/4! + \ldots\right], \text{ so}$$

$$g(z) = 2\left[1 + \left[g^{(2)}(x)\right]z^2/2!g(x) + \left[g^{(4)}(x)\right]z^4/4!g(x) + \ldots\right].$$

In this expansion of $g(z)$, x must not appear, since $g(z)$ does not depend on x. So, for example, the $z^2/2!$ term's coefficient $[g^{(2)}(x)]/g(x)$ must be independent of x—and obviously it cannot depend on z, either. So it must be a constant b. Hence $g^{(2)}(x) = b\, g(x)$. Differentiating twice, $g^{(4)}(x) = b\, g^{(2)}(x) = b^2 g(x)$, so the $z^4/4!$ term's coefficient $g^{(4)}(x)/g(x) = b^2$, and so forth for the other terms. Therefore,

$$g(z) = 2\left[1 + bz^2/2! + b^2 z^4/4! + b^3 z^6/6! + \ldots\right].$$

Letting $b = -a^2$,

$$g(z)=2\left[1-a^2z^2/2! + a^4 z^4/4! - a^6 z^6/6! + \ldots\right].$$

The bracketed expression is the Taylor expansion of cos az.

24. I simplify slightly this step of Poisson's argument, following Young (1834, 252).

25. The core of this argument appears in Barlow (1848, 9).

26. Something like this procedure seems to be suggested by Barlow (1848, 10–11), but the suggestion was not taken up by any later writers (as far as I know).

27. However, electric current (as used in characterizing an electric circuit) is not a vector quantity—despite having a magnitude and being associated with a direction. After all, if two wires are connected to a given pole of a battery, one directed upward and one directed to the right, then it is not true that the net current flow is along the diagonal between them, since no wire points in that direction. The parallelogram law thus does not apply. Not all quantities characterized by a magnitude and a direction combine parallelogramwise. For instance, walking 3 m east and then 4 m north is not equivalent to walking 4 m north and then 3 m east, if "equivalent" journeys must traverse the same ground, pass the same sights, and so forth.

28. I do not intend to be presupposing a sharp distinction between metaphysics and science. Indeed, I have argued elsewhere that metaphysics is continuous with physics and that "philosophical" concerns have been integral to progress in physics (Lange 2002, 201). But I do insist that the dispute over the scientific explanation of the parallelogram law should not be capable of being settled merely by what it is to be a law of nature or a scientific explanation— any more than these philosophical accounts should suffice to preclude a geocentric cosmology.

29. I have omitted some features of Lewis's account (such as the roles of chance and natural properties) that do not affect my discussion.

30. Of course, that law M can be deduced from law L does not ensure that M is explained by L. This is one lesson commonly drawn from the notorious footnote 33 in the classic paper by Hempel and Oppenheim (Hempel 1965, 273).

31. Another strike against the Best System Account (as I have amended it) is that as far as I know, no scientist has defended a statical explanation by arguing that the loss of strength from omission of the dynamical laws is balanced by the increase in simplicity.

32. As far as I can see, an account of laws as metaphysically primitive (as in Maudlin 2007) has no resources in terms of which to elaborate what facts would make the parallelogram law, despite following from dynamical laws, explained by statical rather than dynamical laws.

33. Of course, a *component* force must be the power to cause a mass to undergo a *component* acceleration. The parallelogram law for the composition of accelerations will, in turn, have to be explained by what accelerations are—and, ultimately, by what displacements are.

Some essentialists (e.g., Ellis 1990, 70) instead regard forces as a species of causal relation, not as causes themselves. (Recall note 2.) However, since this view is independent of essentialism, and since the moral I will draw applies beyond forces to other vector physical quantities that all essentialists regard as causal actors, I will construe essentialism as treating forces as causal actors.

34. It is not the case that advocates of the statical explanation (as I understand them) regard the dynamical laws as able to explain why the parallelogram law is *true* and even why it is *a law* (since it follows exclusively from laws), but as unable to explain why it has its characteristic necessity (which is stronger than any necessity possessed by the dynamical laws). Rather, the parallelogram law is true (and has the weaker flavor of necessity characteristic of the dynamical laws) because it is a law (with the stronger flavor of necessity). As I noted in section 4.5, advocates of the statical explanation do not believe that the parallelogram law's truth is *also* explained dynamically.

35. See, for instance, Poisson (1831, 83), where he is concerned with the stresses in elastic materials. This common explainer of parallelogram laws for the various physically diverse quantities I mentioned earlier is not enough to make them *physically* non-coincidental since it is insufficient by itself to explain any of them and their other important explainers are distinct.

36. I ended the passage from Clifton with an ellipsis. The passage goes on to require that the feature of the model corresponding to the explanandum not be "explicit in the definition of the model." Perhaps this requirement would rule out explaining the parallelogram law merely by pointing out that the theory represents forces as vectors and that vectors compose parallelogramwise. But I am unsure since (1) this requirement is "informal," as Clifton says, since the notion of being "explicit" is not precise, and (2) this requirement is motivated by the wish to avoid the model's simply listing all of the phenomena to be explained without genuinely unifying them under a small number of explainers. A general account of forces that includes a few force laws, the laws of motion, and that forces are vectors would achieve genuine unification of many phenomena even if it expressly stipulated that forces can be represented as vectors and that vectors compose parallelogramwise.

37. Railton's thought seems to be that for the star to occupy a smaller volume, two electrons would have to occupy the same quantum state, in violation of the Pauli Exclusion Principle. Whether or not this is true does not matter for my purposes; even if Railton's example is scientifically inaccurate, we can think about what sort of explanation would be involved if it were scientifically accurate.

38. This origin of the electron degeneracy pressure suggests that Skow (2014, 459) is correct in maintaining that the electron degeneracy pressure is a cause of the collapse's cessation. Although Skow (462) mentions briefly the idea that the law fixing the boundary of state space might be "more fundamental" than a dynamical law, he sets this idea aside; he thinks that a philosopher who regards an explanation of the white dwarf's behavior as non-causal would instead regard the boundary-fixing law as "independent" of the dynamics in that had the boundary law not obtained, the dynamics would have been no different. He argues that this counterfactual is implausible. By contrast, I appeal to a different counterfactual: that the boundary law would still have held even if the dynamics had been different. However, there is a point on which Skow and I agree: we both reject the argument that an explanation of the cessation of the white dwarf's collapse qualifies as non-causal by virtue of the fact that the explainer (the boundary law) is a law, not a cause, and the cessation has no cause. As I argued in chapter 1, an event with no cause can have a causal explanation that cites no cause.

Dorato and Felline (2010) regard the uncertainty principle as supplying "structural explanations."

39. The preceding passage appears in Lange (2009a, 11).

■ **Chapter 5**

1. The orthodox view (Prior, Pargetter, and Jackson 1982) is that a disposition does not help to cause its manifestation. Some philosophers (e.g., Sober 1984, 77–78, 84; see Shapiro and Sober 2007, 253) see this view as the wrong conclusion to draw from Molieresque "dormitive virtue" considerations.

2. They have in common the cosmological Big Bang, perhaps the presence of oxygen in the atmosphere above the country, and so forth—but none of these is relevant in the given context. As I mentioned in chapter 1, an explanation need not describe the result's actual causal history in order to qualify as causal, as long as the explanation explains by virtue of supplying relevant information regarding the world's network of causal relations. For instance, Jackson and Pargetter (1992) correctly say that the boiling water in the flask explains why the flask cracked by virtue of the fact that had the given energetic collision between a water molecule and the flask not occurred (or not caused a crack to form), another collision would almost certainly have done so. The preempted "cause" did not actually cause the crack and

so information about it does not describe the crack's actual causal history. But information about it explains by virtue of describing the world's network of causal relations (in particular, by telling us something about what that network would have been like, had it been different in a certain way).

3. The question "Why were the students who did the worst on the first exam by and large not the students who did the worst on the second exam?" is understood in some contexts to be demanding a particular kind of explanation: one appealing to important causes common to many of the students. In that case, the correct reply is to reject the why question as having a false presupposition (that there is such a cause). But the fact that regression toward the mean fails to answer the why question in such a context does not show that it is never an answer—that there are no contexts where the why question lacks this presupposition. (See note 7.)

In section 1.2, I characterized "equilibrium explanations" as causal explanations because they work by supplying information about the world's causal structure. A detailed account of the history of the causes by which a given system has been brought to equilibrium (e.g., the history of the population's changing sex ratio and consequent selection pressure resulting in the population's current approximate 1:1 sex ratio) does not deepen the equilibrium explanation; the system's particular trajectory through state space toward equilibrium does not figure in the equilibrium explanation. Similarly, an explanation in the coin-toss case appealing to regression toward the mean is not deepened by an account of the causal factors responsible for the coin's 50% chance of landing heads (such as the coin's mass distribution) since the coin's 50% chance of landing heads does not figure in the explanation. (By contrast, an account of the causal factors responsible for some of the facts that do figure in the equilibrium explanation (e.g., for the fact that male and female offspring require the same parental resources) would deepen the equilibrium explanation.)

4. Although statistics textbooks commonly present regression toward the mean as answering why questions ("Explain why the rookie of the year in major-league baseball usually does not perform as well in his second season" [Gravetter and Wallnau 2009, 536]), Lipton (2004, 32; 2009b, 622) is the only philosopher I know who has mentioned explanations that appeal to regression toward the mean. He calls such explanations "non-causal" on the grounds that they do not explain by giving some information about the explanandum's causes. However, he says that in being non-causal, an explanation appealing to regression toward the mean is like an explanation that explains why it is that, when a bunch of sticks are tossed upward and then photographed at some instant, more of the sticks in the photo are nearly horizontal than nearly vertical. I discussed this example in chapter 1 and suggested that this explanation is not straightforwardly non-causal; it may appeal to the causal details of the particular stick-tossing mechanism at work. In that case, it would *not* be non-causal. Rather, it would then resemble the explanation that appeals to the coin's 50% chance of landing heads rather than the explanation that appeals to regression toward the mean.

5. That an RS explanation unifies causally diverse cases does not mean that it derives its explanatory power from doing so. Whereas unificationist accounts of scientific explanation take unification to be the source of explanatory power, I think unification results from having similar explanations.

6. Thanks to Chris Haufe for calling this article to my attention.

7. Once again (see note 3), the question "Why was there a higher rate of emission during that period?" may in certain contexts be demanding an explanation *of a certain kind*—so that the correct reply is to reject the why question. Nevertheless, in other contexts, the question does not have such a presupposition. In those contexts, that the fluctuation is "due to chance"

is itself a perfectly good explanation rather than merely telling us that there is no explanation of a certain kind. Here is a similar example: "We want an explanation of the dramatic increase in the number of cases of [Creutzfeldt-Jakob disease] that occurred during the final quarter of 1998. Is it simply a statistical fluctuation attributable to chance, or is it a result of increased awareness and more accurate diagnosis of the disease, or is the disease beginning a trend of claiming more victims?" (Salmon 2001, 61–62).

8. On this point, I may be disagreeing with some philosophers who have described explanations that I would characterize as RS. For example, Walsh (2007, 283–284) gives an example part of which involves taking samples from two collections of apples, Jonagolds and Pippins. Samples of n Jonagolds nearly always weigh more than samples of n Pippins when n is large, but as n diminishes, the frequency with which Pippin samples outweigh Jonagold samples increases somewhat. Walsh says that this phenomenon is explained by the fact that a Jonagold's average weight is greater than a Pippin's, but Pippins vary in weight more than Jonagolds (and enough so that some Jonagolds are outweighed by some Pippins). It seems to me that we might even omit some of these details and explain this phenomenon as the typical signature of a statistical phenomenon (also exhibited by the case studied by Rutherford and Geiger): since a Jonagold is likely but not certain to weigh more than a Pippin, samples can depart from expectation and departures are more likely as samples are smaller. However, Walsh insists that "the effect is explained by the statistical properties of the set-up and not by the causal properties of the apples" (2007, 284; and see 288–289)—that is, not by the weights of the various apples in the two collections from which the samples are drawn. I see no reason to say that the result cannot be explained by the relevant propensities (e.g., the chance of selecting a Jonagold having a given weight) or, in turn, by the grounds of these propensities (which include the weights of the various apples in the collections). Non-causal explanations do not always preclude causal explanations.

9. Some such slogan is quite common. For instance, Galton discovered that across those cases where the two parents' mean height is between 70 and 71 inches (average human height was 68.2 inches), the mean children's height is 69.5 inches. The RS explanation of this fact in terms of regression toward the mean shows that "this is a statistical, not a genetic phenomenon" (Bland and Altman 1994, 1499).

10. Of course, the RS reason why a run of 200 coin tosses has only 20 heads (where the mean outcome is 100 heads) is the same as the RS reason why a run of 200 coin tosses has only 5 heads: such wild fluctuations occasionally happen with runs of independent, identically distributed trials. That both outcomes receive the same RS explanation should not disturb us. It has long been widely (though not universally) accepted that different outcomes can receive the same causal statistical explanation. For instance, if Jones contracts paresis, then the considerations responsible for Jones's likelihood of contracting paresis (such as his having latent untreated syphilis) will explain why he does, and if Jones does not contract paresis, then the same considerations will explain why he does not (Salmon 1989, 62). I see no reason why incompatible outcomes cannot likewise receive the same RS explanation.

11. In the most evenly matched case (that is, where each student has a 50% chance of winning any given round), the chance that one player will be in the lead only once or never is 0.5379 (Feller 1957, 79).

12. The RS explanation does not have to include the mathematical derivation showing this "one-sidedness" to be a characteristic feature of random walks. The RS explanation appeals merely to the fact that it is such a feature. (Similarly, I argued in section 1.5 that distinctively mathematical explanations in science include mathematical facts, of course, but not their proofs.)

13. Matthen (2009) has recently proposed that "statistically abstractive" (SA) explanation is a hitherto neglected form of explanation and that explanations by drift are SA explanations. An SA explanation is not an RS explanation. Rather, it is a statistical explanation of the usual sort, its only distinction being that it derives the chance of the fact being explained by placing the case in a reference class that is not objectively homogeneous. In doing so, it ignores certain statistically relevant factors on the grounds that they are uninteresting to a particular theory in play (such as population genetics).

14. To defend this view properly would take me too far afield. I do wish to note, however, that selection for some trait is a causal *process* (as Shapiro and Sober [2007, 256] call it in a passage I quote shortly), not a *cause*. In selection, various features of the population undergoing selection and of its environment are causes of the outcome frequencies. Selection (like diffusion, erosion, heat flow, and electrical conduction) is a process involving population-level causes and effects, the result being that certain traits are "selected" over others so that a new set of trait frequencies is the effect that is explained (just as temperature differences are causes in the process of heat flow, with a new spatial distribution of heat as the effect to be explained). To say that "selection for properties causes differences in survival and reproductive success" (Sober 1984, 100) is to specify the causal process at work, not to say that selection is a cause in place of or alongside various features of the population and environment. This can easily lead to confusion. To cite one example, McLaughlin (2007, 279–280) interprets Sober's remark above as mistakenly treating selection as a cause; McLaughlin then goes on to insist that selection "just is (nonaccidental, differential) reproductive success."

Though selection for some trait is a causal process rather than a cause, a causal explanation of some change in trait frequency can cite selection for some trait since in doing so, it describes the relevant feature of the causes at work (see Shapiro and Sober 2007, 253). In the same way, a causal explanation for some geological feature can cite erosion. What is a "causal process" in the above sense? Often, a causal process is defined as a sequence of states, each successive state being caused (at least in part) by its predecessor (as distinguished from a "pseudoprocess," such as a shadow moving across a page, where the earlier stage is not a cause of the later one). But to understand natural selection (or erosion) as a causal process, we must recognize that what unifies the states in the sequence as a distinct causal process, and what makes a given causal process a case of natural selection (or erosion), is something about the kind of causes at work at each stage. Part of what unites the stages of a population into a single causal process of natural selection for better camouflage, for example, is an important, stable, causally relevant feature of the causes at work in each stage.

15. Compare "It was drift, not selection" to "This is a statistical, not a genetic phenomenon," quoted in note 9.

16. By adding another population of moths where both light and dark moths happened to land on representative samples of trees, we could turn Beatty's example into my earlier example involving two populations with the same initial frequencies under the same selection pressures but with frequencies that have diverged by the end of a given interval.

17. Sober (personal communication, June 2012) currently believes that drift and selection are not distinct causal processes; rather, there is only one population-level causal process at work. However, drift and selection involve different causes co-occurring (population size and fitness differences, respectively) that jointly influence the trait frequencies, just as in a series of coin tosses, there is only one causal process by which heads and tails are accumulating, but the coin's bias and the number of tosses are distinct causes, separately manipulable.

18. There are other problems with them, too. In some cases, selection is *stronger* insofar as population size is smaller. See Sober (2001).

19. The relevant theorem of the probability calculus is that in n independent trials where the chance of a given kind of outcome in any given trial is p, the chance of i such outcomes is $[n!/i!(n-i)!]\,p^i\,(1-p)^{n-i}$.

20. However, Sober (2011) believes that although the fitnesses of various traits in a population stand in metaphysically necessary connections to the traits' expected frequencies, they are causes of those frequencies; no contingent law of nature is needed to mediate between a cause and its effect. (This may not represent a departure from Sober's prior view of fitnesses as "causally inert" (Sober 1984), since Sober was arguing there that fitnesses are not causes of the survival and reproduction of *individual organisms*; he did not address whether they are causes of trait frequencies in a *population*.) Sober now gives manipulationist reasons for thinking fitness to be a cause of trait frequency, and he says that a contingent law is not needed to mediate a causal relation because (he says, appealing to Davidson) it is an analytic truth that E's cause would cause E (i.e., if E occurs and has a cause, then E's cause caused E). However (I reply), this truth's analyticity does not show that a causal relation requires no contingent law to connect cause and effect, since "contingent" here should be contrasted with "metaphysically necessary" (a modal matter), not with "analytic" (a conceptual matter). Although "E's cause" may be analytically connected to "E," it does not follow that the event that is E's cause is connected to E by metaphysical necessity. By contrast, that trait A is fitter than trait B *is* connected with metaphysical necessity to a relation between A's and B's expected frequencies. This connection holds in virtue of what fitnesses essentially *are*, whereas the event that is E's cause is not essentially E's cause. I do not see how fitness's manipulationist credentials do anything to undermine Sober's previous (1984) argument that fitness is a mere actuarial property reflecting various potential causal factors that may not actually have come into play and so is unsuited to being a cause. That argument, in my view, precludes fitnesses from being causes even of trait frequencies. (Of course, I agree with Sober [1984] that fitness can still figure in causal explanations since it can describe the world's causal relations without figuring in any itself.)

I suggested in chapter 1 that Mother's having 3 children and 23 strawberries were causes of her failure when she tried to distribute her strawberries evenly (without cutting any) among her children. That these numbers of strawberries and children would cause Mother to fail is metaphysically necessary. But (I argued) these numbers of strawberries and children do not function *as causes* in the explanation of Mother's failure. That explanation is non-causal. In contrast, trait fitnesses *are* supposed to figure in causal explanations of trait frequencies. On my view, causal explanations contain no metaphysically necessary statements specifying the causal relevance of certain features of events. (See Lange and Rosenberg 2011.)

21. Walsh (2007) has also argued that the number of tosses is not a cause. Here is his argument, as I understand it. Consider 100 fair coin flips resulting in roughly 50% heads, although in the 10 runs of 10 successive flips each, there were significant departures from 50% heads. Why is that? A drift explanation appeals to 10 flips being much smaller than 100 flips. But if the number of flips is a cause, then (Walsh says) we would have to say that drift as a cause is strong in each subpopulation but weak in the population as a whole—which is a "contradiction" (296) since the 100-flip population is composed of the 10 subpopulations. However, I see no contradiction in taking the number of tosses as a cause: that there were only 10 tosses could be a cause of the outcome for a given subpopulation but plainly is not supposed to be a cause of what happens in the overall population. Walsh generates a contradiction only by

turning the number of tosses into the strength of a "force": drift is weak for the overall population but strong in each subpopulation, which is a contradiction ("drift is objectively both
weak and strong in the population" (296)) considering that the overall population is constituted by the subpopulations. But without treating drift as a force acting on each subpopulation (and perforce the overall population), Walsh generates no contradiction; at least, I see
no contradiction arising simply from $n = 10$ being a cause for a subpopulation but $n = 100$
being a cause for the population as a whole. (Matthen 2009, 409, gives an argument similar to
Walsh's: "How can strong nondirectional (and therefore noncanceling) forces operating on
parts of a population give rise to a weak force operating on the whole?")

22. That an explanation by drift cites no causes does not entail that it is not a causal explanation. As I showed in section 1.2, a causal explanation need not specify any causes. Brandon
(2006, 329) says that drift explanations are causal precisely because they describe what happens by default—that is, in the absence of causes making it happen otherwise. (See my reference to Brandon in chapter 1.) I have argued that drift explanations are non-causal because
they are RS, not because they cite no causes.

23. Explanations by drift are not the only kind of RS explanation in evolutionary biology. Grantham (1999) supplies another example: the explanation of cladogenetic trends in
terms of passive diffusion away from a boundary. Grantham emphasizes a point that I have
also made: that a fact's having such an explanation does not preclude its also having a causal,
selectionist explanation.

■ Chapter 6

1. Among the philosophical works on dimensional analysis are Birkhoff (1950), Bridgman
(1931), Campbell (1957), Causey (1967, 1969), Ellis (1966), Krantz, Luce, Suppes, and
Tversky (1971), Langhaar (1951), Luce (1971), Laymon (1991), and Sedov (1959). None
characterizes dimensional analysis as capable of funding scientific explanations. In contrast,
Batterman (2002a, 2002b) explores the explanatory contributions of dimensional analysis.
Batterman understands dimensional analysis as the simplest species of "asymptotic explanation," and Batterman sees an asymptotic explanation as supplying a kind of understanding that cannot be supplied, even in principle, by a derivation of the same explanandum
from more fundamental laws. There are thus close similarities between Batterman's themes
and mine.

Batterman's "asymptotic explanations" target relationships that emerge in the long run
for a wide range of specific initial conditions (as the influence of those initial details dies
out) and at the macroscopic level (where various microstructural details make negligible difference). Like Batterman, I emphasize (in chapter 10) how dimensional explanations unify
because they can ignore certain physical details. As I will show, dimensional arguments work
by presupposing that (at least to a sufficiently good approximation) a given phenomenon is
independent of various parameters. However, I do not contend that an equation explained
dimensionally must be the result of some more fundamental theory taken to some limit.
I also deny that a dimensional argument that is explanatory acquires its explanatory power by
virtue of capturing the asymptote of some fundamental theory.

Batterman emphasizes that the same asymptotic explanation applies to all simple pendulums, whatever material their bobs are made of. I argue (in chapter 10) that dimensional explanations allow connections to be drawn among much more disparate cases—for
instance, among a pendulum, a body in free fall, and a water wave. These cases have the same
(or relevantly similar) dimensional architecture despite differing profoundly in their physical

features *even when considered asymptotically*—in the limit where the influences of initial transients and microstructural details become negligibly small.

2. Many (e.g., Bridgman 1931, 51) mistakenly identify Fourier as the first to employ dimensional reasoning.

3. I am indebted to Palmerino (1999, 296) for this way of displaying Deschamps's argument.

4. Unfortunately, there are several common definitions of the term "dimensionally homogeneous." Here is a definition that is close to the one that I just gave (but that is defective in not leaving room for a relation to be "dimensionally homogeneous" even if it fails to hold): that a relation is "dimensionally homogeneous" if and only if it holds in any system of units for the fundamental dimensions of the quantities so related. This definition may be found in articles and textbooks concerning a wide range of subjects—for example, coastal engineering (Hughes 1993, 27), engineering experimentation (Schenck 1979, 88), chemical engineering (Zlokarnik 2006, 3), fluid mechanics (Shames 2002, 8), and pharmacokinetics (Rescigno 2003, 23), as well as dimensional analysis (Langhaar 1951, 13 and 18; Laymon 1991, 148). (I will refine this definition in section 6.5 so as to recognize that a given relation is dimensionally homogeneous or not only *for a certain set of fundamental dimensions*, such as {mass, length, and time}.)

A second common definition is that a relation is "dimensionally homogeneous" if and only if every term in the equation has the same dimensions. Such definitions appear in Birkhoff (1950, 80), Bridgman (1931, 41), and Furbish (1997, 116), for example. (However, Bridgman, 37, also says that the assumption that a given relation holds for any system of units for the various fundamental dimensions of the quantities so related "is absolutely essential to the treatment, and in fact dimensional analysis applies only to this type of equation.") In section 6.4, I contrast this second notion (which I term "dimensional consistency") with the first (which I call "dimensional homogeneity"). As a third alternative, "dimensional homogeneity" is sometimes defined directly in terms of the equation's form, as described in section 6.2.

5. That it is *impossible* for the relation among the distances traversed in successive equal time intervals by a body falling freely from rest to accord with Fabri's proposal seems to me the point behind remarks like this: "The dimensions test is the basic logical grammar of physics. Although, unfortunately, it does not ensure that our equations must be true, it does ensure that they do make sense, that they could conceivably be true" (Polya 1977, 126). Of course, the issue (as I see it) is broadly logical possibility, not conceivability or meaningfulness. The claim that Fabri's proposal holds in all systems of units is meaningful; it just cannot be true. Moreover, as I have mentioned, a relation can hold without being dimensionally homogeneous. Nevertheless, Polya's remark nicely expresses the idea that Fabri's proposal does not describe a way that the world might have been. (As Polya also emphasizes, the fact that Galileo's proposal is not impossible on dimensional grounds does not show that it is true, as I will shortly explain.)

6. I am treating expressions like "Fabri's proposal" as rigid designators.

7. For more on Huygens's argument, see Palmerino (1999, 323–324) and Meli (2006, 333).

8. This "motivation" fails to motivate the requirement that $c > 0$, which presumably arises from the thought that two units cannot measure the *same* quantity if one increases while the other decreases (though they might then measure logically related quantities).

9. This criterion for units to specify the same quantity occasionally appears to depart from ordinary usage. For example, degrees Celsius and degrees Kelvin are ordinarily regarded as

measuring the same quantity: temperature. But since their zeros do not coincide, a doubling of degrees Celsius—e.g., from 2°C (275K) to 4°C (277K)—does not coincide with a doubling of degrees Kelvin. However, if K measures how far a temperature departs from absolute zero, then °C does not count as a unit for the same quantity as K. (In laws such as the ideal-gas law [$PV = nRT$], T must be expressed in an absolute scale.) Nevertheless, on this criterion, °C and K are both units of temperature *difference*, since then the arbitrary zeros drop out.

10. See, e.g., Bridgman (1931, 21–22); Birkhoff (1950: 87–88); Luce (1959, 87); Ellis (1966, 204).

11. At least according to classical physics. I will assume classical physics for all of my examples in this chapter.

12. Nor is the explanans one of the non-constraints to which an "explanation by constraint" may appeal, namely, a fact that in the context of the why question is understood to constitute the case with which the why question is concerned. For instance, these facts included the numbers of strawberries and children in connection with the distinctively mathematical explanation of Mother's failure to distribute the strawberries evenly among her children. See chapter 1.

13. By a "derivative law," I mean a logical consequence of natural laws alone (together with mathematical truths and other broadly logical necessities) that is not a fundamental law, but rather is explained by other laws. For example (according to classical physics), the centripetal force law $F = m\omega^2 r$ follows from and is explained by Newton's second law of motion (together with geometric facts).

Some philosophers use the term "derivative law" to encompass some generalizations that do not follow from natural laws alone. For example, that all bodies falling to Earth from a small height in conditions where all nongravitational influences can be neglected (for example, with negligible air resistance) accelerate at approximately 9.8 m/s^2 is sometimes termed a "derivative law." Yet it follows from more fundamental laws (such as Newton's law of gravity and second law of motion) only when they have been supplemented by various nonlaws, such as the accidental fact that Earth's mass is 5.98 x 10^{24} kg. I will be concerned only with "derivative laws" that are naturally necessary rather than accidental. (The above accidental fact specifying the rate of gravitational acceleration is sometimes termed "Galileo's law of falling bodies," though in the previous section, I used "Galileo's law" to refer to a natural necessity: the fact that all such falling bodies cover a total distance proportional to t^2 during the period t after their release.) A given derivative law's scope may be rather narrow; the law may be a consequence of more fundamental laws applied to a certain specific range of conditions.

14. That this derivation is generally regarded as explanatory is evident from common remarks such as Weinberg (1987, 6).

15. Had T depended on the planet's mass, then Kepler's third law (that $T \propto r^{3/2}$ with the same proportionality constant for every planet orbiting the Sun) would not have held.

16. There might seem to be one difference: the salt's being hexed explains nothing whereas the elements of the fundamental laws that do not contribute to explaining $T \propto r^{3/2}$ help to explain other facts. However, the salt's being hexed might indeed explain other facts, such as the way that superstitious people treat the salt.

17. Here, I think, my view disagrees with Campbell's. Although not discussing dimensional arguments as explanations, he says that "for the application of the argument from dimensions everything involved in the dynamical reasoning is required except the numerical values of no-dimensional magnitudes" (1957, 403, and see 422).

18. Analogously, the electrostatic force between a particular pair of point bodies (with certain charges, at a certain separation) is explained by the consequence of Coulomb's law that is restricted to that particular combination of charges and separation. This derivative law, in turn, is explained by Coulomb's law in its full generality. In this way, the full Coulomb's law is explanatorily relevant to the electrostatic force between the pair of bodies.

19. Dretske (1970) makes the same point, using other examples.

20. Likewise Barenblatt (1987, 5): "The dimensions of both sides of any equation having physical sense must be identical. Otherwise, the equation would no longer hold under a change of fundamental units of measurement." Douglas (1969, 3): "An equation about a real physical situation will be true only if all the terms are of the same kind and therefore have the same dimensions."

21. Bridgman (1931, 42) and Birkhoff (1950, 83) give similar examples. Bridgman emphasizes that "=" in the equation should be understood as numerical equality; obviously, if "=" required the same units on both sides, then trivially an equation would have to be dimensionally consistent. (Perhaps we should say that since the equation relates the mere numbers on both sides, the two sides are dimensionless and therefore the equation is in fact dimensionally consistent. But then the requirement of dimensional consistency would be trivially satisfied by any equation.) Some might say that the example, though it follows logically from natural laws alone, is not itself a law, and so it fails to show that laws can be dimensionally inconsistent. In Lange (2000), I discuss the distinction between laws and naturally necessary nonlaws.

22. Nor is dimensional consistency sufficient for dimensional homogeneity. In CGS electrostatic units, charge (like force) is not an independent dimension. It has dimension $L^{3/2} M^{1/2} T^{-1}$. (One "electrostatic unit" is defined as the charge where the electrostatic force between two point bodies so charged, 1 cm apart, equals 1 dyne.) Accordingly, Coulomb's law in these units ($F = q_1 q_2 / r^2$) has no dimensional constant of proportionality. A change to other units would require the introduction of a dimensional proportionality constant. So this expression for Coulomb's law is dimensionally consistent (in CGS electrostatic units) but not dimensionally homogeneous.

23. Shames (2002, 8), for example, invokes a "law of dimensional homogeneity" (that "an analytically derived equation representing a physical phenomenon must be valid for all systems of units") as if it were one among the many contingent laws and metalaws of nature. Likewise, Romeny (2003, 16) characterizes the "law of scale invariance" as "one of the most fundamental laws of physics."

24. In this, I think I agree with Campbell (1957, 366–369) and Ellis (1966, 117). That all laws can be expressed in terms of dimensionally homogeneous relations seems akin to the view (advanced by Reichenbach, Hempel, Carnap, and others) that all fundamental laws can be expressed without proper names or "local predicates" (i.e., predicates defined in terms of particular times, places, objects, events, etc.). Indeed, a similar intuition lies behind both ideas: the laws are too "general" to privilege any particular thing (whether an object or a unit). For more on natural laws and nonlocal predicates, see Lange (2000).

25. Since it is trivial that every law can be expressed in terms of a dimensionally homogeneous relation, I do not understand why those who believe in some nontrivial "principle of dimensional homogeneity" qualify the principle; they say that we need an explanation "of why *(most)* numerical laws of physics are dimensionally invariant" (Krantz et al. 1971, 504, my italics) or "of the *prevalence* of dimensionally invariant laws (Causey 1969, 256, my italics) or of the fact "that *practically* every law of physics is dimensionally invariant" (30, my italics)

or of the fact that "most, if not all, physical laws can be stated in terms of dimensionally invariant equations" (Luce 1971, 157).

26. Having included ρ_s and an unspecified $f(\rho_f / \rho_s)$ in the relation, there is no need also to include ρ_f.

27. This yields the hydrodynamic answer when $f(\rho_f / \rho_s) = (2/9)\,(1 - (\rho_f / \rho_s))$.

28. In contrast, take a case where thermal energy *is* converted to or from another form of energy. In giving a dimensional explanation for the gain in heat h of a body having mass m upon falling to the ground (without bouncing) from rest at height s, we must presume there to be a dimensionally homogeneous relation between h and some subset of g, m, and s where heat is *not* given its own dimension. (No such dimensionally homogeneous relation is possible if heat is given its own dimension.) Dimensional reasoning then yields $h \propto mgs$.

■ Chapter 7

1. In the literature on explanation, the existence of explanations in mathematics is often acknowledged. For one example per decade, see Nagel (1961, 16), Rescher (1970, 4), Sober (1984, 96), Smart (1990, 2), and Psillos (2002, 2). But explanation in mathematics is typically not examined at length. In the five works just cited, either explanation in mathematics is set aside as genuinely not germane to the kind of explanation being examined, or it is given cursory treatment, or it is just ignored after being acknowledged once.

2. Van Fraassen (1977, 1980) has been especially influential in emphasizing the role of context in scientific explanation. Kitcher and Salmon (1987) have convincingly argued against "anything goes."

3. Of course, mathematical facts are often used to explain why certain contingent facts hold, as I showed in chapter 1. (For recent discussions, see Baker 2005; Colyvan 2001, 2002; and Melia 2002; as well as the earlier papers Nerlich 1979 and Steiner 1978b.) But these are explanations of physical facts and so are not "mathematical explanations" of the kind that will form the subject of part III.

Likewise, in a conversation, we might "explain" why (or how) some mathematical proof works (either by giving its overall strategy or by making more explicit the transitions between steps). A textbook might "explain" how to multiply matrices. A mathematics popularizer might "explain" an obscure theorem by unpacking its meaning. However, none of these is the kind of "mathematical explanation" with which part III will be concerned. None involves explaining why some result holds—just as Hempel (2001, 80) pointed out that an account of scientific explanation does not aim to account for what I do when I use gestures to "explain" to a Yugoslav garage mechanic how my car has been misbehaving. (For a similar remark, see Hafner and Mancosu 2005, 217–218.) I am also not concerned with historical or psychological explanations of why mathematicians held various beliefs or how a given mathematician managed to make a certain discovery. Likewise, questions asking for good reasons for some belief are sometimes expressed as why questions, as in "Why do you think that this strategy for proving the theorem is going to work?" and "Why do you think that this mathematical claim is true?" But these questions are not answered by mathematical explanations of the sort that part III will be investigating. Explaining why we should (or do) believe in a theorem is distinct from explaining why the theorem holds (i.e., explaining the theorem). This distinction is familiar from the literature on scientific explanation.

4. To avoid the corrupting influence of philosophical intuitions, I will try to use examples from workaday mathematics rather than from logic, set theory, or other parts of mathematics that have important connections to philosophy. But by focusing on proofs

that mathematicians themselves recognize as explanatory, I do not mean to suggest that philosophers must unquestioningly accept the verdicts of mathematicians. Indeed, some mathematicians (e.g., Gale 1990) have denied that there is any distinction between proofs that explain why theorems hold and proofs that merely show that they hold. (Some philosophers agree; see, for example, Grosholz 2000, 81, and Zelcer 2013. However, Gale later changed his mind; see the text associated with chapter 8 note 23.) But just as an account of *scientific* explanation should do justice to scientific practice (without having to fit every judgment of explanatory power made by every scientist), so too an account of *mathematical* explanation should do justice to mathematical practice. With regard to the examples that I will discuss, the judgments made by various mathematicians of which proofs explain are (I believe) widely shared and easily appreciated by other mathematicians as well as by nonmathematicians. Accordingly, it is especially important that an account of mathematical explanation fit such cases.

Here is an objection to the notion of explanation in mathematics. Consider this fact about explanation generally (whether it be scientific, mathematical, or some other kind): If p explains q, then any p' that is logically equivalent to p also explains q. For p and p' to be logically equivalent is for them to be true in exactly the same logically possible worlds. Now any two mathematical truths are true in exactly the same logically possible worlds: all of them. So if one mathematical truth p explains another q, then any other mathematical truth p' explains q—trivializing the notion of a mathematical explanation.

To this objection, I reply by denying that if p explains q, then any p' that is logically equivalent to p also explains q. Suppose that we are dealing with some scientific explanation where p explains and entails q. (For instance, perhaps p is a fundamental law and q is some derivative law.) Then p is logically equivalent to $p\&q$. But $p\&q$ does not explain why q holds. Likewise, p is logically equivalent to $(q \supset p)\&q$, but this conjunction does not explain q.

5. Although I am interested in the distinction between explanatory and non-explanatory proofs, I do not believe that explanatory proofs are necessarily "better" all things considered; there are many dimensions along which a proof can be evaluated. I also do not believe that a mathematics teacher should always prefer an explanatory proof to a proof that is not explanatory. There are many purposes in pedagogy, and an accessible proof that proceeds by brute force (and hence is not explanatory, in cases where the theorem's symmetry or simplicity is striking) may sometimes be more useful pedagogically, all things considered, than an explanatory proof. Likewise, in mathematics research rather than pedagogy, proofs of different kinds serve different purposes. Therefore, I do not agree with Andrew Gleason's oft-quoted remark, "Proofs really aren't there to convince you that something is true—they're there to show you why it is true" (Alsina and Nelson 2010, xix), if this remark is intended as giving *the* function of proofs in mathematics.

Although an explanatory proof may foster "understanding," I will not appeal to "understanding," "insight," "satisfaction," "illumination," or "enlightenment" in order to capture mathematical explanation, just as these notions are too psychological and too imprecise to figure in an account of scientific explanation. (But I will give examples where mathematicians use these terms to express a proof's explanatory power or impotence.)

6. From the Bay Area Math Meet, San Francisco, April 29, 2000.

7. As Bas van Fraassen kindly pointed out to me, the same calculation is used to derive Carnap's measure function m* (which assigns equal probability to every structure description) from de Finetti's representation theorem and an initial assignment of a flat probability density over all possible objective chances of the given outcome. See, for instance, Jeffrey

1983, 199–200. In fact, the same calculation has an even more venerable pedigree: in the "billiard table" in Bayes's 1764 paper (see Stigler 1986, 124–126).

8. Regarding another method of tackling this integral (using generating functions—another example of which I will discuss in section 7.6), Zeitz (2007, 352) says: "The above proof was a thing of beauty. . . . Yet the magical nature of the argument is also its shortcoming. Its punchline creeps up without warning. Very entertaining, and very instructive in a general sense, but it doesn't shed quite enough light on this particular problem. It shows us *how* these $n + 1$ probabilities were uniformly distributed. But we still don't know *why*."

The proof I gave can be shortened: by integration by parts, as I showed, the total chance of r heads in n tosses is $\binom{n}{r}\int_0^1 p^r(1-p)^{n-r}\,dp = \binom{n}{r}\frac{n-r}{r+1}\int_0^1 p^{r+1}(1-p)^{n-r-1}\,dp = \binom{n}{r+1}\int_0^1 p^{r+1}(1-p)^{n-r-1}\,dp$, which is the total chance of $r + 1$ heads in n tosses. In this way, we show that the chance is independent of r and so must be $\frac{1}{n+1}$. However (as Tord Sjödin noted when he showed me this shortcut), that things suddenly work out here so neatly is no less "magical" than in the longer proof.

9. Zeitz (2007, 353): "The probabilities were uniform because the numbers [generated randomly] were uniform, and thus their rankings [that is, the place of the first generated number among the others, as ranked from smallest to largest] were uniform. The underlying principle, the 'why' that explains this problem, is . . . Symmetry."

10. There are many similar examples where mathematicians characterize a theorem as "explaining" various instantiations of it. For instance, in 1599, Edward Wright published a table of the "perpetuall addition" of secants (in modern terminology: a table of definite integrals of sec x taken from 0 to various angles) for use in constructing Mercator projections of the earth. About 50 years later, Henry Bond "discovered by chance" (according to Edmond Halley) that the entries in Wright's table were nearly identical to the entries in a table of $\log(\tan(x/2 + \pi/4))$. (For more on this episode, see Rickey and Tuchinsky 1980.) As Spivak (1980, 361) says, "the correspondence between the two tables . . . remained unexplained until the invention of calculus," when $\int \sec x\,dx = \log\left(\tan\left(\frac{x}{2} + \frac{\pi}{4}\right)\right)$ was discovered. This theorem, then, explained its near instances in the tables. (The differences between the tables were explained by calculational errors and rounding off.)

11. Kitcher (1985, 637; 1989, 425–426) presents this case as an example of mathematical explanation, but he diagnoses it in terms of his account of mathematical explanation (see section 8.5) rather than in terms of symmetry.

12. See, for instance, Davenport 1999, 82–83.

13. The arrangement may seem asymmetric in one respect: vertex A differs from B and C in being opposite to the only side of ΔABC that is intersected by l_1 along its extension rather than between the triangle's vertices. However, the configuration shown in fig. 7.4 is a special case of Menelaus's theorem since l_1 need not intersect any side of ΔABC between the vertices; l_1 may intersect all three sides along their extensions.

14. Proof of lemma: Complete the triangles (see fig. 7.18) with perpendicular lines; let x be the lengths of the two top perpendiculars and y be the lengths of the two bottom perpendiculars; let the hypotenuses be a on the top left, b on the bottom left, c on the top right, and d on the bottom right.

The two left triangles are similar: both involve right angles, and the top angles of each are corresponding angles. Hence, corresponding parts of the two triangles are in a constant ratio. In particular, $x:y = a:b$. The same argument on the right side yields $x:y = c:d$. Hence, $a:b = c:d$.

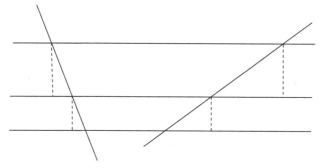

Figure 7.18 Proof of lemma

15. Devlin (2008) writes: "The routine solution by integration . . . gives us the answer, but does not explain what is going on." In contrast, the proof that I have presented as explanatory "helps us to understand what is going on."

16. Another reason why the theorem is remarkable is that apparently, it was not even conjectured by the ancients, but only circa 1900. (Varignon's theorem—which I will discuss shortly—was also apparently not conjectured by the ancients.)

17. Indeed, rather than asking "Why does the napkin-ring theorem hold?" in a context where the result's independence from r and R is salient, we might just as well have asked "Why is the napkin ring's volume independent of r and R?" Likewise, to ask "Why is Zeitz's biased-coin theorem true?" (in a context where its symmetry is salient) is just to ask "Where does the symmetry in Zeitz's biased-coin theorem come from?" (But see the text at note 26.)

Although I will suggest (see the end of chapter 8 and also chapter 10) that salience plays a role in certain *scientific* explanations too, I do not believe that the distinction between a scientific explanation and a non-explanatory derivation of the explanandum always requires that the explanandum display some striking feature.

Is it unilluminating to characterize a "salient feature" partly as a feature that gives content (in the manner I am describing) to a demand for mathematical explanation, while in turn characterizing "mathematical explanation" in terms of a salient feature? I do not think that my proposal is thereby rendered unilluminating. We can say plenty about salience other than through its role in mathematical explanation (namely, by way of paradigm cases, the kinds of features that are typically salient, how features become salient, and so forth—all topics that I will be discussing). We can recognize a feature as salient independent from identifying some particular proof as explanatory. We can likewise say plenty about mathematical explanation apart from its connection to salience.

To appreciate that the connection I propose between salience and mathematical explanation does not trivialize my account, compare my account to van Fraassen's pragmatic approach to scientific explanation. His account characterizes a "scientific explanation" as an answer to a why question specified partly in terms of a contrast class. It also characterizes the "contrast class" in a given case as consisting of the possible occurrences that are understood to be playing a certain role in a given question demanding a scientific explanation (van Fraassen 1980, 127). Nevertheless, van Fraassen's pragmatic account is not trivialized by this connection between explanation and contrast classes because we can say plenty about each apart from its connection to the other.

Hafner and Mancosu (2005, 226) identify a "rather striking" feature of Kummer's convergence test as motivating the question of why the test works. In addition, Hafner and Mancosu

438 ■ NOTES TO CHAPTER 7

(229) seem to say that a given proof (Pringsheim's) of Kummer's test is explanatory when one striking feature of the test is under consideration (namely, that it involves an arbitrary series) but that the proof is not explanatory when another such feature is under consideration (namely, the test's apparent isolation within the general array of convergence tests). Later I will present other examples of this phenomenon.

Regarding a given proof of the intermediate value theorem, Resnik and Kushner (1987, 149) say that "we find it hard to see how someone could understand this proof and yet ask *why* the theorem is true." Even if this claim is true, I think it fails to show that the proof explains why the intermediate value theorem holds. Perhaps the intermediate value theorem in a given context exhibits no striking features and so no one could ask for an explanation over and above a proof of the theorem (and so perforce no one who understands the proof could ask). (Thanks to Finnur Dellsen.)

For more on salience, see especially section 8.6.

18. There may also be cases where the result exhibits a feature that is only slightly salient. If some proofs but not others exploit a similar feature in the problem, this difference would ground only a slight distinction between proofs that explain and proofs that merely prove. Another way for intermediate cases to arise is for a certain feature to be salient in the result, but for various proofs to exploit to different degrees a similar feature in the setup—rather than for any proof to proceed entirely from such a feature.

19. Poincaré (1913, 373–374) says that a brute-force proof is unsatisfying when the result exhibits some noteworthy feature such a symmetry or simplicity: "When a rather long calculation has led to some simple and striking result, we are not satisfied until we have shown that we should have been *able to foresee*, if not this entire result, at least its most characteristic traits. . . . To obtain a result of real value, it is not enough to grind out calculations, or to have a machine to put things in order. . . . The machine may gnaw on the crude fact, the soul of the fact will always escape it." Though Poincaré does occasionally refer to a result's "soul" as "why" it holds (375), he generally emphasizes merely the efficiency of certain proofs and their enabling us to foresee other results.

Dirac (as quoted in Wilczek and Devine 1987, 102) makes a remark along similar lines: "I consider that I understand an equation when I can predict the properties of its solutions, without actually solving it." One way to prove that the solutions have a certain property is actually to solve the equation and then to observe that its solutions possess the given property. But there may be another, less brute-force proof. The former proof, I am arguing, cannot explain why the solutions have this property, whereas the latter proof may be explanatory; the fact that the solutions have this property may display some outstanding feature, and the latter proof may exploit a similar striking feature of the equation.

See also note 8 ("its punchline creeps up without warning") and my remarks about "inevitability" in chapter 9 (in the text associated with note 6) and in chapter 4 note 16. Being "able to foresee" a result's characteristic features seems to me closely related to appreciating a result's "inevitability."

My proposal also seems to reflect the idea expressed by Sawyer (1955, 26): "In . . . an illuminating proof, the result does not appear as a surprise in the last line; you can see it coming all the way." If a result arises from an "algebraic miracle" (as in the first proof I gave of Zeitz's result), then the result appears as a surprise at the end—when the miracle occurs. Sawyer (36) goes on to say: "*where there is pattern there is significance*. If in mathematical work of any kind we find a certain striking pattern recurs, it is always suggested that we should investigate *why* it occurs." Here the connection between explanation and a "striking pattern" is made more explicit. Of course, the remark Sawyer italicizes might be interpreted as saying that any result exhibiting a striking pattern has an explanation. I disagree. In fact, although in some cases (such as Morley's theorem) mathematicians are justified in continuing to seek an explanation despite having found none so far, in other cases (such as the fact that I am about to mention regarding e) mathematicians are justified in believing that there is no explanation.

Sawyer (1955, 164–165) also makes a comment that I read as fitting nicely with my claim that a why question regarding a result is intelligible if and only if the result exhibits a salient feature: "If we had not first of all studied projective geometry and seen the significance of the cross-ratio, we should have thought nothing of it if the expression $(a-d)(b-c)/(d-b)(c-a)$ [the cross-ratio] occurred in the course of a calculation. It would just have been another collection of symbols. But now we say, 'Ah, the cross-ratio! Why does that occur here?'"

20. Perhaps (contrary to the passages I quote) some combinatorial mathematicians regard the proof from generating functions as explanatory just like the simple bijective proof I am about to give. Perhaps, then, I should restrict myself to identifying what it is that makes the bijective proof explanatory and not argue that the generating-function proof lacks this feature, but merely that it is perceived as lacking this feature by those who regard it as less explanatorily powerful than the bijective proof. (See the remark from Stanley in note 22.)

21. The dot diagrams in figs. 7.12 and 7.13 all have their rows weakly decreasing in length (just like the diagram in figs. 7.10 and 7.11), but (unlike that earlier diagram) their rows do not have their centers aligned. (Since the parts are not all odd, some rows do not have center dots.) Rather, each row is aligned on the left. Clearly, the same partition may be displayed in various distinct dot diagrams.

22. I do not contend that any bijective proof (regardless of the bijection's complexity or artificiality) is explanatory, that no generating function proof is explanatory, or that there is never a good reason to seek a generating function proof once a simple, explanatory bijective proof has been found. Each kind of proof may have some value. For instance, a generating function proof may be much shorter or help us to find proofs of new theorems. Also bear in mind that "the precise border between combinatorial [i.e., bijective] and non-combinatorial proofs is rather hazy, and certain arguments that to an inexperienced enumerator will appear non-combinatorial will be recognized by a more facile counter as combinatorial, primarily because he or she is aware of certain standard techniques for converting apparently non-combinatorial arguments into combinatorial ones." (Stanley 2012, 13) See note 20 above and chapter 9, note 5.

It might be suggested that a bijective proof explains by revealing members of the two kinds of partition to be in fact the same abstract object, represented in different ways. According to this suggestion, that these two apparently distinct things are really one and the same explains why the same number of each exists. Other, nonmathematical explanations work in this manner; for example, the reason why Mark Twain has the same birthdate, eye color, and height as Samuel Clemens is that Mark Twain is Samuel Clemens. (See chapter 1.)

However, this suggestion entails that *any* bijective proof explains, whereas I believe that in mathematical practice, only simple bijective proofs explain. That is, if a bijection is sufficiently complicated or artificial, then although the proof goes through, it does not explain. That is because a bijection does not show that an O-partition is really a D-partition in disguise (in the way that Mark Twain is Samuel Clemens). Rather, a bijection reveals that the O-partitions and D-partitions can be used to represent exactly the same abstract objects. If the two kinds of partitions can be extracted with sufficient ease from exactly the same diagrams, then the scheme is simple enough to explain why there are the same numbers of partitions of the two kinds.

23. I have closely followed the description of this example in Bressoud (1994, 72–73).

There are other examples where a contrast with a theorem makes certain features of that theorem stand out. Here is a notable example. Regarding various proofs of the fact that the quintic equation is not generally solvable in radicals, the proof using Galois theory is often cited by mathematicians (e.g., Alperin 1980, 70; Pesic 2003, 94, 108, and 145) and philosophers (e.g., Kitcher 1989, 425–426; Pincock 2015a) as going beyond previous proofs to *explain why* the quintic is not generally solvable (and hence why, despite great efforts, no general algebraic formula for solving it has ever been found). I suggest that the distinction between an explanation and a mere proof of the quintic's unsolvability is grounded in this result's most striking feature: that in being unsolvable, the quintic differs from all lower-order polynomial equations (the quartic, cubic, quadratic, and linear), every one of which is solvable. In the context of this salient difference, we can ask why the quantic is unsolvable. Accordingly, an explanation is a proof that traces the quintic's unsolvability to some other respect in which the quintic differs from lower-order polynomials. Therefore, Galois's proof (unlike Abel's, for example) explains the result. That the distinction between an explanation and a mere proof depends upon the salience of the difference in solvability between quintics and lower-order polynomials is strongly suggested by the why question's typical form: "Why? What happened to the pattern of algebraic equations each having solutions? What is it about the fifth degree that causes the problem? Why does it then go on to affect all higher degrees of equations?" (Pesic 2003, 3)

Let's consider another example where a feature of some result is made salient by a contrast between that result and others. A number n is divisible by 9 iff the sum of n's digits is divisible by 9. The fact that divisibility by 8 (or 10 or . . .) is *not* associated with the sum of the digits being divisible by 8 (or 10 or . . .) gives content to a request for the rule's explanation over and above its proof. In this context, the question "Why is there this rule for divisibility by 9?" means something like "What's so special about 9 that there is a rule like this?" In such a context, an explanation over and above a proof of the rule would show how the rule derives from some other property the possession of which is similarly something "special about 9." Indeed, the divisibility-by-9 rule "results from the fact that" 9 is one less than the base (10) in terms of which n is being represented (Posamentier and Lehmann 2009, 66; Sorensen). This is shown by a proof of the rule that generalizes it to any base B. If n is expressed as ". . . $dcba$" in base B, then $n = a + bB + cB^2 + \ldots = (a + b + c + \ldots) + b(B - 1) + c(B^2 - 1) + \ldots = (a + b + c + \ldots) + (B - 1)[b + c(B + 1) + \ldots]$, and so n is divisible by $(B - 1)$ iff $(a + b + c + \ldots)$, i.e., the sum of its digits in base B, is divisible by $(B - 1)$. This proof derives the divisibility-by-9 rule from something "special about 9" (in base 10). Surely this proof does explain why there is a rule for divisibility-by-9 when there is no similar rule (in base 10) for divisibility-by-8, for example.

Of course, the divisibility-by-9 rule can be proved without exploiting the fact that 9 is one less than the base: $n = a + 10b + 100c + \ldots = (a + b + c + \ldots) + 9b + 99c + \ldots$. But this proof (until we generalize it to any base) does not reveal what is special about 9. The rule just emerges as an algebraic accident.

Zelcer (2013) cites Hume's Philo in his *Dialogues Concerning Natural Religion* (section 9) as offering the divisibility-by-9 rule as exemplifying the fact that for mathematical truths, in Zelcer's (2013, 177) words, "it hardly makes sense to seek out explanations." I am not sure that this is Philo's point; it may instead be that the rule is (as Philo says) not "the effect either of chance or design" but instead "it must forever result from the nature of these numbers," thereby explaining "why it was absolutely impossible that" the rule fail to hold. In any case, I have suggested that the rule *has* an explanation (at least in a context where the contrast with divisibility by 8, 10, . . . is striking).

24. Perhaps another feature that is often salient in mathematical results, and thus often grounds the distinction between proofs that explain and proofs that do not, is a result's being mathematically powerful or important. Here I do not mean that the result is useful for many practical applications, but rather that it is mathematically useful—that is, roughly speaking, useful in proving a wide variety of other (powerful) results or useful in having a wide variety of extensions, generalizations, analogues, abstractions, and so forth to a wide variety of mathematical domains. Though (as the previous sentence made plain) I am not sure what "power" (or "importance") amounts to precisely, I believe that mathematicians care about revealing whether or not various results are powerful, and when they discover that a result is powerful, they want to know *why* it holds and thereby to understand where its power comes from. That is, they want a proof of the result revealing that it follows from premises that are powerful independently of this result. (Without this independence requirement, any proof of the result would do since its premises, in entailing the result, would presumably thereby qualify as powerful.) A result's power can be made especially salient or mysterious when the result is revealed to follow from mathematical premises that seem to hold little independent power. (To reveal that the result follows from the axioms, then, does not suffice to make its power salient or mysterious.)

As an example, consider Cauchy's inequality: that if n is a positive integer and $a_1, \ldots, a_n$ and $b_1, \ldots, b_n$ are nonnegative real numbers, then $(a_1^2 + \ldots + a_n^2)(b_1^2 + \ldots + b_n^2) \geq (a_1 b_1 + \ldots + a_n b_n)^2$. Steele (2004, 1) writes: "There is no doubt that this is one of the most widely used and most important inequalities in all of mathematics. A central aim of this [book] is to suggest a path to mastery of this inequality, its many extensions, and its many applications—from the most basic to the most sublime." (Hardy, Littlewood, and Polya, 1952, 16, likewise characterize Cauchy's inequality as "very important.") Then Steele uses mathematical induction to prove this inequality. The inductive argument turns on the fact that $x^2/2 + y^2/2 \geq xy$, which follows from $x^2 + y^2 - 2xy \geq 0$, which follows from $(x - y)^2 \geq 0$. This provokes Steele (2004, 19) to remark: "one might rightly wonder how so much value can be drawn from a bound which comes from the trivial observation that $(x - y)^2 \geq 0$." In other words, Steele is asking why Cauchy's inequality is so powerful—in other words, for a proof of Cauchy's inequality that reveals where its power comes from. (He is asking not for what makes it so important—not for what constitutes its importance—but rather for what accounts for its importance.) Steele answers his question by pointing out that if $a = x^2$ and $b = y^2$, then $x^2/2 + y^2/2 \geq xy$ is equivalent to $a/2 + b/2 \geq \sqrt{ab}$, i.e., $2a + 2b \geq 4\sqrt{ab}$. Now $2a + 2b$ is the perimeter of a rectangle with sides a and b, whereas $4\sqrt{ab}$ is the perimeter of a square with side $\sqrt{ab}$, i.e., a square of the same area as the rectangle with sides a and b. So the inequality used to prove Cauchy's inequality says that among all rectangles of a given area, the square has the smallest perimeter. This is a powerful result. Steele says that it is the "rectangular version" of the fact that of all planar regions with a given area, the circle has the smallest perimeter. As Steele (19–20) concludes, "we now see more clearly why $x^2/2 + y^2/2 \geq xy$ might be powerful: it is part of that great stream of results that links symmetry and optimality."

25. This proof appears, for example, in Wells (1991, 198). Zeitz (2010, 99) characterizes this proof as explanatory.

26. See note 17.

27. Brown (1997, 177) also suggests that picture proofs are sometimes explanatory, sometimes not—but does not say what contribution a proof's pictorial character might make to its explanatory power. Steiner (1978a, 136–137) also cites one proof's "pictorial aspect" as contributing to its explanatory power, but without further elaboration. A picture proof may allow us to see immediately ("graphically," you might say) that a given theorem holds, or it may

allow us to understand better how a nondiagrammatic proof of the theorem works, and both of these outcomes constitute a kind of "insight" into the given theorem. Nevertheless, this sort of insight should be distinguished from whatever is supplied by an account of why the theorem holds. For instance, consider the famous diagrammatic proof that $1/2 + 1/4 + 1/8 + \ldots = 1$ (Brown 1999, 37; Nelson 1993, 118). I do not think that this proof shows *why* the theorem holds. What would the reason why be?

28. This example is given by Dreyfus and Eisenberg (1986, 3). (Thanks to Manya Sundström for calling this article to my attention.) Dreyfus and Eisenberg do not suggest that the second proof's explanatory power fails to derive from its appeal to a symmetry. They are concerned instead with the reason why "mathematicians generally agree that the second proof is aesthetically more appealing than the first one."

I deny that greater aesthetic appeal is always associated with greater explanatory power. This is illustrated by another example that they give. The distance d from a line $y = mx + b$ to a point (a,c) on the Euclidean plane is given by $d = (ma + b - c)/\sqrt{(1 + m^2)}$. One way to prove this formula is to find the equation for the line through (a,c) perpendicular to the given line, then to solve the two linear equations for the point at which the two lines intersect, and then to find the distance between that point and (a,c). But Dreyfus and Eisenberg (1986, 6) also give an approach that is "clever, slick, and elegant," avoiding this tedious algebra. That approach involves forming a pair of similar right triangles (see fig. 7.19). By the triangles' similarity, $d/1 = (ma + b - c)/\sqrt{(1 + m^2)}$. For all of its beauty and brevity, however, this proof seems to me and Sundström to be no more explanatory than the algebraic one. On my view, this is because the formula for d exhibits no especially striking feature, so there is no distinction between an explanation of it and a mere proof of it.

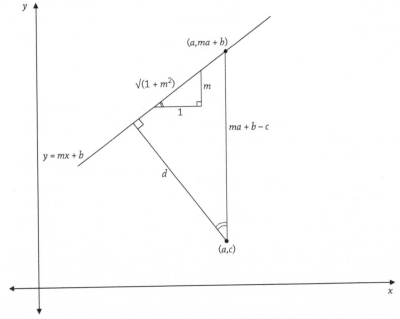

Figure 7.19 Beautiful, brief, non-explanatory proof

29. "Haven't all of us said, and heard other mathematicians say: 'yes, I have checked the proof step by step, and I am convinced it's right, but I don't know *why* it works'? . . . Keep thinking till you understand the abstraction that explains what you have done" (Halmos 1985, 16). Tappenden (2005, 171 and 200) mentions another example where a clever substitution transforms an integral from "nasty" to "nice"; Tappenden calls this transformation "miraculous," a term suggesting that it might become the object of a mathematical explanation. Sandborg (1998, 611–613) gives an example of a proof that Polya says introduces an auxiliary mathematical series as a "deus ex machina"; Sandborg characterizes Polya as asking a why question: Why, in proving the result, does it help to introduce an auxiliary sequence— and why this auxiliary sequence in particular?

30. I will say more about mathematical coincidence in chapter 8.

31. Kitcher (1981) proposes roughly that we make mathematically rigorous arguments in order to explain why certain nonrigorous methods arrived at correct results. In contrast, I have suggested that not all rigorous proofs of those results explain why the nonrigorous methods worked.

32. For a nice example of these distinctions being drawn with regard to Heaviside's operational calculus, see Sumpner (1928–29, 404–405 and 425).

33. For instance, upon learning that a mathematician has proved that for any prime number, there are infinitely many pairs of consecutive larger prime numbers where the members of the pair differ by less than 70 million (McKee 2013), one naturally wonders *why* the proof works for 70 million and not for (e.g.) 60 million. (The threshold has since been diminished.)

34. This sum is $\zeta(3)$, where $\zeta(s) = \Sigma_{n=1}^{\infty} \dfrac{1}{n^s}$ is the Riemann zeta function. $\zeta(s)$ is intractable for any positive odd integer (other than $s = 1$, for which the sum diverges).

35. As another example where a mathematician explains why one problem turns out to be so much more difficult than another, seemingly closely related one, consider these remarks that Hardy wrote in his copy of a letter he had written to Ramanujan: "When r is even $f(xe^{-p\pi/q})$) is an *elementary* function. The same sort of method applies but is *much* easier. Hence we see *why* the odd case is so much harder" (Berndt and Rankin 1995, 152). See also chapter 10 note 9.

■ Chapter 8

1. The article appears (unsigned, as a "gleaning") on p. 283 of the December 1986 issue. Baker (2009a) independently pursues thoughts about coincidence, unity, and explanation that are in some ways similar to mine below.

2. Of course, other numbers besides "calculator numbers," such as 630036, also possess this feature—and hence they, too, are divisible by 37. De Villiers (1993) gives a very similar example and has the same view regarding which proof of it is explanatory. The explanandum is that the sum of any two-digit number with its reverse is always divisible by 11. De Villiers contrasts a proof that checks every number from 10 to 99 with an algebraic proof: If the number is $10a + b$, then $10b + a$ is the result of reversing its digits, and their sum is $11a + 11b = 11$ $(a + b)$. According to de Villiers, the algebraic proof "provides an explanation" whereas the proof that checks every case "provides no explanation or understanding of *why* the result is true; it simply verifies."

3. If a result is remarkable for identifying something common to each case of an apparently diverse lot, then these "cases" may themselves be general results—as when each case is a theorem and the result identifies something common to each of them. Entirely dissimilar

proofs of two theorems would fail to explain why those theorems involve a common element. On the other hand, proofs of each theorem may explain this pattern if the proofs themselves exploit a common element. Note the explanatory language in the following remark (from a mathematician discussing some mathematics that though he calls "trivial"):

> There are lots of 'meta-patterns' in mathematics, i.e. collections of seemingly different problems that have similar answers, or structures that appear more often than we would have expected. Once one of these meta-patterns is identified it is always helpful to understand what is responsible for it. . . . To give a trivial example, years ago while the author was writing up his PhD thesis he noticed in several places the numbers 1, 2, 3, 4 and 6. For instance, $\cos(2\pi r) \in \mathbb{Q}$ for $r \in \mathbb{Q}$ iff the denominator of r is 1, 2, 3, 4 or 6. Likewise, the theta function $\Theta[\mathbb{Z} + r](\tau)$ for $r \in \mathbb{Q}$ can be written as $\Sigma\, a_i \theta_3(b_i\, \tau)$ for some a_i, $b_i \in \mathbb{R}$ iff the denominator of r is 1, 2, 3, 4 or 6. This pattern is easy to explain: they are precisely those positive integers n with Euler totient $\varphi(n) \le 2$, that is there are at most two positive numbers less than n coprime to n. [Two numbers are "coprime" if and only if their only common divisor is 1.] The various incidences of these numbers can usually be reduced to this $\varphi(n) \le 2$ property. (Gannon 2006, 168)

We can understand the general idea here even if we do not know what Jacobi's theta function is (in fact, $\theta_3(b\tau) = 1 + 2\sum_{n=1}^{\infty}(e^{\pi\tau})^{n^2}\cos(2\pi nb)$) or how $\varphi(n) \le 2$ is connected to these two theorems. The general idea is that proofs of the two theorems (one about cos, the other about $\Theta[\mathbb{Z} + r]$) can explain why $\{1,2,3,4,6\}$ figures in both theorems if each of those proofs exploits exactly the same feature of $\{1,2,3,4,6\}$—e.g., nothing about $\{1,2,3,4,6\}$ save that this set contains all and only the positive integers where $\varphi(n) \le 2$. (A proof exploits more if, for instance, it determines which numbers n are such that $\varphi(n) \le 2$, and then proceeds separately for each of the five cases.) Since the striking feature of the two theorems (when presented as Gannon does) is that $\{1,2,3,4,6\}$ figures in both, the point of asking why the two theorems hold is to ask for proofs of the two theorems where (nontrivially) both proofs exploit exactly the same feature of $\{1,2,3,4,6\}$. Even with such proofs, it might still be a mathematical coincidence that the positive integers with one feature (involving cos) are exactly the positive integers with the other feature (involving $\Theta[\mathbb{Z} + r]$). (Perhaps no proof of one theorem automatically proves the other.) Nevertheless, the coincidence that both theorems involve exactly the positive integers n where $\varphi(n) \le 2$ would explain why both theorems involve $\{1,2,3,4,6\}$, and hence involve exactly the same integers.

4. Strictly speaking, that a given result identifies a property common to every single case of a certain sort is just a symmetry in the result—for example, that under a switch from one calculator number to any other, divisibility by 37 is invariant. Accordingly, I have already argued (in the previous chapter) that a proof that works by exploiting the same sort of symmetry in the setup counts as explanatory. My view of mathematical explanation does not require that a theorem's displaying a striking symmetry be sharply distinguished from a theorem's being striking for its treating various cases alike. (I will return to this point in section 10.2.)

5. When I say that such a proof "is absent," I don't mean merely that it has not yet been discovered. I mean that no such proof exists "in Plato's heaven"; such a proof is impossible.

6. On my view, if some mathematical result's salient feature is its identifying a property as common to every case of a certain sort, then the mathematical result is a mathematical coincidence if and only if it has no mathematical explanation. In contrast, although it is a physical coincidence that Presidents Lincoln and Kennedy both had vice presidents named "Johnson", this physical coincidence has a scientific explanation (at least in contexts where

the why question is *not* understood as seeking only interesting common causes). The explanation consists of the relevant causes of Andrew Johnson's becoming vice president together with the relevant causes of Lyndon Johnson's becoming vice president. Although these causes have nothing interesting in common, they do (in certain contexts) explain the physical coincidence by separately explaining its two components. (See, for instance, van Fraassen 1980, 25.) But this kind of explanation is unavailable for mathematical coincidences because there are no causal explanations in mathematics. A mathematical coincidence has no explanation at all, whereas a physical coincidence still has an explanation (in certain contexts) despite having no explanation citing interesting common causes of its components.

This may not constitute a very great difference between mathematical and physical coincidences because very often, when we ask for a scientific explanation of some relation (or of some pair of facts), we are interested only in scientific explanations that reveal interesting common causes of the relata (or of the two paired facts). Consider: "Why is it that the Moon's angular diameter in the Earth's sky is very nearly equal to the Sun's angular diameter in the Earth's sky?" In most ordinary contexts, this question is asking for an important common cause, and so the correct answer is that there is no reason why; it is a coincidence. So in this sense it is true that a physical coincidence has no explanation just as a mathematical coincidence has none.

7. Steiner (1978a, 136) deems the second proof "more illuminating" than a proof of the summation formula that proceeds by mathematical induction. (Steiner does not discuss mathematical coincidences or contrast the second proof with separate proofs of the even and odd cases as in the first proof.) Shortly I will discuss mathematical induction.

8. Strangely, Davis apparently holds just the opposite view: "The existence of the coincidence implies the existence of an explanation" (1981, 320). See Baker 2009a, 155. Davis's remark is less puzzling if he is interpreted as saying that a seeming coincidence cries out for an explanation.

9. Even an indirect proof (a proof by contradiction, a nonconstructive proof) could then qualify as such an explanation; it could constitute a "common proof" of each of the theorem's components. The distinction between proofs that explain and mere proofs does not have any straightforward relation to the distinction between direct and indirect proofs, contrary to Nicole and Arnauld as quoted in section 7.1. (Of course, when the result's salient feature is not its unity but rather something else, then indirect proofs may fail to explain by failing to exploit a similar feature of the setup.)

10. This discussion presupposes that the property of becoming undefined somewhere on the unit circle centered at the origin of the complex plane is a natural property in mathematics and so a respect in which these two functions are alike—rather than a gerrymandered, wildly disjunctive shadow of a predicate. I mentioned this point earlier and I will have more to say about it in chapter 9.

There are many other ways in which my elaboration of a proof that treats all of the components alike is vague at the margins—and in which the notion of a mathematical coincidence is correspondingly vague. For instance, I require that in a "common proof," *any* component of the result is such that its proof can be generalized without further resources to cover every other component. But suppose that only *certain* components are such that their proof can be so generalized—or that only *a single* component permits this. Then the result may fall into some intermediate region; depending on the details, it may not be a complete coincidence, but neither does the proof treat the various components utterly alike. (Consider Duchayla's proof from section 4.3, where the proof of the parallelogram law's holding for the resultant's magnitude needs no further resources to prove its holding for the resultant's direction, but not vice versa. The proof treats the result's two components very differently since the law's holding for direction is used to show its holding for magnitude, but not vice versa.)

Here is another kind of intermediate case. Consider the following four definite descriptions:

(1) The number of points in a plane that uniquely determine a conic section

(2) The degree of the alternating group that is the smallest non-Abelian simple group

(3) The smallest degree general algebraic equation that is not solvable in closed form

(4) The smallest n such that every n^{th} Fibonacci number gains another digit in its decimal expansion

It turns out (I believe) to be no coincidence that 5 is picked out by both (2) and (3). However, for each other pair selected from these four definite descriptions, it is a coincidence that both members refer to 5. Now what about the fact that (1), (2), and (3) all refer to 5? (For each of these conjunctions, its salient feature is obviously that each of its conjuncts picks out the same number.) By my account, it is a coincidence that (1), (2), and (3) all refer to 5, since its three components have no "common proof." However, I think it would sometimes be misleading to characterize this fact as coincidental and simply leave it at that, since it is no coincidence that (2) and (3) both refer to 5. One might be inclined to say that it is not a *complete* coincidence that (1), (2), and (3) all refer to 5. Although it is a coincidence, strictly speaking, there is a sense in which it is not *as much* of a coincidence as the fact that (1), (2), and (4) all pick out 5. My account can accommodate such 'degrees' of being a coincidence.

Another kind of marginal case may be where there is no common proof for every component's truth, but there is a common proof for every component that it is true *if* any other component is true. Perhaps that would suffice to render the result non-coincidental.

Also see chapter 9 note 26 regarding the Taylor series example.

11. Once again, I am grateful to a very brief mention in Sorensen's paper for calling Stewart's discussion to my attention.

12. Leavitt (2007, 182) characterizes the fact that these are all prime as a "coincidence," considering that 333 333 331 is not prime.

13. Thanks to Alan Baker for calling my attention to this example.

14. See note 10.

15. A similar example involves the fact that of any two consecutive nonzero natural numbers and their sum, exactly one is a multiple of 3.

16. Zeitz (2000, 1) mentions this theorem in passing but does not discuss it or give any proof of it. I wonder if he had in mind the proofs I discuss.

17. Some philosophers appear quite confident that proofs by mathematical induction are generally explanatory, whereas other philosophers appear equally confident of the contrary. Kitcher (1975, 265) takes proofs by mathematical induction to be explanatory. Brown (1997, 177; 1999, 42) agrees, at least in number theory. Steiner (1978a, 151) uses his account of mathematical explanation (discussed in section 8.5) to argue that proofs by mathematical induction "usually" are not explanatory. (See note 22.) Hafner and Mancosu (2005) consider a proof by mathematical induction of the formula I gave earlier for the sum of the first n nonzero natural numbers. To deem that proof explanatory, they say, "would indeed be very counterintuitive!' (2005, 234) They elaborate slightly: "it clearly isn't [explanatory] . . . according to the understanding of working mathematicians (some mathematicians even take inductive proofs to be *paradigms of non-explanatory* proofs)" (Hafner and Mancosu 2005, 237). Regarding the same proof, Hanna (1990, 10; see 1989, 48) writes, "This is certainly an

acceptable proof. . . . What it does not do, however, is show *why* the sum of the first *n* integers is $n(n + 1)/2$. . . . Proofs by mathematical induction are nonexplanatory in general." There are also empirical psychological studies (e.g., Reid 2001; Smith 2006) suggesting that students generally regard proofs by mathematical induction as deficient in *explaining why* the theorem proved is true.

Elsewhere (Lange 2009b) I have offered an argument for the explanatory impotence of mathematical induction that differs from the argument I present here. My earlier argument is not limited to certain contexts, but it is limited to theorems where the first instance is not explanatorily prior to any other instance. (See note 19.)

In the text connected to note 12 of chapter 7, I mention another case where mathematicians regard an inductive proof as nonexplanatory.

18. The inductive proof of the triplet theorem is also a far cry from a proof of the triplet theorem that shows that $(n - 1)n(n + 1) = n^3 - n$ is always divisible by 6 by giving separate treatment to each of these 6 cases: $n \equiv 0, 1, 2, 3, 4,$ and 5 (mod 6). (For instance, if $n \equiv 3$ (mod 6), then $\equiv n^3 - n \equiv 3^3 - 3 = 27 - 3 = 24 \equiv 0$ (mod 6).) Thanks to Manya Sundström for suggesting this proof.

19. By "such a proof by induction," I mean a proof that treats only the base case separately. Many inductive proofs prove the inductive step by distinguishing among several cases. Such an inductive proof would then fail to afford uniform treatment even to all but one of the cases. So on my view, such a proof would lack even the modest explanatory power of the triplet theorem's inductive proof.

In a proof by course-of-values induction (a.k.a. "strong induction," "complete induction"), there is no base case. Such an argument uses this rule of inference:

For any property P,
if for any natural number k, if $P(1)$ and . . . and $P(k − 1)$, then $P(k)$,
then for any natural number n, $P(n)$.

Since there is no base case, it might appear that a course-of-values induction explains (in a context where the result's unity is salient), by my lights, since it does not give special treatment to a base case. However, as Baker (2010) rightly says, even though a course-of-values induction contains only the "inductive step," typically it must prove the inductive step by treating at least $k = 1$ as a special case, since the antecedent "if $P(1)$ and . . . and $P(k − 1)$" is empty for $k = 1$. So although any result provable by ordinary induction can be proved by course-of-values induction, the latter has no automatic explanatory advantage over the former.

20. Baker (2010) points out that an inductive-style proof that takes $n = 5$ as the base case, proceeding upward and downward separately from there, does not do as well as an ordinary inductive proof (i.e., a proof that takes $n = 1$ as the base case, proceeding upward from there) in treating all cases alike. I agree, and accordingly, I take such a proof as lying even further away from a fully qualified explanation than an ordinary inductive proof that affords uniform treatment to all but the base case. This represents a more nuanced verdict than I gave in my (2009b), where I said simply that if the argument proceeding upward from $n = 1$ is explanatory, then so is the argument proceeding upward and downward from $n = 5$. I no longer accept that the two proofs must lie in exactly the same spot along the continuum between being an explanation and having no explanatory significance at all. (Thanks to Alan Baker for pressing me on this point.) Suppose, for instance, that the downward induction from $n = 5$ proceeds by showing that if the theorem holds for $n = 5$, then it holds for $n = 4$, and then showing separately (by using specific numerical information about $n = 3$ that differs from the

information used in the previous step) that if the theorem holds for $n = 5$, then it holds for $n = 3$, and then likewise proceeding separately for each of $n = 2$ and $n = 1$. The downward step would then be proceeding by cases and so (in a context where the theorem's salient feature is its unity) would be very much inferior in explanatory power to the inductive proof that proceeds upward from $n = 1$ without any further division into cases. (Thanks to Lars-Daniel Öhman and Olow Sande for suggesting that some downward steps might proceed by cases.)

A given proof by induction may be capable of being reworked very easily into a noninductive proof that does not proceed by cases—indeed, into a proof that is explanatory. In that event, the proof by induction might generously be deemed explanatory by virtue of its close relation to this other proof.

If the inductive step does not proceed by cases (see previous note), then the inductive step explains why it is that *if* the theorem holds for $n = 1$, *then* it holds for all natural numbers $n > 1$; the inductive step gives uniform treatment to all of the cases of this conditional result. Another, related conditional result is that either the theorem holds for all nonzero natural numbers or for none—in other words, that if there is a nonzero natural number for which the theorem holds, then it holds for all n. Suppose that this conditional result's striking feature is its unity (in the consequent's covering all n) and consider an inductive-style proof of it that proceeds upward and downward from the theorem's holding for an arbitrary n. If the upward argument treats all of its cases alike (and the downward argument does, too), then this proof has (on my account) some intermediate degree of explanatory significance (since it divides the cases into only two classes) but falls short of an explanation (since it treats the upward n differently from the downward n). (See my 2009b, 210.)

(Thanks to Hartry Field for suggestions regarding the explanatory significance of inductive proofs.)

21. It might be proposed that a mathematical explanation works by revealing some kind of structure that lies behind the phenomena to be explained, generating them. There may be some truth to this proposal insofar as the "structure" is a feature of the setup that is similar to the salient feature of the result. However, talk of "structure" tends to sound as though it is talking about a feature of the case that, by virtue of underlying the phenomena whatever the context, is explanatory whatever the context. In contrast, my account (especially in the way that a feature's salience can shift with the context) points away from mathematical explanation as working by revealing some kind of structure that is explanatory whatever the context. (See my comments in section 8.6 on mathematical reductions as explanations.)

22. Steiner (1978, 151) says that "inductive proofs usually do not allow deformation," and hence are not explanatory, because by replacing S_1's characterizing property with S_2's in the original inductive proof, we do not automatically replace the original theorem at the start of the inductive step with the new theorem to be proved—and in an inductive argument, the theorem must be introduced at the *start* of the inductive step. It seems to me, however, that if we take the inductive proof that the product of any three consecutive nonzero natural numbers is divisible by 6 and replace the initial reference to three consecutive nonzero natural numbers (the characterizing property: being n, $n + 1$, and $n + 2$) with a reference to four consecutive nonzero natural numbers, then the first step of the inductive proof is automatically that the first case of four consecutive nonzero natural numbers is obviously divisible by their product (1x2x3x4 = 24), and this gives us immediately the new theorem to be proved (namely, that the product of any four consecutive nonzero natural numbers is divisible by 24) for use at the start of the inductive step. So in this case, at least, the inductive proof permits deformation.

Hafner and Mancosu (2005, 234–237) argue that the inductive proof of the formula for the sum of the first n nonzero natural numbers is "generalizable" in Steiner's sense—although (Hafner and Mancosu say) proofs by mathematical induction are widely regarded by mathematicians as failing to explain. I am not certain that their example withstands Steiner's point that the new theorem to be proved does not arise merely from deforming the original proof, since it is unclear to me how much a deformation can change the original proof without departing from its "proof idea."

23. See chapter 7, note 4.

24. Resnik and Kushner (1987, 147–152) likewise argue that the standard proof of the intermediate value theorem (which, they say, is explanatory if any proofs are) simply collapses if any attempt is made to shift it to cover anything besides an interval over the reals (such as an interval over the rationals or a disjoint pair of intervals over the reals).

25. Such a family might, for instance, consist of solutions (to polynomial equations with integer coefficients) of the form $a + b\sqrt{n}$ where $\sqrt{n}$ is not rational. The results analogous to d'Alembert's theorem could be proved by exploiting the group of symmetries of the number field obtained by adjoining the polynomial equation's solutions to the rational numbers (the Galois group). The question is whether the explanatory power of the proof explaining d'Alembert's theorem derives from the possibility of such a family.

26. However, in some cases where we can appreciate a given proof's explanatory power solely from examining details of the proof itself, we can do so only if we already understand which properties are natural properties in mathematics. Whether a given property is natural may depend on its role in other proofs, as I will discuss in the next chapter. With this in mind, let me contrast my view with Kitcher's. Kitcher sees any explanatory proof's power to explain as depending on its relation to other proofs (for its proof scheme's membership in the explanatory store). In contrast, for proofs that explain certain theorems (namely, theorems having as their salient feature that they identify some property as common to a wide range of cases), I see the proofs' explanatory power as depending partly on the "common" properties being mathematically natural, which (according to chapter 9) depends upon these proofs' relations to other proofs. In short, Kitcher and I both make holistic moves, but the wholes appear at different points and do different jobs. (For a brief discussion of "local vs. global notions of explanation" in connection with Kitcher's view, see Mancosu 2009, 153.)

27. "Note that generally speaking, analytic (coordinate) proofs tend to be less *explanatory* than synthetic geometry proofs" (De Villiers 2003, 165). See also the Gowers passage quoted at the end of this chapter as well as the remarks in chapter 9 comparing a coordinate geometry proof of Desargues's theorem to the proof exiting to the third dimension. In the following passage, Ruelle (2007, 18) seems to be expressing the idea that a plug-and-chug coordinate-geometry proof is brute force and therefore is seen by at least some mathematicians as not explanatory. He describes one method of proof as follows: "Use brute force. In fact, for problems of elementary geometry one can always (as we shall see) introduce coordinates, write equations for the lines that occur, and reduce the problem to checking some algebra. This method is due to Descartes. It is effective but cumbersome. It is often long and inelegant and some mathematicians will say that it teaches you nothing: you don't get a real understanding of the problem you have solved."

28. Humphreys (1993, 186) also argues that "unification construed as paucity of argument patterns does not translate directly into increased understanding." Humphreys's examples involve logic rather than mathematics. However, in logic, the "filling instructions" for argument schemata have minimal stringency. On that ground, Kitcher could disqualify any

of those argument schemata from being explanatory, just as he uses this ground to preclude $a\&b \to a$ and $a \to a$ from having explanatory power.

29. Tappenden (2005) offers a similar objection to this "winner take all" feature of Kitcher's account of mathematical explanation. My approach does not have this defect.

30. Another option is that besides the kind of explanatory proof that I am working to analyze, there is another kind of explanatory proof—one that figures in foundational studies in mathematics, logic, set theory, and the philosophy of mathematics. If there is this distinct species of mathematical explanation, then my examples will not have revealed it; recall chapter 7, note 4.

31. Pincock (2015) explores this line of thought, though he is careful not to suggest that all explanations in mathematics work in this way.

32. See chapter 9 note 8.

33. I am grateful to John Roberts for suggesting this example and that I emphasize the material that I discussed three paragraphs above. Section 10.2 will give additional examples of scientific explanations that work like the explanations in mathematics that I have discussed. I will give yet another example in chapter 11 in connection with the reason why the weight of the displaced fluid parcel appears in the expression for the buoyant force.

34. I do not need to claim that this common answer to the why question about mirrors is actually correct. (Perhaps the correct answer instead rejects the explanandum: mirrors do not flip left-right or up-down, but rather front-back.) But even if the common answer that I have mentioned is incorrect, its error is not in the *way* that it purports to explain—and my point is simply to show that some respectable purported scientific explanations aim to work in the same way as the explanations in mathematics that I have examined.

■ Chapter 9

1. Admittedly, this is a radical view. Perhaps the idea that Euclidean geometry is in this respect mistaken about Euclidean points, lines, and planes—and that projective geometry uncovers the truth about the explanation of certain facts about Euclidean entities—is part of what Cassirer is driving at in passages such as the following, which concern "new elements" in mathematics such as points at infinity: "For it is not enough that the new elements should prove equally justified with the old, in the sense that the two can enter into a connection that is free from contradiction—it is not enough that the new should take their place beside the old and assert themselves in this juxtaposition. This merely formal combinability would not in itself provide a guarantee for a true inner conjunction, for a homogeneous logical structure of mathematics. Such a structure is secured only if we show that the new elements are not simply adjoined to the old ones as elements of a different kind and origin, but the new are a systematically necessary unfolding of the old. And this requires that we demonstrate a primary logical kinship between the two. Then the new elements will bring nothing to the old, other than what was implicit in their original meaning. If this is so, we may expect that the new elements, instead of fundamentally changing this meaning and replacing it by another, will first bring it to its full development and clarification. And when we survey the history of the ideal elements in mathematics, this expectation is never disappointed" (Cassirer 1957, 392).

2. Sawyer (1955, 148–149) and Stankova (2004, 175–178) contrast the proof exiting to the third dimension with Euclid-style proofs. I think it is fair to read both authors as seeing the former proof as possessing explanatory power absent from the latter. (See the passage from Stankova quoted above and also notes 4 and 9 below.)

3. Homogeneous coordinates are standardly used because textbook authors are anticipating the fact that (as I will discuss) the theorem's "natural setting" is projective rather than Euclidean geometry, and homogeneous coordinates assign finite coordinates to the points at infinity figuring in projective geometry. (My thanks to Jamie Tappenden for discussion of this point and others in the vicinity and for calling my attention to the passages I cite in note 5.)

4. I read McLeod and Baart as using "insight" here to refer to explanatory power, but admittedly, one might try to argue that they have something else in mind.

5. Actually, matters are somewhat more complicated. Although the coordinate-geometry proof that I gave is plug-and-chug brute force, there are more elegant analytic arguments. (See, for instance, Lord 2013, 34–36, and Borceux 2014, 215–217.) Dieudonné (1985, 9) writes that "by the use of homogeneous coordinates accompanied by a harmonious choice of indexing notation" we can maintain "a symmetry and a clarity in the calculations so that they closely follow the geometric argument." Perhaps, then, a coordinate-geometry proof, despite its metric character, can allow at least a proficient mathematician to see through the calculations to the nonmetric, explanatory proof. (For a similar point, see chapter 7, note 22.) In that event, a coordinate-geometry proof would possess explanatory power for the same reason (to be elaborated in section 9.3) as the proof exiting to the third dimension.

6. Regarding "inevitability," see also chapter 7 note 19.

7. There may be other proofs that also explain why Desargues's theorem holds—especially in contexts where different features of the theorem are salient. Desargues's theorem has many rich connections to other parts of mathematics.

8. This example is usefully compared to the example from section 8.3 involving two Taylor series of real-valued functions, where the similarity in their convergence behavior can be explained only in terms of the complex plane. Just as the third dimension is not artificial to Desargues's theorem in Euclidean geometry, the imaginary numbers are not artificial to those Taylor series. Of course, mathematicians sometimes consider a proof using only the notions that occur in a statement of the theorem to be more "elementary" (or more "natural") than a proof that appeals to "extraneous" notions. But a more "elementary" proof need not be more explanatory, and that mathematicians are seeking a given kind of proof does not entail that they regard that kind of proof as more explanatory. (These points are made effectively by Zelcer, 2009, 167–171, in connection with two proofs of the prime number theorem.) See also the end section 8.5 and section 9.4.

9. Without exiting to three dimensions, the axioms of incidence do not suffice to prove Desargues's theorem in two dimensions. There are non-Euclidean geometries where Desargues's theorem in two dimensions fails but the axioms of incidence regarding two dimensions hold. See Baker 1922, 120, and Arana and Mancosu 2012. The latter presents a passage where "the eminent algebraist" Marshall Hall (1943) says that the explanatory contribution made by exiting to three dimensions is to supply another way of picking out line LMN—namely, as the intersection of two planes. Hall writes that "the kernel of the proof" exiting to three dimensions "lies in the identification of [LM, LN, and MN] with [the two planes' line of intersection] and hence with each other" (233). He says that these "forced identifications" explain "why" Desargues's theorem holds in three-dimensional projective geometry but not in two-dimensional projective geometry. (I shall say more about projective geometry in the following sections.) Hall (232) elaborates: "One way of answering this fundamental question is the following: In a space configuration of three or more dimensions the identification of a line, constructed as the intersection of two planes, with a line, constructed

as the union of two points forces the identification of further constructed elements and the establishment of non-trivial configurations such as the Desargues configuration, while in the plane a line may be constructed only as a union of two points, a point as the intersection of two lines and there are no forced identifications."

That an explanation of Desargues's theorem must be nonmetrical (in a context where the theorem's striking feature is nonmetrical) is similar to the example involving the triangular and square numbers in section 7.6: an explanation of that theorem must be geometrical rather than, say, algebraic (in a context where that theorem's geometrical character is salient).

10. Tappenden (personal communication, June 2015) suggests that part of Gray's point in the passage I quoted in section 9.2 is that it is the ability to visualize the proof that is responsible for giving us a sense of the result's inevitability. I interpret Gray's point in terms of my view that "understanding" the theorem (i.e., knowing its explanation, that is, why it is true) comes from recognizing that all three cases involve the same pair of planes (and how that leads to their all involving the same line), which seeing the figure greatly assists us in appreciating—but this does not mean that the proof's explanatory power derives primarily from its visualizability per se. More important is *what* is visualized: the common pair of planes and how it produces the common line. The figure is a "powerful guide" to understanding the theorem because it helps us to appreciate how the common line comes from the common pair of planes. (For more on my view of visualizability's relation to explanation in mathematics, see section 7.6 at note 27.)

11. But there cannot be exactly one—as I will show in a moment.

12. Here is a typical statement of this familiar view: "In the case of ordinary geometrical elements our intuition makes us feel at ease as far as their 'existence' is concerned. But all we really need in geometry, considered as a mathematical system, is the validity of certain rules by means of which we can operate with these concepts, as in joining points, finding the intersection of lines, etc. . . . the mathematical existence of 'points at infinity' will be assured as soon as we have stated in a clear and consistent manner the mathematical *properties* of these new entities, i.e., their relations to 'ordinary' points and to each other" (Courant 1996, 181). Carnap (1950) is the classic statement of the distinction between internal and external questions.

13. The theorem in projective geometry also allows O to be at infinity (so OA′, OB′, and OC′ are parallel) or some of the vertices (A, B, C, A′, B′, C′) of the two triangles to lie at infinity, whereas Euclidean geometry does not.

14. On Kitcher's account of explanation, the fact that more can be proved by a single proof in projective geometry than by the corresponding single proof in Euclidean geometry counts toward boosting the prospects of these projective proof schemes earning their way into the "explanatory store." However, Kitcher's account can reach this correct result only if the "filling instructions" for the projective proof scheme use exclusively natural properties. As I will explain shortly, the question of what makes the properties in projective geometry natural is a key challenge for my proposal as well. Kitcher (1989) uses projectibility to distinguish natural from nonnatural properties. Whatever we may think of this appeal to epistemic considerations to account for the naturalness of various properties in science, projectibility seems out of place in an account of the naturalness of various mathematical properties, since inductive projection (though occurring in math) does not have the central place in mathematics that it holds in science.

15. In the next section, I will refine this remark in an important way (currently obscured by the "at best" qualification).

16. Hafner and Mancosu (2009, 158) point out that officially, Kitcher's account does not allow competitors for the "explanatory store" to be argument patterns filled by vocabulary expanded beyond the vocabulary of the sentences being systematized. Projective geometry is a good example of how an expanded conceptual repertoire enables mathematical explanations of truths expressible in an antecedent vocabulary.

17. Using the labels from fig. 9.6—though, of course, M does not appear anywhere on that figure! M is the intersection of parallel lines AC and A'C'.

18. "As regards your way of considering parallel lines as if they met at a point infinitely distant, in order to include them in the same genus as those that go toward a point—it's very good . . ."

19. After completing my paper (Lange 2010) on mathematical coincidence, I found that Wilson (1992) also argues that the points introduced by projective geometry are not mere conveniences, prettifying Euclidean theorems, nor is it the case that "any self consistent domain is equally worthy of mathematical investigation" (152). Rather, those theorems "cry out for the extended, projective setting" (153). Although Wilson says that nineteenth-century mathematicians compared appeal to ideal points to "physical explanations by appeal to unseen molecular structures" (151), Wilson does not offer an account of a theorem's "proper setting," much less unpack it in terms of mathematical explanation. His concerns lie elsewhere. Wilson, in turn, notes that Manders (1987, 1989) also argues that points at infinity "unify concepts, in a technical sense which covers widely cited advantages of simplification and clarity" (554). Manders elaborates the conceptual unification and "more systematic understanding" (561) provided by these posits not fundamentally in terms of mathematical explanation, but rather through model-theoretic notions such as "closure" and "completeness" (as when the addition of complex numbers allows all quadratic equations in one unknown to have solutions) that need not bring any increased explanatory power by my lights. Nevertheless, I agree with Manders that "we can have explicit epistemological grounds for commitment to those domains of entities by which certain prior domains of inquiry are made more understandable" (562). Putnam (1979, 73) argues that "the consistency and fertility of classical mathematics is evidence that it—or most of it—is *true under some interpretation.*" His argument differs from mine in several respects. He is giving an argument for wholesale realism regarding (most of classical) mathematics, whereas I am concerned with how the potential for giving particular explanations in mathematics supports the existence of the particular entities invoked by those potential explanations. He focuses on "consistency and fertility" rather than specifically on explanation in mathematics. He is arguing for a certain variety of "realism" regarding mathematical entities, whereas I argue only that explanatory considerations show that projective points have the same ontological status (whatever that is!) as Euclidean points.

After I had largely finished this chapter, Steiner kindly called my attention to his (1983a, 1983b). There he identifies the "epistemic reality" of a mathematical entity with its having several "independent" descriptions (roughly, its figuring in several separate branches of mathematics, such as geometry and statistics). In emphasizing several "independent" descriptions of the same mathematical entity, Steiner comes near to what I term "mathematical coincidences." He also uses the notion of explanation in mathematics to specify what it is for two descriptions to be "independent": it is for there to be no proof that explains why the descriptions are coreferential. On Steiner's view, then, the "epistemic reality" of a mathematical entity consists in its having two descriptions where their coreference is unexplained. Steiner's idea is rather different from mine. The target of explanation with which I am concerned is not a theorem involving multiple descriptions of the entity in question, but rather a theorem that does not involve that entity at all (e.g., a theorem that mentions only Euclidean points, not projective points). Moreover, I argue that it is precisely the explanatory power of projective points that vouchsafes their ontological status—not the absence of certain explanations.

20. In creating a specious unity, the concept of a projective "point" would then be like the property F that applies to all and only things at worlds where a given deductive system of actual truths holds—thereby threatening to undermine Lewis's Best System Account of natural law by allowing a maximally simple formulation of a deductive system of actual truths with maximal strength (Lewis 1983, 367). See also the bogus explanation created by disjunctive properties in the notorious footnote 33 in Hempel's and Oppenheim's classic paper (Hempel 1965, 273).

21. In section 8.3, I mentioned the role played here in my account by the notion of natural properties in mathematics and I issued the promissory note that I hope now to redeem. In other examples, an innovation allows a common proof to be given of results that would otherwise involve several special cases requiring separate treatment, but where (unlike the Desargues example that I am discussing) no innovation is needed to appreciate that the separate theorems regarding these special cases together identify something that these cases have in common. For instance, by appealing to points with imaginary coordinates (nowhere on the Euclidean plane), we discover to be no coincidence a result that without these points would appear coincidental: that for any two circles, there is a line where for any point on the line, the tangent from that point to one circle is equal to the tangent from that point to the other circle. The "coincidence" is that this fact holds whether the two circles intersect on the Euclidean plane in two points, in one point, or nowhere. These cases must be proved separately if no appeal is made to imaginary points. (For a nice, brief account, see Sawyer 1955, 180–181) That two pairs of circles each have such a line can be appreciated as a respect in which the two pairs are similar (despite the circles in one pair overlapping while the circles in the other pair fail to touch) without any recourse to points with imaginary coordinates. (For another case, consider the Taylor series example with the radius of convergence on the complex plane.) Such a case does not involve the circularity (no pun intended) between naturalness and explanatory power that I am about to discuss in the case of Desargues's theorem.

22. As indirect support for this idea, I will argue in chapter 11 that roughly the same idea applies in science: many properties (such as having a given Reynolds number) become natural by virtue of their roles in certain scientific explanations.

23. By this "Insofar as . . ." formulation, I mean to recognize that a given mathematical property's naturalness and a given proof's explanatoriness can be matters of degree. (Lewis likewise regards naturalness as a matter of degree.) Also note that this view leaves room for a property to figure in an explanatory proof without its role there contributing at all toward making the property natural. The property must figure in the proof as a respect in which (if the property were natural) various things would be alike so as to enable the proof to explain by revealing how one (salient) similarity arises from another. Thus, the property cannot figure in the proof merely as the referent of a convenient notational device, for example. Note also that since an entire constellation of proofs is needed to render certain properties natural (and hence to make those proofs explanatory), the proof of Desargues's theorem that I have been examining is not enough by itself to make the property of being a projective point natural. (Nor, of course, have I aimed to give a full account of the mathematical significance of Desargues's theorem.)

24. I say "*seemingly* disjunctive" because although the expression "being a Euclidean point *or* a point at infinity" appears to denote a genuinely disjunctive property, that appearance turns out to be deceptive; the property to which this expression refers was discovered to be mathematically natural. Whether a property is natural or disjunctive is not a matter of the syntax of the predicate picking it out.

25. Other discussions include Lakatos (1976), Corfield (2003, 2005). I am grateful to Professor Tappenden for discussions of his views; of course, I am responsible for any remaining misapprehensions of them.

26. Steiner (1978b, 18–19; 1978c, 141–142; 1990, 105–107) likewise says that this theorem concerning complex power series explains why the Taylor series for $1/(1 + x^2)$ converges at $|x| < 1$ but not at $|x| > 1$—and, as Steiner (1990, 106) notes, Waismann (1982, 29–30) says the same. Neither mentions mathematical coincidence or compares the convergence of the series $1/(1 - x^2)$. Wilson (2006, 313–314) gives the same example and says that expansion to the complex plane brings "understanding." I distinctly recall being thunderstruck by the Spivak passages when I encountered them in my first college mathematics course (using Spivak's textbook).

27. The same point applies in connection with another example from chapter 8. Why does π have so many unreasonably close approximations? Because it is an irrational number and every irrational number does. The theorem proved by Apostol and Mnatsakanian (2002) identifies a natural property possessed by π (namely, that it is irrational) where it is no coincidence that all possessors of this property are alike in the relevant respect (namely, in having so many unreasonably close approximations). In contrast, the property of being π or e is not a natural mathematical property, though all of its cases are also alike in having so many unreasonably close approximations.

Another example of explanation by subsumption under a theorem (suggested to me by the mathematician Edward Frenkel) is the explanation of the four classical theorems of vector calculus (the gradient theorem for line integrals, Green's theorem, the classical Stokes's theorem, and the divergence theorem). These theorems have a striking similarity: each states that the integral, over some object, of some type of derivative of function f is equal to some function of f's values at or some integral of f's values along the object's boundaries. (For the four theorems, the objects are—respectively—a curve, a planar region, a surface in three-dimensional space, and a volume.) An explanation of this similarity is that these theorems are all special cases of the generalized Stokes's theorem from differential geometry, which generalizes these results for arbitrary dimension in terms of differential forms. Frenkel writes (personal communication, January 2014): "Each of [these four theorems] relates two integrals, but the statements seem to be ad hoc; they involve expressions that seemingly have nothing to do with each other. One can prove each statement directly (and this is how they are presented in most calculus textbooks), but this does not give us a good understanding of what's *really* going on. To understand that, we need to consider differential forms and the de Rham differential. . . . Seen through the lens of the de Rham complex, all of the above statements become crystal clear. We now understand *why* they are true."

Ruelle (2007, 117) seems to be referring to roughly the same sort of explanation by subsumption (involving a context-sensitive notion of salience that is not "completely logical") when he writes, "Use of analogy is not a completely logical process, and this will delight some mathematicians, while irritating others. The latter will want to understand why two theories are similar, perhaps by finding a more general theory that contains both as special cases."

■ **Chapter 10**

1. I make a similar point about explanation in mathematics in chapter 7, note 17.

2. Only in juxtaposition does this feature become striking; neither result has an outstanding feature taken in isolation from the other. In chapter 8, I presented this phenomenon in the case of other mathematical coincidences and non-coincidences.

3. Hempel (1965, 435–436) similarly points out that the set of laws governing one phenomenon can be strictly analogous to the set of laws responsible for another phenomenon. Although such an analogy may be helpful in the context of discovery (441), Hempel insists that there is no explanatory work for a "structural isomorphism" (439) to do. Each set of laws explains its own domain: "For the systematic purposes of scientific explanation, reliance on analogies is thus inessential and can always be dispensed with" (439). Hempel seems not to have considered that the explanandum might itself be an analogy: not the derivative law governing one phenomenon or the derivative law governing the other, but the analogy between them. This analogy (it seems to me) is explained by the isomorphism between the two sets of more fundamental laws. In this way, an analogy can be indispensable to a scientific explanation.

4. See chapter 8, note 4.

5. An analogous point could be made regarding the parallel proofs of dual theorems in projective geometry.

Note that the symmetry doing the explaining is a symmetry in the more fundamental electrostatic and thermodynamic laws. Thus the explanation here is not purely mathematical; the contingent laws of nature also play a key role.

Presumably, we could also have an explanation of the kind I am describing where a pair of accidents (rather than a pair of derivative laws) is being explained by some accidents (together, perhaps, with some laws).

6. Commentators on Thomson have overlooked this kind of explanation. Accordingly, they have held that the analogies discovered by Thomson are heuristically valuable but explanatorily irrelevant. In particular, commentators have claimed that in order for the analogy between electrostatics and thermodynamics to be explanatorily relevant, the entities covered by one of these fields would have to reduce to the entities covered by the other—for instance, voltage (electrical potential difference) would have to be temperature difference. Here are passages from two commentators: "When writing about electrostatics, for example, he used the heat diffusion analogy, but he did not reduce electrostatics to the laws of thermal diffusion. . . . Thomson used formal analogy as a heuristic device only" (Roche 2008, 98); "much confusion exists that is unfair to Kelvin, between analogy and explanation. . . . Crystal clear from these early papers is that fact that for him, analogy was a device not of explanation but of discovery" (Everitt 2008, 231).

I certainly agree that we cannot use a feature of thermodynamics to explain a feature of electrostatics unless electrical phenomena are, at bottom, thermodynamic phenomena. But causal explanation is not the only kind of scientific explanation there is. Instead of explaining a derivative law of electrostatics, we may want to explain why certain derivative laws in thermodynamics and electrostatics are so much alike. Analogy between the fundamental laws of electrostatics and thermodynamics is then explanatorily relevant; the explanation is non-causal. (For another example of this phenomenon, see Feynman, Leighton, and Sands 1963, vol. 1, 25-7 to 25-8.) The distinction here is similar to the distinction in section 3.3 between using a bar's length in inertial frame S′ to explain its length in S, on the one hand, and explaining the relation between its lengths in S and S', on the other hand.

Feynman et al. also note (1963, vol. 2, 12-2) that steady heat-flow solutions and electrostatic solutions are mathematically the same and ask why they are (12-12). Feynman seems to suggest that this is *no* physical coincidence because although thermodynamics and electrostatics are not "dealing with the same stuff," there is a common explainer behind (what I termed) the "fundamental" thermodynamic and electrostatic equations: both sets of equations are approximations to even more fundamental equations (separate equations for thermodynamics and electrostatics) and also "are the simplest vector equations that one can get which involve only the spatial derivatives of quantities" where these derivatives vary reasonably smoothly with position. Feynman has been understood as suggesting that the analogy between the "fundamental" thermodynamic and electrostatic equations is no coincidence because their common form has a common explanation: "these formal identities . . . have been beautifully explained. . . . It is through a common process of approximation/ abstraction that different physical phenomena are encompassed by analogous mathematizations" (Lévy-Leblond 1992, 152–153). It seems to me that on Feynman's picture, it remains a physical coincidence that both thermodynamic and electrostatic processes, despite their differences at the level of fundamental equations, can be approximated well by equations of the same mathematical form (i.e., by the simplest possible equations of a certain kind). That scientists tried the same "approximation/abstraction" for both thermodynamics and electrostatics explains why scientists arrived at equations of the same form for both processes but fails to explain why the same approximation works for both processes. (Thanks to Pen Maddy for calling the Feynman passage to my attention.)

7. Of course, the explanation that I have been examining could justly be called a "distinctively mathematical" scientific explanation. My point is simply that it works differently from the distinctively mathematical scientific explanations that I described in chapter 1.

8. "Nihil elegantius est quam consensus quem observasti inter numeros potestatum a binomio et differentiarum rectangulo; haud dubie aliquid arcane subset."

9. Gregory (1837, 32) also argued that the reason why certain differential equations are so much more difficult to solve than others is because they cannot be solved by replacing derivatives with powers because these laws of combination do not apply: "the second law of combination does not hold with regard to these symbols of operation. . . . It is this peculiarity with regard to the combinations of the symbols <x> and d/dx which gives rise to the difficulty in the solution of linear equations with variable coefficients." Recall my remarks at the end of chapter 7 regarding mathematical explanations that aim to account for why certain problems are so much harder to solve than others.

10. "Chemin faisant, d'autres rapports, entre la différentielle, la différence, l'état varié et les nombres, se sont manifestés; il a fallu en rechercher la cause; et tout s'est expliqué fort heureusement, quand, après avoir dépouillé, par une sévère abstraction, ces fonctions de leurs qualités spécifiques, on a eu simplement à considérer les deux propriétés qu'elles possèdent en commun, d'être distributives et commutatives entre elles."

11. If we do not give a common proof that the binomial formula applies to all commutative rings, then the fact that it applies to both real numbers and polynomials in D ("D" for differentiation—polynomials such as $(D^2 + 2D + 3) f(x)$, which represents $f''(x) + 2f'(x) + 3f(x)$) "appears as a strange coincidence," according to Sawyer (1966, 150).

12. Technically, this is the *adiabatic* bulk modulus (rather than the *isothermal* bulk modulus) because although the compressions and rarefactions are associated with temperature changes, they occur so rapidly that little heat can flow.

13. The L line in each case dictates that v is independent of λ—though for different reasons in the two cases. However, we could not have reached this result had we also included the wave's amplitude in characterizing it. (But the M and T lines would have been unaffected.)

14. I could have added a third kind of wave: a torsional wave of twisting and untwisting traveling along a rod with a circular cross-section. It has the same dimensional architecture; its speed is $\sqrt{(G/\rho)}$, where G is the shear modulus.

Of course, unlike the derivations from more fundamental laws, the dimensional explanation does not explain why these systems have waves running through them in the first place. I discussed this in chapter 6.

15. That two facts are naturally necessary does not suffice to make a given consequence of them no (physical) coincidence. For instance, nineteenth-century chemists believed it naturally necessary that all noncyclic alkane hydrocarbons differ in molecular weight by multiples of 14 units, and they also believed it naturally necessary that the atomic weight of nitrogen is 14 units. But they termed it "coincidental" (albeit naturally necessary) that all noncyclic alkanes differ in molecular weight by multiples of the atomic weight of nitrogen. Noncyclic alkanes contain no nitrogen. See, for instance, van Spronsen 1969, 73–74, and Lange 2000, 203–207.

16. As I showed at the end of chapter 7, there are also explanations in mathematics that aim to explain such facts—for instance, why a result regarding finite sums does not extend to infinite sums.

17. I have omitted a column for the angle from which the pendulum is released, since angle is usually taken to be a dimensionless quantity, and so dimensional analysis cannot impose any constraint on how it figures in the equation for the period. That is, dimensional analysis reveals only that T is proportional to $\sqrt{(l/g)}$ times some unknown function of the initial angle.

18. Similarly, Hacking (1990) emphasizes that statistical reasoning identifies new targets of explanation (e.g., normal distributions).

The why question answered by a dimensional explanation may sometimes not be asked until we have carried out the dimensional argument that can answer it. For instance, regarding the orbiting planet discussed in section 6.2, we may not have thought to ask why $T \propto r^{3/2}$ until after seeing that there is a dimensional argument that would answer this question. But this explanandum does not involve any dimensional concepts; it does not constitute a dimensional fact. My point now is that dimensional facts supply new targets for explanation.

19. The constant of proportionality turns out to be $\sqrt{(2\pi)}$. No dimensional explanation explains that.

■ Chapter 11

1. That is, one with a rigid arm to which the two point bodies are secured, the bodies feeling no influences besides the contact force from the arm and a force from an ambient gravitational field that can safely be treated as approximately uniform over the seesaw.

2. Perhaps "*l&c&f*" denotes the same fact as "*l&c*." (I will have nothing to say about fact individuation.) Nevertheless, "*l&c&f* explains why *f*" is not equivalent to "*l&c* explains why *f*." For instance, if causal explanation is understood to be the kind of explanation at issue,

then "*l&c&f* explains why *f*" holds exactly when "*l&c&f*" captures all and only the contextu- ally relevant features of *f*'s causal history (or, more broadly, of the world's network of causal relations). But "*l&c&f*" cannot do this because *f* is not part of its own causal history. (In different contexts, different features of *f*'s causal history—more distal or proximate, more coarse-grained or fine-grained . . . —will be of interest, but there is no context in which *f* is a feature of interest because *f* is not part of its own causal history.) Analogous considerations apply to other kinds of scientific explanation. For instance, consider an "identity explanation" from Achinstein (1983, 236): "The reason that ice is water is that ice is composed of H_2O molecules" is an explanation whereas (Achinstein notes) "the reason that ice is water is that ice is water" is not an explanation, even though the property of being water and the property of being composed of H_2O molecules "are clearly identical" (236). Even if explanation is a relation among facts, evidently it must also be sensitive to the ways in which those facts are expressed. This is an old point; as Mackie (1974, 260) said, "Oedipus' having married Jocasta is the same fact as his having married his mother, and if the latter caused the tragedy, so did the former. Yet the latter description helps to explain the tragedy in a way that the former does not." (See Davidson 1967, 695.)

3. Often I use "properties" to include relations. Furthermore, even if it is logically impos- sible for anything to possess the property of having $m_R x_R - m_L x_L > 0$ but to lack the property of having $x_R - m_L x_L/m_R > 0$, I take these to be distinct properties. Thus I say that a property is *associated with* a class of possibilia, not that a property is *identical to* a class of possibilia or that a class of possibilia is associated with exactly one property.

4. For more on the distinction between laws and naturally necessary nonlaws, see Lange 2000, 201–207.

5. This formulation acknowledges that naturalness comes in degrees. (See section 6.) Once again, however, in using the concept of naturalness to express our question, we must reject the thought that a reducible property cannot be natural (to any appreciate degree) because it is redundant in characterizing the world. Nonredundancy seems to me quite dis- tinct from being a genuine respect of similarity (rather than an arbitrary or gerrymandered "property"), figuring in laws (rather than merely in logical consequences of laws), and being explanatorily powerful. Nevertheless, some metaphysicians simply identify the perfectly natural properties with the fundamental properties.

6. Dennett refers to "center of gravity," which in a uniform gravitational field is identical to center of mass.

7. Perhaps there is another explanation of the tipping law from energy conservation that does not begin from an expression ($U = Mgh$) for the system's gravitational potential energy in which the center of mass's location figures as a unit. Perhaps there is an explanation that begins with the gravitational potential energies of each point particle and then massages the sum of those energies until Mgh emerges.

It is not obvious to me that such an argument is in fact explanatory—that the expression for the potential energy of a configuration derives from the expression for the potential energy of a point particle. The order of explanatory priority might be the other way around, or the two laws may be equally basic. But even if such an argument does explain, it does not undermine the explanatory power of the tipping law's derivation from energy conservation and $U = Mgh$.

8. Notice that it is not circular or trivial to say that W_p is natural enough to join Archimedes's principle in explaining the magnitude of the buoyant force on a given body by virtue of its entering as a unit in some explanation of Archimedes's principle. First, the two explanations have different targets: the former explains the magnitude of the buoyant force on some

particular body, whereas the latter explains Archimedes's principle. Second, the explanation of Archimedes's principle does not itself depend on W_p's naturalness.

9. This conclusion presupposes that all explanations of the derivative law involving μ are like this one. If there were another explanation into which μ entered as a unit, then my account would offer a different verdict. I do not know of such an explanation; the law can be explained by a Lagrangian approach to the two-body problem, for instance, but once again, μ does not enter as a unit into the Lagrangian.

10. The precise explanation of the onset of turbulence is a notorious open question. Scientists justly expect Re (as the ratio of inertial to viscous forces) to enter as a unit into an explanation of whatever derivative laws cover this phenomenon. (See the above passage from Reynolds.) But as of this writing, no general explanation has been found.

11. Suppose we take seriously the idea that the property of having a given value of the Reynolds number qualifies as a natural property (i.e., a genuine respect of similarity) by virtue of its role in dimensional explanations, which are not causal explanations (i.e., do not derive their power to explain from supplying information about the world's network of causal relations). The view (Fodor 1988; Shoemaker 1984) that physical properties qualify as natural by virtue of their causal roles would then have to be amended to "becausal" roles.

12. In chapter 9 note 23, I suggested that the naturalness of properties in mathematics is likewise a matter of degree.

13. For the derivation, see Feynman et al. 1963, vol. 2, 21-1 to 21-11; Janah et al. 1988.

14. This formula is given by Feynman et al. (1963, vol. 2, 21-1); it was first published by Heaviside in 1910 (Heaviside 1912, 438).

15. There are other ways on my proposal for intermediate cases to arise. Suppose that property P fails to enter as a unit into any explanation of any law that, together with some initial conditions that include P's instantiation, entail a given outcome O. However, suppose that P nevertheless enters some explanation of L as a unit, where L is a law that performs considerable explanatory work (though not in explaining O). Then P's role in L's explanation might give P some degree of naturalness—enough for O's entailment from P's instantiation (together with other facts) to possess some power to explain O.

16. There is also an important respect in which the two examples differ. In the case of Re, the explanations in which Re functions as a unit do not depend for their explanatory power, in turn, on Re's naturalness (see also note 8). By contrast, a proof of Desargues's theorem in projective geometry that exits to the third dimension succeeds in explaining that theorem partly by virtue of the naturalness of various projective properties. However, their naturalness (in turn) arises from their roles in other explanations. (See chapter 9.)

17. See chapter 8 note 3. I have not suggested that explanation be understood in terms of non-coincidence. On the contrary, I have tried in various cases to understand coincidence in terms of the absence of a certain kind of explanation.

18. See end of section 10.2.

■ REFERENCES

Abrams, Marshall. 2009. "How Do Natural Selection and Random Drift Interact?" *Philosophy of Science* 74: 666–679.

Achinstein, Peter. 1983. *The Nature of Explanation*. New York: Oxford University Press.

Alper, Joseph S., Mark Bridger, John Earman, and John Norton. 2000. "What Is a Newtonian System? The Failure of Energy Conservation and Determinism in Supertasks." *Synthese* 124: 281–293.

Alperin, Jonathan. 1980. "Groups and Symmetry." In *Mathematics Today*, edited by Lynn Arthur Steen, 65–82. New York: Vintage.

Alsina, Claudi, and Roger B. Nelson. 2010. *Charming Proofs*. Washington, DC: Mathematics Association of America.

Andrews, George E., and Kimmo Eriksson. 2004. *Integer Partitions*. Cambridge: Cambridge University Press.

Angel, Roger. 1980. *Relativity: The Theory and Its Philosophy*. Oxford: Pergamon.

Annamalai, K., and I. Puri. 2002. *Advanced Thermodynamic Engineering*. Boca Raton, FL: CRC Press.

Anonymous. 1829. "Review of Laplace's Celestial Mechanics." *American Quarterly Review* 5: 310–443.

Anonymous. 1837. "Composition." In *The Penny Cyclopaedia of the Society for the Diffusion of Useful Knowledge*, vol. 7, 423. London: Charles Knight and Company.

Anonymous. 1850. "On the Composition and Resolution of Forces." *English Journal of Education*, n.s., 4: 378–381.

Anonymous. 1880. "Composition and Resolution of Forces and Motions." In *Library of Universal Knowledge—A Reprint of the Last (1880) Edinburgh and London Edition of Chambers's Encyclopædia*, vol. 4, 208–209. New York: American Book Exchange.

Apostol, Tom M., and Mamikon A. Mnatsakanian. 2002. "Surprisingly Accurate Rational Approximations." *Mathematics Magazine* 75: 307–310.

Arana, Andrew, and Paolo Mancosu. 2012. "On the Relationship between Plane and Solid Geometry." *Review of Symbolic Logic* 5: 294–353.

Aristotle. 1980. *Minor Works*. Translated by W. S. Hett. Cambridge, MA: Harvard University Press.

Armstrong, David. 1978. *Universals and Scientific Realism*, vol. 1. Cambridge: Cambridge University Press.

Armstrong, David. 1983. *What Is a Law of Nature?* Cambridge: Cambridge University Press.

Armstrong, David. 1997. *A World of States of Affairs*. Cambridge: Cambridge University Press.

Atiyah, Michael. 1988. "How Research Is Carried Out." In *Collected Works*, vol. 1, 211–216. Oxford: Clarendon.

Augustine. 1982. *The Literal Meaning of Genesis*, vol. 1. Translated by John Hammond Taylor. New York: Newman Press.

Azzouni, Jody. 1997. "Applied Mathematics, Existential Commitment, and the Quine-Putnam Indispensability Thesis." *Philosophia Mathematica* 5: 193–209.

Baker, Alan. 2005. "Are There Genuine Mathematical Explanations of Physical Phenomena?" *Mind* 114: 223–238.

Baker, Alan. 2009a. "Mathematical Accidents and the End of Explanation." In *New Waves in Philosophy of Mathematics*, edited by Otávio Bueno and Øystein Linnebo, 137–59. Houndmills, UK: Palgrave Macmillan.

Baker, Alan. 2009b. "Mathematical Explanations in Science." *British Journal for the Philosophy of Science* 60: 611–633.

Baker, Alan. 2010. "Mathematical Induction and Explanation." *Analysis* 70: 681–689.

Baker, Alan. 2012. "Science-Driven Mathematical Explanation." *Mind* 121: 243–267.

Baker, H. F. 1922. *Principles of Geometry*, vol. 1. Cambridge: Cambridge University Press.

Balashov, Yuri, and Michel Janssen. 2003. "Critical Notice: Presentism and Relativity." *British Journal for the Philosophy of Science* 54: 327–346.

Barbour, Julian. 1989. *Absolute or Relative Motion?* vol. 1. *The Discovery of Dynamics.* Oxford: Oxford University Press.

Barenblatt, G. I. 1987. *Dimensional Analysis.* New York: Gordon and Breach.

Barlow, P. 1848. "Mechanics." In *Encyclopaedia Metropolitana*, edited by Edward Smedley, Hugh James Rose, and Henry John Rose, vol. 3, 1–160. London: Griffin.

Barrow, John D., and Frank J. Tipler. 1986. *The Anthropic Cosmological Principle.* Oxford: Clarendon.

Bartlett, D. F., and Y. Su. 1994. "What Potentials Permit a Uniqueness Theorem." *American Journal of Physics* 62: 683–686.

Bartlett, W. H. C. 1850. *Elements of Natural Philosophy*, vol. 1. New York: A. S. Barnes.

Barton, Gabriel. 1999. *Introduction to the Relativity Principle.* Chichester: Wiley.

Batterman, Robert W. 2002a. "Asymptotics and the Role of Minimal Models." *British Journal for the Philosophy of Science* 51: 21–38.

Batterman, Robert W. 2002b. *The Devil in the Details.* New York: Oxford University Press.

Batterman, Robert W. 2010. "On the Explanatory Role of Mathematics in Empirical Science." *British Journal for the Philosophy of Science* 61: 1–25.

Beatty, John. 1984. "Drift and Natural Selection." *Philosophy of Science* 51: 183–211.

Beatty, John. 1992. "Random Drift." In *Keywords in Evolutionary Biology*, edited by E. Keller and E. Lloyd, 273–281. Cambridge, MA: Harvard University Press.

Beebee, Helen. 2004. "Causing and Nothingness." In *Causation and Counterfactuals*, edited by John Collins, Ned Hall, and L. A. Paul, 291–308. Cambridge, MA: MIT Press.

Bell, A. W. 1976. "A Study of Pupils' Proof-Explanations in Mathematical Situations." *Educational Studies in Mathematics* 7: 23–40.

Bell, J. S. 1987. "How to Teach Special Relativity." In *Speakable and Unspeakable in Quantum Mechanics*, 67–80. Cambridge: Cambridge University Press.

Belot, Gordon. 2011. *Geometric Possibility.* New York: Oxford University Press.

Benjamin, Arthur T., and Jennifer J. Quinn. 2003. *Proofs That Really Count.* Washington, DC: Mathematical Association of America.

Bennett, Jonathan. 1970. "The Difference between Right and Left." *American Philosophical Quarterly* 7: 175–191.

Bergmann, Peter G. 1962. "The Special Theory of Relativity." In *Encyclopedia of Physics*, vol. 4, edited by S. Flügge, 109–202. Berlin: Springer-Verlag.

Berndt, Bruce C., and Robert A. Rankin. 1995. *Ramanujan: Letters and Commentary.* Providence, RI: American Mathematical Society.

Bernoulli, Daniel. 1726/1982. "Examen Principiorum Mechanicae, et Demonstrations Geometricae de Compositione et Resolutione Virium." *Commentarii Academiae Scientarum Imperialis Petropolitanae* 1: 126–142. Reprinted in *Die Werke von Daniel*

Bernoulli, vol. 3, edited by L. P. Bouckaert, D. Speiser, and B. L. van der Waerden, 119–135. Basel: Birkhäuser.

Berzi, Vittorio, and Vittorio Gorini. 1969. "Reciprocity Principle and Lorentz Transformations." *Journal of Mathematical Physics* 10: 1518–1524.

Besant, W. H. 1883. "The Teaching of Elementary Mathematics." Paper presented at the annual meeting of the Association for the Improvement of Geometrical Teaching, January 1883, reported in "The Teaching of Elementary Mechanics" [by R.T.], *Nature* 27: 581–583.

Bigelow, John, Brian Ellis, and Caroline Lierse. 1992. "The World as One of a Kind: Natural Necessity and Laws of Nature." *British Journal for the Philosophy of Science* 43: 371–388.

Bird, Alexander. 2007. *Nature's Metaphysics: Laws and Properties*. New York: Oxford University Press.

Birkhoff, Garrett. 1950. *Hydrodynamics*. Princeton: Princeton University Press.

Blaikie, James. 1879. *The Elements of Dynamics (Mechanics)*, 3rd ed. Edinburgh: James Thin.

Block, Ned. 1974. "Why Do Mirrors Reverse Left/Right but Not Up/Down?" *Journal of Philosophy* 71: 259–277.

Bogomolny, A. "Menelaus Theorem: Proofs Ugly and Elegant—A. Einstein's View." Interactive Mathematics Miscellany and Puzzles (website). http://www.cut-the knot.org/Generalization/MenelausByEinstein.shtml#F. Accessed April 12, 2009.

Bohren, Craig. 2004. "Dimensional Analysis, Falling Bodies, and the Fine Art of *Not* Solving Differential Equations." *American Journal of Physics* 72: 534–537.

Bokulich, Alisa. 2008. *Reexamining the Quantum-Classical Relation*. Cambridge: Cambridge University Press.

Bollobás, Béla. 2006. *The Art of Mathematics*. Cambridge: Cambridge University Press.

Bondi, Hermann. 1970. "General Relativity as an Open Theory." In *Physics, Logic, and History*, edited by Wolfgang Yourgrau and Allen Breck, 265–271. New York: Plenum.

Bondi, Hermann. 1980. *Relativity and Common Sense*. New York: Dover.

Boole, George. 1841. "On the Integration of Linear Differential Equations with Constant Coefficients." *Cambridge Mathematical Journal* 2: 114–119.

Borceux, Francis. 2014. *An Algebraic Approach to Geometry*. Cham, Switzerland: Springer.

Bos, H. J. M. 1974–75. "Differentials, Higher-Order Differentials and the Derivative in the Leibnizian Calculus." *Archives for History of Exact Sciences* 14: 1–90.

Brading, Katherine, and Elena Castellani. 2003. *Symmetries in Physics: Philosophical Reflections*. Cambridge: Cambridge University Press.

Braine, David. 1972. "Varieties of Necessity." *Supplementary Proceedings of the Aristotelian Society* 46: 139–170.

Brandon, Robert. 2005. "The Difference between Drift and Selection: A Reply to Millstein." *Biology and Philosophy* 20: 153–170.

Brandon, Robert. 2006. "The Principle of Drift: Biology's First Law." *Journal of Philosophy* 103: 319–335.

Brannan, David. 2006. *A First Course in Mathematical Analysis*. Cambridge: Cambridge University Press.

Bressoud, David M. 1994. *A Radical Approach to Real Analysis*. Washington, DC: Mathematical Association of America.

Bressoud, David M. 1999. *Proofs and Confirmations: The Story of the Alternating Sign Matrix Conjecture*. Cambridge: Cambridge University Press.

Bridgman, Percy W. 1931. *Dimensional Analysis*. New Haven: Yale University Press.

Brown, Harvey. 2005. *Physical Relativity*. Oxford: Clarendon.

Brown, Harvey, and Peter Holland. 2004. "Dynamical versus Variational Symmetries: Understanding Noether's First Theorem." *Molecular Physics* 102: 1133–1139.

Brown, Harvey and Oliver Pooley. 2006. "Minkowski Space-Time: A Glorious Non-entity." In *The Ontology of Spacetime*, edited by Dennis Dieks, 67–89. Amsterdam: Elsevier.

Brown, James Robert. 1997. "Proofs and Pictures." *British Journal for the Philosophy of Science* 48: 161–180.

Brown, James Robert. 1999. *Philosophy of Mathematics: An Introduction to a World of Proofs and Pictures*. London: Routledge.

Browne, W. 1883. *The Student's Mechanics*. London: C. Griffin.

Brunhes, Edmond [Frère Gabriel-Marie]. 1920/1991. *Exercices de Géometrié*. 6th ed. Tours: A. Mame. Reprint, Paris: Editions Jacques Gabay.

Byers, William. 2007. *How Mathematicians Think*. Princeton: Princeton University Press.

Cacciatori, Sergio, Vittorio Gorini, and Alexander Kamenshchik. 2008. "Special Relativity in the 21st Century." *Annalen der Physik* 17: 728–768.

Callender, Craig. 2005. "Answers in Search of a Question: 'Proofs' of the Tri-dimensionality of Space." *Studies in History and Philosophy of Modern Physics* 36: 113–136.

Cambridge University. 1856. *Cambridge Examination Papers—Being a Supplement to the University Calendar for the Year 1856*. Cambridge: Deighton, Bell.

Cambridge University. 1884. *Cambridge University Examination Papers, Michaelmas Term 1883 to Easter Term 1884*. Cambridge: Cambridge University Press.

Campbell, Norman Robert. 1957. *Foundations of Science*. New York: Dover.

Carnap, Rudolf. 1950. "Empiricism, Semantics, and Ontology." *Revue Internationale de Philosophie* 4: 20–40.

Carnot, Lazare. 1803. *Géométrie de Position*. Paris: Crapelet.

Carter, Brandon. 1990. "Large Number Coincidences and the Anthropic Principle in Cosmology." In *Physical Cosmology and Philosophy*, edited by John Leslie, 125–133. New York: Macmillan.

Cassirer, Ernst. 1957. *The Philosophy of Symbolic Forms*, vol. 3. New Haven: Yale University Press.

Castelvecchi, Davide. 2004/2005. "Fine-Tune This." *Symmetry: Dimensions of Particle Physics* 1/2 (December/January): 8–9.

Causey, Robert L. 1967. *Derived Measurements and the Foundations of Dimensional Analysis*. Measurement Theory and Mathematical Models Reports, technical report no. 5. Eugene: University of Oregon.

Causey, Robert L. 1969. "Derived Measurements, Dimensions, and Dimensional Analysis." *Philosophy of Science* 36: 252–270.

Challis, James. 1869. *Notes on the Principles of Pure and Applied Calculation*. Cambridge: Deighton, Bell.

Challis, James. 1875. *Remarks on the Cambridge Mathematical Studies and Their Relation to Modern Physical Science*. Cambridge: Deighton, Bell.

Chang, Kung-Ching, Yiming Long, and Eduard Zehnder. 1990. "Forced Oscillations for the Triple Pendulum." In *Analysis, et Cetera*, edited by Paul Rabinowitz and Edward Zehnder, 177–208. San Diego: Academic Press.

Chasles, David. 1837. *Aperçu Historique sur L'origine et le Developpement des Methods en Géométrie*. Paris: Gauthier-Villars.

Church, I. P. 1908. *Mechanics of Engineering*, New York: Wiley.

Clifton, Robert. 1998. "Structural Explanation in Quantum Theory." Unpublished manuscript. PhilSci Archive. http://philsci-archive.pitt.edu/91/.

Cockle, James. 1879. "Notes Bearing on Mathematical History." *Memoires of the Literary and Philosophical Society of Manchester*, ser. 3, 6: 10–15.

Colyvan, Mark. 1998. "Can the Eleatic Principle Be Justified?" *Canadian Journal of Philosophy* 28: 313–336.

Colyvan, Mark. 2001. *The Indispensability of Mathematics*. New York: Oxford University Press.

Colyvan, Mark. 2002. "Mathematics and Aesthetic Considerations in Science." *Mind* 11: 69–78.

Colyvan, Mark. 2007. "Mathematical Recreation versus Mathematical Knowledge." In *Mathematical Knowledge*, edited by Mary Leng, Alexander Pasneau, and Michael Potter, 109–122. Oxford: Oxford University Press.

Connes, Alain. 2004. "Symmetries." *European Mathematical Society Newsletter* 54: 11–18.

Corfield, David. 2003. *Towards a Philosophy of Real Mathematics*. Cambridge: Cambridge University Press.

Corfield, David. 2005. "Mathematical Kinds, or Being Kind to Mathematics." *Philosophica* 74: 30–54.

Corry, Leo. 1997. "Hermann Minkowski and the Postulate of Relativity." *Archive for History of Exact Sciences* 51: 273–314.

Corry, Leo. 2010. "Hermann Minkowski, Relativity and the Axiomatic Approach to Physics." In *Minkowski Spacetime: A Hundred Years Later*, edited by Vesselin Petkov, 3–42. Dordrecht: Springer.

Courant, Richard, Herbert Robbins, and Ian Stewart. 1996. *What Is Mathematics?* 2nd ed. Oxford: Oxford University Press.

Cox, J. 1904. *Mechanics*. Cambridge: Cambridge University Press.

Crombie, A. C. 1952. *Augustine to Galileo: The History of Science ad 400–1650*. London: Falcon Press.

Dauben, Joseph W. 1988. "Abraham Robinson and Nonstandard Analysis: History, Philosophy, and the Foundations of Mathematics." In *History and Philosophy of Modern Mathematics*, edited by William Aspray and Philip Kitcher, Minnesota Studies in the Philosophy of Science, vol. 11, 177–200. Minneapolis: University of Minnesota Press.

Davenport, Harold. 1999. *The Higher Arithmetic: An Introduction to the Theory of Numbers*. 7th ed. Cambridge: Cambridge University Press.

Davidson, Donald. 1967. "Causal Relations." *Journal of Philosophy* 64: 691–703.

Davies, Paul. 1986. *The Forces of Nature*. Cambridge: Cambridge University Press.

Davis, Philip J. 1981. "Are There Coincidences in Mathematics?" *American Mathematical Monthly* 88: 311–320.

De Morgan, Augustus. 1859. "On the General Principles of Which the Composition or Aggregation of Forces Is a Consequence." *Transactions of the Cambridge Philosophical Society* 10, pt. 2: 290–304.

De Morgan, Augustus. 1864. "Duchayla." *Notes and Queries*, 3rd ser., 5 (130): 527–528.

De Villiers, Michael. 1993. "Computer Verification vs. Algebraic Explanation." *Pythagoras* 31 (April): 46.

De Villiers, Michael. 2003. *Rethinking Proof with The Geometer's Sketchpad 4*. Emmeryville, CA: Key Curriculum Press.

Dennett, Daniel C. 1983. "Intentional Systems in Cognitive Ethology: The 'Panglossian Paradigm' Defended." *Behavioral and Brain Sciences* 6: 343–390.

Dennett, Daniel C. 1991. "Real Patterns." *Journal of Philosophy* 88: 27–51.

Dennett, Daniel C. 2000. "With a Little Help from My Friends." In *Dennett's Philosophy: A Comprehensive Assessment*, edited by Don Ross, Andrew Brook, and David Thompson, 327–388. Cambridge, MA: Bradford.

Denyer, Nicholas. 1994. "Why Do Mirrors Reverse Left/Right and Not Up/Down?" *Philosophy* 69: 205–210.

Descartes, René. 1639. Letter to Girard Desargues. In *Œuvres Complètes de René Descartes*. Connaught Descartes Project, Past Masters database, vol. 01: Correspondence: 1619–1650, Correspondence1639,II,554–556.http://www.library.nlx.com/xtf/view?docId=descartes_fr/descartes_fr.00.xml;chunk.id=div.descartes.Correspondence.1619.pmpreface.pm.1;toc.depth=2;toc.id=div.descartes.Correspondence.1619.pmpreface.pm.1;hit.rank=0;brand=default. Accessed July 24, 2009.

Devlin, Keith. 2008. "Lockhart's Lament—The Sequel." Devlin's Angle, May. Website of Mathematical Association of America. www.maa.org/external_archive/devlin/devlin_05_08.html. Accessed June 29, 2013.

Dieks, Dennis. 2009. "Understanding in Physics: Bottom-Up versus Top-Down." In *Scientific Understanding: Philosophical Perspectives*, edited by Henk W. de Regt, Sabina Leonelli, and Kai Eigner, 230–248. Pittsburgh: University of Pittsburgh Press.

Dieudonné, Jean. 1985. *History of Algebraic Geometry*. Monterey, CA: Wadsworth.

DiSalle, Robert. 2006. *Understanding Space-Time*. Cambridge: Cambridge University Press.

Dobbs, W. J. 1901. *A Treatise on Elementary Statics*. London: Adam and Charles Black.

Dorato, Mauro, and Laura Felline. 2010. "Structural Explanations in Minkowski Spacetime: Which Account of Models?" In *Space, Time, and Spacetime: Physical and Philosophical Implications of Minkowski's Unification of Space and Time*, edited by Vesselin Petkov, 193–207. Berlin: Springer-Verlag.

Douglas, John F. 1969. *An Introduction to Dimensional Analysis for Engineers*. London: Pitman.

Dretske, Fred. 1970. "Epistemic Operators." *Journal of Philosophy* 67: 1007–1023.

Dretske, Fred. 1977. "Laws of Nature." *Philosophy of Science* 44: 248–268.

Dreyfus, Tommy, and Theodore Eisenberg. 1986. "On the Aesthetics of Mathematical Thought." *For the Learning of Mathematics* 6: 2–10.

Duchalya, C. D. M. B. 1804. "Demonstration du Parallèlogramme des Forces." *Bulletin des Sciences par la Société Philomathique de Paris* 4: 242–243.

Duffin, W. J. 1980. *Electricity and Magnetism*, 3rd ed. London: McGraw-Hill.

Dugas, René. 1988. *A History of Mechanics*. New York: Dover.

Duhem, Pierre. 1991. *The Origins of Statics*. Boston Studies in the Philosophy of Science, vol. 123. Dordrecht: Kluwer.

Dunham, William. 1991. *Euler: The Master of Us All*. Washington, DC: Mathematical Association of America.

Earman, John. 1989. *World Enough and Space-Time*. Cambridge, MA: MIT Press.

Earnshaw, Samuel. 1845. *A Treatise on Statics*. 3rd ed. Cambridge: Cambridge University Press.

Eddington, Arthur S. 1920. *Space Time and Gravitation*. Cambridge: Cambridge University Press.

Ehrenfest, Paul. 1917. "In What Way Does It Become Manifest in the Fundamental Laws of Physics That Space Has Three Dimensions?" *Proceedings of the Amsterdam Academy* 20: 200–209.

Einstein, Albert. 1905/1989. "On the Electrodynamics of Moving Bodies." In *Collected Papers of Albert Einstein,* vol. 2, translated by Anna Beck, 140–171. Princeton: Princeton University Press.

Einstein, Albert. 1907/1989. "Comments on the Note of Mr. Paul Ehrenfest: 'The Translatory Motion of Deformable Electrons and the Area Law.'" In *The Collected Papers of Albert Einstein,* vol. 2, translated by Anna Beck, 236–237. Princeton: Princeton University Press.

Einstein, Albert. 1911/1993. "'Discussion' Following Lecture Version of 'The Theory of Relativity.'" In *The Collected Papers of Albert Einstein,* vol. 3, translated by Anna Beck, 351–358. Princeton: Princeton University Press.

Einstein, Albert. 1919/1954. "What Is the Theory of Relativity?" *Times (London),* November 28, 1919. Reprinted in *Ideas and Opinions,* 227–232. New York: Bonanza.

Einstein, Albert. 1921. "The General Physical Theory of Relativity." *Nature* 106 (2677): 791–793.

Einstein, Albert. 1935. "Elementary Derivation of the Equivalence of Mass and Energy." *Bulletin of the American Mathematical Society* 41: 223–230.

Einstein, Albert. 1949. "Autobiographical Notes." In *Albert Einstein: Philosopher-Scientist,* edited by P. A. Schilpp, Library of Living Philosophers, vol. 7, 1–96. Evanston, IL: Open Court.

Einstein, Albert. 1955/1956. "Letter to Carl Seelig (2/19/55)." In Max Born, *Physics in My Generation,* 194. London: Pergamon Press.

Ellis, Brian. 1966. *Basic Concepts of Measurement.* Cambridge: Cambridge University Press.

Ellis, Brian. 1990. *Truth and Objectivity.* Cambridge: Blackwell.

Ellis, Brian. 2001. *Scientific Essentialism.* Cambridge: Cambridge University Press.

Ellis, Brian. 2002. *The Philosophy of Nature: A Guide to the New Essentialism.* Montreal: McGill-Queen's University Press.

Elster, Jon. 1983. *Explaining Technical Change.* Cambridge: Cambridge University Press.

Everitt, C. W. Francis. 2008. "Kelvin, Maxwell, Einstein and the Ether: Who Was Right about What?" In *Kelvin: Life, Labours, and Legacy,* edited by Raymond Flood, Mark McCartney, and Andrew Whitaker, 224–252. Oxford: Oxford University Press.

Fayngold, Moses. 2008. *Special Relativity and How It Works.* Weinheim, Germany: Wiley-VCH.

Feller, William. 1957. *An Introduction to Probability Theory and Its Applications,* vol. 1, 2nd ed. New York: Wiley.

Fermi, Enrico. 1956. *Thermodynamics.* New York: Dover.

Feynman, Richard. 1967. *The Character of Physical Law.* Cambridge, MA: MIT Press.

Feynman, Richard. 1987. "The Reason for Antiparticles." In Richard Feynman and Steven Weinberg, *Elementary Particles and the Laws of Physics,* 1–60. Cambridge: Cambridge University Press.

Feynman, Richard. 1998. "The Development of the Space-Time View of Quantum Electrodynamics." In *Nobel Lectures: Physics, 1963–1970,* 155–179. Singapore: World Scientific.

Feynman, Richard, Robert Leighton, and Matthew Sands. 1963. *The Feynman Lectures on Physics.* Reading, MA: Addison-Wesley.

Field, J. V., and J. J. Gray. 1987. *The Geometrical Work of Girard Desargues.* New York: Springer-Verlag.

Fine, Kit. 2005. "The Varieties of Necessity." In *Modality and Tense,* 236–259. Oxford: Oxford University Press.

Fisher, R. A. 1930/1983. "Letter to J. S. Huxley, 6 May 1930." In *Natural Selection, Heredity, and Eugenics. Including Selected Correspondence of R.A. Fisher with Leonard Darwin and Others*, edited by J. H. Bennett, 222–223. Oxford: Clarendon Press.

Fodor, Jerry. 1974. "Special Sciences." *Synthese* 28: 97–115.

Fodor, Jerry. 1988. *Psychosemantics*. Cambridge, MA: MIT Press.

Fourier, Joseph. 1878. *The Analytical Theory of Heat*. Translated by Alexander Freeman. Cambridge: Cambridge University Press.

Francis, Richard L. 2002. "Modern Mathematical Milestones: Morley's Mystery." *Missouri Journal of Mathematical Sciences* 14 (1) (Winter): n.p.

Furbish, David J. 1997. *Fluid Physics in Geology*. New York: Oxford University Press.

G., A. G. 1890. "Our Bookshelf." *Nature* 42: 413.

Galbraith, J., and S. Haughton. 1860. *Manual of Mechanics*. London: Longmans, Brown, Green, Longmans, Roberts.

Gale, David. 1990. "Proof as Explanation." *Mathematical Intelligencer* 12 (1): 4.

Gale, David. 1991. "Mathematical Entertainments." *Mathematical Intelligencer* 13 (1): 40–42.

Galilei, Galileo. 1974. *Two New Sciences*. Translated by Stillman Drake. Madison: University of Wisconsin Press.

Galton, Francis. 1886. "Regression towards Mediocrity in Hereditary Stature." *Journal of the Anthropological Institute of Great Britain and Ireland* 15: 246–263.

Gannett, Joel. 2007. "Nothing but Relativity, Redux." *European Journal of Physics* 28: 1145–1150.

Gannon, Terry. 2006. *Moonshine beyond the Monster*. Cambridge: Cambridge University Press.

Gardner, Martin. 1979. *Mathematical Circus*. New York: Knopf.

Gardner, Martin. 1988. *Hexaflexagons and Other Mathematical Diversions*. Chicago: University of Chicago Press.

Gasking, Douglas. 1955. "Causation and Recipes." *Mind* 64: 479–487.

Gibbons, John. 2006. "Mental Causation without Downward Causation." *Philosophical Review* 115: 79–103.

Gödel, Kurt. 1949. "A Remark about the Relationship between Relativity Theory and Idealistic Philosophy." In *Albert Einstein, Philosopher-Scientist*, edited by P. A. Schilpp, Library of Living Philosophers, vol. 7, 555–562. La Salle, IL: Open Court.

Goldhaber, M., P. Langacker, and R. Slansky. 1980. "Is the Proton Stable?" *Science* 210: 851–860.

Goodeve, T. M. 1874. *Principles of Mechanics*. London: Longmans, Green.

Goodman, Nelson. 1983. *Fact, Fiction, and Forecast*. 4th ed. Cambridge: Harvard University Press.

Goodwin, Harvey. 1846. *An Elementary Course of Mathematics*. Cambridge: Deighton.

Goodwin, Harvey. 1849. "On the Connection between the Sciences of Mechanics and Geometry." *Transactions of the Cambridge Philosophical Society* 8: 269–277.

Gowers, W. T. [Timothy]. 2000. "The Two Cultures of Mathematics." In *Mathematics: Frontiers and Perspectives*, edited by V. Arnold, M. Atiyah, P. Lax, and B. Mazur, 65–78. Providence, RI: American Mathematical Society.

Gowers, W. T. [Timothy]. 2007. "Mathematics, Memory, and Mental Arithmetic." In *Mathematical Knowledge*, edited by Mary Leng, Alexander Paseau, and Michael Potter, 33–58. Oxford: Oxford University Press.

Graham, L. A. 1959. *Ingenious Mathematical Problems and Methods*. New York: Dover.

Grantham, Todd. 1999. "Explanatory Pluralism in Paleobiology." *Philosophy of Science* 66: S223–S236.

Grattan-Guinness, Ivor. 1990. *Convolutions in French Mathematics, 1800–1840*, vol. 1. Basel: Birkhaüser.

Gravetter, Frederick, and Larry Wallnau. 2009. *Statistics for the Behavioral Sciences*. 8th ed. Belmont, CA: Wadsworth.

Gravina, Maria Alice. 2008. "Dynamical Visual Proof: What Does It Mean?" ICME 11 [11th International Congress on Mathematical Education]—TSG [Topic Study Group] 22. tsg. icme11.org/document/get/233. Accessed June 29, 2013.

Gray, Jeremy. 2007. *Worlds out of Nothing*. London: Springer-Verlag.

Greene, Brian. 2005. *The Fabric of the Cosmos*. New York: Vintage.

Gregory, Duncan. 1837. "On the Solutions of Linear Differential Equations with Constant Coefficients." *Cambridge Mathematical Journal* 1: 22–32.

Gregory, Duncan. 1841. *Examples of the Processes of the Differential and Integral Calculus*. London: Deighton.

Gregory, Oliver. 1826. *A Treatise of Mechanics*, vol. 1, 3rd ed. London: F.C. & J. Rivington.

Gregory, Richard L. 1987. "Mirror Reversal." In *The Oxford Companion to the Mind*, edited by Richard L. Gregory, 491–493. Oxford: Oxford University Press.

Grosholz, Emily R. 2000. "The Partial Unification of Domains, Hybrids, and the Growth of Mathematical Knowledge." In *The Growth of Mathematical Knowledge*, edited by Emily Grosholz and Herbert Breger, 81–91. Dordrecht: Kluwer.

Gross, David. 1996. "The Role of Symmetry in Fundamental Physics." *Proceedings of the National Academy of Sciences USA* 93: 14256–14259.

Gross, David. 2004. "The Future of Physics." Lecture at Kavli Institute for Theoretical Physics, Santa Barbara, CA, October 9. online.kitp.ucsb.edu/online/kitp25/gross/rm/qt.html. Accessed September 16, 2013.

Guy, Richard K. 1988. "The Strong Law of Large Numbers." *American Mathematical Monthly* 95: 697–712.

H., A. 1848. "[Review of] Whewell's Mechanics—Last Edition." *Mechanics' Magazine* 48 (July 29): 103–107.

Hacking, Ian. 1990. *The Taming of Chance*. Cambridge: Cambridge University Press.

Hafner, Johannes, and Paolo Mancosu. 2005. "The Varieties of Mathematical Explanation." In *Visualization, Explanation and Reasoning Styles in Mathematics*, edited by P. Mancosu, K. F. Jørgensen, and S. A. Pedersen, 215–250. Dordrecht: Springer.

Hales, Thomas. 2001. "The Honeycomb Conjecture." *Discrete and Computational Geometry* 25: 1–22.

Hall, Marshall. 1943. "Projective Planes." *Transactions of the American Mathematical Society* 54: 229–277.

Halmos, P. R. 1985. "Pure Thought Is Better Yet." *College Mathematics Journal* 16: 14–16.

Halonen, Ilpo, and Jaakko Hintikka. 1999. "Unification: It's Magnificent but Is It Explanatory?" *Synthese* 120: 27–47.

Hanca, Jozef, Slavomir Tulejab, and Martina Hancova. 2004. "Symmetries and Conservation Laws: Consequences of Noether's Theorem." *American Journal of Physics* 72 (4): 428–435.

Hanna, Gila. 1989. "Proofs That Prove and Proofs That Explain." In *Proceedings of the 13th International Conference for the Psychology of Mathematics Education*, vol. 2, edited by G. Vergnaud, J. Rogalski, and M. Artigue, 45–51. Paris: Laboratoire PSYDEE.

Hanna, Gila. 1990. "Some Pedagogical Aspects of Proof." *Interchange* 21: 6–13.

Harari, Orna. 2008. "Procus' Account of Explanatory Demonstrations in Mathematics and Its Context." *Archiv für Geschichte der Philosophie* 90 (2): 137–164.

Hardy, G. H., J. E. Littlewood, and G. Pólya. 1952. *Inequalities*. 2nd ed. Cambridge: Cambridge University Press.

Harman, Gilbert. 1973. *Thought*. Princeton: Princeton University Press.

Harman, Gilbert. 1986. *Change in View*. Cambridge: Bradford.

Haugeland, John. 1993. "Pattern and Being." In *Dennett and His Critics*, edited by Bo Dahlbom, 53–69. Cambridge, MA: Blackwell.

Healy, Lulu, and Celia Hoyles. 2000. "A Study of Proof Conceptions in Algebra." *Journal for Research in Mathematics Education* 31: 396–428.

Heaviside, Oliver. 1893. *Electromagnetic Theory*, vol. 1. London: Electrician.

Heaviside, Oliver. 1912. *Electromagnetic Theory*, vol. 3. London: Electrician.

Hempel, Carl G. 1965. *Aspects of Scientific Explanation and Other Essays in the Philosophy of Science*. New York: Free Press.

Hempel, Carl G. 2001. *The Philosophy of Carl G. Hempel*. Edited by James Fetzer. New York: Oxford University Press.

Herschel, John F. W. 1850. "Quetelet on Probabilities." *Edinburgh Review* 42: 1–57.

Hertz, Heinrich. 1999. *Die Constitution der Materie*. Edited by Albracht Fölsing. Berlin: Springer-Verlag.

Hertz, Heinrich. 1950. *The Principles of Mechanics Presented in a New Form*. New York: Dover.

Hilbert, David, and Stefan Cohn-Vóssen. 1952. *Geometry and the Imagination*. New York: Chelsea.

Hildebrandt, Stefan, and Anthony Tromba. 1985. *Mathematics and Optimal Form*. New York: Scientific American.

Hodge, M. J. S. 1987. "Natural Selection as a Causal, Empirical, and Probabilistic Theory." In *The Probabilistic Revolution*, vol. 2, edited by Lorentz Krüger, Gerd Gigerenzer, and Mary S. Morgan, 233–270. Cambridge, MA: MIT Press.

Hoffman, Johan, and Claes Johnson. 2007. *Computational Turbulent Incompressible Flow*. Berlin: Springer.

Horsley, J. 1743. *A Short and General Account of the Most Necessary and Fundamental Principles of Natural Philosophy*. Glasgow: Andrew Stalker.

Howard, Don. 2010. "'Let Me Briefly Indicate Why I Do Not Find This Standpoint Natural.' Einstein, General Relativity, and the Contingent a Priori." In *Discourse on a New Method*, edited by Mary Domski and Michael Dickson, 333–355. La Salle, IL: Open Court.

Hughes, R. I. G. 1989a. "Bell's Theorem, Ideology, and Structural Explanation." In *Philosophical Consequences of Quantum Theory*, edited by James Cushing and Ernan McMullin, 195–207. Notre Dame, IN: University of Notre Dame Press.

Hughes, R. I. G. 1989b. *The Structure and Interpretation of Quantum Mechanics*. Cambridge, MA: Harvard University Press.

Hughes, Steven A. 1993. *Physical Models and Laboratory Techniques in Coastal Engineering: Advanced Series on Ocean Engineering*, vol. 7. Singapore: World Scientific.

Humphreys, Paul. 1993. "Greater Unification Equals Greater Understanding." *Analysis* 53: 183–188.

Icke, Vincent. 1995. *The Force of Symmetry*. Cambridge: Cambridge University Press.

Isaacs, I. Martin. 2001. *Geometry for College Students*. Providence, RI: American Mathematical Society.

Jackson, Frank, and Philip Pettit. 1990. "Program Explanation: A General Perspective." *Analysis* 50: 107–117.

Jackson, Frank, and Philip Pettit. 1992. "In Defense of Explanatory Ecumenism." *Economics and Philosophy* 8: 1–21.

Janah, A. R., T. Padmanabhan, and T. P. Singh. 1988. "On Feynman's Formula for the Electromagnetic Field of an Arbitrarily Moving Charge." *American Journal of Physics* 56: 1036–1038.

Janssen, Michel. 2009. "Drawing the Line between Kinematics and Dynamics in Special Relativity." *Studies in History and Philosophy of Modern Physics* 40: 26–52.

Jeans, James. 1920. "Contribution to "Discussion on the Theory of Relativity." *Proceedings of the Royal Society of London* 97: 66–79.

Jeans, James. 1951. *The Growth of Physical Science*. 2nd ed. Cambridge: Cambridge University Press.

Jeffrey, Richard. 1983. *The Logic of Decision*. 2nd ed. Chicago: University of Chicago Press.

Johnson, W. E. 1889. "Proof of the Parallelogram of Forces." *Nature* 41 (December 19): 153.

Jones, Alexander. 1986. *Pappus of Alexandria, Book 7 of the Collection, Part 2*. New York: Springer-Verlag.

Keeports, David. 2002. "How Does the Potential Energy of a Rising Helium-Filled Balloon Change?" *Physics Teacher* 40: 164–165.

Keyton, Michael. 2004. "Theorems of Mystery." Illinois Mathematics and Science Academy, staff.imsa.edu/~keyton/Talks%20and%20Papers/10%20Favorite%20Theorems%20of%Mystery.doc. Accessed June 29, 2013.

Kibble, T. W., and F. H. Berkshire. 1996. *Classical Mechanics*. 4th ed. Harlow, Essex: Longmans.

Kiernan, B. Melvin. 1971. "The Development of Galois Theory from Lagrange to Artin." *Archive for History of Exact Sciences* 8: 40–154.

Kim, Jaegwon. 1974. "Noncausal Connections." *Noûs* 8: 41–52.

Kim, Jaegwon. 1998. *Mind in a Physical World*. Cambridge, MA: MIT Press.

Kimura, Mootoo. 1991. "The Neutral Theory of Molecular Evolution: A Review of Recent Evidence." *Japanese Journal of Genetics* 66: 367–386.

Kitcher, Philip. 1975. "Bolzano's Ideal of Algebraic Analysis." *Studies in History and Philosophy of Science* 6: 229–269.

Kitcher, Philip. 1981. "Mathematical Rigor—Who Needs It?" *Noûs* 15: 469–493.

Kitcher, Philip. 1984a. "1953 and All That: A Tale of Two Sciences." *Philosophical Review* 93: 335–373.

Kitcher, Philip. 1984b. *The Nature of Mathematical Knowledge*. Oxford: Oxford University Press.

Kitcher, Philip. 1985. "Two Approaches of Explanation." *Journal of Philosophy* 82: 632–639.

Kitcher, Philip. 1989. "Explanatory Unification and the Causal Structure of the World." In *Scientific Explanation*, edited by Philip Kitcher and Wesley Salmon, Minnesota Studies in the Philosophy of Science, vol. 13, 410–505. Minneapolis: University of Minnesota Press.

Kitcher, Philip. 1993. *The Advancement of Science*. New York: Oxford University Press.

Kitcher, Philip. 2003. *Science, Truth, and Democracy*. New York: Oxford University Press.

Kitcher, Philip. 2011. "Epistemology without History Is Blind." *Erkenntnis* 75: 505–524.

Kitcher, Philip, and Wesley Salmon. 1987. "Van Fraassen on Explanation." *Journal of Philosophy* 84: 315–330.

Kittel, Charles, Walter P. Knight, and Malvin A. Ruderman. 1973. *Mechanics—Berkeley Physics Course*, vol. 1. New York: McGraw-Hill.

Kline, Morris. 1972. *Mathematical Thought from Ancient to Modern Times*. New York: Oxford University Press.

Kment, Boris. 2015. "Replies to Sullivan and Lange." *Philosophy and Phenomenological Research* 91: 516–539.

Koppelman, Elaine. 1971. "The Calculus of Operations and the Rise of Abstract Algebra." *Archive for History of Exact Sciences* 8: 155–242.

Kosso, Peter. 2000. "Fundamental and Accidental Symmetries." *International Studies in the Philosophy of Science* 14: 109–121.

Krantz, David H., R. Duncan Luce, Patrick Suppes, and Amos Tversky. 1971. *Foundations of Measurement*, vol. 1. *Additive and Polynomial Representations*. New York: Academic Press.

Krauss, Laurence. 2011. *Quantum Man*. New York: Norton.

Kuhn, Thomas. 1977. "Objectivity, Value Judgment, and Theory Choice." In *The Essential Tension*, 320–339. Chicago: University of Chicago Press.

Kyburg, Henry E., Jr. 1965. "Comment." *Philosophy of Science* 32: 147–151.

Lagrange, Joseph-Louis. 1813/1881. "Théorie des Fonctions Analytiques." 2nd ed. In *Œuvres de Lagrange*, vol. 9, edited by J.-A. Serret, 13–413. Paris: Gauther-Villars.

Lagrange, Joseph-Louis. 1826. "Note XIII: Sur la Résolution des Équations Algébriques." In *Traité de la Résolution des Équations Numériques de Tous les Degrés*, 3rd ed., 242–272. Paris: Bachelier.

Lagrange, Joseph-Louis. 1869. "Refléxions sur la Résolution Algébrique des Équations." In *Œuvres de Lagrange*, vol. 3, edited by J.-A. Serret. Paris: Gauthier-Villars, 205–421.

Lakatos, Imre. 1976. *Proofs and Refutations*. Edited by J. Worrall and E. Zahar. Cambridge: Cambridge University Press.

Lanczos, Cornelius. 1986. *The Variational Principles of Mechanics*. New York: Dover.

Lange, Marc. 2000. *Natural Laws in Scientific Practice*. New York: Oxford University Press.

Lange, Marc. 2002. *An Introduction to the Philosophy of Physics: Locality, Fields, Energy, and Mass*. Malden, MA: Blackwell.

Lange, Marc. 2004. "Would Direct Realism Resolve the Classical Problem of Induction?" *Noûs* 38: 197–232.

Lange, Marc. 2007. "Laws and Meta-laws of Nature: Conservation Laws and Symmetries." *Studies in History and Philosophy of Modern Physics* 38: 457–481.

Lange, Marc. 2009a. *Laws and Lawmakers*. New York: Oxford University Press.

Lange, Marc. 2009b. "Why Proofs by Mathematical Induction Are Generally Not Explanatory." *Analysis* 69: 203–211.

Lange, Marc. 2011. "Conservation Laws in Scientific Explanations: Constraints or Coincidences?" *Philosophy of Science* 78: 333–352.

Lange, Marc, and Alex Rosenberg. 2011."Can There Be *a Priori* Causal Models of Natural Selection?" *Australasian Journal of Philosophy* 89: 591–599.

Langhaar, Henry. 1951. *Dimensional Analysis and Theory of Models*. New York: Wiley.

Laymon, Ronald. 1991. "Idealizations and the Reliability of Dimensional Analysis." In *Critical Perspectives on Nonacademic Science and Engineering*, edited by Paul T. Durbin, 146–180. Bethlehem, PA: Lehigh University Press.

Leavitt, David. 2007. *The Indian Clerk*. New York: Bloomsbury USA.

Lederman, Leon, and Dick Teresi. 1993. *The God Particle*. New York: Dell.

Lee, A. R., and T. M. Kalotas. 1975. "Lorentz Transformations from the First Postulate." *American Journal of Physics* 43: 434–437.

Lee, Chunghyoung. 2011. "Non-conservation of Momentum in Classical Mechanics." *Studies in History and Philosophy of Modern Physics* 42: 68–73.

Leibniz, Gottfried Wilhelm. 2004. *Sämtliche Schriften und Briefe*. Edited by Deutsche Akademie der Wissenschaften. Darmstadt/Leipzig/Berlin: Akademie-Verlag, ser. 3, vol. 6, pt. A.

Leng, Mary. 2005. "Mathematical Explanation." In *Mathematical Reasoning, Heuristics, and the Development of Mathematics*, edited by Carlo Cellucci and Donald Gillies, 167–189. London: King's College Publications.

Leroy, Bernard. 1985. "Archimedes Principle: A Simple Derivation." *European Journal of Physics* 6: 56.

Levi, Mark. 2009. *The Mathematical Mechanic*. Princeton: Princeton University Press.

Lévy-Leblond, Jean-Marc. 1976. "One More Derivation of the Lorentz Transformations." *American Journal of Physics* 44: 271–277.

Lévy-Leblond, Jean-Marc. 1992. "Why Does Physics Need Mathematics?" In *The Scientific Enterprise*, edited by Edna Ullmann-Margalit, 145–161. Kluwer: Dordrecht.

Lewis, David. 1973. *Counterfactuals*. Cambridge, MA: Harvard University Press.

Lewis, David. 1983. "New Work for a Theory of Universals." *Australasian Journal of Philosophy* 61: 343–377.

Lewis, David. 1986a. *On the Plurality of Worlds*. Oxford: Blackwell.

Lewis, David. 1986b. *Philosophical Papers*, vol. 2. New York: Oxford University Press.

Lewis, David. 1999. "Humean Supervenience Debugged." In *Papers in Metaphysics and Epistemology*, 224–247. Cambridge: Cambridge University Press.

Lewis, David. 2007. "Causation as Influence." In *Philosophy of Science: An Anthology*, edited by Marc Lange, 466–487. Malden, MA: Blackwell.

Lipton, Peter. 2004a. "What Good Is an Explanation?" In *Explanations: Styles of Explanation in Science*, edited by John Cornwell, 1–21. Oxford: Oxford University Press.

Lipton, Peter. 2004b. *Inference to the Best Explanation*. 2nd ed. London: Routledge.

Lipton, Peter. 2009a. "Understanding without Explanation." In *Scientific Understanding: Philosophical Perspectives*, edited by Henk W. de Regt, Sabina Leonelli, and Kai Eigner, 43–63. Pittsburgh: University of Pittsburgh Press.

Lipton, Peter. 2009b. "Causation and Explanation." In *The Oxford Encyclopedia of Causation*, edited by Helen Beebee, Christopher Hitchcock, and Peter Menzies, 619–631. Oxford: Oxford University Press.

Lock, J. B. 1888. *Elementary Statics*. London: Macmillan.

Lock, J. B. 1891. *Elementary Dynamics*. London: Macmillan.

Lodge, Oliver. 1890. *Elementary Mechanics*. Rev. ed. London: W. & R. Chambers.

Loewer, Barry. 2007. "Laws and Natural Properties." *Philosophical Topics* 35: 313–328.

Loney, S. L. 1891. *The Elements of Statics and Dynamics*, vol. 2. Cambridge: Cambridge University Press.

Lord, Eric. 2013. *Symmetry and Pattern in Projective Geometry*. London: Springer.

Lord, Nick. 2007. "An Amusing Sequence of Trigonometric Integrals." *Mathematical Gazette* 61 (521): 281–285.

Luce, R. Duncan. 1959. "On the Possible Psychophysical Laws." *Psychological Review* 66: 81–95.

Luce, R. Duncan. 1971. "Similar Systems and Dimensionally Invariant Laws." *Philosophy of Science* 38: 157–169.

Luchins, Abraham S., and Edith H. Luchins. 1990. "The Einstein-Wertheimer Correspondence on Geometric Proofs and Mathematical Puzzles." *Mathematical Intelligencer* 12 (2): 35–43.

Lycan, William G. 1981. "Psychological Laws." *Philosophical Topics* 12: 9–38.

Lyon, Aidan, and Mark Colyvan. 2008. "The Explanatory Power of Phase Spaces." *Philosophia Mathematica* 16: 227–243.

Macaulay, William H. 1900. "The Laws of Dynamics, and Their Treatment in Text-Books (continued)." *Mathematical Gazette* 1: 399–404.

Mach, Ernst. 1960. *The Science of Mechanics.* La Salle, IL: Open Court.

Mackie, J. L. 1974. *The Cement of the Universe.* Oxford: Oxford University Press.

Malouf, Janice. 1992. "An Integer Sequence from a Rational Recursion." *Discrete Mathematics* 110: 257–261.

Mancosu, Paolo. 2008. "Mathematical Explanation: Why It Matters." In *The Philosophy of Mathematical Practice,* 134–150. Oxford: Oxford University Press.

Manders, Kenneth. 1987. "Logic and Conceptual Relationships in Mathematics." In *Logic Colloquium '85, Studies in Logic and the Foundations of Mathematics,* edited by the Paris Logic Group, vol. 122, 193–211. Amsterdam: Elsevier.

Manders, Kenneth. 1989. "Domain Extension and the Philosophy of Mathematics." *Journal of Philosophy* 86: 553–562.

Martin, Robert M. 2002. *There Are Two Errors in the Title of This Book.* Peterborough, Ontario: Broadview Press.

Matthen, Mohan. 2009. "Drift and 'Statistically Abstractive Explanation.'" *Philosophy of Science* 76: 464–487.

Maudlin, Tim. 2007. *The Metaphysics within Physics.* Oxford: Oxford University Press.

Maxwell, James Clerk. 1856/1890. "On Faraday's Lines of Force." In *The Scientific Papers of James Clerk Maxwell,* vol. 1, edited by W. D. Niven, 155–229. Cambridge: Cambridge University Press.

Maxwell, James Clerk. 1860/1990. "Inaugural Lecture at King's College, London." In *The Scientific Letters and Papers of James Clerk Maxwell,* vol. 1, edited by P. M. Harman, 662–674. Cambridge: Cambridge University Press.

Maxwell, James Clerk. 1860/1890. "Illustrations of the Dynamical Theory of Gases." In *The Scientific Papers of James Clerk Maxwell,* vol. 1, edited by W. D. Niven, 377–409. Cambridge: Cambridge University Press.

Maxwell, James Clerk. 1871. *Theory of Heat.* London: Longmans, Green.

Maxwell, James Clerk. 1873. *A Treatise on Electricity and Magnetism,* vol. 1. Oxford: Clarendon.

Maxwell, James Clerk. 1881. *An Elementary Treatise on Electricity.* Oxford: Clarendon Press.

McKee, Maggie. 2013. "First Proof That Infinitely Many Prime Numbers Come in Pairs." *Nature News,* May 14, 2013. doi: 10.1038/nature.2013.12989. www.nature.com/news/first-proof-that-infinitely-many-prime-numbers-come-in-pairs-1.12989. Accessed May 16, 2013.

McLaughlin, Brian. 2007. "On Selection Of, For, With, and Against." In *Thinking about Causes,* edited by Peter Machamer and Gereon Wolters, 265–283. Pittsburgh: University of Pittsburgh Press.

McLeod, Robin J. Y., and M. Louisa Baart. 1998. *Geometry and Interpolation of Curves and Surfaces.* Cambridge: Cambridge University Press.

McMullin, Ernan. 1978. "Structural Explanation." *American Philosophical Quarterly* 15: 139–148.

Medvedev, F. A. 1998. "Nonstandard Analysis and the History of Classical Analysis." *American Mathematical Monthly* 105: 659–664.

Meli, Domenico Bertoloni. 2006. *Thinking with Objects.* Baltimore: Johns Hopkins University Press.

Meli, Domenico Bertoloni. 2010. "The Axiomatic Tradition in Seventeenth-Century Mechanics." In *Discourse on a New Method*, edited by Mary Domski and Michael Dickson, 23–41. La Salle, IL: Open Court.

Melia, Joseph. 2002. "Response to Colyvan." *Mind* 111: 75–79.

Mermin, N. David. 1990. "Relativity without Light." In *Boojums All the Way Through*, 247–265. Cambridge: Cambridge University Press.

Mermin, N. David. 2009. *It's About Time: Understanding Einstein's Relativity*. Princeton: Princeton University Press.

Miller, Arthur I. 2005. *Empire of the Stars*. Boston: Houghton Mifflin.

Miller, Richard. 1987. *Fact and Method*. Princeton: Princeton University Press.

Millstein, Roberta. 2002. "Are Random Drift and Natural Selection Conceptually Distinct?" *Biology and Philosophy* 17: 33–53.

Millstein, Roberta. 2006. "Natural Selection as a Population-Level Causal Process." *British Journal for the Philosophy of Science* 57: 627–653.

Minkowski, Hermann. 1908/1952. "Space and Time." In H. A. Lorentz et al., *The Principle of Relativity*, notes by A. Sommerfeld, translated by W. Perrett and J.B. Jeffery, 73–91. New York: Dover.

Mitchell, W., J. R. Young, and J. Imray. 1860. *The Circle of the Sciences*, vol. 9. *Mechanical Philosophy*. London: Richard Griffin.

Morrison, Margaret. 1995. "The New Aspect: Symmetries as Meta-laws—Structural Metaphysics." In *Laws of Nature: Essays on the Philosophical, Scientific, and Historical Dimensions*, edited by Friedel Weinert, 157–188. Berlin: de Gruyter.

Moulton, F. R. 1914. *An Introduction to Celestial Mechanics*. 2nd rev. ed. New York: Macmillan.

Mudaly, Vimolan, and Michael de Villiers. 2000. "Learners' Needs for Conviction and Explanation within the Context of Dynamic Geometry." *Pythagoras* 52 (August): 20–23.

Mumford, Stephen. 2004. *Laws in Nature*. London: Routledge.

Nagel, Ernest. 1961. *The Structure of Science*. New York: Harcourt, Brace.

Nahin, Paul. 2009. *Mrs. Perkins's Electric Quilt*. Princeton: Princeton University Press.

Ne'eman, Yuval. 1999. "Symmetry as the Leitmotif at the Fundamental Level in the Twentieth Century Physics." *Symmetry: Culture and Science* 10 (1/2): 143–162.

Ne'eman, Yuval, and Yoram Kirsh. 1996. *The Particle Hunters*. Cambridge: Cambridge University Press.

Nelson, Roger B. 1993. *Proofs without Words: Exercises in Visual Thinking*. Washington, DC: Mathematical Association of America.

Nerlich, Graham. 1979. "What Can Geometry Explain?" *British Journal for the Philosophy of Science* 30: 69–83.

Nerlich, Graham. 1991. "Hands, Knees, and Absolute Space." In *The Philosophy of Left and Right*, edited by James Van Cleve and Robert Frederick, 151–172. Dordrecht: Kluwer.

Nerlich, Graham. 1994. *The Shape of Space*, 2nd ed. Cambridge: Cambridge University Press.

Nerlich, Graham. 2006. Review of *Physical Relativity* (2005), by Harvey Brown. *Australasian Journal of Philosophy* 84: 634–636.

Newman, Donald J. 1996. "The Morley Miracle." *Mathematical Intelligencer* 18 (1): 31–32.

Newton, Isaac. 1687/1999. *The Principia: Mathematical Principles of Natural Philosophy*. Translated by I. B. Cohen and A. Whitman. Berkeley: University of California Press.

Newton, Isaac. 1979. *Opticks*. New York: Dover.

Nickel, Bernhard. 2010. "How General Do Theories of Explanation Need to Be?" *Nous* 44: 305–328.

Nicole, Pierre, and Antoine Arnauld. 1717. *Logic; or the Art of Thinking*. Translated by Ozell. London: William Taylor.

North, Jill. 2009. "The 'Structure' of Physics: A Case Study." *Journal of Philosophy* 106: 57–88.

Norton, John. 1992. "Philosophy of Space and Time." In Merrilee Salmon et al., *Introduction to the Philosophy of Science*, 171–231. Englewood Cliffs: Prentice-Hall.

Norton, John. 2008. "Why Constructive Relativity Fails." *British Journal for the Philosophy of Science* 59: 821–834.

Nummela, Eric. 1987. "No Coincidence." *Mathematical Gazette* 71 (456): 147.

Owens, David. 1992. *Causes and Coincidences*. Cambridge: Cambridge University Press.

Pais, Abraham. 1986. *Inward Bound*. Oxford: Clarendon.

Pal, Palash. 2003. "Nothing but Relativity." *European Journal of Physics* 24: 315–319.

Palmerino, Carla Rita. 1999. "Infinite Degrees of Speed: Marin Mersenne and the Debate over Galileo's Law of Free Fall." *Early Science and Medicine* 4: 268–328.

Pars, L. A. 1921. "The Lorentz Transformation." *Philosophical Magazine*, 6th ser., 42: 249–258.

Pears, David. 1952. "Incongruity of Counterparts." *Mind* 61: 78–81.

Pearson, Karl. 1911. *The Grammar of Science, Part I—Physical*. 3rd ed. New York: Macmillan.

Penrose, Roger. 1987. "Newton, Quantum Theory, and Reality." In *Three Hundred Years of Gravitation*, edited by Stephen Hawking and Werner Israel, 17–49. Cambridge: Cambridge University Press.

Perkins, G. 1842, "Solution of a Functional Equation, Which Has Been Employed by Poisson in Demonstrating the Parallelogram of Forces." *American Journal of Science and Arts* 42: 69–71.

Pesic, Peter. 2003. *Abel's Proof*. Cambridge, MA: MIT Press.

Peskin, Michael E., and Daniel V. Schroeder. 1995. *An Introduction to Quantum Field Theory*. Boulder: Westview.

Pincock, Christopher. 2007. "A Role for Mathematics in the Physical Sciences." *Noûs* 41: 253–275.

Pincock, Christopher. 2015a. "The Unsolvability of the Quintic: A Case Study in Abstract Mathematical Explanation." *Philosophers' Imprint* 15 (3): 1–19.

Pincock, Christopher. 2015b. "Abstract Explanations in Science." *British Journal for the Philosophy of Science* 66: 857–882.

Planck, Max. 1948. "Ansprache des Vorsitzenden Sekretars, Gehalten in der öffentlichen Sitzung zur Feier des Leibnizschen Jahrestages, 29 June 1922." In *Max Planck in Seinen Akademie-Ansprachen*, 46–48. Berlin: Akademie-Verlag.

Plutynski, Anya. 2007. "Drift: A Historical and Conceptual Overview." *Biological Theory* 2: 156–167.

Pnueli, David, and Chaim Gutfinger. 1992. *Fluid Mechanics*. Cambridge: Cambridge University Press.

Poincaré, Henri. 1905/2001. "On the Dynamics of the Electron." *Comptes Rendus* 140: 1504–1508. Reprinted in A. A. Logunov, *On the Articles by Henri Poincaré "On the Dynamics of the Electron."* Translated by G. Pontecorvo. Dubna: Joint Institute for Nuclear Research.

Poincaré, Henri. 1908. *Thermodynamique*. 2nd ed. Paris: Gauthier-Villars.

Poincaré, Henri. 1913. "The Future of Mathematics." Chap. 2 of *Science and the Scientist*, bk. 1 of *Science and Method*, in *The Foundations of Science*, translated by George Bruce Halsted, 369–382. New York: Science Press.

Poinsot, Louis. 1847. *The Elements of Statics*. Pt. 1, translated by T. Sutton. Cambridge: Cambridge University Press.

Poisson, Siméon Denis. 1811. *Traité de Mécanique*, vol. 1. Paris: Courcier.

Poisson, Siméon Denis. 1831. "Mémoire sur les Equations Générales de l'Équilibre et du Movement des Corps Élastiques et des Fluids." *Journal de l'École Polytechnic* 13 (20): 1–174.

Poisson, Siméon Denis. 1833/1842. *A Treatise of Mechanics*, vol. 1, 2nd ed. Translated by H. H. Harte. London: Longmans.

Pólya, George. 1954. *Mathematics and Plausible Reasoning*, vol. 1. *Induction and Analogy in Mathematics*. London: Geoffrey Cumberledge.

Pólya, George. 1977. *Mathematical Methods in Science*. Washington, DC: Mathematical Association of America.

Posamentier, Alfred S., and Ingmar Lehmann. 2009. *Mathematical Amazements and Surprises*. Amherst, NY: Prometheus.

Post, Scott. 2011. *Applied and Computational Fluid Mechanics*. Sudbury, MA: Jones and Bartlett.

Potter, Merle, David Wiggert, and Bessem Ramadan. 2012. *Mechanics of Fluids*. 4th ed. Stamford, CT: Cengage Learning.

Pratt, J. H. 1836. *The Mathematical Principles of Mechanical Philosophy*. Cambridge: Deighton.

Price, Bartholomew. 1862. *A Treatise on Infinitesimal Calculus*, vol. 4. *The Dynamics of Material Systems*. Oxford: Oxford University Press.

Price, Bartholomew. 1868. *A Treatise on Infinitesimal Calculus*, vol. 3. *A Treatise of Analytical Mechanics*. 2nd ed. Oxford: Clarendon.

Prior, Elizabeth, Robert Pargetter, and Frank Jackson. 1982. "Three Theses about Dispositions." *American Philosophical Quarterly* 19: 251–257.

Psillos, Stathis. 2002. *Causation and Explanation*. Chesham, UK: Acumen.

Purcell, Edward. 1965. *Electricity and Magnetism—Berkeley Physics Course*, vol. 2. New York: McGraw-Hill.

Putnam, Hilary. 1979. "What Is Mathematical Truth?" In *Mathematics, Matter and Method—Philosophical Papers*, vol. 1, 2nd ed., 60–78. Cambridge: Cambridge University Press.

Railton, Peter. 1980. "Explaining Explanation: A Realist Account of Scientific Explanation and Understanding." Ph.D. diss., Princeton University.

Railton, Peter. 1981. "Probability, Explanation, and Information." *Synthese* 48: 233–256.

Rankine, W. J. M. 1872. *A Manual of Applied Mechanics*. 6th ed. London: Charles Griffin.

Rayleigh (Lord). 1915a. "The Principle of Similitude." *Nature* 95: 66–68.

Rayleigh (Lord). 1915b. "The Principle of Similitude." *Nature* 95: 644.

Reese, K. M. 1987a. "Intriguing Result of Really Long Division." *Chemical and Engineering News* 65 (43) (October 26): 96.

Reese, K. M. 1987b. "Result of Really Long Division Is Not a Fluke." *Chemical and Engineering News* 65 (46) (November 16): 88.

Reid, D. A. 2001. "Elements in Accepting an Explanation." *Journal of Mathematical Behavior* 20: 527–547.

Reisman, Kenneth, and Patrick Forber. 2005. "Manipulation and the Causes of Evolution." *Philosophy of Science* 72: 1113–1123.

Rescher, Nicholas. 1970. *Scientific Explanation*. New York: Free Press.

Rescigno, Aldo. 2003. *Foundations of Pharmacokinetics*. New York: Kluwer.

Resnick, Robert, David Halliday, and Kenneth Krane. 1992. *Physics*. 4th ed. New York: Wiley.

Resnik, Michael, and David Kushner. 1987. "Explanation, Independence and Realism in Mathematics." *British Journal for the Philosophy of Science* 38: 141–158.

Reynolds, Osborne. 1883/1901. "An Experimental Investigation of the Circumstances Which Determine Whether the Motion of Water Shall Be Direct or Sinuous, and of the Law of Resistance in Parallel Channels." In *Papers on Mechanical and Physical Subjects*, 51–105. Cambridge: Cambridge University Press.

Riabouchinsky, Dimitri. 1915. "The Principle of Similitude." *Nature* 95: 591.

Rickey, V. Frederick, and Philip Tuchinsky. 1980. "An Application of Geography to Mathematics: History of the Integral of the Secant." *Mathematics Magazine* 53: 162–166.

Rindler, Wolfgang. 2006. *Relativity: Special, General, Cosmological.* 2nd ed. Oxford: Oxford University Press.

Robison, John. 1803. "Dynamics." In *Supplement to the Encyclopaedia or Dictionary of Arts, Sciences, and Miscellaneous Literature*, vol. 1, 581–629. Philadelphia: Thomas Dobson.

Robison, John. 1822. *A System of Mechanical Philosophy*, vol. 1. Edinburgh: John Murray.

Roche, John 2008. "Concepts and Models of the Magnetic Field." In *Kelvin: Life, Labours and Legacy*, edited by Raymond Flood, Mark McCartney, and Andrew Whitaker, 94–121. Oxford: Oxford University Press.

Romeny, Bart M. ter Haar. 2003. *Front-End Vision and Multi-scale Image Analysis: Multi-scale Computer Vision Theory and Applications.* Dordrecht: Kluwer.

Rosen, Gideon. 2010. "Metaphysical Dependence: Grounding and Reduction." In *Modality: Metaphysics, Logic, and Epistemology*, edited by Bob Hale and Aviv Hoffmann, 109–135. New York: Oxford University Press.

Routh, Edward J. 1896. *A Treatise on Analytical Statics*, vol. 1. Cambridge: Cambridge University Press.

Rudiak, V. M. 1964. "A Proof of Archimedes' Principle." *Physics Teacher* 2: 293.

Ruelle, David. 2007. *The Mathematician's Brain.* Princeton: Princeton University Press.

Rutherford, Ernest, and Hans Geiger. 1910. "The Probability Variations in the Distribution of a Particles." *Philosophical Magazine*, ser. 6, 20: 698–707.

Rutherford, T. 1748. *A System of Natural Philosophy*, vol. 1. Cambridge: J. Bentham.

Salmon, Wesley. 1977. "A Third Dogma of Empiricism." In *Basic Problems in Methodology and Linguistics*, edited by Robert Butts and Jaakko Hintikka, 149–166. Dordrecht: Reidel.

Salmon, Wesley. 1984. *Scientific Explanation and the Causal Structure of the World.* Princeton: Princeton University Press.

Salmon, Wesley. 1989. "Four Decades of Scientific Explanation." In *Scientific Explanation*, edited by Philip Kitcher and Wesley Salmon, Minnesota Studies in the Philosophy of Science, vol. 13, 3–219. Minneapolis: University of Minnesota Press.

Salmon, Wesley. 1998. *Causality and Explanation.* New York: Oxford University Press.

Salmon, Wesley. 2001. "Explanation and Confirmation: A Bayesian Critique of Inference to the Best Explanation." In *Explanation: Theoretical Approaches and Applications*, edited by Giora Hon and Sam Rakover, 61–91. Dordrecht: Kluwer.

Sandborg, David. 1998. "Mathematical Explanation and the Theory of Why-Questions." *British Journal for the Philosophy of Science* 49: 603–624.

Sawyer, W. W. 1943. *Mathematician's Delight.* Harmondsworth: Penguin.

Sawyer, W. W. 1955. *Prelude to Mathematics.* Harmondsworth: Penguin.

Sawyer, W. W. 1966. *A Path to Modern Mathematics.* Harmondsworth: Penguin.

Schenck, Hilbert. 1979. *Theories of Engineering Experimentation.* 3rd ed. New York: Hemisphere.

Sedov, L. I. 1959. *Similarity and Dimensional Methods in Mechanics.* London: Infosearch.

Servois, François-Joseph. 1814–15. "Réflexions sur les Divers Systèmes d'Exposition des Principes du Calcul Différentiel, et en Particulier, sur la Doctrine des Infiniment Petits." *Annales des Mathématiques Pures et Appliquées* 5: 141–170.

Serway, Raymond, and John Jewett. 2008. *Physics for Scientists and Engineers*, vol. 1, 7th ed. Belmont, CA: Thomson.

Seth, Suman. 2010. *Crafting the Quantum*. Cambridge, MA: MIT Press.

Shames, Irving H. 2002. *Mechanics of Fluids*. 4th ed. New York: McGraw-Hill.

Shapiro, Larry, and Elliott Sober. 2007. "Epiphenomenalism: The Dos and the Don'ts." In *Thinking about Causes*, edited by Peter Machamer and Gereon Wolters, 235–264. Pittsburgh: University of Pittsburgh Press.

Shoemaker, Sydney. 1984. "Causality and Properties." In *Identity, Cause, and Mind*, 206–233. Cambridge: Cambridge University Press.

Silvester, John R. 2001. *Geometry: Ancient and Modern*. Oxford: Oxford University Press.

Skertchly, J. Alfred. 1873. *Natural Philosophy, Part I. Mechanics*. London: Thomas Murby.

Sklar, Lawrence. 1977. *Space, Time, and Spacetime*. Berkeley: University of California Press.

Skow, Bradford. 2014. Are There Non-causal Explanations (of Particular Events)? *British Journal for the Philosophy of Science* 65: 445–467.

Sloane, N. J. A. 2007. *The On-line Encyclopedia of Integer Sequences*. www.research.att.com/~njas/sequences/. Accessed August 24, 2009.

Smart, J. J. C. 1990. "Explanation—Opening Address." In *Explanation and Its Limits*, edited by Dudley Knowles, 1–20. Cambridge: Cambridge University Press.

Smith, J. 2006. "A Sense-Making Approach to Proof: Strategies of Students in Traditional and Problem-Based Number Theory Courses." *Journal of Mathematical Behavior* 25: 73–90.

Sober, Elliott. 1983. "Equilibrium Explanations." *Philosophical Studies* 43: 201–210.

Sober, Elliott. 1984. *The Nature of Selection: Evolutionary Theory in Philosophical Focus*. Cambridge, MA: MIT Press.

Sober, Elliott. 2001. "Two Faces of Fitness." In *Thinking about Evolution: Historical, Philosophical, and Political Perspectives*, vol. 2, edited by Rama S. Singh, Costas B. Krimbas, Diane B. Paul, and John Beatty, 309–321. Cambridge: Cambridge University Press.

Sober, Elliott. 2011. "*A Priori* Causal Models of Natural Selection." *Australasian Journal of Philosophy* 89: 571–589.

Sorensen, Roy. N.d. "Mathematical Coincidences." Unpublished manuscript.

Speiser, David. 1987. "The Principle of Relativity in Euler's Work." In *Symmetries in Physics (1600–1980): Proceedings of the 1st International Meeting on the History of Scientific Ideas held at Sant Feliu de Guixols, Catalonia Spain, 20–26 September 1983*, edited by Manuel G. Doncel, Armin Hermann, Louis Michel, and Abraham Pais, 31–50. Barcelona: Universitat Autonoma de Barcelona.

Spivak, Michael. 1980. *Calculus*. 2nd ed. Berkeley: Publish or Perish.

Stachel, John. 1995. "History of Relativity." In *Twentieth Century Physics*, vol. 1, edited by Laurie Brown, Abraham Pais, and Brian Pippard, 249–356. New York: American Institute of Physics Press.

Stachel, John. 2002. "'What Song the Syrens Sang': How Did Einstein Discover Special Relativity?" In *Einstein from 'B' to 'Z': Einstein Studies*, vol. 9, 157–170. Boston: Birkhäuser.

Stankova, Zvezdelina. 2004. "Geometric Puzzles and Constructions—Six Classical Geometry Theorems." In *Mathematical Adventures for Students and Amateurs*, edited by David F. Hayes and Tatiana Shubin, 169–184. Washington, DC: Mathematical Association of America.

Stanley, Richard P. 2012. *Enumerative Combinatorics*, vol. 1, 2nd ed. Cambridge: Cambridge University Press.

Stanley, Richard P., and Anders Björner. 2010. *A Combinatorial Miscellany*. Geneva: L'Enseignement Mathématique.

Steele, J. Michael. 2004. *Cauchy-Schwarz Master Class: An Introduction to the Art of Mathematical Inequalities.* Cambridge: Cambridge University Press.

Steiner, Mark. 1978a. "Mathematical Explanation." *Philosophical Studies* 34: 135–151.

Steiner, Mark. 1978b. "Mathematics, Explanation, and Scientific Knowledge." *Noûs* 12: 17–28.

Steiner, Mark. 1978c. "Quine and Mathematical Reduction." *Southwestern Journal of Philosophy* 9: 133–143.

Steiner, Mark. 1983a. "Mathematical Realism." *Noûs* 17: 363–385.

Steiner, Mark. 1983b. "'Under a Description.'" In *How Many Questions?*, edited by Leigh S. Cauman, Isaac Levi, Charles Parsons, and Robert Schwartz, 120–131. Indianapolis: Hackett.

Steiner, Mark. 1990. "Mathematical Autonomy." *Iyyun* 39: 101–114.

Stevin, Simon. 1955. *The Principal Works of Simon Stevin*, vol. 1, edited by E. J. Dijksterhuis. Amsterdam: C. V. Swets & Zeitlinger.

Stewart, Ian. 1975. *Concepts of Modern Mathematics.* Baltimore: Penguin.

Stewart, Ian. 1996. *From Here to Infinity.* Oxford: Oxford University Press.

Stewart, James. 2009. *Calculus.* Belmont, CA: Thomson.

Stigler, Stephen M. 1986. *The History of Statistics.* Cambridge, MA: Harvard University Press.

Strevens, Michael. 2008. *Depth.* Cambridge, MA: Harvard University Press.

Sturgeon, Nicholas. 1985. "Moral Explanations." In *Morality, Reason and Truth*, edited by David Copp and David Zimmerman, 49–78. Totowa, NJ: Rowan and Allanheld.

Sumpner, W. E. 1928–29. "Heaviside's Fractional Differentiator." *Proceedings of the Physical Society* 41: 404–420, 425.

Sylvester, J. J. 1882. "A Constructive Theory of Partitions, Arranged in Three Acts, an Interact and an Exodion." *American Journal of Mathematics* 5: 251–330.

Tait, Peter Guthrie. 1885. *Lectures on Some Recent Advances in Physical Science.* 3rd ed. London: Macmillan.

Tappenden, Jamie. 2005. "Proof Style and Understanding in Mathematics I: Visualization, Unification, and Axiom Choice." In *Visualization, Explanation, and Reasoning Styles in Mathematics*, edited by P. Mancosu, K. F. Jørgensen, and S. A. Pedersen, 147–214. Dordrecht: Springer.

Tappenden, Jamie. 2008a. "Mathematical Concepts and Definitions." In *The Philosophy of Mathematical Practice*, edited by P. Mancosu, 256–275. Oxford: Oxford University Press.

Tappenden, Jamie. 2008b. "Mathematical Concepts: Fruitfulness and Naturalness." In *The Philosophy of Mathematical Practice*, edited by P. Mancosu, 276–301. Oxford: Oxford University Press.

Tarasov, Lev, and Aldina Tarasova. 1973. *Questions and Problems in School Physics.* Moscow: Mir.

Tate, T. 1853. *The Principles of Mechanical Philosophy.* London: Longmans, Brown, Green, and Longmans.

Teller, Paul. 1991. "Substance, Relations, and Arguments about the Nature of Space-Time." *Philosophical Review* 100: 363–397.

Terletskii, Yakov. 1968. *Paradoxes in the Theory of Relativity.* New York: Plenum.

Thomson, William [Lord Kelvin]. 1845/1872. "On the Mathematical Theory of Electricity in Equilibrium." *Cambridge and Dublin Mathematical Journal*, 1: 75–95. Reprinted in *Reprint of Papers on Electrostatics and Magnetism*, 15–37. London: Macmillan.

Thomson, William [Lord Kelvin], and Peter Guthrie Tait. 1888. *Treatise on Natural Philosophy.* Cambridge: Cambridge University Press.

Todhunter, Isaac. 1876. *William Whewell, DD. An Account of His Writings*, vol. 1. London: Macmillan.

Todhunter, Isaac. 1878. *Mechanics for Beginners*. London: Macmillan.

Trefil, James. 2003. *The Nature of Science: An A–Z Guide to the Laws and Principles Governing Our Universe*. Boston: Houghton Mifflin.

Van Fraassen, Bas. 1977. "The Pragmatics of Explanation." *American Philosophical Quarterly* 14: 143–150.

Van Fraassen, Bas. 1980. *The Scientific Image*. Oxford: Clarendon.

Van Fraassen, Bas. 1989. *Laws and Symmetry*. Oxford: Clarendon.

Van Spronsen, J. W. 1969. *The Periodic System of Chemical Elements*. Amsterdam: Elsevier.

Vinner, Shlomo, and Evgeny Kopelman. 1998. "Is Symmetry an Intuitive Basis for Proof in Euclidean Geometry?" *Focus on Learning Problems in Mathematics* 20 (2/3): 14–26.

Waismann, Friedrich. 1982. *Lectures on the Philosophy of Mathematics*, ed. Wolfgang Grassl. Amsterdam: Rodopi.

Walsh, D. M. 2007. "The Pomp of Superfluous Causes: The Interpretation of Evolutionary Theory." *Philosophy of Science* 74: 281–303.

Walsh, D. M., Tim Lewens, and André Ariew. 2002. "The Trials of Life: Natural Selection and Random Drift." *Philosophy of Science* 69: 452–473.

Watkins, John. 1984. *Science and Scepticism*. Princeton: Princeton University Press.

Weinberg, Steven. 1987. "Newtonianism and Today's Physics." In *Three Hundred Years of Gravitation*, edited by Stephen Hawking and Werner Israel, 5–16. Cambridge: Cambridge University Press.

Weinberg, Steven. 1995. *The Quantum Theory of Fields*, vol. 1. Cambridge: Cambridge University Press.

Weisbach, J. L. 1875. *Theoretical Mechanics*, vol. 1. Translated by E. B. Coxe. New York: Van Nostrand.

Wells, David. 1991. *The Penguin Dictionary of Curious and Interesting Geometry*. London: Penguin.

Weyl, Hermann. 1952. *Symmetry*. Princeton: Princeton University Press.

Whewell, William. 1832. *The First Principles of Mechanics, with Historical and Practical Illustrations*. Cambridge: L. and L. L. Deighton.

Whewell, William. 1840. *The Philosophy of the Inductive Sciences*, vol. 1. London: John W. Parker.

Whewell, William. 1841. *The Mechanics of Engineering Intended for Use in Universities, and in Colleges of Engineers*. Cambridge: Cambridge University Press.

Whewell, William. 1847. *An Elementary Treatise on Mechanics*. 7th ed. Cambridge: Deighton's.

Whewell, William. 1858. *History of Scientific Ideas*, vol. 1, 3rd ed. London: J. W. Parker.

Whewell, William. 1874. *History of the Inductive Sciences*, vol. 1, 3rd ed. New York: Appleton.

White, Colin. 2011. *Projectile Dynamics in Sport: Principles and Applications*. London: Routledge.

Whitehead, Alfred North. 1907/1971. *The Axioms of Descriptive Geometry*. New York: Hafner.

Whittaker, Edmund. 1953. *A History of the Theories of Aether and Electricity*, vol. 2. *The Modern Theories*. London: Thomas Nelson.

Wigner, Eugene. 1949. "Invariance in Physical Theory." *Proceedings of the American Philosophical Society* 93: 521–526.

Wigner, Eugene. 1952. "On the Law of Conservation of Heavy Particles." *Proceedings of the National Academy of Sciences USA* 38: 449–451.

Wigner, Eugene. 1972. "Events, Laws of Nature, and Invariance Principles." In *Nobel Lectures: Physics 1963–70*, 6–19. Amsterdam: Elsevier.

Wigner, Eugene. 1985. "Events, Laws of Nature, and Invariance Principles." In *How Far Are We from the Gauge Forces*, edited by A. Zuchichi, 699–708. New York: Plenum.

Wigner, Eugene. 1992. *Collected Papers of Eugene Paul Wigner*, vol. 3. Berlin: Springer.

Wilczek, Frank, and Betsy Devine. 1987. *Longing for the Harmonies: Themes and Variations from Modern Physics*. New York: Norton.

Wilf, Herbert. 2000. *Lectures on Integer Partitions*, under the auspices of the Pacific Institute for the Mathematical Sciences at University of Victoria. www.math.upenn.edu/~wilf/PIMS/PIMSLectures.pdf. Accessed September 24, 2009.

Wilkinson, T. T. 1864. "Duchayla." *Notes and Queries*, 3rd ser. 6, 132: 39.

Wilson, Mark. 1992. "Frege: The Royal Road from Geometry." *Noûs* 26: 149–180.

Wilson, Mark. 2006. *Wandering Significance*. Oxford: Clarendon.

Woodall, Douglas R., and Robin J. Wilson. 1978. "The Appel-Haken Proof of the Four-Color Theorem." In *Selected Topics in Graph Theory*, edited by Lowell W. Beineke and Robin J. Wilson, 83–101. London: Academic Press.

Woodward, James. 1989. "The Causal Mechanical Model of Explanation." In *Scientific Explanation*, edited by Philip Kitcher and Wesley Salmon, *Minnesota Studies in the Philosophy of Science*, vol. 13, 357–383. Minneapolis: University of Minnesota Press.

Woodward, James. 2003. *Making Things Happen: A Theory of Causal Explanations*, New York: Oxford University Press.

Wussing, Hans. 1984. *The Genesis of the Abstract Group Concept*. Cambridge, MA: MIT Press.

Young, J. R. 1834. *Elements of Mechanics*. Philadelphia: Carey, Lea & Blanchard.

Yourgrau, Wolfgang, Alwyn Van der Merwe, and Gough Raw. 2002. *Treatise on Irreversible and Statistical Thermophysics*. New York: Dover.

Zeitz, Paul. 2000. "Graph Theory." *Handout for Berkeley Math Circle*, http://mathcircle.berkeley.edu/index.php?options=bmc|bmcarchives|Circle%20Archives, October 8.

Zeitz, Paul. 2007. *The Art and Craft of Problem Solving*. 2nd ed. Hoboken: Wiley.

Zeitz, Paul. 2010. *The Art and Craft of Mathematical Problem Solving*. Chantilly, VA: Teaching Company.

Zelcer, Mark. 2013. "Against Mathematical Explanation." *Journal of General Philosophy of Science* 44: 173–192.

Zlokarnik, Marko. 2006. *Scale-up in Chemical Engineering*. 2nd ed. Weinheim: Wiley-VCH.

■ INDEX

Printed in the USA/Agawam, MA
March 14, 2018

671456.002